Invisible
Writer

Other Books by Greg Johnson

FICTION AND POETRY

I Am Dangerous (stories, 1996)
Pagan Babies (novel, 1993)
Aid and Comfort (poetry, 1993)
A Friendly Deceit (stories, 1992)
Distant Friends (stories, 1990)

CRITICISM

Joyce Carol Oates: A Study of the Short Fiction (1994)
Understanding Joyce Carol Oates (1987)
Emily Dickinson: Perception and the Poet's Quest (1985)

Invisible Writer

A BIOGRAPHY OF

Joyce Carol Oates

GREG JOHNSON

A DUTTON BOOK

—for Dedrick, Paul, and David Burch

DUTTON
Published by the Penguin Group
Penguin Putnam Inc., 375 Hudson Street,
New York, New York 10014, U.S.A.
Penguin Books Ltd, 27 Wrights Lane,
London W8 5TZ, England
Penguin Books Australia Ltd, Ringwood,
Victoria, Australia
Penguin Books Canada Ltd, 10 Alcorn Avenue,
Toronto, Ontario, Canada M4V 3B2
Penguin Books (N.Z.) Ltd, 182–190 Wairau Road,
Auckland 10, New Zealand

Penguin Books Ltd, Registered Offices:
Harmondsworth, Middlesex, England

First published by Dutton, an imprint of Dutton NAL, a member of Penguin Putnam Inc.

First Printing, April, 1998
10 9 8 7 6 5 4 3 2 1

 REGISTERED TRADEMARK—MARCA REGISTRADA

LIBRARY OF CONGRESS CATALOGING-IN-PUBLICATION DATA:

Johnson, Greg.
    Invisible writer : a biography of Joyce Carol Oates / by Greg Johnson.
      p.   cm.
    ISBN 0-525-94163-0 (alk. paper)
    1. Oates, Joyce Carol, 1938–   —Biography.   2. Women authors,
American—20th century—Biography.   I. Title.
PS3565.A8Z685   1998
813'.54—dc21
    [B]   97-34996
                                                              CIP

Printed in the United States of America
Set in Transitional 521
Designed by Eve L. Kirch

This book is printed on acid-free paper. ∞

What is the ontological status of the writer *who is also a woman?*

She is likely to experience herself, from within, as a writer primarily; perhaps even a writer exclusively. She does not inevitably view herself as an object, a category, an essence—in short, as "representative." The individual, to the individual, is never a type. And in the practice of her craft she may well become bodiless and invisible, defined to herself fundamentally as what she thinks, dreams, plots, constructs.

—"(Woman) Writer: Theory and Practice" (1988)

... at home, in the privacy of my work, I *am* virtually no one, at all.   —*Journal*, February 12, 1994

CONTENTS

PREFACE

During the five years I spent researching and writing this book, many individuals and institutions provided invaluable assistance. For granting extensive interviews and other help, I wish to thank Joyce Carol Oates; her husband, Raymond Smith; and her parents, Frederic and Carolina Oates. I'm particularly grateful for Fred and Carolina's guided tour through their daughter's childhood environment: the landscape surrounding the Tonawanda Creek in Millersport that figures so powerfully in the fiction of Joyce Carol Oates.

I also wish to thank Kathleen Manwaring, manuscripts supervisor at the Department of Special Collections, Syracuse University Library. Kathleen offered friendly, enthusiastic, and indefatigable assistance at all stages of my research. During my visits to the Joyce Carol Oates Archive, I benefited from Kathleen's prodigious feat of sorting and cataloging Oates's papers; as I wrote the book, my work was aided immeasurably by her prompt responses to my countless queries and requests.

Librarians at other institutional collections also guided me to material crucial to my research. I wish to thank the highly professional staff at the following institutions: the University of Detroit Libraries, the Detroit Public Library, the University of Windsor Library, the University of Michigan Library, the Butler Library at Columbia University, the Firestone Library at Princeton University, the Library of Congress, and the Harry Ransom Research Center for the Humanities at the University of Texas. The library personnel at the following newspapers also provided significant material: the *Detroit Free Press*, the *Detroit News*, and the *Windsor Star*. A special thanks to Beverly Brasch at Kennesaw State University, who promptly handled my interlibrary loan requests, and to the KSU administrators who supported my work by granting me release time from teaching duties. I am also grateful to Robert Hollenbach, Randy Souther, and Brandon Stickney for their research assistance, and to Lori Krise for her help in transcribing dozens of taped interviews.

The following individuals made an enormous contribution to this book. Many provided detailed personal recollections and granted access to their correspondence with Joyce Carol Oates, while others offered significant information and leads: William Abrahams, Alice Adams, Max Alberts, Dick Allen, Lori Allen, Frank Aronson, Colin Atkinson, James Atlas, Russell Banks, Robert J. Barnes, Alice L. Birney, Madison Smartt Bell, Joe David Bellamy, Pinckney Benedict, Henry Bienen, Terry Bird, Steven Bloom, Rebecca Bragg, Karen Braziller, Gertrude Bregman, Victor Brombert, Dan Brown, Richard Burgin, Patricia Hill Burnett, Dr. Bruce Burnham, Margie Carlin, Ellen Shapley Comerford, Joel Conarroe, Ed Cone, Lee Cooke-Childs, Frank Corsaro, Janet Cosby, Gary Couzens, Frank Coward, Molly Eimers Dee, Nicholas Delbanco, Cheryl DeNero, Sally Daniels Dike, John Ditsky, Carol Dixon, Linnea Ogren Donahower, Margaret Drabble, James Dubro, Sandy Gillan Dwenger, Charles East, David Ebershoff Jr., Mark Eccles, Emory Elliott, Herb Evert, Robert and Lynne Fagles, Susan Feinstein, Lucinda Franks, Ellen G. Friedman, Sharon Friedman, Jean E. (Windnagle) Fritton, Donn Fry, Paul Fussell, David Galef, Robert G. Gaylor, Reginald Gibbons, Gail Godwin, Laurence Goldstein, Elizabeth Graham, Richard Gregory, John Grube, Robert G. Hagelman, Daniel Halpern, Jeannie Halpern, Betsey Hansell, Klaus Harpprecht, Kevin Harris, Guy Henle, Mary Ellen Henle, Jack Hewson, William Heyen, Arthur Hoffman, Jim Holleran, Thomas Jackson, Tama Janowitz, Howard Junker, Alfred Kazin, Edmund Keeley, Richard Kostelanetz, Maxine Kumin, George Kunz, Nora Leitch, Elmore Leonard, John L'Heureux, Marj Levin, Philip Levine, Marilyn Lyman, David Madden, Rosemary Mancini, Mary Marshall, John Martin, Gail Paxson Mates, Jack Matthews, Jerome Mazzaro, Jim McDonald, Norman McKendrick, Eugene McNamara, Robert McPhillips, Jeffrey Meyers, Diane Middlebrook, Charles Murrah, Don O'Briant, Frederic J. Oates Jr., Alicia Ostriker, Cynthia Ozick, Matt Phillips, Robert Phillips, George Pitcher, Thomas Porter, Lucie Prinz, Nelia Pynn, Ruth Rattner, John Reed, Ruth Reed, Marinelle Ringer, Ned Rorem, Sally Rosenbluth, Philip Roth, Henry B. Rule, Leslie A. Rutkowski, Nancy Dalton Sanders, Robert J. Schaefer, Thomas Schaub, Susan Shreve, Evelyn Shrifte, Elly Sidel, Ruth E.

Sinclair, Leif Sjoberg, Lois Smedick, Dave Smith, Jared Smith, Gordy Stearns, Scott Stein, Richard Stern, Robert Stone, Harry Strickhausen, Dabney Stuart, Walter Sutton, Deborah Tannen, R. B. Thomas, Richard Trenner, Lewis Turco, Jim Tuttleton, Frank Tuzzolino, Anne Tyler, Michael Upchurch, John Updike, Bette Weidman, Mark Weimer, Ted Weiss, Gloria Whelan, Jenny Whelan, Milton White, Faith Whittlesey, Gwenan Wilbur, Colin Wilson, Eleanor G. Wilson, Judith Wynn, Herb Yellin, Matthew J. Zeiler, Dan Zins.

Finally, I wish to acknowledge the work my editors at Dutton, Audrey LaFehr and Rosemary Ahern; of the copyeditor, Shelly Perron, and the associate manuscript editor, Kari Paschall; and of my agents at Sanford J. Greenburger Associates, Theresa Park and the late Diane Cleaver. A special thanks to Dede Yow, and again to Kathleen Manwaring and Randy Souther, for reading a near-final version of this book and making valuable suggestions.

A note on punctuation: Joyce Carol Oates frequently uses ellipsis dots as a stylistic device in her writing. All ellipses in quoted material are her own; when I have deleted material in a quotation, I have placed my own ellipses in brackets.

INTRODUCTION

*And so my life continues through the decades . . . not
connected in the slightest with that conspicuous other
with whom, by accident, I share a name and a likeness.
The fact seems self-evident, that I was but the door
through which she entered—'it' entered—but any door
would have done as well.*

—" 'JCO' and I" (1994)

On April 21, 1976, Joyce Carol Oates gave a reading from her work at
Miami University in Oxford, Ohio. At thirty-seven, Oates was already one
of the most celebrated writers in the United States, but for almost a decade
she had taught at the University of Windsor, maintaining on the Canadian
side of the Detroit River a discreet distance from the violent American reality
she had dramatized so powerfully in her fiction. She gave few interviews and
declined most invitations to read from her work on college campuses. A professor in the Miami University English department, Milton White, had invited her to Oxford several times, but Oates had explained politely that she
was simply too busy with her writing. White persisted, sending letters that
Oates found touching in their expression of admiration for her work. Finally
she had relented, agreeing to the April visit.

As Oates approached the stage, the packed auditorium grew quiet. Her
face was familiar, of course, from her dust jackets and from the cover story
Newsweek had published four years earlier. In the opening paragraph of that
article, Walter Clemons had defined a paradoxical quality to Oates's personality that helped account for public fascination about her: "If you met her at
a literary party and failed to catch her name, it might be hard to imagine
her reading, much less writing, the unflinching fiction that has made Joyce
Carol Oates perhaps the most significant novelist to have emerged in the
United States in the last decade." To the audience in the Miami University

auditorium—including her future biographer, who was seeing Oates in person for the first time—this observation must have seemed particularly apt. Oates approached the stage shyly, arms folded across a small sheaf of papers she clasped tightly to her chest. Dressed simply in a dark orange dress, Oates was thin and surprisingly tall, moving with a willowy grace toward her chair near the podium, where she sat to await her introduction. Her features were striking: dark hair parted neatly in the center and brushed flat along her temples; a delicate, pallid complexion; enormous dark eyes trained on the papers in her lap but occasionally lifted for a brief, inquisitive glance into the audience. As Milton White introduced her, Oates looked distinctly shy and ill at ease, as if discomfited by the recitation of her achievements and prizes, the proclamation of her "literary genius." Oates might come forward to give her reading, I thought, when the introduction was concluded; but it seemed just as likely she would decide not to go through with it, escaping offstage with the folder of poems still clutched to her chest.

When Oates took the podium, her manner changed abruptly. Thanking Milton White for his gracious introduction and many kind letters, she described the pleasant drive she and her husband had taken from Windsor and their leisurely stroll through the campus grounds that afternoon. In sharp contrast to the timorous-seeming woman who had approached the stage, Oates now appeared confident and genuinely pleased to be there. She planned to read poetry, she said, so that she could talk informally between the poems; a long piece of fiction would be too wearing for the audience. Apart from her casual but practiced manner, there were other surprises. She spoke in a flat midwestern drawl that seemed at odds (to my southern ears, at least) with her graceful appearance. Even more unexpected was her spontaneous and lively sense of humor. After numerous rereadings of such novels as *them* (1969) and *Wonderland* (1971), I had expected an intense, unsmiling, uncompromisingly *serious* presence. Although her casual remarks after she read each poem included references to Nietzsche, Jung, Lawrence, and Yeats—not surprising from a university professor and a wide-ranging literary critic—they were also peppered with droll asides that elicited bursts of uproarious laughter from the audience. At one point, introducing her next poem, she offered an apologetic warning—at eleven thousand lines, the poem was rather long. The audience stayed silent. Pausing a beat or two, Oates said, "Of course, I'm only joking." Again the audience broke into laughter. "You people at Miami University are so *polite*," she added, smiling. "If I'd announced an eleven-thousand line poem back in Detroit, there would have been gunfire."

During the next several years, I attended several more of Oates's readings: at Johns Hopkins University in 1977, at the Philadelphia Public Library in

1981, at the New York West Side YMCA in 1982. As a graduate student in English at Emory University in the late 1970s, and as a fledgling assistant professor in the early 1980s, I had continued to follow her work closely. I had begun reviewing books for literary journals and often wrote about her books and about critical studies of her work. After a decade of reading Oates, I considered her the most talented, most inventive, and most exciting of American fiction writers. Occasionally I wrote to her, usually after a new book of hers had come out, and I was gratified by her prompt, often lengthy replies. A kind of long-distance friendship developed, particularly as my professional involvement with her work increased. In addition to reviews and essays, I eventually published two critical studies on Oates: *Understanding Joyce Carol Oates* (1987) and *Joyce Carol Oates: A Study of the Short Fiction* (1994).

When, in 1991, I first suggested the idea of writing her biography, Oates was skeptical. She was only in her mid-fifties, after all, and continued to publish at least two books each year. Her quiet routine of teaching, writing, and occasional public readings did not lend itself, she thought, to a particularly vivid or dramatic biographical account. She informed me, however, that in 1990 she had established an archive at her alma mater, Syracuse University, for the maintenance of her dozens of manuscripts, several thousand letters, and the personal journal she had kept regularly since 1973. For my critical work, she suggested that I could peruse the manuscripts—but not the letters or journal, which were kept in a "restricted" part of the archive. She would grant me access to the journal and to most of the letters (the permission of each correspondent was also required) if I did decide to pursue a biographical project.

I had long been curious about the relationship between Oates's work and her life. If her fiction had a central theme, it was the riddling nature of human identity, what she called in *Wonderland* "the phantasmagoria of personality." Like Jesse Vogel in that novel, most of Oates's major protagonists endure transformations of being that suggested the author's obsession with the self in its struggle to achieve definition, usually in the face of inimical and even violent psychological, familial, and societal forces. In what ways did this artistic preoccupation reflect Oates's own personal experiences? What biographical issues underlay her fascination with twins, for instance, a subject explored in her mystery novels published under the name of her literary doppelgänger, Rosamond Smith? And how did her characteristic themes relate to her legendary productivity as a writer?

Observing Oates's career from a distance, I had long viewed her life as bearing a paradoxical relationship to her writing. She pursued a quiet, disciplined daily routine, yet wrote about people floundering in personal chaos and social disorder. A famous writer in an age of celebrity, she shunned publicity, keeping such a low profile that many journalists considered her a recluse. A frail-appearing woman with gentle manners, she wrote energetically and expertly about the violent sport of boxing. A writer who often expressed a yearning toward "invisibility," she published more visibly than any other American writer: her name had been ubiquitous in magazines for more than three decades and her work in various genres filled more than sixty published volumes.

As I delved into biographical sources, including her letters and journal, the paradoxes only multiplied. The woman often perceived as timid and shy, I learned, was actually quite strong-willed and outspoken. The writer possessed of unlimited vitality had struggled with anorexia, at times seeming literally to starve herself into "invisibility," and occasionally voiced the astonishing complaint that she was "staggeringly indolent." Despite her reputation as a lively, engaging teacher and public speaker, many people found her aloof and otherworldly, almost as if the "real" Joyce Carol Oates were indeed invisible, or wished she were.

In a 1989 letter, Oates related her own sense of invisibility to her gender: "the social self, the person people encounter, is almost irrelevant. I think this must be particularly true for women writers, though not necessarily for the traditional reasons—the masking of the writerly self by, say, Jane Austen, Edith Wharton, Emily Dickinson, in the service of maintaining an acceptable feminine image in others' eyes." But my initial supposition that Oates's life story followed patterns similar to those of other major American women writers quickly dissolved. Certainly the relationship between Oates's placid routine and the emotional intensity of her work recalled the Emily Dickinson who saw herself as "Vesuvius at home." Like Kate Chopin, Oates had been attacked for employing a stark realism that even in the late twentieth century had struck some critics as "unseemly" in a woman writer. Her Roman Catholic background and work-centered, puritanical temperament resembled those of Flannery O'Connor, another outwardly quiet person whose fictions were typically resolved through acts of violence. Yet the contrasts with the lives of these female literary forebears were at least as notable as any similarities. Unlike Dickinson, Oates had led a prominent career as a professional "woman of letters"; unlike Chopin, she had ignored critics who suggested that she write less and concentrate on the domestic subject matter that traditionally had been the province of women's writing; and unlike O'Connor, she repudiated Catholicism and adopted a nonjudgmental stance toward her fictional characters. Nor did Oates fit neatly into the contemporary stereotype of the "woman writer." Although self-defined as a feminist, Oates had written as frequently and sympathetically about men as about women, and in fact had cited male authors almost exclusively as her significant literary influences. Oates viewed herself not as a woman writer but as a "(woman) writer," a key distinction that insisted upon the invisibility—that is, the irrelevance—of gender in relationship to art.

The historical contours of Oates's life had a paradoxical quality of their own. The rural, economically straitened environment of her childhood, in the bleak heart of the upstate New York snowbelt, seemed an improbable setting for intellectual and artistic achievement. Oates went to the same one-room schoolhouse her mother, Carolina, had attended in the 1920s. A scholarship winner, Oates became the first member of her family to attend college and ultimately became valedictorian of her two-thousand-member senior class at Syracuse University. By then, her writing career was already launched: she had claimed the same prestigious writing prize, in a competition administered by *Mademoiselle* magazine, that Sylvia Plath had won a few years earlier. Soon her graduate seminar papers were being printed in prominent academic journals. Within a few years, she was winning O. Henry awards for her short stories on an annual basis and publishing the books that made her, in the opinion of one critic, "the finest American novelist, man or woman, since Faulkner." By the early 1970s, Oates's literary success suggested a feminist version of the archetypal pursuit and achievement of the American dream.

As her career progressed, not the least notable feature of her success, especially in the context of American literary lives, was its sustained intensity. Unlike many American writers, she was not a likely subject for that subgenre of literary biography Oates herself has scornfully termed the "pathography." The brilliant early books, unlike Melville's or Salinger's, did not give way to a disappointing, decades-long silence; unlike Fitzgerald or Jean Stafford, there was no descent into the creative dead end of alcoholism; unlike Stephen Crane or Flannery O'Connor, there was no tragically early illness and death, cutting off a career in its prime; and unlike Sylvia Plath or Anne Sexton, there was no grave psychological disorder, no attraction to suicide. Instead Oates seemed in the tradition of Hawthorne, Henry James, Edith Wharton, and John Updike, a writer who worked regular hours and kept writing as the central focus of daily life.

In Oates's journal and letters, she often expressed the concern—as if issuing periodic warnings to her biographer—that a relatively uneventful literary life might prompt an urge toward embroidery, if not outright "confabulation," on the part of a biographer seeking to lend drama or controversy to his subject's life. She disagreed, for instance, with Leon Edel's assertion that a biographer must seek out a "hidden personal myth" in a writer's experiences. By dabbling in psychoanalysis, she suggested, the biographer "will quite naturally project his own 'personal myth' onto the subject." She also worried about the biographer who "fails to see that the quality of the subject's achievement, and not certain quirks or eccentricities of his life, deserves our attention." Rather than indulging in speculations about a writer's unknowable "inwardness," she argued, a biography should be "solidly grounded in fact."

Oates's view of biography was undoubtedly shaped, at least in part, by the numerous myths and misconceptions about her own life that had developed during a quarter-century of literary fame: Joyce Carol Oates was withdrawn and humorless; her dozens of books were the result of trancelike "automatic writing" that required little or no revision; she had a mysterious, somewhat austere personality, living purely in her own world of intellect and imagination. Some of these misconceptions, of course, had basis in fact. Except when adopting a friendly, teacherly persona during her readings, she did strike many people as forbidding and unapproachable; in her early interviews and letters, she did claim that she seldom revised her work. But most people who came to know Joyce, as opposed to "Oates," found a lively, accessible woman who loved to gossip and to write long, chatty letters; who had a sharp wit and a gift for mimicry; who balanced her work life with regular, quite gregarious socializing; who enjoyed numerous friendships with both men and women; and who had developed a reputation as a generous source of aid and inspiration to younger writers.

Even Oates's close friends, however, were puzzled by the mysterious intensity of her engagement with her work. As I conducted interviews, people who had known her for years sometimes turned the tables and questioned me, most often to make a single perplexed inquiry: "How does she do it?" The answer was quite simple, in fact; she had been offering it to interviewers for years. Oates worked daily at her writing, even during her travels. On a typical day she worked from eight in the morning until one or two in the afternoon; took a break for jogging, bicycling, and doing errands; then worked again from about four until dinnertime. Occasionally she might work after dinner, though evenings were typically reserved for seeing friends or reading at home.

To her biographer, the most interesting question became not "How does she do it?" but "Why does she do it?" Her devotion to work could be explained by her family circumstances: the Depression-era background and toilsome lives of her parents combined with a cultural work ethic dating back to American puritanism. One could emphasize psychological factors: literature became an escape from the threatening world of her childhood and from the turbulent social reality of America, the means of creating an imaginative "counterworld" that reflected a violent society but kept the writer safely cocooned inside the aesthetic constructs over which she exerted a godlike control. Or one could accept the answer Oates herself often gave: she loved her work, and in fact didn't consider it "work" at all. Quite simply, she lived for her writing; it was her "life's commitment."

Like Henry James, Oates had long insisted that the true expression of her personality lay not in the random, anecdotal contours of her personal experiences but in the deep counterminings of her art. Along with personal documents and interviews, therefore, the massive collection of her manuscripts in the Joyce Carol Oates Archive seemed crucial to understanding the complex relationship between her experience and her writing. My careful study of her manuscripts revealed, in fact, that many of the accepted notions about her work, and her work habits, were mere fabrications by critics and so-called literary journalists who had, for more than three decades, tirelessly speculated, complained, and gossiped about the phenomenon of "Oates." When I first visited the archive, my overwhelming impression was of the sheer amount of labor represented by the manuscripts, for they betrayed the stereotype of Joyce Carol Oates as an author who wrote rapidly or carelessly—or easily. The novel manuscripts in particular were astonishing in their complexity, their evidence of ceaseless revision and, of course, their sheer volume.

Even more than the manuscripts, however, Oates's massive, typewritten journal, begun in 1973, provided a rich source of insight into her creative process and her personal life. The journal reveals the extent to which Oates has *lived* her art. Her lengthy, meditative entries ponder the philosophical issues she dramatizes in her fiction and describe in detail the technical challenges and daily frustrations of producing individual novels and stories. The journal is extraordinarily varied: on one day, Oates will recount a disturbing dream of the night before, then try to assess its significance; on another, she will respond to a book she is reading, conducting a kind of dialogue with the author; on another, she will record ordinary, quotidian events such as a trip to New York, a public reading that went well or badly, a quarrel with a colleague. There are vivid accounts of classes she has taught, parties she has given and attended, new people she has met. Perhaps most revealing, at least for a biographer, are the many passages given over to memory: a random incident in her present life often serves as a kind of Proustian trigger, leading to nostalgic recollections of childhood and adolescence, of deceased friends and relatives, of particularly happy or trying experiences in earlier phases of her public career.

Above all, the journal conveys the same quality that many readers have sensed in Oates's fiction: a limitless passion to explore, by way of language, the complex interaction of an individual consciousness with the changeable, often fearsome world it confronts on a daily basis. It is Oates's passion, finally, that has prompted her to create one of the richest legacies in American fiction. "If I had to do it all over again, I'm not sure that I could," she told one interviewer. Elsewhere she remarked that her epitaph might read: "She Certainly Tried." Although this biography attempts to elucidate the process by which the Joyce Carol Oates canon has come into being, it seems likely that a quotation Oates once pinned to the bulletin board over her desk best expresses her own ultimate view of her life and her writing. Not surprisingly, the words are from that other prolific American novelist, Henry James: "We work in the dark—we do what we can—we give what we have. Our doubt is our passion, and our passion is our task. The rest is the madness of art."

1

In the North Country

*Trees—grass—stones—river—
our steaming breaths:
the ice-drowse is upon us, the
hypnosis
of ancient sleep.*
—"Ice Age" (1978)

In May 1980, while visiting Hungary as part of a tour organized by the U.S. Information Agency, Joyce Carol Oates felt an unexpected sense of homecoming. At forty-one, an internationally famous writer already mentioned as a candidate for the Nobel Prize in literature, she had not expected that her eight days in Budapest—one of many stops in a grueling six-week tour involving dozens of talks, receptions, and meetings with her European publishers and translators—would result in a poignant distraction from the immediate concerns of her career.

Joyce had felt apprehensive about the Hungarian visit, knowing that her mother's family had emigrated from Budapest at the turn of the century. Memories of her grandparents' peasant origins and temperaments, which might "sound flamboyant and colorful," she noted wryly in her journal, "if seen through the retrospective of years and the prudent filter of language," suggested a possibly discomforting encounter with her own heritage. "Most of what was Hungarian in my life," she admitted, "was ignored, or denied, or repressed." Yet Budapest proved to be a pleasant surprise, "a jewel of a city." Walking the streets with her husband, Joyce was struck by "the disquietingly familiar look of strangers glimpsed on the streets: the eyes, the cheekbones, skin coloring, the general bearing. Several of the Hungarians to whom I have been introduced [. . .] resemble me more closely than my brother does, and far closer than either of my parents. Uncanny sensation!—as if I had stepped into a dream. A few days later she noted, "Lovely Budapest: I don't know where I am, but I think I am at home."

This note of surprised discovery has often characterized Joyce's reflections upon the details of her family history. Some of these recollections, previously denied or repressed, have struck her with the force of revelation. As a young writer, she had refused to discuss her background with journalists, claiming that the material was too personal. Even her friends and academic colleagues recalled her unwillingness to talk about her early years or her family. Joyce's immigrant heritage, the hardscrabble early lives of her parents during the Depression, and her own childhood in the upstate New York countryside seemed to her, as a young English professor and aspiring novelist, part of a world best left "back there"—a rich fund of memories and material for her writing, but related only in a private, oblique way to the intellectually oriented young writer she had become.

As she grew older, however, Joyce's expressions of nostalgia for her family heritage appeared often in her private journal, and by the 1990s her parents' and her own recollections became the focus of several autobiographical essays. These "confessional" pieces included details about her childhood and family that, twenty years earlier, she would not have shared with her closest friends, much less have committed to print. She had become particularly obsessed with the early lives of her parents, in part because, as she wrote in 1995, "we carry our young parents within us, so much more vivid and alive, pulsing-alive, than any memory of ourselves as infants, children."

Joyce had also become fascinated by her grandparents' experiences, which were marked by the same dark turnings of fate that regularly befall the characters in Joyce Carol Oates's fiction. Her maternal grandparents, she learned, had been forced to give her mother, Carolina, up for adoption because the family had grown too large; her paternal grandmother, to whom Joyce was extremely close as a child, had been abandoned by her husband when Joyce's father, Frederic, was only a toddler. There were other surprising details: Joyce's paternal great-grandfather was a German Jew who had changed his name from "Morgenstern" to "Morningstar" in the 1890s. Years later, in a fit of jealous rage, he beat his wife severely with a hammer and then shot himself. Joyce's maternal grandfather, Stephen Bush, also met a violent end: he was murdered in a tavern brawl.

Although Fred and Carolina Oates provided a safe and nurturing home environment for their children, Joyce's early years had held their own terrors, including an instance of "semi-molestation" and constant bullying that prompted her, years later, to describe her childhood as "a daily scramble for existence." In 1995, she observed: "How ironic, as a writer I've been constantly queried why do you write about violent acts? what do you know of violence? and my replies are polite, thoughtful, abstract and even idealistic. I might say that my entire life, indeed the lives of both my parents, have been shaped by 'violent acts.' "

It was perhaps inevitable that a novelist obsessively concerned with the mysteries of personality and identity should finally long to piece together what could be recovered of her past, with its eerily blended elements of terror and beauty. For many of Joyce's earliest impressions were imbued with a magical sense of wonder that inspired an intense nostalgia: "what romance, in that world," she wrote in a letter to Carolina. "Because you inhabited it, you and Daddy, it's transformed." To focus exclusively on the unsavory and violent details of her background, she observed, would be no less misleading than to deny them. Joyce often felt willingly "pulled back into that world as into the most seductive and most nourishing of dreams. I'm filled with a sense of wonder, and awe, and fear, regret for all that has passed, and for what must be surrendered, what we can imagine as life but cannot ever explain." To Joyce, her family background continued to represent a tantalizing mystery, "like a door opening to a shadowy passageway, but only just opening a few inches, never to be budged any further."

Joyce's maternal grandparents, Stephen and Elizabeth Bush, had come to the United States from Budapest in 1902. Like most immigrants, they "Americanized" their names. (Their Hungarian surname, "Büs," translates into English as "melancholy.") Stephen, born in Lovasz Patona, Hungary, sometime in 1874, and Elizabeth, born in Budapest on October 17, 1878, had been urged to emigrate by family members already living in Buffalo, New York. The couple settled near the Black Rock section of the city, a bleak waterfront area dominated by the Niagara River.

Though their relatives had written that conditions were far better in America than in Hungary, immigrant life was difficult for the young couple, especially as the size of the family increased. In Black Rock, crowded dwellings shared space with numerous taverns, where a diverse and often fractious population of immigrant Hungarians, Germans, Poles, and other ethnic groups gathered at the end of the day. The clash of languages and cultures, combined with heavy drinking and the frustrations of poverty, led to frequent outbreaks of violence. Little is known about Stephen Bush except that he was notorious for his short temper, a trait that poverty, alcohol, and the stress of caring for a large family did nothing to assuage. One night in early 1917, when Stephen was forty-three, his life ended violently. Though the precise circumstances of the tavern fight are not known, it seems likely that the violence erupted spontaneously, out of a sudden argument, since neither of the men was armed. Stephen's assailant grabbed the nearest available blunt object—

either a shovel or a poker, according to family recollections—and beat him to death. Stephen Bush left behind Elizabeth and their nine children, six boys and three girls. The youngest child, Carolina—born November 8, 1916—was only six months old.

Carolina Oates recalled that her grandparents had emigrated to America along with her parents, but had been so disillusioned by the conditions in Black Rock that they returned to Hungary almost at once. Her aunt Lena often recounted the difficulties of the Atlantic crossing, in steerage; when the boat arrived, the family was infested with lice. Settling in Black Rock among other recently arrived Hungarians, the Bushes clung to their language and heritage with a tenacity their granddaughter Joyce would later associate with "a peculiar sort of Old World obstinacy and self-defeat."

After her husband's violent death, Lena's sister Elizabeth found herself in an unwelcoming industrial city with little idea of how to care for her large family. Since Lena and her husband, John, had no children, they volunteered to take in the six-month-old Carolina; already burdened with eight other children, Elizabeth agreed to this informal adoption—a transaction that Carolina would later come to resent deeply. John Bush, possessing marketable skills as a blacksmith, was in better economic circumstances than his widowed sister-in-law to care for the baby girl. John and Lena also took in Carolina's older sister Mary, a girl of high intelligence whom they wanted to help educate.

Deciding on Carolina's adoption, all three adults were undoubtedly well intentioned. Carolina's mother knew her infant daughter would have a more stable life with John and Lena than she could provide, and certainly Carolina's new parents, both blood relatives, treated her well. "I was close to them. They were very, very good to me," Carolina recalled. "They had no other children, so I was special." As she grew older, however, she came to perceive the adoption as an abandonment by her mother. "I was never really part of the family," she remarked, the sadness audible in her voice more than half a century later. "I was sort of left out and I always felt really bad. I just couldn't understand why my mother couldn't handle one more child."

When Carolina was still a small girl, John and Lena left Buffalo for the countryside south of Lockport, in Erie County, buying an old farm in the tiny settlement called Millersport. The property was bounded on one side by the Tonawanda Creek, on the other by a two-lane dirt road that ran north to Lockport and south into the outskirts of Buffalo. This rural area that Joyce Carol Oates, in her early novels and stories, would one day mythologize as "Eden County" was certainly a better setting for raising a child than the crowded industrial sections of Buffalo, yet Carolina's emotional life remained troubled by the relationship between her natural and adoptive families. Her mother, Elizabeth, "had moved up" a little economically, thanks to a cash settlement resulting from her husband's death. Elizabeth's oldest son, Leslie, insisted they use part of the money to buy their own small farm, only three or four miles from where John and Lena lived. The close proximity of Carolina's natural mother and siblings reinforced her feelings of rejection and made for some painful visits. To make matters worse, Carolina's siblings felt jealous over her relatively comfortable home life. Carolina continued visiting her mother and siblings but "there wasn't any closeness."

Though Carolina's adoptive parents had more economic stability than her natural family, Carolina's own upbringing was far from affluent. John and Lena's place, dating from 1888, was no longer a working farm; their vegetable crops and fruit orchards were primarily for the family's own consumption. But as the 1920s came to an end, the demand for John's skills as a blacksmith decreased, though he maintained a forge in the old barn and did whatever blacksmithing his neighbors required. Often such work was done on the barter system: the swing on which Carolina played had come from a farmer for whom John had done some work.

Carolina's teenage years coincided with the Great Depression, and along with the rest of the country the Bush family suffered bleak times. John went to work in a steel foundry in Lackawanna, outside Buffalo—a rough and exhausting job that left his skin pitted with steel filings. Like most men of that era, he consoled himself at the end of his long days by smoking cigarettes he rolled himself and by drinking, often bringing home a quart of whiskey on payday. Behind his back, Lena would sometimes pour out part of the bottle and dilute the rest with water. Though John lacked the kind of violent temper that had led to his brother's death, "he could be very unpleasant when he had something to drink," Carolina remarked. Joyce, who called him "Grandpa Bush," recalled that John "began his day, at his early breakfast, with swigs of hard cider from a stoneware crock placed on the floor by his heel. That was just the beginning." Toward afternoon he might disappear with his cider jug into the privacy of the barn. Joyce's father remembered that John sometimes would start out drinking coffee in the morning, then grumble that "this goddamn coffee is too hot" and switch immediately to his hard cider—a tactic repeated so often it became a family joke. "He had all the vices," Joyce admitted, and at times the results could be humorous. She recalled one memorable day when Grandpa Bush "got drunk and started his Model-T and it got away from him, plowed through my grandmother's laundry drying on the clothesline, and continued on into a neighbor's yard."

Born on March 6, 1882, John had enlisted in the navy at age twenty-two; he worked as a blacksmith aboard the USS *Cleveland* and was honorably discharged in 1907, after serving almost three years. He was short of stature at five feet five inches, but was burly and sometimes pugnacious. Though John had gotten into his share of trouble as a young man, in later life he was well liked in the Millersport area and was particularly admired for his strength: if a horse tried to get away while he was shoeing it, John would wrestle it down. Known for his generosity, John was the kind of gruff but kindhearted man "who would give the shirt off his back." Generosity and family solidarity were part of the Bushes' working-class Hungarian heritage; when Carolina Bush married Frederic Oates during the worst years of the Depression, the new son-in-law was welcomed into the household, and except for a brief period when Fred moved his wife and first child to Lockport, the extended family remained intact in the old farmhouse throughout Joyce's childhood.

John died when Joyce was twelve; as an adult, she paid tribute to her Grandpa Bush in a poem called "First Death, 1950." Though recognizing that their starkly different temperaments and backgrounds precluded any real closeness—"False to say now that I loved you, / or that I even knew you"—the poem offers a compassionate summary of John's grueling work life, his primitive sense of humor, and the physical toll exacted by poverty:

> You crossed the heaving ocean with no pity for your own flesh,
> unmindful of the flame-rimmed smokestacks of the New World,
> that gave no heat, but paid a surprising wage.
> And you had no time to observe the storm of steel fragments
> about your head like gnats, or your eyes socketed with grime,
> or your face and hands and forearms encrusted with filth
> that could never be wholly scrubbed away.

Though sometimes repulsed by Grandpa Bush as a girl, Joyce later acknowledged that she couldn't "guess how your tender lungs bled, in secret," and suggested that his vivid presence, however boisterous and rough-edged, was nonetheless missed after his death:

> the coarse gray soap you used was thrown away,
> and your filth-stiffened clothes,
> and the jaunty 'railroad' cap,
> and there were no more drunken shouts on Friday night,
> no more barks of laughter,
> jokes and quarrels and flights of whimsy in Hungarian,
> no more nights disturbed by your angry hacking cough.

Both John and Lena had strong Hungarian accents, but in most respects they differed little from other inhabitants of that rural area known in Buffalo as "the north country." Lena Bush, whom Joyce later described as a simple woman with a "peasant" mentality, was passive and dutiful, her heritage that of the nineteenth-century working-class European housewife. As a young woman she had been plump, pretty, and curly-haired, but Joyce remembered her as a "sometimes querulous, 'nervous' person" who wore "her graying hair in a cabbage-like bun"; on Sundays, she was "cruelly corseted" and smelled of soap, seeming to the young Joyce "so old as to be beyond calculation, or curiosity." A black-and-white home movie taken outside the farmhouse by Frederic Oates, probably in the late 1940s, shows Lena standing at the kitchen door, a stout, smiling, plainly dressed woman; she waves briefly toward the camera, then quickly retreats into the kitchen. Lena kept an extremely neat house—a trait she would pass on to her adoptive daughter and granddaughter—and she enjoyed preparing traditional Hungarian dishes, including "rich, heavy, sour cream-dolloped goulashes." Lena made her own noodle dough, Joyce recalled, "rolling the stiff dough into flat layers on the kitchen table, stacking the layers carefully together, cutting them briskly with a long-bladed knife into noodles which were then set aside, on cloth, to dry." She also concocted Hungarian pastries of such complexity that Carolina never learned to prepare them.

Carolina's childhood and adolescence, while marred by her sense of alienation from her natural family and the limited educational opportunities of rural New York in the 1920s and 1930s, was nonetheless relatively tranquil. The winters could be brutal, but the presence of the wide, slow-moving creek, the pear and apple orchards, and the various farm animals made the place a child's paradise in the summer. Carolina attended Erie County District School No. 7, the same one-room schoolhouse—in walking distance of the farm—where her daughter Joyce would get her own elementary education. Since John and Lena were Roman Catholic, they sent Carolina to St. Mary's in Swormville, about three miles south of the farm on Transit Road, for junior high school.

Like millions of other American children of that era, however, Carolina never graduated from school, quitting after the eighth grade. The Depression had struck, times were hard, and she was now old enough to work. Not far from the Bush farm, at an intersection of three byroads, was a small diner and beer joint called Hass Cafe; because alcohol was served inside and she was under age, Carolina worked at an outside concession adjacent to the cafe. "It was just a hot dog place," she recalled. After she turned eighteen she began working inside, serving beer and food to local farmers and laborers. Carolina's future at this point in her life might have seemed uncertain, even grim, but she had a number of personal advantages: a lively disposition, formidable energy, and a natural talent for the domestic arts of cooking, housekeeping, flower arranging. And she was strikingly pretty. Photographs from that time show a slender young woman with curly auburn hair and a gentle smile. Not surprisingly, she attracted the attention of young men in the area while working at the cafe, and one evening a local man brought a friend of his specifically to meet her: a dark, good-looking city boy, from Lockport, named Frederic Oates.

At twenty-one, Fred was three years older than Carolina and had at least one trait in common with her murdered father: he had a hot temper. He liked to fight and had even boxed for a while. A studio photograph of Fred at age twenty-one showed him strong-looking, swarthy, and handsome. Clean-shaven, he had thick dark hair and brows, and dark eyes that looked resolutely into the distance. The young Fred had a sharp sense of humor, too, and there was a teasing quality to his courtship of Carolina. He remembered that once when he visited her at the cafe, "she was so angry with me because I told her I wanted my hot dog burned better than that. I guess she thought I was just being nasty, which I probably was." Yet they soon realized that they had much in common, and after a two-year courtship, Fred making the nine-mile trip down from Lockport regularly to see her, the couple were married.

In 1986, when Joyce Carol Oates published *Marya: A Life*, she described the novel as a blending of her mother's early life and her own. Despite the superficial dissimilarities between Carolina and Joyce in terms of educational and professional opportunities, Carolina's influence upon her daughter's life has been profound, as is suggested not only by this artistic blending of their life experiences in *Marya* but also by Joyce's other sympathetic portraits of maternal figures. In her 1996 novel *We Were the Mulvaneys*, for instance, the abundantly generous and nonjudgmental Corinne Mulvaney has many of Carolina's personal traits; even her physical descriptions recall early photographs of Joyce's mother. In *Marya*, the emotional matrix of Marya's childhood is virtually identical to Carolina's. First Marya loses her father at a young age: "A death in a tavern brawl, a man savagely beaten, a certain alcoholic content in his blood, a certain reputation in the area for making trouble." Marya likewise experiences maternal abandonment and dislocation (as a child Marya overhears her stepmother remark callously, "she's not my kin"), and spends her life on a farm that is virtually identical to the one where Carolina passed her childhood. Lockport becomes the more romantic-sounding "Innisfail," Transit Road becomes "Canal Road," Millersport and the Tonawanda become "Shaheen Falls" and "Shaheen Creek." Descriptive passages in the novel evoke both the austere natural beauty and the underlying sense of menace at the heart of Joyce Carol Oates's world:

> Along the Innisfail Pike the countryside changed: now it was acre upon acre of farmland, sloping hills, woods, fields of wheat, rye,

corn, soybeans, acres of apple trees, pear trees, the wide mud-
colored Shaheen Creek. . . . Marya remembers the Canal Road
stretching between Innisfail and Shaheen Falls: nine miles of un-
paved dirt and gravel, all but impassable in winter, so dusty by mid-
June it had to be oiled. . . . Fields, pastureland, barbed-wire fencing.
Then the old bridge above the Shaheen Creek that so frightened
Marya she frequently dreamed of it: the planks rattling beneath the
car's wheels, the rust-streaked girders trembling.

In her 1987 essay "Beginnings" Joyce claimed that she wrote the novel before she learned how Carolina's father had died, and was later astonished to
learn that "the story I believed I had invented recapitulated an incident in
my mother's early life." She found this intuitive process fascinating and mysterious: "Somehow, without knowing what I did, without knowing, in fact,
that I was doing anything extraordinary at all, I had written my mother's
story by way of a work of prose fiction I had invented." What Joyce did not
mention is that a similar instance of her novelistic "intuition" had occurred
almost twenty years earlier. In A Garden of Earthly Delights (1967), she had
written a scene that also bears a striking resemblance to the circumstances of
her grandfather's murder. Centered upon Clara Walpole, who is born into a
family of migrant workers, the novel devotes several of its early chapters to
Clara's father, Carleton. A man whose youthful strength has been drained by
poverty and the struggle to support his large family, Carleton slips away from
the workers' camp with a friend for a night of drinking in a local tavern. In a
powerful scene that capitalizes on Joyce's strengths as a young writer—her
sense of pacing and drama, her ability to dramatize the complex, often
violent psychological conflicts of uneducated and inarticulate characters—
Carleton becomes involved in a brutal fight with his friend Rafe. Like Joyce's
grandfather, Carleton is attacked with a blunt object, but in the novel the
outcome is reversed: it is Carleton who wins the fight, knifing Rafe in the
chest and escaping any serious physical injury. Since "Carlton" was the name
of Joyce's paternal grandfather, and since the character suffers an experience
similar to that of her mother's father, Carleton Walpole suggests an intriguing composite of both men, an emblem for the background of poverty and
violence on both sides of her family.

A Garden of Earthly Delights, with its title's grimly ironic reference to the
famous triptych of Hieronymous Bosch, also represents an early, extended portrait of an American "Eden" whose economic system relies on the exploitation
of impoverished migrant workers. Although the scene of Carleton's barroom
fight is set in Florida, it is based on Joyce's early memories of the workers
who passed through upstate New York during her childhood. Frederic Oates

remembered that area farmers started bringing people up from the South, sometimes building small shanties for them as temporary housing. Desperately poor, these people worked for extremely low wages, and their situation made an impression on Joyce, leaving her with "a strong memory of those migrant workers" more than forty years later. These memories also figure in one of her most powerful early stories, "First Views of the Enemy," in which a middle-class woman suffers a delusional, near-hysterical fear of the workers in her area, whom she perceives as the "enemy" threatening her economic and psychological security. Whether dealing with impoverished rural areas or inner-city slums, Joyce's fiction would always exhibit a special sensitivity to the plight of economically disenfranchised Americans, a trait that came directly out of her own early life and the far greater deprivations experienced by her parents and grandparents.

Joyce has often said that a primary motive behind her writing is her yearning to memorialize the past, especially the lives of her mother and father. The rural world of her mother's childhood and the youthful aspirations of both her parents inspired in their daughter a romantic longing to cast the turbulent flux of a lost era into the enduring shapeliness of art. In A *Garden of Earthly Delights* and in other early novels such as *them* (1969) and *Wonderland* (1971), Joyce reached back to the 1930s as the dramatic focus of her narratives, evoking the world of the Depression and its aftermath as a landscape marked by the passionate energies and sharp deprivations out of which her young protagonists tried to forge their own identities and control their own fates. In contrast to the heroines of her later, more explicitly feminist work, Joyce cast young males in these novels as her autobiographical counterparts, or soul mates. Out of her own early sense of self she created sensitive, highly intelligent idealists who experience a variety of fates: suffering defeat by the materialistic forces of midcentury American culture, like Swan Revere in A *Garden of Earthly Delights*; pursuing the American dream through love and violence, like Jules Wendall in *them*; or forging a self through the sheer force of will, like *Wonderland*'s Jesse Vogel, a Depression-era orphan who becomes a celebrated neurosurgeon.

At the heart of these early protagonists' experiences, however, is their author's insistent homage to the bedrock natural and social reality from which they arose. In an early interview, Joyce remarked that behind all her fiction lay an "imperishable sense of reality" derived primarily from the natural settings and economically straitened circumstances of her family background—a reality she has transcribed faithfully and sometimes obsessively in her fiction. "The real clue to me," she added, "is that I'm like certain people who are not really understood—Jung and Heidegger are good examples—people of peasant stock, from the country, who then come into a world of literature or philosophy. Part of us is very intellectual, wanting to read all the books in the library—or even wanting to *write* all the books in the library. Then there's the other side of us, which is sheer silence, inarticulate—the silence of nature, of the sky, of pure being."

Though Joyce identified with her highly intelligent young heroes in the early novels, she placed them in a family context that included such earthy characters as Clara, Swan's mother in A *Garden of Earthly Delights*, and Loretta, Jules's mother in *them*. Shortly after *them* was published Joyce told an interviewer, "I have a great admiration for those females who I know from my own life, my background, my family—very strong female figures who do not have much imagination in an intellectual sense, but they're very capable of dealing with life." If Joyce's protagonists, including the heroines of such later novels as *Marya* and *Because It Is Bitter, and Because It Is My Heart* (1990), move like Jesse Vogel out of their rural backgrounds and into the world of academia and the arts, their emotional trajectory often resembles that of F. Scott Fitzgerald's boats against the current, beat back ceaselessly into the past. Similarly, one of Joyce's distinctive fictional worlds—Eden County, "the north country"—has continued to fascinate her primarily because of the ongoing conflict between the bleak reality of its economic and social conditions on the one hand, and the author's identification with the quixotic, passionate strivings of its people on the other. Joyce's sense of the beauty—even the poetry—of that survival has its major paradigm for Joyce in the experience of her parents, Carolina and Frederic: their early hardships, their ultimate endurance. It lends to her work, too, its pervasive sense of mystery, its awareness of "the phantasmagoria of personality," which in her parents' case has represented a personal efflorescence to which the word "survival" scarcely does justice.

The facts of Frederic Oates's early life, when compared with those of Carolina Bush, suggest the basis of their initial attraction and their long, solid marriage. Like his wife, Frederic Oates—born March 30, 1914—suffered an early life marked by poverty, abandonment, and violence.

The Oates family had emigrated from Ireland in the late nineteenth century. Frederic's great-grandfather, Dominic, had married Mary Mullaney; the couple had six children, three sons and three daughters, and the family came to America after Dominic's death, settling in the Buffalo area. Dominic and Mary's youngest son, James, married Caroline Spedding; their son, Carlton, was Frederic Oates's father. As with Carolina's ancestors, there was little in the Oates family background that suggested literary aspirations.

Fred's childhood and adolescence were spent in Lockport, a setting that would become the emotional wellspring of his daughter's fiction. The city of

Lockport lies in the heart of the north country, twenty miles northeast of Buffalo and east of Niagara Falls, and about the same distance south of Lake Ontario. Bisected by the Erie Barge Canal, the city grew up around its original five flights of locks. The locks officially opened on October 26, 1825, when the first two boats passed from the canal's lower level, through the new locks, and into the upper level. (The area was visited that year by General Lafayette, who called the locks "the greatest engineering marvel of the world.") The canal was enlarged by 1862, and a third expansion was completed in 1917; by this time the locks were 328 feet long and 45 feet wide, with a 12-foot depth of water over the sills that permitted boats as long as 300 feet and carrying up to two thousand tons of freight to pass through.

This city and its "engineering marvel," a centerpiece of Joyce's early memories, figure importantly in several of her major novels. *Wonderland* employs the city's actual name, whereas in *Marya: A Life* it becomes Innisfail; in *You Must Remember This* (1987), Port Oriskany; in *Foxfire: Confessions of a Girl Gang* (1993), Hammond (although Hammond has a river instead of a canal). In *Wonderland*, Jesse ponders his own identity while standing on the bridge above the locks, staring down at the rushing, turbulent water that seems an emblem of his own patternless existence. While writing *You Must Remember This*, in which certain features of Lockport, including the canal, dominate the landscape of "Port Oriskany" and the life of the novel's heroine, Enid Stevick, Joyce taped a map of her fictional city to the wall above her desk (she followed this procedure for other novels as well) so that in her imagination she could "traverse its streets, ponder its buildings and houses and vacant lots, most of all the canal that runs through it, as it runs through Lockport, New York ... the canal that, in Enid's heightened and often fevered imagination, as in my own, seemed an object of utter ineffable beauty." By using the word "beauty," Joyce added, she "did not mean mere prettiness but something more brutal, possessed of the power to rend one's heart."

A sense of place is important to most novelists, but in Joyce's work the setting is profoundly linked to each major character's sense of self; her fiction is often a means of recovering worlds she has lost, especially the rural setting of her childhood and the city of Lockport. As an adult, she would devote many passages in her journal to recording in precise detail the rooms, houses, neighborhoods, and natural landscapes in which crucial events of her life had transpired. In 1985, after a five-day visit with her parents, Joyce wrote in one entry that she felt "caught in that odd hypnotic trance of (what can I call it? the spell—surely inexplicable to anyone else—of Lockport, NY) the past not quite remembered." During the second night of her visit home, she wrote:

I drove by myself around the city. At dusk. Very slowly. Those streets:
Grand St., Transit St., Green St., Hawley St. (the old ruin—it *is* a
ruin—of the Hawley St. school where, 60 years ago, my father was a
student), Outwater Park, Ontario St.... The old Niagara Hotel,
seedy, run-down. Walking along streets I'd walked 35 years before
looking for—. Lost emotions. Lost feeling. That elusive lost self.
Three times I drove along Grand St., past the house my grandmother had rented.... Yet to think of approaching it as it was in,
say, 1953, or earlier, is to feel a clutch of emotion almost too powerful to contain. And to ascend those stairs! And to enter that small
living room! the kitchen! my grandmother's bedroom & sewing room!

Characteristically, Joyce made pragmatic use of this burst of nostalgia in
her novel *You Must Remember This*, published two years later. Thanking John
Updike for his glowing review of the novel in *The New Yorker*, Joyce wrote
that she was especially pleased Updike had quoted a passage featuring a footbridge, "the very image that was the first thing I had written, in a sort of
white heat, imagining the novel as a recasting of my early adolescence spent
in Lockport.... [M]y grandmother with whom I was extremely close lived on
a street very like the Stevicks', in a house very like theirs." The footbridge, she
recalled, was "high above the Erie canal and precariously close, as it seemed
to me, to a railroad bridge." So haunting to the young Joyce that she often
dreamed about it, the Lockport footbridge makes numerous appearances in
her fiction.

Surrounded by farming communities, Lockport in the 1930s and 1940s
was a city of less than twenty thousand inhabitants; it was dominated by
heavy industry and the workings of the canal. Residential areas featured rows
of plain, sturdy-looking frame houses, little changed today from the years of
Joyce's childhood. Transit Road divided the town in half, north to south; a
portion of the state transit line first established in 1798 for surveying pur-
poses, Transit remains the longest straight-line road in western New York,
leading directly southward to the farming area where Carolina grew up, and
where she and Frederic Oates raised their three children.

Frederic's father, Joseph Carlton Oates, was born July 15, 1892, in Lockport. In 1917 he married Blanche Morningstar, a dark-eyed beauty of eighteen. Blanche would live virtually all her life in Lockport, dying there in 1970
at the age of seventy-six. No photograph of Carlton survives, but there are
several of Blanche, including some from her early life. As Joyce noted in her
journal, they show a "shadowy young woman whose features I seem to have
inherited, in part ... the slightly sunken eyes, the quizzical expression, the
sobriety, stubbornness, penchant for secrecy." Like the home movies taken

when Blanche was in her sixties, these early photographs also suggest the quality of serenity and self-possession, an almost regal poise, that she would maintain throughout her life. Carolina remembered that when she first met her mother-in-law, Blanche was so dignified and well dressed that Carolina felt intimidated.

Yet Blanche's early years were far from placid. She was born April 30, 1894, in Hartland, New York; her family members had changed their name from "Morgenstern" around the time of her birth, and later kept their Jewish background a secret not only from their neighbors but from Blanche and their other daughters as well. In those days, according to Fred Oates, German Jews were placed on a level "just one notch above the blacks." Blanche's marriage was not a happy one: in 1916, Carlton abandoned his wife and two-year-old son, forcing Blanche to move back in with her parents and numerous siblings, who included a brother two months younger than Frederic. (Whenever Blanche was asked about her husband, she would say simply: "The man was no good.") Fred experienced the same sense of alienation in his new household that Carolina had felt as a child when visiting her own siblings.

The household was not a peaceful one. Like Carolina's family, the Morgensterns had little money, and Frederic's childhood was marked by constant moves from one rental property to another. "We moved all over hell's creation—maybe because the rent was due," he recalled. For a while, his mother was forced to work as a maid, and later she found a job in a factory that made fiber tubing. This factory was located in the semi-industrial, working-class area of Lockport known as "Lowertown." Frederic remembered visiting her there when he was five or six, and seeing a maze of belts and pulleys: "The place scared me to look at it." Economic insecurity was compounded by severe family conflicts. Blanche's parents' marriage was a miserable one, plagued by constant arguing. The smoldering bitterness between the couple finally erupted in a scene of such horrific violence that it recalls one of Joyce Carol Oates's more turbulent fictions.

According to both Frederic and Carolina, who knew Blanche's mother well, Grandma Morgenstern was a malicious, hateful woman—"simply nasty," Frederic claimed—who deliberately baited her husband's pathologically jealous temperament. She tormented him by locking the door to her bedroom and, when her husband arrived home, pretending to entertain a lover inside. "She drove him nuts that way," Frederic remembered. One of his uncles owned a shotgun, which he kept hidden; but the volatile Grandpa Morgenstern eventually found it. "I used to come home nights and he would be sitting on the stairway next to Grandma's bedroom, and it scared the devil out of me. I remember going up the stairs once and almost falling over him— I couldn't imagine what he was doing there." On one of these occasions, while locked out of his wife's bedroom, Grandpa Morgenstern sat with the shotgun cradled on his knees.

One evening Blanche arrived home from work to find the front door locked; she could hear a violent argument raging between her parents upstairs. Grandma Morgenstern was screaming—her husband had begun beating her with a hammer. "My mother started pounding on the front door," Fred remembered. "She'd known something was wrong because the door was never locked, never at any time of the day or night. My grandfather heard her pounding on the door and he quit beating my grandmother and ran down to the basement and shot himself." He had placed the gun barrel beneath his chin and died instantly. Blanche's mother, seriously wounded, hobbled downstairs and unlocked the door for Blanche, who took her mother to the hospital.

It was typical of his grandmother, Frederic Oates observed, that in the aftermath of her husband's suicide she thought only of herself. When he came to visit her in the hospital, she blamed him for what had happened, whining to her grandson, who was about fifteen at the time, "Frederic, why did you ever go away and leave me to that madman?" Upset, Frederic told his uncles what she had said, but they assured him that she'd made exactly the same accusation to each of them. "That's the kind of woman she was," Frederic recalled bitterly. Other family members were similarly unstable. Joyce remembered one of Frederic's uncles as having "that sort of male-Irish-immature-charming-feckless-man-among-men-heavy-drinker-angry-good-natured-unreliable" personality that she would re-create in Corky Corcoran, hero of her 1994 novel, *What I Lived For*. When Joyce was in her late forties, she learned an additional, rather macabre fact about her father's family: asking what Grandpa Morgenstern had done for a living, she was told that he was a gravedigger.

Given this family background, it seems astonishing that Blanche could function as the loving, nurturing mother and grandmother that she did, a paradox that would lead Joyce to wonder if there was any meaningful relationship between personal history and personality. Yet Blanche not only endured but prevailed: she stayed in Lockport, remarried, and pursued her interests in needlework and reading. Unlike the first marriage, her second—to Leo H. Woodside—was a happy one, and she would always be known to Joyce as "Grandma Woodside." Extremely devoted to her grandmother as a child, Joyce remained close to Blanche until her death in 1970. Grandma Woodside, Joyce would later say, was the one person she had loved most after her parents. Their common interest in literature made their bond especially close. It was Blanche who gave Joyce her most important childhood book, an illustrated copy of Lewis Carroll's *Alice in Wonderland* and *Through the*

Looking Glass. When Joyce was fourteen, Blanche gave her a more practical but equally significant gift: her first typewriter.

Blanche's son Frederic had inherited his mother's artistic inclinations, though like her he had little time to develop them. In sixth grade, he started violin lessons in school, then briefly took private lessons with money he earned selling newspapers. Blanche had bought him a violin, and as a high school freshman he played in the school orchestra. But the family's unstable economic circumstances soon dictated that he spend most of his time work-ing, and he was unable to pursue his love of music and reading until after his retirement. Ironically, his artistic aptitude helped him decide to drop out of high school. In his freshman year, Fred had a teacher named Mr. Zimmerman who taught mechanical drawing and art. Fred did so well in the class that Zimmerman recommended him to a former student who worked as a sign painter for the Lockport theaters and who needed an assistant. Fred got the job, working after school and all day on Saturday and Sunday. "They kept pil-ing the work up on me so I didn't go back to school for the second year," he recalled, though he was making only $2.50 a week at first. Tired of working so hard for such low pay, Fred tried to return to school but went only another half-year before quitting again in order to work. Learning the sign-painting trade proved to be a bonus, however, in the hard economic times to come.

Fred worked for several years in a commercial sign shop, then got a better job in the punch press department of the Harrison Radiator Company, a divi-sion of General Motors, in November of 1936; he was twenty-two. Estab-lished in 1910, Harrison's had enjoyed considerable growth through the 1920s by developing a ribbon cellular-type radiator that helped prevent en-gine overheating; the company expanded further in the 1930s, when it began to manufacture heaters and thermostats. Fred felt lucky to have his new job: "I thought when I got a job at Harrison's, I was set." He married Carolina in 1937, and Joyce was born on June 16, 1938.

But Fred's job at Harrison Radiator did not end the young family's eco-nomic worries. The effects of the Depression were especially severe in west-ern New York, and there were constant work layoffs. Soon after Joyce's birth, Fred found himself unemployed. Other families dependent on Harrison's went on welfare, but the Oateses never requested public assistance. Thanks to his early work experience, Fred always had his sign painting to fall back on. For a while he set up shop at home, taking jobs where he could find them. But such employment was far from steady, and at one point, while Joyce was still a toddler, one of his layoffs from Harrison's lasted so long that he moved his family out of John and Lena's farmhouse and into Lockport, where he had found work at a sign shop. The family rented a small apartment on Main Street, but they were forced out when the landlord decided to renovate the building. World War II had begun, and there were housing shortages. "We couldn't find anything else, so we decided to go back to Millersport again and rebuild the farmhouse." Fred planned to alter the structure so that it would accommodate the two families comfortably. But, he remembered, "Money was too short to do any work right then."

As a sign painter, Fred had developed a distinctive style; Joyce observed that "Daddy's signs were always discernible" in the area. (An example of his work survived into the 1990s: on Fred and Carolina's Transit Road mailbox.) Despite Fred's talent, there was little artistic satisfaction in painting the signs. During the long winters he often had to work outside, in brutal cold, doing lettering on the sides of trucks, old barns, and garages. Sometimes his work would be washed away by a sudden rainstorm, and he would have to do the lettering all over again. There was a great deal of competition, so that Fred often had to lower his prices to the point where he was practically giving his work away. He was always glad to get rehired by Harrison's, where both the pay and the working conditions were better.

Joyce's dominant recollection of her father's life during her childhood is this constant scrambling for work. The focus of life, she remarked, was much more on economics than would be the case for a middle- or upper-class family. There was constant talk and anxiety "about the salary, the raises and overtime, whether there would be a strike or a layoff."

On one occasion Fred tried to make extra money on the side, but the results were both comical and disastrous. He'd decided to start raising pigs, and quickly discovered that he couldn't control the animals. Years later he told his grown-up daughter about "the pigs burrowing under the fence, running out onto Transit Road, his catching them by hand after much difficulty, and throwing each of them (large creatures) back over the fence so that they landed heavily on their sides and the 'earth shook.' Shortly afterward he killed them, and slaughtered them, and 'cured' them with some sort of salt-gun injection; and hung the meat up in the barn; and the meat rotted." Joyce noted in her journal that Fred's telling of this story to Joyce and her husband in 1977, while visiting some of Joyce's friends in an affluent suburb of Detroit, made the anecdote seem hilarious: "I know, however, that the situation wasn't funny. He tried to raise pigs because we were very poor. It was poverty behind the desperation . . . and it was a sort of tragedy that, after all the humiliating effort, the meat rotted."

Fred's work-oriented life meant there was little leisure time left over for reading or music, but there was one interest that he never relinquished: his fascination with airplanes. As a teenager, in the years after World War I, he recalled standing out and watching an old war plane flying over. "It was the most beautiful sight I ever saw. You could see the struts, the wings—it was great." He was working at a sign shop, making five dollars a week by then, when a barnstormer set up business on the outskirts of Lockport. "I took my five dollars out there—my whole week's pay. The flight was only eight or ten minutes, just up and around the city, but boy, I felt it was well worth it." Years passed before he could get up enough money for flying lessons, but eventually he earned his license and would sometimes rent a small plane on Sundays for fifteen dollars an hour, taking up family members for rides around the Lockport and Buffalo areas. He and his flying buddies also enjoyed flying low to "buzz" friends' and neighbors' houses. In a poem dedicated to Fred, "Abandoned Airfield, 1977," Joyce later evoked the romance of her father's flying, recalling "the jarring thud of the plane's wheels / and the rightness of the cindery earth / and the sunburnt alarm of children who must witness / their fathers riding the air, / garish and frail as kites." She surely had her father in mind, too, when she placed Gideon Bellefleur, the hero of her novel *Bellefleur* (1980), in the cockpit of a Hawker Tempest for his last, suicidal flight, during which he experiences the euphoria of the plane's speed and power before deliberately crashing into the stone walls of Bellefleur Manor. In *Man Crazy* (1997), the portrayal of Ingrid Boone's father, a Navy pilot and flying enthusiast, also draws upon Fred's youthful love of aviation.

Another early pursuit that fed more directly into his daughter's work was Fred's interest in boxing. Before he married Carolina, Fred remembered, "a friend of mine used to be in the Golden Gloves, and he used me for a punching bag a few times." He acknowledged that he was prone to get in fights as a teenager, sometimes making an unwise choice of opponents and getting badly beaten. "I had a little trouble holding back, I'll tell you that. I used to blow up real easily." This friend, Archie Burley, was a fairly good middleweight boxer who hoped for a professional career; it was Burley who taught Fred "to pick my opponents like any smart person would." Unfortunately for Burley, he failed to take his own advice. "He was hurt very badly—he was mismatched," Joyce remembered. "He had a manager who didn't really care much about him." Some years later, Burley committed suicide. Joyce would draw upon Burley when developing one of her most complex characterizations: Felix Stevick, the failed boxer in her novel *You Must Remember This*. "Archie Burley and his failure, his suicide, gave me the sense of boxing being about failure," she observed. Being a titleholder may be wonderful, she added, but the losing side of such contests was what engaged her as a writer of fiction.

Another, more shadowy relationship in Frederic's life also raised the possibility of physical combat, though in a completely unexpected way. Fred's awareness of his father had always been darkened by Carlton's early abandonment of the family and by vague hints of even more sinister transgressions.

By the time Fred was a teenager in Lockport, Carlton was known to be living in Buffalo, and the young Fred was told, "If any man had done to my mother what your father did to *your* mother, I would kill him. I'd look him up and kill him." Yet no one, including Blanche, would ever tell Fred exactly what Carlton might have done. Preoccupied with raising his own family, he simply put his father out of his mind until the mid-1940s. One night, while Fred was visiting the cafe where Carolina had once worked, he was accosted by an angry-looking man who said, "I understand you were looking for me," and who then challenged him to a fight. Fred, now a married man of thirty, was astonished to learn that the man was his father. "I found out who he was and wouldn't fight," Fred recalled. "He was in his fifties. I wouldn't hit the guy, even if he had been a stranger." Fred and Carlton kept in touch after that, until Carlton's death in 1956, but they never developed a close relationship.

Fred's interests in flying and boxing were put aside almost wholly during the early 1940s. On Christmas day, 1943, when Joyce was five, Fred and Carolina's second child, Fred Junior—nicknamed "Robin" as a boy—was born; in addition to the economic strains of a growing family there was concern that Fred might be called up for service. Fortunately, he had been rehired at Harrison Radiator shortly after World War II began. The company had become involved in defense work, manufacturing war materials such as heat exchangers, oil coolers, radiators, and thermostats for use in ships, tanks, and gun carriages. Involved in this work, Fred had a deferment, but there was always the chance that it might be canceled.

Fred managed to avoid the war, continuing to do defense work at Harrison's. Another major job also kept him busy during this period: gradually the war had brought better economic times, and he was finally able to begin renovation work on John and Lena's old farmhouse, creating a dwelling with separate apartments for the two families. Fred did most of the reconstruction work himself, learning as he went along through trial and error, and Joyce recalled hearing the sound of her father crawling around the attic and hammering on the roof. Fred gutted the house and took the inside stairs completely out, adding an exterior stairway so that the house would have two private entrances. The outside walls, visible in family photographs, were covered in artificial siding, made of asphalt. "It was supposed to be fireproof composition board," Fred remembered. "It had speckles on it and grit, like roofing material." (In *Marya: A Life*, Marya's adoptive parents "nailed up asphalt siding so clever in its design and grainy texture it looked from the road like genuine red brick.") After the work was done, Fred and his family took the quarters upstairs, while John and Lena stayed downstairs. Both families had more privacy after the renovation, cooking and eating their meals separately until after Grandpa Bush died in 1950. At that time, Joyce was "farmed out down-stairs" into a larger and more private bedroom.

Having suffered early abandonment by his father and an unstable family environment as a child, Fred had determined to take the opposite route with his own children. He became an extremely protective father; he gave an impression of sternness to neighborhood children and was still capable of losing his temper. One winter, when Joyce was three or four, Grandpa Bush had decided impulsively, and perhaps under the influence of hard cider, to enhance the thrill of little Joyce's snow sledding. He started to attach her sled to the rear bumper of Fred's car in order to pull her along Transit Road (already, by then, a fairly busy highway), but Fred came running out before this adventure could get under way. "Jesus, I was so mad at him I could have killed him. I laid him right out, that day. . . . I could just see him stepping on the brakes and what would happen to her—she would just shoot underneath. Oh, God." Another glimpse of Fred as a young father appears in fictional form in Joyce's novel *Wonderland*. Fleeing the oppressive household of his adoptive father, Dr. Karl Pedersen of Lockport, Jesse Vogel stops along a country road, where he sees a young family "who lived in a nearby farmhouse on the highway." Jesse sees Carolina's old swing, and the chickens picking in the grass; he then glimpses Joyce at age three or four, talking with her mother. As Jesse gets closer to Joyce and Carolina, however, the young Fred Oates appears: "He was tall, husky, with his shirtsleeves rolled up past his elbows. His hair was black. . . . Jesse saw a cautious, springy threat to his step, in the very look of his arms." Backing away, Jesse thinks, "In such a way . . . does a man protect himself and his family. In such a way does a man, a normal man, exclude the rest of the world."

In a 1992 afterword to the novel, Joyce verified that hers is the "young family in a green swing behind a farmhouse," adding: "The uses we make of our homesicknesss!" Mythologizing her parents' and grandparents' Erie County world as "Eden County" in her earliest fiction, and populating the north country with her fictional towns of Yewville, Derby, Marsena, and Port Oriskany in much of her later work, Joyce wrote out of an intense nostalgia for her parents' vanished world and also from a desire to evoke the "imperishable reality" that lay behind it. In an early interview, questioned about the mythical overtones of "Eden County," Joyce said bluntly that the area was hardly a "paradise lost. It's pretty bad, as a matter of fact." She added that intellectuals and writers "have forgotten if we ever knew the toughness of the world where there isn't any money. This is the basic reality. It's economic."

Yet Joyce's nostalgia for the distant past has only intensified with time, partly because of the difficult struggles her family endured. Her awareness, like her writing, seems always to include and revere the past, both its places and its people. In her letters and journals, and most important in her fiction, Joyce would remain a pilgrim who returned often to the north country of upstate New York. As one of her poems, "Our Dead," put it, "nothing surrenders / there is no forgetting / the head is a net dragging decades / dustballed and frayed." The poem's most moving stanza suggested the poignant way in which Joyce's childhood would continue to nourish her imagination:

> it is immortal, this rustling of childhood
> the odor of damp wool
> of sickrooms sour and pleasant
> the disorder of blankets imagined as tents
> the dampness of newspapers and a father's wintry embrace.

In another poem, "Dreaming America"—which is dedicated to Carolina—Joyce memorialized the vanishing of her mother's rural world in a way that makes it similarly representative of a major swath of her writing. The poem begins, "When the two-lane highway was widened / the animals retreated," and "When the cornfields were bulldozed / the farmhouses turned to shanties; / the barns fell; / the silos collapsed." Joyce herself would become, as an adult, one of the poem's travelers, amazed and bemused by the north country's changing landscape: "*Where did the country go?*—cry the travelers, soaring / past."

2

"The Girl Who Wrote on the Edges"
1938–50

Within a few minutes I can transport myself to that world, Millersport when I was about 5 or 6, but I can't recall myself in it, very little dialogue, few meetings with other people. It's all a scene, a setting, a landscape awaiting population. Which perhaps accounts for my conviction that in most good writing the setting is one of the characters, one of the most important characters. It speaks. It lives.

—*Journal*, April 6, 1976

Although Joyce Carol Oates enjoyed a childhood anchored by an emotionally secure family life, her early years were punctuated by physical and psychological terrors that would haunt her as an adult and inform much of her fiction. Life on the Millersport farm offered many of the same idyllic qualities that had eased the pain of Carolina's own childhood, but the harsher realities of the north country—especially to a child as sensitive as Joyce—would produce lasting effects and help account for the portrayal of an unstable and often fearsome reality that characterizes her work and that has bewildered, and at times even repulsed, some critics and readers, even as others have applauded her willingness to deal with the complex and sometimes painful nature of working-class life. Her childhood experiences clearly gave rise to the paradoxical apprehension of the world that marked her adult sensibility: we inhabit a random, often frightening reality marked by ceaseless flux, violent dislocations, ugly surprises; and yet we manage, in D. H. Lawrence's sense of the phrase, not only to "come through," but to experience a nostalgic adult yearning to revisit and re-create that early, turbulent world, to recall its austere beauty as well as its anxiety and terror.

Like most people, Joyce retained a handful of images from her first few years, even from the time when Fred and Carolina were living in Lockport. In

1978, she wrote in her journal: "Sometimes I have such vivid memories! Going back to the first year, evidently, so my mother says, when I describe certain impressionistic scenes . . . the kitchen of an old, rented, forgotten house, the stairway, etc." In 1982, she again reached back to the distant past: "My mind fixes upon old memories. Snatches of conversations. A mystery about to be revealed. The glimpse of a back yard from a forgotten window or doorway. . . . Living on Main Street, Lockport. Visiting my grandmother on Grand Street. Then elsewhere. Always rented flats, apartments. Woodframe houses." She also recalled her "handsome father with his head of thick black hair, leaning against a glider in some forgotten meadow, on some forgotten festival Sunday afternoon."

Such early memories were pleasant ones, but she acknowledged that she tended to block out uglier recollections. One day when Joyce was seven, she and her father, along with two-year-old Robin, were returning from a visit to Grandma Woodside's house when they noticed a crowd had gathered around the Erie Canal bridge, at Richmond Avenue. They stopped just in time to witness a man's body pulled from the water by a large hook, "and the hook sank into the man's body, into his back . . . and one of the policemen had turned aside, gagging." Many years later, when Joyce was forty, her father recalled this early event and "seemed surprised that I didn't remember, but indeed I didn't—don't—because, he said, it seemed to have made an impression on me at the time." Twelve more years would pass before, in 1990, the memory would be recast as the powerful opening scene of *Because It Is Bitter, and Because It Is My Heart*, when "Little Red" Garlock's body is hauled out of the Cassadaga River. Like the unconscious awareness of her grandfather's murder that she dramatized in *A Garden of Earthly Delights* (1967), this incident suggests a suppression of violent memories that later found their way back into consciousness through the workings of her novelistic imagination.

This process of deliberately recalling the pleasant memories of childhood while blocking out more painful incidents may account, in part, for the sharp divergence between Joyce's autobiographical commentary on her childhood, most of which stresses its positive, idyllic aspects, and her dramatizations of childhood experiences in her fiction, which often feature harrowing scenes of violence, molestation, and other forms of victimization at the hands of adults. In a 1990 *Life* magazine article, for instance, Joyce meditated on a snapshot of herself at age six, posed in front of a Christmas tree. Though acknowledging that in 1944 the war news was monitored anxiously by her parents, she writes that "Christmas 1944 is, for me, a time of family happiness." Some of the details seem drawn from a Norman Rockwell painting: "I remember the excitement of Daddy bringing home the Christmas tree . . . and the ceremony of trimming it. I remember the pungent aroma of the tree's needles, and I remember the box of Christmas ornaments taken from a closet shelf. . . . Was anything, except the spectacle of Christmas presents, more wonderful than this box of ornaments, to be added to over the years? Was any family activity more thrilling than the annual trimming?" In a similar essay Joyce meditated on another snapshot, this one from a summer day in 1949, when she was eleven. The photograph had been taken in the rear yard of the farmhouse, and she comments that "by way of the snapshot, as if unlocking its mysterious power, I can 'see' into other parts of the yard . . . I can 'see' the old barn; the fields beyond. . . ." She closes by expressing gratitude for the photographs, exclaiming: "What wonders the lowly 'snapshot' yields!"

Other snapshots from the 1940s, most of them taken with Fred's box-style Brownie camera, verify that Joyce enjoyed many of the typical childhood pursuits of her time and place. A wintertime shot pictures her, at age four or five, perched atop a sled, bundled in a parka with a pointed hood framing her smiling, elfin face; others, taken in the summer, show her sitting on a flat white rock ("Joyce's rock," as Fred and Carolina came to call it) in Tonawanda Creek, or doing the backstroke in the pool at Lockport's Outwater Park. In others, Joyce and Robin play in the family swing. There is also a shot taken in May 1941, when Joyce was nearly three: she sits on the grass with Carolina, her attention taken by a kitten her mother holds in her arms—suggesting an early beginning to Joyce's lifelong love of cats.

In 1975, when Joyce was thirty-six, she would reflect in her journal on the essential happiness of her early childhood: "I begin to see as I grow older how very fortunate I was in my early years: a mother, a father, a grandmother (my paternal grandmother) who loved me very much. And rural surroundings, beautiful surroundings . . . beautiful in their simple way." As she has remarked often, the family might have lacked money, but Joyce wasn't really aware of being deprived, since almost everyone in the area lived in similar circumstances. By the mid-1940s, Fred's job at Harrison Radiator had brought his family out of poverty and "into a sort of part-middle-class as a consequence of that great force, the American labor movement." Fred had managed to get transferred out of the punch press department and into the engineering tool room; always energetic and ambitious, he began going to night school, taking courses in trigonometry and related subjects, so that he could go into tool-and-die design. Fred had owned a secondhand, canary-yellow Studebaker President, but by 1948 he had bought a late-model Pontiac sedan, of which he was extremely proud. And life wasn't all work: he continued to enjoy airplanes, and sometimes even flew in gliders that were borne up by plane to a height of 1,500 feet, then released. Carolina began to enjoy such leisure-time activities as gardening and flower arranging, occasionally winning prizes for her arrangements in local contests. Joyce took part in 4-H and other activities, and in a 1989 letter to John Updike she recalled that she was able to take piano lessons through most of her childhood and adolescence, reaching "a plateau of enthusiastic incompetence at about age 17."

Even as a young girl, Joyce preferred solitary pursuits. Her love of hiking, bicycle riding, and exploring, which she would retain as an adult, had their beginnings in childhood idleness. "I recall myself as a girl," she wrote in her journal, "hiking/wandering/prowling for hours, along the creek; through woods, pastures, farmland; nearly always alone, and drawn to aloneness. The old farmhouses/barns. . . . The Tonawanda Creek, the eerie underside of the bridge. Tramping for miles. No thought to it. And, in Lockport, much of the same—just walking, walking." In a 1993 letter she noted, "Because, I assume, I grew up in the country . . . most of my waking life when I wasn't actually in school was in 'nature'—meaning primarily silence, and solitude." Joyce particularly enjoyed exploring the farm and the surrounding landscape: the old barn (her parents later used it as a garage) and the chicken coop, the pear orchards, the field where Fred grew potatoes, the family vegetable garden. She felt a particular attraction to the many abandoned houses in the area, with their half-rotted barns, silos, and corncribs. In 1995, comparing these vivid recollections to the paintings of Edward Hopper and Charles Burchfield, she remarked that "I have never found the visual equivalent of these abandoned farmhouses of upstate New York, of northern Erie County, in the area of the long, meandering Tonawanda Creek and the Barge Canal."

The Tonawanda and the Erie Canal were particular sources of fascination. Like the lake-effect weather, the creek was unpredictable. Though placid and slow-moving in the summer, it could also be dangerous: "a child could drown in it. Because in flood time it has the power to uproot trees, docks, even parts of houses, and to bear them away in a fury of mud-brown churning water"— a phenomenon she would dramatize in her prize-winning early story, "Upon the Sweeping Flood." As for the canal, it was the dominant, bisecting topographical feature of Lockport: "To walk along the canal's high banks, on cracked and littered pavement, gazing down at the foaming, black water below, is mesmerizing," she recalled.

Since most of Joyce's childhood wanderings were conducted in solitude, she reflected that "I must have been a lonely child." Though Robin was only five years younger, Joyce's life was essentially that of an only child, since they shared few interests. Fred Oates Jr. (who later shed his childhood nickname) said that "I remember very little of [Joyce]. The only thing that really stands out in my mind was that she was always in her room doing her homework." Joyce herself once wrote, "My own brother and I share virtually no interests and do not speak the same language at all apart from our upstate New York accents." Although Joyce later could not recollect her baby brother's arrival on Christmas day, 1943, Carolina reminisced about that day during a holiday visit to her daughter in 1987: "I remember it as if it had happened yesterday. Robin was born, and Daddy brought you down to the hospital to see us, and you were wearing a green coat Grandma Woodside had made you, and when I saw your coat was buttoned crooked I knew your father had buttoned it. You looked frightened . . . excited."

Though Joyce and her brother were not close, there were neighborhood kids with whom Joyce shared childhood adventures, mostly out of doors. Her first and closest childhood friend was Jean Windnagle, whose family lived in a house adjacent to John and Lena's property. Unlike Joyce and her family, the Windnagles lived in outright poverty. Jean's father was alcoholic, abusive, and chronically unemployed; her mother was a factory worker who bore the entire burden of caring for her husband and five children. Since the Oateses were better off financially, Jean remembered, Joyce "usually had more things than I did. Sometimes, she would give me some of her things, such as erasers or pencils." Jean had a sharp awareness, however, that her family was held in low regard by Fred and Carolina. "[Joyce's] mother was friendly and nice," Jean noted, "but gave the impression of being a little snobbish. She used to get upset if I picked any apples off her Delicious apple tree. [Joyce's] father was quiet and reserved. He had a stern, distinguished look about him that made me keep my distance from him. I felt like he was going to scold me for something, although he was never mean. . . . Her family was good to me, but I knew not to overstep my boundaries."

A year older than Joyce, Jean shared her sense of daring and love of mischief, though she also remembered Joyce's absorption in reading and writing. Jean, on the other hand, "was more into playing baseball, climbing trees and being a tomboy." Since both Joyce and Jean were plagued by little brothers, "We used to think of ways to stop our brothers from always following us. We had a spot in the woods that we made into a fort. We would make holes in the ground and cover [them] up with blankets and hope that our brothers or Joyce's cousin would fall into [the holes] if they tried to get into our fort. At Halloween we would make a dummy person and stuff him with leaves. We would take him to somebody's doorstep and leave him and then knock on the door and run." Sometimes the two best friends would simply roam through the fields, looking for snakes and mice. Jean also remembered that they would throw rocks into Tonawanda Creek, wanting to scare the fish away so the fishermen couldn't catch them. "The fishermen would get very upset with us."

Carolina Oates recalled being frightened by one of Joyce and Jean's adventures. The girls had decided to camp out one night down by the creek. Then "it was starting to rain and thunder . . . and I was really worried, so I went down and here they were in this little fort. It was just something they had made to keep the rain out. . . . I brought Joyce home. I couldn't believe they were doing that." For all her apparent shyness, Joyce was a daring child: "Until the relatively mature age of 11," she recalled, "I did many absurd, pointless, dangerous things while 'exploring' the countryside near my family's farm in upstate New York, and I marvel that I didn't seriously injure or kill myself."

In her journal, Joyce once mused that she would like to write "one of my 'crystallizations-around-a-theme' essays: THE SECRETS OF CHILDHOOD. Activities of children of which parents know nothing." One of her childhood secrets was a hiding place she kept in a lilac tree, not far from the back door and the window of the washroom; an oddly shaped branch formed "a kind of seat, or swing." The recollection of this particular secret came to her in 1982, in May, when "the scent of lilacs is overpowering. Sensuous and intoxicating but also ethereal. 'Pure.' " This "pure" memory, however, suggests a model for one of Joyce's most disturbing early stories, "The Molesters," which begins with the child-narrator perched in a lilac tree. Gradually, the story reveals her molestation by a fisherman at a nearby creek—an event drawn from perhaps the darkest incident in Joyce's own childhood. In "The Molesters," the girl has "a little chair in the lilac tree made by three branches that come together. I like to sit here and hide." Another of the autobiographical details is the girl's indifference to a doll she received from her grandmother: "I never remember it or think about it," the girl says, and she describes "its eyes staring as if they saw something that frightened them." Carolina Oates remembered that her daughter, unlike most girls, had no interest in dolls. Grandma Woodside gave Joyce a large, expensive doll for Christmas when Joyce was five, but "Joyce was really afraid of the doll. It just wasn't her thing." Joyce gave the doll away to another girl.

Joyce incorporated another of her childhood "secrets" in a much later story, "Why Don't You Come Live with Me It's Time." Based in part on Joyce's relationship with Grandma Woodside, it includes a scene in which the girl narrator negotiates a dangerous bridge crossing late at night; the bridge, only partway completed, comprises a few ten-inch steel beams, with a river far below. This stunt "has its exact parallel in things I'd done, usually with other children," she wrote in her journal. In an autobiographical essay, she recalled the incident: "I remember crawling on hands and knees across the skeletal, rusted girders of an old bridge above Tonawanda Creek, trying not to glance into the creek bed below, where jagged rocks and boulders poked above the water's surface, a possibly fatal place to fall." On another occasion, when Joyce was ten or eleven, she was playing with Jean Windnagle and another neighborhood child, David Judd, when the children began daring each other to jump off the Judds' roof. Joyce recalled that only she had been foolhardy enough to take the dare. "And what if I'd shattered my legs? broken my neck? twisted my spine? banged my silly head? to what purpose?" She recalled that when she hit the ground, "I felt the force through the soles of my feet like a sledgehammer blow reverberating up through my spine, neck, head. My friends changed their minds about jumping and I was left with a dazed, headachy elation."

Joyce also remembered exploring a boarded-up cider mill built on a bank of the Tonawanda. "I would push through a rear cellar window into the mill, frequently cutting myself on broken glass and exposed nails. Everywhere inside were cobwebs, grime, fantastical machines in various stages of rust and decrepitude." (This incident would form the basis of her short story "In the Warehouse," in which a young girl murders an older bully by pushing her from a second-floor ledge.) Joyce recalled the thrill of "getting to a window, jumping up to balance myself on my forearms, staring from this height at the creek below, or at the very house I lived in. Thinking with childish satisfaction, *So, this is how it is!*"

Until she was twelve, the focus of Joyce's life beyond the farm was the one-room schoolhouse she attended with Jean Windnagle and a motley assortment of other children in the area, including some hulking farm boys more than twice Joyce's size. There was a great deal of bullying, and even the short walk to the school—sometimes accompanied by Jean—became a test of Joyce's survival skills. "The other students, particularly the boys, were very rough, really cruel kids. A lot of things frightened me, but I had to face it day after day." Because the area was rural and "everybody intermarried," Joyce said, many of the kids were mentally retarded and the older kids would bully the younger. In her journal, she recalled witnessing "So many brutal, meaningless acts . . . incredible cruelty, profanity, obscenity . . . even (it was bragged) incest between a boy of about 13 and his 6-year-old sister . . . things done to animals." Merely riding to school on the bus became a hellish experience:

> Retarded children grown big and nasty. The extraordinary things they would say on the school bus, to very young children, about sex, sexual behavior . . . giggling, gloating, rolling their eyes. Only by focusing upon the stupidity (and the inaccuracy) of such things have I been able, over the years, to draw out the poison drop by drop; for this was an underworld, a child's world of which my parents knew nothing. Even when I and a few others were tormented at school, our fears were disregarded by adults who simply didn't *know*.

In dealing with bullies, Joyce's assets were her cunning and her speed: "I could run very fast. 'She runs like a deer,' I can remember one of my tormentors exclaiming." Joyce used the memory in her 1969 novel, *them*, in which Jules Wendall "got constant practice in running because older kids chased him for long, breathless, speechless minutes. They gave up in sullen admiration, never catching him. They said, 'He runs like a deer!' Sometimes he turned back upon them with his fierce eyes." In *Marya: A Life* (1986), Marya contemplates the terrors of certain unsafe areas, "no-man's-lands, limbos of a sort, places where language did not prevail and the only protection was flight, if you could run fast enough; or submission, if you couldn't."

The primitive nature of the school and the roughness of her older male classmates encouraged the already bookish and introverted Joyce to follow her solitary inclinations. Even though the quality of education in the school "wasn't too wonderful," Joyce would later report, she managed to distinguish herself at a very young age and to begin her lifelong habit of winning prizes. She entered a church contest at age ten that involved the memorization of Bible verses; Joyce memorized three hundred of them, beginning with the Book of John, and won a week at a Methodist Bible camp near Lake Ontario. (The camp turned out to be a "dreadful place: the other children weren't very Christian.") She also won a spelling bee sponsored by the *Buffalo Evening News*, but this time the prize was more to her liking: her first dictionary, which quickly became a source of fascination. And she excelled in her schoolwork. "She was always above average," Jean Windnagle recalled. "I don't remember her getting anything less than an A or B+." Another friend from the one-room schoolhouse, Nelia Pynn, remembered that Joyce was ten when they met: "My very first impressions of Joyce were of her extremely high intelligence and her gentleness, kindness and helpfulness. . . . She was different from the other students because of her intellect. I knew it was rare to have such a gifted student in our small rural school." She added that Joyce was "a voracious reader" and "always had a book under her arm."

Except for the addition of electricity, the school was little improved from the years when Carolina had attended. Joyce recalled it as "a rough-hewn, weatherworn, uninsulated clapwood building on a crude stone foundation." It lacked indoor plumbing; the students used insect-ridden outside toilets that the larger kids deliberately tipped over during play periods. Inside the schoolroom, the wood-frame walls were decorated with a spelling chart, a display of world flags, a portrait of Abraham Lincoln. Coats and jackets hung from a hook on one wall; there were several high windows with shades, two blackboards, a supply shelf partly covered by a makeshift curtain. Nelia Pynn remembered that the room was so cold in the winter that the children often wore their coats and gloves during the day, sitting at wooden desks fastened together in rows. "The boys outnumbered the girls," she added. "Most of us came from lower middle-class families whose fathers were laborers or farmers and whose mothers were homemakers."

Jean Windnagle recalled their teacher, Mrs. Dietz, as "a nice matronly lady, and pleasant." Joyce liked Mrs. Dietz, too, remembering her as "very husky, very big," physical qualities that probably came in handy, since she managed all eight grades by herself and spent much of her energy in controlling the bigger, more boisterous students. A photograph taken inside the schoolroom shows Mrs. Dietz as a round-faced, capable-looking woman, surrounded by twenty of her students—including Joyce at about age ten, smiling and attractive with long, wavy dark hair.

It was in the fourth grade, about the time this picture was taken, that a sexual assault against Joyce took place, an incident she later recalled as a "semi-molestation." One morning before school, a group of the dreaded farm boys cornered her near the schoolhouse. She remembered that "[to] be dragged, terrified, desperately resisting, in the direction of the boys' outhouse, to the accompaniment of collective jeering and laughter, was a nightmare experience for younger girls." Joyce was "mauled" rather than raped, and the incident "was one of psychic violence primarily"; but even in 1993 the assault was still "so vivid in my memory, surrounded by such powerful inchoate emotions, it's as if it happened only a few years ago." After the attack, Joyce was verbally threatened, "ordered not to tell." The incident left her "with so profound a sense of helplessness and estrangement that I seem to accept the ill-will of others as a natural fact of life." It later served as the basis for the terrifying attack on Marya Knauer before she goes off to college: "She remembers, afterward, one of them prying her legs apart—she remembers him prodding and jabbing at her—trying to enter her—trying to force his penis in her—but she might have squirmed free, arching her back, or one of the others hauled him away." The assault surely fueled, as well, the wrenching accounts of molestation in such stories as "Blindfold," "Hostage," and "The Molesters," as well as the aura of sexual menace plaguing so many female characters in Joyce's fiction. "It was extremely important for me," Joyce claimed, "to have these early experiences of being a helpless victim, because it allows me to sympathize—or compels me to sympathize—with victims."

Apart from her ability to outrun her bullies, Joyce also had vigilant parents. "My father more or less protected us from what might have been violence in the raggedy rural area in which we lived," she wrote to her friend Bob Phillips. "I think there must be a profound amnesia about childhood because now and then I remember something vaguely, usually to do with school, and then I forget; but there's very little emotion attached." This remark suggests a measure of denial, but still the bullying she endured made a lasting impression: "Such systematic, tireless, sadistic persecution had the consequence of making me love with a passion the safe, even magical confines of *home* and *schoolroom* (cynosures of gentleness, affection, calm, sanity, books) and, later, *library*. For outside these magical confines, the true brutes, or merely brutish Nature, await us."

During these years, home was the most reliable haven for Joyce. Here the only teasing came from Grandpa Bush, who nicknamed her "Dolly" and often expressed his affection by pulling her hair. Tense or violent moments around the farm were relatively few, and incidents that did occur were typical of life generally in that part of the world. Carolina remembered that one time a drunken man pulled onto the property, parking just outside the house; he promptly fell asleep in the car. The family became increasingly worried, Fred being off at work, but eventually the man woke up and simply drove away. Another incident involved the family next door, the Windnagles. One August afternoon Mr. Windnagle, drunk, became annoyed with his son's dog and gutshot the animal with a .22 rifle. In a poem, "Back Country," Joyce recalled the incident: "Nellie had fled into the road, / yipping pain in ribbons, bright red confetti, / we had never heard anything like it before." Nellie dragged herself to the Oates farmhouse, snapping at Robin when he tried to help. The poem captures the sense of threat posed by Mr. Windnagle's drunkenness and his possession of a gun: "We can't call the police, my mother says, we can't make / trouble my grandmother says, they are thinking of our neighbor's wife / they are thinking of the children, and of the gun." This incident, like many others in Joyce's family history—her grandfather's murder, Grandpa Bush's erratic behavior, random violence in the countryside—were all associated with the abuse of alcohol. "In that world," Joyce has said, "everybody drank," so it isn't surprising that Joyce herself became a lifelong teetotaler.

There were safe havens in Lockport as well. Joyce often visited Grandma Woodside's house, where she basked in Blanche's unconditional love. When Joyce was in her thirties and living in Windsor, Ontario, she and her grandmother were still maintaining a warm, loving correspondence. In one letter, written when Joyce was thirty-one, Grandma Woodside offered a recollection from Joyce's childhood that says much about their relationship: "When you were a little girl 2 or 3 and your mother had occasion to scold you, perhaps telling you you had been naughty, you would always say, 'Grandma says I'm the loveliest girl in all the world' and indeed you still are, darling." In the poem "Snapshot Album" Joyce mourned her grandmother in lines embodying the fierce nostalgia characteristic of her childhood memories:

    In one snapshot there's a dark
squirmy child posed on your grandmother's lap

and who holds the camera?—fixing you there
in a dead woman's arms. It is 1942.
So fleshy, warm. That powdery
smell like waking from a dream you begin
to lose even as you wake, sliding away
swift, anonymous.

Another sacred place in Lockport was the public library. Like Maureen
Wendall in *them*, who feels protected from the violence of her daily existence
when she escapes to the library, Joyce found solace in the presence of books
and the sense of safety the library atmosphere provided. Because her family
could not afford to buy books, the library also became an important source
for her education and her preparation for her own writing career. "Among my
early childhood memories," Joyce wrote, "are hours spent in the children's
section of the Lockport Public Library, a splendid Carnegie-endowed land-
mark building on Main Street. . . . It is not an exaggeration to say that this
handsome and well-stocked library—and by extension the American tradition of the free public library—made my life as a writer possible."

Despite her love of nature, her pranks and explorations with Jean Windnagle, and her typical childhood activities such as piano lessons and 4-H, the
world of books and writing lay at the center of Joyce's childhood experience.
Witnessing and sometimes experiencing the violent unpredictability of life
in the north country, Joyce began cultivating at an early age a literary counter-
world that not only seemed safer but also more focused, dramatic, and compelling than the "raggedy" reality that surrounded her at home and school.
Her early, energetic involvement in literary pursuits, at the expense of more
typical childhood activities, would ultimately lead to her adult sense of herself as an "invisible woman" whose only significant identity lay in her writing
and would help lay the groundwork for her spectacularly productive career.

Among her many beloved childhood books, Joyce has often singled out
Lewis Carroll's *Alice in Wonderland* and *Through the Looking Glass*. The
cherished Christmas gift from Grandma Woodside to her eight-year-old
granddaughter was the focal point of her earliest awareness of literature. She
called her 1946 Junior Library edition, published by Grosset & Dunlap with
oversized pages, large type, and illustrations by John Tenniel, "the first great
book of my life." Carolina remembered that Joyce memorized whole sections
of the book and would walk around the house gleefully reciting them. "I
might have wished to be Alice, that prototypical heroine of our race," Joyce
has written, "but I knew myself too shy, too readily frightened of both the unknown and the known (Alice, never succumbing to terror, is not a real child),

and too mischievous." Later she recognized that she did not really want to be Alice: she wanted to be Lewis Carroll. Clearly, a major theme of Joyce Carol Oates's later fiction was beautifully embodied in Alice's stories: "She managed not simply to survive some very odd, alarming experiences, but to triumph. Everything shifts and changes about her, nothing is very stable . . . but Alice asserts herself." Carroll's achievement, Joyce added, "obviously inspired me in some deep, fundamental way, or in any case affirmed the sovereignty of the imagination."

Beginning at age three or four, even before she could read or write, Joyce had already begun telling stories by way of drawings. She remembered that after "tirelessly" executing her stories in pictures, she would simulate handwriting at the bottom of the page, "being eager to enter adulthood. Wasn't handwriting what adults did?" Some of the drawings were done in ordinary writing tablets, which Joyce filled with human and animal figures "acting out complicated narratives—surprises, chase scenes, mistaken identities, happy endings." Some drawings were brightly colored, in paints or crayon ("I loved my crayolas," she said, "I loved the smell of them"), and executed on whatever kind of paper was available—including a large number done on sandpaper appropriated from her father, who kept it on hand for household repairs.

By the time Joyce was eight and had read the Alice books, she "tried to compose Alice-like novels of my own, with drawings to accompany them." (For a long while, she assumed that books always contained drawings.) "It was all play, sheer whimsical experimentation," she recalled, though she approached her play with a characteristic intensity, producing "several thousand pages of prose" on tablets her parents bought her, then on "real paper" when she received the gift of a toy typewriter. Joyce often read in the poetry anthologies given to her father by Grandma Woodside, and around this time she began writing her own poetry, one example of which is contained in a letter she sent to Grandma Woodside in Lockport. The letter and poem (which are reproduced with misspellings intact) are the first by Joyce that survive:

East Amherst, New York
March 10, 19—

Dear Grandma,

   I wrote these verses for you and Mommy.
   I gave Mommy one.
   But it was a little different. The verses are here, Grandma. There're about numbers up to 13.

   Number's Troubles
      One had to stay in the house,

Two ran away from a mouse,
Three couldn't find her bluse,
Four had to wait for a bus,
Five had to run to the store,
Six made too many fusses,
Seven fell down and made his leg sore,
Eight ate ice cream and wanted more
Nine loved to eat crust,
Ten bought a nice new hat,
Eleven picked some pretty flowers,
Twelve had a pussy cat,
Thirteen sat down and thought
For hours.

> Your loving Granddaughter,
> Joyce Oates.
> P.S. There's a picture for you, too.

The illustration, at the bottom of the sheet, is an elephant carrying a banner in his trunk that proclaims the author's name, "Joyce"; underneath the elephant Joyce wrote the words "Trade Mark" and signed her name. The manuscript shows even at this early age a self-consciousness about her writing: the literary affectation of the date, "19—," the "trademark" implying ownership, the letter's reference to revisions she has made to the poem, and the poem itself with its clever rhymes, varying rhythms, and unexpectedly serious closure. Another manuscript written a couple of years later, a song titled "Up in Joe's Garet," also displays a sense of ownership, Joyce having written on the back: "This song has been written by Joyce Oates and has not been copied from any published pieces."

Even as a young child, Joyce had a fiercely proprietary attitude about her work. On one occasion, Joyce wrote a story to be read aloud in school, but her parents suggested she change the title. "Joyce was headstrong as a child," Fred remembered. "She didn't want to change it." Finally, he had to explain to his daughter why "The Cat House" was not an appropriate title for a story about cats.

Joyce did some writing, too, in Jean Windnagle's autograph book, including this poem in the "friendly insult" genre composed on January 13, 1950, when Joyce was eleven:

Dear Jean,
    Roses are red,
    Violets are blue,
    I've seen pretty girls,

But Who Hoppen to you?!

> Your Friend, Joyce Oates

About a year later, in March 1951, she wrote a similar verse:

Dear Jean,

> Roses are red, (*and*)
> Weeds are green,
> You are the *scariest thing*
>   I've seen!! (*oohh!!*)
>
> (Never a moment *dull*,
> If you know Jean *Windnagle*!!)
>
>> Yours, Joyce Oates

The most interesting entry in Jean's autograph book, though, is an encoded message composed of both words and pictures, written on March 7, 1951. Along with girlish sentiments such as "UR 2 good 2 Be 4gotten" and "May your joys be as deep as the ocean, and your sorrows as light as the foam," Joyce laboriously appended an additional message around the four sides of the sheet: "*When you go to the woods / To gather hedges / Remember the girl / Who writes on the edges.*" The little poem is remarkably suggestive: it forecasts her sense of personal marginality, her adult view of herself as an "invisible woman"; and it also predicts the physical appearance of her later worksheets and manuscripts, which often lack margins entirely, crammed at all four edges with a torrent of words.

Apart from their childlike exuberance and humor, the number of Joyce's early manuscripts suggests that high productivity and intense devotion to her work came naturally. Carolina remembered that her daughter was "always working, always busy," and that she had little interest in radio or television. Even when she did watch a television program, Joyce would read avidly during the commercials. Unlike her younger brother, who was more easygoing, Joyce also had a competitive streak, and would lose interest in playing games at which Robin excelled. Fred and Carolina remembered that during her teenage years Joyce became furious when Robin beat her repeatedly at chess; finally she refused to play the game with him any longer. In a letter to her college friend Carol North, Joyce admitted that "most of my games with Robin ended with my knocking all the pieces off the board and onto the floor while he would sit gloating over his literal and moral victory."

Joyce's combination of innate drive, a love of literature, and a yearning for achievement naturally set the stage for her spectacular academic and literary careers. During her childhood years, however, drawing and writing were simply "spontaneous and fun" for her; she was neither hindered nor prodded by her parents, who didn't see her intense activity as anything extraordinary. As Fred has observed, Joyce was "our firstborn, you know. We thought all children were like her, so it didn't seem unusual to us." Even when a project gave her trouble, Fred noted, "she didn't give up. She would dig right in and stay with it." Because there were few other families within walking distance of the farmhouse, Joyce seldom had visits from school friends or other diversions. In any case, Fred added, "I wouldn't say that she was much of an outgoing girl." By 1953, the Windnagles had moved away, so even her old next-door playmate was no longer present as a distraction from her reading and writing.

Joyce's habit of flight from the terrors of childhood into a private world—in her case, the bodiless realm of literature—is reflected in the experiences of several of her later heroines: Enid Stevick in *You Must Remember This* (1987), Iris Courtney in *Because It Is Bitter, and Because It Is My Heart*, Maddy Wirtz in *Foxfire: Confessions of a Girl Gang* (1993), and especially Marya Knauer in *Marya: A Life*. These fictional alter egos also share Joyce's childhood doubleness: a "good girl" exterior concealing a mischievous nature. In 1978 Joyce told an interviewer: "I was always, and continue to be, an essentially mischievous child. This is one of my best-kept secrets." The similarly deceptive Marya, credited by her friends with finding the most ingenious hiding places, develops a canny ability to become invisible: "She slipped away, she was there but not there, *not-there* became a place familiar to her. . . . There, she had nothing to do but breathe and feel her heart beat quietly. She couldn't be surprised and she couldn't be hurt." Despite her shy appearance, however, Marya preserves a kernel of quiet cunning that remains carefully hidden and protected. Iris Courtney shares this trait, impersonating an above-average student and "good girl" for her sixth-grade teacher, Mrs. Rudiger, who understands that Iris "only pretends to be shy and well-behaved. It is a pose, a ruse, a game, an artful befuddlement. In spirit, Iris Courtney sides with the outlaws." For Enid Stevick of *You Must Remember This*, the split identities require separate names: Enid Maria is the model schoolgirl who gets high marks and goes to confession, while "Angel-face" is the mischievous rebel who was "sly wriggly hot-skinned treacherous, with . . . an innocent watchful expression, delicate-boned as a bird (hadn't some old fool said, eyeing her?) and sneaky." And Maddy Wirtz of *Foxfire* has not only the buried rebelliousness but also the verbal ability and even some physical traits of her author as a child, having a "skinny wiry frame, my crimped-kinky dark-brown hair lifting like a crest from my forehead, something sly-shy, simian and pushed-together in my narrow face. . . . Maddy Wirtz was the one perceived as having the power of words. Thus of intelligence, cunning."

Although Joyce's experience of molestation enabled her to feel compassionate toward powerless victims—the young girls in "The Molesters" and "Blindfold," the teenage victims in such stories as "Where Are You Going, Where Have You Been?," "How I Contemplated the World from the Detroit House of Correction and Began My Life Over Again," and "Testimony," among many others—her work is more distinctly autobiographical when portraying the clever doubleness of such girls as Marya, Enid, Iris, and Maddy. In an earlier novel, *Childwold* (1976), Laney Bartlett is a young girl from the country whose innate shrewdness enables her to deal with Kasch, a middle-aged man infatuated with her. Similarly, in one of her most powerful early stories, "Small Avalanches," the thirteen-year-old Nancy avoids a would-be molester by forcing him to chase her up a steep hill, then kicking rocks down upon her pursuer. Overcome by exhaustion from the chase, the man collapses while Nancy looks down in triumph: "I had to laugh at the way he had looked, the way he kept scrambling up the hill and was just crouched there at the end, on his hands and knees. He looked so funny, bent over and clutching at his chest, pretending to have a heart attack or maybe having one, a little one, for all I knew. This will teach you a lesson, I thought." Returning home to her shrill, hectoring mother, who tells her she looks "like hell," Nancy says nothing about her experience, knowing instinctively that her own vigilance and cunning are her only protection against the world's random dangers.

Inherent in female experience in midcentury America is this taboo against speaking out about rape, molestation, incest. In "Blindfold," when Betsy's uncle dies after years of molesting her, she finally tells her mother what happened, but her mother accuses her of making up lies and forces her to apologize. Regarding her own molestation, Joyce has remarked that she had no recourse because "there was no consciousness then. Molested, battered children were in a category that was like limbo. There were no words, no language. . . . Then there was a certain amount of hesitancy, if not actual shame, to say anything about your body." Not surprisingly, a number of Joyce's autobiographical portraits—especially that of Marya Knauer—stress the girls' contempt for their own bodies (Marya refers to "her unspeakably disgusting body"), sometimes to the point that they suffer anorexia, and their cultivation of a "stoniness of soul" in relationships with others. Like other of Joyce's heroines who have learned to manipulate men after suffering abuse—Maureen Wendall of *them* is an example—Marya does not even like to be touched by another person.

Joyce's childhood years taught her the lessons that most "nice girls" learned in the 1940s and 1950s: to hide mischievous or aggressive inclinations behind a mask of docility; to feel ashamed of sexual feelings and of their bodies; to avoid male predators through constant vigilance and avoidance; to look inward, rather than to the social world, for a sense of self. Her clear-eyed apprehension that she lacked any sort of power fueled her impulse to create a private domain of language and imagination that she could rule absolutely. At this stage, of course, her writing existed only "on the edges" of the real world; when, in her late teens and early twenties, her work would begin to garner recognition, she would react with a sense of astonishment. Beginning to write in the 1940s, Joyce exhibited a childlike playfulness but also a certain degree of ambition and self-consciousness, as the early manuscripts show. She could not have avoided feeling, however, that her writing was unlikely to have any added significance as she grew older. There was little educated awareness of literature in her family or her school environment; for economic reasons, her educational opportunities appeared limited; and perhaps most delimiting of all, she was female. Her heritage, her culture, her own introverted personality and modest sense of self—all precluded any likelihood, even in fantasy, that she might enjoy "success" in the larger world.

It should not be surprising, then, that Joyce never planned to "become a writer." For a girl of her time and place, it was a sufficiently large and difficult dream to imagine she would teach school one day—a suitable "female" occupation—and this was the hope that Joyce cherished in her early years. The socially supported and economically stable life of a teacher, in addition to the personal rewards brought by relationships with students and colleagues, would continue to hold a strong appeal for Joyce long after her literary success might have enabled her to leave academic life. This is partly the natural result of her cautious, working-class background, an economic pragmatism born of the Depression and the strong work ethic of her family. Teaching would also provide a continuation of her childhood identity as a "good girl," an aspect of herself that developed into the adult to whom she referred as "Joyce Smith, a professor of English, a wife, a woman, with certain friends, certain duties"—a visible, accountable woman distinct from the "invisible woman" who imagined and composed the work of Joyce Carol Oates. In her writing, however, she would always retain her childhood sense of spontaneity, inventiveness, experimentation, mischief—everything that had belonged to the hidden, private Joyce, a girl who not only wrote on the edges but, in a very real sense, lived there.

3

The Romance of Solitude 1950–56

Strange sense of . . . of what? . . . loneliness, melancholy, romance. I would get up and walk outside, at 2 or 3 in the morning, and watch the cars go by on Transit Road, wondering who was in them. Never very many. And trucks; buses. An almost overwhelming sense of— of curiosity, exhilaration. Loneliness. Wonder.
—*Journal*, June 5, 1976

On November 27, 1950, when Joyce was twelve, her Grandpa Bush died. Although Joyce had not felt close to him, his death was the first disruption of the extended family that had lived together in the Transit Road farmhouse since Joyce was a baby. "Our household was traumatized," Joyce later said. One unanticipated effect of John's death was that the family, urged by the widowed Lena, started attending mass; there was a Catholic church called Good Shepherd in Pendleton, a small town about two miles from home. Fred and Carolina, lapsed Catholics, began going regularly and, Joyce remarked, "my brother and I were more or less hauled in the net with them." Joyce herself could never accept any organized religious belief, or even belief in God: "It just seemed so . . . fantastical. But perhaps I would have believed if I'd been involved in Catholicism at a young, vulnerable age. ('Give me a child before he's seven, and I will have him all his life'—the chilling watchword of the Jesuits.)" Even as an adolescent, Joyce was extremely strong willed and not likely to accept unquestioningly a supernatural system of belief. For this energetic, ambitious twelve-year-old, however, another facet of Catholic ritual was even less acceptable: the mass was "surpassingly dull."

Joyce's parents also lost interest in the Church, but not until they had attended regularly for more than a decade. Fred, always interested in music, enjoyed singing in the choir and playing the church organ. But he gradually became disgusted by the arbitrary nature of Church rules. Although John had long before stopped attending mass, "they did allow," Fred remarked, "and I use the word *allow*," Grandpa Bush to be buried in the church cemetery. The priest, a man with "big dollar signs in his eyes," sold them a grave. The priest also asked Fred and Carolina, who had been married by a justice of the peace, to get married again in the Church. They obeyed, but Fred, sharing his daughter's skeptical nature, felt resentful. His doubts only increased with time, yet Fred and Carolina remained in the Church throughout Joyce's adolescence and into her early twenties. As late as 1961, when she was a graduate student at the University of Wisconsin and had become engaged to Raymond Smith, Joyce's parents were against the marriage at first because Ray was a lapsed Catholic.

As an adult, Joyce's dominant recollection of her teenage religious experience was "the numberless, so fatiguing and unrewarding Catholic masses I'd been forced to endure when I lived at home. I don't think most people comprehend how onerous 'religion' can become when it's shoved down a child's or a young person's throat week after week; what resentment builds up. The more imaginative you are, the more rebellious—the more restless and miserable." Joyce came to view churches as organizations interested primarily in consolidating power. "I think people have been brainwashed through the centuries," she later remarked. "The churches, particularly the Catholic Church, are patriarchal organizations that have been invested with power for the sake of the people in power, who happen to be men. It breeds corruption."

Ironically, Joyce's first teaching job would be at the University of Detroit, a Jesuit institution, where she met priests whose intellects she respected. For the Church itself, however, she continued to express nothing but scorn. In a 1993 essay on the "sin" of despair, commissioned by *The New York Times Book Review*, she wrote, "What mysterious cruelty in the human soul, to have invented despair as a sin!" Falling into despair, "The alleged sinner has detached himself even from the possibility of sin, and this the Catholic Church, as the self-appointed voice of God on earth, cannot allow." Joyce received a number of letters in response to the essay, including one from a Catholic priest. "You're very nice to write so temperately regarding my 'Despair' essay," she responded. "As a former Catholic, I do tend to think of the Church reproachfully. Also, perhaps, as a woman and a feminist. . . . What I could not comprehend—I'm sorry, this sounds so aggressive, but I don't mean it to be so—is how, in contemporary times, knowing what we do of the earth's evolution, and the universe, and mankind's penchant for fantasizing all manner of gods to guarantee 'immortality' as well as to punish enemies and to justify earthly imperialism, an intelligent man or woman could be 'religious,' let alone Catholic."

Like many other literary former Catholics, Joyce would turn to artistic profit her early ordeal of sitting through the mind-numbing rituals of the mass and hearing a theology she could not even respect, let alone believe. Yet the Catholic liturgy surely contributed to her firm sense of novelistic structure and provided a system of belief against which to measure and develop her own philosophical views. Some of her finest early stories—"At the Seminary," "In the Region of Ice," "Shame"—would bring a humanistic focus to Catholic characters and settings. A number of autobiographical protagonists, from Karen Herz in Joyce's first published novel, *With Shuddering Fall* (1964), to Marya Knauer of *Marya: A Life* (1986) and Enid Stevick of *You Must Remember This* (1987), would feel estranged from their Catholic heritage, finding its philosophy alien and false to their own experience of the world.

But the most sustained use of her religious background came in a novel that deals not with Catholicism but with a charismatic fundamentalist preacher. In the spring of 1950, about six months before Grandpa Bush's death, Joyce had accompanied a girlfriend of hers to a Methodist church in Pendleton. Unlike her passive and resentful attendance at Catholic masses, Joyce's participation in the Methodist service was more active and engaged; for a while, she even played the organ—"an ancient, wheezing, foot-pedal instrument"—while the congregation sang. She was impressed by the "raw, unmediated emotion" she felt in the church, "the sense that people really believed God, or Jesus Christ, was present. It was fascinating for me to see, too, adult men and women shift in and out of what I perceived to be a kind of communal insanity. They surrendered their sanity, then returned to it."

In *Son of the Morning* (1978), Nathan Vickery inspires his followers to this fever-pitch of emotion. Shortly after completing the novel, Joyce remarked that intense religious emotion, as evidenced particularly in fundamentalist Christianity, relates to the essentially "adolescent" quality of the American national character. To prepare for writing the novel, she spent hours in reading and rereading the Bible, which she hadn't done since memorizing those three hundred verses for the church contest. Getting into the mind-set of a biblical literalist, she said, was a "shattering experience." But religion had become a source of fascination to her as a writer and a social chronicler—not as an individual. Even at age twelve, she recalled, "I was an emotional child, yet frequently detached, strangely analytical, judging." When Fred and Carolina took Joyce back to Catholic services after Grandpa Bush's death, "I would look around in church and see people praying and sometimes crying and genuflecting, saying the rosary, and I never felt any identification."

If religion brought little of value into Joyce's life as she reached adolescence, there were other changes at the time of Grandpa Bush's death that were more meaningful. In the fall of 1949 she had transferred from the one-room district school to attend sixth grade at John Pound Elementary School in Lockport. Located on High Street, less than two blocks from Transit Road, the school was a massive, red-brick structure near the center of town, strikingly different from the little wooden schoolhouse. Since the school did not bus children from the rural areas, Joyce took a Greyhound Bus to Lockport and for years afterward would recall the excitement she felt at the approach of the bus. She would also take a bus into town on weekends, to see movies or visit the library. "Riding buses has been so much a part of my life," she recalled; "it was fraught with such great emotion. Jean [Windnagle] and I would sometimes go into Lockport, and we'd go out and we'd wait for the bus. You'd see the Greyhound bus come and stop at a stop light way up the road, and then it would come down. This Greyhound bus coming was always a sign of something exciting . . . an adventure."

Spending more time in Lockport also allowed for frequent visits to her beloved Grandma Woodside and for the exploration of new friendships. Although most of Joyce's classmates and teachers from her adolescent years recalled her extreme shyness, she made at least one close friend during sixth grade, Marilyn Mason, and another during junior high, Bette Pancoe, to whom she stayed close until high school graduation. (In *You Must Remember This*, she memorialized two of her school friends, Nelia Pynn and Bette Pancoe, by naming a minor character "Nelia Pancoe.") Another, more unusual friendship, with a black boy named Roosevelt Chatham, would inspire Joyce's short story "Concerning the Case of Bobby T." and her 1990 novel, *Because It Is Bitter, and Because It Is My Heart*. Roosevelt lived in the shabby section of Lockport known as "Lowertown," and Joyce remembered him as a likable troublemaker, "very charismatic, unpredictable, smart, funny, daring." In junior high school, he took on a somewhat protective, older-brother stance toward frail-looking Joyce, and would become the primary model in *Because It Is Bitter* for Jinx Fairchild, who has a similar relationship with Iris Courtney. The racial abyss between Iris and Jinx approximates the one Joyce remembered existing between her and Roosevelt; like Iris, she never knew what happened to her black friend after she left the Lockport area for high school. "And I don't want to know," she wrote. "I'm sure it would be heartbreaking." (In "Concerning the Case of Bobby T.," Frances Berardi's uneasy friendship with Bobby T. Cheathum is charged with sexual tension, erupting in a fight that gets Bobby sent to a mental hospital for twenty years.) The bittersweet nature of Joyce and Roosevelt's friendship is suggested not only in the novel but also by its dedication to her memory of "R.C." (Some people mistakenly assumed the initials referred to the short-story writer Raymond Carver, whom Joyce knew slightly and who had recently died when the novel came out.)

Perhaps Joyce's most important relationship of these years was with the city of Lockport itself. In her journals and letters, she focuses especially on her memory of the railroad trestle-bridge over the Erie Canal, where she often walked after school and on Saturdays. Her Lockport wanderings made such a profound impression that the city's unique character would be memorialized in several of her major novels and dozens of short stories. As she wrote to her friend Bob Phillips,

> It's solely Lockport, NY that figures in my imagination; I really don't know why. Maybe our most intense emotional experiences are lived before the age of 12 or so. Or, at any rate, memories are intensely imprinted in us, obsessively so. Lockport is a place of mystery for me. I always think there is a secret that will be revealed to me there. . . . It seems that these streets, these scenes, bridges over the canals, etc., are irrevocably imprinted in my memory.

One day in 1983, after recalling her early adolescent walks around the city, she wrote of becoming "enormously excited at once, extremely nervous," as the idea for *You Must Remember This*—the novel that would appear four years later—"swept over me."

There were adventures at home as well. Joyce remained close to her parents, often helping her mother with the cooking and sharing likewise in Fred's interests in boxing and flying. Assisting Carolina with the kitchen work was a pleasure rather than a chore, especially since much of the food they ate was grown on the farm. The family always had chickens, Rhode Island Reds, which supplied them plentifully with eggs. Although Joyce, like a number of her fictional heroines, was disgusted by the filth and smell of the chicken coops, she had a favorite bird, a kind of pet, that she named "Happy Chicken." The Oateses grew their own potatoes, corn, carrots, and tomatoes; and the pear, apple, and cherry trees provided an abundance of fruit, some of which was sold by the roadside in bushel baskets.

Although Joyce would maintain an interest in cooking and housework into adulthood, she responded with more excitement to the traditionally male pursuits of her father, especially since these often involved the adventure of travel outside the familiar rural boundaries of Joyce's childhood. Around the time Joyce began attending school in Lockport, her father began taking her on outings to Buffalo, another city that would figure prominently in her fiction, partly inspiring (along with Lockport) the intimately detailed city of Port Oriskany, where the Stevicks live in *You Must Remember This*, and also serving as the model for Union City, home of Corky Corcoran in *What I Lived For* (1994). Buffalo was the city where Joyce went Christmas shopping with Grandma Woodside and where she occasionally visited a bakery whose specialty was "Freddie's Doughnuts . . . immense, sweet, doughy, covered in confectioner's sugar and filled to bursting with whipped cream." With her father, she went to Buffalo for boxing matches; these father-daughter outings would have a lifelong impact on Joyce. Unlike most girls of eleven or twelve, she was attracted rather than repelled by the drama of the ring, perhaps apprehending in its combination of violence and structure, pain and art, the paradigm for her own developing responses to the world. Once she asked her father, at a Golden Gloves tournament, why the boys wanted to fight and get hurt. Fred responded, "Boxers don't feel pain quite the way we do." She recalled also that the family, along with millions of other Americans, often watched the Friday night fights on television. During one particularly bloody match, she remembered that even Fred, former amateur boxer and avid fan of the sport, had had enough: "It's over!" he cried. "It's over! What's the point!"

Joyce was apparently less fascinated with flying, though she gamely went along on weekend outings when Fred would rent a Piper Cub, Cessna, or Stinson for an hour or two, using a small country airport near Lockport. She remembered one exciting trip in an open-cockpit, 175-horsepower Fairchild training plane: "I wore a helmet and goggles, but no parachute, for the very good reason that I wouldn't have known how to use a parachute." But during one of these trips it was Joyce's primary interest—reading—that took precedence over her father's "romance of the air." Fred recalled that Joyce had taken a comic book along for the plane ride, and he had to scold her because she stayed so absorbed in her reading that she had neglected to fasten her seat belt. He was paying fifteen dollars an hour for the plane and felt annoyed that Joyce was more interested in the comic book.

But Joyce's love affair with reading had grown only more intense as she got older. After completing sixth grade at Pound Elementary, she transferred to Lockport's North Park Junior High school—a sprawling, flat-roofed, rather plain-looking building of pale brown brick with high, narrow windows. She acknowledged that her reading at this time did include comic books— " 'Tales of the Crypt' is the title that comes to mind, to my shame"—in addition to genre mysteries, adventure and science fiction stories, volumes in the "Black Stallion" series, even *Mad* magazine. But she was also developing a taste for serious literature. She recalled puzzling over Edgar Allan Poe's "The Gold Bug" and reading a long list of classics: *The Yearling, Wuthering Heights, Green Mansions, Oliver Twist, David Copperfield, Great Expectations, Our Town, Dracula*. (Around this same time Joyce also saw, and was profoundly impressed by, the classic film of *Dracula*, starring Bela Lugosi; she speculated that Lugosi, in "his ethnic exoticism," must have reminded her of Grandpa Bush, whose wedding portrait, taken in his twenties, had shown him as a "dashingly handsome, Magyar exotic.") Sara Glover, one of Joyce's English teachers at North Park, remembered that "We read a lot of literature— poetry, plays, fiction, everything. [Joyce] was an avid reader, and we always had supplementary lists. She would get things from the library; she would give very good book reports." Though Joyce was energetic in her class work, Mrs. Glover recalled her as a "very quiet girl; she was not outgoing . . . she was sort of a loner." Joyce didn't contribute much to the class discussion, but she was always insightful when she did speak: "You could always count on her for knowing the right answer."

Even in junior high, Joyce's favorite activity was writing. "She wrote profusely," Mrs. Glover remembered. "She was writing compositions, really about anything. She just loved to write and she was forever bringing up things that she had written for me to look at, and to give her my opinion, and she did more than what I would assign. She would always do extra. She kept me busy correcting, I'll tell you that." One of Joyce's classmates, Gordy Stearns, remembered one particular class: "Mrs. Glover asked Joyce to read a story she had written. Somewhat reticently, Joyce stood up and began. It was a story of unrequited teenage love; the scene, a skating rink; the ending, poignant." He added that "when Joyce finished, Mrs. Glover was absolutely beaming. I think Mrs. Glover knew Joyce had real talent." Joyce paid homage to her teacher in her 1996 novel, We Were the Mulvaneys; Marianne, a character who is in many ways an emotional self-portrait, also has an English teacher named "Mrs. Glover."

Joyce excelled in her schoolwork that first year at North Park, earning an A average in all but one of her courses; she received a 96, her highest grade, in her reading, art, and language classes; her one B grade, an 83, was in physical education. From several of her teachers, she also earned special notice for taking initiative and assuming responsibility. (Along with everyone else, she also patiently endured that ritual familiar to most students of the 1950s: "emergency" drills in case of an atomic bomb attack. "Did I really live through that?" she would ask in her journal, recalling the "degrading demeaning ineffably funny" nature of such experiences, in retrospect.) Joyce's industry at North Park brought special recognition by the end of that year. In a letter dated June 15, 1951, and signed by the principal, Kenneth A. Fuller, and the guidance counselor, Rachael F. Flagler, Fred and Carolina received the news that "Joyce Oates has been judged the Outstanding Girl in seventh grade for 1950–51. This all-around award is one of which she can be proud." The distinction brought Joyce her first press attention: her picture and a brief story about the award appeared in the Lockport newspaper.

Her eighth-grade marks were similarly impressive. Her average for the 1951–52 school year was 93 percent, though in physical education she received an 81 and a written critique citing her "low preparedness." Her other teachers, little knowing how prescient their remarks would seem in the context of Joyce's adult career, noted that she was a "good worker" and "shows interest in work." She also participated in a number of extracurricular activities

during her years at North Park—the choir, the music council, the news club—
and served as council secretary during both seventh and eighth grades.

If Joyce's pattern of academic excellence and "good girl" behavior was
already evident in her junior high school record, she also had experiences
during these years that forced her to confront the darker side of human nature. Once again she became the object of harassment, but ironically enough
the perpetrators were not the bullying farm boys she had known at the district school, but some of the very teachers who praised her academic work.
The honor of serving as class secretary, for instance, led in eighth grade to an
experience of nightmarish humiliation. (Later she would re-create the incident in *them* [1969], in one of the most compelling chapters devoted to
Maureen Wendall.) One day, on the bus, Joyce lost the secretary's notebook
in which the class records were kept. The teacher tormented her for days afterward, insisting that she find the notebook, but she could not. For Joyce, so
intent on performing well at school and earning the praise of her teachers,
this minor lapse assumed tragic proportions. "Poor silly helpless Joyce!" she
recalled in her journal. "Nearly as bad as Maureen Wendall." In *them*, the lost
notebook becomes for Maureen "the worst experience of her life. . . . It
seemed to Maureen that her life was coming undone. The world was opening
up to trap her, she was losing her mind, she was coming undone, unfastened.
It was like that time her period had begun in school, a hot flow of blood, a
terrible sickening surprise." Like Joyce, Maureen never finds the notebook,
but the teacher's cruelty becomes one of the many childhood incidents that
gradually harden her, helping create the rather cold, manipulative young
woman she has become by the end of the novel.

Joyce suffered persecutions by other teachers at North Park as well. One
of these, a gym teacher who has been re-created several times in Joyce's
fiction—most notably in an uncollected 1978 story published in *Mademoiselle*, "First Death"—began to harass her. "You seem so alone," the woman
told her. In her journal, Joyce wrote that the teacher's face (though she had
forgotten her name) remained vivid in her mind's eye: "a spiteful, smiling,
somehow teasing and accusing look . . . dark skin, dark eyes, dark curly or
kinky hair." Though the gym teacher had seemed to like Joyce at first, she
had unaccountably turned against her; when Joyce misplaced her gym outfit
one day, the woman used the mistake as an excuse for stepped-up harassment. Joyce remembered her "relentless persecution of me for weeks." Laney
Bartlett in *Childwold* (1976) suffers a similar experience: "Miss Flagler, the
girls' gym teacher: calling you into her cubbyhole of an office. Small, swarthy-
skinned, alert, close-cropped black hair like a boy's, sardonic, mocking. . . .
She was nice and then she got irritated with you, lost her patience." Ironi-

cally, Rachael Flagler, the guidance counselor at North Park, had signed the letter to Fred and Carolina that praised Joyce's accomplishments.

In a similar incident, Joyce missed the bus one morning when she'd been expected at a special school event: "my homeroom teacher and my English teacher never 'forgave' me for that, as if it had been deliberate." Joyce wrote in her journal that such persecutions, at the hands of the very people she worked so hard to please, combined "to make my eighth grade experience a sort of nightmarish delirium for months." In another entry she added, "I remember my sickened feeling of guilt and unreasonable terror re. the authorities of that absurd little school. . . . I was such a good, studious, hard-working girl . . . a perfect victim, being shy, and over-scrupulous." Joyce mused that she could easily have "drifted into simply not caring about my teachers' trivial expectations," noting that a "certain violent sullenness lies in us all, awaiting release." Instead, "I kept on making the effort to be a 'good girl.' "

Why did these women teachers persecute Joyce? Despite her shy demeanor, Joyce's other qualities—her energy, drive, and ambition—might have struck them as excessive or unseemly, especially in a young girl from the country, in the early 1950s. Perhaps they also sensed the strong-willed, rebellious nature she kept concealed beneath her docile exterior. (By contrast, Joyce seems to have had no difficulty with her male teachers at North Park; as a girl, she might have been "invisible" to them, subject to their benign neglect despite her excellent work. One of her English teachers, Mr. Nixon, remembered that she wrote a great deal, but failed to notice whether she possessed any talent.) There were other kids at North Park, after all, who might more reasonably have been the focus of these teachers' reproaches. Some of the children were, Joyce remembered, "really vicious," including several who used heroin, and some students were sexually promiscuous. One seventh-grade girl ran away with an adult man, a heroin addict. "It was quite a scandal," Joyce said. She would dramatize these darker facets of her junior high school years in her 1993 novel, *Foxfire: Confessions of a Girl Gang*. Soon after the novel appeared, she reminded an interviewer that the 1950s were "a period of extremes, of myths and false impressions. But there was this other world—dark, exciting and turbulent—that was inhabited by kids who were really tough." (Even as early as *them*, she had created one of these "tough kids" in the sensitive Maureen Wendall's amoral, bratty younger sister, Betty.) Maddy Wirtz, the narrator of *Foxfire*, becomes like Joyce the only girl in her group of friends to get a college education, thus acquiring the skills to become their chronicler.

Despite the sometimes "nightmarish delirium" of her time at North Park, there were consolations as well. Visiting her grandmother was perhaps Joyce's favorite escape from the occasional stresses of school life. Grandma

Woodside's house, at 188 Grand Street, was less than a mile from the school, and at the end of the day Joyce could walk directly to her most cherished haven. But even this short walk brought reminders of the darker side of adult experience, for the way to Grandma Woodside's led past a "mystery house" where, it was rumored, a girl had been imprisoned by some local men and sexually abused—a horror Joyce would later dramatize in her story "Little Wife." By contrast, Grandma Woodside's house remained the source of her most pleasant memories. In 1977 she reminisced: "Thinking of the walk to and from school, to and from her house, arouses in me a powerful emotion . . . almost a sense of awe, of chill. The apartment upstairs, the living room & small kitchen & my grandmother's bedroom (always so neat, so attractive, smelling of lavender sachet), the back stairs, my step-grandfather's room, the science fiction magazines he read . . . detective magazines too, I think." In 1973 she had remembered her grandmother's "selfless love, uncomplaining, all-forgiving," and four years later called her "a warm, marvelous, generous person . . . truly an exceptional person."

Apart from providing uncritical love and a sense of family identity, Grandma Woodside nurtured Joyce in another crucial way: she encouraged her reading and writing. Although Joyce had owned a toy typewriter as a child—"marvelous zany invention," she called it—Grandma Woodside's gift of a real typewriter when Joyce was fourteen marked a symbolic milestone in Joyce's self-awareness as a writer. From that point on, her manuscripts would be executed not in her large, childish handwriting but with a professional finish that corresponded to her increasing engagement with her work. Not surprisingly, Joyce promptly decided to type out a novel. Inspired partly by a book she had been reading about stallions, she plotted a story deliberately aimed at readers her own age. Aware of the kids at North Park who used heroin at the ages of eleven or twelve, she composed a book about a young boy addicted to drugs who is then " 'redeemed' by coming to live in the country and acquiring, somehow, a horse." Pleased with her work, Joyce decided to make her first formal submission to a New York publisher. Ironically, the editor to whom she sent the typewritten manuscript "seemed not to know that she was dealing with so young and naive a writer," and she rejected the book as too depressing for the juvenile market.

Joyce's increasing absorption in her writing coincided with her transfer to yet another school at the end of ninth grade: Williamsville Central High School. In 1949, the state of New York had reconfigured some of its school districts, creating a Central District east of Buffalo that necessitated the construction of a new high school to serve the towns of Williamsville, Amherst, Clarence, and a number of outlying areas, including the north country bordered by the Tonawanda Creek. The new Williamsville school, a stately Georgian structure, opened in the fall of 1951. One of the teachers hired that year, George Kunz, remarked that "no expense had been spared to construct a showplace school of which the community could be proud." The new superintendent, W. J. Herrington, had "highly eccentric, Dickensian manners and strong religious convictions." He believed that American moral values in 1951 were corroding and began each assembly with scripture readings. Teaching jobs were scarce at the time, since schools were still affected by the low birth rate of the Depression years. An English and Latin teacher, Kunz remembered that he was hired because he was Jesuit-educated, and that the superintendent sought out other teachers with similarly conservative backgrounds.

Although the city of Williamsville actually predated Buffalo—for many years, the open fields between the two were connected only by a small commuter trolley—suburban Buffalo had grown northward by 1950, turning the once autonomous smaller city into a Buffalo suburb (a transformation of identity that irked Williamsville residents). A relatively affluent city of professionals and businesspeople, Williamsville was a thriving, cosmopolitan area in the early 1950s, a striking contrast to the shabby, working-class Lockport. The kids from the north country who would now be bused down to Williamsville were clearly a different breed from the children of doctors and executives who immediately became the social arbiters of the new school.

To Joyce, the product of a wood-frame country schoolhouse and Lockport city schools, this sparkling new campus with its well-dressed students represented an alien environment. Molly Eimers, one of Joyce's new classmates, recalled that before the district was expanded "our school was much smaller and consisted of only kids from the village—a rather 'elite' group." People from the rural areas to the north were thought to be "hicks," and the phrase "the north country" was always a dismissive term when used by Williamsville residents. Another of Joyce's new classmates was Ellen Shapley, who recalled that the Williamsville students would say, "Here comes another bus from the north country" as if referring to an influx of countrified refugees. "You had all these people coming in from that area who were farm children," she remembered, "and they just didn't seem to mingle with the others. I would think they were intimidated." Frank Coward, hired that first year to teach at the new school, had the same perception: "It had to be difficult for many from the north country."

Although Joyce was remembered as neat and well groomed, she lacked the other girls' expensive clothes, wearing mostly the handmade outfits sewn by Carolina and by Grandma Woodside. Joyce was acutely aware that she dressed differently: "As a young girl I attached a great deal of importance to clothes," she noted in her journal. "Because we were relatively poor, no doubt. The purchase of a sweater or a skirt was an *event*." She remembered that the other kids "were solidly middle/upper-middle class. I really didn't belong to their world of expensive Tartan plaid pleated skirts, matched sweater sets, 'professional' fathers and 'volunteer' mothers, but they were kind enough to behave toward me as if I did." Frank Coward, a popular teacher known for his bow ties and sharp wit, remembered Joyce at fifteen as "rail-thin with a tendency toward plain, older-looking clothes. The appearance and personality as presented were of a piece, colorless, and a decided contrast to most of her classmates." Joyce struck him as "an introverted loner," and he felt concerned enough to ask the school guidance counselor to do a "home check." But the counselor reported that Joyce's home life was nothing out of the ordinary.

Not surprisingly, the girl who had been known in the Lockport schools as quiet and shy made the same impression in the bustling, intimidating new school. One classmate, Lee Cooke, remembered Joyce as "a little eccentric," a girl who never cared about her own lack of popularity in the school's somewhat cliquish atmosphere. For Molly Eimers, "the vision that comes to me most frequently is Joyce with a shy smile clutching an armload of books to her chest, as one might guard a treasure." Another friend, Gail Paxson, considered Joyce to be "shy, almost apologetic, very neatly but not stylishly dressed; she smiled, but I don't remember a laugh." Although Gail suffered from polio, Joyce never referred to her classmate's disability. Perhaps she sensed a kinship, perceiving Gail as another outsider: "She often was interested in talking to me. She was incredibly introspective—she appeared unhappy and haunted much of the time. She asked if I'd ever thought about serious things like life, death, moral issues."

Another classmate, Dick Gregory, remembered a less somber Joyce, especially in the literature classes taught by Frank Coward: "He seemed to be able to draw out Joyce better than anybody. She seemed very receptive to his wit and humor." One of the school's most popular girls, Linnea Ogren, recalled Mr. Coward saying to a group of chattering students, "Quiet down, boys and girls, and listen to Miss Oates. She will go far." The class read such books as *The Brothers Karamazov* and *Wuthering Heights*, works that urged Joyce into "talking more—about the books and the characters and plots that we were studying." Gregory remembered that "Joyce had large eyes which bulged out a little, giving them a very prominent and expressive quality. She also had very expressive dimples," and "a sort of head-tilted coy expression which was very attractive. Once I started looking at Joyce, I found it very difficult to look away."

Throughout her high school years, Joyce remained shy and showed little interest in dating, popular music, or other typical teenage pursuits. But she did gradually find her niche at Williamsville, joining clubs and participating in a number of activities. In her sophomore year, she made the volleyball team, and as a junior she worked on the school newspaper, *The Billboard*. She also joined Quill and Scroll, an honorary society for students interested in writing;

played on the basketball team; and joined both the French Club and Hi-Y, an organization whose goal was "to create, maintain, and extend throughout the home, school, and community high standards of Christian character." By her senior year, Joyce had become one of the most active students in her class: she sang in the chorus, played basketball and field hockey, worked on the yearbook, served as associate editor of *The Billboard*, became president of Quill and Scroll and vice president of the French Club, and for good measure also joined the Drama Club, the Debate Club, the International Club, and even the Bowling Club. One of her classmates, Faith Ryan, remembered that everybody liked Joyce. "She was always very accommodating to everyone else, and if there would ever be a disagreement, she would always back off—she was not assertive but very sweet, no malice, no enemies, nothing like that." Gradually Joyce had dispelled her image as an eccentric loner and by her senior year had been given an affectionate nickname: "Oatsie."

Joyce had also succeeded in joining the cliquish high school sorority known as the Tri-Delts, from which she had been blackballed in previous years; the club considered itself "pretty exclusive," Ellen Shapley noted, and favored "the squeaky clean look—the pincurls, the crinoline skirts, saddle shoes, cinched belts." Faith Ryan recalled that the girls were generally divided into those who "were pretty and had all the boyfriends and were the cheerleaders and that sort of thing—very nice clothes, nice houses," and the less popular girls from poorer families who were "achievers" in their studies. The Tri-Delt girls could be "very dominant and cruel to people who weren't 'in.' " But Joyce's involvement in this club added little to her high school experience. Foreshadowing her unhappy experiences as a sorority member in college, the club's activities were superficial and unmemorable. Many years later, Joyce remarked: "We were all very good friends in this club—which must have 'met' once a week?—but I can't remember a single occasion, nor can I remember, or even guess, what on earth we talked about so earnestly."

Despite all this activity, Joyce's studies always came first. During all three years of high school, she made the honor roll and excelled in her courses. As a sophomore, her load included English, world history, plane geometry, biology, and French, in addition to driver's education, and in her junior year she took English, American history, chemistry, French, and a health class. As a senior she took a different load each term, including a number of electives: literature, journalism, algebra, physics, and third-year French in the first term; creative writing, citizenship, drawing and painting, and a continuation of physics and French in the second. Her overall average for the three years was 93.3 percent and her one perfect score, predictably enough, was in creative writing, in which she earned a 100 on the final exam and an A+ in the course. Joyce was part of an exceptionally bright class that included a future college president (Steve

Lewis, now at Carleton College) and a U.S. ambassador to Switzerland (Faith Ryan Whittlesey, the highest-ranking woman in the Reagan administration); ultimately Joyce finished twelfth out of 143 students in the academic rankings.

Joyce may have seemed shy to her outgoing fellow students, but it is unlikely that they understood the intensity—or the excitement—of her private engagement with her intellectual pursuits, her writing above all. Her teachers, of course, quickly recognized that she was exceptional: "the quality of her writing," Frank Coward noted, "the nature of subject matter and the depth for which she was striving, set her and her writing apart." He began reading her work regularly, "but when it became clear how very personal, self-exploring her work tended to be, I was hesitant." He recalled her avid interest in the craft of writing, the development of style. Another English teacher, Harold Stein, was a short, balding, soft-spoken man, less popular than Mr. Coward and a favorite victim of student pranks; sometimes the kids would tie the doorknob to an outside stairway so he couldn't get out of the classroom. But Stein shared Joyce's love of writing and became one of her mentors. An ardent admirer of her work, he would allude to her essays and short stories during class. Faith Ryan remembered that Stein spent "a disproportionate amount of time" with Joyce. "He obviously had found a kindred spirit in her, who loved the language as much as he did." Even George Kunz, an English teacher who never had Joyce in his classes, remembered that other teachers "had spoken of her great talent and her dedication to writing."

Despite this recognition, the peculiar intensity of her dedication remained private. None of her classmates or teachers knew that she had written a novel while still in junior high, or could have guessed that she had now begun a deliberate apprenticeship, "consciously training myself by writing novel after novel." For the time being, the fifteen-year-old Joyce put aside any notion of publication, throwing away her apprentice novels as soon as she completed them: "I seem to have written them as a pianist practices scales and exercises." Some of the novels—she wrote roughly a dozen of them—were deliberate imitations of the masters she read in her classes. Faulkner's *The Sound and the Fury*, for instance, inspired Joyce to write "a bloated trifurcated novel." Gail Paxson remembered that Joyce also "was taken at the time with Hemingway's style. She wrote some exceptionally powerful short stories that were shared with some of us." During her sophomore year, Joyce later recalled, she "accidentally opened a copy of Hemingway's *In Our Time* in the public library one day and saw how chapters in an ongoing narrative might be self-contained units. . . . So I apprenticed myself, with my usual zeal, to this beautiful and elusive new form. I wrote several novels in imitation of Hemingway's book." Hemingway's disaffected posturing did not appeal to her— "that ironic burnt-out voice being merely monotonous to my adolescent ear"—but his structural device of arranging short stories into a novel would influence several of her mature works, including such otherwise dissimilar novels as *Bellefleur* (1980), with its maze of interlocking tales, and *Marya: A Life*, each of whose chapters first appeared in story form. Conversely, she would also write collections of stories that resembled loosely structured novels, such as *Crossing the Border* (1976), much of which concerns the troubled marriage of a young Canadian couple, and *All the Good People I've Left Behind* (1979), which includes several stories and a novella dealing with the romantic misadventures of Annie Quirt.

Although Joyce was captivated by the bold experiments of Faulkner and Hemingway, she met with a roadblock when seeking out the work of another noted modern author, James T. Farrell. The public librarian, perhaps sharing the archconservative standards of the school superintendent, balked when the fifteen-year-old Joyce tried to check out Farrell's *Studs Lonigan*, and refused to let her have the book. (Coincidentally, Farrell was then the "star" author of Vanguard Press, which would become Joyce's first publisher.) But Joyce read just as avidly in nineteenth-century literature, developing an especially passionate admiration for Thoreau's *Walden*. Although she would write a play in the early 1990s based on Thoreau's life and work, *The Passion of Henry David Thoreau*, his influence on her fiction is less easy to discern. In her essay "Looking for Thoreau" she wrote that "it is difficult for me to speak of him with any pretense of objectivity." In her journal, she added: "Thoreau is mysteriously intimate, very much bound up with my soul, my adolescent-self." It seems likely that the philosophical richness of his work and his prizing of solitude particularly appealed to her in high school, the time when she first began brooding about "life, death, and moral issues" and fiercely valued her own solitude. For Joyce, *Walden* was "suffused with the powerfully intense, romantic energies of adolescence, the sense that life is boundless, experimental, provisionary, ever-fluid, and unpredictable; the conviction that, whatever the accident of the outer self, the truest self is inward, secret, inviolable."

If Joyce's most serious reading and writing were kept private, she did share her literary abilities and ambitions—to a carefully controlled extent—with her high school peers. One of her duties as a member of the newspaper staff was to write occasional movie reviews and other reportage, and these pieces show the playful, ironic side of Joyce's writing that would later surface in some of her satiric fiction and plays. Her more serious literary ambitions were also acknowledged at "Billsville," as the students nicknamed the school. In a list of "Senior Secrets" printed in the Williamsville yearbook, *The Searchlight*, Joyce Oates is especially noted for "her book"—probably the group of Hemingway-inspired stories she showed to Ellen Shapley and others. Ellen hoped to become a painter, and in her copy of the yearbook Joyce wrote: "If I *ever* (this is a joke) write a book, you can help illustrate it—if you would have time for such things." Most of her classmates viewed her as someone with a special destiny in store. In a *Billboard* article called "Senior Alphabet," the good-natured Linnea Ogren is placed under "S" for "smile" and Molly Eimers is "E" for "effervescent"; but Joyce is classified under "U," for "unique."

Joyce's decision to let people read the Hemingway-inspired novel ultimately brought a hostile reaction to her "uniqueness"; and once again, as at North Park, it was a woman teacher who caused the problem. Joyce had given the woman her manuscript of stories, but "she never gave it back to me. She just kept it." Joyce "asked for it a few times, but I never got it back—and I just stopped asking. I wouldn't say she stole it—she just probably lost it—but it was gone, and I had no copy, and no carbon. It was just gone." The incident caused Joyce to reflect again that "when you're a young person, you just don't have any power," especially when a person in authority "does something to you." Eventually Joyce might have disposed of the novel on her own, as she did with the other apprentice novels she wrote in high school, but nonetheless the experience was disillusioning.

One story from the manuscript lost by her Williamsville teacher does survive, since it was published in a 1956 student literary magazine called *Will O' the Wisp*. Entitled "A Long Way Home," the story is interesting not only as Joyce's first printed work but also because it suggests the thematic and technical issues that were engaging Joyce during her apprenticeship. Clearly indebted to "Soldier's Home" in Hemingway's *In Our Time*, "A Long Way Home" features a young male narrator named Jack whose family is preparing for his older brother's homecoming from the war. Narrated in a simple but efficient style, the story shows a flair for pacing, structure, and dialogue; it focuses on Jack's yearning simply to go fishing with Albie when he gets home (the fishing notion probably gleaned from the "Big Two-Hearted River" narratives in *In Our Time*), in marked conflict with their mother's desire to make a fuss over his homecoming. Like most student fiction, the story falters in its characterizations: Jack's narrative voice is bland and curiously genderless, the mother is shrill and unconvincing, and Albie's appearance is somewhat anticlimactic. Nonetheless "A Long Way Home" exhibits a sophisticated degree of control in dramatizing its theme of denial, evoking the two brothers' instinctively shared longing for a return to boyhood innocence. Decades later, rereading the story, Joyce felt "strangely impressed" and even "a little amazed" by this early effort: "It seemed to have so much detail in it. I think I would have been quite astounded if a student of mine had written that story. I wouldn't have thought I could have written that well at that age."

In contrast to her writing and her schoolwork, Joyce's home life in Millersport had changed little, and there was little interaction between the two spheres. Only Joyce's closest friends who happened to live in the countryside near her, such as Linnea Ogren and Gail Gleasner, knew much about her home and family. Linnea, an attractive, dimpled girl elected cheerleader three years in a row and voted "most popular" by the senior class, served as something of a social conduit for the less gregarious Joyce. Linnea remembered that Joyce would sometimes come to her house on Friday nights when there was a football or basketball game at the school, and after the game Fred Oates would arrive to take his daughter home again. Gail, a sweet-natured girl who became Joyce's closest friend in high school, shared her academic seriousness and actually placed several notches higher than Joyce in the final rankings. Although Gail's family was well-off financially, the girls had much in common, especially since "Gail was an intellectual, and wasn't interested in boys and clothes." Gail occasionally visited Joyce at home, and Carolina remembered that the Gleasners, "very nice people," would sometimes take Joyce out to dinner with them. Like Joyce, Gail belonged to the Tri-Delt club during their senior year, and Gail's mother would drive them down to the school for meetings. Joyce and Gail remained close; they roomed together at Syracuse University, and later kept in touch and occasionally visited until Gail's death in 1990.

Despite the driver's ed courses Joyce and Gail took, there was no question of their owning or driving a car, since car ownership for teenagers in the 1950s was almost exclusively the province of boys. But a cousin of Joyce's named Vinnie owned a memorable two-door sedan he had fondly named "Lightning Bolt." The car had a cracked windshield and emitted poisonous clouds of exhaust, but it sported "glamorous red zigzag lightning-arrows on its sides shakily painted by Vinnie himself; pockmarked bumpers; no fenders; five-dollar tires." As Joyce later remarked, "I'd like to claim that I rode with him and his friends after school" in the car or that she participated in the "lurid happiness it aroused." As a younger cousin, and a girl, Joyce was excluded from Vinnie's escapades, but in Foxfire: Confessions of a Girl Gang she would appropriate Vinnie's car for the use of Maddy Wirtz and her fellow gang members, transforming this traditionally male symbol into an instrument of feminist will. Maddy announces proudly: "FOXFIRE acquired a car—baptized LIGHTNING BOLT once we got it home and painted it, all the exquisite colors of the rainbow pierced along both sides by bronze-gold lightning zigzags."

Foxfire may be read partly as an elaborate fantasy of the intimate sisterhood Joyce never had in adolescence. The geographical and social distance between Joyce and the other Williamsville students meant that she had little company in Millersport. Nor was much thought given to boys: "the idea of dating," Joyce admitted, "or even the word, or the term, would have been somewhat odd" to her. The prospect of sexual experimentation likewise held no appeal. In 1977 Joyce wrote in her journal, "My inclination toward chastity, my prolonged (one can only call it that, in 1977!) virginity *as a matter of conscious principle* weren't, aren't, symptomatic of the morality of the 50's but symptomatic of my own morality, my own self." The culture did exert a negative influence, however, since Joyce felt a sense of physical disgust and worthlessness concerning the normal bodily changes of adolescence, especially menstruation, that only compounded the residual shame of her earlier sexual abuse. As an adult, she recalled her youthful distaste for the physical realities of female life. Her shame over menstruation, she wrote in her journal, "I suppose is quite normal, not only in this culture but in all cultures. Shame being in a sense built into the female: biological rather than conditioned. But of course it is exaggerated by conditioning. . . . As a young teenager the experience of menstruation wasn't a very pleasant one for me."

When Joyce wasn't at school or taking the bus into Lockport, she simply stayed at home and worked at her writing, patiently continuing the apprenticeship that would begin bearing fruit in only a few short years. Joyce never recalled her adolescence as a period of social deprivation, however, but as a time fraught with intense excitement and an air of romance—the fleeting romance of adolescent solitude and wonder. One result of Joyce's excited absorption in her writing was the severe insomnia she suffered throughout her high school years. Sometimes, overstimulated by reading and unable to sleep, she would turn on the radio:

> Country & Western music. All-night shows. Strange sense of . . . of what? . . . loneliness, melancholy, romance. I would get up and walk outside, at 2 or 3 in the morning, and watch the cars go by on Transit Road, wondering who was in them. Never very many. And trucks; buses. An almost overwhelming sense of—of curiosity, exhilaration. Loneliness. Wonder.

Often during her busy adult career Joyce would think back to these years and feel a powerful tug of nostalgia. Although she was frequently alone as an adolescent, her gym teacher was wrong in assuming she was lonely; rather, the apprentice writer prized her opportunities to encounter and contemplate the sweeping flood of impressions that adolescence brings, and to translate them into the fictional forms and techniques she was learning so rapidly. Her teenage romance with solitude became the part of her life to which she returned most often in her journals and letters; she would claim at times that her interior self remained youthful even as her adult identity often felt beleaguered by the demands of her multifaceted career. Quite often, in fact, the adult Joyce longed "simply to be alone for a while," she told an interviewer wistfully in 1972, "even if only to think dark thoughts and recall with amazement simpler times."

4

Syracuse
1956–60

Nothing was worthwhile, really worthwhile, except studying; getting high grades; and her own reading, her own work. . . .

—*Marya: A Life* (1986)

When asked if she had been the first person in her family to attend college, Joyce Carol Oates once observed that the question, considering her background, was wrongheaded. In the working-class world of Millersport, where most people lived a paycheck or two away from outright poverty, college had never been an option for anyone before the 1950s. In fact, Joyce told the interviewer, she was the first person in her family to finish high school. Even though Fred Oates's hard work had kept his family off the dole in the late 1930s and 1940s, and had even afforded them a minimal degree of financial security by the time Joyce was a teenager, his brilliant daughter was able to continue her formal education only because she was among the fortunate 11 percent of her high school class who won a college award. Some of Joyce's affluent Williamsville classmates were accepted by prestigious, expensive schools such as Princeton, Cornell, Williams, and Antioch. A larger number entered the state university system at Buffalo, while several others went to Syracuse University, which had offered Joyce matching funds to supplement her New York State Regents scholarship. For this reason, Syracuse seemed a natural choice, since it had a good reputation and was only about 150 miles from Millersport.

Although Joyce felt she would probably become a teacher, a "Directory of Graduates" published in her high school newspaper lists her future occupation as "writer," and most of her high school classmates seemed aware of her ambition. Joyce's career goal is particularly interesting in the context of the directory as a whole, which shows a dramatic (though not surprising, in 1956) divergence of ambitions along gender lines. By far the most popular career goal named by Joyce's female classmates was "secretary" (listed by twenty-three girls), followed by "teacher" (twelve), "housewife" (five), and "nurse" (four). Other female ambitions in the class included becoming a grocery store clerk, a beautician, an airline stewardess. Only a small group of girls dared hope to enter a profession or the arts—there is one listing each for "psychologist," "commercial artist," and "musician." Dozens of their male counterparts, by contrast, confidently planned careers as doctors, engineers, architects, and businessmen.

Joyce remembered that above any professional goals, "in those years girls *hoped* to become engaged directly out of high school, as a way of being shielded from seeking a 'career.'" The few girls from Joyce's senior class who did aspire beyond menial jobs and housewifery were "anomalies." In an essay called "An Unsolved Mystery," Joyce recalled the fate of another Williamsville senior, Betty Miller, who had been, like Joyce, "intellectually advanced" and relatively shy. "We did not resemble each other physically at all," Joyce wrote. "Yet in some mysterious way we were like sisters. Or twins." Betty had received a scholarship to Cornell, where she intended to study chemistry, but for reasons Joyce never discovered her friend committed suicide near the end of her freshman year, swallowing a corrosive chemical she had obtained in a science laboratory. Joyce had tried to maintain the friendship through letters, but Betty was a poor correspondent and had finally stopped writing altogether. On one occasion Joyce telephoned her, but "was hurt by her affected coolness." Like many college students, Joyce would lose track of most of her high school friends, forming more enduring friendships once she arrived at Syracuse University.

The reputation of Syracuse was "on the rise" in the mid-1950s, according to the poet Dick Allen, another undergraduate with literary ambitions whose future wife, Lori Negridge, roomed with Joyce during part of their sophomore year and again when they were seniors. Students and faculty alike were consciously attempting to enhance the school's reputation, which "had been blurred by our success in football and by our being called, sometimes, the 'Miami University of the North.'" The insular world of English majors and would-be journalists was stimulated by famous visiting writers—Robert Frost, Ayn Rand, e.e. cummings, and many others—and by the intense activity surrounding the student newspaper, *The Daily Orange*, and the literary magazine, *Syracuse 10* (until 1958, the magazine was called *The Syracuse Review*). A number of Syracuse undergraduates contemporary with Joyce went on to have similarly distinguished careers, including the news anchorman

Ted Koppel, the actress Suzanne Pleshette, and the writer Michael Herr. The school was also the setting for political agitation, including protests against the nuclear bomb and civil rights activities.

Joyce began her freshman year with a quiet but fierce determination to excel. Freshmen had the option of living either in large dormitories or aging Victorian houses on the campus that were called "freshman cottages." Joyce chose the latter option, since the houses were less expensive and offered a more homelike, protective environment (including a resident adviser) and a quieter setting for her studying and writing. (The only drawbacks were the curfews—strictly enforced for women students, but not for men—and the mandatory house meetings on Sunday night, during which the girls would hear lectures from a professor or other adult member of the community.) Arriving in Syracuse on the hot, muggy afternoon of September 23, Joyce was assigned to Walker Cottage; located on Walnut Avenue, it was the smallest of the cottages and housed about fifteen girls. Joyce later recalled her arrival at Syracuse as "an event of such psychic upheaval" that she could "still remember the dazedness of it—and the half-melancholy, half-manic atmosphere of the freshman cottage I lived in."

One of her housemates that year, Carol North, became one of Joyce's closest college friends. Like Joyce, Carol was an English major with literary interests; the girls also shared a rural upbringing, Carol having grown up on a farm near Rochester. Initially Joyce was placed on the third floor, along with Carol and three other girls; there were three bedrooms on the floor, but all five girls shared a single bathroom. Another of Joyce's freshman housemates, Sandy Gillan, remembered that the third-floor arrangement didn't last: "If you lived under her room, there was this ongoing thunder of a manual typewriter, and it went on until one, two, three o'clock in the morning." Joyce finished out her freshman year in a downstairs room, a single, where the "thunder" of her writing would be less bothersome to the other girls.

Like most college freshmen, Joyce and her housemates felt "terribly homesick," and Joyce recalled "how red-eyed we were after telephone calls in the not-quite-privacy of the little telephone alcove downstairs." But her most vivid memory was the excitement of her first year away from home, especially "the strange, inexplicable romance of waking before dawn in the winter . . . hearing the snow being blown against the window . . . trudging to the dining-hall, which would be nearly deserted at 7 AM." She felt "infatuated, my mind swirling with people, books, ideas, experiences." Her life during those first few months was hectically busy: aside from her course load and her writing, she took a job at the university library, working as a page back in the stacks and earning ninety cents an hour. She recalled "Waking so very early—the alarm going off at 6:45—everything dark & freezing. The cafeteria a block away in a dormitory. Plodding through the snow, groggy from lack of sleep, always rather insecure re. schoolwork despite my grades." College, she quickly saw, wasn't merely a continuation of her Williamsville experience, since it had "a kind of sanctity that high school didn't have. Ritual. Ceremony. Reading & rereading texts. Extra assignments. Books on reserve. A curious insatiable love of learning." After her early-morning visit to the cafeteria, she had an 8 A.M. French class; her other courses that first semester were in English, journalism, botany, and philosophy, in addition to required courses in physical education and "responsible citizenship."

Although Joyce had played basketball well in high school, her freshman P.E. class was the scene of a frightening episode that first year. One day on the basketball court, Joyce suddenly collapsed. Her heart had begun racing, and she couldn't get her breath. "The gym teacher almost fainted," Joyce recalled. "She was ashen white; I don't know what I looked like, but she really thought she was going to lose a student right in front of her eyes." Later Joyce would learn that her collapse was the first manifestation of tachycardia, a malformation of the heart valve that causes the victim to hyperventilate: "It's like a mimicry of death. It's terrifying because you feel that you are dying." The episodes came without warning, and her collapse on the basketball court was only the first of more than fifty attacks that would strike in subsequent years. This physical condition, as it turned out, would enhance rather than hinder her productivity: "It's because of these attacks that I have a heightened sense of mortality and time," she told an interviewer. "That's why I'm always working and why I'm concerned with wasting time."

That initial attack may well have been brought on by the sudden stress of her new environment. She would later write in her journal: "I remember the excitement of each day at Syracuse, the intense nervousness re. exams & papers; a kind of marvelous dread; expectation. At the same time it was hellish to be so young and undefined, to be at the very foot of what appeared to be a hill but was in fact a mountain. If I had known all that lay ahead—! To be 21 again would be a trauma, to be 18 again would be unthinkable. I couldn't bear it." Financially, at least, Joyce's freshman ordeal was eased somewhat by assistance from home. Grandma Woodside occasionally sent checks, while Carolina continued making Joyce's clothes and even did her laundry, which Joyce mailed back to Millersport every week in a metal-banded box. Sandy Gillan remembered that the freshly done laundry would often come back with baked goods packed inside: "Everybody looked for Joyce's laundry box. She did this for years. I don't think she ever went near a washing machine."

Hoping to find a pragmatic outlet for her interest in writing, Joyce began as a journalism major, but quickly transferred into the English department, which was known for its excellent faculty and a number of talented students.

The department was then housed on the bottom floor of the Hall of Languages, an immense, turreted, Gothic structure looming majestically atop one of the campus hills; the building would become both the intellectual and emotional nexus of her time at Syracuse. Three decades later, this looming, idiosyncratic structure with its semicircular stairway remained a powerful image for Joyce, a building she could "practically traverse in my imagination, upstairs and down, including the antiquated ladies' room in the basement."

One of the professors she sought out her freshman year was Walter Sutton, an Americanist and one of the department's most popular teachers. Appearing in his office dressed in a blue reefer coat and a bright red stocking cap, Joyce fixed her large, dark eyes on Sutton and asked if she might do an independent project on Kafka. Explaining that Kafka wasn't quite in his field, Sutton was nonetheless impressed by her, and suggested she take a course with him first. By the time Joyce enrolled in one of Sutton's American literature classes, during her junior year, she was already something of a legend on campus, both for her academic achievement and her fiction prizes. "She was also capable, I thought, of very precocious statements and judgments," Sutton remembered. Near the end of a course in nineteenth-century American literature, she remarked to him that it seemed, collectively, that the great American authors in the 1800s "were learning to write, over the course of a century," a comment that showed the critical sophistication of her reading and also suggested that she read from a writer's point of view. In private conversations with Sutton, Joyce could be pointed and even caustic in her remarks, sometimes expressing her opinion, though an undergraduate herself, on "what faculty members she thought should, or should not, be teaching graduate courses."

Another of Joyce's English professors, Arthur Hoffman, recalled her shy disposition, but part of her quietness in Hoffman's class may be explained by the subject matter: eighteenth-century English literature. An admirer of turbulent, passionate authors such as Lawrence and Dostoevsky, and of the modernist experimentations of Kafka and Faulkner, Joyce has often expressed impatience with the decorous artificiality of Augustan writing. Hoffman himself admitted that his class, offering a detailed investigation of the rhymed couplet, "may have bored the hell out of some students," Joyce among them. She remained "totally silent" throughout the course, though she later credited her professor with teaching her to respect the achievement of eighteenth-century authors. (When writing a series of academic satires in the 1970s, however, she couldn't resist poking fun at the kind of scholarship "inspired" by literature of that period. In a journal called *Augustan Studies*, one of her characters publishes articles with the titles "The Decline of the Enjambed Couplet in the Early Eighteenth Century" and "The Return of the

Enjambed Couplet in the Late Eighteenth Century.") Hoffman was also the faculty adviser to the student literary magazine and a close friend of Donald Dike, the creative writing professor who became Joyce's most important influence at Syracuse. Hoffman remembered that Dike also commented on her shyness, saying that "she brought these manuscripts to him and offered them in the most shy and modest way, as though they were nothing."

By the end of her freshman year, Joyce had adjusted to the intensity of her new environment; during her first semester she earned four A and three B grades, but in her second she made A's in all her courses except physical education (an uninspiring class in badminton). She had also overcome her shyness and modesty about her fiction enough to submit stories to the *Syracuse Review*, the student-edited magazine, and to join the literary staff. Joyce remembered feeling intimidated by the other staff members, three young Jewish women from upper-middle-class families. "I was in awe of these very bright women. That they should want to publish my work just seemed amazing." To Joyce as a wide-eyed, hopeful freshman, the *Syracuse Review* office in the Hall of Languages had a rarefied, even sacred aura. It was "fraught with mystery, a place of sacred events." Only as an adult did Joyce look back and realize that it was really just a windowless closet with a tattered sofa, an old carpet, a table with coffee rings.

Joyce's stories published in *Syracuse Review* that first year show the dramatic progress she had made as a fiction writer in the two years since "A Long Way Home," written when she was sixteen. "Lament Cantabile," in the January 1957 issue, and "Synchronal," in the April 1957 issue, demonstrate not only a precocious technical proficiency but also the fascination with psychological disturbance, the tendency toward allegorical structures, and the bleak and dispassionate portrayal of modern society that would characterize much of Joyce's mature work.

"Synchronal" describes the chance meeting of two teenaged boys on a country road: the viewpoint character, Paul, and a boy named "Bethlehem" whose clothes are spattered with blood. The story labors under the influence of Faulkner, both in substance and style. Bethlehem's eyes are described as "two pieces of shiny coal pressed into his face, lifeless, immobile"—a description borrowed almost verbatim from "A Rose for Emily." Faulkner's mannerisms intrude in other descriptive passages, as in a house that "leaned skyward out of the brazen and sunfilled air with a look at once tragic and comic, forlorn, grotesque, and prevailing." "Synchronal" suggests the influence of Flannery O'Connor, whose most famous stories were appearing during Joyce's college years in quarterlies such as *Sewanee Review* and *Kenyon Review*— exciting new magazines Joyce had discovered in the library's periodical room. (Joyce would dramatize this discovery in "The Death of the *Kenyon Review*," a quirky story she published under the pseudonym "Rae Jolene Smith" in the spring 1978 issue of *Yale Review*.) Like O'Connor's The Misfit in "A Good Man Is Hard to Find," Bethlehem is guilty of mass murder and indulges in philosophical asides referring to Christ, the end of the world, and the motiveless malignity of human beings in the twentieth century.

Narrower in scope and ambition, "Lament Cantabile" tells of the wasted emotional life of a self-deluded woman who has allowed her father (again like Faulkner's Emily) to keep away gentleman callers. Like "Synchronal," which had stressed the vacant, lifeless qualities of its characters and setting, "Lament Cantabile" portrays the woman's pathetic fixation on her pet bird, which sits in its cage "like something stuffed full of lumpy cotton, barely living." As in much of her later fiction, Joyce resolves the plot through violence: a young boy reaches inside the cage and kills the bird with a pair of scissors. "Lament" is more controlled in language and execution than "Synchronal," but both show that Joyce apprehended very early the direction her work would take. Despite their unassimilated influences, both display a remarkable blend of ambitious, serious themes with carefully deliberated technique, qualities so rare in undergraduate fiction that the admiration of Donald Dike and of Joyce's colleagues on the literary staff is easy to understand.

Despite all her frenetic academic and literary activity during her freshman year, Joyce found some time for social life, including her close friendships with Carol North and with Bob Phillips, another freshman who was also an aspiring writer. With Carol, Joyce attended free lectures and concerts sponsored by the university, and they occasionally ventured into town for movies or shopping. Joyce had also begun attending sorority "rush" parties. Her primary motive was pragmatic rather than social, since a sorority would provide a living situation much more congenial than the alternative—life in a crowded, noisy dormitory.

Unlike most of the girls, Joyce waited until the second semester to pledge a sorority, choosing Phi Mu at the urging of her friend Lori Negridge, who "rushed" Joyce. Lori later admitted that Phi Mu was "lowly regarded" on campus. "We were mainly the kind of people who couldn't fit in anywhere else." Next door to the Phi Mu house was the Phi Pi sorority, which Carol North had pledged. Carol maintained her friendship with Joyce but remembered that other friends "would look at me askance" for even socializing with a Phi Mu. The Phi Mu girls were considered neither particularly bright nor good-looking, just "sort of nondescript." At this time Joyce had long, wavy dark hair, and Bob Phillips recalled another attractive feature: "her enormous big brown eyes, very liquid, very intelligent." But like many student intellectuals of the time Joyce wore imposing black-rimmed glasses and plain, dark clothes. Soon enough it became clear that she had little in common with the other Phi Mu girls and that the sorority would prove a hindrance to her academic goals rather than the sanctuary she had envisioned. The English department's Shakespeare professor, Mary Marshall, saw Joyce as "a hawk among the pigeons" at Phi Mu: "her sorority sisters were mostly not very impressive. Joyce was of a different order of sensibility altogether." Joyce would later refer to the "despairing" nature of her sorority experience, saying that her decision to join was "a mistake from the start."

Joyce had decided to room with Lori Negridge in the Phi Mu house, and Lori recalled that they had "a large room, and we each had our own walk-in closets. The walls were pink. We went out and bought without arguing matching gray cord bedspreads. That was the last time we agreed on anything for a while." Joyce likewise remembered that she and her new roommate had serious conflicts. "We didn't get along. Lori smoked; she was a chain-smoker." The girls agreed to change their quarters, and as she had done in Walker Cottage, Joyce moved into a room by herself. The private, slant-ceilinged room, located at the top of the house, appears in much of her writing. Alone in her new quarters, "I was *so* happy," she recalled.

The Phi Mu house itself was attractive and comfortable. Built of white-washed stone, it featured a spacious porch spanning the front with large French doors. Inside were a foyer, a reception room, and a well-furnished living room whose centerpiece was a grand piano. The food was adequate, if sometimes rather bland. On Sunday nights the British house mother, Mrs. Hodson, presided over a formal dinner, for which the girls were expected to appear punctually in full dress, including stockings and heels. Mrs. Hodson's favorite meal for such occasions was roast chicken, mashed potatoes, and cauliflower; one evening, surveying this colorless repast, Joyce called it their "white dinner." The name stuck, and the girls jokingly referred to their Sunday evening meal as "the white dinner" from that night forward.

The principles and requirements of sorority life, however, thwarted Joyce's happiness almost from the beginning. She became aware that one of the more sinister aspects of Greek life was its bigotry, both racial and religious. "Joyce was more adamant than some of the rest of us," according to Sandy Gillan, who served as vice president of Panhellenic in her senior year and made some progress in changing the regulations. "She had probably spent a great deal more time thinking about it." Joyce found the racism on campus generally to be "enormously disturbing," partly because in the late 1950s it "went unacknowledged, unspoken." (She would filter some of these emotions into her heroine Iris Courtney's college experiences in *Because It Is Bitter, and Because It Is My Heart* [1990].) Joyce remembered "a powdered and perfumed alum explaining the sorority's exclusion of Jews and blacks: 'You see, we have conferences at the Lake Placid Club, and wouldn't it be a shame if *all* our members couldn't attend. . . . Why, it would be embarrassing for them, wouldn't it?' " The dull meetings and mindless activities—decorating floats, singing sentimental songs for a Christmas chorale—seemed a waste of time, and the sorority fined members who failed to attend. When they joined Phi Mu, the girls were told there would be one meeting each week, lasting two to four hours; but often there were three or four meetings. Lori Negridge remembered that the float decoration involved spending hours "stuffing toilet paper into chicken wire"—an activity so inane that Joyce refused to participate. "Instead of working with Nietzsche or Kant," she recalled, "I was expected to put crepe paper over wire, and to like doing it. Everybody would be down in the basement working on the float, and Joyce would be upstairs. And this was perceived as some kind of violation of the order of the universe." Remembering her adolescent boredom when forced to attend church, Joyce remarked that "the sorority functions and the utterly insipid 'Greek ceremonies' made the Catholic mass look positively exciting by contrast."

Though "feminism" was not yet in her vocabulary, she also found it difficult to accept the other girls' unconscious but slavish adherence to patriarchal codes of female conduct. As time passed, the "Greek" system came to represent much of what she detested in American culture at the time. In 1978, she indicted virtually all aspects of her sorority experience: "The racial and religious bigotry; the asininity of 'secret' ceremonies, the moronic emphasis upon 'activities' totally unrelated to—in fact antithetical to—intellectual exploration; [. . .] the aping of the worst American traits—boosterism, God-fearing-ism, smug ignorance, a craven worship of conformity; the sheer *mess* of the place once one got beyond the downstairs." By 1978, of course, Joyce was a world-famous author, but at age eighteen she had no way to fight the organization she had joined so casually. Joyce did make efforts to leave the sorority, but she met with immediate resistance. Appealing to the dean of women, Mrs. Marge Smith—her nickname was "large Marge"—Joyce learned that university policy did not permit deactivization. The housing agreement Joyce had signed when joining Phi Mu amounted to an enforceable contract, in which Joyce had agreed to pay room and board for three years. She was told that if she really intended to leave Phi Mu, she had better seek out a lawyer. Joyce had no choice but to remain in the sorority house, where she participated in its functions and "sisterhood" as minimally as possible until her graduation.

The combination of overwork and disillusionment contributed to a breakdown during December of Joyce's sophomore year. She had earned grades of A in all her courses during the fall term (this time, even in badminton) but her state of exhaustion and her newly discovered heart condition forced her to quit her library job. As always, Joyce retreated into her writing. Her sorority sisters would congregate in the common room, "smoking, screaming with laughter about boys, and eating, and I would be typing. So I was thought of as very strange."

Aside from knowing Joyce to be extremely private, some of the other Phi Mu girls also considered her manipulative and unnecessarily tight with her money. Although Joyce had a savings account, she would borrow from friends rather than make a withdrawal and lose interest, even when the friend had to tap her own savings account to grant the loan. When Lori Negridge pointed out to Joyce that now the friend was losing interest, "she just smiled." In a letter to Carol North, Joyce commented mischievously that one of her friends was "rather spoiled and with a little too much money for *my* good (she expects me to spend my money too, which is an outrageous thing)." Beneath her humor, however, lay the economic poverty of Joyce's early life that had helped to encourage her frugal habits. Since Joyce seldom talked about her family background to friends, they had no way of knowing that Joyce's reluctance to spend money had deep-rooted causes.

Joyce was also disinclined to perform chores that she found unrewarding, and occasionally talked friends into helping her. Gail Gleasner, her close friend from Williamsville, had transferred from a private Catholic college to Syracuse during Joyce's sophomore year. According to Carolina Oates, Gail would often be talked into doing laundry or sewing by the overworked Joyce. "She was very strong-willed in that way," Carolina recalled. According to Sandy Gillan, Joyce had a limited interest in friendship, always placing her academic work and her writing first. "She very much wanted to be writing, wanted to protect her time, but she also wanted to belong—and was reluctant to."

Joyce's compulsive working habits at Syracuse might have helped her academically, but they continued to keep her under considerable emotional strain. In *Marya: A Life*, Marya's overwork results in this same kind of personal turmoil, making her susceptible "to tears at odd unprovoked moments, to eating binges, to outbursts of temper"; there are times when she isolates herself altogether, keeping her door "closed for days on end and speaking to no one." Even during "vacations," Joyce worked constantly; her brother remembered "the sound of a typewriter coming from her room all day because she was constantly writing one of her stories." Adopting a facetious tone in her summertime letters to Carol North, Joyce nonetheless reported that she was working hard. Writing from the viewpoint of a semiliterate fictional character, "Bethlehem J. Hollis," she described her own work habits: "Most of the time she sits at her desk, from 10 to 5, doodling on bits of scrap paper. Occasionally she tries to write somethin but is aghassed at the thot that some eng.

professor named Donald Dike or Donald Duck is goin to leer over it in the near future & has to date done circa 190 pp of short stories & goin on 300 pp of some novel." In another letter to Carol, she adopted the tongue-in-cheek persona of her brother, signing the letter "Robin J. Oates." In the letter, "Robin" noted that he was sometimes called "the Plague of Millersport" and that he had encountered, in his sister Joyce's room, "a lot of junk-papers mostly with scribblin on them—faces & designs & things & some writin all crost out."

Carolina Oates and Grandma Woodside worried that Joyce worked too hard and neglected to eat enough—concerns that would form a persistent theme in their communications with Joyce well into her adulthood. To their distress, Joyce had begun exhibiting signs of the anorexia that would continue to plague her for many years. Her weight fluctuated dramatically, and during visits home she would often appear gaunt and pale. "Joyce was never heavy," according to Lori Negridge, "although she thought she was and often complained about being too fat." Joyce's letters to Carol North often commented on her weight: in August 1957 she boasted that she had dieted for two weeks and planned to lose fifteen pounds; a year later, she remarked similarly that "I, Joyce Oates, have been on a diet for a week or so and have done marvelously, having lost nine pounds." Marya Knauer experiences anorexia as a kind of perverse triumph: "Her puritan spirit blazed; she thought it an emblem of her purity that the waistbands of her skirts were now too loose, her underwear was a size too large." Although most anorexics exhibit symptoms during their adolescence and early twenties, Joyce's most serious bout with this disorder—to which she sometimes applied a more euphemistic term, "fasting"—would occur in her early thirties, during the most stressful period in her life.

Prompted by feelings of inferiority regarding her background, by her desire to excel, and by her intense drive to explore simultaneously her own talent and the vast body of world literature and philosophy, Joyce remained so intensely focused on her college work that her physical identity seemed insignificant, its needs ignored. Her reputation for overwork became legendary among her fellow students. Lori Negridge remembered Joyce complaining that she was unprepared to take a test because she'd read one of the required books only four times. "Unless she read a book five times, she did not truly have it." Joyce admitted that if a professor assigned a ten-page paper, she would turn in thirty pages instead. Yet Joyce often joked about her devoted studying, as in this passage from a letter to Carol North about her absorption in philosophy: "I am now in the midst of being de-Spinozaed because now I am reading Immanuel Kant and he is converting me from Spinoza's pantheism in the same way Spinoza converted me from John Stuart Mill's hedonism, and before him Thomas Hobbes converted me from Butler's God-liness, which was, however, already quite ruint by Nietzsche's Will to Power!!!"

Joyce was even more obsessive about her writing. According to Bob Phillips, "The rumor on campus was that she'd take a ream of paper, write a novel on one side, then turn the sheets over and write another novel on the back. When both sides were covered, she'd discard it all." The mystique surrounding Joyce's work habits was only intensified by her love of privacy. If anyone happened into her room while she was writing, Sandy Gillan recalled, "she very deliberately would put something over the manuscript. She was not open with it—it was hers. As you got to know her better, you respected that."

Joyce's scant leisure time was spent with friends like Bob Phillips, with whom she took long walks around the elm-shaded campus. But her closest friend was her sorority sister Dottie Palmer, another "renegade" from typical activities at Phi Mu. Dottie was a tall, energetic, witty blond with whom Joyce developed an intense, good-humored camaraderie that excluded their other friends. "With Dottie, [Joyce] was not only open, but silly," Lori Ne-gridge recalled. "They seemed to live in their own little world, with tightly interlocked wavelengths, and they found the greater world hilarious." Some-times Lori would become part of the clique, and she found it "very warm, comfortable and accepting, much like sisterhood is supposed to be." Joyce re-spected Dottie's independence and her refusal to conform to others' expecta-tions—including Joyce's own. Occasionally Dottie would side with Lori against Joyce, especially where Joyce's constant writing was concerned. The three girls moved into a room together during their senior year. According to Lori, "Dottie and I would be trying to sleep and Joyce would be madly typing away. I solved it—with Dottie goading me on—by cracking my toes. Joyce couldn't handle the sound," and would agree to stop writing for the night.

One major distraction from Joyce's writing was the romantic relationship she developed with Frank Aronson, a biochemistry major whom she dated regularly from her sophomore year until graduation. A studious, dark-haired Jewish boy from Brooklyn who loved opera, Frank had the intellectual ability and low-keyed temperament that made him an ideal complement to Joyce's more intense personality. They discussed Bergman and Fellini films, listened to classical music, and took a German conversation class together. Frank was dependable and unthreatening; the couple went out regularly, sometimes four or five times a week, occasionally double-dating with Dick Allen and Lori Negridge. Although Dick felt that Joyce and Frank's relationship lacked passion, Joyce's roommate Lori remembered otherwise: "Much to my embar-rassment, I came upon Frank and Joyce on more than one occasion and can testify that their relationship contained a great deal of passion." Another of Joyce's sorority sisters, Sandy Gillan, claimed that Joyce's having a boyfriend "surprised the daylights out of all of us." Occasionally Joyce would bring him to sorority functions, "but not very often. It was a very different kind of relationship." Joyce, always extremely private, didn't indulge in boy talk and refused to discuss Frank with her friends.

"We were fairly 'serious' about each other," Joyce later recalled. "I remember Frank as extremely intelligent, thoughtful, cultivated. Visiting his family in Brooklyn, however, I did not feel that they looked upon me with much enthusiasm. A little Catholic girl." She remembered only one serious breach in the relationship. One Saturday Frank hadn't arranged a date with Joyce, and she was furious: "I was so vexed, on a mean-spirited level, by him, it seemed to unravel our entire relationship." They continued to go out, but Frank's brief defection had threatened Joyce's sense of stability and control: "how odd, how sad, that in three years of friendship with Frank I seem to recall only that incident that upset me," she wrote in her journal. Joyce's involvement in her imaginative work required even in college an absolute control over her personal life, a control that sometimes necessitated an exercise of the "strong-willed" nature her mother had observed. The incident with Frank seemed, to Joyce, to reveal a chink in her boyfriend's shining armor, making her aware that their friendship probably would not last beyond her college years. As late as June of 1960, however, after Joyce had graduated, she considered marriage to Frank Aronson a real possibility. "I might be going to convert to Judaism," she confided to Carol North, "depending upon circumstances."

More significant than her fairly quiet, "safe" romance with Frank Aronson was the relationship she developed with her creative writing professor, Donald Dike, who nurtured Joyce's writing from the moment she enrolled in his workshop as a sophomore. Impressed by the quality of Joyce's fiction and perplexed by her modesty about it, Dike not only offered praise and feedback but also became vocal on campus about the shy new talent he had discovered. He told his colleague Walter Sutton that the English department might have "another Katherine Anne Porter" on its hands. Bob Phillips, too, recalled that "Dike was positive he'd discovered a genius in Joyce," and Dike's wife concurred: "Donald felt a very deep respect and affection for her. He considered her a genius." Heartened by his praise and admiring of his intelligence, Joyce in turn idolized her teacher.

Dike was also well liked by colleagues and other students, despite his complex personality. A heavy drinker, a passionate admirer of Faulkner and Conrad, he often gave the impression of being uncomfortable in the professorial role. He struck Carol North as "one of those very creative people who doesn't quite have the talent to make it" as a writer, but who felt some bitterness about functioning as a mentor to students more talented than he. Dike's

colleague Arthur Hoffman admired him "without bound," though acknowledging that he was a man "of considerable emotional temperature who could
get pretty loud on occasion." Bob Phillips found him "an overwhelming personality, loud, contentious, almost demonic," and Joyce herself remembered
her teacher as "a most forceful, complex, ambiguous personality." While
Joyce basked in his praise, other students resented him for not appreciating
their ability. "I had the uneasy feeling that he overestimated my putative talent," Joyce remarked. "His praise and encouragement (he wanted me to be a
'writer,' not a teacher) seemed to me dangerous, feeding a young person's capacity for self-delusion. . . . I felt that his singling me out for praise isolated
me from my friends and classmates, and made me singularly disliked."

Joyce's fellow students were certainly aware of Dike's admiration for her
work. Bob Phillips recalled that she was too shy to read her own fiction in
class, so Dike would read it enthusiastically for her, while Joyce "hung her
head." According to Dick Allen, Dike seldom offered much negative criticism
to his students, preferring to let them develop in their own way without imposing his judgments. Dike felt that Joyce "could do no wrong," and often
said that he had nothing to teach her. The result was "a cordial teacher-
student relationship, he praising, she encouraged by the praise but realizing,
even then, that she didn't really need his advice." But Joyce came to depend
on his unqualified approval, so that she felt betrayed when, on one occasion,
he did make negative comments on one of her stories. Like the incident with
Frank Aronson, Dike's unexpected criticism violated Joyce's strictly defined
view of their relationship. Lori Negridge remembered that Joyce became "so
upset she confronted him, although confrontation was not normally her
way." Dike responded by salving Joyce's wounded ego, and they resumed
their posture of mutual, unqualified admiration.

One key contribution Dike made to Joyce's literary development related
to the sometimes violent and sordid subject matter in her fiction. She confided to him that she worried about her parents' reaction to her work, fearing
they might consider it "not nice," and Dike tried to reassure her. Fred and
Carolina acknowledged that they were shocked by some of their daughter's
stories, at first. Carolina would say to Fred, "Where did she learn about
that?" But Fred reasoned that Joyce had always "had her eyes open" to the
world around her, after all, and had been reading incessantly since childhood.
He understood that "she wasn't any longer a twelve-year-old little girl" and
that her work simply reflected the turbulent society she'd been carefully observing all her life. Joyce's parents were heartened when Dike took the time
to write them a letter on June 28, 1959, at the end of her junior year. Dike
wanted Fred and Carolina to know that Joyce had "gifts of the mind and the
imagination which are extraordinary," and was "probably the most brilliant

student" he had ever taught at Syracuse. Although Joyce would make a fine critic, Dike insisted that "my deepest concern is with her rarer—and possibly very important—talent for fiction and poetry."

By June 1959, Dike had reason to believe that his confidence in Joyce's gifts might soon be affirmed by the literary establishment. As a sophomore and junior she had continued earning straight A's, an average marred only by a B in physical education in the fall of her junior year. Moreover, her course load was ambitious: in addition to her writing and literature classes, she had decided to minor in philosophy, taking courses in classic, contemporary, and religious philosophy. (She was discouraged from pursuing graduate study in philosophy, however, "by a kindly professor who pointed out that it was, and is, hardly a field for a woman.") For Dike's class alone, she had written count-less stories, several of which had won the fiction prize of Rho Delta Phi, the English honorary society, and had been published in *Syracuse 10*. In addition, Joyce had turned in several novels. Encouraged by Dike's praise, she began submitting her work to national magazines and contests.

One of the most prestigious competitions open to college students in the 1950s was the *Mademoiselle* College Fiction contest, which Sylvia Plath had won in 1952 as a Smith undergraduate. Early in her junior year, Joyce entered a story in the competition called "In the Old World." (She liked the title so well that she gave it to another, entirely different story published in the March 1959 issue of *Syracuse 10*.) Although none of her fellow English ma-jors were surprised, Joyce herself was astonished when she learned from *Mademoiselle* that she had been chosen, along with one other girl, as a cowin-ner of the prize, their manuscripts culled from more than six hundred en-tries. "I remember the shock, the slow-dawning pleasure," she wrote in her journal years later, "the sense of *But I don't deserve this*." She blurted out the news to some of her sorority sisters, then ran up the steep hill to the Hall of Languages, where a flyer about the contest had been posted on a bulletin board outside Dike's office. The letter from *Mademoiselle* hadn't mentioned the dollar amount of her prize; she had thought it was $250, and was thrilled to learn that it was $500. Twenty years later, she remembered vividly the "fluttery heart-racing sensation of success, the pleasure of calling home, of telling Dike the next day, etc., etc." Soon another story was accepted by the prestigious literary magazine *Epoch*. Although she didn't recognize it at the time, Joyce's professional career had begun in earnest.

The stories Joyce wrote in her junior and senior years showed her increas-ing ability to articulate her unique vision of the world around her. Complex in both theme and execution, such stories as "Rapport," "Sweet Love Re-membered," "A Confession," and the two different narratives published under the title "In the Old World" convey both the natural and socioeconomic harshness of the western New York countryside; they portray characters who, like Flannery O'Connor's, battle losing odds in the struggle against their environment and often cannot articulate or even understand that struggle. Moreover, Joyce's fascination with philosophical issues prompted her to construct allegorical narratives that balance the reader's attention between the individual dramas being portrayed and the larger, more abstract questions about the modern world raised by the characters' experiences.

"Rapport" features an encounter between a physician named Morgan and a young girl who are traveling through a countryside ravaged by brushfires; Morgan is forced to recognize his inability to "save" anyone, including himself. ("Rapport" seems to be an Ur-version of "Upon the Sweeping Flood," the O. Henry–winning title story of Joyce's second collection, in which a man in circumstances similar to Morgan's navigates a flood-ravaged rural area.) Moral confusion also lies at the heart of "A Confession," which narrates the journey of two men on their way to tell a black migrant worker's family that the worker has been lynched (the man had confessed to setting the workers' camp on fire). By the end of this oblique, riddling tale, their epistemological despair leads to one of the men's decision to murder the other.

In the Kafkaesque 1959 version of "In the Old World," a young man named Nathan finds himself on trial with no awareness or memory of his crime. Again Joyce stresses the precarious moral underpinnings of the "new world" in which Nathan finds himself: "All things that happen are more than you, you can't touch them, they just keep on an' on after you—die— How can one of them just say this thing happenin' now has somethin' to do with what happened sometime *else*?" Set in a courtroom, the story is based on a trial Joyce had attended in Lockport in June 1957. She later recalled the trial as a capital murder case: "two young men had murdered a man, had stolen his money and had murdered him." She couldn't remember the verdict, but she did recall that the courtroom proceedings were tedious, such "a contrast with the reality of the murder." This contrast prompted Joyce to "philosophical broodings upon what a tenuous hold reality has with any other previous time. The young men in the courtroom were clearly not the young men who committed the murder." Instead of crazed-looking killers, she had sat staring at well-behaved young men in neckties. "I think I was sort of impressed by that." In a letter to Carol North, Joyce wrote jokingly about the trial, but her lifelong fascination with human psychological complexity, especially the kind of Jekyll-and-Hyde doubleness often apparent in her characters, had one of its earliest and most dramatic manifestations in this trial she witnessed at age nineteen.

The biblical cadences, the depiction of apocalyptic fires, floods, and judgments, the contrast in values between the "old world" and a confused modern landscape—such features give these stories the impersonal, mythic power that would be noted in reviews of Joyce's first collection, *By the North Gate* (1963). Two other stories written at Syracuse, "Sweet Love Remembered" and the *Mademoiselle* version of "In the Old World," would be included in that collection. That these stories, revised only slightly for book publication in 1963, had been completed in 1958, during Joyce's junior year, testify to the doggedness with which she worked as a college student to develop her distinctive narrative voice and to map out her fictional terrain.

These two nationally published stories also show her breaking out of the somewhat static, prolix forms of allegory that were notable in some of her earlier fiction. "Sweet Love Remembered" describes the casual relationship of a young waitress, Amie, and an older man, both of whom feel adrift in a world devoid of meaning. Amie lives with her "knowledge that the world was false and painful" and that "she would always be alone with this knowledge," while her lover complains that "What we say has a meaning only for now, and for this place, and as soon as we go off somewhere else it all changes, it can't even be remembered correctly." The one anchor in Amie's life, referenced in the Shakespearean allusion of the story's title, is her recollection of her brother coming toward home from the woods, his leg bleeding—a memory that seems emblematic of the wounding nostalgia Amie suffers almost constantly. A mere thirteen pages long, "Sweet Love Remembered" is one of Joyce's most powerful early stories, evoking a young woman's sense of loss and hopelessness at the very moment her adult life is beginning. Since Amie's youthful circumstances strongly resemble Joyce's—Amie's rural home sounds exactly like Joyce's in Millersport, even including a creek bordering the property—it is tempting to read the story as depicting Joyce's own fierce nostalgia about her early home life and her apprehensions about her future in the larger world.

Relatively little of Joyce's earliest fiction, however, features women as protagonists: just as she would experiment with a male-sounding version of her name by publishing early work as "J. C. Oates," she seems not yet to have considered herself a "woman writer" empowered to deal forthrightly with feminist concerns. She would occasionally assume a male alter ego later in her career, including such notable portrayals as Jesse Vogel in *Wonderland* (1971), Xavier Kilgarvan in *Mysteries of Winterthurn* (1984), and Judd Mulvaney in *We Were the Mulvaneys* (1996), but male characters dominate her undergraduate fiction. Even in her first published volume, *By the North Gate*, only three out of fourteen stories have women as central characters.

One male alter ego she wrote about frequently while at Syracuse was named "Swan Walpole," the central character of the *Mademoiselle* prizewinner "In the Old World" and also a major figure in her second novel, A *Garden of Earthly Delights* (1967). Carol North read a number of stories about Swan, and remembered that Joyce's identification with him was so strong that she once sent a letter to Carol signed "Swan" rather than "Joyce." In the *Mademoiselle* story, Swan comes into town seeking the sheriff, but finds instead a callow deputy lacking a badge; also present, working in the deputy's office, is a black boy with a bandaged eye. Like most of Joyce's early protagonists, Swan has a philosophical turn of mind and a fascination with a Bible-dominated "old world" of absolute moral values. He speculates about how the town's founders must have felt, creating a new society, a new world: "they couldn't resist; a place where all things might be different, where nothing had anything to do with anything else." But then Swan tells the increasingly puzzled deputy about a violent incident that happened recently, out in the country: a black boy had been chased by several white boys, who then cut out the black boy's eye. Swan wonders aloud (while taking a knife out of his pocket) what happened to the idea of "an eye for an eye," since no one had been punished for the crime. Finally understanding Swan's guilt, the deputy puts on his tarnished badge and tells him to go home, but the narrative has conveyed in a powerfully ironic way Swan's awareness of his society's racial injustice and its lack of a moral center.

Focusing obsessively on a world that lacks any discernible moral structure and concerned with themes of sin and guilt, hypocrisy and injustice, natural catastrophe and human violence, Joyce attempted to work out in her undergraduate fiction many of the philosophical riddles she studied in the turbulent novels of Melville, Faulkner, Kafka, and other authors she read under the tutelage of Donald Dike and Walter Sutton. Her fiction was perhaps most powerfully influenced, however, by a writer she had discovered on her own during her freshman year. Arriving early for a class in the Hall of Languages, she found a paperback anthology left behind by another student and began reading from the work of Friedrich Nietzsche. Her reaction was immediate and powerful; fascinated by a philosophy that aspired to the condition of literature and by a thinker who was also a poet, a mystic, and an "antiphilosopher," Joyce sensed in the freedom and daring of Nietzsche's thought a corollary to her own imaginative plunges. At an age when most young adults are feeling their way toward independence, Nietzsche's example gave Joyce permission to exercise her own developing artistic will. Years later, she recalled the exciting impact of her discovery: "Late adolescence is the time for love, or, rather, for passion—the conviction that *within the next hour* something can happen, will happen, to irrevocably alter one's life. [. . .] To have read Nietzsche at age eighteen, when one's senses are most keenly and nervously alert, the very envelope of the skin dangerously porous; to have heard, and been struck to the heart, by that astonishing voice—what ecstasy! what visceral unease!—as if the very floor were shifting beneath one's feet."

During her sophomore year Joyce's confidence had risen to the point that, with Donald Dike's enthusiastic support, she made a gesture toward book publication, the first since she had submitted her full-length novel at age fifteen. Thumbing through a writer's magazine, Joyce saw a listing for Vanguard Press, which included the encouraging information that the publisher was interested in new writers. She knew little about Vanguard and certainly had no idea that the company had published such celebrated novelists as Saul Bellow and James T. Farrell. "If I had known they had published James Farrell I would have been intimidated," she recalled. "I would probably have felt that I shouldn't send them anything." Though Joyce did submit a novel, she met with another rejection; but the editorial head at Vanguard, James Henle, expressed an interest in seeing further work. In August 1958 Joyce sent a second manuscript, this time a collection of her stories. Her letter accompanying the submission—neatly typed on stationery decorated with tiny flowers and the scripted monogram "J"—suggests the self-deprecating modesty that Dike had noted. "Enclosed are the stories," she wrote to Henle, "which I suppose will seem queer to you, but which I hope won't be entirely a waste of time." She closed by inviting Henle "to take as long a time as you want; there is certainly no hurry about this." A Vanguard reader's note to Henle, scrawled along the borders of Joyce's letter, notes that they should probably reject the stories because "they're depressing" and dealt with characters "living in a fantasy world. As the author says, they're queer." The reader added that Joyce wrote with "a curious skill & is, undoubtedly, a talent," but that the stories were "half sheer genius, the other [half] sheer Kafkaesque fudge." Joyce's manuscript was returned, and again she was invited to send future work. Suffering the editorial gambit of encourage-and-reject throughout the following year, Joyce added a postscript to an August 1959 letter to Bob Phillips in New York: "Do go over to Vanguard Press and break a window or something." Another three years would pass before she finally received good news from Vanguard.

During her junior year Joyce applied for, and received, a summer school fellowship to Harvard University. Recommending her, Walter Sutton remarked that she was "extremely intelligent and mature in her perceptions," with the ability to write "unusually well in both creative and critical modes." Aided by the scholarship and the money from her *Mademoiselle* prize, Joyce made the most of her time at Harvard, rooming with her close friend Gail Gleasner in Weld Hall, an aged building imbued with the sanctity of Ivy

League tradition. Hoping to solidify her background in classic English literature, she took a course in Chaucer from a professor she described as "the
most difficult in the English department, with a 40% failure expected." She
also took a class in Shakespeare, audited a course in the modern novel taught
by Allen Tate, and attended poetry readings given by Stanley Kunitz and
Richard Wilbur. On a weekend visit to Dartmouth College, Joyce attempted
a literary encounter of another kind. Having heard that J. D. Salinger was researching a new book in the Dartmouth library, she and a friend "blundered
into the library, looking brightly around; it then occurred to me that I did not
know what Mr. Salinger looked like." After finding his photograph in a reference book, Joyce continued the search but never laid eyes on the elusive
Salinger.

Despite the sprightly, ironic tone of her letters from Harvard, Joyce also
used her time away from Syracuse to reflect on her own literary development.
Even with her awards and her teachers' praise, she continued to have doubts
about the kind of writing to which she felt drawn, especially since she hoped
for a teaching career. Her economic background—which included memories
of her father's uncertain employment during her childhood—contributed to
her pragmatic, conservative view of her job prospects.

Her gender added to the sense of insecurity, since few women were encouraged to pursue graduate study in the 1950s. One of her Harvard professors was the prominent critic Dorothy Van Ghent, whose course in the
English novel Joyce audited. Joyce wrote to Carol North that Van Ghent was
"really fine, and an inspiration for those who might aspire to samelike positions." But there were few such encouraging role models at Harvard, Syracuse, or elsewhere. Fortunate as Joyce was to have supportive teachers like
Donald Dike, she felt acutely the lack of a female mentor. "If I had had a
'JCO' with whom to talk, aged 18 or 19," she wrote, "I think I would have
been enormously grateful. But, then, 1956–60, there were only men." Despite this frustration, however, Joyce later remarked that "though there were
few women professors at Syracuse, women students were extremely re-
spectably treated and encouraged. It might not have been like that elsewhere,
Harvard or Columbia for instance. I was fortunate."

If women were not expected to pursue academic careers, Joyce knew they
were certainly not expected to write violent stories about the seamy underside of American life. "I am beginning to wonder about the wisdom of a great
deal of some really vicious writing of mine which has been published in
relationship to the future," she wrote, referring to her *Syracuse 10* stories.
Surprisingly, she considered it "quite likely that I will not be doing too much
writing anymore." After this stunningly inaccurate prediction, Joyce repeated
the idea that her work was "simply vicious," adding that "I am tired indeed of

this particular climate of thought" and that she found one of her own poems "disgusting." At other times, she tried making light of her subject matter, as in the generally facetious letters she sent to Carol North: "I would have one of my characters write you," Joyce quipped, "but they are too out of sorts, it has been hot and humid lately, and what with several months since the last murder they are getting a little restive and a little bored."

Such comments show that Joyce possessed an uneasy awareness of the kind of writer she was destined to be, if she intended to write at all. Remarking on a debut collection of stories just published by the young John Updike, *The Same Door*, Joyce added that she hadn't yet read the book because "I have the idea he is not my kind of writer." Perceiving the contrast between Updike's subject matter and her own, she cited a review that had claimed Updike was unconcerned with "the catastrophes of life." But underlying Joyce's concern about the subject matter of her fiction lay an instinctive fear of her own imaginative power and energy, especially the sense of unreality that descended whenever she plunged obsessively into her writing. Joyce later articulated this fear through her alter ego Marya Knauer, who tells her best friend in college that she "feared to write anything that wasn't academic or scholarly or firmly rooted in the real world: once she began she wouldn't be able to stop: she was afraid of sinking too deep into her own head, cracking up, becoming lost." One of the strongest passages in *Marya: A Life* describes one of these fearful plunges:

> Lately her "serious" writing frightened her. Not just the content itself—though the content was often wild, disturbing, unanticipated—but the emotional and psychological strain it involved. She could write all night long, sprawled across her bed, taking notes, drafting out sketches and scenes, narrating a story she seemed to be hearing in a kind of trance; she could write until her hand ached and her eyes filled with tears and she felt that another pulse beat would push her over the brink—into despair, into madness, into sheer extinction. Nothing is worth this, she told herself very early one morning, nothing can be worth this, she thought, staring at herself in the mirror of the third floor bathroom—a ghastly hollow-eyed death's head of a face, hardly recognizable as Marya, a girl of nineteen.

Joyce's time at Harvard kept her busy with exactly the kind of "safe" academic writing that Marya preferred, and she did well in her courses, earning an A in Chaucer and a B+ in Shakespeare. She returned for her senior year at Syracuse as a nationally published writer—her *Mademoiselle* story appeared in the August 1959 issue—and with the intention of pursuing a master's degree immediately after graduation. Her only stumbling block continued to be her extreme shyness. She applied for one of the coveted Woodrow Wilson graduate scholarships and again was aided by Walter Sutton. Echoing Dike's letter to Fred and Carolina, Sutton wrote that Joyce was "the most capable undergraduate student of literature I have encountered" and possessed a mind that was "both imaginative and orderly." Sutton warned the scholarship committee that Joyce's "shyness of manner" might seem a drawback, but noted that "extroversion is not essential to success" in the academic world. The application process included personal interviews, and it was here that Joyce faltered. Mary Marshall remembered conducting a practice interview with Joyce, during which she suggested that Joyce should try to be assertive and outgoing when interviewed by the scholarship board. But Joyce expressed dismay at the notion of pretending to be other than she was, and during the actual interview at Cornell University she gave quiet, monosyllabic replies to her questioners. "The committee was very sympathetic to her," Sutton remembered, "but they could not get her to speak." As a result, she was denied the scholarship. She had also been "hobbled," she later said, by a sexist regulation governing the awards: out of the four scholarships available, only one could be given to a female student, giving her "a 75 percent disadvantage. It's one of those odd things that today would be considered shocking."

Despite her performance for the Woodrow Wilson committee, Joyce's Syracuse professors and fellow students noted a distinct change in both her appearance and behavior during her senior year. Most dramatic was the change in Joyce's physical appearance. Though she remained as devoted to writing and studying as ever, she decided to compromise somewhat with 1950s standards of feminine attractiveness by giving herself a startling "makeover." Arthur Hoffman remembered that Joyce's new appearance amazed him: "she suddenly changed and began to wear a good deal of makeup," growing long fingernails and carefully painting them. "I had to do a double take when I saw her," he added. Carol North also remembered Joyce's wearing makeup "and trying to look a little prettier," and Sandy Gillan recalled that Joyce's long fingernails clashed dramatically with her typewriter keys. Her nails were "incredibly strong, the kinds of fingernails everybody gets very jealous over," and as the months passed they made visible indentations in the keys.

During her senior year, Joyce made all A's despite an ambitious load that included European philosophy, German, and the usual litany of English courses: literary criticism, American poetry, American fiction, eighteenth-century English literature, and Milton. Her hard work resulted in some exciting news from the university: not only would she graduate summa cum laude; she had also been named class valedictorian. But, inaugurating a pattern that she would observe frequently in later years (when honorary degrees and other "awards" would include hidden obligations, usually a requirement that Joyce accept the degree in person), the honor conferred an unwanted duty: the shy Joyce Oates would be required to make a valedictory address during the 1960 commencement exercises. To the girl who had been unable to read her fiction in the supportive environment of a writing workshop, the idea of giving a formal address before several thousand people—including Supreme Court Chief Justice Earl Warren and University Chancellor William Tolley—seemed paralyzing. Nor was she encouraged much by the professor assigned to advise her about the speech: remember, he cautioned, as soon as you begin speaking, everyone will be ready for you to sit down again. Joyce asked if there were any way she could possibly avoid giving the speech, but the professor was not encouraging. "Only if it rains," he told her.

Learning that the outdoors commencement in Archibald Stadium had never been rained out, Joyce understood that the odds were against her and apprehensively began writing her speech. As her adviser suggested, she kept it short. The ultimate aim of a university education, she wrote, was "the cultivation of a quality of mind" that could recognize the highest social and moral ideals. Several of Joyce's phrases in the speech suggest the major themes of her fiction: "The world into which we are drifting is a precarious world, nor would any of us be alarmed at the thought that we will probably accomplish few miracles there—save perhaps the miracle of survival." She criticized the sterile conformism of the 1950s and stressed the importance of individuality, warning against "a perverse pride in what is immediate and shallow."

Though Joyce had worked hard on the speech, she still hoped fervently for rain in the days before graduation. Giving the valedictory address was "such a sophomoric thing to do," she complained to Sandy Gillan. "Why do I have to do this?" Lori Negridge remembered that Joyce's fearful complaints became "a mantra" during that last week: "I don't want to give a speech, I don't want to give a speech." Joyce said that if only it would rain, she would come back to the house and give the speech to her sorority sisters. Even after the commencement ceremony began, Joyce waited uncomfortably in her cap and gown and "continued making a fuss," repeating her mantra over and over.

Fred Oates had come to his daughter's graduation, and he began recording the proceedings with his movie camera. The film shows Chief Justice Warren and other dignitaries filing onto the field, followed by the solemn procession of white-robed graduates. At first, the sun was shining. Lori Negridge recalled that when clouds appeared and a few drops of rain began to fall, shortly after the ceremony began, "The officials were not concerned. No Syracuse graduation had ever been rained out. It was a rule." But soon the scattered raindrops turned into a steady drizzle. The heavy wool robes worn by the graduates began to smell, and families in the stands started opening their umbrellas. According to Sandy Gillan, Joyce began to cheer up considerably: "She was sitting up on the podium, grinning from ear to ear." The rain grew heavier. Reminiscing to Carol North, Joyce wrote that "I had by that time compromised myself to about five hundred rosaries and any number of candles in return for the favor of having the rain increase, which it did, giving one some reason to believe in extra-terrestrial patterns." Lori recalled that her father, Tony Negridge, was the first parent to leave the bleachers and run out onto the field with his umbrella to protect his daughter. "He was not the last. Soon we were deluged with parents and umbrellas." The situation became so chaotic that Chancellor Tolley finally interrupted his own speech and shouted, "You're all graduated!" The rain began to pour, everyone fled the stadium, and after visiting with her parents Joyce hurried back to the Phi Mu house with her sorority sisters, giddy with relief.

"Joyce was giggling all the way," Sandy Gillan remembered. When they reached the sidewalk going into the house, somebody reminded Joyce that she had agreed to read her speech to the sorority. One of the girls shouted, "You don't get in the house until you give us the first three lines." But Joyce refused. She had found a new mantra: "I got away with it!" she cried. "I got away with it!" Inside the house, she again refused to give the speech. Instead, happily graduated, she went alone to her upstairs room and shut the door.

5

New Directions 1960–62

*The continent takes us on
begins to dream us:
worlds shading into worlds. . . .*
—"Fertilizing the Continent" (1974)

*We love, we have loved, we touch
and wander
and draw together puzzled in
the dark.*
—"Marriage" (1968)

The three years following Joyce's graduation from Syracuse University were among the most frustrating of her life. She attended a graduate school, the University of Wisconsin, whose professors and academic methods she disliked, and which worked her so hard that she was too drained and demoralized to write fiction. After getting her M.A. at Wisconsin she lived for a year in a small southern city—Beaumont, Texas—whose racism, cultural backwardness, and physical ugliness repelled her, and then moved to Detroit, Michigan, a city notorious for violent crime and its own racial problems. Yet these years of long-distance moves and frequent disappointments also brought Joyce some of her happiest experiences: in Wisconsin, she fell in love with a fellow graduate student named Raymond Smith, and married him; in Beaumont, she completed her first short-story collection, *By the North Gate,* and sold it to a New York publisher; in Detroit, she began her professional career as a teacher and, more important, found the setting and themes of her most powerful early fiction.

Joyce chose to attend Wisconsin because the school had offered her a substantial fellowship; whereas most students worked their way through school and required two years to complete the M.A., Joyce's award would permit her to study full-time and complete the degree in a mere nine months. Other considerations affected Joyce's decision. Her college boyfriend, Frank

Aronson, planned either to remain at Syracuse for graduate school or transfer to Cornell; having decided to break off the relationship, Joyce deliberately did not apply to either school. And she had heard that Wisconsin was an excellent place to study American literature—a reputation that her experience there did not bear out. According to Ray Smith, who was finishing his Ph.D. the year Joyce arrived, "the faculty at Wisconsin had been very good at one time. But they were a little bit over the hill—they were older, they weren't exciting the way the professors were at Syracuse." Among graduate students, the school was nicknamed "Harvard West" because faculty who couldn't get jobs in the Ivy League would come to Wisconsin instead.

The campus, situated on Lake Mendota, was physically attractive: the student union featured a large lakefront, with terraces, piers, and an inviting beach. The school was also much larger than Syracuse, boasting three thousand graduate students and a total student body of eighteen thousand. But Joyce, who knew no one when she arrived, applied herself to studying and took little time to enjoy the social activities on campus. Nor did she arrive with any expectation of romance; she was focused wholly on the exciting goal of an academic career. She had moved into a campus dormitory, Barnard Hall. "I have a single room, which is a blessing," she wrote to Carol North. "I have all kinds of fears, etc. about Wisconsin, but I hope things turn out well." Joyce's dormitory mates included two Catholic nuns. Writing to Walter Sutton, she remarked wryly that "the climate of respectability they give us is of much value."

Disillusionment with the school set in almost at once. Joyce discovered that most of the graduate faculty in English were extreme conservatives who discouraged students from studying either American literature or creative writing—the two fields in which she was most interested. Instead she was forced to take dull, poorly taught seminars in Old English and sixteenth-century British literature. In the latter course Joyce was criticized by the professor, Merritt Hughes, for writing an essay on Spenser and Kafka, "because he hadn't read Kafka; had no idea who Kafka was; but felt quite certain that Kafka wasn't important." (Kafka, like Nietzsche, remained one of Joyce's literary idols; she later wrote that during her college years "I *was* Franz Kafka for a while.") Unlike Syracuse, where she had studied with "enthusiastic, brilliant professors," the University of Wisconsin was a place "where 'primary' materials were simply there to be footnoted, where everything was dull, gray, one-dimensional . . . 'scholarly.' "

Joyce's friend Bob Phillips had stayed at Syracuse for graduate work, and her letters to him from fall 1960 were filled with nostalgic recollections of her undergraduate experience and horror stories about her new life at Wisconsin. She reminisced about her glory days of publishing stories in *Syracuse 10,* pleading with Phillips to send her new issues of the magazine as they came out. By contrast, even the student literary magazine at Wisconsin was "a lamentable thing," a seedy journal controlled by "beat" writers on campus. Joyce was appalled by the brutal competitiveness among the graduate students, so different from the generally supportive atmosphere she had enjoyed at Syracuse. She wrote to Phillips that she dreaded an oral presentation of her research on the Puritans: "after innocent first year graduate students finish their feeble papers, the older students, with condescending expressions, proceed to rip apart not only the thought, the conclusion, the words, the method, but the whole conception of the paper—in other words, back to the simple naked mind of the student himself." The previous year, she noted, one student had committed suicide after failing his preliminary examinations. Joyce also complained that she'd had no time for writing since she arrived in Madison. She told Carol North that she had produced 322 pages of a novel and six short stories the previous summer; but she would write no fiction at all during the Wisconsin academic year. If she decided to pursue an academic career, she remarked, "I will probably never write again."

Despite Joyce's grim absorption in her uncongenial studies, she took time on October 23 to attend a departmental social hour for graduate students. She was sitting at a table with some other students "when this handsome, older man came and sat down." This older man, all of thirty, was Raymond Smith: "he was very warm," Joyce recalled, "and we just got to talking and we hit it off very well. I think he probably liked it that I didn't know anything," whereas Ray, in his last year at Wisconsin, "knew all the ropes." Ray remembered that his initial attraction to Joyce "was an emotional and romantic one, but more importantly, I found Joyce a very open and warm and yet modest young woman. It was easy to talk with her—our conversations seemed effortless." Like Joyce, Ray had no particular interest in getting married, "but when you hit it off with someone, it's intuitive." In her journal, Joyce later noted that her and Ray's romance "happened rather quickly, yet not dizzyingly. I had anticipated from the first that we would be married."

Apart from their shared interest in literature, Joyce Oates and Raymond Smith had other things in common. Both had a Roman Catholic background, and both had rejected Catholicism. Like Joyce, Ray had wanted to write fiction, and like many would-be novelists of the day had moved to Greenwich Village in his early twenties, supporting himself with day jobs such as clerking in an export office and proofreading. But his fiction "never panned out," he recalled. "I wrote some stories that I thought were fairly good, and a couple of novels I just about completed. But I lost interest in them." His only fiction publication had been in his high school newspaper— a piece "I thought was a story." Deciding that graduate school was imperative if he hoped to make a living, Ray brought his fiction with him to Madison but never worked at it, getting caught up in his studies instead. Unlike Joyce, he enjoyed graduate school. Admiring the department's Jonathan Swift specialist, Ricardo Quintana, Ray focused on the eighteenth century and was writing his dissertation on Swift when he met Joyce.

Ray's family background had been somewhat more affluent than Joyce's. Ray and his family escaped the worst effects of the Depression because Ray's father—also named Raymond—was a successful automobile salesman. His mother, Elizabeth M. Doyle, had taught elementary school before her marriage. Born in Milwaukee on March 12, 1930, Ray was the third of four children; he attended the local Catholic elementary school and a Jesuit high school. During World War II Ray's father suffered unemployment due to the halt of automobile manufacturing, but saw the family through by working at a low-paying job with the IRS. Although the family did not share Ray's interest in serious literature, his parents—like Joyce's—were interested in music. They sent Ray's two sisters for piano lessons and purchased a piano, which both of Ray's parents enjoyed playing during their leisure time.

But literature was the art form that brought Ray and Joyce together. During Ray's first conversation with his future wife, she announced that she was a writer. When Ray asked, "But have you published?" Joyce modestly told him she had, but gave no details. "Later I found out that she had won the prestigious *Mademoiselle* short-story contest," he remembered, "and some weeks later she gave me an offprint of her article on Samuel Beckett (one of the first) and I glimpsed the quality of intellect and imaginative boldness of the girl I was to marry. I was awed."

On the night of their first meeting, Ray and Joyce had dinner with some other graduate students in the student union, then proceeded to a local pub for more of their "effortless" conversation. They began dating regularly, going to concerts and movies, occasionally visiting a local supper club where they could dance. Taking advantage of the attractive lakeside campus, they also bicycled and hiked, spending a good deal of time outdoors. At night, they would cook dinner at Ray's studio apartment and spend the rest of the evening studying together. Joyce was having difficulty with Old English and Ray helped her get through the course. He also helped indoctrinate Joyce into the politics of graduate school. Two weeks after meeting Ray, Joyce wrote to Bob Phillips, "I have become fairly well acquainted with a Ph.D. candidate here, who will get his degree this spring, and the revelation into the inner workings of the academic polity is one which would disillusion anyone." Later that month, she wrote that she and Ray had become engaged: "My meeting him had the aura of one of the more suspiciously idyllic romance narratives, or suspiciously convenient." She added that Ray was a "most agreeably intelligent person." Joyce also sat down and wrote a "cold, brief, emotionless letter," as she later described it, to Frank Aronson, breaking off their relationship. She recalled in her journal that, for all its limitations as a graduate school, she had "made the right decision to go to Wisconsin, rather than remain at Syracuse in order to be near Frank." The relationship "would certainly have drifted into an engagement and into marriage, a disaster for us both." On the other hand, Ray was the ideal choice for her, as she made clear in sketching the personal qualities that so perfectly complemented her own:

> Ray's sense of humor. Intelligence. Kindness. Patience. (Though he is not *always* patient.) Easily hurt; but not inclined to brood; not at all "philosophical" (as I am); perhaps a sunnier nature; or at least a less dense one. My conviction, the first evening we met, that I would marry this man, that I would fall in love with him. . . . An uncanny certainty.

Originally Joyce and Ray set their wedding date for June, but since they were spending all their free time together anyway, they decided to marry during the break between semesters and moved the date up to January 23—choosing that day because they had met on October 23 and become engaged on November 23. Almost everyone Joyce knew was surprised by her precipitous engagement. When she phoned Carol North, now attending graduate school in Rochester, Carol felt "absolutely shocked." She remembered that Joyce expressed nervousness about her impending marriage, telling Carol that she was frightened. But, she added, she looked forward to leaving Madison; her M.A. would be completed after spring semester, and Ray was scheduled to complete his Ph.D. Ray *would* graduate that spring, Joyce remarked, even if she had to write his dissertation for him.

Joyce's parents were also shocked by the engagement. Carolina was alone when she got the news, and waited until Fred got home from work to tell him. Fred remembered that Carolina blurted out, "Joyce is getting married" as soon as he walked in the door. Affecting nonchalance, he replied, "Oh, really?" and took a cigar out of his cigar box, as he did every evening after work. But Fred's distress was betrayed when he lit the cigar: he had forgotten to remove the cellophane wrapper. Though this later became a fondly recalled family anecdote, Fred and Carolina were both seriously concerned about the marriage at the time. They were still practicing Catholics, and not knowing that Joyce had lost interest in Catholicism, they were unhappy that Ray had left the church. Hearing of her parents' concern, Joyce decided that Ray and her father should meet before the wedding. Since Ray would be in Philadelphia during Christmas week, interviewing for teaching jobs at the

Modern Language Association convention, Fred arranged to drive down and meet with him. Both men were extremely nervous—especially Ray, who in the same day was interviewing both for jobs and as a potential husband—but they hit it off well, enjoying a cheeseburger and a few beers together at the Benjamin Franklin hotel. The two men "had similar tastes," Ray remembered, and during that meeting Fred decided that he not only approved of his future son-in-law but also liked him a great deal.

Joyce and Ray were married in Madison, in a small Catholic chapel. Despite the anxiety she had expressed to Carol North, Joyce had no cause for regret: "I went about afterward," she later recalled, "thinking, and occasionally even saying aloud, how marvelous marriage was—how one couldn't imagine, beforehand—simply couldn't imagine. The transition from 'I' to 'we.' No, one simply can't imagine." The couple moved into a spacious five-room apartment (the second floor of a private home) on University Avenue, not far from the campus. Their new home featured a modern kitchen, including a much-admired garbage disposal, and a separate study where they could work. Joyce remembered rising each morning "at dawn, leaving my sleeping husband to sit in an oversized chair by a window in the living room, there to study, study, study." Eight days after her marriage, Joyce wrote that she had attained "at least the comfortable solidarity of a bourgeois middle-class backdrop . . . which is, I have come to think, more and more important for those who do, ultimately, discover in themselves a faint straining away from the normal and traditional." This remark recalls Joyce's frequent quotation of Flaubert's assertion that a writer must remain a bourgeois in his living habits, so that he can be wild in his art. Although Joyce had temporarily stopped writing while she pursued her M.A., she understood from the outset that her stable marriage and the maintenance of comfortable middle-class surroundings were essential conditions under which to pursue her work as a writer.

Joyce looked forward more than ever to leaving Madison, since Ray had been successful in finding a job during the MLA convention. After doing well in several interviews, he accepted an assistant professorship at Lamar State College of Technology in Beaumont, Texas, partly because the college had promised to find some part-time teaching for Joyce as well. But Joyce's own professional future seemed uncertain. Like most women at that time, especially married women, she received little encouragement to work toward a Ph.D. She detested the pedantic approach to literature favored by her Wisconsin professors and had no interest, she remarked, in "turning into those people." The one teacher she admired that year was a woman, Helen White, who taught Joyce's course in medieval literature. "She was *human*—had human, emotional responses to the literature she taught," Joyce wrote in her journal. But Joyce wanted to be a writer, not a scholar. She told Bob Phillips that she had "dozens of ideas sort of buzzing around" for new fiction, but no time to execute them. Though she had achieved some further acceptances of her work—the Beckett essay she'd shown to Ray and a section of her Melville paper had been taken by academic journals, and her story "A Legacy" was accepted by *Arizona Quarterly*—her firmly entrenched modesty combined with her awareness of the sexist nature of the academic/literary establishment gave her little reason to be hopeful about a writing career.

Joyce's final rite of passage at Wisconsin—her oral examination for the master's degree—clarified the obstacles she faced both as a woman in the male-dominated academic world and as a critic more interested in exploring the passionate experience of literature than in contributing further "footnotes" to the dull, droning pile of scholarship her teachers were producing. Though Joyce had earned A grades in all but one of her graduate courses (she received a B+ in Old English), she had reason to worry about the oral exam. She described the process to Bob Phillips:

> There has never been anything so brutal as the method of getting MA's here at Wisconsin. You have three people on your examining board, who make or ruin your subsequent career. You may be dedicated to the teaching profession—want to teach in college above all—but if someone on the panel decides you aren't quite good enough, down it goes on your record and you are about finished, save at some Mississippi girls' school. In 50 minutes they are supposed to "know" how good a student you are, by questioning you orally. If you happen to be a genius at writing they would not know it.

She related various horror stories: a young woman had been penalized because she could not answer a question put to her *in Latin* by the Milton scholar Merritt Hughes; another female student was thrown out of the graduate program because an elderly, unmarried female instructor resented young married women. Though Joyce informed Bob, in a breezy aside, that "my exam couldn't have been better," actually the opposite was true. Perhaps she wanted to preserve her stellar academic reputation in Bob's eyes, or perhaps she simply preferred to put the ordeal behind her, but in reality Joyce's exam had been a nightmare.

As usual, there were three examiners—all male—on Joyce's committee. One of them, a young professor named G. Thomas Tanselle, "had a very narrow concept of literature," Joyce remembered. "He was mainly interested in literary history, bibliography." Despite Joyce's brilliant academic record and her already burgeoning list of publications, Tanselle began grilling Joyce on Walt Whitman, and not on the poetry itself but "about the dates of Whitman's different publications, and what was privately printed, and which poem was in this edition or that edition." Joyce was stymied. She could have spoken eloquently about Whitman as a poet, "but this other side of it really hadn't even come up. So I just kept saying, 'Well, I'm afraid I don't know . . . I'm afraid I don't know.' " Although Joyce passed the exam, the committee wrote in her record that "Miss Oates should not be allowed to continue for a Ph.D."

The incident was upsetting, but it was not surprising. "They had to winnow out some people," Joyce reflected, "and I think to be a woman, a young married woman, put me in a category that was expendable." She believed that Tanselle had purposely directed impossible questions at her, "so that I *would* have to say that I didn't know." Though the unpleasant exam had no real effect on Joyce's career, since she was already making plans to leave for Texas with Ray, it certainly sharpened her awareness that her gender and her approach to literature would not find acceptance easily in the academic world of 1961. So it was with a sense of weary relief rather than triumph that Joyce wrote to Bob Phillips, "My husband and I will both get our degrees— his Ph.D., mine a lowly M.A.—June 5." Soon they would be leaving for Texas, where Ray would work at lecture notes for his first year of teaching and Joyce, at last, would return to writing fiction.

After finishing their degrees, Joyce and Ray made their first visit to Millersport as a married couple. Beaumont, Texas, their destination for the fall, was more than 1,500 miles from the world of Joyce's childhood, and it seemed unlikely that she would often see her parents after the move. Joyce had finally gotten her driver's license the previous summer, at the age of twenty-two, but she was no longer willing to fly in airplanes. In the past, she had flown often with her father and had taken several commercial flights between Madison and Buffalo for visits with her parents. But during one of these, the turbulence was so intense that "everyone thought we would crash and the stewardesses looked green." Joyce "decided quite *rationally* not to fly again for a while." In fact, she would not resume regular airplane travel for nearly two decades. (As her writing became well known, she saw her fear of flying as a blessing rather than an inconvenience: "I must admit that it has made my life awfully simple," she wrote. "I am just not available most of the time; everywhere on earth is too far to drive.")

The summer visit with Joyce's parents went well. As they got to know Ray better, Fred and Carolina liked him even more and felt confident that Joyce had married wisely. An ongoing family problem helped draw Ray into the family circle. In 1956, on Joyce's eighteenth birthday, Carolina had given birth to her third child, a daughter named Lynn Ann. By 1961, when Lynn was five, her severe developmental problems had been diagnosed: the child was autistic. Ray remembered that during his and Joyce's visit to Millersport, they spent a great deal of time talking about Lynn and discussing the various options for treatment. Lynn, whose pale complexion, dark hair, and large, dark eyes gave her a startling resemblance to Joyce, manifested the hyperactivity combined with an inability to communicate that is characteristic of severe autism. Fred's home movies of Lynn, taken throughout her childhood and adolescence, not only document her physical resemblance to Joyce but even show Lynn using some of her older sister's distinctive mannerisms.

Yet the illness, little understood at the time, bore a terrible stigma, and Joyce seldom discussed her sister with colleagues and friends. The conventional perception of autism was dramatically expressed in a 1965 *Life* magazine article on the malady, which referred to autistics as "mental cripples." Joyce's discomfort with the issue surfaced on those rare occasions when she did mention her sister in letters. She confided to Bob Phillips that her home situation in Millersport sometimes resembled a scene in Hawthorne's *The Scarlet Letter*, since Lynn and her manic behavior reminded Joyce of Hester Prynne's wild young daughter, Pearl. Writing to Carol North in 1959, Joyce had humorously described the three-year-old Lynn's antics: "my little sister, whimsical as always, just put her head with a monstrous amount of curls, shoulder-length, down into a mud puddle she made by emptying a sprinkler into the dirt." In her journal, Joyce later recalled that "Lynn was never animal-like: only non-human, perversely anti-human. Would not look anyone in the eyes, would not sit still; but of course I mean could not—*could not* do these things." In a 1993 interview, Joyce would remark that she hadn't visited her sister in many years because Lynn "wouldn't know me." There were degrees of autism, and Lynn's was "in the most severe 10 percent."

The extraordinary fates of Carolina Oates's two daughters—both born on June 16 and virtual twins in physical appearance, but one brilliantly gifted, the other severely disabled—contributed to Joyce's fascination with twins, as manifested in her pseudonymous "Rosamond Smith" novels and some of her short fiction, and to her lifelong interest in the theme of "doubleness" in human nature. "That Lynn was born on my birthday, resembles me, and has never spoken a coherent sentence while I am blessed/damned as 'prolific' has not escaped my awareness and my sense of irony," Joyce remarked. In the early 1980s, she wrote a pair of moving poems about her sister. In "Mute Mad Child," the speaker notes the "Silence coiled inside the jabber, the high-pitched humming and keening," and presents the autistic girl's thoughts in italics: "*I desire nothing of you,* the child says. *Who are you? . . . Did you confuse me with yourself?*" In "Autistic Child, No Longer Child," Joyce states the paradox of her and Lynn's relationship:

I cannot look into you
as into a mirror, though you mirror me, sister
and were born on my birthday eighteen years after me
and late, very late.

By the time Lynn was fifteen, she had become too much for Carolina to handle and was placed in an institution close enough to Millersport that she could be brought home each Sunday for a family visit. "Autistic Child," recalling one of these visits, describes Lynn as a "Flywheel, whirligig, hummingbird, singing the same / cruel tune, a drone, a dirge, a nursery tune":

Now you crackle with spirit, on Sundays most dead,
now you navigate the room, left to right, the relentless tune,
the moon-blank stare, what year have we now, what weather?
how far it carries, your cheerful baby-dirge!

Inside Lynn's "empty stare" Joyce sensed the "voltage" of human emotion, but the poem's last two lines poignantly state the sisters' inability to communicate: "To touch you, sister, is to feel that voltage. / To touch you, sister, is not our privilege."

Although Joyce and Ray would maintain a close relationship with Joyce's parents throughout their marriage, one of their motivations in accepting the Texas appointment was its distance from the midwestern world of his upbringing. In addition, the couple cherished some "romantic notions" about Texas, though these would quickly be dispelled when they confronted the tawdry reality of Beaumont. The general unattractiveness of this small coastal city—especially its racism, so much more overt than in the North—made Joyce and Ray understand almost immediately that they'd made a mistake. Several years later, writing *them* (1969), Joyce would send Jules Wendall and his lover Nadine to Beaumont in a scene that suggests a harrowing of hell. During his brief time there, Jules suffers high fever and severe diarrhea; waking up one morning, he discovers that Nadine has abandoned him. The city seems the logical setting for these degrading experiences: "The air in Beaumont stank. It must have been gas from refineries; there was a faintly sickish taste borne on one wind and a faintly acrid taste born on another. . . . A heavy, cobweb-like dampness hung over everything." Even in 1993, more than thirty years after leaving Texas, Joyce would write, "just the realization WE'RE NOT IN BEAUMONT, TEXAS lifts us to a transcendental plane."

Like most first-year faculty couples, Joyce and Ray had very little money. Arriving in Beaumont, they had no car and no furniture, and moved briefly into a downtown hotel while they hunted for a furnished apartment. The southeast Texas weather, in July, was almost unbearably hot and humid. After finding a small place on Sweet Gum Lane, Joyce was appalled to discover the apartment was infested with roaches. One of her new colleagues, Henry Rule, remembered that "Joyce expressed horror at the size, boldness, and number of the creatures." Nor did Ray and Joyce seem to enjoy socializing with the Lamar faculty. Ray was perceived as well qualified for his job, but quiet and reserved, while Joyce gave the impression of "extreme, almost pathological shyness." Charles Hagelman, the English department chairman who hired Ray, noticed that "they did not mix much with either the people in the community or on the faculty." Ray taught his classes and kept his office hours, but spent the rest of his time with Joyce, who felt isolated in the apartment.

When Joyce and Ray arrived, Lamar Tech was experiencing some difficult transitions. The school had been integrated only two years before, and there had been considerable infighting among the faculty. Another English professor, Robert Barnes, recalled that the faculty as a whole was "suspicious, clannish, and not very friendly. Thus, there was little interaction with faculty members for Joyce and Ray." Barnes and his wife did invite the Smiths over a few times; they discussed such books as Golding's *Lord of the Flies* and earned Joyce's trust to the point that she showed them some of the short-story manuscripts she'd been writing. Both were impressed by her talent. Henry Rule and his wife, new arrivals like the Smiths, also invited Joyce and Ray for dinner, though the Rules were still using packing crates for furniture. "Joyce and Ray must have been as poor as we were," Rule remarked, "because we loaned them our ancient panel truck with a hole in its floor for transportation. Every time the truck splashed through a puddle of water, passengers were in danger of getting their feet wet."

Despite their social isolation, the Smiths became embroiled in a departmental controversy that fall. Ray had begun a grueling work load, teaching two sections of freshman composition in the second summer session and three more in the fall, in addition to a sophomore literature course; like many beginning instructors, he was given an uncongenial schedule that included 8:00 A.M. classes. That fall, according to his chairman, "Ray's effectiveness in the classroom was seriously questioned by his students," and his teaching was investigated by a departmental committee. Ray's difficulties were compounded by his extremely tough grading: he was failing the large majority of his freshman composition students. Lamar maintained an open admissions policy, and many of the students were poorly prepared for college. But, meeting with the committee that looked into his teaching, Ray told his colleagues that "the low grades were not his fault because his wife corrected and graded his papers for him." Ray defended this practice by claiming that Joyce knew more about writing than he did. Joyce, who occasionally observed Ray's classes that fall, wrote to Bob Phillips that "he teaches very well," but "rather coldly and impersonally," and she acknowledged that he was failing 85 percent of the class. "He may well be out of a job," she remarked, "but refuses to compromise." Wanting to ease the situation for Ray and hoping to keep him on the faculty, Hagelman adjusted his teaching load for the spring term and had no more complaints about Ray's work.

But Joyce and Ray's initial disillusionment with Beaumont only deepened as the months passed. Joyce's dominant impressions were the "persistent chemical smell to the air; a hard glaring pitiless blue sky; dead or dying snakes on the roads." She wrote to Walter Sutton that the city was "very provincial, made up mostly of Baptists, a sect for which I have little patience." The city was "honeycombed by slums": the black section of town consisted of filthy huts, dead dogs and armadillos in the road, and on one occasion a "gigantic dead steer" that forced Joyce and Ray's car into a detour. To the white populace of Beaumont, Joyce wrote, "all this horror might be happening in Africa. It has a ghostly unreality." Despite the recent integration of the college, she added, black students "choose to disdainfully segregate themselves." Virtually all the black students were near-illiterate, speaking "a garbled, bestial sort of talk" (a remark that would not have sounded racist in these years preceding the civil rights era and that revealed Joyce's lack of contact with southern blacks). She concluded that "the situation of the Negroes in this part of the south . . . is hopeless, and it would take nothing short of a moral earthquake to change matters."

Joyce had suffered another disappointment that fall. Although she had been promised that she could teach a section or two of freshman composition, the chairman reneged on this offer, leaving her with no professional affiliation. Only weeks after their arrival, Joyce wrote to Bob Phillips that they were already planning their move back north. She felt guilty, she wrote, because the English department at Lamar was quite good, despite the poorly prepared students and uncongenial city. She acknowledged that she, not Ray, had insisted on leaving because "I've changed my mind about what I wanted to do. . . . It is too difficult to make the transition from a student to a wife; that is, purely a wife, without anything more." She felt that she should be working, both for personal and financial reasons. As a beginning assistant professor, Ray's salary for the year was only $5,400, plus an additional $900 for the two summer courses. But Joyce was earning no money at all; her only connection with the profession she loved was through the mail, for she had continued to submit some of her unpublished articles and stories. She stayed busy, she wrote, "mailing out some three or four innocuous offerings, back and forth, to the pity and terror of the Negro mailman."

Joyce did try out one other option that fall: she applied to the Ph.D. program at Rice University and was promptly accepted. Attending classes presented a problem, however, since Rice, located in Houston, was about seventy miles west of Beaumont. Joyce took a bus to the campus for her classes, staying overnight in a hotel; the next day, Ray would drive out to pick her up (they had recently acquired a used Volkswagen) and they would have dinner in Houston before returning to Beaumont. The routine quickly grew tiresome, and though Joyce liked her Rice professors well enough, they were "hardly stimulating." She was offered both a teaching fellowship and a graduate scholarship, but lost interest in pursuing a Ph.D. within a few weeks, partly because of a serendipitous incident in the Rice University library. Browsing among the new books one day, she came upon the latest volume of the *Best American Short Stories* anthology, then edited by Martha Foley. Her story "A Legacy" had been cited in the "Honor Roll" at the back of the book. "I hadn't known about it until I just picked it up and saw it," she later told an interviewer. "I thought, maybe I could be a writer. I went back to Beaumont on the bus and stopped thinking about a Ph.D."

Back in the apartment, alone all day while Ray taught his classes, Joyce once again plunged into her writing. Living in her imagination, "scarcely in Texas at all," she worked at fiction constantly, "in a trance of oblivion." By March of 1962, she could report that "I have written at least a thousand stories, it seems, lately, some of them inspired by the local language." (The fact that she set most of the stories in "Eden County," located in upstate New York, but was gleaning some of the language from the way people talked in southeastern Texas, may account for some critics' impressions, throughout the 1960s, that Joyce was a southern writer.) In addition to the many stories, she noted that she was about one-fourth of the way into a new novel. Years later, Joyce recalled that this long manuscript—which would become her first published novel, *With Shuddering Fall*—had an unusual inspiration. One day, while Ray was teaching his classes, Joyce sat at home reading a novel by Shirley Ann Grau, *The House on Coliseum Street.* Joyce found the novel so poorly written, she later said, she decided she could do better and set to work on *With Shuddering Fall*. The incident was a classic example of how one could be inspired by bad art, she said. A novice writer who read only great books might be too intimidated to try writing at all.

But publication remained elusive: aside from the three stories already published in *Mademoiselle*, *Epoch*, and *Arizona Quarterly*, she had placed only one more manuscript—*The Literary Review* had taken "The Fine White Mist of Winter." The rest of her stories had been continually rejected. She observed that "I am tremendously excited about the writing, not, however, in terms of its being published—that's the unpleasant part about writing."

By now, Joyce had more than enough stories to form a strong collection; since most were set in the north country, she titled her manuscript *By the North Gate*, alluding to an Ezra Pound translation of the eighth-century Chinese poet Rihaku. The relevant passage, which she appended to the book as an epigraph, suggested the bleak tonality of the stories and the "barbarous" nature of Eden County: "By the North Gate, the wind blows full of sand, / Lonely from the beginning of time until now! / Trees fall, the grass goes yellow with autumn. / I climb the towers and towers to watch out the barbarous land."

Especially for a first collection, Joyce's manuscript was remarkably unified. Most of the stories dealt with Eden County's dispossessed citizens, narrating in swift, suspenseful prose their hard and sometimes violent struggles. Like Faulkner's Yoknapatawpha, Joyce's Eden County clearly represented her own postage stamp of native soil, its bitterly ironic name suggesting a microcosm of the economically deprived and psychologically troubled humanity she wished to explore. Adopting Faulkner's mythmaking stance, Joyce began some of the stories with the same phrase—"Some time ago in Eden County . . ."—and dramatized the struggles of her north country people in their clashes with the land and with their own powerful, unarticulated emotions. A few years later, Joyce would note that the stories "were written to demonstrate a certain theme or obsession I had at that time: the relationship between the individual and the unknown, whether unpredictable and uncontrollable forces within himself or in other men, or in nature."

Many of the hallmarks of Joyce's mature work were already present here. The stories featured acts of vicious, random violence, the perpetrators recalling the bullying farm boys who had tormented Joyce at school. In the title story, an old farmer's only companion, a hound named Nell, is tortured and killed by a pack of local boys, and in "Boys at a Picnic" another gang of boys brutally murders a young girl inside a church. There are moments when seemingly "ordinary" people drift into madness, as when Grace in "Pastoral Blood" leaves her affluent home and her fiancé to pursue her own self-destruction. She degrades herself sexually, picking up a hitchhiker and servicing him in her car, and invites her own gang rape by a group of black sailors at a riverfront tavern. (There is also a knife fight in the tavern, again recalling the circumstances of Joyce's grandfather's murder.) More generally, the stories convey Joyce's vision of a barbarous natural and social reality. In Eden County, she portrays the agrarian "old world" of her north country heritage as it clashed with a fearsome modern world marked by a rapacious industrialized economy and an absence of moral principles. Beleaguered by poverty, Joyce's people live out their violent struggles against an indifferent, often cruel natural landscape. In "Swamps," a homeless woman drowns her own baby in a muddy creek, and in "The Fine White Mist of Winter" a merciless blizzard forces a racist sheriff into a shelter with several black men. Inimical natural forces and economic factors combine powerfully throughout the stories to destroy the essential humanity of Joyce's characters.

Having completed and arranged the collection, Joyce decided to try submitting again to Vanguard Press. One day that spring, alone in the apartment while Ray was teaching, Joyce received Vanguard's response, opening "an ostensibly ordinary letter to read that my book of stories *By the North Gate* was accepted for publication. My vision blotched, my tongue actually went cold. Numb. I remember that absurd and almost immediate sensation: my tongue going numb." The letter was from Vanguard editor Evelyn Shrifte: she "wrote such a lovely little letter," Joyce recalled, "and I read it over several times. Usually the first sentence would say, 'We are so sorry, this is certainly promising.' I kept looking for those words, but they weren't there. It was, 'We're happy to accept the book.' I felt like turning upside down—I just couldn't believe it."

Joyce and Ray hadn't been able to afford a telephone, so Joyce ran out of the apartment to a phone booth on the corner and called her husband. She also shared the exciting news with her parents and her Syracuse mentor, Donald Dike. On April 9, she wrote to Bob Phillips, "Perhaps [Dike] happened to tell you that I'll be having a book published? After many tries—a book of short stories. . . . I'm very excited but—increasingly—worried about it." Although she didn't specify the nature of her worry, it was likely that Joyce was still concerned about her subject matter and the way it might be perceived by her family, by critics, and by potential employers. Once again the issue of her gender arose to mar what should have been an entirely happy occasion. For the past two years, she had been publishing even her scholarly work under names deliberately chosen to disguise her identity as a woman. As she had written to one friend in 1960, she "hid under the charming name J C Oates, so they wouldn't suspect I am only a girl, hence not on a level with the masculine mind." After marrying Ray, she used the name "J. Oates Smith" for some of her academic essays (and continued to use that name in scholarly journals as late as 1967). She employed a gender-neutral name for some of her stories as well: "The Fine White Mist of Winter" appeared under the name J. C. Oates both in *The Literary Review* and in the 1963 volume of *Best American Short Stories*. Having at times expressed her own distaste for her bleak subject matter, she naturally worried what the world would think of a writer—especially a writer who was young, married, female, and nominally a Catholic—who published a first book of stories that featured rapes, beatings, madness, suicide, and a number of brutal murders.

Despite her worries about the debut collection, Joyce's future looked increasingly bright that spring. Her career as an author had been launched, and she and Ray had achieved the goal they had set from the moment they arrived in Beaumont: they would soon be leaving Beaumont. The previous December, they had attended the MLA convention in Chicago. Ray and Joyce had both snagged a number of interviews, and both were offered jobs at universities in Detroit. Ray's job was at Wayne State, where his teaching load would be considerably less onerous than his assignment at Lamar had been. Joyce, though she had only an M.A., was helped by her publications and was offered both the instructorships for which she applied. Having accepted an offer from the University of Detroit, she noted that the English department there had twenty men on the faculty, a combination of Jesuit priests and lay-men, and "only two women: a nun and me." Joyce would teach both fresh-man and sophomore courses, which she reported was "unusual for someone without any experience." She added, "We don't really expect to stay in De-troit long, but it promises to be an exciting two or three years."

Joyce and Ray had been especially fortunate in that the hiring situation in English departments, always grim, was especially difficult for married couples seeking jobs in the same city. She later gave the credit for their success to the department chairman who had hired her, Clyde Craine. She wrote to Craine's daughter, "Clyde was singlehandedly responsible for bringing Ray and me up from Texas, in 1961; he interviewed me, offered me a job at U.D., and arranged for Ray to be hired at Wayne. The move transformed our lives, and, for me, as a novelist, it allowed me to imagine from the inside the conscious-ness of a great American city, at a time of enormous social turmoil and change." Of the three long-distance moves Joyce had undertaken in the past three years, the move to Detroit was by far the most important to her career as a writer. Except in a handful of scattered, stray scenes, both Madison and Beaumont are virtually absent from her fiction: only the most atypical story in *By the North Gate*, "The Expense of Spirit," deals with her graduate school experience at Wisconsin, in the satiric manner she would later employ in her collection of academic tales, *The Hungry Ghosts* (1974).

Joyce and Ray were so excited about their new jobs and their new lives in Detroit that they left Beaumont within days after classes ended. Ray had not even graded his students' exams: he did his grading on the way to Michigan and mailed the results back to Beaumont. Joyce humorously described their 1,200-mile journey northward in a letter:

> We had an interesting though hectic trip, ascending from purga-
> tory (summer has been in since March down south) to the Ohio
> River. We passed within twenty or so miles of Faulknerland and did
> actually see sharecroppers and Negro "workers," men, women, chil-

dren, out in the cotton fields, though this is 1962, in the sun. . . . Somehow we made it out of the south. We got lost at the border and kept driving back into Tennessee all the time. We would drive a few miles and see a sign of a colonel with mustaches welcoming us back into Tennessee all the time. It was very traumatic but we finally got out.

Arriving in Detroit, they spent two days apartment hunting, finally choosing an orange brick apartment house on Manderson Road, only about five minutes from the University of Detroit. Joyce found it ironic that they should now be living in an affluent section of Detroit, since both she and Ray were unemployed until the fall. They had investigated their respective employers and had found that while Wayne State seemed progressive, the University of Detroit, being Catholic, remained staunchly traditional. Clyde Craine told Joyce that she should be prepared to come across snipped-out material in the library, since the university employed a censoring board. Despite such "horrors," Joyce remained upbeat. Craine was interested in her writing, she noted, "and will be startled to see pages snipped out of it, no less will I be."

Having explored the city, Joyce wrote to Walter Sutton that "we are enormously pleased with Detroit." After feeling isolated in the alien environment of Beaumont, Joyce's happy return to the Midwest and her excitement about her teaching job temporarily obscured the darker aspect of her new surroundings, which she would soon begin dramatizing in her fiction. By 1968, when she left the city for Windsor, Ontario, she would have experienced thoroughly the violent unrest of mid-1960s Detroit, seeing it as a microcosm for many of the social evils in America as a whole. Her opinion of the city would change drastically during the six years she lived there. Recalling her initial, ecstatic reaction to Detroit, she would look back and see the 1962 move— and her own youthful self—in somewhat jaded terms. "When you're young and naive," she told an interviewer, "you might end up in Detroit."

6

"An Entirely New World": Detroit, 1962–64

Ceaseless motion, the pulse of the city. The beat. The beat. A place of romance. The quintessential American city.
— "Visions of Detroit" (1986)

By the early 1960s, the city of Detroit had developed a misleading aura of prosperity and forward-looking optimism. A sparkling contemporary cityscape—dominated by large-scale additions to the downtown Civic Center, numerous architecturally striking bank buildings and hotels, and new expressways recently cut through the heart of the city—drew attention away from the rundown areas cluttered with dilapidated warehouses, trash-filled vacant lots, razed or abandoned small businesses. A recession in 1953 and 1954 had brought widespread unemployment by striking at the heart of Detroit's economy, the automotive industry, but there were few outward signs of the severe economic and racial problems that would erupt in the 1967 riot. Despite its architectural face-lift and civic boosterism, however, Detroit had experienced a loss of population throughout the 1950s, when more than half a million people, most of them middle-class whites, left the city for the suburbs. At the same time, the numbers of blacks and poor whites rose substantially, creating an urban core population described by one historian as "the old, the very young, the black, the unskilled, and the fearful." Not surprisingly, the crime rate had begun to soar by the time Joyce and Ray Smith arrived to begin their new teaching jobs. Joyce would later note that Detroit, for years called "Motor City," was to become better known as "Murder City, U.S.A."

Unlike Ray's new employer, Wayne State University, which Joyce described as "more or less carved into an old slum," the University of Detroit was situated in a quiet, upper-middle-class neighborhood. Writing to Walter Sutton, Joyce stressed the positive features of her new surroundings. "The University of Detroit has an idyllic-looking campus," she noted. Despite the library censorship board, about 40 percent of the roughly ten thousand students were not Catholic, and the school was "not very strictly controlled by the Jesuits." Though Joyce, as an ex-Catholic and a woman, was something of an anomaly on the faculty, she had the strong support of her lay department chairman, Clyde Craine, who recognized her talent. Craine was a native Detroiter from a wealthy family who had been educated at Oxford and maintained a spacious home and country club membership in the affluent suburb of Bloomfield Hills. Always nattily dressed and articulate, he was a worldly, amiable man well liked by his colleagues at the university, to which he had devoted himself wholeheartedly. Craine had hired several other new faculty around the time he hired Joyce, and she enjoyed the camaraderie and friendly competition of these younger colleagues—all of them, like Joyce, at the beginning of their careers and trying to establish themselves in their profession.

Because of the several highly regarded universities in the area—Wayne State, Oakland, and the University of Michigan campuses in Ann Arbor and Dearborn—the University of Detroit, known locally as "U.D.," had begun taking aggressive steps to remain competitive. At the urging of its young new president, Father Laurence V. Britt, S.J., whose tenure spanned the years 1960 to 1966, the university was making strong efforts to acquire distinguished lay faculty. Britt succeeded in raising salaries by 66 percent in five years, dramatically increasing the volume of research grants, and reducing teaching loads. At the same time, admission standards were raised and graduate programs planned for several departments, including English (though its doctoral program wouldn't begin until 1967, the year Joyce left the school). One of Joyce's colleagues at U.D., James Holleran, recalled the atmosphere of "academic excitement" as the university made this "deliberate effort to improve itself." Young faculty members "were strongly encouraged to publish," so it appeared that Joyce, with her ever-expanding bibliography, would have no trouble establishing her niche in the department.

Joyce and Ray, grateful simply to have jobs in the same city, were especially pleased when their schools offered them the chance to teach summer courses, which would provide temporary income before their official appointments began in the fall. Ray had two courses at Wayne State and Joyce was given a section in freshman composition, the usual assignment of a beginning faculty member. But Joyce reported that she found her first venture into teaching "very pleasing and rewarding—I do feel it is the right profession for me, despite Eng. 1 and its dutiful parade of themes." In the fall, though she would have a heavy load of four sections, she was pleased that they included two sophomore courses in short fiction and drama.

Despite her excitement and general busyness that summer, Joyce noted that she'd continued "writing and reading like mad." Her reading focused on such contemporary authors as Saul Bellow, Iris Murdoch, and Mary McCarthy, though she was also reading the novels of Henry Fielding, since she and Ray had decided they would both write essays on the eighteenth-century novelist. Yet her own fiction writing, renewed in earnest during her lonely months in Beaumont, hardly seemed to suffer: "I've finished a novel," she told one friend, "which began as a kind of attack on Beaumont but levelled off to a conventional story, or unconventional; it's easy to see, now, why the Southern writers are so forceful." She'd already begun another book, "an academic novel," finding the project irresistible even though "my talent is hardly for parody or satire." She'd also continued working hard at shorter fiction: "Upon the Sweeping Flood," one of her finest early stories (it would appear in *Best American Short Stories 1964* and become the title story of Joyce's second collection), had been accepted by *Southwest Review* and "The Fine White Mist of Winter," published the previous year in *The Literary Review,* was to be reprinted in *Prize Stories 1963: The O. Henry Awards*—a bit of good news, Joyce reported, that she couldn't "quite comprehend."

When summer school ended, Joyce and Ray drove east for a long vacation: they visited with Fred and Carolina in Millersport, went to New York City to meet with Joyce's new associates at Vanguard Press, and stopped briefly in Syracuse to see Bob Phillips and favorite professors such as Walter Sutton and Donald Dike. Joyce's only anxiety about the trip was her and Ray's plan to stay with Dike and his wife, who lived in a farmhouse out in the "hinterlands" more than thirty miles from Syracuse. The visit went well, though Joyce noted that Dike drank heavily and that "his personality at home seems to me no less formidable than it always did in school." The Dikes insisted that Joyce and Ray take the master bedroom, a gesture Joyce found touching. She wrote a comical description of the bucolic but somewhat noisy atmosphere at the Dikes' farm:

> About half an hour after we went to bed some ghastly screaming began—just the bantam roosters, who proceeded to crow, both competitively and in choruses, all night long. Somehow we got accustomed to it. In the early morning (they rise rather early) we looked out the window to see all the horses grouped by the fence, waiting to be taken care of. It was really a beautiful scene, in fact their life there

is beautiful, comparatively, and we returned with muted enthusiasm
to our apartment life here in Detroit.

They also returned with muted finances: in addition to seeing plays in Manhattan, they'd spent a day in Cape Cod and had driven home by way of Concord, Middlebury, Lake Champlain, and the Adirondacks. They experienced
car trouble with their black Volkswagen ("luckily most of the trip was down-
hill," Joyce noted wryly), and arrived back in Detroit with only fifty cents.

Once the fall term began, Joyce stayed busy teaching and getting to know
her new colleagues and surroundings. One of her most autobiographical early
stories, "In the Region of Ice," written a couple of years later, focuses on Sister Irene, whose emotions reflect Joyce's own at the start of her time at U.D.:
"This was a new university and an entirely new world. She had heard—of
course it was true—that the Jesuit administration of this school had hired
her at the last moment to save money. . . . She had no trouble with teaching
itself; once she stood before a classroom she felt herself capable of anything.
It was the world immediately outside the classroom that confused and
alarmed her, though she let none of this show—the cynicism of her colleagues, the indifference of many of the students, and, above all, the looks
she got that told her nothing much would be expected of her."

Despite her promise as a fiction writer, Joyce had reason to feel insecure as
a newly hired university instructor. With only an M.A. degree at a time when
most beginning academics either had the Ph.D. or were working toward it,
she had little hope for promotion beyond her present rank. Despite her disillusionment with the Ph.D. program at Rice, she continued to ponder the
idea of seeking a doctorate elsewhere, perhaps at Wayne State. Knowing that
her short stories brought less prestige than more conventional academic publications, she continued producing scholarly essays in addition to her steady
stream of fiction manuscripts. During her first year at U.D., Joyce published
essays on Beckett, Melville, Renaissance tragedy, and the English and Scot-
tish ballads (she continued to use the gender-neutral name of "J. Oates
Smith"). But she had a frustrating awareness—already well developed after
her experiences at Wisconsin—that as a woman her progress in the male-
dominated academic world would be difficult no matter what she achieved,
especially at a staunchly conservative Catholic university. Her colleague Jim
McDonald noted in particular Joyce's anxiety about the impending Ph.D.
program. Not having a doctorate herself, she viewed the department's plans
"as a threat to her continuing employment." Joyce "was repeatedly assured
that her value to the department lay primarily in her writing of fiction and
criticism, that she was indispensable here," McDonald recalled. "I don't
think she believed this was true."

But, grateful for her new job and eager to prove herself, Joyce continued to work hard at both teaching and writing. By February 1963, the academic novel she'd begun the previous September was already completed and she was "planning vaguely the next one." The new book, she reported, would be a deliberate attempt to employ a "Jamesian technique," though she wondered "how many misguided writers have pondered upon that." Though her own first book wasn't yet released, Joyce's letters from this period show her assessing her competition among contemporary writers, commenting incisively, and quite critically, on the work of Philip Roth, John Updike, and J. D. Salinger. A new book by Salinger, for instance, a writer she had seldom admired, was "unbearably bad, self-parody." Despite all her reading and writing, however, Joyce claimed to be bored with the vacation between fall and spring semesters, feeling "anxious to return to teaching." She was elated by the news that she would teach her first advanced literature course that summer—an American literature survey that would be open to graduate students, a prestigious assignment for a twenty-four-year-old instructor—and she began immersing herself in the American classics, especially the novels of Herman Melville.

As the spring semester came to a close, Joyce and Ray felt established enough to consider buying a house. They were tired of throwing away rent money, and by May they had found a four-bedroom, two-story colonial on Woodstock Drive, in a neighborhood known as Green Acres. Situated on a large corner lot and surrounded by trees, the house with its white aluminum siding and blue shutters represented a dramatic improvement over their roach-infested apartment in Beaumont just a year before. Now Joyce and Ray would each have a separate study, an arrangement they'd wanted ever since they were married. Although, in 1963 terms, the price of $17,900 gave them pause, they "decided to be brave and go ahead," taking out a thirty-year mortgage after learning that the payments compared favorably to what they'd been spending for rent. They quickly set to work improving the property, building a small patio in the back, planting bushes and trees, and putting in grass. They found this work "a wonderful change," Joyce remarked, "from the reading and writing we do most of the time."

The only negative feature of their quiet new neighborhood was Joyce's troubled awareness that the area was racially segregated. Shortly before the move, she'd quipped to Bob Phillips that "Automatic membership in the White Citizens' Council" came with the house, but by that summer she'd begun expressing her growing concern about the city's racial tensions. "The racial problem is a large one in Detroit," she observed. "People tend to react hysterically, both Negroes and whites," but she hoped that integration would come about peacefully. Having written to Walter Sutton in November 1961 about the deplorable racism in Texas, she now discovered that racism in Detroit, though more covert, was equally virulent. "Perfectly nice people often turn unbelievably nasty over the question of integrated neighborhoods," she wrote.

There were disappointments of a more personal nature, too. Joyce was upset that Vanguard Press kept postponing publication of *By the North Gate*. Originally scheduled for the spring, then the summer, the book had now been delayed until October. Joyce complained that if she lived for writing alone, she would feel "completely frustrated. So much of it is out of the writer's hands, in the control of whimsical people." Her sense of futility was only reinforced by the quixotic nature of her novel-in-progress. Neither the manuscript nor its title has survived, but Joyce called it a "long, long tedious Jamesian novel, very leisurely, with a lot of people strung together, the sort of thing written not for any audience and certainly not destined to be published." She enjoyed this project even though she knew the world she was evoking, where everything was "somehow ordered, civilized, and meaningful," was alien to her own developing vision; at one point, she joked that "the ghost of Henry James is really writing it."

Deciding to give James's ghost a rest, she and Ray took a brief vacation when summer school ended. Their itinerary was virtually identical to the previous year's: they visited Joyce's parents in Millersport, Bob Phillips and his wife, Judy, in Syracuse, and then drove into New England. Staying in Nantucket, they enjoyed such diverse attractions as a whaling museum (having just taught Melville, Joyce was fascinated by the diaries and logs of sea captains) and a local production of *The Bald Soprano* by Ionesco, one of her favorite playwrights. They also rented bicycles and explored the island, which Joyce liked so well that she daydreamed about eventually buying a summer place there. The vacation concluded with another visit to New York, where they attended an orchestral concert in Greenwich Village and took long walks around the city.

Despite her frustration at the dilatory ways of her publisher, Joyce liked her editor, Evelyn Shrifte, and now visited with Evelyn and other Vanguard staff whenever she came to New York. Evelyn recalled that Joyce and Ray's money was limited in those days, so she began inviting them to stay at her apartment on Central Park West. There were two rooms in the rear that were "like a separate apartment," Evelyn remembered, "so they stayed there and went about their business as they chose to . . . it was very pleasant." Evelyn had a piano in one room, and sometimes in the morning Joyce would enter it, close the door, and play her favorite Chopin etudes. What Evelyn found most remarkable about Joyce was her extreme shyness: "she spoke in a small, whispery voice," so that Evelyn had trouble understanding everything Joyce said. Later, once her books began appearing, Joyce's shyness made her unwilling to do interviews or other publicity: "she just refused, she would never say anything to anybody." And Joyce was awed by New York: "Oh, her eyes were as wide as an ocean," Evelyn recalled. "I can see her now. The bells were ringing at St. Pat's and it was magic for her." One evening Evelyn treated the Smiths to dinner at an expensive hotel dining room, but Joyce seemed uncomfortable and awkward in the splendid surroundings. It was clear that both Ray and Joyce preferred simpler pleasures. "We would sit around at night," Evelyn said, "and I would read and they would read and then, at 11 P.M., we would have Tab and a cookie."

Vanguard had taken a chance on the unknown young author, but Evelyn was certain of Joyce's talent: "I thought she was a genius." As Joyce was now aware, the small firm had developed a reputation for publishing quality fiction and a wide range of other books. Established in 1926, Vanguard initially had been funded by an idealistic young millionaire, Charles Garland, who saw the need for an American publisher that would reprint classic works of economics and philosophy (Darwin, Hegel, Marx, and others) at low prices, so that good books could be disseminated among the working class. Vanguard was first headed by James Henle, who had purchased the firm in 1928 after Garland's endowment had been depleted; he still held the title of publisher when Joyce's first manuscript was accepted, though the day-to-day workings of the firm had been managed by Evelyn since the early 1950s. (Evelyn had joined the firm in 1929, as a recent college graduate.) As its list expanded, Vanguard had prided itself on discovering new talent and was the first to publish Saul Bellow, Nelson Algren, James T. Farrell, and other prominent novelists. Later, as Joyce's awareness of Vanguard's reputation and her fondness for Evelyn Shrifte grew, Joyce would find it difficult to contemplate leaving Vanguard for a larger publisher, even though her career would have benefited from such a move. Vanguard might be understaffed and often inefficient, but the firm had believed in Joyce from the beginning and published her work with dignity, inspiring Joyce's loyalty for the next fifteen years.

When Joyce and Ray returned home from their summer vacation, good news awaited Joyce: her story "Stigmata," published in the spring 1963 issue of *Colorado Quarterly*, would be reprinted in *Prize Stories 1964: The O. Henry Awards* as the second prize story, bringing her $200 in addition to the considerable prestige of appearing in that anthology for the second year in a row. Again she was looking forward to the new school term—classes would begin for Joyce on September 16—and in a few weeks her first book would finally appear.

Starting her second year at U.D., Joyce maintained a low profile in the

English department despite her growing reputation. James Holleran remembered Joyce in the early 1960s as "quiet, reserved, polite, and charming," a young woman not inclined to call attention to herself. She remained conscientious in performing her academic duties, yet she had little in common with her U.D. colleagues, most of whom were male, Catholic, and strongly interested in sports and drinking. "Obviously, none of this was Joyce's cup of tea," Jim McDonald remarked. "She must have felt excluded from this frame of reference and experience (most of us, including the graduate students, were married with kids and/or kids on the way)." To McDonald, Joyce seemed not only reserved but "evasive, remote, almost stand-offish" around male colleagues who seemed more interested in Detroit Lions football than in Sartre or Nietzsche. "As far as the department, as a unit, was concerned, Joyce was on the fringes—perhaps by nature, perhaps by choice."

But Joyce did develop one significant new friendship during her first two years in Detroit. Dan Brown, also an instructor at U.D. and exactly Joyce's age, was working on his doctorate at Wayne State. Unlike the other young male instructors, Dan shared Joyce's interest in writing; he would later publish several novels and short-story collections, dealing primarily with homosexual themes, under the name "Daniel Curzon," though in the straitlaced early 1960s he was not yet "out" as a gay man, even to his closest friends. Joyce and Dan Brown's friendship would suffer a dramatic breach a decade later, but throughout her years at U.D. Joyce considered him one of her closest friends. They occupied adjoining offices and soon began having lunch together and enjoying long telephone conversations. "We talked easily," Dan recalled, especially about literature and teaching. (Their friendship had begun in earnest when Joyce called Dan, who was active in the university theater group, to ask his advice about teaching plays in her classes.) Years later, in a short story based on their relationship, Dan wrote that the character based on Joyce "liked his company as an intimate *friend*, someone interested in literature as much as she was, someone to be intellectual with in the generally sterile, Catholic atmosphere of their university and its Jesuits, with its Eisenhower residue of the 1950's." Yet his new friend also intimidated him: "Sometimes she made me stammer because she seemed so intelligent," he wrote in a 1986 memoir. Their friendship thrived despite what Dan considered Joyce's puritanical, "iron-maiden" quality; she would become upset if Dan or another male colleague told an off-color joke. (Jim McDonald likewise recalled that departmental humor among the young instructors was largely "of the locker room variety," which held no appeal for Joyce.) But the two had much in common, including similar economic and family backgrounds. Dan's parents, like Fred and Carolina Oates, had not finished high school: "We were trying to escape our semi-literate pasts," Dan wrote. "This and our commitment to writing gave us a bond."

Joyce remembered her friendly relations with Dan Brown and her other U.D. colleagues as growing out "of an egalitarian, sibling sort of atmosphere. We were all young instructors. We were the lowest level, and we made $4,900 a year. . . . Dan was writing fiction and he'd have me read some of it." Dan was the only friend at the time with whom she discussed her own creative work. Jim McDonald remembered her as "unapproachable" on the subject, and Joyce had already developed her longstanding policy of not foisting her proliferating manuscripts on Ray. Since Ray had become especially busy with his job at Wayne State, which operated under the rigorous quarter system and was causing him considerable stress, Joyce's friendship with Dan helped fill the few hours she could spare for socializing. Jim McDonald remembered that Dan was the only colleague with whom Joyce spent much time and that she adopted "a defensive shield" when interacting with the other instructors.

According to Dan's somewhat embittered memoir, Joyce "had selected me as a presentable young man—a little stocky maybe, with a beard when men didn't have beards, but tall and possessed of a car—and we went to plays and concerts and readings, as well as drives out to the rich suburbs of Detroit, to look at all the fancy houses, houses Joyce always noticed as being empty in the daytime." They also took long walks and often played tennis together. But Dan insisted that Joyce was always a "prickly" friend, easily offended by kidding. When she had the jacket photograph taken for her first book, he remembered, Joyce asked him, "Don't I look pretty?" When Dan responded, "Yeah, it doesn't look like you," Joyce became enraged. Dan considered Joyce's appearance enigmatic and changeable. "Joyce was always one of those people who may or may not be attractive. Everybody noticed her eyes; they were fascinating."

Even after Joyce and Dan had been estranged for years, he singled out the qualities he'd admired in Joyce. One was her dedication to teaching: "she seemed to care a lot about her students, at least her smart students," he wrote. "She'd have them over to her house and spend time talking with them in her office." He also recalled Joyce's mordant sense of humor. On one occasion, Joyce gave a talk near the U.D. campus on Jorge Luis Borges, and afterward a priest in the audience asked her "a very convoluted question, which she answered with a very convoluted response. Afterwards I asked her how she'd been able to answer so well." Her reply: "I didn't know what he asked, so I answered the same way. It doesn't matter what's said, only how it *sounds*." On another occasion Joyce and Dan were strolling around the campus when they saw "a man gibbering to himself, obviously mentally disturbed. 'I get paid for doing that,' Joyce smiled." Dan also stressed that "she was never egotistical about her writing, as her career began to take off. If any-thing, she lived as though at any moment it might all be taken away by the gods."

In October 1963, however, it seemed that the gods were smiling. Unlike most first books by unknown authors, *By the North Gate* received wide atten-tion and near-unanimous praise. In *Saturday Review* for October 26, Haskel Frankel (who referred to the author as "Mrs. Oates") set the tone for subse-quent reviews: "In story after story she fuses realism with poetry to reveal life as something always a little larger than those who live it." Though stressing the violent subject matter, Frankel acknowledged (as some reviewers of Joyce's later books would not) that "violence is never the author's sole con-cern." Other glowing reviews appeared in *Time* and *Book Week*. Though Joyce had worried that her stark realism might be considered shocking in some conservative quarters (or "not nice," as she had put it to Donald Dike), even the Catholic press welcomed the book. A priest whose review appeared in the *Michigan Catholic* wrote that *By the North Gate* "contains some of the best stories in modern fiction," adding a wry conclusion that directly addressed Joyce's earlier fears: "Because of the occasional grotesqueries, violence and sex, some readers may find Miss Oates' stories quite unladylike. And no criti-cism, I think, would give her more satisfaction. . . . Highly recommended."

But the most significant critical notice—one that Joyce's Vanguard editor Evelyn Shrifte, thirty years later, would still remember as the review that had launched Joyce's career—was Stanley Kauffmann's thoughtful analysis in *The New York Times Book Review* on November 10. According to Kauffmann, these debut stories "attack large-scale emotion with a fearlessness all the more admirable for her success." Noting the influence of Flannery O'Connor, he added perceptively that Joyce "sometimes seems determined to prove that the 'Southern' story can be written in the North."

Joyce had been influenced by O'Connor's violent themes and cutting sense of irony, and the southern writer had served to some degree as the liter-ary mentor Joyce had lacked in her personal life. Joyce agreed that *By the North Gate* owed an "obvious" debt to O'Connor, but she added that they had both "come down from Faulkner ... and it may be the feminine-Catholicism aspect that has overshadowed my stories, so that they are like hers in certain ways." Her letters to college friends had been peppered with references to O'Connor's new stories as they appeared in literary magazines and prize anthologies during the late 1950s and early 1960s. After the publi-cation of the novel *The Violent Bear It Away* in 1960 Joyce had even sent a fan letter, to which O'Connor replied ("though briefly," Joyce said; neither letter has survived). But Joyce later pointed out a key difference between them: O'Connor's work always has a religious dimension, "whereas in my writing there is only the natural world."

Yet more often than not Joyce's remarks about O'Connor were grudging and critical, as if she were feeling some "anxiety of influence" in the face of her powerful southern contemporary: "I don't know what there is exactly about her that I admire," she wrote to Bob Phillips, complaining that O'Connor was "too strenuously brittle, an obviously nice little old-young Southern woman who has never in her life had any startling experiences but who has read a great deal and is quite anxious to show you that she is not sentimental." But when O'Connor died of lupus the next year at age thirty-nine, Joyce exclaimed, "Is it really true about Flannery O'Connor's death?" She felt that the prominent critic Granville Hicks should do an essay in tribute to the writer: "It isn't just literary affinities that make me feel this way," Joyce added, "but I've always felt a certain interest or even closeness about her, I don't know why, perhaps because I had the idea, perhaps mistaken, that she was a very lonely person." Many years later, after O'Connor's letters were published in *The Habit of Being*, Joyce would marvel that O'Connor's folksy, disingenuous letter-writing style so closely resembled Joyce's own manner in her letters to Carol North in the late 1950s, though there could have been no possibility of direct influence.

With the publication of Joyce's first book, there were already signs that her reputation, like O'Connor's, might be destined to become controversial. A negative review of *By the North Gate* appeared in the literary magazine *Critique*, whose reviewer, while acknowledging the "professionalism of Miss Oates's prose," complained that her fictional world was devoid of meaning: "her obsessive pursuit of the single truth that the inevitable condition of all life is senselessness and brutality puts her in danger of embracing a falsehood. . . . We view these characters, as Miss Oates does, from a distance, without much compassion." The contention that Joyce simply dramatized a horrific world without supplying a shaping moral or aesthetic vision would, like the complaints about her violent themes, become amplified as Joyce published further story collections and novels throughout the 1960s. It was a criticism with which Joyce herself would come to agree (though in a measured, qualified way) by the early 1970s, when the tenor of her work underwent a dramatic change.

Perhaps buoyed by the positive reviews, Joyce agreed to an interview for the *Detroit News*, despite the disinclination for publicity she'd expressed to Evelyn. The interviewer, Edwina Schaeffer, found Joyce "reticent" and willing to give only "careful brief remarks" about herself or her writing. "In appearance, Miss Oates reminds one of a sorrowful madonna in a painting," Schaeffer wrote, with "long black hair hanging loosely about her white oval face; eyelids closed halfway over large dark eyes." Joyce told Schaeffer that "it's hard to talk about one's own writing. It's like talking about your face . . . how do you describe your own face? I know I'd be unhappy without my writing." Asked about her home life with Ray, Joyce would say only that it represented "a study in conventionality." After "forcing" a few more words from her reluctant celebrity, Schaeffer concluded that Joyce Carol Oates was "not her own favorite subject."

Once the glowing notices of By the North Gate had come in, Joyce claimed to find the entire process of publicity and reviews "very dull and tedious," remarking that "I don't think any more of [Kauffmann's] positive remarks than I would have (would have let myself) if they had been negative remarks." Such comments set the tone for Joyce's future ambivalence about critical reception of her work: though always nervously aware when a major review was impending, she would attempt to offset possible hurt by affecting nonchalance or indifference.

After the excitement over By the North Gate had died down, Joyce returned to her usual routine of writing, enthusiastic teaching, and voracious reading. She also formed several new friendships, one that would have a profound effect on both her personal life and her writing. Through a U.D. colleague Joyce met Marjorie Jackson Levin, a reporter for the Detroit Free Press and herself a professional writer of short stories whose work had appeared in McCalls and Cosmopolitan. Through Marj Levin, Joyce would be introduced to the Detroit Women Writers club, an active and respected organization that sponsored readings, benefits, and various other literary events. Established in 1900, it was "the largest and oldest club for professional women authors in the U.S.," wrote another member, Marilyn Lyman.

Although Marj Levin became a good friend, Joyce would grow even closer to two other members of Detroit Women Writers during the next decade: Kay Smith, a lively and charismatic woman whose many activities included writing gardening books and historical accounts of the Detroit area, and the stylish and talented Elizabeth Graham, a professional writer and former fiction editor at Ladies' Home Journal. Though sharing Joyce's literary interests, these new friends were quite different from Joyce in another respect: Kay, Elizabeth, and Marj all lived in the affluent suburbs north of Detroit whose neighborhoods Joyce and Dan Brown had investigated the previous year, as if exploring an alien environment. (Kay was married to Joseph Smith, an investment banker; Elizabeth Graham's husband, Jim, was a high-level executive at Gulf & Western; and Marj's husband was a prominent local physician, Herbert G. Levin.) In these women Joyce found the female friendships that were unavailable at U.D.; she was also introduced to an elegant suburban world far removed from her hardscrabble north country background that she had portrayed so vividly in *By the North Gate*. Joyce's introduction to the suburban ethos of sprawling homes, luxury cars, and country clubs would have a strong influence on much of her writing in the 1960s, inspiring the novel *Expensive People* (1968) and such now-famous early stories as "How I Contemplated the World from the Detroit House of Correction and Began My Life Over Again."

When Marj Levin met Joyce, she was astonished that this shy, self-effacing young U.D. instructor had already published an acclaimed book of stories, had won national awards, and had appeared in such magazines as *Mademoiselle*—and all without the benefit of a literary agent. "I couldn't believe it," said Marj, who immediately called her own agent, Blanche Gregory. "There's this English teacher here who has written this book," Marj told Blanche. "You should call her, she needs an agent." At first, Joyce didn't seem enthused by the idea—she was accustomed to mailing out stories herself and had already established a relationship with Vanguard Press—but finally she accepted Blanche's offer to represent her. The head of her own agency, Blanche Gregory had a long-established reputation as a fine agent and later in her career would represent other well-known authors such as Ann Beattie, Annie Dillard, and Paul Theroux. Joyce liked and admired Blanche; recommending her to Bob Phillips, she added, "Don't let her mild, ladylike manner fool you; she is a shrewd businesswoman. Nothing awes her." Apart from her skill as an agent, she was "rather classy," Joyce said later, "a beautiful woman, with very defined cheekbones." Joyce immediately sent Blanche a story entitled "The Accident," which Blanche began circulating among the major magazine editors in New York. In her modest first letter to Blanche, Joyce welcomed criticism of the story, "since I do not consider most of my stories precious art that cannot be touched by rational judgment, my own or anyone else's." She added that she hoped Blanche's "involvement with me would not result in a rather penniless waste of time on your part."

Although "The Accident" was rejected by three editors, all were enthusiastic about Joyce's talent: the *Saturday Evening Post* asked to see "anything else she writes," *McCalls* was "impressed" but found the story "too difficult" for their audience, and *Redbook* likewise considered it "beautifully done," although "too special and oblique for a mass magazine such as ours." But Blanche was successful on her fourth submission. *Cosmopolitan* accepted "The Accident" on January 4, 1964 (it appeared in the July issue, with the title changed to "Why Did You Cry for Me?") and paid $1,000, far more than Joyce had received for any of her previous stories. "I was just amazed," she later remembered. She was especially happy, she noted on January 22, "because it isn't actually a bad story," though she added that it "isn't anywhere nearly as good as 'By the North Gate,' which was turned down icily by 17 publishers of no-payment literary quarterlies. (If you sense a satirical note, you are correct.)" That same day Joyce wrote gratefully to Blanche about the "wonderful news. . . . I owe it entirely to you, without a doubt. I had not even considered my writing remotely marketable on such levels."

Though buoyed by the magazine sale, Joyce continued to feel frustrated by the editors at Vanguard Press, who persisted "in their usual state of non-communication" despite their young author's excellent reviews. As with most short-story collections, the positive notices had not translated into much sales activity (the book had sold only a thousand copies, and many years would pass before the modest first printing was depleted), and Joyce speculated that her editor probably wasn't enjoying the long "Jamesian horror" she had completed in November, "in a series of yawns." The novel was "really dull, really a failure," she insisted. Yet Blanche, the first person to read the new novel, had responded positively and submitted the manuscript to Vanguard, suggesting only a few revisions to Joyce. With the new submission, Vanguard now had three book-length manuscripts by Joyce to consider. Before meeting Blanche, Joyce had submitted two previous novels: *With Shuddering Fall* in mid-1962 (it would finally appear in 1964 as her first novel) and another, shorter novel in late 1962 called *Sleepwalker*, which Joyce described as a love story whose protagonist was a blind man. It was now 1964 and Vanguard still had not responded to the 1962 submissions, much less the lengthy new manuscript. About this same time, Joyce asked Blanche what to do about a request she'd received from the Actors Studio in New York, who felt that several of the stories in *By the North Gate* could be translated successfully into dramatic form. "I am very shaky about playwriting," Joyce told Blanche.

The self-deprecating tone in such letters had become an established pose; in fact, Joyce continued writing confidently and prolifically despite her full-time teaching, establishing a pattern that would remain consistent from that time forward. (Apart from her duties at U.D., Joyce had even taken on a night course at Wayne State, teaching writing to adult students.) In addition to the Jamesian novel, Joyce kept Blanche busy with new stories that winter. Two of these, "The Psychoanalytical Love Affair" and "Archways," were sold to *Cosmopolitan* for $1,000 and $1,250, respectively, and another went to the prestigious *Virginia Quarterly Review*. (Joyce herself had already placed several other stories to be published that spring, in the literary magazines *Prairie Schooner*, *Southwest Review*, and *MSS*, a new publication edited by the young John Gardner.) Joyce also decided to take the challenge posed by the Actors Studio, adapting a seventy-page novella she'd written the previous

year, "The Sweet Enemy," into an absurdist—and to some readers, quite baffling—play. (Joyce had been teaching Beckett and Ionesco in her classes.)
Gertrude Bregman, an agent who worked closely with Blanche and who handled most of Joyce's shorter manuscripts, remembered that Joyce, visiting the
agents' offices in New York, called *The Sweet Enemy* "a comedy of the absurd
with a capital A." Though both Blanche and Gertrude (whom everyone
called "Gert") enjoyed meeting their new client, they were "completely puzzled" by the play. One evening, determined to understand *The Sweet Enemy*,
Gert "began to analyze the play character by character and scene by scene,"
staying up all night and even then not feeling that she had grasped its meaning. But the director of the Actors Studio, Frank Corsaro, wrote Joyce an enthusiastic letter, calling the play "fascinating" and saying that she was indeed
"a playwright." The studio wanted to schedule the play for production and
Corsaro invited Joyce to come to New York for rehearsals later that year.

Although Joyce had complained that there were "so many novels of mine
in my study that I am discouraged from writing any more," by April 1964 she
was submitting another short novel to Blanche. In her accompanying letter,
Joyce wrote that *The Killer* (an early version of *Expensive People*) might seem
displeasing to some readers; the story focused on a young boy in an upscale
Detroit suburb who murders his callous, social-climbing mother. But Joyce
added: "My theme is one I feel very strongly about—the disintegration of
free will in our society and the increasing difficulty an individual faces in trying to assert his moral 'freedom.'" Echoing her earlier anxieties over *By the
North Gate*, she acknowledged that it was a "uniformly bleak" novel, though
hardly different from stories she read daily in the newspapers. Again she welcomed Blanche's suggestions for revising the manuscript.

Joyce's teaching career was also thriving: she learned she would receive a
thousand-dollar raise for the following year, and she'd been asked to teach an
upper-level course in European writers including Dostoevsky, Mann, Kafka,
and Camus. These were "people I've admired passionately for ages!" she exclaimed. For Ray, however, this second year in Detroit, which had seen such a
blossoming of Joyce's career, had been a time of depression and ill health;
having given up his own literary ambitions, he lacked the ego-sustaining ballast of creative achievement and recognition that Joyce enjoyed. There were
family sorrows as well: Ray's father, in Milwaukee, had undergone several unsuccessful operations for cancer and was now dying. But Joyce attributed
most of her husband's troubles to his job: "The Wayne quarter system with
its relentlessness has exhausted many people, including students, and this is
evidently the main reason for Ray's ill health." But early in 1964 Ray received
some good news of his own: he was offered a position at the University of
Windsor (located just across the Detroit River), where he'd been teaching a

night course in eighteenth-century English literature. His new job, an assistant professorship, would involve a substantial raise and a reduced teaching load. He was especially pleased that he would begin that summer, teaching an upper-level Shakespeare course. Joyce, relieved and gratified by this positive turn in Ray's fortunes, was also happy that the University of Windsor was in commuting distance from their Detroit home.

The only interruption of this sense of well-being that spring came in the form of a burglary: while Joyce and Ray were both at school, someone broke into the house, "threw things around upstairs, looking in vain for money," but ultimately took only Joyce's wristwatch and an old typewriter of Ray's whose worth Joyce estimated at ninety cents. Yet the violation of Joyce's ordered, bookish world had been upsetting. She wrote a story about the incident, "The Thief," and later recalled the "psychological shock" of the burglary: "we returned to a mess—bureau drawers yanked out, clothing tossed onto the floor—my modest jewelry strewn about (and very little taken: the thief's shrewd judgment), curious bloodstains on the parquet floor in the dining room." The fearful and sometimes violent world of Joyce's north country childhood had naturally caused Joyce to cherish the peace and privacy of her present middle-class "sanctuary," as she called it, to which she and Ray had gained access through years of hard work. Shortly after the burglary, they purchased a handgun, which they kept in a bedside table. Joyce's psychological antennae would remain sensitively attuned to Detroit's increasingly violent atmosphere later in the 1960s, which would become a crucial factor in motivating her to leave both U.D. and the city for the comparative calm across the river in Canada.

The positive developments in Joyce and Ray's life that spring and summer helped relegate their concerns about Detroit to the background. As they'd done the previous year, they relaxed by gardening in the back yard—feeling "comfortably bourgeois," as Joyce put it; they took up tennis, attended concerts, and even bought a piano and enjoyed "stumbling" through their attempts at the keyboard. They had also acquired a pair of Persian cats, Kitty and Fluffy, the first of a long series of feline companions that Joyce and Ray would enjoy through the years. And some gratifying good news came in May, when her apparently somnolent Vanguard editors finally accepted one of her longer manuscripts: Joyce's "first" novel, *With Shuddering Fall*, would be published later that year. Especially after her long and earnest apprenticeship—the practice novels written in high school, the several novels shown to Donald Dike during her years at Syracuse, and the additional novels written since her marriage to Ray—this was an exhilarating breakthrough, although Joyce's habit of self-deprecation prompted her to write to Phillips in mock-horror: "they're publishing my horrendous novel—yes, Bob!—about the racing maniacs—at long last!—how awful!—ugh!—due in fall 1964—translated to Anytime—a poor novel but what can I do?"

Apart from her usual tendency to downplay her accomplishments, especially with writer-friends like Phillips (who had been sending manuscripts of his own stories and poems for Joyce to critique), Joyce's facetious claim that *With Shuddering Fall* was "a poor novel" might have been based in her awareness that, like many writers (including Flannery O'Connor), her present ability as a novelist didn't compare favorably with her already high achievement as a short-story writer, even though she'd been working at novels for a much longer period. Though not received with the uniform praise that had greeted the stories, *With Shuddering Fall* would garner serious attention, suggesting to critics that Joyce Carol Oates was an ambitious and energetic new talent whose future work would be awaited with keen interest. And though dealing superficially with "racing maniacs," the novel portrayed Joyce's passionate, conflicted relationship with her own early life, prompting her later admission that the book was highly personal and "in many ways, very autobiographical."

With Shuddering Fall also embodied the prominent features, in both its form and subject matter, of Joyce's later and far more accomplished novels. The story of Karen Herz, a passive and "icily beautiful" teenager growing up in the same Eden County countryside Joyce had depicted in *By the North Gate*, had the tripartite structure that Joyce would employ in *A Garden of Earthly Delights* (1967), *them* (1969), *Wonderland* (1971), *Do with Me What You Will* (1973), and *The Assassins* (1975). With its allusions to Nietzsche, Kafka, Mann, and countless other writers, the novel also displayed Joyce's considerable erudition in world literature and philosophy, and suggested the way in which her fiction would attempt a synthesis of, and an ongoing dialogue with, her intellectual and artistic masters, even as it articulated her own developing vision. *With Shuddering Fall* also combined a focus on intense psychological experience with the type of larger, mythological framework through which Joyce would often attempt to clarify the cultural significance of her narratives. Just as *Wonderland* would contain pervasive allusions to Lewis Carroll's Alice books and *Angel of Light* (1981) would attempt a modern retelling of the Atreus legend, *With Shuddering Fall* had its structural analogue in the biblical myth of Abraham and Isaac. Everything in the novel was "parallel—very strictly parallel" to the Bible story, Joyce later said, calling *With Shuddering Fall* "a religious work." Thus the novel represented a milestone in its author's intellectual and spiritual development in her early twenties. Repudiating her family's Catholicism had not been easy for Joyce, after all, and even after marrying Ray she had occasionally slipped off to Sunday mass by herself. In the novel, Joyce said, "I was working myself out of the religious phase of my life," trying to show that merely "having faith" in a supernatural reality "leaves one really nowhere."

Much of the naturalistic and psychological detail in *With Shuddering Fall* likewise supports Joyce's later assessment that the novel was "very autobiographical." Like Joyce, Karen Herz attends a one-room country school, endures the torments of hulking farm boys ("they did what they wanted . . . ripped your clothes half off," Karen recalls), and develops a reserved, cautious manner: Karen "was proud of her ability to withdraw from the presence of others so completely that her indifference was not even feigned." Karen grows up dominated by her strong-willed father and by her own generalized and crippling fear. In conveying Karen's psychological makeup, Joyce used another fearsome memory from her childhood—the bridge over the Tonawanda Creek that she later described as "an old, old bridge, a nightmare bridge, rusted, with a plank floor" that rattled when she crossed it, causing her to "shut my eyes and cease breathing . . . too frightened even to pray that the bridge not collapse." Similarly, Karen "screamed" whenever her father, driving, approached "an old rusted bridge," prompting Mr. Herz to swear that "it would never collapse while she was on it." This image of the perilous, potentially collapsing bridge (sometimes inspired by other significant bridges in Joyce's youth, especially those over the Lockport canal) would pervade Joyce's future fiction, providing her autobiographical characters a possible escape route but also a potential dissolution, a fall into the abyss. Clara Walpole in *A Garden of Earthly Delights*, Jesse Vogel in *Wonderland*, Enid Stevick in *You Must Remember This* (1987), and Judd Mulvaney in *We Were the Mulvaneys* (1996) ponder their fates while staring down from bridges to the swirling waters below, while the pregnant title character in "Silkie" stands on a bridge with a boy she does not love, manipulating him into marriage and thus assuring her own future security. For Joyce, these fictional versions of the bridges she remembered from childhood became a powerful means of evoking the precarious social and psychological conditions of her characters.

In *With Shuddering Fall*, Joyce's portrayal of Karen Herz' natural environment likewise contributes to the novel's pervasive aura of fear and insecurity. In her ironically named Eden County, the natural world is a place of extremes, savage and beautiful at once, anticipating the imagery of the novel *Childwold* (1976) and such essays as "Against Nature" (1988): "Winters here in the northwestern hills of Eden County were long and brutal. . . . In the worst days the snow looked like an incredible sifting of earth and heaven, blotting out both earth and heaven, reducing them to an insane struggle of white that struck at human faces like knives. Summers reeked with heat, and heaven pressed downward so that the sun had to glare through skies of dust. Sometimes there would be holocausts of fire in the woods, churnings and twistings of white smoke." Repelled by this frequently hellish environment, a Darwinian world where brute power reigns tyrannically over the physically weak, Karen develops a hatred for physical life itself, recoiling in disgust from the natural processes of sexuality, childbirth, and eating. Shar Rule, a local boy who had left Eden County to become a race car driver and whose tormented, doomed relationship with Karen becomes the novel's central focus, recalls that even when Karen was a small child she'd witnessed a dog giving birth and became "sick with watching it," telling Shar to get rid of the puppies. Having sex with Shar, Karen surrenders physically but withdraws emotionally, thinking that "she might have been fleeing her body": "Karen closed her eyes and felt her soul contract itself into a tiny pebble-like thing safe in her brain." At a fairground, Shar and Karen witness a macabre scene (an early example of the Oatesian grotesque) when they visit a freak show, with its horrific mutations of nature and a proudly displayed jar filled with human embryos. Later, wandering down the midway, Karen notes that "[t]he smell of flesh was in the air, and food, and filth," the alliterative linking of flesh, food, and filth signaling her horrified withdrawal from the physical realities of her life.

That Karen has endured a kind of psychological and emotional death is clarified when she falls asleep one night and, "abruptly, she was dreaming. A child had died. It had been growing inside a closet, on the dusty floor, a clothes closet with bright summer dresses in it: tubes ran in and out of the child's body, plastic veins, queer bright colors of red and blue and yellow, a transparent chest so that no one could see the damp red heart. A plastic heart." In characteristic Oatesian language, Karen views her life as "a darkness that was really an open, straining mouth, a vast waiting hole that claimed her!" The dream is prophetic. Dissociating herself from any genuine connection with other people even as she plunges into a masochistic love affair that leads to pregnancy and a painful, life-threatening miscarriage, Karen Herz ("caring hurts") anticipates later Oates heroines such as Elena Howe of *Do with Me What You Will* (also a passive blond); Marya Knauer of *Marya: A Life* (1986); Enid Stevick of *You Must Remember This*; and Iris Courtney of *Because It Is Bitter, and Because It Is My Heart* (1990). These women, along with their numerous counterparts in Joyce's short stories (in *By the North Gate*, the gang-raped Grace in "Pastoral Blood" is a key early example), develop strategies of withdrawal and manipulation when their perception of physical life, especially sex, has become a proven or potential threat to their own integrity of self. Yet ironically, as in Karen's case, they often pursue a self-destructive course by surrendering their own power and inviting their own degradation.

Karen's disgust with food and the process of eating suggests another fearsome natural horror, one that is personified in the obese and morally corrupt "businessman," Max, a racing promoter whom Joyce describes as "a bloated, insatiable spectator, a product of a refined civilization." Anticipating the grossly overweight and megalomaniacal Dr. Pedersen in *Wonderland*, Max has an obsessive (and possibly homosexual) fixation on Shar and uses his economic power to assume the role of puppetmaster over both Shar and Karen, as well as a motley group of other drivers, mechanics, and hangers-on. ("I am the only owner who follows his men around," he tells Karen.) This well-read and generally "refined" monster, like the various freaks Karen witnesses at the fairground, embodies nature gone amok. Watching Max eat, Karen feels "a swirling of nausea." As Joyce would assert in an essay many years later, again using the metaphor of food and eating, the natural world "lacks a moral purpose. . . . It eludes us even as it prepares to swallow us up, books and all."

For all these similarities to Joyce's later work, it was the use of violence in *With Shuddering Fall* that critics, linking the novel to *By the North Gate*, would quickly define as Joyce's most characteristic trait. The novel's primary instrument of violence is Karen's lover, Shar, a would-be Nietzschean *Übermensch*, a "dark, surly" back-country Byronic hero motivated by a concentrated rage that makes him effective as a driver but crippled as a human being. Described as "itching for violence," Shar beats Karen's father severely with the butt of a shotgun, burns down the cabin where his own father has just died, and has unfriendly sexual encounters with Karen that are more like wrestling matches than acts of love: "They grunted together, Karen squirming backward in the damp earth, Shar grinding himself against her." Unable either to love or to escape his need for connection, Shar finally commits suicide, driving his racing car into a retaining wall (ironically enough, the race occurs on Independence Day) while Karen lies alone in a hotel room, recovering from her miscarriage of Shar's baby.

As in the later story "Golden Gloves" and the novel *You Must Remember This*, Joyce dramatizes male violence in terms of athletic contests (racing, boxing) and female victimization in terms of the bloodletting and pain that attend sexual experience. As the novel closes, Karen has recuperated in a mental institution and meekly returns to Eden County, the domination of her father, and her family's Catholicism, still puzzling over the central conundrum of her life: "It is insane to look for meaning in life, and it is insane not to; what am I to do?" Two years later, Joyce would summarize her novel's intentions by suggesting the inevitable doom attending Karen's attempt to conduct a life based on "existential" passions. The novel, Joyce observed, was "a dramatization of the tension between two opposing philosophical commitments: one to a classical, conservative, and impersonal recognition of the 'pattern' of life, the other to a freer, more existential style of living. The novel's structure demonstrates the inevitability of the classical victory, though it is not an inevitability I have any particular enthusiasm for." This duality suggested a pattern that would become common for Joyce as she sent her fictional protagonists along perilous courses of experience even as her own way of living—"classical, conservative"— enabled Joyce Carol Oates to write the books and through them achieve an "impersonal recognition of the 'pattern' of life."

During the summer and fall of 1964, with the novel in press, Joyce plunged into new writing projects. Two of these, uncharacteristically for Joyce, would not be completed. Having placed both their essays on Henry Fielding with an academic journal, Joyce and Ray hit upon the idea of writing a critical study of Fielding together. Ray was feeling the pressure to publish a book, and the two essays they'd already written could work as chapters of a longer study. But they simply lost interest in the project. Years later, Ray acknowledged that writing a book together "wouldn't have worked—Joyce would have ended up writing the whole book." (Ray later published a critical study of eighteenth-century English poet Charles Churchill.) Joyce, as if she weren't busy enough with her fiction, had in the meantime contacted an academic publisher about the possibility of writing a book-length study of the American poet Howard Nemerov and was promptly offered a contract. Nemerov was a poet Joyce had "admired for years and years but who remains inexplicably unknown to a general public," Joyce wrote in October. But only a few weeks after beginning, she felt intimidated by Nemerov's difficult recent poetry and his erudite essays: "I used to like him but now fear him," she confessed. Soon that project also was abandoned, and Joyce sent an apologetic letter to her editor. She'd stayed busy instead rewriting the "academic novel" she'd completed two years before.

A trip to New York during Thanksgiving vacation helped to end 1964 on an upbeat note for Joyce. Frank Corsaro had written that the Actors Studio had begun working on her play and wanted her assistance with rehearsals. Since Ray, now on the Canadian academic schedule at Windsor, was busy teaching, Joyce asked Dan Brown to accompany her. Though Joyce still had doubts about her first venture into playwriting, she looked forward to the challenge and was pleased to be visiting the city, where she could see her old high school friend Gail Gleasner (with whom she would be staying) and sample some off-Broadway plays. She was less sanguine about the series of luncheons and cocktail parties that her agent, Blanche, had arranged, wanting Joyce to meet editors of the various women's magazines who had been responding enthusiastically to her stories. Dan Brown remembered going along to these parties, where he and Joyce "pretended to be cosmopolitan, but we weren't making it." They also attended a dinner given by Joyce's Vanguard editor Evelyn Shrifte, at Evelyn's apartment. According to Dan, both he and Joyce felt out of place: "A couple of wine snobs were the other dinner guests, and they . . . bragged and pontificated about wines so much Joyce and I felt like strangers from the planet Detroit."

Nor did Joyce feel especially comfortable working with Corsaro and his actors on rehearsals for *The Sweet Enemy*. Joyce was "ferociously shy and monosyllabic, almost," Corsaro remembered. "I think she approached the problem of revision with great trepidation, not having had the opportunity to do it before. I felt that she was under terrible strain." But Dan Brown, who also attended rehearsals, believed that Corsaro and the actors seemed to take the play more seriously than Joyce did. According to Dan, Joyce had "forgotten that she'd made the father in the play black and the daughter white—as a joke. When we got to NYC, Corsaro and the others talked in hushed tones about the 'significance' of the mixed racial theme. Joyce and I made mouths to each other behind their backs." But for all its problems and ironies, the trip was "a highlight of both our lives up to then," Dan added. Writing to Bob Phillips, Joyce likewise remarked on how much she had enjoyed herself in New York. And, as if to add the ending punctuation to a year that had seen so many positive career developments, on December 8 Joyce received the annual "Author of the Year" award from the Detroit Women Writers organization, a special distinction in that she was the group's youngest member.

She was also pleased by the reviews of *With Shuddering Fall*, which had been published on October 26. Earlier that month she'd expressed anxiety over its reception: "I don't have much faith in [the novel]," she wrote, "and hope the reviewers will be merciful." Compared with the enthusiastic reception *By the North Gate* had enjoyed the previous year, the praise for Joyce's first novel was somewhat restrained, but the book had its admirers. Fortunately, the reviewer for the influential *New York Times Book Review*, John Knowles (author of *A Separate Peace*), was among them. "One of the excellent qualities of this novel by the talented young writer Joyce Carol Oates," Knowles wrote, "is an unswerving fidelity to its theme." Knowles praised the "fascinating portrait of two characters locked in a baffled love," also noting the vividly rendered atmosphere and the "clarity, grace and intelligence of the writing." Like reviewers of the short-story collection, Knowles mentioned Faulkner as a likely influence on Joyce. He criticized only the frequent shifts in narrative viewpoint and the portrait of Karen, which was "not really in focus. She sifts through her thoughts and feelings and fate at great length, but not always to much purpose." Negative response to *With Shuddering Fall* was typified by the notice in *Harper's*. While acknowledging that the novel had power, the reviewer found the narrative "hysterically incoherent." Remarking on the many "violent scenes," she concluded: "The episodes are often individually impressive but they lack the single point of view, the careful sense of order in confusion needed to lend conviction to the whole."

Though Joyce had expressed her own doubts about the novel, she objected to the *Harper's* review: "Really the novel was most carefully planned," she wrote, "with parallels between characters, incidents, etc., all dull and orderly and *not* incoherent." Yet she insisted, rather oddly, that she "wasn't bothered at all by the review—I think it's because the reviewer was a woman." Complimentary reviewers in *Book Week* and *Saturday Review* had also been women, but Joyce's remark underscores the degree to which literary criticism (at least the criticism that counted, as the critic who called herself "J. Oates Smith" well understood) was a male-dominated field. Although Joyce had associated herself recently with a number of literary women, including her editor, her agent, and her new friends in the affluent suburbs north of Detroit, the writers she most admired were male: apart from revering Nietzsche and Kafka as an undergraduate, she remembered being "bowled over by Faulkner" when she first read him, and when asked to name her influences, she responded: "Freud, Nietzsche, Mann—they're almost real personalities in my life. And Dostoevsky and Melville. Stendhal is a later discovery. And Proust." (By contrast, and despite her recent essay on Virginia Woolf and one she would write in early 1965 on Flannery O'Connor, her letters from the early 1960s are critical of both novelists.) Remarking on her kinship to Melville, she noted in her own fiction "a certain blindness toward excess which I think I share with him," and later summoned up the prodigiously energetic and far-ranging French novelist Balzac in attempting to define her own artistic aims: "I have a laughably Balzacian ambition," she confessed, "to get the whole world into a book."

Although the year had ended well with her New York trip and the respectable notices of her first novel, Joyce had reason to feel apprehensive as a young woman who was attempting to ease quietly into the male bastion of Great Literature. Only a few weeks later, her first venture into yet another genre—her play *The Sweet Enemy*, which opened in February 1965—would bring Joyce not only her first barrage of critical slings and arrows, but also a sharp awareness that just as women were not expected to compete with Melville and Balzac, neither would they be welcomed into the world of Shakespeare, Ibsen, and Tennessee Williams. Joyce was already a highly praised, prizewinning writer and a full-time college instructor, but that wouldn't prevent a local newspaper from reviewing *The Sweet Enemy* under a heading that, with its probably unintentional insult, spoke volumes: "Detroit Housewife Writes a Play."

7

"Violence All Around Me": Detroit, 1965–67

But why these shouts,
*   why thunder of fists and feet*
Why children's faces
*   mesmerized into a Negro dune*
Of shifting tumbling sand? Why the
*   savage fleet*
Flash of knife? Why this noontime jazzed
*   to murderous heat?*
                                    —"Detroit by Daylight" (1968)

In the first weeks of 1965, as the Actors Studio readied its production of *The Sweet Enemy* for the February 15 premiere, Joyce Carol Oates's mood was buoyant. "I've been writing like a fiend," she told Bob Phillips, "stories of my own and stories slanted for commercial markets." *With Shuddering Fall* had been purchased by publishers in England and Germany, and Blanche was optimistic about selling the movie rights. Joyce had also received the flattering offer of a teaching job from Syracuse University. Though honored by the prospect of joining her former English professors as a peer—an unusual opportunity for a young woman of twenty-six with no plans for a Ph.D.—she remarked that she was "more astounded than pleased" by the offer, which she turned down at once. She was puzzled that the university had not also suggested an appointment for Ray, who had begun his new position at the University of Windsor the previous fall. The offer was tangible proof that Joyce's stock had risen dramatically, but for now her primary concern lay with her writing rather than academic prestige. Not surprisingly, she took a step that same month that held both practical and symbolic import: retiring the manual typewriter she'd received from Grandma Woodside at age fourteen, she purchased a new electric model. She lamented the necessity of putting the old machine "out to pasture," exclaiming: "It must have typed millions of words!"

She did take a break from her new Smith-Corona long enough to attend the previews of her play, an experience that was disillusioning but instructive. The negative critical reception of *The Sweet Enemy* might have been less painful if Joyce's recent success as a fiction writer hadn't assured that the play (presented in the small, 149-seat Actors Playhouse in Greenwich Village) would be widely reviewed. It closed after a few performances, bludgeoned to death by a chorus of hostile notices. On February 16, the day after the opening, the drama critic for UPI set the tone, calling *The Sweet Enemy* a sophomoric "charade": "just what the play is about or why [the producers] would choose to present it, even in an off-Broadway house, is a mystery." One reviewer claimed the dialogue was "meaningless" and that the play "should not have been foisted on a paying audience," while another insisted it was "neither a theatre-of-the-absurd offering of passing interest nor a bitter satire on that type of stage writing—although at times it seems to be striving for both goals." The *New York Post* critic made one of the few positive comments the play received—"Miss Oates can really be funny"—but he added that even the humor "ceases to be hopeful and grows tiresome and rather flat," suggesting that the play could most charitably be viewed as an "unintentional satire." The final blow came when the powerful *New York Times* reviewer agreed with his colleagues: "It is difficult to distinguish through the smokescreen of words," he wrote, "where [the play] is heading and why."

In the weeks after the play closed, Joyce drew a valuable lesson from these scorching reviews: in the future she would follow her own instincts about writing and not be drawn into projects conceived by others, however well intentioned. "I was talked into writing *Sweet Enemy*," she told a Detroit reporter. She had enjoyed getting to know Frank Corsaro (who insisted on the play's merits) and claimed it "was almost worth the horrendous reviews to work with someone so unaffected, so dedicated, and so intelligent." Still, the experience had been painful. Dan Brown remembered trying to comfort her: "With her eyes puffy, undershadowed, she sat downcast and abject in a cheap restaurant across from the University, saying, 'You probably won't want to sit with me, after this.'" Joyce had "felt bad at first," she admitted, "but [I] have since become philosophical; I never wanted to write for the theater anyway!" She recalled the fate of Henry James's *Guy Domville*, which had been booed off the stage, and she took some consolation from the fact that America's greatest living playwright, Tennessee Williams, had praised her effort. Williams remarked that *The Sweet Enemy* "catches and distills into a wild sort of dramatic poetry the world of the leather-jacket hero, the swinging chick and the pop art heart. It is staged and performed with terrifying insight and humor." (Williams had planned to attend a party that Evelyn Shrifte gave for Joyce during the previews, but a sudden illness kept him away.) Joyce's experimental play, at least, had been given its chance; Williams was in New York attempting to get financing for two absurdist plays of his own but ultimately failed in the effort.

Although the script of *The Sweet Enemy* has not survived, Joyce's fictional version suggests the play's structure and tone, in addition to the "flashes of mad humor" that one reviewer had noted. (Joyce had already initiated her unusual habit of presenting some works as both plays and stories: her future plays *Sunday Dinner, Black,* and *Bad Girls,* among others, would be published in fictional versions as well.) Joyce's novella, with deadpan straightforwardness, tells the story of a near-imbecilic teenage girl, Eva, and her father, Emanuel, with whom she travels from town to town because Emanuel lives in paranoid fear of an unnamed "enemy." As in the play, he pretends to be a mute so he can avoid potentially dangerous interactions with others. (In the novella, Eva's father is white; as Dan Brown had noted, Joyce raised the absurdist ante in the stage version by giving Eva, with her whitish blond hair, a black father.) During their travels, Eva and Emmanuel encounter some equally eccentric characters—a pseudointellectual named Dr. Wolf, who lectures them on philosophical matters, and a young motorcyclist, Rhone Lee, who rapes Eva shortly after meeting her. We also learn that Eva's father has molested her regularly for years, "grunting and heaving over her night after night."

The novella has traits reminiscent of *With Shuddering Fall.* Like the novel, *The Sweet Enemy* features a passive, victimized white-haired young girl and her domineering father, while the motorcyclist/rapist, Rhone Lee, and the pontificating "intellectual," Dr. Wolf, superficially resemble Shar and Max. But unlike Karen's dramatic story, the novella retains an offbeat, comic tone throughout. A typical moment is Eva's recounting to Dr. Wolf that her father was once assaulted by a blind man: " 'His eyes were all white, no eyeball or anything to see with, and he beat up Pa with his white cane. He said "Kill all the niggers!" But Pa said, laying on the ground, "I ain't no nigger!" The man kept on beating him and said, "Everything looks black to me!" ' Eva adds, " 'It's blind people like that that give the group a bad name.' "

Although Joyce was eager to put *The Sweet Enemy* behind her, she learned within a few weeks that one negative experience with the press could lead easily to another. After the failure of the play, the *Detroit Free Press* published the first lengthy newspaper feature on Joyce and her work, a cover story in the paper's Sunday magazine, *Detroit.* Joyce already had some experience with sexist newspaper coverage: apart from the notorious headline "Detroit Housewife Writes a Play," other brief pieces on Joyce had appeared in the "Women's" rather than the arts section of the Detroit papers. But the *Detroit* magazine story, published on March 16, 1965, assumed a tone from its opening line that was both superficial and condescending: "To meet Joyce Carol Oates," the article began, "is to wonder how a nice girl like her can write about such awful people." The male author went on to describe Joyce as a "tall, cool girl, with a voice like wind whispering in the willows" and a "pious" demeanor. In passing, the reporter referred to Karen Herz of *With Shuddering Fall* as a "nutty teenager." Yet he also elicited information that further suggests Joyce's view of her own life as "a study in conventionality." She remarked that "People are disappointed when they meet a normal writer. They try to bend you into a pattern they can associate with. I have no psychological problems. I like to write and play tennis and play piano in about the same way." Joyce added that she and Ray considered themselves "conservative pessimists and do not claim very much. We are liberals by faith only. We don't think man is perfectable but we like the idea." Although this article itself probably contributed to Joyce's pessimism, at least where press coverage of her career was concerned, it also helped confirm her longstanding attitude (already expressed to Evelyn Shrifte at Vanguard) that she preferred staying home and producing new work to participating in self-promotion, a process that often led to egregious press distortion.

Armed with her new typewriter, Joyce now returned to writing with a vengeance. By mid-March she had written 170 pages of a new novel, which she described as a book she was writing "just for fun." Perhaps as a reward for having withstood the *Sweet Enemy* experience, she "decided to try writing something purely for enjoyment, not bothering to make it good, original, well-written, uncorny, or whatever we generally try to do. For the first time in ages I really enjoyed writing." This novel, she insisted, "won't ever be seen by anyone except myself." She wrote at top speed, producing a bulky manuscript in only a few weeks. During this time Jim Holleran, her U.D. colleague, remembered that Joyce and Ray gave a small party at their house. Holleran, a scholar in English Renaissance literature, had begun working on his own novel, and was grateful to Joyce for offering tips and making suggestions. On the day of the party, Holleran had enjoyed what he considered "a good writing day. I had written two 'finished' pages of my novel, and I was anxious to tell Joyce." She congratulated him, and then Holleran asked how her own work was going. "I had a good day, too," Joyce told him. He asked how much she'd written, and she replied: "About forty pages." When Holleran expressed amazement, Joyce responded, "Oh Jim, I just bought an electric typewriter." But by the time she finished the 625-page manuscript in late April, she admitted that "the fun disappeared, I don't know where. Anyway I wrote something simply for the enjoyment of it and won't ever have to worry about some cranky reviewer finding things wrong with it." Not long afterward, she put the manuscript out with the trash.

Even as Joyce was writing this novel, she was thinking ahead to more serious work. A fervent admirer of Thomas Mann, she remarked that a rereading of *Buddenbrooks* helped her realize that she'd been unnecessarily limiting herself, "along with most modern writers," to a relatively small scope in her novels, which had usually dealt with "just a few characters and a short period of time." She felt it would be challenging to attempt a larger canvas, a novel "with an epic scope—covering a period of time and a number of people." Eventually this ambition would result in Joyce's next published novel, A *Garden of Earthly Delights* (1967), only the first of many similarly large-scale works spanning decades of American history and several generations of fictional characters: *them* (1969), *Wonderland* (1971), and *Bellefleur* (1980), among others. But Joyce would not begin *Garden* for some time and was now staying busy with short stories and with book reviews for the *Detroit Free Press*. During the summer of 1965 she also wrote what she called on July 21 an "incidental novel"; she had already written 240 pages but felt that "it isn't too good. Not commercial, either, but not literary." Yet the novel seemed to "write itself " and was finished by September, when she mailed it off to "poor Blanche." Like the novel she had written "just for fun," the "incidental novel" was thrown away.

Now that she had paid her dues with courses in freshman composition, Joyce's teaching also had grown more interesting and challenging during her third year at U.D. That spring she'd been assigning the great Continental writers—Mann, Kafka, Flaubert, Stendhal, Chekhov, and Dostoevsky—whom she found more compelling and teachable than the standard English classics, and she'd been asked to teach two other advanced courses the following summer and fall. The summer assignment would be an upper-division reading course called American Literature Studies: Psychological Fiction, and in the fall she would teach Existential Literature. The content of these courses would prove significant: during the spring and summer Joyce discussed the authors she was teaching (Harold Frederic and Albert Camus, for example) with a brilliant but deeply troubled graduate student, Richard Wishnetsky. These conversations forged a relationship that inspired one of her finest and most widely read stories, "In the Region of Ice," a narrative that would poignantly evoke both the heartbreak and excitement that the experience of teaching held for Joyce.

Happier in her teaching assignments, Joyce had grown more comfortable with her U.D. colleagues, partly out of necessity: she now shared an office with three other teachers, including the English department's elderly nun, Sister Bonaventure. Two new faculty members had arrived at U.D. the previous fall: Tom Porter, a Jesuit priest who had recently finished his doctoral work at North Carolina; and John Ditsky, a young poet and critic who would become one of Joyce's closest university friends. Porter remembered that by the 1964–65 academic year, Joyce was "an established member of the department, teaching comparative literature." They first met at a small diner across Livernois Road from the liberal arts building, a favorite faculty hangout, and during that initial encounter discussed one of the British authors Joyce didn't particularly admire, D. H. Lawrence. "She didn't think much of his novels," Porter said. "I agreed, but indicated I thought he was a terrific short-story writer." Not having read Lawrence's stories, Joyce quickly followed the recommendation and told Porter she had indeed admired them. As time passed, Joyce would become an avid reader of Lawrence, producing appreciative essays on both his novels and his poetry.

Apart from Joyce's enthusiasm over literary matters, Porter noted her lively sense of humor. Their colleague Sister Bonaventure, he recalled, was "indefatigably and cheerfully pious," and would paste signs around the crowded office with sentiments such as "Smile—God loves you." For her part, Joyce "remonstrated with quotations from Nietzsche and Sartre, et al. Sister Bonaventure simply bounced on her cheery way and Joyce quietly enjoyed the slogan-war." John Ditsky remembered Sister Bonaventure as both deeply religious and abstemious to a fault. "She would spend her lunch hour dining on a thermos of tea and saltines," Ditsky said. "That was her lifestyle. She devoted everything to religion and teaching." But unlike Porter, Joyce recalled that Sister Bonaventure had a censorious, "crabby" side as well: "We'd be making jokes and laughing and she'd be bristling." The nun became particularly upset when a photographer from the *Detroit News* came into the office to photograph Joyce: "she was so angry, and finally grabbed her books and just stomped out, with a rustling of her black habit." Sister Bonaventure later apologized for her behavior, but it was clear to Joyce that "she didn't like me at all."

Although Sister Bonaventure's personality was not the model for Sister Irene in the story "In the Region of Ice," written later that year, Joyce said that "the idea of her was." Temperamentally, Sister Irene was more like Joyce herself—"as if I were a nun." In the story, Sister Irene develops an uneasy relationship with Allen Weinstein, a Jewish graduate student who singles her out as the only professor on campus with whom he can talk. Weinstein's impetuous nature, his passionate love of ideas, and his emotional and intellectual neediness put the reserved Sister Irene on guard. Ultimately, the nun becomes terrified when she understands that Weinstein "was trying to force her into a human relationship," something from which her austere life as a nun has shielded her. When her student breaks down and is committed to a mental institution, he sends her a letter including a quotation from Shakespeare's *Measure for Measure* that she correctly interprets as a suicide threat. (In the play, Claudio longs for death, the "thrilling region of thick-ribbed ice.") She tries to help him, pleading with his parents for their support, but when Weinstein visits her again after his discharge from the hospital, he insists that only she understands him. When the nun, frozen in her own "region of ice," cannot respond, Weinstein becomes enraged and leaves for Canada, where he commits suicide. The story concludes with Sister Irene's dazed reaction: "She was only one person, she thought, walking down the corridor in a dream. Was she safe in this single person, or was she trapped? She had only one identity. She could make only one choice. What she had done or hadn't done was the result of that choice, and how was she guilty? If she could have felt guilt, she thought, she might at least have been able to feel something."

The story powerfully evokes the conflicted emotions Joyce experienced in her dealings with Richard Wishnetsky, who had simply wandered into her university office one day in spring 1965. Unlike most of Joyce's students, Richard was well dressed and clean-cut, an attractive young man working toward his master's degree in sociology, and during that first encounter they talked for about an hour. At twenty-three, only four years younger than Joyce, Richard had "a certain urgent, harassed, slightly embarrassed look," Joyce remembered, and he told her frankly that he considered the other U.D. students his intellectual inferiors. He had graduated with honors from the University of Michigan and had won a Woodrow Wilson fellowship to attend graduate school. While at Michigan, he'd touched President Kennedy after Kennedy gave a speech about founding the Peace Corps, a moment Richard considered the high point of his student life; he spoke often about wanting to join the Peace Corps himself, about his hope to make the world a better place. Joyce was both impressed and alarmed by Richard's extreme seriousness about religious and philosophical matters, an intensity she tried to offset with flippant rejoinders. "I told him that ideas have but a tenuous relationship to real life and that one should not become deranged over them; they are not that important. He dismissed this contemptuously. Ideas were the highest creations of man, the only reality." (In the short story, Sister Irene complains to another nun that Allen "thinks ideas are real." Sister Irene silently disagrees, believing that "only reality is real.") Although Joyce admired Richard's intellect and his "brilliant, keen sense of humor," she sensed a disturbing, unarticulated need in Richard: "He seemed to want something from me, an answer or consolation or perhaps affection, something that —as he was to say in another context—would identify him as a human being."

That first hour inaugurated a series of talks between Joyce and this unusual student, who continued visiting her office for the next several months. Their conversations were "long, sometimes tedious, sometimes exhilarating," Joyce recalled. One day, Joyce returned from class to find Richard sitting at her desk, rifling through her papers; seeing her, he turned with "his manic gleeful laugh and said something vaguely intimidating." On another occasion Richard visited her summer course in American psychological fiction. Joyce remembered that he "shocked the class—which probably felt sorry for me— by talking wildly and with dizzying generalizations, wrenching the discussion from *The Damnation of Theron Ware* to Goethe, Shakespeare, Aristotle. What stays in my mind about that class period is his aristocratic, contemptuous dismissal of the other students—they really did not exist for him." Shortly after this incident she wrote to Dan Brown, who was traveling in Europe, that Richard had left the classroom after a few minutes, alarmed that Joyce had made a sarcastic remark about his attitude. She told Brown that despite Richard's loud and threatening behavior, he reminded her of a homeless puppy who kept turning up at her door. She was uncomfortable, she added, because she didn't quite know how to handle the situation.

During their private conversations, Richard gradually revealed the intellectual and emotional torment underlying his passionate involvement with ideas. He discussed Nietzsche and the "Death of God," telling Joyce that if God did not exist, then life was not worth living and he would commit suicide. Joyce replied, "with a casualness I might now regret, that he perhaps believed in God, then, simply to save himself from suicide." On one occasion Richard brought a copy of Albert Camus's *The Myth of Sisyphus* to her office, a book Joyce considered excellent reading for him: "Camus saw the central problem of philosophy as this: should one live, or commit suicide? His answer, happily, is that one should live, for by killing himself he surrenders to the absurdity of the universe and extends it. All very clear, rational, highly sane"—exactly the kind of thinking Joyce wanted to encourage in Richard.

But like Allen Weinstein in Joyce's short story, Richard grew more and more irrational: he left school and was admitted to a series of mental institutions that summer and fall. He was treated briefly in two private local hospitals, but according to his father, Richard refused extended treatment. On July 29, Edward Wishnetsky filed a legal petition to have his son committed, insisting that Richard had become hostile and belligerent, threatening to burn his parents' car and home. Mr. Wishnetsky added that his son's moods alternated between extreme depression and "very agitated, frenzied behavior" (suggesting that Richard suffered from manic-depression, now more commonly termed a bipolar disorder). Richard refused to sleep, made phone calls day and night, and boasted that he would soon begin dating one of President Lyndon Johnson's daughters. (Richard had also bragged to Joyce of his success with women, stories Joyce considered "wholly mythical.") Mr. Wishnetsky's petition was successful, and Richard was committed to Ypsilanti State Hospital on August 19. But on September 9, after a period of cooperation during which he was given the freedom to wander the hospital grounds, Richard simply walked away. By late November, he had begun outpatient therapy, and soon was described by his psychiatrist as "very well controlled."

Yet Richard suffered relapses during the winter, leaving his parents' home several times without saying where he was going. Richard's psychiatrist remarked that "there was something in him—he was going through hell—that was bizarre, something hidden. This inner process expressed itself in religiosity." According to one of his friends, Richard would frequently throw violent tantrums, knocking over furniture and tearing up the friend's apartment. Joyce felt "greatly moved by his suffering," she later recalled. She understood that in her intellectual debates with Richard during the spring and summer, she had been somewhat deluded: "I could not understand that what I as a professor talked about all the time—every teaching day—these grandiose problems of life, death, God, fate, etc., etc., were being taken in absolute seriousness by Richard. He was really living these problems out, while my colleagues and I made coin by them, so to speak—transforming writers' personal anguish into refined classroom discussions among students with good teeth and good manners and highly ordinary plans for the weekend. In this world, Richard was entirely alone." What had most disturbed Richard about his experience in the mental hospitals, he told Joyce, was that he hadn't been respected as a human being.

Richard had seldom confided in Joyce about his personal life, and only after his release from the mental hospitals did he mention his difficult relationship with his father. (In the story, Allen Weinstein's father is portrayed as a heartless boor who considers his son "crazy," an ungrateful "little bastard.") John Ditsky, sharing office space with Joyce, remembered Richard's accounts of his miserable home life: "[Joyce] would be talking to him two feet behind me, and I was quite aware that this was a troubled, brilliant young man who had an overbearing father: he couldn't satisfy him in any way." Joyce remarked that, like a psychiatrist, she had only the truth as Richard presented it, "no objective truth." But even though Joyce had sensed "latent violence" in Richard all along, it was neither the violent manner of his death nor his mental illness that Joyce later emphasized when she pondered Richard's tragedy: "To say that Richard Wishnetsky was sick," she insisted, "is to say perhaps the most obvious and least significant thing about him." Instead Joyce linked Richard's temperament to that of Dostoevsky, whom he had greatly admired: like the novelist, Richard was "violent, righteous, a 'punisher' . . . a religious person without any specific religion, a Messianic figure with a message only of destruction."

Richard Wishnetsky delivered that message on February 12, 1966, less than a year after he first walked into the office of Joyce Carol Oates. On February 10, he had again left his parents' home with no explanation, just as he had wandered from the grounds of the state mental hospital. Earlier that week he had attempted to join the U.S. Army, but had been rejected; Richard had also made a brief trip to Toledo, Ohio, where he purchased a .32 caliber revolver (laws controlling gun sales were less strict in Ohio than in Michigan). Apparently he spent the nights of February 10 and 11 at a friend's apartment near Wayne State University. At about 11:45 on Saturday morning, February 12, Richard walked into the Shaarey Zadek synagogue (located in the affluent Detroit suburb of Southfield), where his family had worshiped for many years, and approached fifty-nine-year-old Rabbi Morris Adler, who had just given a sermon focused on Abraham Lincoln to the packed congregation of about 750 people. Richard had received his religious education at Shaarey Zadek and had often expressed deep admiration for Rabbi Adler, whom he had sought out for counseling and for long philosophical discussions similar to those he'd had with Joyce at U.D.

Richard's parents and his younger sister were also present at the synagogue that morning. They watched in horror as Richard pulled the revolver from his pocket, fired it into the ceiling, and ordered several people (including a young boy celebrating his bar mitzvah) off the platform, instructing Rabbi Adler to stay seated. Speaking into the microphone, Richard told the congregation to keep calm and they would not be hurt. Because Rabbi Adler was in the habit of taping his sermons and the tape recorder was still running, Richard's last words were preserved. Reading from a prepared script, he said in a firm, determined voice, "This congregation is a travesty and an abomination. It has made a mockery by its hypocrisy of the beauty and spirit of Judaism." At that point, a man in the congregation started toward him, and Richard yelled, "Off!" Rabbi Adler tried to maintain order, saying faintly to the man, "Go back down. I know this boy." Then Richard continued: "This congregation is composed of people who on the whole make me ashamed to say that I am a Jew. . . . It is composed of men, women and children who care for nothing except their vain, egotistical selves." He ended his speech by announcing, "With this act I protest a humanly horrifying and hence unacceptable situation."

Richard turned to Rabbi Adler and shot him twice—once through the head, once in the left arm—then pointed the gun at his forehead and shot himself. In the pandemonium that followed, Rabbi Adler's wife told everyone to remain calm, insisting that Richard was sick and could not be blamed. Richard and the rabbi were rushed to local hospitals, but both had sustained extensive brain damage. Richard never regained consciousness and died four days later. Rabbi Adler underwent two brain operations but remained comatose for almost a month, dying on March 11.

During these weeks Joyce had thought deeply about the tragedy; she published her meditative essay in the *Detroit Free Press* on March 6, insisting that the shootings represented "an intellectual act, no matter how much we might want to reject its premises." She concluded that Richard had unknowingly placed himself, he with his idealism and his passionate sincerity about the future of the world, on the side finally of the Hitlers, the Inquisitors, the righteous and avenging throughout history. Normality endures because it does not think, especially; the abnormal, like Richard, think themselves or others to death. It would be absurd to suggest that his act was totally claustrophobic, that there was no vanity and egoism in that congregation. But this would distinguish that congregation from no other congregation in the world. Richard wanted to destroy them all with his Messianic hatred, and by extension he wanted to destroy the whole world—it is "fallen," it is hypocritical, and it did not love him.

For Joyce, one of the personal ironies of Richard's tragedy was that her story "In the Region of Ice," written several months earlier, had predicted Richard's suicide. An early version (titled "Unheard Melodies," suggesting that Allen Weinstein must originally have quoted Keats rather than Shakespeare when writing to Sister Irene) was rejected by several magazines before *The Atlantic* accepted the revised and retitled manuscript in late February 1966, two weeks after the shootings. Worried that her negative portrayal of Allen Weinstein's parents might be offensive to the Wishnetsky family, Joyce wrote to Blanche asking whether the story could appear under a pseudonym. But either Blanche or the magazine demurred, and ironically enough, considering Joyce's concern that she was "making coin" through the personal anguish of others, the story represented a major advance in Joyce's literary reputation. Published in the August 1966 issue, it won first prize in the 1967 *Prize Stories: The O. Henry Awards* and became one of her most anthologized stories. It would also be made into an excellent, Academy Award–winning short film by Peter Werner. Yet Joyce noted in her journal that Richard had never sought her help as Allen sought Sister Irene's: "had he made an appeal," she asked herself, "what might I have done?—how could I have responded? After his death his other professors wondered aloud how they might have 'saved' him. They spoke of feeling 'guilty.' I never did: I hadn't that much power over him."

Joyce would continue writing about Richard Wishnetsky, approaching his tragedy from a variety of perspectives. "The confrontation between this deeply troubled boy and myself has made a most permanent impression upon my life," she noted more than a year after Richard's death. She published a poem about him, "In Memory of an Ex-Friend, a Murderer," and the title story of her 1984 collection *Last Days* attempts to re-create Richard's state of mind just before his death, incorporating many facts of the case precisely as they'd been reported in newspaper accounts. While working on the story, she remarked that at age 43 she felt "an uncanny identification with my old, former, long-dead student . . . a more powerful identification than I felt at the age of 27." Even in 1993 she would still feel haunted by "the poor feeble ghost of Richard Wishnetsky, who should be living today, a professor of philosophy somewhere, passionately quibbling with upstart students."

After completing "In the Region of Ice" in September 1965, Joyce finally began the long, ambitious novel she'd been contemplating since the previous April. A *Garden of Earthly Delights* "will take me a long, long time," she wrote on October 25. "I can get very excited about it, but also worried—I know that whatever turns up on the page will be far different from what I'm trying for." In the meantime, she was discussing a possible filming of *With Shuddering Fall* with a Hollywood producer, Jerry Bick; she had written the screenplay during the summer, a project on which she spent only a week. "It was a lot of fun," she wrote, "though painful for me when I looked at the novel—I should have rewritten or at least revised that novel. I am supposed to be paid $5,000 for the screenplay." At Bick's request, she did revise the new manuscript, which he said would be fine as a play, but was not really a screenplay. She had also put together the final list of contents for her second collection of short stories, scheduled to appear the following spring. Since all this activity had been combined with summer school teaching, writing her "incidental novel," and her long conversations with Richard Wishnetsky, it's not surprising that on August 3 Joyce had written jokingly to Dan Brown that she sometimes feared her many responsibilities might drive her crazy. Her minimal spare time was spent playing tennis with Ray, John Ditsky, and Ditsky's wife, Sue, and driving out to Birmingham to visit her new friend Elizabeth Graham. Elizabeth and her husband, Jim, had taught Joyce and Ray to play bridge, which Joyce described as an overly complex game that required too much thinking.

Though the 1965 fall term began in August, earlier than usual, Joyce was relieved that her teaching load would be fairly light: only two courses, plus an honors tutorial. But she was hardly idle. She placed several new stories with literary magazines (not liking to bother Blanche with "noncommercial" manuscripts), and corresponded frequently with Evelyn Shrifte at Vanguard about her forthcoming collection, *Upon the Sweeping Flood*. The "doddering" publishing house was again delaying publication; originally planned for October 1965, the volume was rescheduled for January 1966, then March, and then May. Joyce maintained the polite and modest tone characteristic of her letters to Evelyn, though allowing herself the comment that she felt "a little disappointed" by the delay and hinting to Blanche that she might consider changing publishers. Always anxious to see her work in print, Joyce knew that the collection included some of the best stories she had yet written. Though Evelyn had suggested including Joyce's play *The Sweet Enemy* as well, she declined: "I would prefer that it not be published," she wrote, "since I still feel disappointed over it and would not want to see the same kind of reviews again." Once the contents were finalized in November, Joyce felt proud of the book and wrote to Evelyn that the dedication should read, "To my parents, Caroline [sic] and Frederic Oates, and my grandmother, Blanche Woodside." She added, "I hope that isn't too corny—but my family is so proud of my writing, especially my grandmother."

Joyce herself had reason to be proud, since the new collection, both in its technical assurance and its broad range of characters and situations, marked a distinct advance over *By the North Gate*. At the same time, Joyce had again achieved the unity of vision that reviewers had noted in the earlier collection. Throughout *Upon the Sweeping Flood*, Joyce portrayed a shifting, chaotic landscape, its inhabitants poised at the edge of the Nietzschean abyss and engaged in a desperate search for identity, self-assertion, and meaning. Though the weaker stories were sometimes overwritten, including passages in which an intrusive narrator explains the characters' motivations and the story's theme, for the most part Joyce marshaled her narrative elements so that they embodied their own meaning. The influence of early masters, particularly Nietzsche, Faulkner, and O'Connor, was still present, but Joyce had now assimilated them into her own distinctively passionate but ironic narrative voice.

Though pleased with the collection, Joyce was alarmed when Vanguard expressed interest in publishing the "incidental novel" she'd written during the summer, which she described flippantly as "an extravaganza (yes) . . . about a psychiatrist and some love affair and a death (of course)." But that manuscript would soon be supplanted by a longer, more substantial work. Aided by her lighter teaching schedule, Joyce had made steady progress on A *Garden of Earthly Delights*, having written 170 pages by December 13 and considering the partial manuscript "the best thing I've done." During Christmas break, apart from work on the novel, Joyce attended the MLA convention in Chicago, where she was scheduled to participate in a panel discussion of short fiction. As her reputation grew, invitations to speak had become more numerous; though she was still not entirely comfortable talking before groups outside the classroom, she began to accept such engagements more readily. She also received a job offer that fall from the University of Oregon, a position as a "writer in residence" and professor of creative writing. The salary was considerably more than Joyce earned at U.D., but Joyce felt that she and Ray were too settled in their present jobs to consider a long-distance move. Instead, they began looking around for a new home in Detroit. Joyce had become disillusioned with their house on Woodstock, calling it one of "the usual economy-built cardboard-walled colonials people buy as their first home and then rapidly outgrow."

Joyce read proof for *Upon the Sweeping Flood* in December and at the end of the month left for the Chicago convention. She enjoyed visiting with some of her former Syracuse professors, such as Walter Sutton, and she attended readings by Norman Mailer and Ralph Ellison, who "brought down the house." Joyce stressed that Mailer "made an excellent impression, even on people like myself who more or less had come not liking him." Returning to Detroit, Joyce again became absorbed in her long novel. On February 23, she wrote to Bob Phillips: "I am working stolidly on my novel, which has attained a protoplasmic, fierce 440 pages at present and is nowhere near the (gasp) end." She also expressed a sentiment she would repeat many times during her career, as she pursued the arduous completion of a lengthy work: "Never, never again will I undertake an 'epic'! It isn't worth it." She finished the novel in March, and by late April she reported to Evelyn that a "retyping" was in progress: "I do hope you will like this novel," she added, "which has a large span of time and space, many characters, and takes in a variety of activities."

Writing A *Garden of Earthly Delights*, Joyce had employed a method of composition she had followed for many years. " 'It's mainly daydreaming,' " she told one interviewer. " 'I daydream about a kind of populated empty space. There's nothing verbal about it. Then there comes a time when'—she snapped her fingers soundlessly—'it's all set and I just go write it. With a story it's one evening, if I can type that fast.' " In sharp contrast to the habit of endless revision she would adopt later in her career, Joyce did little rewriting. Years later, she recalled the general method of composition she employed in her twenties: "I wrote a first draft straight out, laboring and blundering through difficult scenes, passages, transitions . . . going from Chapter 1 and page 1 to the last chapter and the last page. . . . Then, with the first draft completed, I went through it with a pen and X'd things out and wrote in the margins and added extra pages and plodded and toiled and made my way through what I believed to be (but I was deceived) my *final* vision of the novel. . . . With the first novels I was almost religiously faithful to the early draft, changing only words here and there, usually shortening, condensing." Throughout the 1960s she worked in this same way, directly on the typewriter, with thirty to forty pages not uncommon for a day's work on a novel. After the corrections were completed, Joyce would type out the final draft of her manuscript, a process she considered pure drudgery. When she finally mailed her manuscripts off to Blanche, it was always with a great sense of relief. "How did Fielding and Richardson and Dickens *ever* do it," she exclaimed, "with pencils yet?"

With *Garden* completed and sent off, Joyce undertook a new short story that would become her most famous, reprinted in countless anthologies in the coming years. Like "In the Region of Ice," "Where Are You Going,

Where Have You Been?" was based on a real-life tragedy. In early March, Joyce had picked up a copy of *Life* magazine and begun reading an article about Charles Schmid, an Arizona serial killer of teenage girls whom the article dubbed "The Pied Piper of Tucson." Joyce immediately saw material for fiction in Schmid's story, which included many grotesque elements: only five three, Schmid stuffed rags and tin cans in the bottoms of his boots to make himself appear taller. Yet Joyce had read only part of the article, not wanting "to be distracted by too much detail." With her usual impulse toward blending realism and allegory, she connected Schmid's exploits to mythic legends and folk songs about "Death and the Maiden," and "the story came to me more or less in a piece." Focusing on Connie, an ordinary teenage girl who succumbs to the demonic Arnold Friend, the story was originally titled "Death and the Maiden," but Joyce decided the title was "too pompous, too literary." After the story's first appearance, in the fall 1966 issue of *Epoch*, Joyce dedicated the story to Bob Dylan. While writing "Where Are You Going, Where Have You Been?" she had been listening to Dylan's song "It's All Over Now, Baby Blue," which struck Joyce as "hauntingly elegiac," similar in tone to the story she had written.

Joyce spent her leisure time that spring enjoying her new house. She and Ray had found a place on Sherbourne Road, located in a genteel older neighborhood called Sherwood Forest that was only a five-minute drive from U.D. Their house was even larger than the four-bedroom colonial on Woodstock: made of brick and stone, it featured a downstairs library, a recreation room with fireplace, and a modern kitchen. Again there were separate studies for her and Ray. Joyce wrote to Evelyn that while painters worked on the house, she and Ray enjoyed gardening out in the yard, which boasted apple, maple, and birch trees, and a view of a beautiful magnolia in the lot next door. "Why anyone should bother typing" in the midst of such beauty, Joyce said whimsically to a friend, "I haven't any idea. . . . My typewriter clatters, clatters on."

Ray Smith remembered that their new place "was a good house for parties," and that he and Joyce began entertaining more often. Colleagues from both U.D. and Windsor would be invited, along with nonacademic friends. "Those parties usually ended," Ray recalled, "with me and some of the other men (perhaps I should say boys), including one of the deans (a Jesuit), playing a version of touch football in the street or, later in the year, pushing the cars of our guests through drifted snow in the driveway." Joyce's husband and her male colleagues—including Clyde Craine, John Ditsky, and the Jesuits Tom Porter and Norman McKendrick—all enjoyed drinking at these parties. Porter remembered that on one occasion, when abundant alcohol combined with touch football, "Joyce expressed horror and alarm at [our] conduct; I strongly suspect that her reaction was largely feigned for our benefit. She fussed especially over Ray and the possibility of permanent damage. He paid scant attention and I think, on the whole, she enjoyed the whole episode."

Quite apart from her boisterous academic colleagues, Joyce had begun socializing often with her affluent women friends from the Detroit suburbs, especially Kay Smith, Elizabeth Graham, and Marj Levin. According to Marj, Kay felt an affectionate, almost maternal bond with Joyce. Kay was forty-one to Joyce's twenty-eight, but despite the disparity in age and the two women's sharply different personalities, their friendship developed rapidly. Joyce had struck some of the Detroit Women Writers members as enigmatic and aloof, but Kay was extremely outgoing, gregarious, and well liked. Kay was "very exquisite, a beautiful, beautiful woman," Marj Levin remarked; she was also a lifelong Catholic and devoted to her five children. Though Kay was in some ways a typical suburban matron, tending to her large house and family, she energetically pursued literary interests: she directed an annual creative writing conference held at Oakland University, served as president of Detroit Women Writers, and was a member of the Literature Advisory Panel of the Michigan Council of the Arts. Kay aspired to write fiction, Joyce remembered, but she worked primarily as a freelance newspaper writer and a local historian. Active in civic affairs, she was well known in the area for her book-length history of Bloomfield Township. Despite her age, Kay resembled "a young, shiny-eyed girl who loved books, just arrived at the dormitory," Joyce said fondly, many years after Kay's death. "It was like she had a young girl inside her, as well as being a somewhat mature woman . . . she was like an older sister."

Yet there was a dark aspect to Kay's seemingly enviable life in the suburbs, and before long Joyce would begin satirizing, in *Expensive People* and some of her short stories, the often crass and emotionally sterile world she viewed firsthand in Birmingham, Bloomfield Hills, and Grosse Pointe. "There was a side of Kay that was really repressed," Joyce noted, a repression understandable in a young Catholic woman who had come of age in the 1940s. Only gradually would Joyce become aware that Kay had developed an addiction to alcohol, stemming in part from her unhappy marriage. According to Marj Levin, Kay's husband was "domineering to Kay, totally, and she was totally under his thumb." Another of Joyce's friends agreed that Kay's husband "gave her no room at all to do any thinking of her own. When she'd talk about her husband and his attitude toward her, she protected him, but you could see right through it." As a Catholic, Kay did not believe in divorce; her lively, energetic disposition served to mask her private unhappiness, which she assuaged with alcohol. When Joyce would meet Kay and her other women friends for lunch, Kay would drink several Manhattans, then return home in the evening to have martinis with her husband. Kay's death at fifty-five in 1980, of a liver ailment for which she refused medical treatment (only a few of her closest friends even knew about the illness) would haunt Joyce for years, inspiring her compassionate but harrowing accounts of women's alcoholism in the uncollected story "Blue Skies" and in her 1990 novel, *Because It Is Bitter, and Because It Is My Heart.*

In the early months of 1966, however, such a tragic outcome to the privileged life of someone like Kay Smith—who lived in "Cheeverland," Joyce said—would have been unthinkable. Kay, Liz Graham, Marj Levin, and other suburban friends invited Joyce and Ray to cocktail parties, dinner parties, and country club events. "Ray and I have acquaintances and friends in the 'business' world," she told Bob Phillips, "executives whose wives have befriended me—the wives are writers, well-read, intelligent, former editors of *Ladies Home Journal* etc., who I think are languishing in a way in their $80,000 homes." But even as Joyce enjoyed her forays into the suburbs, she was writing "a kind of comedy" she had entitled *Expensive People*, a new version of the manuscript once called *The Killer*. She had frequently been "having lunch and going to Luncheons," she remarked. Such outings were "a very entertaining but potentially deadening routine, though I like the women very much. All of which is put to good use in the 'comic' novel." The scholarship girl from Millersport enjoyed rubbing shoulders with the wives of corporate executives and wealthy physicians (just as they enjoyed having a much-heralded young novelist to their homes), but her frequent socializing was also a search for new material. John Ditsky, Joyce's U.D. office mate and friend, remembered that Joyce "had a lot of contacts among the people in the wealthier suburbs just north of Detroit and for a while she was very much their darling." When she returned to Detroit, "she would tell us various anecdotes and then later we would see them in print." In her journal, Joyce later wrote that, after being taken up by her new suburban friends, she "felt very faintly the tinges of romantic snobbishness, and exorcized them playfully in *Expensive People.*" Her central perception about her suburban friends' lives related to the emotional and psychological instability she sensed beneath the glittering surface of affluence: "these people, who have everything they want, drive expensive pieces of machinery they in no way can handle or even deserve, are floating on top of a complex society that unfortunately keeps shifting and changing." But even though Joyce found much to observe and write about (for the most part satirically) in the Detroit suburbs, she greatly valued her friendships with the small group of highly intelligent and attractive women she knew there.

Another close friend was Patricia Burnett, a former Miss Michigan whose glamour and gracious personality had made her seem representative of the feminine ideal in the 1950s, especially after she found a wealthy husband and became the mother of four children. Harry Burnett was president of the pharmaceuticals firm Parke-Davis, and Patty went through a period in which she acted the part of a rich man's wife, wearing expensive furs and enormous diamond rings. By the time she met Joyce, however, she'd begun to feel frustrated in her conventional role, and her friendships with Joyce and the other women in their circle ultimately inspired her to seek fulfillment as an artist (she found considerable success as a portrait painter and sculptor) and to become one of the early leaders of the feminist movement. Burnett remembered having ardent discussions with Ray Smith about her feminist ideas in the 1960s and early 1970s, and Ray telling her, " 'You're proposing a total revolution, but you can't do it, Patricia, you're not angry enough.' He didn't know how angry I was underneath." After the National Organization for Women was founded in 1969, Burnett was president for two years, and then served on the organization's National Board for five years. She later became the international chair for NOW and eventually organized twenty-seven chapters in twenty-one countries. Patty Burnett's complex, evolving character—from beauty queen to accomplished artist and ardent feminist—fascinated Joyce. She wrote to Dan Brown that Patty seemed such a wholly successful individual that she considered her a role model. Ironically, Joyce's suburban friends envied her literary success, while she envied their seeming versatility as beautiful women and mothers who maintained a strong interest in the arts.

Though Joyce remained close to Kay, Liz, and Patty for several years, Joyce's important literary friendships were still with men. Though she and Bob Phillips never lived in the same city after they graduated from Syracuse, they kept up an avid correspondence and saw each other whenever Joyce visited New York. Phillips had become a father and had taken a job in advertising to make ends meet, but he'd continued writing fiction, poetry, and criticism. Joyce had also maintained her friendship in Detroit with Dan Brown, who was now teaching at Wayne State while completing his Ph.D. Joyce continued trading manuscripts with both Phillips and Brown, even after her career began to take off, and she often tried to help them, introducing them to Blanche Gregory (who agreed to represent both men) and suggesting her own publisher as a market for their books.

In Brown's case, a rivalry had developed that would later destroy the friendship. He admitted that his pleasure in Joyce's success was "mixed with envy." When Joyce began placing her stories with mass-market magazines like *Cosmopolitan* and receiving thousand-dollar checks in the mail, Brown "got all fired up," Joyce remembered. "He said, 'If Joyce can do that, I can do that.' So he was writing stories aimed at women's magazines which were very unconvincing. Naturally they didn't get accepted, so that started some of the bitterness." Brown also submitted a novel to Vanguard, which was rejected and which Joyce had found "amateurish." Joyce felt that Brown, who was coping with a homophobic mid-1960s marketplace, was "just too angry about a few subjects to make a good writer, at this time." Brown said having Joyce read this unpublished novel, which dealt frankly with homosexual themes, "was my way of coming out to her," and he claimed that after reading it, "Joyce didn't talk to me for six months." Even after the friendship resumed, he added, "something had gone out of the relationship—my availability as a fantasy sex object, I suspect."

The national attention Joyce's fiction had received was also putting her into contact with writers outside her intimate circle of friends. The opportunity to meet her peers often motivated her attendance at various literary conventions and conferences. One writer she met through such networking was the novelist David Madden, who served as fiction editor of the prestigious *Kenyon Review* during the 1960s and had published Joyce's stories "At the Seminary" and "Gifts" in the summer 1965 and fall 1966 issues. He also wrote one of the first in-depth critical essays on her fiction and would later solicit her critical essays on James M. Cain and Harriette Arnow for books he was editing. Madden met her several times in the mid-1960s, at MLA conventions and once at a writers' conference in Detroit. On the first occasion, "I had noticed her sitting on this couch, in a hotel room where people were having a kind of party, and she seemed rather nondescript." But once they began talking Madden found her "very interesting, very striking." Joyce had written similarly to Bob Phillips about her "excellent, lengthy talks with David Madden. . . . He is a fine person." Madden observed Joyce speaking in public and was "struck by how quiet and reserved she was, and how like a teenage girl she was; when she got up to speak she put her knee on a chair and kind of swayed back and forth and dipped her head, and seemed rather immature. But then when you realized what she was saying, it was extremely witty and extremely sharp, and very, very articulate. . . . There was always this disparity, it seemed to me, between the way she appeared and the way she actually conducted herself when she was 'on.' " Madden's feelings toward Joyce cooled somewhat, however, when he experienced firsthand her "very incisive and cutting way" of speaking her mind. After the movie *Bonnie and Clyde* came out, Joyce told Madden that he looked like C. J. Moss, the oddball character played by Michael J. Pollard. The actor was "very unusual, weird-looking," said Madden, who didn't appreciate the comparison. "I could have said that she looked like Olive Oyl in *Popeye*," he added, "but it never would have occurred to me to say anything so insulting. I've never quite gotten over that."

Joyce could also be cutting in print, sometimes responding acidly to contemporary writers and critics with whom she disagreed. One critic she particularly disliked was Stanley Edgar Hyman, husband of the famous author of "The Lottery," Shirley Jackson. In June 1966, after Hyman had given fulsome praise in *The New Leader* to Vladimir Nabokov's *Despair*, calling it the finest novel of the season, Joyce fired off a letter to the editor: "Very amusing, and accidentally so, are many of Stanley Edgar Hyman's reviews," she wrote. Insisting that Nabokov's novel was "flatulent," she pointed out that "Nabokov himself states that the novel contains almost no ideas and that Freudians are warned not to grub around in it, but that hardly stops Hyman (who, incidentally, makes readers who admire Freud ashamed of themselves)." Delivering her final punch, Joyce concluded: "Hyman is beginning to romp around sweatily and hysterically in a game few other serious readers are interested in." Perhaps aware of Hyman's power as a critic, Joyce disguised her identity under yet another version of her name, signing the letter "J. O. Smith." But she continued her attack on Hyman in fictional form, parodying his reviews in her novel *Expensive People* and, in her story "Accomplished Desires," using him as the basis for the philandering, egotistical professor who drives his brilliant wife (based on Shirley Jackson) to suicide.

Joyce could be equally incisive when responding to writers of the past. In college she had developed the habit of heavily annotating the works of literature and philosophy she read so avidly. One much-marked book from 1965 is particularly interesting for the glimpse it affords into Joyce's active, thoughtful engagement with her reading and into her strongly held, sometimes impatiently expressed literary opinions. Edited by Richard Ellmann and Charles Feidelson Jr., *The Modern Tradition: Backgrounds of Modern Literature* was an anthology of literary criticism by nineteenth- and twentieth-century writers. Next to T. S. Eliot's passage about the "objective correlative" in Shakespeare's *Hamlet*, Joyce wrote, "false & silly"; when Ezra Pound discussed symbolism in his essay "Vorticism," she responded in the margin, "No! misunderstood." She was similarly critical of passages by Joris-Karl Huysmans ("how surpassingly silly!"), and when Kierkegaard and Heidegger glorified angst by defining it as an emotion earned by one who has shed habitual behavior and begun to understand his existential condition, Joyce (herself a creature of habit and "conventionality" at age twenty-seven) retorted, "But why is a frame of mind outside 'habit' more reliable, more real, more *representative* than any other . . . ? Perhaps, being shaken and alarmed, one can't judge very well how things are 'existentially.' "

Despite the public recognition she'd begun receiving and her lively, sometimes gossipy interest in the week-to-week activities of contemporary writers and critics (manifest in her chatty letters to Bob Phillips and Dan Brown), reading remained for Joyce an intensely private and serious act. Reading was "the greatest pleasure of civilization," she remarked to one interviewer, and in a later essay titled "Literature as Pleasure, Pleasure as Literature," she argued that "reading constitutes the keenest, because most secret, sort of pleasure."

Since her teenage years Joyce had turned her chronic insomnia into the opportunity to perform what had become, for her, a "sacramental" act, one that represented an intimate and profound communion with another consciousness: "It is the sole means," she wrote, "by which we slip, involuntarily, often helplessly, into another's skin; another's voice; another's soul."

For all her idealism about reading and literature, Joyce had developed a keen, pragmatic interest in the progress of her career. Settling into the new Sherbourne Road house in the summer of 1966, she prepared for the critical response to *Upon the Sweeping Flood*, which had finally appeared in May. The reviews were somewhat mixed, and disappointingly scarce. "I'm sorry [. . .] it hasn't received any more reviews," Joyce wrote to Blanche Gregory. "I guess it just managed to escape notice, or to be eclipsed by other books." The prepublication notices had been positive, though they took note of the book's violent subject matter: *Library Journal* called the volume "brilliantly written . . . though at times the death and violence become almost sickening," while *Publishers Weekly* characterized most of the stories as "bizarre or horrifying" and filled with "painful violence." Subsequent reviews took up this theme at greater length. Fortunately, a major review that was wholly positive appeared in *The New York Times Book Review*. Millicent Bell argued that *Upon the Sweeping Flood* was even stronger than the first collection, exhibiting "Miss Oates as a storyteller with a unique viewpoint rooted in her sense of the explosive power and mystery in human beings."

But this prominent review did not help sales: Joyce's second collection sold even fewer copies than the first. Joyce complained to her agent that Vanguard had done little to promote the collection, and she looked forward apprehensively to the publication of her novel the following year: "I will be so terribly disappointed if *Earthly Delights* disappears at once," she wrote to Blanche, "without reviews or advertisements, the way this book did, that I will certainly want to change to another publisher, for better or worse." Blanche had sent the bulky manuscript of *A Garden of Earthly Delights* to Vanguard in May. "I hope you enjoy it, in spite of its length!" Joyce wrote to her editor, repeating the sentiment she had expressed to Bob Phillips: "I feel that it is the best thing I have done yet and I grew rather attached to it."

Joyce had spent eight months writing *Garden*, a novel whose enormous ambition and smoothly textured prose represented a higher order of achievement altogether than the brief and rather emotionally claustrophobic *With Shuddering Fall*. Opening in the 1920s with the birth of its central character, Clara Walpole, and ending some forty years later with the tragic defeat of this vital, attractive woman, the novel developed a number of major themes: the plight of migrant farm workers, the realities of the Depression and World

War II and their relationship to American capitalism, and the myth of America as a social and economic paradise (again Joyce had set her novel in Eden County). Dividing the novel into three sections, Joyce presented Clara in relationship to her baffled, angry father; then her cynical lover; then her intelligent and sensitive son. Clara was the most complex and moving character Joyce had yet created, the trajectory of her life suggesting a tragic vision of the American dream gone awry.

As she had done with Karen Herz, Joyce layered much of her own personal experience into Clara's portrait. Like Karen, Clara is a highly sensitive child (both girls' whitish blond hair suggests their natural innocence) who attends a one-room schoolhouse, where she endures the abuse of older farm boys; she is also harassed by a potential molester but manages to escape him. In one poignant scene Clara, possessed of a dime, can afford nothing in a five-and-ten store but "an ugly little doll without clothes," recalling Karen's dream of the child with a plastic heart. Clara's instinctive hatred of the naked doll also recalls Joyce's own firm rejection of the doll her Grandma Woodside gave her as a child. Already Joyce's fictional heroines had begun to follow a distinct pattern: denied sufficient nurture and protection as children, suffering molestation and abuse, they fail to develop their own nurturing instincts, perpetuating the cycle of familial disconnection into subsequent generations. The pattern also includes their view of sexuality not as a Lawrencian opportunity for transcendence but as a means of further degradation. Clara's sexual encounter with Lowry, her lover, on the banks of the Eden River recalls Karen Herz's with Shar: emotionally Clara dissociates herself from the sex act, feeling "as if her body were being driven into the ground, hammered into it." When their lovemaking is over she feels "as if she had been opened up and hammered at with a cruelty that made no sense," and "as if he had gone after her with a knife." Just before this encounter, which represents Clara's passage into a new phase of her life, Joyce again used one of her favorite autobiographical motifs: Clara and Lowry had stood discussing their relationship on a rusted bridge, looking down into the river "with its slow-moving water, its film of sleek opaque filth."

Acclimating to her environment, Clara comes to view her life in terms of aggression, acquisition, and conquest, as she unwittingly colludes with the materialist society that has destroyed her impoverished parents. Ultimately Clara's emotional dissociation takes a much different turn than Karen Herz's, since Clara rejects organized religion, runs off at age fourteen with her much older lover, and develops a tough, pragmatic exterior as a way of dealing with her harsh environment. Yet the novel achieves its great pathos through the reader's awareness that Clara, viewing herself as tough and independent as she tries to get what she needs, both materially and emotionally, from the men in her life, actually remains an innocent but doomed child whose values have been distorted by her early experience of poverty, ostracism, and violence. She finally becomes not an outcast from the American garden but its embodiment, an emblem of its rampant excesses, its spiritual emptiness. First as the mistress and later as the wife of Revere, a wealthy Eden County landowner, Clara manipulates her way into economic security for herself and Swan, her son by Lowry.

The highly intelligent and reflective Swan becomes Joyce's central—and autobiographical—character in the final third of the novel, since the hardened Clara now spends most of her time leafing through magazines on interior decoration and ordering bric-a-brac for the house, having become a soulless exponent of American materialism. (Her ultimate fate does recall Karen Herz's, for Clara likewise ends up in an institution.) Feeling powerless and adrift, Swan becomes a tormented young man who kills his stepfather, striking out blindly and madly toward the masculine world he feels unable to emulate; he can emulate only the primary method of that world, which is violence. Thus the story comes full circle, since we recall the economic forces that had helped drive Clara's own father, Carleton, into an early grave. The novel's title, alluding to the famous Hieronymous Bosch triptych with its tortured antipastoral vision, was actually "Swan's title for the story of his life," a claim suggesting the extent to which Joyce felt a deep and abiding identification with her characters.

Vanguard scarcely had time to read A *Garden of Earthly Delights* before Joyce, in the summer of 1966, completed her thorough rewriting of *Expensive People*, which she would come to view as the second panel of her own triptych: just as *Garden* dealt with rural life and *Expensive People* satirized suburbia, her next published novel, *them* (1969), would portray the wretched conditions of inner-city Detroit, whose racial and economic problems were becoming more urgent and potentially threatening with each passing year.

As she worked on *Expensive People*, Joyce was also teaching summer school—"for fun, I guess, rather than money," she said. "I don't know why I always elect to teach summer school. Certainly the money is nothing, just ludicrous." Although Joyce's teaching income had increased from $4,900 in 1962 to her present salary of $8,650 (she had also been promoted from instructor to assistant professor), she decided late that summer to apply for a grant from the John Simon Guggenheim Memorial Foundation. Having taught almost nonstop for four years, she wanted a block of time she could devote entirely to her writing. Asked by the Guggenheim Foundation to give an account of her career, Joyce summarized her three published books, her play, and her critical writing. Perhaps feeling that she might appear too inexperienced for such a major award, Joyce pointed out that although "my external career as a writer begins in 1959, with my first publication, I had been concerned with writing for many years before this. I wrote thousands of pages of fiction before I began to be published."

While waiting for the results of her application, Joyce learned that the movie possibility for *With Shuddering Fall* had apparently dissolved, while the "academic novel" she'd written several years earlier, submitted by Blanche to Harper's, was rejected by a "very, very slow and inconsiderate editor." Even worse news came in September, when Vanguard accepted *A Garden of Earthly Delights* but asked her to cut the long novel by 30 percent, a request that made Joyce "quite unhappy [. . .] one cannot cut anything by 30% and retain the original work." Joyce had continued to feel dissatisfied with the way Vanguard handled her fiction, again instructing Blanche Gregory to pursue the possibility of changing publishers. Though the Harper's rejection had been disappointing, editors at other major houses— Knopf and Atlantic Monthly Press—had also begun courting Joyce, who wrote to Evelyn Shrifte that she could not make the requested cuts to *Garden* "since I have difficulties in seeing a work objectively after I have been with it for so long." Instead she asked that the Vanguard editors make suggestions for cutting, and she would try to comply.

Evelyn's sister, Bernice Woll, who also worked at Vanguard, set to work on the manuscript, which she returned to Joyce on November 21. Joyce completed the suggested revisions in two days. Her attitude had changed dramatically because Bernice Woll, she wrote to Blanche, "did a truly marvelous job of editing," making her realize "what a difficult and important job editing is, something writers rarely think about." In addition to making cuts in the novel (though nowhere near the original suggestion of 30 percent), Joyce agreed with her editors that the animal imagery should be employed with greater subtlety; she had wanted continual references to the Bosch painting, "with its surrealistic intermingling of human and animal, but of course I see that I overdid it." Joyce also agreed to reduce Clara's use of profane language, though pointing out that "for a person of her background, she speaks much too genteely [*sic*]. The real conversation of real people like her (girls I remember from my childhood) utilizes profanity of all kinds as exclamatory devices— to them this kind of talk is not 'profane,' it is just the way people talk." Joyce also responded to the complaint that Swan, Clara's son, seemed overly precocious: "He is supposed to be unusually intelligent," she argued. "There is a literary tradition of unusually intelligent and sensitive children—in the non-naturalistic novel. This is not a naturalistic novel though it sometimes seems like one."

Though Joyce decided to stay with Vanguard for the time being, she had grown unhappy with her situation at U.D. Again she was teaching one of her favorite courses, Existential Literature, and she remained fond of her students. But by now, at the beginning of her fifth year, she'd begun to tire of the "relentless, cyclical pattern" of teaching, and she had no interest in the English department's impending doctoral program. She acknowledged to Walter Sutton that "I don't have associates who are particularly interesting, at the University of Detroit," and she applied that fall for advertised positions at Bryn Mawr and Swarthmore. In December, an offer came that she could not refuse: the University of Windsor, which had rescued Ray from Wayne State, also agreed to hire Joyce. On December 12 Joyce wrote humorously to Liz Graham, who had moved with her husband to Philadelphia, "Windsor offered me a position and I decided to accept, Ray agreeing to this with the provision that I never call him 'Honey' at school." The new job was especially attractive in that she and the Windsor poet Gene McNamara would start planning a master's program in creative writing soon after her arrival. The job at Windsor "will be substantially better" than her present one, Joyce concluded, though she acknowledged feeling "very sentimental about leaving U.D." She soon had reason to feel angry rather than sentimental. During her last semester at U.D., as a deliberate retaliation against her defection to Windsor, she was given a five-day teaching schedule that included 8:00 A.M. classes. She later confided to her journal that "the schedule grew tiresome and tiring and I really couldn't wait for it all to end."

Apart from her dissatisfaction with U.D., Joyce had other reasons to look forward to her new job in Windsor. By 1967, Detroit had become an increasingly unstable and threatening environment, even in bucolic-sounding neighborhoods like Sherwood Forest. The potential for violence in Detroit, Joyce said, was "so transparent, you can hear it ticking," and the slightest sound in the house aroused "animal terror." As she later told an interviewer, "I was aware of hatreds and powerful feelings all around me." One of her U.D. colleagues, Father Norm McKendrick, remembered that Joyce experienced this generalized hatred in a frighteningly personal way. Evoking memories of her experience with Richard Wishnetsky, another troubled U.D. student focused his anger on Joyce and began making threats on her life. "He was leaving her notes," McKendrick said, "and she was really terrified." The priest recalled that after getting one of the student's letters, Joyce "came right into my arms" for comfort. "And I thought, 'This is not the Joyce Carol Oates I've known.' She was really quite frightened." On another occasion, walking along a deserted downtown street toward her car, Joyce was aware of being followed by two young black men. As the men drew closer, Joyce calculated that she did not have sufficient time to run to her car, still some distance away. She fought down the panic, and just as the men reached her, a police cruiser appeared out of a nearby alley and the men quickly turned and fled. This menacing episode would haunt Joyce for years. "Sometimes I think how my life might have been irrevocably altered, at least my interior life," she wrote, "if that police car hadn't turned in." The situation of a frightened woman being followed by a stranger appeared in many of her short stories in the late 1960s and early 1970s.

Such incidents occur in any large city, of course, but for Joyce they seemed emblematic of the grave social malaise Detroit was suffering at the time. According to one historian, the city's black population lived "in a constant state of agitation" in the mid-1960s. The public schools had deteriorated, the median income for inner-city blacks was less than half the Michigan average, and the escalating Vietnam War had caused a reduction in federal aid. In the fall of 1966, a riot was barely averted when a group of black nationalists clashed with police on the city's east side. Black leaders accused police of routine brutality, and the police responded with the first blue-flu strike since 1919. Though city officials had insisted that the L.A. Watts riot of 1965 and other disturbances in Chicago and Cleveland could not happen in Detroit, it was a police raid on a group called the United Community League for Civil Action on Sunday, July 23, 1967, that finally sparked the Detroit rioting. Arsonists, looters, and snipers turned the city into a combat zone, and by Monday night President Lyndon Johnson made a television appearance to declare a state of emergency in Detroit that required federal troops. The violence continued for several days, prompting the city's mayor, Jerome Cavanaugh, to remark that Detroit looked "like Berlin in 1945." By the time peace was restored, 44 people had died, 5,000 more were left homeless, 1,300 buildings had been destroyed, and 2,700 businesses were looted. The mayor insisted that what happened was not truly a race riot (there had been looting by both blacks and whites) but a more general "rebellion of people who have no stake in society, people in both races."

Joyce, who had long sensed the "ticking" of the city's time bomb, had been fortunate: she and Ray were on a lengthy summer vacation when the violence broke out. But the rioting had come perilously close to home. After returning to Detroit Joyce wrote to a friend that "a large building a block and a half away looks as if an atom bomb hit it, and every store along the block parallel to ours (two blocks over) was looted." The situation only reinforced Joyce's eagerness to begin her new job in Canada. The only potential difficulty in timing regarded Joyce's grant application: on March 15, 1967, the Guggenheim Foundation informed her that she had been granted an award of $5,000, but recipients were not allowed to pursue other employment during the grant period. Joyce's salary at Windsor would be $12,000, so she could hardly postpone the start of her new job. To her delight, the Foundation agreed to pay out the $5,000 between May and September, allowing her to accept the grant and relinquish teaching only during the summer months.

While enduring her difficult last semester at U.D., Joyce had taken a break from writing novels. With A *Garden of Earthly Delights* coming out in August and *Expensive People* not yet scheduled, Joyce reported to Liz Graham that "I am at work on various stories and seem to be grinding them out at the rate of about one a week," adding: "This is to prevent my beginning another novel, when I have so many lying around underfoot in my study, turning yellow and moldy." The spate of short stories was highly successful, both artistically and commercially: while a few of the manuscripts, including the powerful Vietnam story "Out of Place," went to literary quarterlies, Joyce's agents sold "A Love Story" and "A Girl Worth Two Million" to *Cosmopolitan* for $1,500 each; "Love and Death" and "Shame" to *The Atlantic* for $800 and $750; "Accomplished Desires" to *Esquire* for $700; and "All the Beautiful Women" to *The Saturday Evening Post* for $2,000. (Originally titled "Fashion," "All the Beautiful Women" resulted from a country club fashion show Joyce attended with her suburban friends, but the story's characters were Jewish. One magazine had rejected "Fashion" with the remark, "No more Jewish stories for a while, please," and the *Post* had accepted the piece with the provision that the characters' names be changed: the ladies originally called Jacobsen, Simon, Abrams, and Baumberger were renamed, in the published version, Jackson, Stone, Elson, and Oliver.)

This group of stories marked a departure for Joyce in that she had temporarily abandoned the rural characters and themes that had dominated her two published collections. She told a *Detroit News* reporter that she now intended to concentrate on more urban, upper-middle-class subjects. "Higher-income people are more sophisticated, have more freedom of choice and therefore more psychological problems to write about," Joyce explained. Her friendships with affluent suburbanites helped give verisimilitude to these new stories and sometimes they provided her with a ready-made plot as well, as had happened with "A Girl Worth Two Million." At a party Joyce attended with Marj Levin and her physician-husband, Herb, the Levins pointed out a woman patient of Herb's whom he'd saved from a suicide attempt. Joyce never talked to the patient and Marj later remarked that it was "incredibly eerie, how she captured the essence of this woman" and her problems after the Levins had given her only a few details. Ironically, Dr. Herb Levin, the suicidal woman's "savior," himself committed suicide some years later, reinforcing Joyce's perception of the quiet desperation just beneath the surface of her suburban friends' successful careers and glib sociability.

Joyce made another significant departure in her writing that spring: for the first time, she plunged into the writing of poetry. Although she'd composed a few poems in her college days, she always considered herself primarily a writer of prose. Her friendship with Gene McNamara, the University of Windsor poet who would become her new colleague in the fall, helped encourage her in this new direction. She noted that poetry seemed to "come easily to me," McNamara remembered. "She took a certain amount of courage from that and began to attempt poetry." (She later credited McNamara with this impetus and dedicated her first volume of poetry, *Anonymous Sins*, to him.) Joyce approached the genre with her usual seriousness and energy. On March 21, she wrote that "I find poetry entirely different from prose—I mean, the writing of it—and much more exciting, at least this week. I've only been writing one week. I've turned out twenty-eight poems, some of them rather long." For the next six weeks, Joyce concentrated wholly on poetry, telling the *Detroit News* that she sometimes wrote as many as twenty poems in a single day. By early May, her "spasm" of poetry, as she termed it, had passed, resulting in more than eighty finished poems, several of which she promptly placed with literary journals. Most of the poems, however, were rejected "quite swiftly and breathlessly." As with her plays, Joyce recognized that poetry was not her major genre, remarking humorously to a friend that "I've stopped writing poems, I guess, out of respect for the medium." Instead, she added, "I'm back to great quantities of prose."

With her last semester at U.D. finally concluded, Joyce had the entire summer free for writing. She was distracted from her work, however, by an unsettling experience. She had already perceived that her growing literary reputation was beginning to attract the envious and outright hostile notice of others (a problem that would only intensify in the coming years). Earlier that spring, a local member of the John Birch Society had sent Joyce two "hate notes," calling her "immoral and criminal" in her writing, and this was followed during the summer by a systematic campaign of harassment conducted by one of her former Syracuse classmates, an aspiring but unsuccessful author. After sending Joyce several angry notes, one of them accusing her of plagiarism, he began addressing hateful letters to the magazine editors who published her, sometimes signing the letters with Joyce's name in the evident hope of damaging her reputation. "I'm really afraid that he is mad in a special, selective way," she wrote worriedly in August, after nearly three months of this harassment, "and that I will be his target for life. . . . I am awfully afraid of him." She added that the man reminded her of Richard Wishnetsky, "who had also a tremendous power for hatred and revenge."

Despite this unpleasant incident, Joyce made good use of the time afforded her by the summer grant. She had told the Guggenheim Foundation that she planned to write "a novel of moderate length, dealing with contemporary America" (a description vague enough to cover whichever novel might actually be published next) and by July 10 she had completed 340 pages of what she called "a love story, sort of "; on August 14 she wrote to Liz Graham that she had finished the novel—which she titled *The Wheel of Love*—but lacked "the energy to type it onto good paper." Much of her energy had been drained not by the writing itself, but by the long car trip she and Ray took in July and by her anxiety over the rioting that had taken place during their absence. Although "the rioting is all over," she wrote to Evelyn Shrifte on August 12, "the city does not seem to me very healthy. There are many rumors in all parts of the city and in the suburbs." Two weeks later she added, "Detroit is a mess: people are anxious to move out, realtors are doing no good by fanning this panic, prices are low and (bad) expectations are high." And there were continuing problems with Vanguard: publication of *A Garden of Earthly Delights* had been scheduled for June, but had been delayed, and when Vanguard sent the proposed art for the dust jacket, Joyce was furious. Inspired by the name of Clara's son, the artist had produced an awkward rendering of a young man's face perched atop the body of a swan. "I am very disappointed in it," Joyce wrote to Evelyn, "and alarmed that a professional artist would draw such an old-fashioned picture. *Please* don't use this or anything resembling it!" Joyce proposed the depiction of a "rich, lush, green stylized garden" as a replacement, and Evelyn, who also disliked the original sketch, instructed the artist to follow Joyce's suggestion. But the incident only reinforced Joyce's fear that Vanguard might continue to mishandle her work. She wrote to Blanche that perhaps the two novels she had written since *Garden*, *Expensive People* and *The Wheel of Love*, should be sent to Peter Davison at Atlantic Monthly Press, a publisher Joyce considered more knowledgeable about contemporary writing.

When *Garden* was finally published on September 7, however, Joyce was pleasantly surprised both by Vanguard's promotional efforts and by the extraordinary amount of review attention her ambitious, "epic" novel received. Although the reviews were again mixed, several of them asserting that Joyce had failed, in the final third of the novel, to sustain the extraordinary power of the early sections focused on Clara, most of the critics recognized that *Garden* heralded not merely a good writer but a potentially major one. Elizabeth Janeway summarized this viewpoint in *The New York Times Book Review*: "This isn't the best book that Joyce Carol Oates is going to write," Janeway accurately predicted, "but if you want to see a big, solid talent getting under way, I suggest you read it." Though finding the book overlong and occasionally clumsy (like other reviewers, she compared Joyce to Theodore Dreiser), Janeway acknowledged that "when Miss Oates is good she is very, very good." Yet she found Clara's tragedy somewhat contrived, as if "the author, rather than life, is denying Clara her full scope. . . . Miss Oates should not let her fictionalizing trap Clara in a preordained fate."

The major newsmagazines concurred with Janeway's assessment. *Time* found "a magical naturalistic quality in this book" but criticized the closing chapters: "What promises to be one of the most acridly realistic novels since Dreiser never quite takes the prize." *Newsweek* agreed that "the book tends to trail off" toward the end, adding: "No one else has brought off a major social novel lately either, but this near miss suggests we may not have long to wait." In *Saturday Review*, the influential critic Granville Hicks (whose rather ponderous prose style Joyce would parody, along with Stanley Edgar Hyman's, in her next published novel, *Expensive People*) praised the complexity of Joyce's characters: "these people are real. They often seem mysterious to us, as, for that matter, they do to themselves; but we accept their existence. They are real to me in exactly the same way as are my neighbors."

Joyce was elated by the response, taking the negative remarks in stride: "I am pleased that the novel is receiving attention from reviewers," she wrote to Evelyn, adding that the reviews, "though not entirely favorable, seemed to take the novel seriously and to be judging it on a fairly high level." (Evelyn, always warmly supportive in her letters to Joyce, had written, "I hope the reviews will bring you some pleasure; at least the book is getting space and praise, though I should have written different reviews myself.") Joyce was also pleased that Vanguard had advertised the book prominently, buying a full-page ad in *The New York Times Book Review*. In the meantime, Joyce met personally with Peter Davison of Atlantic Monthly Press, who had traveled to Detroit in the hopes of convincing Joyce to change publishers. Although she liked Davison a great deal, the notion of finally leaving Vanguard—which had, after all, launched her career and continued publishing her books despite meager sales—left Joyce in an agonizing position. "I like Evelyn very much and I feel that Vanguard has done a great deal for my current novel," she told Blanche. "I am really quite undecided." She pleaded for her agent's advice, and they ultimately took what Joyce considered "a conservative and reasonable course," submitting *Expensive People* to Vanguard with a sixty-day decision clause. Vanguard promptly accepted the novel and agreed to publish it the following year. Relieved that the period of indecision was over, Joyce wrote philosophically to Blanche, "I think that ultimately I will remain with Vanguard, and that my books will do as well there as elsewhere."

Joyce and Ray had also decided, for the time being, to "stay firm" against the panic that had gripped many Detroiters in the wake of the July riot. Increasingly, however, it began to seem pointless for them to live in Detroit any longer, since both were now teaching at the University of Windsor, located "a hardy commuting trip" away. By the end of 1967, Joyce and Ray found themselves, as Joyce put it humorously to Liz Graham, "uneagerly looking forward to next summer's riots" and planning to put their house on the market. "I think, generally, that the atmosphere of such a large city with its numbers and its bad air," she wrote, "apart from any racial problems, is enough to make people want to move out."

The imminent move to Windsor would place Joyce in an environment of relative quiet and safety, but Detroit—with all its physical ugliness, social tensions, and rampant violence—would dominate her imagination for years to come. Just as she felt a piercing nostalgia for the raggedy upstate New York countryside where she spent her childhood, she would come to feel imaginatively "addicted" to the cityscape of Detroit:

> Hazy skylines. Chemical-red sunsets. A yeasty gritty taste to the air. . . . Much motion—Brownian, ceaseless—mesmerizing—a landscape of grids interrupted by sharp-slanted drives, freeways snaking through neighborhoods, cutting streets in two. A city of streets. Freeways. Overpasses, railroad tracks, razed buildings and weedy vacant lots and billboards, and houses, houses, blocks and acres and galaxies of houses, stretching out forever. I shut my eyes and suddenly I am there again. . . .

After Joyce left Detroit, the city would provide not merely the setting but the mood, the tone, and in a real sense the central subject, of some of her finest work: the novels *them* (1969) and *Do with Me What You Will* (1973), and many of the short stories in her next two collections. Like most writers, Joyce could portray a setting much more objectively and powerfully after she had left it behind; feelings of loss and nostalgia have remained a major source of inspiration throughout her career. But her personal removal from the places she writes about extensively in her fiction was also necessitated by her longing for a safely controlled and ordered environment. After she left rural upstate New York, she could consider dispassionately the social and economic conditions that had contributed to her own victimization as a child; after departing Syracuse, she could dramatize the exhilaration of college life and satirize the sorority system. Similarly, having removed herself from the acutely felt dangers of Detroit's urban unrest, she could view the city as a major wellspring of her art and as a cruciblelike environment that had helped shape her development as a writer. But even as she portrayed the city in careful naturalistic detail, she would also attempt an allegorical rendering of Detroit as a "place of romance, the quintessential American city." Two decades later, she recognized that although she lived in Detroit for only a few years, those years represented "a lifetime, in fact, a sentimental education never to be repeated for me." She concluded that "Detroit, my 'great' subject, made me the person I am, consequently the writer I am—for better or worse."

8

A House in Windsor
1968–70

We are so happy with our new home. . . .
—letter to Evelyn Shrifte, July 15, 1968

Joyce Carol Oates's new position at the University of Windsor coincided with her suddenly heightened fame as the author of *A Garden of Earthly Delights*. Unlike her previous books, *Garden* had respectable sales in addition to critical acclaim: within a few months of publication, the novel had sold more than ten thousand copies. Having completed the new novel called *The Wheel of Love* during the summer (she later destroyed the manuscript), she'd already begun to have ideas for another long work but joked to a friend that she kept "beating them back. No, no, no . . . not another novel." Instead she wrote short stories and continued seeing her friends in the Detroit area, especially Kay Smith. She also attended a benefit cocktail party hosted by her friend Marj Levin to finance newspaper advertisements protesting the Vietnam War. "The party was quite pleasant," she remarked to Liz Graham, "though the whole procedure seems to be futile." The painful social issues of the late 1960s were deeply troubling to Joyce, especially since she saw no way to deal directly with them: "The whole racial situation is pretty hopeless, I think," she wrote. "Along with Vietnam and other situations about which I've given up thinking. I haven't got the steadfastness of the *New Republic* people, who write and publish articles week after week after week on Vietnam, Black Power, the Ghetto, Education, etc., over and over, the same issues, the same problems, nothing solved, everything gradually worse, have faith, keep going, don't look back, and so on. . . . Sad."

As always, Joyce preferred dealing with social issues through her writing: her story "Out of Place," written the previous spring, had searingly dramatized the human costs of Vietnam. But her new base of operations in Canada was a welcome respite from the social tensions in Detroit, and her position at Windsor held other advantages as well. Though Joyce's teaching at the University of Detroit certainly hadn't hampered her productivity, she was elated that her course load at Windsor would allow much more time for pursuing her writing career. During her first semester there, fall 1967, she had only eighteen students to teach (seven of them graduate students), compared to 118 during her previous term at U.D. In addition to seminars in creative writing, she taught a course similar to one of her favorites at U.D.—an honors course in existential literature. Though she and Ray were still commuting from their home in Detroit that first year, Ray's job as department chairman kept him in Windsor, so Joyce spent an unusual amount of time in the library and in her office, waiting for Ray to finish his work. Still, she was much happier in the relatively calm and undemanding atmosphere at Windsor.

She received another invitation from Syracuse University that fall, this time for a brief stint as a "visiting writer," which she accepted. Joyce remained uncomfortable about public speaking, however, and her duties included a formal lecture in Maxwell Auditorium on one of her literary heroes, Thomas Mann. Though she suffered twelve hours in a "state of panic" before the lecture, the event went well: introduced by her longtime champion Donald Dike, Joyce talked informally about Mann's *Dr. Faustus*. Both Dike and Walter Sutton gave parties for Joyce during her time there, and she enjoyed visiting classes in the very rooms where she had attended lectures a decade before. "I felt rather homesick, walking around the campus," she remarked. Though she concluded that the visit had been pleasant enough, she was aware that such events put an unusual strain on her: feeling "quite exhausted from the stay," she vowed not to accept such invitations in the future.

Unlike Joyce, Ray was having a difficult time at Windsor, primarily because he had taken on the duties of department chairman shortly after Joyce was hired. He was soon suffering an exhaustion reminiscent of his difficult years at Wayne State, and by the time the spring 1968 term began, Joyce had talked him into resigning. She wrote to Liz, "It will be a tremendous relief for Ray to escape from the pressures of a whole horde of neurotics, madmen, egomaniacs, and blunderers," though she added wryly that "there *are* other people in the English department, I can think of two offhand, who are quite normal and pleasant to get along with." Free of administrative responsibilities and recently tenured, Ray could now simply teach courses in his field and get back to his long-delayed book on Charles Churchill. But Joyce and Ray faced a major hurdle: by late February their Detroit house still had not sold.

Though they dreaded the work of moving, they were eager to become established in Windsor and to avoid both the troublesome commute and the growing unrest in Detroit. Even the relatively quiet U.D. campus, five minutes from their home, had become a focus of disturbance: "Would you believe that the University of Detroit has had big student demonstrations???" she wrote incredulously to Liz Graham. "My sheep-like students at U.D.?" Teaching in Canada, Joyce saw evidence of social turmoil only in the form of long-haired, draft-dodging American students who enrolled for her classes.

Despite Joyce's comical description of her new colleagues, both she and Ray found a more congenial department in Windsor than Joyce had known at U.D. There was a firmer sense of an academic community there, Ray remembered, and "we got along well with most of our colleagues." Joyce had continued developing her friendship with Gene McNamara, with whom she worked not only on the new M.A. program but also on *The Windsor Review*, a literary magazine edited by McNamara and other department members. Joyce had also been instrumental in getting a friend from U.D., John Ditsky, added to the creative writing staff. By March, Joyce was writing that "I really like Windsor, even the crazy people." She told Bob Phillips that "there are several other first-rate and unstuffy people" in the department. "This first year is going by all too quickly."

Another colleague she befriended immediately was Lois Smedick, a specialist in medieval literature and the only other woman in the department. Lois was a young, likable person with a Ph.D. from Bryn Mawr; though not familiar with contemporary literature, she immediately read some of Joyce's work and found it extraordinary. Years later, Smedick imagined "how difficult it would be for a person of Joyce's gifts to come into an ordinary English department." Although Joyce clearly had confidence in her creative ability, "she did not come across as a confident person in her dealings with her new colleagues," Smedick added. "She seemed shy, definitely shy." The department head, John Sullivan, agreed. At university gatherings, Joyce could be charming and witty, he said, "but just when you think you've got close to her as a person, she turns it off again." Joyce also felt somewhat distanced from the department as a whole, Smedick believed, because many of the faculty didn't acknowledge Joyce's achievements as a writer. "I've always had the sense that people feel more comfortable denigrating talent," Smedick said. Some of Joyce's less amiable colleagues would eventually serve as subjects for her fiction. As she told Phillips, "We seem to have a surplus of troubled, aggressive, neurotic people in the English department—they do make life more interesting, I suppose, than the people in the relatively soporific department at University of Detroit."

By January 1968, comfortably settled in her new job, Joyce could no longer resist beginning another long novel. During a bout with the Asian flu, she'd passed the time reading some of the gargantuan masterpieces of nineteenth-century fiction, such as Dickens's *Our Mutual Friend* and Dostoevsky's *The Possessed*. Despite her admiration for Faulkner, Lawrence, and other modernists, she believed that the nineteenth century had produced "the best novels." Having successfully used Mann's *Buddenbrooks* as "a kind of model" for *A Garden of Earthly Delights*, she considered using *The Possessed* as a model for her new book, but decided that Dostoevsky's novel was "too wild and bizarre." Remarking that she was "better off flailing about on my own," she wrote on January 10 that it felt "exciting to be going into a long work with many characters, many events, a jagged and unlean plot, closely tied in with 'reality' (the setting is Detroit and it will all culminate in the 1967 riot)." This was Joyce's first mention of the novel she would later title *them*, a book that would win the National Book Award and confirm Joyce's reputation as a major American novelist.

According to Dan Brown, Joyce got the idea for *them* after he drove her through the impoverished section of Detroit where he'd grown up, on Lycaste Street. "She was struck by the atmosphere of it all," Brown remembered. " 'Lycaste' is even mentioned in the book." In addition to the inner-city setting, a more recent experience of Brown's also found its way into the novel: "I had a student at Wayne State—either black or mulatto—who told me in conference that she'd been raped by somebody and had gone into a decline, a semi-coma for a year or more." When he told Joyce about the conference, she questioned him eagerly about the girl and also asked him about the 1967 race riot. "She was actually in New Hampshire when it took place," he said. In the novel, the suffering of Brown's student became that of Maureen Wendall, who is savagely beaten by her stepfather. Not surprisingly, when the novel came out Joyce inscribed her gift copy to Brown: "for my dear friend Dan—without whom this book would never have been imagined!"

Another significant influence on the novel was Joyce's recent reading of Stendhal, whose hero Julien Sorel in *The Red and the Black* served in some ways as a model for the penniless but ambitious young hero of *them*, Jules Wendall. In a January 1967 book review, Joyce had written that "the great drama of capitalist society always has been, in the writer's imagination, the penetration into that society from without by a young man of no background, little means, but a great deal of charm and intelligence." As if predicting the novel she would begin a year later, she added: "The finest novel of this genre probably will always be Stendhal's *The Red and the Black*, but there are many contemporary works to suggest that the fascination with this subject is as strong as ever." Though viewed by critics and reviewers in the late 1960s as a Dreiserian naturalist, Joyce told an interviewer in 1969 that

"I'm really a romantic writer in the tradition of Stendhal and Flaubert." While commentators focused on the violent and tragic elements of her work, Joyce emphasized her characters' resilience and spirit, their ability to survive despite extremely difficult conditions.

Following her usual pattern, Joyce worked steadily and sometimes obsessively on the novel once its essential story and structure had coalesced in her mind. In late February, she reported to Liz Graham that she was progressing "slowly and languidly," but by July she had accumulated, "with the speed of a glacier," 570 pages. A few weeks later, the first draft of 700 pages was complete, suggesting that Joyce's concept of time, as always, differed markedly from other people's. But this novel, Joyce said, had been particularly compelling: "we writers like to exploit our own worst fears and agonies. I have all sorts of crazy dark things, private fears, in my writing, with the great density of them in the current novel."

Joyce's progress with *them* was undoubtedly encouraged by the recognition her work received in the early months of 1968. In February, she learned that A *Garden of Earthly Delights* had been nominated for the National Book Award. "I was astonished when Evelyn called me to tell me the news, and can't get over it yet," Joyce wrote. Though acknowledging that William Styron's *The Confessions of Nat Turner* was the favorite, she was pleased simply to be nominated along with such acclaimed writers as Styron, Norman Mailer, and Thornton Wilder. (Wilder was the surprise winner, for *The Eighth Day*.) Despite her disinclination to travel, she planned to attend the ceremonies in March, primarily so she could meet the fiction judges— Granville Hicks, Josephine Herbst, and John Updike. That same month, Joyce made her first television appearance on a book-chat show, an episode that paired her with the well-known critic Norman Podhoretz (whom Joyce found "immensely egotistical but somehow charming in spite of that"). And the month ended with extraordinary good news: on February 28, John Cheever wrote to congratulate Joyce on winning the Richard and Hinda Rosenthal Foundation award, which had been established in 1957 to honor an American "literary work, published during the preceding twelve months, which though not a commercial success, is a considerable literary achievement." Administered by the National Institute of Arts and Letters, the award included a $2,000 prize and a ceremonial, followed by a luncheon, to be held in New York on May 28. Ironically, the National Book Award nomination and its attendant publicity had ensured that Joyce's novel *was* a commercial success. As Joyce described it, "Evelyn managed to sell Fawcett the paperback rights to *Garden of Earthly Delights* for a sum paltry to Harold Robbins but amazing for me."

Along with the honors heaped upon her novel, Joyce received good news that spring about some of her newer work. She had put together a collection of the critical essays she'd been publishing over the years, focusing the volume on tragic and comic literature. Although Oxford University Press had rejected the book, entitled *Existential Modes of Tragedy and Comedy*, it was accepted in April by the University of Chicago Press. She had also put together a volume of poems from the large mass of poetry she'd written the previous year. Entitled *False Confessions*, the manuscript was accepted by Louisiana State University Press and scheduled for spring 1969. When Joyce's agent Blanche Gregory informed her Vanguard editor about the new acceptances, however, "Evelyn was quite unhappy at my giving two books to other publishers." As a result, the collection of essays was withdrawn (it finally appeared from Vanguard in 1972, in a revised version entitled *The Edge of Impossibility: Tragic Forms in Literature*), though L.S.U. did publish the book of poetry on schedule and with a new title, *Anonymous Sins*.

Joyce thoroughly enjoyed the National Institute of Arts and Letters luncheon on May 28. She was especially impressed by John Updike, and their meeting inaugurated a literary friendship—and an extensive, lively correspondence—that would last for decades. Updike was "most gracious," she told Liz Graham. "Someone said that he used to be bony and shy, but over the years has fleshed out and is suntanned and sociable. He looks like a basketball player, actually." Joyce went on to describe her other encounters with well-known writers, evoking the humorous self-caricature of a literary ingenue rubbing shoulders with the gray eminences of American letters:

> John Cheever is a bouncy little man, very jolly and pleasant. Kenneth Burke was quite drunk and excused himself, saying he "had to get another drink before it was too late." I don't know what he meant by that. Marianne Moore was looking for the lady's room and I directed her. Robert Lowell shook my hand (!) and Howard Nemerov was around. . . . You'll be pleased to learn that I didn't stumble on stage. Howard Moss ([poetry editor of] *New Yorker*) and I both received awards; he has been turning down my things for years; so we eyed each other nervously and edgily for many minutes.

In all, that spring had brought Joyce extraordinary good fortune: aside from the new level of recognition this luncheon and other such events represented, she could now feel, at age twenty-nine, solidly established as a respected American writer. She had a celebrated, recently published novel, another one (*Expensive People*) forthcoming later that year, and a third major novel that was rapidly nearing completion. With the recent acceptances of her two additional manuscripts, it appeared that she would soon be recognized as an accomplished critic and poet. And Joyce's agents continued to sell her stories to important markets. Though the *Atlantic* had already scheduled "Shame" for the June 1968 issue, the magazine now purchased another long story, "Love and Death." *Esquire*, which had published "The Wheel of Love" in October 1967 and "Accomplished Desires" in May 1968, now purchased a third manuscript, "An Interior Monologue." Other stories Joyce wrote in 1968 would appear in major women's magazines: "Wild Saturday" in *Mademoiselle*, "Bodies" in *Harpers Bazaar*. Clearly, Joyce's work was now avidly sought by the major magazine editors, and she had no trouble meeting the demand. Blanche Gregory recalled that as soon as she and her associate Gert Bregman would sell an Oates story, another would arrive in the mail. Quite often, according to Gert, Joyce sent two or three stories in a single mailing.

There was also good news in her domestic life: after months on the market, her and Ray's Detroit house had finally sold. In Windsor, they'd found a house on the Detroit River; Joyce described it to Liz Graham as "quite small, with only two bedrooms, but otherwise quite nice." A single-story, white brick house with a back terrace and a lawn sloping down to the river, it had a view of Belle Isle and, in the far distance, the Detroit skyline. According to Ray Smith, their Riverside Drive home had a unique charm that set it apart from the larger but more conventional houses they'd owned in Detroit. He recalled that "the river (and surrounding waterways) was a flyway for migrating birds," and he and Joyce bought their first "bird book" soon after moving there. "The side of the house facing the river was mostly glass, and from our dining room and library, we could watch the Great Lakes freighters slide noiselessly by with their running lights twinkling in the night. In the winter the shifting ice on the river would sound like the crack of a rifle. It was, overall, a highly romantic setting." Joyce agreed, writing to Liz after they'd moved in, "We love the new home—we may do nothing except look at the water all summer." With its white shutters and walls of white and pale yellow, the house reminded her of Nantucket, she added, and seemed an ideal place to write.

After completing the lengthy first draft of *them* during the summer, Joyce immediately began revising and retyping the novel. Settled into her quiet new house, she had few distractions. Since there were only two bedrooms, Ray took the second as his study and Joyce now worked in their bedroom, setting up her electric typewriter on a card table in one corner. But her less spacious surroundings didn't faze Joyce, who had always liked a spartan atmosphere for writing. Her U.D. colleague Norm McKendrick remembered seeing Joyce's study in the Sherbourne Road house, and had been "pretty impressed" by her plain, uncluttered work area. "She had her electric typewriter, her stack of blank paper on one side, and a stack of typed manuscript on another. She said that was the only way you can do it—you come up, sit down, and you start." In a 1991 essay, Joyce recalled her temperament as a young writer: "I was puritanical then, stubborn and self depriving. [. . .] I did not believe in any kind of distraction, let alone beauty, in my corner. Not even a clock—a plain alarm clock, or a wrist watch. Nor a calendar with an attractive picture." Her monastic devotion to literature represented a kind of "willed chastity," she said, and it somehow added to her sense of seriousness that she wrote on "an inexpensive card table, with an easily scratched chestnut sheen and legs that sometimes buckled" and that she worked, "often in a fever of concentration, in a corner of our bedroom. Two blank walls, and no distractions."

One day that summer, contemplating her friend Kay Smith's hectic life in a letter to Liz Graham, Joyce stressed this absence of distractions in her own daily routine. With five children, Kay had "so many things to do," she wrote, "many of them involving driving the children back and forth, that I really don't know how she manages. My life seems smooth and serene as the desert sands compared to hers." By now, having turned thirty, Joyce had deliberately created the kind of structured, disciplined, and somewhat isolated life that would preserve most of her time for writing. Although Joyce always insisted that she and Ray never made a conscious decision about whether to have children—"We never really thought about it much," she told one inter-viewer—it seems unlikely that the little girl who hated dolls, and who grew into a young woman obsessed with literary achievement that required a "willed chastity," would ever have been open to the notion of motherhood. "Certainly my work would not have precluded children—most writers do in fact have children," she said in 1993, "But my maternal instinct is not, one might say, at the governing center of my being." Marj Levin, whom Joyce saw often in the late 1960s, remarked that Joyce had no "emotional room" for children: "she's too sensitive, and if something was wrong with her child she wouldn't be able to handle it. Her personal life—I'm not going to say [it's] barren, but it's pretty placid. All of her emotions seem to come through her writing and her characters."

Another significant consideration underlay Joyce's disinclination to con-sider having children: since she had an autistic sister and one of Ray's sisters had undergone a lobotomy, Joyce speculated to Bob Phillips (with her typi-cally mordant humor) about the "alarming concoction" she and Ray might produce. She congratulated Phillips, whose first child had recently been born, then added: "Your baby sounds delightful. Ray and I think vaguely of such things at times, but I am an awful coward. . . . And what would the baby look like? Another matter: Ray and I are convinced that any issue of ours would carry the worst traits of both families, which is *quite* an accomplishment.

(Retardation, madness, orneriness, ugliness, etc.)" Years later, at the age of forty-three, Joyce would reflect more seriously, in her journal, on her decision to remain childless:

> I feel odd, almost apologetic (though why?), because I never wanted children. . . . Have never wanted to have a baby; or to have grown children; or any sort of large, bustling family. Though, if I think about it, I don't *not* want a more conventional sort of life. . . . The maternal instinct seems lacking in me. [. . .] After a period of time, in the presence of children or inordinately simple-minded people, I want to escape to my own privacy, to my own thoughts. . . . I find the task too tiresome, too unrewarding, to *pretend* to be more congenial than I am. Overhearing mothers talking baby-talk in the A & P (or, almost as frequently, scolding), I think—how can they keep it up? Days, weeks, months? Years? . . . But then of course they don't all keep it up. Having children doesn't confer blessings of any sort; doesn't make one "normal." Consider Plath, Sexton, et. al. [*sic*] If anything, such added responsibilities, such added burdens of thought and worry, must have made things worse for these unhappy women.

What maternal feelings Joyce did have, she lavished on the two Persian cats she and Ray had acquired. Unlike children, cats fit well into the disciplined routine of Joyce's working life, which demanded that she retain absolute control. She wrote to Dan Brown that she felt perplexed by the idea of a child growing up and asserting its individuality. Such a loss of control over her personal life might have negatively affected her work, and for Joyce, as always, her writing came first.

The novel Vanguard was preparing for fall 1968 publication, *Expensive People*, was also part of Joyce's dialogue with herself about the prospect of motherhood. A striking departure in both form and technique from *A Garden of Earthly Delights*, Joyce's abrupt venture into postmodern experimentation featured a notably unreliable narrator named Richard Everett, an obese teenager who claims to have murdered his calculating, social-climbing mother, Nada. (Nada is also a writer, and the novel includes one of "her" stories entitled "The Molesters"—actually a story Joyce had published that same year in a literary magazine.) Joyce later remarked that this unique, deliberately skewed narrative viewpoint had been the genesis of *Expensive People*: "I would imagine that not even Nabokov could have conceived of the bizarre idea of writing a novel from the point of view of one's own (unborn, unconceived) child, thereby presenting some valid, if comic reasons for it remaining unborn and unconceived." Not only is Nada Everett a serious fiction writer; she also has a family background and physical appearance that are virtually identical to Joyce's. Nada comes from an upstate New York town called "North Tonawanda"—Joyce's ironic homage to the Tonawanda Creek bordering her family's property—and is described as having "solemn dark eyes . . . fine clear skin, rather pale . . . short hair [that was] very dark, almost black." Since the novel culminates in Nada's murder by the brilliant but deeply troubled Richard (it was surely no accident that he bore the name of Joyce's troubled former student, Richard Wishnetsky), it suggests a bizarrely exaggerated autobiographical projection on Joyce's part, with her monstrous antihero coming to literary life as the "alarming concoction" Joyce had imagined when speculating about her own possible identity as a mother.

The novel had another, apparently unintended autobiographical dimension. Rereading it years later, Joyce remarked that its "thinly codified secret (having to do with the execution of an ambitious woman writer as fit punishment for having gone beyond the 'limits of her world'—upstate New York) strikes me as sobering and not, as I'd surely intended, blackly comic." Though the matricide was based, like many of the events in Joyce's fiction, on an incident she read about in the Detroit newspapers, one of its basic motives was to exorcise the part of Joyce that had sometimes enjoyed for the wrong reasons her participation in the upper-class suburban world of Birmingham and Bloomfield Hills. Those stirrings of "romantic snobbishness" had combined with Joyce's disinclination during that period of her life to discuss her family background, especially with her affluent suburban friends. Both Marj Levin and Patricia Burnett recalled that Joyce never talked about her upbringing. Lois Smedick, Joyce's new Windsor friend, also had the impression that "her childhood background was forbidden territory." Burnett even had the mistaken impression that Joyce herself had come from a wealthy family: "She always said, 'I had a perfect childhood.' I felt she resisted discussing her family background." (In the novel, Nada Everett invents a shadowy, exotic past as the Russian émigré "Natashya Romanov" as a way of covering her humble midwestern roots as "Nancy Romanow.") As Nada's name suggests, her aristocratic pretensions amount to nothing, and since she remains absorbed in her dual compulsions, writing fiction and social climbing, she has nothing to offer her son in the way of nurture or moral guidance.

Joyce later reported that *Expensive People* had been one of the most fluid, near-effortless writing experiences of her career. She had felt dissatisfied with her 1964 manuscript, *The Killer*, also a first-person confession narrated by an adolescent boy. That 250-page novel, she recalled, had been written in a "subdued, naturalistic key." The new version came easily once Joyce found the flamboyant, darkly comic "voice" for her narrator. A hectoring, hostile storyteller, this desperate eighteen-year-old (who plans to commit suicide once his tale is told) refuses to surrender the reader to the story itself or to permit the illusion of reality, the reassuring verisimilitude, commonly sought in the realistic novel. Instead, his story parodies such an approach, relentlessly calling attention to its own artifice. "It's possible that I'm lying without knowing it," Richard says frankly. Joyce later remembered "giving voice to the doomed Richard Everett in long unbroken mildly fevered sessions," creating the new novel at a rate of forty to fifty pages each day. Once it was completed, the earlier manuscript "was quickly and unsentimentally tossed away."

With publication of the new novel scheduled for October 1968, Joyce ended the summer with "a blaze of activity." In addition to typing out the revised version of her long, "elephantine" novel *them* and rereading the works of Yeats in preparation for a fall graduate seminar on modern poetry, Joyce took the train to New York to meet with her Vanguard editors and to help publicize *Expensive People*. As usual, Evelyn Shrifte gave a party to celebrate the new book at her Central Park West apartment. At Evelyn's suggestion, Joyce even went shopping for clothes (an activity she loathed, preferring to wear the hand-sewn clothes her mother sent from Millersport) and remarked that she "finally managed to buy a dress" at Lord & Taylor. Although Joyce still dreaded interviews—"I'm just not interesting, like LeRoi Jones or Truman Capote or Gore Vidal," she complained—she tried to cooperate with her publisher's promotional efforts. Warren Bower, interviewing Joyce for *Saturday Review*, described her as "a slender, soft-voiced young woman who talks about herself with reluctance." When the conversation turned to her work, however, she made "precise and thoughtful observations about how she works and what she writes." Regarding the composition of *Expensive People*, Joyce told Bower that the work had been "a joy," compared to her other novels. "I found it easier and more exciting to write. This feeling lasted throughout the whole book, and there was less rewriting to be done than ever before. I don't say I'm not going to write any more novels after the manner of *Buddenbrooks*," she added, knowing that her completed next novel would return to the realistic manner of *A Garden of Earthly Delights*, "but at least I can with confidence choose the structure that seems best suited to the story I want to tell." More generally, she told Bower that "I am obsessed with the mysteries of human relationships. I like to think my writing has no 'ideas' in it at all, only human emotions."

Once again, Joyce enjoyed positive reviews for her new book. *Publishers Weekly* proclaimed that "Joyce Carol Oates is completely her own woman, writing in a style that cuts to the bone in its chilling effectiveness." Granville Hicks pointed to the novel as evidence of its author's versatility: "She has proved that she can do something different and do it wonderfully well." John

Knowles, who had reviewed *With Shuddering Fall* in *The New York Times Book Review*, now wrote in the same publication that "Miss Oates has no trouble becoming a semi-insane, boy-genius murderer," though he felt that the first-person viewpoint precluded a full characterization of Richard's mother. By contrast, Louis T. Grant in *The Nation* found Nada a "brilliant" character, and praised the novel for avoiding the "self-conscious, affected, trivial and artificial" nature of much contemporary experimental fiction.

The reviews were particularly interesting in light of a chapter in the book entitled "Reviews of *Expensive People*." Through her narrator, Joyce got her revenge on critics she considered pompous, such as Stanley Edgar Hyman— whom she fictionalized as "Hanley Stuart Hingham"—and poked fun at such powerful institutions as *Time* magazine and *The New York Times Book Review*. The *Time* parody is particularly effective, mocking the self-consciously glib, trendy style the magazine affected in the late 1960s: "Confused and confusing tale of a child with a famous madcap socialite mother and a dear doddering foolish father, set in that well-covered terrain, Suburbia. Everett sets out to prove that he can outsmarte Sartre but doesn't quite make it." The actual *Time* review of *Expensive People*, claiming that the modern Gothic is the "forte of frail, large-eyed women novelists," reads as an only slightly less successful parody: "Author Oates has but one message in her demonic little tale: behind the suburban facade lie corruption and madness. To hear her tell it, American husbands and wives are nice clean-cut vampires planting stakes in each other's hearts. And there is always the monster in the playroom." As Joyce remarked to Evelyn, the *Time* review was "even more foolish than the parody I had made up!"

As with *A Garden of Earthly Delights*, Joyce's growing reputation translated into encouraging sales: *Expensive People* sold more than eleven thousand copies in hardcover (within the next two years, Fawcett would print two hundred thousand copies in paperback). On October 27, Vanguard again bought a full-page ad for Joyce's new novel in *The New York Times Book Review*. Years later, Evelyn Shrifte would recall that Joyce's earlier books "did pretty well, but when we got to *Expensive People*, sales started looking better." Her reputation continued to look better, too; like *A Garden of Earthly Delights*, *Expensive People* was nominated for the National Book Award. (The award went to Jerzy Kosinski's *Steps*, which Joyce considered "an awful novel.")

Joyce's increased fame created even more demands on her time. National literary competitions—the Hopwood Awards at the University of Michigan, the short fiction contest sponsored by the National Endowment for the Arts, Sciences, and Humanities—asked her to serve as a judge. A publisher of high-quality limited editions, George Bixby of Albondocani Press, requested a group of her new poems (the small book appeared in late 1968, under the title *Women in Love and Other Poems*). She began reviewing books for *The New York Times Book Review* and the *Washington Post Book World*. There were also frequent trips to New York, where Joyce continued to meet prominent editors, critics, and writers. Such ancillary activities were always draining, however, and she remarked to Liz Graham that "the New York literary life, consisting mainly of expensive lunches and cocktails . . . just isn't for me." For the present, the attention was gratifying, but Joyce was now putting the finishing touches on *them*, a novel that would thrust her toward the kind of literary fame enjoyed by only a handful of big-name authors. However, Joyce would find the effects of her fame to be unpleasant and, within a short time, almost overwhelming.

With *them*, her most ambitious novel to date, Joyce had completed her informal trilogy of novels dealing with rural, suburban, and inner-city American life. *them*, which she called her "Detroit novel," was a large-scale attempt to dramatize the full reality of contemporary American life by focusing on the city Joyce perceived as a microcosm—in its racial problems, its extremes of poverty and affluence, its capitalistic identity as "Motor City"—of the national culture. She found in Detroit a powerfully dramatic example of the "vibrating field of other people's experiences," as she called it, that had begun to inform her vision of American social history. Now living in Windsor and having achieved a more detached, objective view of the city where she had lived for six years, she came to see Detroit as a mythic force, "larger and more significant than the sum of its parts," and wanted to create characters who represented the struggling, anonymous masses of poor and working-class people in major American cities. At the same time, her principal characters—Loretta, Maureen, and Jules—became such distinct individuals in Joyce's imagination that she thought about them constantly, and at night even dreamed about their lives instead of her own.

Working on *them* through most of 1968, she remained "very deeply into, very obsessed with" the Wendalls. She saw them as "participants in a vast social drama—the complexity (and the tragedy) of which they barely grasped." As in *A Garden of Earthly Delights*, such ambition had required an epic sweep and length; it also dictated the traumatic, often violent experiences endured by the Wendalls since, as the narrator notes approximately halfway through the novel, "all of Detroit is melodrama, and most lives in Detroit fated to be melodramatic." Beginning in 1936, the book introduces us to sixteen-year-old Loretta, whose youth and penchant for daydreaming about the future help her endure an impoverished and rather sordid family life. But her initiation into her unstable social environment is swift: the dreamy teenager poring over the Sunday supplements soon experiences the murder of her boyfriend by her own brother; a sexual assault by the policeman she eventually marries, Howard Wendall; an abrupt move to the country along with Howard's domineering mother, Mama Wendall, followed by an escape to Detroit with her two young children after Howard goes off to war; an arrest for soliciting once she gets to the city, desperate for money; and a gradual immersion in the daily trauma and uncertainty of living in Detroit—moving constantly, living mainly on welfare, becoming involved with a series of shadowy men. Loretta develops a thick-skinned, knowing, sardonic exterior; like Clara in *Garden*, she is a spontaneous, sensual woman who learns to survive day by day, another in Joyce's gallery of women characters drawn from her memories of older female family members who had few educational advantages but had become adept at dealing with life.

The remainder of the novel, focusing on Loretta's children Maureen and Jules, dramatizes the struggles of two sensitive young people as they, too, try to cope with their harsh and unpredictable urban environment. As a girl, Maureen is wholly passive, an eternal victim. She suffers the harsh discipline of the nuns at school, the casual cruelty of her mother, and a brutal physical assault by one of her mother's lovers, which sends her into prolonged catatonia (like the student Joyce's friend Dan Brown had described). As a teenager, Maureen begins prostituting herself because her accumulation of money provides a sense of empowerment, all the more valuable for remaining secret, and she grows into a cool, manipulative young woman who views life as a power struggle and resolves to get what she wants on her own terms. Deliberately seducing another woman's husband and marrying him, Maureen gradually hardens herself to her environment, and even to her family members, as a defense against further suffering.

By contrast, Maureen's brother, Jules, opposes himself to his own world in the manner of a romantic hero: he is the archetype of the character Joyce (in discussing Stendhal) had described as the "young man of no background, little means, but a great deal of charm and intelligence." By turns naive and shrewd, loving and violent, Jules is the most complex and memorable character Joyce had yet created. His personal charisma embodies the energy and idealism of a potentially heroic figure, but his impoverished background has helped create a more sinister Jules: the petty criminal, the world-weary cynic, and ultimately the murderer. In the course of his adventures, Jules is chased through the night-shrouded slums and almost killed by a policeman; he is beaten and perhaps sodomized at a juvenile detention center; and he succumbs to an erotic obsession with Nadine, a dark-haired beauty from a wealthy Grosse Pointe family whose name, like Nada's in *Expensive People*, suggests a moral void. (Nadine, too, attempts to murder him.) Equating money with power, like his sister Maureen, Jules seeks advancement through a sinister "businessman" (akin to Max in *With Shuddering Fall*) and again almost loses his life. In the novel's final chapters, Jules is a temporarily enervated, cynical figure, on the fringes of political radicalism in Detroit just before the 1967 riots. Reentering the bleak reality of his native city, he seeks redemption not in love but in violence. Killing a policeman during the chaos of the riots, Jules achieves an ironic liberation and at the end of the novel is heading for California with a renewed idealism about the future.

Joyce had originally called the novel *Love and Money*; though she rejected this title as "too explicit," it names the two major forces governing her characters' fates. A confusion of love and money, to some degree, helps defeat both Maureen and Jules: Maureen sells her "love" in exchange for money and, ultimately, a stable middle-class life; while Jules views success in Hollywood terms (fast cars, gorgeous women, great wealth) in his pursuit of the American dream. The siblings' different paths are partly dictated by gender, of course, since Maureen uses sex and Jules uses violence as the means of obtaining power and self-definition.

Apart from the novel's social themes, the Wendalls' story dramatizes some of the ongoing concerns in Joyce's own life. Several incidents are directly autobiographical: as noted earlier, Maureen's loss of a secretary's notebook in junior high school, and her subsequent persecution by a teacher, is virtually identical to the humiliation Joyce suffered at North Park middle school when she lost a similar notebook. But perhaps more significant is the way in which Joyce had split two distinct aspects of her own personality and characterized each of them fully in Maureen and Jules. For Maureen is the "good girl" who ultimately escapes her environment through her own shrewd efforts, achieving a conventional home and marriage, while Jules is the daring romantic, the adventurer who bids farewell to his sister with "an ironic, affectionate bow" before pursuing the ongoing, exciting experiment his life has become. Thus Maureen and Jules suggest the polarities of Joyce's own adult experience, the balance she had achieved between the outwardly stable, conventional routine of her married life and the experimental, quixotic pursuit of literature that dominated her private world. (Not surprisingly, she later confessed to a special, abiding affection for Jules, among all her characters.) Recalling the loss of the secretary's notebook, Joyce remarked that both she and Maureen "responded in a very weak, rather victimized way . . . I'm not a strong person, she's not either." As a writer, however, Joyce identified with Jules's strength and cunning, and would later note how many of her major male characters had names, like hers, beginning with *J*: Jules, Jesse Harte in *Wonderland* (1971), Jack Morrissey in *Do with Me What You Will* (1973), Jerome Corcoran in *What I Lived For* (1994), Judd Mulvaney in *We Were the*

Mulvaneys (1996). As "J. C. Oates," of course, Joyce had given her own literary identity a male-sounding name early in her career.

Like many of her protagonists, Maureen and Jules suggested "lives I might have led" if her own circumstances had been different; her actual experience might include brief impulses toward the "snobbishness" of Nada, the conventionality of Maureen, or the wayward romanticism of Jules, but as an artist she used these characters to live out extreme, tragic versions of certain typical American pathways. In *them,* Maureen's "bourgeois" stability leads her into a narrow, spiritually impoverished existence, and Jules's questing spirit prompts him toward sexual obsession and violent criminal behavior. Yet the two characters represent values that Joyce had constructively assimilated into her own experiences. She continued to cite Flaubert's dictum, "Live like the bourgeois, so you can be wild in your imagination." Joyce noted that "I was living like that long before I came across Flaubert's remark."

Many of the short stories Joyce wrote in the late 1960s likewise dealt with the kinds of extreme emotions from which her own carefully structured life shielded her; she would later collect some of these in her aptly named volumes *The Wheel of Love* (1970)—its title suggesting a torturous, inescapable cycle—and *Marriages and Infidelities* (1972). According to Dan Brown, Joyce was particularly fascinated with marital infidelity. He recalled that she told him about "a handsome book salesman who had taken her out to lunch and then had asked her to run away with him. She was positively thrilled. . . . She saw herself as a 'brain' and sort of unpretty, and here was this sexy man giving her the chance to 'change her life completely.' " Now that Joyce was focusing her stories on upper-middle-class experience rather than the rural ethos of her earliest stories, some of her most powerful work featured externally successful men and women whose personal lives were fraught with the intense emotions infidelity can bring: euphoria, desperation, guilt, suicidal impulses. As Joyce later told an interviewer, the "bizarre paranoia" found in such stories "isn't anything to cultivate, but I evidently needed to write about it. Then, seeing these things externalized, out of my own imagination, they seemed to be totally foreign, freakish . . . but, like old snapshots that distort and don't flatter and yet are obviously of yourself, they must be claimed."

In "Unmailed, Unwritten Letters" and "I Was in Love," for instance, Joyce employed a macabre, often ironic tone in which the narrators discussed their emotional and sexual lives. Joyce's subject matter prompted her toward technical "infidelities" as well, resulting in some brilliant formal experimentation. "Unmailed, Unwritten Letters" reworked the epistolary mode to reveal the unnamed narrator's desperate need to release her emotions, while "I Was in Love" parodied confession-magazine melodrama from its opening sentence: "I was in love with a man I couldn't marry, so one of us had to die." In these and other stories such as "Accomplished Desires," "What Herbert Breuer and I Did to Each Other" (later retitled "A Premature Autobiography"), "Scenes of Passion and Despair," "Love and Death," "Puzzle," and "To My Lover, Who Has Abandoned Me . . . ," Joyce wrote obsessively about infidelity and its emotional cost, as if the girlish side of her, who had been "positively thrilled" by the proposition from a sexy book salesman, were being sternly lectured on the wages of sin by the rather puritanical adult fiction writer. Recurring situations in such stories include a woman entrapped in a safe but passionless marriage who is attracted to a charismatic, verbose man (often a brilliant academic); a woman feeling victimized and powerless as she endures an affair and its inevitably unhappy ending; and an innocent child (Bobby in "I Was in Love," Buchanan in "Wild Saturday") who suffers both psychological and physical violence as a result of his parents' behavior. Similar stories from this time such as "Normal Love," "Bodies," and "Demons" also featured paranoid and frequently violent lovers. Not surprisingly, some of the women's magazines to whom Joyce's agents submitted the manuscripts found them impossible to publish: *McCalls* commented that "Normal Love" was "fine, bone-chilling, but no," while *Ladies Home Journal*, in an unintentionally humorous response, considered "Wild Saturday" powerful, "but too depressing for our ladies."

Apart from her own experiences, Joyce's observations of her friends' marriages also contributed to her fiction about romantic love, particularly where the female character's identity was concerned. While Joyce admired Liz Graham's husband, Jim, she disliked the overbearing, egotistical men whom Kay Smith, Marj Levin, and Patricia Burnett had married. Patty Burnett remembered that Joyce was "very very curious about my life and what I was doing, and how I felt about men, and the women's movement." In 1969, Patty painted Joyce's portrait and remembered that as Joyce sat there, perfectly motionless, she remarked that "women should be utterly independent in their marriage, and lead their own lives, and not be the pawn of husbands." An academic couple Joyce befriended in the late 1960s, John and Ruth Reed (then both teaching at Wayne State), also recalled Joyce's strong opinions about women's independence and the importance of a healthy marriage. The Reeds had met Joyce through a mutual friend, the poet Jerome Mazzaro, and like most people on their first encounter with Joyce, they had found her withdrawn and shy. But a friendship between the two couples developed quickly. "One of the reasons," Ruth Reed recalled, was that Joyce and Ray "liked being with another married couple who enjoyed one another, and got along." Ruth remembered attending a dinner party during which a man had verbally abused his wife, and "Joyce in particular was very critical of his behavior, when we were alone together, later; she was eager to talk about it." It was clear to Ruth that both Ray and Joyce "strongly believed in marriage, in fidelity," and that they enjoyed a relationship "built on mutual trust, love, affection, respect—they seemed to see themselves very much as a partnership."

Despite her belief in women's independence of men, many years would pass before Joyce's work would be discussed in the context of feminist literature. The often passive and even masochistic nature of her heroines did not conform to the doctrinaire feminist image of a strong, independent woman. Joyce's public image as a frail, shy young novelist with a little girl's voice likewise disqualified her from sisterhood with the outspoken leaders of the women's movement. But in the sphere of her personal relationships, Joyce retained the strong will her parents had observed in Millersport and remained the independent thinker who had refused to participate in her sorority's inane activities at Syracuse. Enjoying her marriage, her friends, and her university colleagues throughout her twenties, Joyce had remained stubbornly focused on her own personal and artistic goals.

By the end of 1968, Vanguard had read and enthusiastically agreed to publish *them*, paying an advance of $2,000. With each new book, Joyce's publishers had grown more certain that their young author was a genius. "We consider her one of the most brilliant writers of our time," Evelyn Shrifte told a reporter, shortly after accepting the new novel. "Her narrative sense and the overtones in her work are extraordinary; and her keen perception and compassionate understanding incredible in one so young." Shrifte had been contacted by the *Detroit News*, since the newspaper had now decided (as the *Detroit Free Press* had done in 1965) to publish a cover story about Joyce in its Sunday magazine section. The resulting article again typified the sexist coverage Joyce received at this point in her career, even after publishing several acclaimed books: the male interviewer referred to Joyce (who was now thirty years old) as "a literary pixie" and as "that rare female creature who doesn't talk much." But Joyce used the interview to address a question that reviewers of her books had posed with increasing frequency: why did her fiction merely dramatize nightmarish contemporary problems, without attempting to suggest any solutions? Echoing her previous position that she liked to think her work contained no "ideas," only human emotions, Joyce insisted, "I have no message, no cause, no backs to scratch. If there are problems to solve, that is for others. I am not a problem solver."

Beginning with this same issue of the *Detroit News*, Joyce had agreed to become a regular contributor to the Sunday magazine. According to the newspaper's book editor, Joyce would use the magazine as a forum to "comment on any and everything that hits her fancy." In a column accompanying her interview, Joyce wrote a review of the John Cassavetes film *Faces* in which she elaborated her own theory of art: " The most powerful moral art is not the kind that preaches goodness, but the kind that shows the sickening, corrosive effect of various kinds of 'evil.' " Joyce's stint as a contributor to the magazine was short-lived: she produced a few more brief essays, including one "On the Student Revolution" and another on "The Masculine Mystique" in films such as *Bullitt*, starring Steve McQueen.

The essay on student revolutions is particularly noteworthy in revealing Joyce's essential conservatism. Although she often criticized corrupt systems of power (especially the excesses of American capitalism) in her fiction, she also respected the necessity for organizational structures and hierarchies (whether in the political, business, or academic sphere) that were based on genuine achievement, experience, and seasoned maturity. She had sympathized with student protests against the Vietnam War, but she now castigated the student movement's "unrealistic goals—autonomy without experience—and a mysterious quality to its imagination which appears to be suicidal." She insisted that "Universities, like all institutions, cannot operate democratically. A university is absolutely committed to a sense of professionalism, a hierarchy of knowledge and experience." Like the later scenes of her forthcoming novel *them*, which parody the illogical, self-serving extremes of political revolution in 1967 Detroit, she criticized the "suicidal hysteria, a desire to annihilate all structures, all institutions," adding: "The spirit of the revolution is betrayed by this stupidity—a half-conscious, eerie, unfocused desire for failure."

Joyce's decision in early 1969 to write these newspaper columns followed an already familiar pattern. Having finished a long novel, she typically looked around for shorter, less ambitious projects, and often used other forms—essays, plays, and poetry—as a means of amplifying themes she had treated only partially in the longer work. As her career progressed, her poetry in particular would serve this function (in addition to providing a restorative consolation after the sustained, arduous labor required by a novel). As she would later tell an interviewer, her "poems are nearly all lyric expressions of larger, dramatic, emotional predicaments, and they belong to fully developed fictional characters who 'exist' elsewhere. The poems are therefore shorthand, instantaneous accounts of a state of mind that might have been treated in a 400-page work." Perhaps inspired by the intensely erotic affair between Jules and Nadine she had portrayed in the later chapters of *them*, Joyce returned to poetry writing that spring, even though she continued to express doubts about her ability as a poet. "I've been writing a lot of poems, airily," she remarked to Bob Phillips on June 2. "I've written so many—I really love to write poems!—that it would be unlikely that even a few might be good." Unlike her first volume, *Anonymous Sins*, her new "surge" of poetry—which would be collected under the title *Love and Its Derangements* in 1970—was composed "during a period of intense concentration, so that it is like a novella." The poems dealt with the intense emotions of romantic love and infidelity.

Joyce had also become a tireless letter writer during this period. As she became more successful, she felt the need to remain connected to close friends. Writing to Liz Graham, Dan Brown, and Bob Phillips, she reported in detail her activities and good news, while simultaneously taking pains not to appear egotistical and risk putting strain on the friendships. Joyce sometimes revealed her dependence on her friends when the quantity or quality of their own letters didn't match her expectations. After she sent Phillips a long letter accompanying her first volume of poems, *Anonymous Sins*, and Phillips was slow in replying, Joyce fired off this unusually curt, two-sentence note: "Some time ago I sent a copy of my book of poetry to you; did you ever receive it? Or were you so disappointed in it you couldn't bring yourself to acknowledge it . . . ?" Her many letters to Dan Brown, who was traveling in Europe that summer, urged him to write longer and more frequent replies.

Despite her busyness and frequent exhaustion, Joyce retained her uncanny ability to concentrate intensely on a single project. On one occasion, she found that she could apply this talent to an unaccustomed challenge: doing absolutely nothing. In July 1969, when Patty Burnett asked Joyce to sit for a portrait, Joyce found to her surprise that "I can sit without moving for forty-five minutes, in a kind of daze, perfectly content to daydream in silence." Burnett marveled at this ability: "I remember her sitting in my studio, with her eyes shut, and she could literally stop breathing; she just existed; I almost felt like holding a mirror to her nostrils to see if she was breathing. She said she could almost transport herself into a sort of trance." A poem Joyce later wrote about the experience suggested that the sitting allowed her an escape from her own identity—a need she would feel more often as her celebrity grew, and that would inspire her interest in Zen meditation in the early 1970s. In "Portrait," which is dedicated to Burnett, Joyce wrote: "I can see the face growing, my face / growing free of me— / it is floating free of me in the room / . . . the lips have nothing to declare. / It is at peace, being immortal."

Joyce also escaped into other leisure-time activities: she and Ray had taken up jogging along the Detroit River, they occasionally went boating or biking, and after a two-year lapse they'd resumed playing tennis, and sometimes played badminton as well. Ray's sporty mood that summer is evident in the birthday present he bought Joyce in June: a bright red Fiat convertible, replacing the staid little black Volkswagen she'd been driving for years. "Ray and I have a new image now around Windsor," Joyce wrote humorously to Evelyn Shrifte.

Soon after the fall term began, Vanguard began preparing for the October publication of *them*. Reporters from both the *The New York Times Book Review* and *Time* magazine flew to Windsor for interviews with Joyce, and she began to feel anxious about the imminent reviews. L.S.U. Press had also scheduled *Anonymous Sins* for October, so Joyce would soon get public reaction to both her first effort at poetry and her most ambitious novel to date. In late September, Joyce and Ray went to New York for a further round of interviews, which Joyce found "exhausting."

Joyce's boundless energy, her capacity for work, and her tendency to take on more and more projects lend her letters from this time a frenetic, uncomfortable tone, as though she had mounted a treadmill but couldn't bring herself to step off. As she told her friends, she lacked the ability simply to take vacations or travel for pleasure. Even on her trips, she took work along, and was constantly jotting down notes for new poems and stories. Rather than taking a break from teaching once the spring term ended, she accepted an invitation from the University of Michigan to teach summer school, which meant commuting once a week for long, exhausting days of classes and student conferences. Apart from her work, much of her "nonsensical activity," as she had described it to Liz, included frequent socializing with colleagues from both U.D. and Windsor, and especially with her friends in suburban Detroit. Joyce's increasing fame made her and Ray a particularly attractive catch to party givers; though Joyce usually found such occasions taxing rather than enjoyable, the 1950s "good girl" lodged firmly inside rendered her unable to say "no." Occasionally her letters expressed a concern with her weight and a need to rid herself of the "complications"—especially the constant demands on her time, both professionally and socially—that were sapping her vitality. Though Joyce was five foot nine, she sometimes weighed as little as ninety-five pounds. To many observers, she appeared "spectrally thin." Years later, in her journal, Joyce would speculate that she had been suffering a form of anorexia and would destroy photographs from this time that showed her looking gaunt and unhealthy.

In fact, Joyce's increasingly hectic life had begun to take a considerable physical toll. After the New York trip, she wrote that she was extremely busy and worried that despite attending dinner parties and eating in New York restaurants, she was unable to gain any weight. For Joyce, periods of stress had begun causing a near-total loss of appetite. In her letters, Joyce sometimes expressed a revulsion toward food and toward parties generally, describing an event at the Detroit Golf Club where she had witnessed heaping displays of food that she found disgusting. Though she added that such displays were so ostentatious they could not be parodied, she would soon accept her own challenge, composing for her next novel, *Wonderland*, the notorious dinner-table scene—both the funniest and most macabre in all her fiction—in which the obese Pedersen family stuffs itself relentlessly.

Negative images of food recur with a peculiar frequency and intensity throughout her work. Her female protagonists in every decade of her career—Karen Herz in *With Shuddering Fall* (1964), Elena Howe in *Do with Me What You Will* (1971), Marya Knauer in *Marya: A Life* (1986), and Marianne Mulvaney in *We Were the Mulvaneys* (1996)—disdain the process of eating and nurture. In *them*, a girlfriend of Jules's remarks that "I hate food. It's disgusting, when you consider it. And the need for food, having bodies and being reduced to *eating food*—did you ever think about that?" In the story "Unmailed, Unwritten Letters," the woman narrator's doctor asks, "Why are you trying to starve yourself?" She replies: "*To keep myself from feeling love, from feeling lust, from feeling anything at all.*"

This drive toward anorexia is often coupled with a portrayal of female sexual experience in wholly negative and destructive terms. Especially considering the huge body of Joyce's work, it is striking that the vast majority of her women experience sex as degrading and even horrific; rarely do lovers in Joyce's fiction experience genuine tenderness and communion in the sexual act. Karen Herz, Clara Walpole, Maureen Wendall, Marya Knauer, Enid Stevick, Marianne Mulvaney, and Ingrid Boone are only a few examples of the dozens of Joyce's heroines who suffer sexual molestation, incest, or rape, permanently altering their sense of self and their ability to form fulfilling sexual relationships.

In his study of anorexia and bulimia, Dr. Richard A. Gordon notes that anorexic women often recoil from even nonabusive sexual activity, "which is experienced as 'disgusting' or 'painful.' " The literature of anorexia stresses this link between the denial of food and the avoidance of sexual maturity and its attendant risks. Psychologically, a refusal of food is linked with an attempt to forestall womanhood, so that, as the feminist historian Joan Jacobs Brumberg writes, "[the anorexic's] body remains childlike." This denial of adult female sexuality is surely related to the disdain for dolls and other symbols of maternity that Joyce exhibited as a child and later built into the characterizations of many of her protagonists; it also accounts for the numerous portrayals of emaciated, boyish-looking young women whose degradation and lack of nurture make them into doll-like, unsexed automatons. Shelley Vogel, Elena Howe, and Ingrid Boone are only the most prominent examples.

Although Joyce herself sometimes dismissed her personal issues with food, claiming that she simply preferred working to eating, it seems clear that the frequent and occasionally intense anorexic impulses that mark her life and are often dramatized in her fiction have deep psychological roots. The career-related stresses that began intensifying in 1969 could be seen in her emaci-ated appearance and in her alternating bouts of manic productivity and extreme exhaustion. While some people overeat in times of stress, Joyce al-ways went to the opposite extreme and even told an interviewer that "I find it boring to eat, and would not do it except for social reasons." One friend from the late 1960s remembered that food was always "a very sensitive area" for Joyce. "I felt in a position of trust that I was invited to eat with her. Eating was somehow potentially problematical." The social gatherings Joyce herself hosted were notably spartan. Ruth Rattner, an artist and art history professor Joyce had met through Marj Levin, remembered that "it was so funny, we would go over to their house on Riverside Drive, and there would be nothing to eat. We'd all bring things. Because Joyce didn't care about eating." This indifference to food was noted by several of Joyce's friends, beginning in the late 1960s and continuing through the 1970s. The artist Betsey Hansell, whom Joyce met in the mid-1970s, remembered the lunches Joyce some-times prepared: "there would be maybe a half a canned peach, with a little cottage cheese, and maybe a glass of iced tea . . . it would be so spartan—you know, she eats very little." Even in the late 1970s, after Joyce and Ray had moved to Princeton, the poet Maxine Kumin noted that Joyce "cared very lit-tle for food and drink and offered a rather abstemious table to guests."

What personal issues underlay Joyce's anorexic impulses during these years? Both medical and feminist authorities on anorexia have defined a number of causative factors, many of which correspond to the facts of Joyce's early life and her psychological makeup. According to one expert, an experi-ence of sexual abuse such as Joyce suffered as a young girl often leads to the development of an eating disorder; for a girl who has felt victimized, fasting "begins to yield a particularly powerful sense of control . . . it provides a sense of mastery." Dr. Hilde Bruch, one of the pioneering theorists on the etiology of eating disorders, notes that "most anorexics are outstanding students who are praised for their devotion to work, enthusiasm in athletics, and helpful-ness with less advantaged schoolmates," a profile that accurately describes Joyce's personality as a student in middle school and high school. Another expert similarly characterizes the typical young anorexic as highly intelligent, polite, and "demanding of herself." Such a young woman can also be "stub-born, rigid, and strongly defensive about her behavior, displaying perfection-ism, excessive orderliness, meticulous attention to detail," and striking others as "a 'good girl' who alternates between compliance and rebellion." Another priority for the anorexic, Dr. Bruch adds, is "not giving into fatigue," since "the body and its demands have to be subjugated every day, hour, and minute." In her journal, Joyce occasionally expressed this notion: "I love to be fatigued, malnourished," she wrote.

Like other forms of addiction, the predilection for fasting relates to a denial or suppression of the painful, chaotic emotions that arise from early experiences of abuse. In 1971, Joyce wrote that "I should be a rational, contained person, I guess, but really I am very emotional—I believe that the storm of emotion constitutes our human tragedy." According to the feminist psychotherapist Susie Orbach, "submitting her body to rigorous discipline is part of [the anorexic's] attempt to deny an emotional life. . . . She attempts to control it so that she will not be devoured by her emotions." The physical body itself "is experienced as an object that must be controlled, or it will control. The emaciated body demonstrates that *she* controls her body whereas the average-sized body controls *her*." Especially relevant to Joyce's physical self-perception is Orbach's observation that the anorexic has "a shaky corporeal sense of herself": "There is no notion or sense of the body as an integrated aspect of self."

Throughout her life, Joyce has made comments that are notable for expressing an uncertain sense of her physical self, leading her repeatedly to use the metaphor of her own "invisibility." Many of Joyce's self-descriptions suggest a willfully abstracted woman who, like a grown-up version of her childhood alter ego, Lewis Carroll's Alice, has all but vanished into the wonderland of her imagination. She told one interviewer that "there's this kind of empty blur that must be where I exist"; she told another that she saw herself as a "mere vapor of consciousness." She added: "I don't really identify with my physical self that much." Friends and journalists often had a similar impression of Joyce. Betsey Hansell observed that Joyce seemed "all spirit and no flesh," while Ruth Rattner noted an "ethereal quality" about her. When Alfred Kazin interviewed her in 1972, he remarked that although his subject politely answered all his questions, "Joyce Carol Oates is not exactly here."

In her journal, Joyce would later reflect on her dislike of eating, which had become particularly troublesome in the years 1969 to 1971. She recalled that she simply "had no appetite: or, rather, what should have been an appetite for food went into an 'appetite' for other things." She added that "The appeal of 'anorexia' is no mystery. Perhaps a number of mysteries. A way of controlling and even mortifying the flesh; a way of 'eluding' people who pursue too closely; a way of channeling off energy in other directions." Yet she recognized that "[a]norexia is a controlled and protracted form of suicide, literally. But figuratively & symbolically it means much more. No one wants to be *dead*—! But there is the appeal of Death. The romantic, wispy, murky, indefinable, incalculable appeal." As she would later write in the essay "Food Mysteries," "Without appetite, steadily losing weight and noting with a grim pleasure how readily flesh melts from your bones, you experience the anorexic's fatally sweet revelation: *I am not this*, after all." Whatever psychological or stress-related causes lay behind Joyce's distaste for food were only reinforced by the innate puritanism of her temperament, which also encompassed her dislike of vulgarity, her immense reserve, and her rigorous work ethic. What Joyce has called her "class anger" was also relevant here: she had been a child of the Depression, empathized with the poor in her early fiction, and would never feel comfortable with any of the trappings of affluence.

Clearly, Joyce never fasted to the degree that her health was seriously threatened; in fact, she prided herself on maintaining her regular teaching and writing schedule even during times of illness. Yet her unwillingness to cancel one of her classes or to stop writing when she became ill or exhausted was itself an example of the rigid control characteristic of the anorexic personality. (This trait remained in place well into the 1990s, when she told an interviewer that "[a]lmost every minute of my life is plotted out.") It seems likely that in 1970 and 1971, as Joyce's visibility as a public figure brought sudden, intense, and unwanted pressures into her life, her unwillingness to eat normally related to this overwhelming need for control. Her sense of being exploited by the press and by many of her social acquaintances perhaps rekindled the feelings of victimization she had known as a child. Hilde Bruch observes that when women succumb to anorexia they are "engaged in a desperate fight against feeling enslaved and exploited," an emotion that Joyce confronted with increasing frequency during this stressful period of her life. Just as she had eluded her childhood molesters by running fast, she would soon escape her adult terrors by "running" away from America altogether and spending a year in England.

As if Joyce's increasing fame had not created enough problems, she suffered another source of stress at this time. The Windsor English department, relatively quiescent when Joyce first joined the faculty, had now become embroiled in a controversy centering on an assistant professor named Phil London and his involvement with student protests, an endemic late 1960s phenomenon that had finally reached Windsor. Along with Gene McNamara and other of her "semi-conservative" colleagues, Joyce had voted not to grant tenure to London, whom she considered unprofessional. Falling in with the ultraliberal politics of the time, London had begun giving A's to all his students and joining in their demonstrations against the university administration. Gene McNamara recalled one occasion when a group of students occupied the Religious Studies building, bringing sleeping bags and forming a barricade. London happily joined them. Joyce wrote to Dan Brown that her outspoken, often abrasive colleague had a small clique of students who remained devoted to him. After the department denied him tenure, London brought a lawsuit and the faculty split along political lines. The situation was complicated by the nervous breakdown of another male colleague, whom London had accused of making sexual advances toward him. The turmoil "created a climate of horror and tension," McNamara remembered, one that negatively affected Joyce.

Joyce had always preferred order and stability in her working environment, and this prolonged controversy, involving endless arguments and meetings among the faculty, had another unhappy consequence. A rift developed between Joyce and her only female colleague, Lois Smedick, who was sympathetic to London. "I was young, foolish, and rash," Smedick admitted, "but I felt that the department was acting high-handedly" in terminating London. In retrospect, Smedick saw that the issue for Joyce was less political than professional: "she was a serious academic . . . she took seriously the activity of grading a paper," and could not sympathize with "this rhetoric of the 1960s that grades were a matter of indifference." Ultimately London lost his court battle and moved to Toronto, and Joyce handled the residue of bitter feelings in the way she handled most problems: through her writing. Her story "Pilgrims' Progress"—published in *Playboy* under the title "Saul Bird Says: Relate! Communicate! Liberate!"—was the first of the academic satires she would gather in a volume called *The Hungry Ghosts* (1974); many were thinly disguised portrayals of her Windsor colleagues. Lois Smedick's friendship with Joyce was further strained because Wanda, the London character's dupe in Joyce's story, was based on her. Joyce insisted to Lois that Wanda was an "attractive" character, but in parodying London, she later claimed, she could have gone much further: "The real 'Saul Bird' of the story is, in real life, much *worse*—but fiction can't absorb the foolish, disgusting extremes of reality."

By the end of 1969, Joyce had put the London affair and its related worries behind her. That fall, perhaps as a way of coping with the anxiety and pressure, and inspired by the example of her artist-friend Patty Burnett (whom she continued to see often that year), Joyce decided to channel her creativity in a new and possibly therapeutic direction: she began taking art lessons. All her life, Joyce had been in the habit of drawing faces; the margins of her manuscripts are often covered with such sketches. ("Each novel calls forth hundreds or perhaps thousands of these simple unfinished drawings," she later wrote. "The activity seems to have something to do with my groping for a visual representation of a character whom I 'see' in my mind's eye.") She told Dan Brown that she'd decided she might as well try to paint the faces. With her usual zeal, she began painting intensively, considering it merely a pleasant hobby. Her artwork was particularly relaxing, she said, because there was no pressure to excel: she knew that she had no real talent for painting.

(For similar reasons, she had long enjoyed playing the piano, happy to remain "an enthusiastic amateur.") What she enjoyed about painting, she said, was a joyous quality in the work that formed a sharp contrast to the somber themes of her fiction. In her writing, she said, stories could not have happy endings.

Despite its attendant stresses, the ordeal of bringing *them* to publication did end happily. Joyce's fiction had always enjoyed positive reviews, but the critical acclaim that greeted *them* was the high point of her career. Comparing her to Steinbeck, Robert M. Adams in *The New York Times Book Review* called *them* "a vehement, voluminous, kaleidoscopic novel" that represented "a fine performance—psychologically more subtle than *A Garden of Earthly Delights*, structurally less predictable, but with the same strong flow of verbal and imaginative energy." *Time* proclaimed that Joyce was "that rarity in American fiction, a writer who seems to grow with each new book." In *The Nation*, Calvin Bedient wrote that "when Miss Oates's potent, life-gripping imagination and her skill at narrative are conjoined, as they are preeminently in *them*, she is a prodigious writer, one of the best we now have." Even *The New Yorker*, which had ignored Joyce's career to this point and remained the only major magazine that declined to publish her short fiction, printed a long, largely positive review by L. E. Sissman. Though he found Jules "a fitfully realized character," he concluded that "Oates is a writer of daring, discipline, and talent. Her taste is almost unerring; few writers have her gift for handling sexual scenes with masterly tact and suggestion, avoiding the wrenchingly explicit and the bathetically lyrical. Her skill in realizing character is rare and growing." Among reviewers for major publications, the only dissenting voices were those of Benjamin DeMott in *Saturday Review* (who complained that all Oates's fiction, including *them*, showed the author's "inability to perceive or create meaning" in her narratives) and Elizabeth Dalton in the conservative magazine *Commentary* (who claimed the author suffered from "violence in the head" and called *them* "a failure of literary intelligence, of structure and style"). These negative comments, however, were all but lost in the nationwide chorus of praise.

As 1970 began, Joyce resumed her usual routine of writing short stories and book reviews, and found that she was enjoying her teaching duties more than ever. (She had recently been given tenure at Windsor, while Ray was promoted to full professor.) She wrote to Dan Brown that her classes were going well, partly because she was able to blend her ironic habits of thought with an enthusiastic classroom persona. She found that as she gained experience, she required very little time to prepare her classes. As a teacher, Joyce had always been a natural: she never "lectured" or spoke from prepared notes. Her enthusiasm for literature and her love of the spontaneous give-and-take of literary discussion helped inspire a responsive energy in her students. When Dan Brown sent her some essays he'd written about the art of teaching, Joyce remarked that she taught naturally, without requiring any theories. As she would later note in her journal,

> Unwritten, untouched: the temptations of teaching, of giving oneself so completely to the vital immediacies of the classroom that nothing else remains. Commonplace but misleading, the skeptical attitude toward teaching. I can't understand it. From the first, at the University of Detroit [. . .] the temptation was to lose myself in the teaching, in the fascinating complexities of the students, in the oddly jovial, frantic social context of the college. Very real temptations, these, because the rewards are so immediate—so emotional. After a long exhausting day—at the University from 10 until after 6—little spirit left for what is private (my own writing), yet much left for a continuation of the same bright rapid flow of consciousness. Euphoric, could teach hour after hour.

For all her enjoyment of teaching, Joyce now marshalled her primary energies for work on another major novel. She told Dan Brown that she was pleased by the response *them* had received because readers seemed to have grasped the novel's major themes. Her new success had brought financial rewards as well: Fawcett paid $62,000 for the paperback rights. But now that Joyce had started a new novel, she said, she wanted to proceed very slowly and deliberately. Having begun the manuscript she would eventually call *Wonderland*—her working title was *The Madness of Crowds*—Joyce again had an uncanny experience of seeing reality mirror what she had already concocted in fictional terms. *Wonderland* begins with the murder of the boy Jesse Harte's mother and siblings by his deranged father, who then commits suicide. On February 3, Joyce wrote to Brown that she was alarmed to see a newspaper report that was eerily similar to her plot, involving a family with exactly the same number of children and even a young boy who had escaped slaughter and was only a year younger than her character Jesse. Although critics had begun complaining of excessive violence in her work, labeling her a modern Gothic novelist, such coincidences showed that her imagination was simply responding to the violent reality of America. As she had told *Time* magazine, "Gothicism, whatever it is, is not a literary tradition so much as a fairly realistic assessment of modern life."

Though the early months of 1970 were focused on *Wonderland*, Joyce and Ray did a considerable amount of traveling, most of it career-related. Their destinations were close to home. Joyce was "visiting writer" at Northwestern University for two days, gave a poetry reading at Eastern Michigan University, participated in a Twentieth-Century Literature Conference in East Lansing, and accompanied Ray to a conference on eighteenth-century English literature in Toronto; they also made a brief visit to Milwaukee to visit Ray's family. (On their way to Northwestern, Joyce's Fiat broke down; soon afterward, she and Ray purchased a more practical Pontiac.) They also began making plans for a more ambitious trip: a summer tour of Europe. Since Joyce still refused to fly, they would travel by ship. Joyce planned to visit her publishers in London and Paris, but they were going primarily as tourists, having never crossed the Atlantic before. Writing to Dan Brown, Joyce expressed a comic apprehension of the numerous museums they would visit in their highly compressed two-week visit.

In early March, Joyce's already busy schedule accelerated to a dizzying pace in her own country: she learned that *them* had won the National Book Award for fiction. As with *Garden*, she had been pleased by the nomination but had not expected to prevail. She wrote to Dan Brown that she had assumed Jean Stafford would win. Evelyn Shrifte called to say that Joyce should prepare a five-hundred-word speech for the ceremony on March 4. For Joyce, who had prayed for rain on the day of her valedictory address, even losing a National Book Award was preferable to making a speech. But Joyce gamely typed out her remarks, and she and Ray went to New York to face another round of interviews and receptions. Though she turned down many interview requests and refused to appear on television, she did submit to an interview for *Newsweek*. Asked the question that had already become routine—Why was there so much violence in her novel?—Joyce answered quietly, "Things like that happen every day in Detroit." Asked about her writing habits, she remarked that first drafts came "in a state of high psychic energy," and then afterward "these disembodied hands that write my stories" typed out the narrative.

Interviews aside, Joyce enjoyed her time in New York. She gave the required speech in Lincoln Center, alongside fellow winners Lillian Hellman (drama), Erik H. Erikson (philosophy and religion), and Isaac Bashevis Singer (children's literature), and after the ceremony Evelyn Shrifte gave one of her celebratory dinners. Though Joyce may have dreaded giving her speech, it contained—in sharp contrast to her minimal remarks in interviews—an eloquent defense of the novelist's role in twentieth-century America. "Writing fiction today sometimes seems an exercise in stubbornness and an anachronistic gesture that goes against the shrill demands of the age," she insisted, but she argued that writers were "tough, meticulous people, dedicated to a systematic analysis of the life of sensation and of the electronic paradise that threatens to make language itself obsolete." Like her essay about student revolts, she offered a conservative warning against "the style of the new decade," which she called "accelerated and deathly." The emphasis upon sensation, including drug taking, was "a speeding up of the ordinary process of life. It is a gravitation toward death." She concluded with a statement of her personal mission:

> In the novels I have written, I have tried to give a shape to certain obsessions of midcentury Americans—a confusion of love and money, of the categories of public and private experience, of a demonic urge I sense all around me, an urge to violence as the answer to all problems, an urge to self-annihilation, suicide, the ultimate experience and the ultimate surrender. The use of language is all we have to pit against death and silence.

A few weeks later, Joyce was pleased that her ordinary, quiet routine had resumed once again. She told Dan Brown she was relieved that the media frenzy surrounding the NBA was concluded; she was weary of being congratulated, she added, insisting (in a note she'd begun sounding with increased frequency) that she needed to slow her pace and reduce her level of anxiety. In New York, she had told an interviewer that "I've lost about 20 pounds lately because I've been so busy." Two weeks later, she complained to Dan about the numerous bizarre letters she'd begun receiving and about people who recognized her in public and approached her. She was also annoyed by the flood of bound galleys, sent by publicity departments who wanted a quote from Joyce, and by requests for aid from countless acquaintances and colleagues. She was growing tired of all the fringe activity that attended literary fame, she said, unaware that her indoctrination into the American publicity machine was only now beginning.

Joyce and Ray's plans for a summer trip to Europe were canceled when Joyce received tragic news: her beloved paternal grandmother, Blanche Woodside, had been diagnosed with terminal cancer. Joyce and Ray made a trip to Lockport in mid-May, and for Joyce the visit was extremely stressful. Aside from Grandma Woodside's illness, Joyce's parents were still attempting to care for their autistic daughter, Lynn, now almost fourteen and increasingly difficult to control; she had been on a waiting list for state hospitalization for more than three years. Joyce wrote to Liz Graham that the situation at home was "such a strain on both Ray and me—more on me than on Ray, I think, because I'm miserable with hoping *he* isn't being too miserable— which makes *him* unhappy—and on and on." The stress again affected Joyce's health. Fearing that she had contracted mononucleosis, Joyce sought a doctor's advice and vowed to stop accepting invitations. At times, she and Ray even refused to answer the telephone. Though she had once been eager to investigate the day's mail, she added, she was now quite happy that Canada was "in the throes of a mail strike."

Joyce seldom mentioned Mrs. Woodside's illness in her letters that summer, maintaining her droll, upbeat persona; she remained disinclined to discuss her family or any genuinely personal matters, even with her closest friends. But the impending loss of her grandmother was a serious blow. Despite her busy schedule, Joyce had always written regularly to her, sending along gifts of flowers and books, clippings about her literary activities, and bits of domestic news. Blanche Woodside's responses reveal her unconditional love for her favorite grandchild (there are frequently expressed worries that Joyce works too hard and doesn't eat enough) and suggest the pride Joyce's accomplishments had brought to the family. When the profile appeared in *Time* after publication of *them*, Mrs. Woodside informed Joyce that several "Big Wheels" at Harrison Radiator, where Joyce's father still worked, "came to congratulate him, and there was so much excitement, there was very little work done in Engineering the rest of the day." After Joyce won the National Book Award, Mrs. Woodside reported humorously that her son had "a field day" at Harrison's. "Everybody came to shake his hand, to talk, and some came just to look at him." But halfway through this letter, Mrs. Woodside abruptly and matter-of-factly mentioned a recent hospitalization: "I have a malignant growth on the left breast, and under [my] arm. Surgery is not possible because of my heart condition. I am not in any pain yet, and feel pretty much as usual, tho of course this won't last." Then she continued narrating the usual family news.

The final group of letters Mrs. Woodside wrote to Joyce suggests a kind-hearted, courageous woman utterly lacking in self-pity. She discusses the imminent wedding of Joyce's brother, Fred Jr., and makes typical grandmotherly requests for more letters and a visit home; but she uses most of her space to praise Joyce's accomplishments, just as she'd done when Joyce was a little girl. Her final letter, on May 11, came after one of Joyce's visits, and focused on Joyce's health rather than her own: "I received the beautiful grandmother card yesterday. Thank you darling. It was also good to see you and Ray again, altho you are still too thin, your face is just as lovely as ever. Last summer you looked tired out." She then apologized if she had seemed "absent-minded" during Joyce's visit, blaming her fatigue on the hot weather, and anticipated that soon she "may not be able to get around so well." During the next few weeks, Mrs. Woodside's condition deteriorated steadily; she died on July 25.

During her grandmother's illness, Joyce's routine had become manageable again, since she and Ray had decided to pare back their social life. As she'd done the previous year, she agreed to teach summer school at Ann Arbor, which again involved intense, day-long sessions each Wednesday that were so tiring, she told Liz Graham, "I practically have to be carried home by poor Ray when it's all over." But the rest of the week was free for writing. As she had vowed, she was proceeding slowly on *Wonderland*. She'd written to Liz that she'd managed to write "the first one hundred pages without arriving at the story yet, which takes some doing." By mid-July, she told Bob Phillips that she was "beyond the 200-page mark, plodding sluggishly and hideously onward, onward. I really enjoy writing it, though." Since her hero, Jesse, would grow up to become a brain surgeon, she'd been doing research into the medical profession. One of her Detroit-area friends, Gloria Whelan, was married to a neurosurgeon, who loaned Joyce his professional journals. The world of doctors, she wrote, was "so different from our world of the academy, literature, ideas . . . there, everything is *real*, horribly real. I don't know if I could survive long in so physical an element." Becoming increasingly absorbed in Jesse's story, however, and perhaps using work to cope with her grandmother's death, Joyce had begun writing compulsively by the end of July, abandoning her resolve to proceed "slowly." She later recalled "all the excitement and dread and exhaustion" of those long days of summer 1970 when, as her narrative momentum increased and she was producing from fifteen up to forty pages each day, she brought the long manuscript to completion. By August 28, she was writing to Phillips that "I've been working on my novel almost constantly and have finished it, about 600 pages." She described the experience to an interviewer: "It was just like a hallucination. I just felt that this was coming from somewhere, and I really should write it. And I felt as though I were in a daze and I would hardly know where I was. I'd look up and wonder what time it was—it was very exciting."

Wonderland had been the most intense and absorbing experience of her writing life: "Much of this novel was written in a great fever, hour after hour, so that I was almost in a daze and had to be brought back to reality by going out for a walk or a game of tennis with Ray," she wrote. "I'm afraid it could be rather easy to stay in that other world." Though Joyce had enjoyed working on the novel, she later told an interviewer that "while writing *Wonderland* I found it difficult to keep up the barriers, to keep myself going as Joyce Smith, a professor of English, a wife, a woman, with certain friends, certain duties." The novel had involved meditating on the human brain, she added, which had led "again and again to the most despairing, unanswerable questions." Another problem was the novel's near-exclusive focus on its hero, Jesse; citing the difficulty of this approach, she predicted that *Wonderland* "might be my last novel, at least my last large, ambitious novel, where I try to re-create a man's soul, absorb myself into his consciousness, and coexist with him." Jesse's story also affected Joyce psychologically because it departed from the pattern of her previous novels: "It's the first novel I have written that doesn't end in violence, that doesn't liberate the hero through violence," she said, "and therefore there is still a sickish, despairing, confusing atmosphere about it." This sense of incompleteness would haunt Joyce for more than a year, finally prompting her to revise the ending of *Wonderland* for the paperback edition.

Because the first draft had been written in such "a fever," Joyce now proceeded to a careful revision, "consciously re-thinking each scene, nearly each page," and cutting unnecessary exposition and dialogue. Whereas the retyping of her earlier novels had seemed pure drudgery, she had now begun to enjoy revising her work: "I don't think there's anything more pleasurable, in a mildly hedonistic way, than working out little annoying problems of construction and development," she observed. Since Vanguard planned that Joyce's next two books would be the collection of essays on tragedy and a volume of short fiction called *Love Stories* (later retitled *The Wheel of Love*), there was no hurry in sending the new novel: she spent the rest of 1970 on a slow, meticulous revision of the manuscript. In a September letter to Evelyn Shrifte, she described *Wonderland* as a work about "domestic and demonic love," a modest phrase that barely suggests the thematic range and the combination of realism and allegory Joyce had attempted in her most ambitious novel to date. Neither did it express Joyce's personal uneasiness with the dark philosophical brooding at the heart of *Wonderland*, which she later speculated was "probably an immoral novel." The phrase recalled her college teacher Donald Dike's recollection of Joyce worrying that her fiction might be perceived as "not nice," but it also suggested that in the face of her sprawling, "demonic" new novel, the author of what reviewers had often termed her "unflinching" fiction had herself begun to flinch. For years, Joyce's critics had accused her of creating narratives of contemporary Gothic horror that lacked moral coherence, and Joyce herself would soon see *Wonderland* as a pivotal work: "With *Wonderland* I came to the end of a phase of my life," she said, "though I didn't know it. I want to move toward a more articulate moral position, not just dramatizing nightmarish problems but trying to show possible ways of transcending them." In a lighter tone, Joyce remarked to Liz Graham that her Vanguard editors "told me excitedly that the novel just about makes them sick . . . which isn't exactly a compliment, but they seem to mean it to be."

Wonderland was conceived and written during a transformative period in Joyce's literary development: maturing as both a woman and a writer, and aware of her growing audience and influence, she longed to communicate to her readers the balance she had achieved in her own personal outlook. It was possible to acknowledge the horrors of contemporary life while maintaining high standards of ethical conduct and anticipating the likely development of an American culture she viewed as unformed and immature. Partly because of her strong identification with her protagonist as he struggles with his own transformations, *Wonderland* was her strangest, most haunting novel, and for some critics it remains her finest achievement. Juxtaposing the realistic and the grotesque, presenting the physical, psychological, and spiritual transformations of its protagonist with unblinking thoroughness, and written with a feverish intensity that no other Oates novel can quite match, *Wonderland* goes to the heart of those basic philosophical riddles that haunt all her fiction: How can the self be defined in relation to a shifting, unreliable phenomenal and social reality? What is human "personality"? (Joyce dedicated the novel "to those of us who pursue the phantasmagoria of personality.") Are our personalities defined by our brains, and what is the distinction between the brain and the "mind"? Are we tragically limited by our physical selves, especially our brain chemistry, or are we capable of transcending this fate, escaping our entrapment in a universe of flux and in bodies that must inevitably die?

Spanning the years 1939 to 1971, *Wonderland* tells the harrowing story of Jesse Harte, a boy of working-class background (again Joyce used the upstate New York countryside of her childhood) who eventually becomes a celebrated brain surgeon, his ambition fueled by the need to exert control over his own destiny, his "fate." After his father massacres the family and commits suicide, Jesse seeks a series of alternate fathers: the first and most memorable, Dr. Pedersen, is an obese and diabolically controlling "diagnostician" who presides over a helpless alcoholic wife and two gifted but miserable children, all three as grotesquely fat as Pedersen himself. Representing patriarchal greed and tyranny raised to a level of grotesque insanity, Pedersen adopts Jesse in the hope of casting the boy in his own image. Again Jesse escapes a potentially murderous father, and as a young medical student replaces Pedersen with Dr. Perrault, a brilliant but coldly pragmatic brain surgeon who pursues knowledge through pure science and views human personality as an unstable "illusion." But as Jesse attempts to define himself through other relationships—a companionable but passionless marriage; a friendship with another young doctor, "Trick" Monk, who mocks Jesse's seriousness; an obsessive extramarital affair that forces Jesse to confront his own repressed passions—he perceives his reality as a shifting "wonderland" that will not yield to his longing for stability and control. In the climactic scenes of the novel, Jesse's agonized search for his runaway teenage daughter, Shelley, who has become lost in the psychedelic American wonderland of the late 1960s and early 1970s, becomes his personal struggle against the forces of darkness and chaos that have threatened all his life to destroy him.

As Joyce had done in *them*, she sought in her new novel to portray more than three decades of American experience. But apart from its grounding in realism, *Wonderland* marked an ambitious combination of other techniques, for the novel employs imagery and allusion that powerfully convey an irrational, dreamlike reality counterpointing Jesse's own pragmatism and his longing to conduct his life according to the dictates of reason. Allusions to Joyce's favorite childhood book, Lewis Carroll's *Alice in Wonderland*, pervade the novel, as when Jesse becomes obese while growing up with the Pedersens, then returns to normal size when he escapes them; Alice had likewise undergone changes in physical size when plunged into an irrational environment. Further, as the critic Gordon Taylor has astutely noted, the novel's structure replicates its central symbol of the human brain, creating "inwardly tightening circles of mental experiences" and moving toward "a terminus in Jesse's baffled brain." The novel's brilliant fusing of realistic and fantastic modes, combined with its wholly convincing portrayal of its male protagonist, brought Joyce's fictional art to a distinguished new level of achievement.

As she worked at revising *Wonderland* during the fall of 1970, Joyce returned to her pleasant routine of teaching and working at shorter projects. At the university, she told Liz Graham, she had "a fairly hectic three-day schedule" of teaching; and because the story satirizing her colleague Phil London had just appeared in *Playboy*, she joked that she'd "been hiding around corners at school." Her courses that term were especially enjoyable: a graduate seminar in creative writing and an ambitious course of her own devising entitled "Natural and Unnatural Man," the syllabus ranging from Thoreau, Emerson, and Freud to several of her favorite modern novelists, Lawrence, Faulkner, Kafka, and Camus. She also prepared for the October publication of *The Wheel of Love* (her book of essays had been delayed), and worked at a new group of stories that attempted to reimagine several classics of the genre. She had already completed "The Dead" and "The Lady with the Pet Dog," in homage to Joyce and Chekhov (though giving both stories contemporary settings and adopting the female characters' viewpoint), and was now attempting to rework James's "The Turn of the Screw." "It's a lot of fun to reimagine these famous old stories," she told Liz Graham. "There is no question of anyone writing stories as good as those, so in a way one is free to try almost anything."

Joyce's new collection of stories fared well with reviewers. Since *Upon the Sweeping Flood* appeared in 1966, Joyce had written more than seventy new stories, enabling her to include only her very best work in the new volume. At 440 pages and containing twenty stories, *The Wheel of Love* was almost as long as her first two collections put together, and Joyce's advance in technique and storytelling power was immediately apparent. Many of the stories had won national prizes and would remain among her most-anthologized titles: "In the Region of Ice," "Where Are You Going, Where Have You Been?," "Accomplished Desires," and "How I Contemplated the World from the Detroit House of Correction and Began My Life Over Again." In *Library Journal*, John Alfred Avant called the book "one of the finest collections of short fiction ever written by an American," adding that "one must really call Joyce Carol Oates, at the outrageous age of 32, a great writer." The best stories, wrote Richard Gilman in the *The New York Times Book Review*, "create a verbal excitement, a sense of language used not for the expression of previously attained insights or perceptions but for new imaginative reality," and Daniel Stern in the *Washington Post Book World* cited the volume as "powerful proof of her stature" as "a first-rate short story writer." As usual, there were a few grudging responses. In a hostile review entitled "A Time for Silence," Pearl K. Bell insisted that Oates "seemed in therapeutic need of a spell of silence" and that reading *The Wheel of Love*, Bell "felt as though I were the captive audience of an intelligent and articulate but dementedly garrulous woman." But even Bell acknowledged that "Oates can make superb use of her incontestably fecund talent."

Once again, Joyce had run the gauntlet of reviews and come away relatively unscathed. As the fall semester ended, Joyce and Ray were planning a Christmas vacation to Key West and anticipating a long tour of Europe the following summer, to make up for the trip they'd been forced to cancel during Blanche Woodside's illness. "Ray hopes to take his sabbatical next year," Joyce told Liz Graham, "and I have applied for a leave of absence, so we tentatively plan on spending two or three months in London." Later they would decide to extend their London stay to an entire year, largely as a means of escaping the constant demands on Joyce's time.

For now, Joyce relaxed by rereading the novels of Charles Dickens, and in mid-December she and Ray left for Florida. "How Ray and I managed to get to the farthest Southern tip of the U.S., I don't know," she wrote to Bob Phillips, "but we're delighted to be here." She told Liz Graham that the trip was "quite an adventure for us," and that she admired "the sane, sensible, fortunate people" who lived there. They visited Hemingway's Key West house and enjoyed the miles of deserted white beaches, the palm trees, the sandpipers and pelicans. The word "*vacation*," however, always held a different meaning for Joyce than for other people. She had brought the manuscript of *Wonderland* with her to Florida, she admitted, and she continued her painstaking revisions of the novel. They might be on vacation, she told Phillips, but "I have my typewriter to occupy me most evenings."

9

Transformation of Being: Hollywood and London, 1971–72

We really love London—I can't express my feelings too strongly. It is all that New York City and Los Angeles should be. . . .
—letter to Kay Smith, October 1, 1971

By 1971, Joyce often felt that her life was slipping out of her control. Literary fame had brought financial and personal rewards, but it had also fostered a daily barrage of phone calls, letters to answer, requests for interviews and publicity quotes for other writers' books, and countless other claims on her time and energy. Most troubling of all were the clamorous demands of social acquaintances who were not really friends. She complained to Bob Phillips that she felt "besieged by responsibilities. I am going to have to cut back on my commitments and my relationships with people (some of whom I don't even know personally); I am getting into a maze of problems." To Liz Graham, she remarked that she felt "at a loss to understand why so many people have taken it in their heads suddenly to bother me. . . . If I didn't have Ray, I think I would just disintegrate, or perhaps run away." She added that the stress had begun causing "vague unnamed unnameable terrors that are probably the heralds of a total breakdown."

Through a combination of discipline, concentration, and a strict avoidance of the distractions that plague most writers, Joyce had managed for years to juggle her two full-time careers as an author and university professor; but in the past she had enjoyed a degree of anonymity (on campus, she was still known as "Mrs. Smith") that had shielded her from public scrutiny. Temperamentally reserved, she felt increasingly victimized as a variety of individuals—some of them well meaning, others openly hostile—made Joyce the focus of their intense, obsessive interest. She had begun receiving anony-mous, vaguely threatening letters, presumably from strangers. Even more troubling were the constant demands of supposedly friendly acquaintances: "Social life, whatever it is, has become a kind of monster in my life," she wrote to Liz Graham in early March. "I can't handle it, can't handle the com-pulsive need some people have to intrude upon my life, to be possessive and even jealous." One woman in particular, an overbearing artist with whom Joyce had become friendly, had developed an unwanted maternal interest in Joyce, phoning her constantly, letting the phone ring up to fifty times if she didn't answer. Joyce told Kay Smith that the woman's "excessive concern, her interest in what I am doing, how I feel (whether I am sleeping well enough—eating well enough—dressing warmly enough!) is almost driving me mad." Feeling debilitated by all the attention focused on her, both from the media and from her countless acquaintances, Joyce wrote to Liz that she'd decided life in Windsor "is spiritually exhausting and depressing . . . it isn't quite worth it." Soon enough, the notion of "running away" seemed not only desir-able but practicable. Ray was scheduled to take his sabbatical during the next academic year, so Joyce applied for an unpaid leave of absence: they would escape North America and spend two or three months in London, where they knew virtually no one. Before long, they had decided to stay away for an en-tire year.

Though they wouldn't leave until August, the certainty of a coming re-prieve helped Joyce to cope with the remaining months in Windsor. Even so, she confessed to Liz that "there are times when I'm afraid I am really going to have a nervous breakdown." Only a few years before, this relatively quiet Canadian university had seemed a sanctuary from the turbulence of Detroit, but her new job had brought its own problems. Joyce now found herself in-creasingly isolated among her colleagues. In the wake of the controversy over Phil London, her relations with Lois Smedick remained distant, and now that Joyce's literary reputation overshadowed that of her longtime friend and colleague John Ditsky, she found that Ditsky had become "self-conscious and abrasive"; she now considered him an "ex-friend." (Before Joyce left for En-gland, she and Ditsky patched up the friendship.) Though Joyce had always enjoyed teaching, even students had become a source of stress. After she taught summer school at Michigan, a graduate student took a fifty-mile taxi ride to Joyce's house in Windsor, demanding to talk with her. Later that year, safely in London, she was able to joke about the situation, recalling that even her Windsor students "had taken to coming out to visit me, unannounced. Ray would have to pull me out by the ankles from under the bed, saying in his gentle, urgent voice, 'There's a student to see you. . . .' " But in early 1971 the stress was real, and painful. Even the weather wasn't cooperating: this was "the most miserable winter we've endured yet," Joyce told Bob Phillips. "Ray and I stare out our back window toward the river, which isn't visible any longer, and wonder what on earth we are doing here."

To some extent, Joyce had contributed to her own discomfort in the English department by continuing to write satires about her colleagues and publish them in such high-profile magazines as *Playboy*. Having weathered the displeasure of Lois Smedick and others over the "Saul Bird" story, Joyce had placed another manuscript with *Playboy* that featured a portrait of the only black member of the English department, Ed Watson; some of her colleagues read the story in manuscript. "The Loves of Franklin Ambrose" (later retitled "Up from Slavery") was extremely unflattering to Watson and to the department generally, but Joyce insisted that it "really happened." She added, "People are mad at me [. . .] & I won't even let Ray read the story. Oh dear. But if I had it to do again I'd do it again, of course." Joyce was relieved that the story would not appear until after she and Ray left for England.

Joyce's isolation and feelings of entrapment by her own career surfaced in many of her letters during that winter and spring, and are also evident in some of the writing she was doing, notably her story "The Dead"—her reimagining of James Joyce's classic work—with its account of a woman writer's psychological disintegration. Although Joyce, happily married, didn't have the physical aloneness of her character Ilena, she did have some of her loneliness. Joyce's closest male and female friends of the late 1960s, Dan Brown and Liz Graham, had now left the Detroit area, and her letters to both suggested how keenly she missed the pleasures of genuine friendship. Confessing to Liz on February 8 that both she and Ray were "tired of Windsor," Joyce closed her letter on a plaintive note: "*please* write sometime soon, even if just a postcard. You are very real to me whether you write or not, however."

Joyce's letters to Dan Brown similarly expressed the importance she placed on friendship. She told Dan that after Ray and her family, Dan was one of the few people she considered important. She hoped their friendship could continue with the same degree of openness and enjoyment, and she expressed regret that he lived so far away. Joyce did not yet know that her friendships with both Liz and Dan were essentially finished. Liz's letters would gradually become less frequent, then cease altogether; when Liz and her husband returned to Birmingham the following year, she and Joyce seldom saw each other. Joyce's friendship with Dan would soon suffer a much more abrupt and painful collapse. Joyce was also hurt by the loss of her closest college friend, Dottie Palmer, who had simply stopped answering Joyce's letters, without explanation. Several years later, Joyce would come to a philosophical acceptance of such losses: "I tried to keep up the relationships," she remarked, "but distance and radically different lives made it quixotic, at best." She acknowledged that "friendship is a mystery as baffling as love" and that even the closest friendships can "reverse themselves, and what was warm and intimate becomes bewilderingly hostile. I am inclined to accept the biblical wisdom about matters of the psyche—the spirit moves as it will, and no one can consciously direct it."

Although she continued to see Kay Smith, who remained a warm and sustaining force in her life, Joyce had increasingly turned to letters as a way of maintaining her friendships, even with people who still lived in the Detroit area such as Kay, Patty Burnett, and Gloria Whelan. When possible, Joyce drove over to Detroit to meet these women friends for lunch, but her hectic life in Windsor made such get-togethers increasingly difficult to arrange. In any case, Joyce at times preferred letters to personal visits: "writing letters is sometimes more interesting than talking," she had observed, "at least it stimulates different areas of the mind." Her long letters, chatty and frequently humorous, showed the open, relaxed, gregarious, and sometimes mischievous side of Joyce's personality, which she did not reveal to people until she knew them well. They also functioned as a release of leftover energy after she had finished her serious writing for the day.

One of Joyce's most enjoyable friendships of these years was conducted entirely through the mail; in late 1969, she'd received a fan letter from a writer, Gail Godwin, who had just begun to publish her own fiction. Then working on her doctorate at the University of Iowa, Godwin told Joyce that she'd been composing letters to Joyce Carol Oates in her head for several years. Joyce responded promptly, noting that "it does seem that we have much in common." The two women's lively, warm correspondence would continue for many years. When Godwin's first novel, *The Perfectionists*, appeared in 1970, Joyce reviewed it enthusiastically for *The New York Times Book Review*, and Godwin responded in kind with a lengthy appreciation of *Wonderland* in the prominent literary magazine *North American Review*. Within just a few months, the tone of the correspondence grew humorous and confiding: Joyce and Gail discussed new books, swapped manuscripts, talked shop, and traded gossip about New York magazine editors and other writers. Joyce later remarked that Gail's "literary likes and dislikes, as well as her general 'style' of interpreting life, are remarkably similar to my own. At the same time, she is totally original and sees things I don't see."

Though Gail was a year older than Joyce, she clearly viewed Joyce as a kind of mentor and literary idol, and Joyce issued warnings to her not-yet-famous friend about the perils of literary celebrity. When Gail mentioned a feature story on Joyce that had appeared in *Vogue*, Joyce sent a lengthy anecdote whose jocular tone, typical of her letters to Gail, barely concealed the anxiety her celebrity had brought:

When I get into New York I always have to see someone for lunch, someone after lunch, someone in the late afternoon, someone for dinner, someone after dinner, someone squeezed in somewhere else, it's just terrible. I don't look like my picture in *Vogue* or like any of those pictures [. . .], which seem to show a rather weird person, whom I wouldn't like. I was having breakfast at the Plaza with my agent, my husband, some producer/director and as usual in NY I began to have violent stomach aches, apocalyptic seizures, but all carried out in a feminine gentle way. [. . .] Then it got to be time for my appointment with the *Vogue* photographer. They sent a limousine with a chauffeur in livery, who came in to find me, and rising ghastly and pathetically serious I excused myself for a minute, dashed to the elegant Plaza ladies' room, tried to be sick or something, while out in the plush corridor my husband waited nervously and down a few yards from him my agent wrung her hands. The pains did not subside, but I became more stoical and hearty, so I ventured out again. [. . .] I was whisked at five miles an hour through Manhattan traffic down to Greenwich Village, helped out of the limousine (by my husband, I think), where a very gentle, kindly, understanding photographer took my photograph, not showing any of the violent stomach seizures, the earthshaking spasms of pain a lady just naturally doesn't complain about, etc. That's how you end up in *Vogue* looking weird!

The incident had clearly troubled Joyce: she detailed it again in another letter to Godwin about eighteen months later. Noting that she routinely coped with a psychologically stressing experience by writing a story about someone having a similar experience, she remarked that the *Vogue* incident resulted in her story "Plot," which she described as "an attempt to record second by second the experience I thought I was having of going crazy."

The tongue-in-cheek references in the earlier letter to "feminine gentle" behavior and remaining "a lady" pointed to another cause of stress. Unlike Norman Mailer or Truman Capote, who frequently "acted out" in public, Joyce knew the kind of behavior that was expected of her as a woman (and that was in fact dictated by her own natural reserve). While her writing was always a positive outlet, much of her stress was driven inward, causing such alarming physical symptoms as relentless insomnia and sudden, eerie sensations in her head that made her fear that she suffered a tumor or some other brain dysfunction. Finally Joyce consulted a neurologist, she told Gail, and endured "a series of awful tests at a hospital." She was told that her brain showed signs of a hormonal imbalance, a potentially dangerous condition that could cause a deterioration of thinking processes. Fortunately, her hormone levels soon returned to normal, and having nervously consulted books and neurological journals about her condition and about the brain generally, she incorporated the material into her "novel about brains," *Wonderland*, and described her fear of psychological breakdown in "Plot." Since the story focused on a young, drug-addicted man, she recalled to Gail that she'd felt "immensely clever that while people read the story, if they ever did, they would *think* the hero's symptoms were all fiction, but in fact they were *real*." When she came across the story in *Paris Review*, she thought to herself, "My God!—was that me, I?—and did I get through it, did I triumph over it? Yes, indeed."

In "The Dead," a more recognizably autobiographical story, Joyce described Ilena Williams as an alter ego, "a way I could have gone. Sometimes a crossroad appears and one can go one direction or the other. Sometimes just writing a story about it, mapping out these directions, saves one from doing it." Like Joyce, Ilena is an English professor and a critically acclaimed novelist whose life has veered out of control. Joyce told Gail that "The Dead" had "some authentic details and some invented ones, but the general tone is sincere enough." But unlike Joyce, Ilena copes with her stress through frantic love affairs and drug addiction, which lead finally to a lethal overdose. In her journal, Joyce later recollected that one of the doctors she consulted about her stress and insomnia had prescribed barbiturates: "Enormous dosage, so powerful I could barely wake for hours the following day." She had taken the pills for several months, but one day she simply threw them into the toilet, deciding that the doctor was "really a criminal" and that such drugs were dangerous. "If drugs or alcohol damage sleep, thereby damaging dreams," she wrote, "they guide the helpless individual toward death—toward his own suicide"—exactly the fate of Ilena Williams. After discarding the pills, Joyce sensed her own "instinct for survival—tremendous relief afterward, feeling I had escaped something dangerous." In "The Dead," as in "Plot," she had dealt with her psychological difficulties more directly and therapeutically, overcoming them by writing about them.

Never again would Joyce succumb to the temptation of coping with her problems through drugs. In a brief essay published in *McCalls*, "The Fact Is: We Like to Be Drugged," Joyce did not discuss her own experiences but noted a remark by one of her students: life was so boring and difficult, he insisted, "that only artificial stimulants could make it worth living." Joyce acknowledged that "there is something terrible about consciousness; it is too much for us," but warned that America's drug-saturated society seemed "to be going out in a din of discordant voices, shrill demands for instant gratification." Joyce ended with a stern warning, though her readers could not have known that she had earned this wisdom through a bitterly difficult personal struggle: "It is suicide, this obliteration," she wrote. "This fear of intelligent, rational consciousness is suicide. If we can recognize this danger, will we cease to drug ourselves? Are we brave enough to take on consciousness fully, with lidless eyes?"

Now that *Wonderland* was at Vanguard and scheduled for October 1971 publication, Joyce stayed busy with shorter projects. "I've been writing stories and a few uninspired poems," she remarked to Bob Phillips in March. She and Ray had taken time out to attend an Irish Studies conference in Toronto, where they heard W. H. Auden read his poems, and they were busy planning a more extensive trip to the western United States, a region they wanted to explore thoroughly by car. They'd decided to leave as soon as the spring semester ended. The two-week trip would be a typically Oatesian "vacation": "We'll both be taking work along," she noted, "and one typewriter."

Among many other destinations, Joyce and Ray planned to visit Hollywood, since earlier that year Joyce had been asked to write an original movie script. Initially begun at the suggestion of Frank Corsaro, this screenplay, entitled *Dawn*, had been purchased by Paul Newman's production company as a possible vehicle for Joanne Woodward. With her usual zest, Joyce had plunged into the project by first composing a 110-page novella to prepare herself, then writing two drafts of a screenplay based on her fictional treatment. The script told the story of an interracial relationship: Dawn Steigner, a divorced woman who quits her job at a Los Angeles welfare office, disgusted by the racism and petty bureaucratic tyrannies of her superiors, becomes romantically involved with one of her former clients. (Sidney Poitier had been slated to play opposite Woodward.) Though Joyce felt somewhat hesitant at first, she soon found it "very exciting to work in a new medium." While writing the script, Joyce had several telephone conversations with Paul Newman, but confessed that "we generally can't think of much to say to each other."

Another notable encounter had occurred around this time between Joyce and the prominent critic Alfred Kazin, who had journeyed to Windsor for a lengthy interview with Joyce for *Harper's* magazine. Though Joyce seldom granted interviews, she knew that Kazin was a serious critic, not merely a journalist out to exploit her. But Joyce's and her interviewer's accounts of their visit varied widely; Joyce was unaware of the effect her quiet, reserved demeanor had on Kazin, who seemed to expect that any celebrated writer must necessarily be a vivid, larger-than-life "personality." After the visit, Joyce told Bob Phillips enthusiastically that "Kazin is very gentlemanly, very soft-spoken and pleasant. It wasn't an interview so much as a four-hour conversation that rarely faltered. He is, of course, an intimate friend of such people as

Saul Bellow, and has many fascinating anecdotes about them." But when Kazin's interview was published, a somewhat chastened Joyce reported to Gail Godwin that "I liked him immensely, but I don't think he liked *me*." In fact, Kazin reported that Joyce was "shy, doesn't drink or smoke, has no small talk, no jokes, no anecdotes, no gossip, no malice, no verbal embroidery of the slightest kind, and is as solemn as a graduate student taking an oral examination." He added that she seemed to have "no ego, no sense that Joyce Carol Oates is important." Though Kazin had come to Windsor "seeking out a young woman who will not be sought out," he did like Joyce once he adjusted to what he viewed as her "unbelievable 'old-fashionedness.' " He described her as "a square, a lovely schoolmarm," and noted perceptively that "her life is in her head": "My deepest feeling about her is that her mind is unbelievably crowded with psychic existences, with such a mass of stories that she lives by being wholly submissive to 'them,' the others." Yet Kazin ended his piece by asserting that Joyce's writing was "not artistically ambitious enough."

The incident revealed an ingrained characteristic of Joyce's social personality: to people she didn't know well, she often appeared rigid and aloof, even though she didn't intend any rudeness and wasn't necessarily conscious of the impression she gave. Friends from different periods in her life all remarked on her visible distress during social encounters that Joyce herself would insist she had enjoyed. This disparity related in part to Joyce's characteristic lack of interest in food and drink, and to her concern with wasting time. Kazin complained that Joyce had not offered him even a glass of water during a four-hour visit, and according to Joyce he was offended when she refused his invitation to lunch. (She had a story to write, she told him.) Part of what Kazin interpreted as excessive humility simply related to Joyce's habit of deference to older literary men; Kazin was roughly the same age as Joyce's former professors at Syracuse. (He had described her as "absurdly respectful to the middle-aged critic who is trying to draw her out.") Yet Kazin's widely read article in *Harper's* was influential in confirming the standard view of Joyce Carol Oates as forbidding and unapproachable.

In the ensuing years, both writer and critic would remain wary of the other. Soon after Kazin's interview appeared, Joyce published a long story entitled "The Sacred Marriage," which she dedicated to Kazin. Recalling Henry James's "The Aspern Papers," Joyce's story described a critic's visit to the home of a famous poet's attractive widow; he works with the poet's papers during the day and conducts a passionate affair with the widow at night. "What a creative transformation of that rather stilted and barren Sunday morning visit!" Kazin later remarked. For her part, Joyce always insisted that she had been friendlier and more hospitable than Kazin remembered.

Not surprisingly, Joyce was happy when the spring semester ended and she could leave behind her unpredictable colleagues, demanding students, bewildered interviewers, and "monstrous" social life for a peaceful driving vacation with Ray. Though they had recently bought a Mercedes, they were now leery of foreign cars and took their Pontiac on this long, meandering trip out west; it would total more than eight thousand miles. (Contemplating her wanderings through the country, Joyce wrote to Gail Godwin that she felt "like a character in a youth movie or a 1950s novel.") She and Ray left Windsor on April 22 and by the end of the month had reached Colorado, where they were awed by the spectacular terrain: "my head is filled with contrasts and visions—almost more than can be absorbed," she wrote to Gloria Whelan. "The Rockies turned out to be even more magnificent than I had hoped." To Dan Brown, she exclaimed that her vision was seared by the extraordinary sights America had to offer. She and Ray visited the D. H. Lawrence shrine at Taos, New Mexico, then made their leisurely way through Arizona and southern California. Arriving in Palm Springs, where they stayed for a week, they made several drives out into the Mojave Desert, which looked spectacular in the clear spring air. Then they drove to Los Angeles, where Ray did research at the famed Huntington Library and Joyce, with some trepidation, began a series of meetings with the movie people involved with her screenplay.

On the whole, Joyce was pleasantly surprised by her Hollywood experience. Though she had shied away from meeting Paul Newman, who was filming on location in Tucson when Joyce and Ray drove through, they had dinner twice with Joanne Woodward and the director Martin Ritt. Woodward also gave a small party for Joyce at her Beverly Hills home. Joyce had warmed immediately to the actress, telling Kay Smith that she was "very nice, doesn't seem at all self-conscious and glamorous; in fact, most of her conversation is about her children (5 daughters and 1 son!)." Newman and Woodward's home, she reported, was "large and sunnily decorated," filled with a variety of pets, and entirely unpretentious. Joyce also spent time consulting with Ritt about revisions of the screenplay; she liked the director as well, finding him sensitive and hard-working.

The only unpleasant part of Joyce's Los Angeles stay was her meeting with her Hollywood agent. The legendary H. N. Swanson had represented the movie work of such luminaries as F. Scott Fitzgerald, William Faulkner, and John O'Hara. Swanson took Joyce and Ray for an obligatory lunch at the Brown Derby, but she found the agent "a blustering, mercenary man," almost a caricature of the stereotypically aggressive Hollywood deal maker. "Mr. Swanson is the number one Hollywood agent," Joyce told Kay, "but I hope never to meet him again personally!" However, Joyce did get another taste of the financial rewards Hollywood can offer, earning more for her brief screenplay than the combined advances for all her books thus far: in addition to an initial payment of $17,500, Joyce received a "salary" of $5,000 daily for working with Ritt on revisions. She finished a new draft of the screenplay on May 17, but ultimately Newman's company decided against filming *Dawn*. In the early 1970s, a major film about an interracial love affair was deemed "too controversial," especially since the script featured a climactic scene of trademark Oatesian violence when Dawn's black lover beats and rapes her.

Leaving Hollywood, Joyce and Ray slowly made the beautiful drive up the coast toward San Francisco. They toured the Hearst Castle in San Simeon, and stopped every hour or two along the coast near Carmel and Big Sur. "Ray and I had never seen such beautiful countryside," she wrote to Kay. "The Pacific Ocean—the rocks and mountains—the millions of wildflowers—the perfect weather—we just can't believe our good luck." After a visit to San Francisco, where Joyce noted the city's "intensity and rather aggressive people," they drove northward through the California redwood forests, a region Joyce found particularly serene and peaceful. They proceeded into Oregon and visited Victoria, British Columbia, then began the trip homeward, stopping at Yellowstone Park. They drove the last 1,200 miles in two days, encountering a snowstorm in Wyoming: "I drove 50 desperate miles behind a snowplow," Joyce wrote to Phillips. Though she felt "shellshocked from night driving in snow, wind, rain, small floods, glaring lights of 50-ton trucks, Big Boy hamburger signs, depressing air of Chicago and Detroit, etc.," she acknowledged that the trip as a whole had been wonderful. Now, she said, "Ray and I realize how truly amazing this country is. The 'country' isn't Nixon, or Agnew, or Abbie Hoffman, or Norman Mailer. It's just *there* and it's unbeatable."

Back in Windsor, there was a huge backlog of mail, along with several literary projects Joyce wanted to complete before she and Ray left for London. By the end of July, she was writing to Liz Graham that "things seem to get more hectic every day." There would be family visits before their ship departed in late August: Joyce's parents came for a few days, and shortly afterward Ray's mother and brother came out from Milwaukee. Joyce was spending most of the summer preparing three book manuscripts, two of which were scheduled for 1972: a new collection of stories, *Marriages and Infidelities*, and an anthology of contemporary short fiction she was editing for Random House. The third manuscript, a volume of poems called *Angel Fire*, would not appear until 1973, but with *Wonderland* coming out in October, soon to be followed by the long-delayed collection of essays *The Edge of Impossibility* in spring 1972, Joyce's reputation as a prolific writer would soon escalate dramatically. She acknowledged to Liz that her publishing schedule "sounds like inflation, indeed," and that Vanguard's annual list could not accommodate all the manuscripts Joyce had been producing. For her more experimental, less commercial work Joyce would soon begin working with a third publisher, Black Sparrow, a small literary press best known for publishing acclaimed poets such as Charles Bukowski and Diane Wakoski.

For the time being, Joyce was satisfied to be published by Vanguard. She thanked Evelyn Shrifte for her new contract, whose terms—an advance of $12,500 for *Wonderland* and an additional novel—she called "very generous. Ray and I both appreciate all that you have done for me, now and in the past." Joyce's National Book Award and her increased fame had helped boost her sales: *The Wheel of Love* had sold more than thirteen thousand copies in hardcover, a surprising number for a volume of stories, and Fawcett had agreed to bring out all three of her collections in paperback. For the year 1970, she had paid $60,000 in income taxes. She told Dan Brown that she considered the figure unreal, adding that the money did not really affect her personal life. But Joyce's success had brought her increased clout with her publisher: as Evelyn had done with *A Garden of Earthly Delights*, she asked Joyce to shorten the manuscript of *Wonderland*, but this time Joyce refused. Once a book was finished, Joyce was still disinclined to make any changes. When Gail Godwin mentioned that she was revising the manuscript of a novel, Joyce responded: "I don't make many revisions at all (in fact none for any book) . . . so can't give advice."

Joyce was exaggerating a little, since in fact she'd recently done some fairly extensive revisions of *Wonderland*, but at this point in her career Joyce helped to foster her image as an inspired "Cassandra" (as Alfred Kazin had called her) rather than the meticulous craftsman she actually was. That summer, in an interview by mail with Joe David Bellamy, Joyce remarked that on some days she had written forty or fifty pages on both *Expensive People* and *Wonderland*, and that for the latter novel she had worked "in a kind of trance, elated and exhausted, for many hours at a time. I wasn't creating a story but simply recording it, remembering it." (In 1976, rereading the Bellamy interview, she admitted she had employed a "persona" and allowed herself some "leg-pulling" replies to Bellamy's questions: "Even as I typed out those responses I must not have meant them, not even in a hypothetical way. I invented a persona that would seem impressionistic, uncalculating, naive, 'inspired'.") Critics would soon use such remarks against Joyce, portraying her not as an inspired genius but as a shoddy craftsman. By claiming in several prominent, early interviews that she seldom revised her work, she had unknowingly done considerable damage to her reputation. It would take many years for Joyce to correct the perception that she was a careless writer. By the 1980s, her work habits had changed dramatically and she began to discuss openly her laborious process of revision. (When the Bellamy interview, first published in 1972, was reprinted in *Conversations with Joyce Carol Oates* in 1987, Joyce deleted her remark about writing "forty or fifty pages a day" and added a new sentence: "Then, of course, there is revision.") But in 1971, with her National Book Award and countless short-story prizes in hand, a critical backlash was already brewing. By the mid-1970s, she would suffer acutely from that peculiar phenomenon of the American publicity machine: its eagerness to create "stars" and then, at a certain point, begin attacking them.

Even before Joyce and Ray left for England, however, there were indications that *Wonderland* would not receive the critical acclaim *them* had enjoyed. Prepublication reviews were mixed, admiring of Joyce's ambition but also put off by the dark themes in her new effort. Even so, two major book clubs, including the Literary Guild, had purchased the novel, and Vanguard had pledged $25,000 for a major advertising campaign. Joyce's own energies were focused on completing and mailing off her three new manuscripts, and preparing for her and Ray's imminent departure (most of the work fell to her, since Ray had recently been hospitalized for minor surgery).

Joyce and Ray left on August 27, boarding the steamship *The Empress of Canada* for the six-day crossing. Joyce felt an immediate relief to be out of the country: "I am so spiritually exhausted [. . .] by all the abuse and acclaim that I would like to arrange a funeral for 'Joyce Carol Oates' and escape with the bit of protoplasm I have, in what's left of this body I somehow got born into, to some foreign place," she wrote to Gail Godwin. London provided exactly the haven she sought. After waiting four hours on the Liverpool dock for their Mercedes to be unloaded, Joyce and Ray began a leisurely two-week tour of the British Isles, staying in bed-and-breakfasts along the way. At each stop, Joyce reported to Kay Smith, they were treated warmly by their landladies, and by avoiding hotels they'd "gotten to know, however haphazardly, the way life is lived in quite ordinary homes in Great Britain." They visited Scotland, Ireland, North Wales, and the Highlands. Joyce particularly loved the Highlands, which were "eerie, uncanny," she told Kay. "They are very *close* as you drive along, unlike the mountains of the West. Everything is accessible, yet aloof and inhuman." Though Joyce was dismayed to find much of Ireland "shabby and dirty," they explored the country thoroughly, visiting Dublin, Cork, Limerick, Galway, and Kilarney. Joyce told Gloria Whelan that they'd spent "an extraordinary hour" at Yeats's tower in Thoor Ballylee, near Galway: "Absolutely lovely—in beautiful, isolated Irish hills, with a stream nearby—and throwing light vividly upon so much of Yeats' poetry, which takes its symbolism largely from Ireland. I reread all of Yeats' poetry immediately afterward." Not surprisingly, much of their trip was a literary pilgrimage:

they'd been "very moved" by their visit to St. Patrick's Cathedral, the burial place of Jonathan Swift.

Joyce and Ray had spent most of September exploring Great Britain, but were now eager to get settled. After several weeks, the stresses of travel—"glorious moments," she told a friend, alternating with "moments of sheer depression and demoralization"—had begun to fray Joyce's nerves. They had hoped to rent a country place, in Surrey, but the plumbing and heating in all the houses they inspected were primitive, the interiors cold and stark, so they decided abruptly to take a London flat instead. "We realized that central London would be ideal," she wrote to Kay, "so in about a day we located the flat we are now in." Their new home, on Dunraven Street in Mayfair, overlooked Hyde Park and featured a balcony running the length of their living room; in the evening, they could draw their chairs up to the French windows and "gaze out dreamily at Hyde Park and the traffic going by down below. Of course, we do have books in our laps now and then."

The flat reminded Joyce of her editor Evelyn Shrifte's apartment overlooking Central Park. The neighborhood, only a few blocks from the American Embassy, was lined with attractive town houses and small shops. After long days of writing and reading, she and Ray took lengthy walks. (They avoided using their car, having discovered that London traffic was worse than Detroit's.) They also went often to plays and movies, a luxury they seldom allowed themselves back home, and even rented a television set, though they didn't own a set in Windsor. Joyce found that television in England was actually worth watching. Though she did meet with her English agent, Murray Pollinger, and her publisher, Livia Gollancz, she was determined to avoid the superficial kind of socializing she had found so stressful in Windsor. By September 30, happily settled in the Mayfair flat, she wrote exuberantly to Bob Phillips: "How great it is to be in London! It's a truly magnificent city. From this distance, Windsor looks trivial and inconsequential indeed." To Gail Godwin she wrote: "Thank God . . . for the anonymity here! Back in Windsor/Detroit my life was a circus." She added that it was "a vast relief to be here where no one can get me . . . because we don't answer the telephone."

Joyce's distance from the United States also made the impending publication of *Wonderland* easier to contemplate, though she confessed to feeling "edgy, as always, about reviews of my novel." Having won the National Book Award for her previous book, she knew that *Wonderland* would be reviewed widely. In early October the barrage of notices began, and they were decidedly mixed. Some critics noted a distinct advance in both her technique and ambition, but others were repelled by the physical violence and psychological intensity of this long novel, viewing it as a mere catalog of horrors. The *Newsweek* reviewer felt that Joyce was beginning to repeat herself and had descended into melodrama. Most damaging was Geoffrey Wolff's all-out assault in *The New York Times Book Review*. Complaining that "Miss Oates loves to splash blood on us," he added that her new book was "as entertaining as a fatal plane crash."

Joyce took the negative reviews philosophically, recalling that she had given a "tepid" notice to Geoffrey Wolff's novel *Bad Debts* the previous year, which may have accounted for the unusually hostile tone of Wolff's review. "As time goes on we all accumulate many enemies," she remarked, "some lying low with maniacal grins, some springing robustly forward." Joyce's editor, Evelyn Shrifte, wrote to console Joyce about the Wolff review: "It is so angry a review of *Wonderland*, one can only think the writer was envious and wielded an axe to try to do away with the object of his envy." Though *Wonderland* sold only fifteen thousand copies in hardcover (little more than half the sales of *them*), there were other consolations: Fawcett had paid $110,000 for the paperback rights. Joyce had thought such sums "reserved for Olympians like Capote or Roth (though no doubt their prices have soared higher), and if I return to teach, which I think I want to, I will either be working for nothing or, in some terrible reverse-Malthusian way, paying for the privilege of working." To Dan Brown, who was also spending the year in London, she complained cheerfully that she was supporting dozens of welfare families with her income taxes.

Happily settled in London, Joyce had returned to her disciplined regimen, spending long hours at her typewriter each day. In addition to her usual short stories, she became involved in a longer manuscript loosely inspired by the Charles Manson case in Los Angeles. Soon after arriving in England, she read in *Esquire* an excerpt from Ed Sanders's book on Manson, an account she found "horrible and compelling." Joyce's recent trip to California also helped inspire the novella, which she called *The Triumph of the Spider Monkey*. Sending the manuscript to John Ditsky, she remarked that "it's about one of *the* California experiences." This highly experimental work, which she later transformed into a stage play, attempts to intuit the psychological workings of a mass murderer (an experiment she would repeat many years later in *Zombie* [1995], based on serial killer Jeffrey Dahmer) and suggests Joyce's ongoing fascination with the relationship between notorious criminals and the society that produces them.

That summer and fall Joyce had been meditating on both the psychological aspects of criminal behavior and on the codification of American law. The ambitious new novel she was planning, *Do with Me What You Will*—its title evoking the legal principle of nolo contendere—would focus on the American legal system, just as *Wonderland* had examined the medical profession.

Joyce had been following newspaper accounts of a Detroit court case: a young White Panther had been sentenced to fifteen years for possession of a single marijuana cigarette. The case prompted many discussions between Joyce and Ray about the legal system. Before leaving Detroit, Joyce had interviewed a local judge, Peter Spivak, and she'd begun reading numerous books on American jurisprudence. She had also visited Detroit's City-County building, peering into courtrooms and eavesdropping on lawyers' conversations. As had happened with *Wonderland*, her composition of the novel flowed swiftly once its structure, characters, and themes had coalesced. Freed from teaching and the other duties that had besieged her in Windsor, she found the writing of *Do with Me What You Will* one of the smoothest and most pleasurable experiences of her career.

Though *Do with Me What You Will* featured lawyers as major characters and culminated in a trial, Joyce saw her new novel primarily as a love story. Its protagonist, Elena, is another passive, beautiful, pale blond heroine like Karen in *With Shuddering Fall* and Eva in *The Sweet Enemy*. Like the early lives of Clara in *A Garden of Earthly Delights*, Maureen in *them*, and Jesse in *Wonderland*, her childhood is marked by victimization: after a bitter divorce, her crazed father, Leo Ross, kidnaps the seven-year-old Elena from school in the novel's dramatic opening scene. Though Elena is rescued after Leo takes her to California, she is then transferred to the "care" of her aggressive, insensitive mother, Ardis, an attractive woman who makes her living variously as a prostitute, a model, and a television personality, and who grooms her beautiful young daughter for a modeling career and for a lifetime of pleasing men. Ultimately Ardis picks out Elena's husband, the powerful attorney Marvin Howe (Elena is only seventeen when she marries him) and the remainder of the novel dramatizes Elena's gradual awakening from the fatal enchantment of her own prescribed feminine role as the passive, decorative wife of a wealthy man. The critic Ellen Friedman has astutely noted the ways in which Joyce's characterization of Elena—who is described as a young princess with Rapunzel-like long hair and is almost literally a "sleeping beauty"—derives from classic fairy tales. The novel's first section, "Twenty-eight Years, Two Months, Twenty-six Days," details Elena's life until the moment when she meets her Prince Charming, the handsome young married lawyer Jack Morrissey, with whom Elena has a long, anguished, but ultimately liberating relationship.

Joyce began the novel with the crime of kidnapping, and in the opening scene of part two she described another desperate act: the 1953 murder of a Detroit businessman by Jack Morrissey's disturbed father, Joseph. In a narrative that has many parallels with Elena's, Joyce then described Jack's own troubled childhood and brought the lovers together through Elena's husband

Marvin Howe, who represents Joseph Morrissey and achieves a verdict of not guilty (by reason of insanity), and who serves as a sinister "model" of his profession much as the megalomaniacal physicians, Pedersen and Perrault, functioned in *Wonderland*. In their love affair, Jack and Elena try to free themselves from the effects of various domestic crimes committed against them. Joyce was attempting, she remarked, to produce "a love story that concentrates upon the tension between two American 'pathways': the way of tradition, or Law; and the way of spontaneous emotion—in this case, Love. In the synthesis of these two apparently contradictory forces lies the inevitable transformation of our culture." One of her models for the novel, she said, was Dostoevsky's *Crime and Punishment*, since she wanted to "construct the exact imaginative equivalent, hour-by-hour, thought-by-thought, of an experience both shattering and transforming, in order that the reader will have lived through the event himself."

Do with Me What You Will also marked an advance in Joyce's narrative technique. Without sacrificing her expertise in psychological realism and sociological observation (as in *them*, the carefully detailed Detroit setting grounds the novel convincingly in time and place), Joyce employed an innovative structure outwardly conforming to, but artistically subverting, that of a legal proceeding, a technique evoked by the title of part two: "Miscellaneous Facts, Events, Fantasies, Evidence Admissible and Inadmissible." (The epilogue is titled "The Summing Up.") Incorporating the viewpoints of many characters and employing letters, court transcripts, and italicized interior monologues, the novel suggested Joyce's ongoing interest in formal experimentation and displayed the narrative poise she had developed through the many innovative stories in *The Wheel of Love* and *Marriages and Infidelities*. Another structural principle, Joyce told Evelyn Shrifte, was the shape of a "mandala," a Zen object of meditation, which for Joyce was the "central 'invisible' core" of the novel. She even suggested that the jacket design could incorporate a stylized version of a mandala, "in which the secret of the universe is described as a mystical marriage of male and female." (Vanguard did not adopt this suggestion.) For Joyce, however, the most unusual aspect of the novel was its "happy ending": she viewed the entire narrative as a replay of events in which the newly liberated lovers Elena and Jack recall their personal histories and the ways in which each has transcended a seemingly preordained tragic fate. After completing the first draft, she joked to Gail Godwin about the response she anticipated from reviewers: "a 'positive' novel! a Love Story! a valentine of a novel, in fact—so that all the critics who disliked my other fiction can say eagerly, 'Bad as the gory writing was, the sentimental writing is far worse.'"

In portraying Elena, Joyce had drawn upon much of her own psychological experience. Like the young Joyce, the frequently victimized Elena becomes a quiet, introverted child. Emotionally malnourished, she has no interest in dolls and acts out her deprivation by showing symptoms of anorexia even as a young child: she is "never hungry" and when forced to eat she often vomits shortly afterward. In one of her interior monologues, Elena says that she tried to tell her father "*how the eating was bad, how it hurt me*"; when Elena is a teenager, her mother Ardis's only concern is with her daughter's attractiveness to men. But the novel as a whole, Joyce insisted, was not about victimization but "about a young woman's 'liberation'—the evolution of her consciousness." The extremely dark tonality of *Wonderland* had marked a terminus, she felt, in her urge to portray a tragic vision of contemporary life and personal destiny. Joyce herself soon felt that *Wonderland* had been an unnecessarily extreme vision. She told an interviewer the following year that with *Do with Me What You Will* and everything afterward, she intended "to move toward a more articulate moral position, not just dramatizing nightmarish problems but trying to show possible ways of transcending them."

In London, near the end of 1971, one of the most dramatic and transformative experiences of Joyce's life brought her to this turning point.

By the middle of December, she had already typed about two hundred pages of *Do with Me What You Will*, reaching the opening chapter of part two. On December 12 she wrote humorously to John and Sue Ditsky that "someone in my novel is committing a murder a few blocks from your house—but don't worry, it's in 1953." But later in the month she "hit a snag" in the novel, and this difficulty with her writing coincided with some troubling personal conflicts.

She was still grieving, she realized, over her Grandmother Woodside's death the previous summer, which she had "no idea how to deal with, how to mourn." And more recently, in early October, she'd experienced the sudden, unexpected loss of a much-valued friend. Dan Brown, to whom she'd been so close during her University of Detroit days, was also living in England that year, and Joyce had looked forward to renewing their old camaraderie. She was pleased that Dan, after years of rejection, had placed a novel, *Something You Do in the Dark*, with Putnam's. She'd written to congratulate him, noting that although publication would not make him happy, it would certainly help. Published around the same time as *Wonderland*, Dan's novel dealt frankly with the then-controversial subject of homosexuality; on the advice of Joyce and his London house mate, he'd published the book under a pseudonym, "Daniel Curzon." Blanche Gregory (now Brown's agent as well as Joyce's) had asked Joyce to provide a blurb for the dust jacket. Joyce agreed, calling *Something You Do in the Dark* "engrossing, powerful, and disturbing."

Frederic Oates, Joyce's father, in 1935 (age 21).

Blanche (Morgenstern) Oates (later "Blanche Woodside"), Joyce's paternal grandmother, c. 1917 (age 23).

Carolina Bush, Joyce's mother *(back row, far left)*, c. 1928 (age 11), in front of Rural District School No. 7 (a one-room schoolhouse), Niagara County, New York.

Joyce *(standing, far right)* with her classmates, inside the same schoolhouse her mother, Carolina, attended, 1948 (age 10).

Joyce Oates (age 2), winter 1941.

Frederic and Joyce Oates (age 3), 1941.

Carolina and Joyce Oates (age 3), 1941

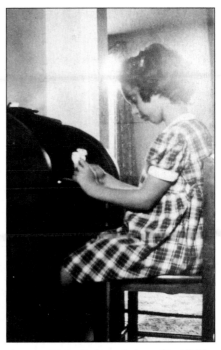

Joyce at her first desk (age 5), 1943.

Joyce in a school photo (age 11), 1949.

Joyce (age 11) and her brother, Fred, Jr. (age 6), 1949.

Joyce Carol Oates, a winner of the 1959 *Mademoiselle* College Fiction Contest.

Joyce on her high school graduation day, 1956.

Ray Smith in 1961, shortly after marrying Joyce and moving to Beaumont, Texas.

Studio photo of Joyce, 1965.

Richard Wishnetsky, the troubled graduate student Joyce befriended at the University of Detroit.

Ray and Joyce's first house, 2500 Woodstock Drive, Detroit. PHOTO COURTESY OF GREG JOHNSON

Joyce and Ray's Sherbourne Road house, near the University of Detroit. PHOTO COURTESY OF GREG JOHNSON

Joyce and Ray in Key West, Christmas, 1970.

The Detroit skyline, seen from Windsor, Ontario. PHOTO COURTESY OF GREG JOHNSON

Joyce on the "beach" behind her home on Riverside Drive, Windsor, 1970.

Joyce and Ray's home on Riverside Drive, Windsor.

Joyce and Ray (with Kay Smith), at their 10th anniversary party, 1971.

This haunting study of Joyce was taken by Graeme Gibson in 1973, when Joyce was 35.

Newsweek

Love and Violence:
A Vision of America

*Novelist
Joyce Carol
Oates*

The *Newsweek* cover story on Joyce in 1972 marked an important milestone in her career. COURTESY OF *NEWSWEEK* MAGAZINE

Joyce and Margaret Drabble in Hampstead, London, 1972.

Joyce on a London Street, 1972.

Joyce and Ray's apartment building on Dunraven Street *(center)*, overlooking Hyde Park in Mayfair, London. They lived here from September 1971 to March 1972.

Joyce at a Fawcett publicity event, New York, 1976.

Joyce with her Detroit friends Elizabeth Graham and Kay Smith *(seated on ground)*, Sissy Jackson *(in chair)*, Marj Levin and Patricia Burnett *(standing)*, 1977.

Joyce with Gail Godwin and Robert Starer, Woodstock, New York, 1976.

Joyce with her Windsor friends Gene McNamara, Charles Harte, and John Ditsky, outside Harte's bookstore, 1978.

Joyce with her Windsor friend Lois Smedick and her new Princeton friend Elaine Showalter, 1980.

Joyce with her cat Misty, in her backyard in Princeton, 1980.

Bob Phillips, Joyce's friend since her undergraduate days at Syracuse.

Lynn Ann Oates, Joyce's sister, in 1981 (age 24). Eighteen years younger than Joyce, Lynn bore a striking resemblance to her sister at that age.

Joyce with her Princeton colleagues Russell Banks and Toni Morrison, on the occasion of Joyce and Morrison being given their "endowed chairs" by the university, 1989.

Joyce and Ray's "glass house" in Princeton, where they have lived since 1978.
PHOTO COURTESY OF GREG JOHNSON

Joyce with Henry and Leigh Bienen in August 1987 at Lana Lobell farm in Bedminster, New Jersey, just after Joyce and Ray purchased their filly, Impish.

Joyce and Ray with John Updike at the Swedish Book Fair, 1987.

Ray, Joyce, Carolina, and Fred in London, 1989.

A section of the Joyce Carol Oates archive, just before leaving Princeton for its permanent home at Syracuse University.

Joyce and Ray with novelist Richard Ford *(left)* and poet Daniel Halpern, at the 92nd Street "Y," 1992.

Joyce and Ray with Princeton friends at a 1994 PEN benefit dinner *(left to right)*: Ray, Chase Twichell, Russell Banks, Joyce, Mike Keeley, Mary Keeley, Paul Auster.

Fred and Carolina Oates, in front of their Millersport home, 1993.
PHOTO COURTESY OF GREG JOHNSON

Joyce and Ray with Dutton editor William Abrahams, San Francisco, 1995.

Joyce's workroom in her Princeton home. PHOTO COURTESY OF GREG JOHNSON

On October 1, just a few days after Joyce had gotten settled in the Mayfair flat, she and Dan met for lunch, and Joyce presented him with a copy of *Wonderland* bearing a warm inscription: "For Dan—with admiration for your talent—and gratitude for your friendship. Love, Joyce." During the meal, Dan had planned to ask Joyce for some additional help. After years of eking out a living by teaching English in Far Eastern countries, he'd moved to London to write full-time and was now almost penniless. Despite Joyce's blurb, his novel had been published to a resounding silence, and his next two manuscripts had been rejected by Putnam's. According to Dan, the *New York Times* had a blanket policy of either ignoring books by gay writers or reviewing them negatively (an opinion that is borne out by Joseph C. Goulden's 1988 biography of the notoriously homophobic *Times* editor A. M. Rosenthal). In his 1986 memoir, Dan recalled that he hadn't "had the nerve to ask Joyce directly for assistance" during their lunch together. Instead, he wrote her a letter, asking if she would attempt to review his novel in *The New York Times Book Review*.

Joyce was furious. He had destroyed their friendship, she wrote him on October 3, adding that she hadn't received any help with her own first book. Joyce believed that Dan was trying to exploit her, while Dan felt that Joyce, now enjoying both financial and critical success, had betrayed him by denying help to her former "best friend." He also believed that Joyce was homophobic and that her attitude toward him had changed dramatically after he revealed his sexual orientation. Yet Joyce felt she had done enough by providing a blurb and had no intention of using her influence to try and "rig" a prominent review, either by her or someone else.

Clearly, Dan's request had come at exactly the wrong time. One of the reasons Joyce had come to London was to avoid the importunities of friends seeking her help and more generally to escape her identity as "Joyce Carol Oates." For his part, Dan was feeling desperate about his prospects after years of struggling and believed that his novel about gay identity was being deliberately suppressed by the establishment media. Neither Joyce nor Dan was in a frame of mind to understand the other's position, and the quick unraveling of their friendship seemed all but inevitable.

Dan sent Joyce a second letter on October 5, attempting to apologize and explain his current problems. But for Joyce, the damage was done. She sent back the letter, writing on the envelope that she was returning the letter without opening it because his first letter had upset her too deeply. She added that their friendship had always been somewhat one-sided, since she felt that she'd been more interested than Dan in their spending time together. To John and Sue Ditsky, Joyce wrote that her "single, and last, meeting with Dan Brown turned out to be disastrous," but declined to discuss any of the details. For now, Joyce simply wanted to put the entire episode behind her.

Adding to Joyce's anxiety was her increasing awareness that London wasn't really the ideal cosmopolitan haven she had first supposed. As she recalled in her journal, the winter weather had begun to dampen her spirits: "constant rain, constant rain-clouds, the sun either hidden all day or shining for a few minutes and then setting rather abruptly at about 4 o'clock." Their neighborhood, too, had lost much of its charm as she became annoyed by "the bustle and noise and apparent *pointlessness* of all that activity on Oxford Street and Park Lane . . . not to mention the frankly stupid materialism of Mayfair, the ugly moronic trash for sale." She'd found Mayfair "exciting at first, then depressing, that eternal impersonal flux of taxi-cabs and double-decker buses—tourists, sight-seekers, spectators, people with money, parodies of themselves"; she'd also begun noticing the many "vagrants, the old men and women, alcoholics, dying creatures wrapped in rags, carrying shapeless bundles, half-human." By late December, the depression that had prompted Joyce to escape Windsor had returned in full force. She later acknowledged that this period represented "the very nadir of my psychological life."

The turning point came unexpectedly. One day, alone in her flat, she had a mystical experience that she would attempt many times to describe in her journal, but which she acknowledged lay beyond the scope of language. A new and frightening depth of awareness abruptly flooded her mind. At first she resisted, but "then I gave in as if to death," she recalled, "to a dissolution of the spirit." The primary feature of the experience, which lasted for several minutes, was the sensation that her individuality, her "ego," had surrendered to a larger, transcendent reality: "the experience of feeling that my body was about to dissolve or explode: each atom in it about to fly off, no longer held together. Absolute loss of 'ego,' selfness. About five to eight minutes of this unforgettable experience in which I realized that 'I' did not exist and had never existed, in the way I had always supposed. Afterward, complete recovery in a matter of minutes . . . personality or conscious attitude completely changed." No single word could adequately describe this "wildly transcendent experience": "Transformation. Conversion. Can these things really happen so quickly . . . ? Indeed they can, indeed they can." She added, "A violent re-organizing of the psyche is involved. An upheaval. What was valued is torn away, and new values arise. What one *was* is torn away and a new personality comes to light."

Though Joyce's awareness of transformation had been dramatic and sudden, there had been signs within the past year that a major change was coming. As she noted to Evelyn Shrifte, the introduction Joyce had written to her collection of essays on tragedy had hinted at her imminent shift in viewpoint: "When I wrote the 'introduction' to *The Edge of Impossibility* I was groping about for this sense of certainty, though I didn't know it at the time," she said. In the introduction, Joyce had written: "The art of tragedy grows out of a break between self and community, a sense of isolation. At its base is fear." After a discussion of classical tragedy, she ended by stressing the visionary, or "hallucinatory," as a communal mode of perception available in the future: "If communal belief in God has diminished so that, as writers, we can no longer presume upon it, then a redefinition of God in terms of the furthest reaches of man's hallucinations can provide us with a new basis for tragedy."

Though Joyce's critical and philosophical thinking on others' work suggested a new direction, one of her own experiences as a writer had offered more immediate and dramatic evidence that the isolated, "existential" self Joyce had dramatized in her earlier fiction had been part of the Western Romantic delusion she was beginning to reject. In November of 1970, while revising *Wonderland*, she had begun "to dream about and to sense, while awake, some other life, or vision, or personality." Prompted by this mysterious sense of otherness, Joyce sat down and wrote a short story that was wholly unlike her typical work: it was "a highly abstract story set nowhere at all; I did not understand the story and in a way felt it was not my own. I could not make sense of it." She put the story aside, but the dreamlike otherness that had prompted the first story grew stronger: "There seemed to be a great pressure, a series of visions, that demanded a formal, aesthetic form." She wrote more of the brief, riddling stories seemingly dictated by this "other" self; she called her literary alter ego "Fernandes" and became aware that Fernandes was Portuguese. "If I did not concentrate deliberately on my own work," she recalled, "or if I allowed myself to daydream or become overly exhausted, my mind would move—it would seem to swerve or leap—into 'Portugal.'" Before long, Joyce felt "besieged by Fernandes—story after story, some no more than sketches or paragraphs that tended to crowd out my own writing." The nature and setting of the stories were especially puzzling in that Joyce had never visited Portugal or had any particular interest in going there. Eventually, after transcribing more than twenty of these mysterious, otherworldly tales, "Fernandes retreated when his story seemed to be complete." (Joyce published the stories in the same literary magazines where she sent her usual work, but Fernandes was listed as the author, Joyce herself as the "translator.")

During the Fernandes experience, she had shared it with only one close friend, Kay Smith. Unlike Joyce, Kay did have a strong interest in Portugal and had visited there frequently. Joyce, having developed her awareness of the "other" personality that had begun assailing her, excitedly questioned Kay about the Portuguese people and their customs. On October 29, 1970, she had explained to Kay, "I woke up with this gentleman in the back of my mind—he is in his fifties, refined, a bachelor, narrowly intelligent, perhaps a little snobbish, and he writes strange little stories." A couple of weeks later, after setting down some of the Fernandes tales, Joyce called them "mainly metaphysical and surreal. [. . .] They are a kind of anti-matter to my other fiction, which gets very emotional and melodramatic." At Joyce's request, Kay had sent photographs and written reminiscences of Portugal, and Joyce had gotten further material from the library. Even in these surrealistic stories, she wanted the same kind of verisimilitude that she gave to her fiction set in Detroit.

Viewed in retrospect, the Fernandes stories are not Joyce's best work: some of the stories are too brief (only two or three pages) to have much impact, and their rather stilted, abstract style seldom conveys the excitement of visionary experience. They appear to be strongly influenced by the parables of Jorge Luis Borges, but they lack Borges's complexity and erudition. Ironically, the better stories, such as "Letters to Fernandes from a Young American Poet" and "Plagiarized Material," are those more recognizably Oatesian in their style and subject matter.

The Fernandes experience—which Joyce viewed as a kind of "possession"—had not really disturbed her, though she did begin reading extensively in parapsychology, mysticism, and the occult. She wrote to an interviewer that the stories had grown out of "hypnogogic" images, "inexplicable flashes of another world, blinding lights, turquoise sky, everything heightened and unnatural." Years later, publishing the Fernandes stories under the title *The Poisoned Kiss*, she would remark: "I have not been able to comprehend, to my own satisfaction, what really happened. . . . My fairly skeptical and existential attitude toward life was not broad enough to deal with the phenomenon I myself experienced, and yet, at the present time, I find it difficult to accept alternative 'explanations.' "

Joyce's dramatic, life-altering mystical experience in her London flat clarified somewhat the "groping toward certainty" she'd described to Evelyn. Both the introduction to *The Edge of Impossibility* and the Fernandes stories suggest an increased, if not yet fully conscious, longing to probe the boundaries of the ego, both in her writing and in her personal life. Seven years later, shortly after writing her novel about a religious seeker, *Son of the Morning*, Joyce outlined the philosophical relevance of her own intensely visionary experience in London:

> I saw that the Void is primary; the Void underlies the sensual, phenomenal world; it *is* that world, transformed by our sensory ap-

paratus. But we mistake the temporal, colorful, sensual world for the original one, which is a grave error. Mistaking the superficial for the profound, the secondary for the primary. . . . I "saw" (it's only a metaphorical expression) that our temporal lives, which seem so important to us, are rather like images on a screen with which we identify. We're fireflies, in the Void. [. . .] The vision is, simply, that everything is ordained; time is a solid thing, an essence, in which we move "forward" but could as easily move backward. . . . Whatever happens to us can't be avoided. We can only control, to some extent, our attitude toward it. Hence there is no "negative" side, everything is there, from the beginning, irrefutable. But we can alter our perception of it through certain conscious disciplines, like intensive meditation . . . the purging of the soul of trivia. . . . I saw no "creator" in the Void, and certainly no evidence of a personality. It's an inhuman vision—outside the sphere of "humanity."

In late December 1971, Joyce's first response to this mystical apprehension was to recognize that she'd made a "grave error" in her own artistic life. She realized that when completing *Wonderland,* she had forced the novel to a falsely tragic conclusion, imposing her predetermined design upon the final scene instead of following her instinctive awareness that the ending was not artistically or emotionally satisfying. Putting aside her current manuscript, she returned to *Wonderland* and created an entirely new ending. A few days later, she wrote anxiously to Evelyn Shrifte at Vanguard: "I have just not felt right about *Wonderland,* about the ending especially—it has really disturbed me, to the point at which I can't bear to think about the novel and feel a kind of revulsion toward it. I think it is a very dark, relentless work, and I wonder if you might not be receptive to a modified ending . . . ? [. . .] Could further editions of the novel actually be altered? Would you at least consider this, since it means so much to me?" Joyce enclosed her new ending for the novel, remarking that it was "more ambiguous than the other, but not nearly so dark," and even offered to pay for changing the printer's plates herself. "I can't emphasize strongly enough my feelings about this," she added. "I have felt terribly guilty and even depressed about the novel as it stands." To Joyce's relief, Evelyn agreed, and the ending of the novel was altered for the British hardcover edition and the American paperback.

Apart from this letter to Evelyn, Joyce kept her sudden "conversion" a private matter: none of the letters she was writing to her close friends mentioned the mystical experience, though it had vaulted her into a sudden and exhilarating new stage of being. But in a philosophical essay published the following year, she described in general terms the kind of personal, crucial moment of transformation during which people "approach the end of one segment of their lives and must rapidly, and perhaps desperately, sum up everything that has gone before." Her books published during this period clearly reflected this dramatic change of viewpoint, toward which she'd already been moving instinctively with her planned "positive" resolution of *Do with Me What You Will*. The book of essays currently in press, *The Edge of Impossibility: The Tragic Experience in Literature*, may be viewed as a critical "summing up" of her own preoccupation with tragic themes, but even before the book appeared her reading had verged abruptly in a new direction. She had begun an intensive study of visionary literature—she became particularly absorbed in D. H. Lawrence's poetry—and began a new series of critical essays focused on spiritual transcendence. (These would be collected in 1974 under the title *New Heaven, New Earth: The Visionary Experience in Literature*.) Contributing to Joyce's psychological healing was a series of "numinous dreams" she experienced in the days after her mystical experience (these would continue for the next several years). These dreams—some of them terrifying, others consoling—confirmed Joyce's belief that personal salvation lay in escaping the illusion of the Romantic, isolated ego and participating in what her 1972 essay called a "communal consciousness." She wrote that "Our intelligence, our wit, our cleverness, our unique personalities—all are simultaneously 'our own' possessions and the world's. This has always been a mystical vision, but more and more in our time it is becoming a rational truth. It is no longer the private possession of a Blake, a Whitman, or a Lawrence."

Energized by her psychological breakthrough, Joyce returned excitedly to her new novel. She was no longer blocked: working intently for the rest of December and January, she managed to complete a seven-hundred-page draft by the first week of February. She immediately began revising and retyping the novel, forcing herself to go more slowly: "I've disciplined myself not to write so much, to cut back," she confessed to Gail Godwin on February 18; "10 pp. or so a day on [revising] the novel, then reading & letters." But this "discipline" didn't last. Joyce's optimism about the future had accessed enormous reserves of new energy, and she later told Bob Phillips that during the rest of that winter and spring she had never worked harder in her life. "I find that I'm rising earlier and earlier, to make the days more productive, and I've never felt so good about writing," she said. After mailing the final draft of *Do with Me What You Will* to Blanche Gregory, Joyce had "immediately rushed into half a dozen new projects" that included short stories, book reviews, and long essays on D. H. Lawrence, Sylvia Plath, and James Dickey. To Evelyn Shrifte, Joyce wrote: "I feel a completely new, exhilarated certainty about much that has bewildered me in life, and my writing from now on will be somewhat different." She added, "I hope I don't sound mystical—I'm just very enthusiastic and have been pouring out my 'new' ideas to poor Ray for the past week!" She wrote similarly to John and Sue Ditsky that she felt, "in some strange mystical way," that the political and social turbulence in America "will shortly get better" and that "all this despair, this 'literature of exhaustion' has about run its course—I think—I hope. At least my own death trip seems to have run out."

Despite her intent focus on writing, Joyce had abundant energy left over for traveling and socializing. In January 1972 she and Ray traveled to France, getting by on Joyce's halting "schoolgirl French." They visited countless museums and caught colds by walking around in the wintry drizzle of Paris, which they found to be "an extraordinarily beautiful city, probably more beautiful than London." They took the train to Nice, where they stayed several days and enjoyed the Riviera. In both Paris and Nice they found the people quite friendly, but because they were avoiding tourist spots and staying in out-of-the-way hotels, Joyce found it draining to try and communicate with her minimal French. "I realized how terrible it is to be reduced to the rudiments of a language," she wrote to Gloria Whelan, "to have one's I.Q. cut back to about 50." Though Joyce and Ray were glad they had seen France, they returned to London with a sense of relief.

In March, having had enough of Mayfair and wanting to acquaint themselves with another section of the city, they moved to a two-level penthouse maisonette in Belgravia. Though they would miss the view of Hyde Park, their new neighborhood was much quieter; bordering Chelsea and only a block from Sloan Square, the area was "lovely—the way Greenwich Village might have been decades ago, and should be now." Their new quarters, occupying the top two floors of "a quaint crooked Englishy building," featured a large outdoor terrace where she and Ray planted flowers despite the cold spring weather. "I feel I could stay here forever," Joyce wrote cheerfully to Gail Godwin, "in spite of three-foot corridors & a crooked kitchen." Joyce had a large study, with a panoramic view of "spires, domes, chimneys." After their work day, they enjoyed strolling through Chelsea and along Kings Road, "settling nicely into the Bohemian life we somehow missed, Ray and I, having jumped from being graduate students to being bourgeois, without any transition." Joyce and Ray had never been happier, and even had fantasies of becoming British citizens. Joyce told Gail that she "wept to think we probably must go back, to 690 murders in Detroit in 1971 (London had 70), crossfires of feuds in the English Department, the old arias, the old costumes." (She and Ray had recently seen *The Marriage of Figaro*, prompting Joyce to exclaim that "life *is* a comic opera.") With her new sense of well-being, even Joyce's lifelong insomnia had disappeared.

While she and Ray had declined invitations and even avoided answering the telephone during their first months in London, they now became more sociable and saw a number of other Americans either residing in or traveling through London that year. Her good friends Bob Phillips and Patty Burnett both came through town, and Joyce socialized with several prominent American writers: Paul Theroux, Robert Coover, John Gardner, John L'Heureux, and Stanley Elkin, among others. She especially liked Gardner, another highly energetic writer who, like Joyce, disdained the more self-indulgent kinds of experimental writing that had become popular since the late 1960s. Joyce wrote to John Ditsky that she and Gardner "get along awfully well, and I'm envious of his new extravaganza, which will be 1500 pages"; she found Coover "awfully nice" and also liked Theroux, whom she found "even more intense, hyper-, brilliant, energetic than I had feared. . . . I have never felt before how deeply fascinating it can be to meet—but not at great length—people of accomplishment who are not egotistical, certainly not famous, but who somehow carry their talents with them, effortlessly, generously." Joyce impressed her writer friends in much the same way. John L'Heureux recalled meeting the Smiths for drinks at the Cafe Royal: "What impressed me most was her energy, of mind and body. She was electric, leaping in conversation from remarks about films to analyses of Tolstoy and Dostoevsky and on to the pleasures of living in Chelsea and the relative ease of writing. . . . She did not seem in the least impressed with her productivity or her evident genius." Among the writers she met, Joyce's only disappointment was Stanley Elkin, whom she disliked intensely. "I had looked forward to meeting him," she wrote, "but he turns out to be almost proudly ignorant (hates music), a weak, vulgar bully (interrupts, contradicts), and somewhere, somewhere inside him there must be the real Elkin, who can write so well."

Joyce also met several of England's most respected writers during that spring and summer, and she liked them all. After meeting the eminent novelist Iris Murdoch, Joyce wrote to Kay Smith that she was "*the* most unpretentious person I've ever met." Joyce became especially friendly with Margaret Drabble, whose novel *The Needle's Eye* she had admired greatly. She felt an immediate rapport with "Maggie," as though they were long-lost girlfriends from high school. Drabble recalled that Joyce and Ray came twice for dinner to Drabble's home in Hampstead: "my children called her 'the thin lady' as she was strikingly, almost alarmingly, slim: she had a very pale, white skin, and dramatic red lips, and was an exotic figure." Though Joyce was shy at first, Drabble remembered that she would "become more animated in conversation as the evening went on." There were also larger parties: Joyce invited Drabble and several other writers to the Mayfair flat, and Drabble threw a large party attended by more than fifty people, including Alison Lurie and Doris Lessing. Joyce brought along a bouquet of long-stemmed red roses, a gift that charmed Drabble.

Joyce had been eager to meet Doris Lessing. She had sent a friendly letter to the world-renowned novelist, who responded by inviting Joyce to lunch. Joyce was somewhat apprehensive, since she revered the author of *The Golden Notebook*. "I am a shameless hero-worshipper," she confessed to Gail Godwin. In the past, she added, most of her heroes had been men: "I very early in life latched onto spiritual, intellectual, visionary fathers, all kinds, and had there been many women of comparable achievement in history, I would surely, happily, have latched onto them." Doris Lessing was one of these few "heroic" women writers. After their first meeting, Joyce wrote: "She is very warm, gracious, and yet formidable. I began to feel awfully insubstantial next to her and am looking forward to seeing her again." In her account of the two-hour visit, published the following year, Joyce recalled that "I felt almost faint—certainly unreal—turning transparent myself in the presence of this totally defined, self-confident, gracious woman." The two writers discussed their backgrounds, comparing the violent political climates of the United States and Lessing's native Rhodesia. Joyce described her new interest in mystical experience to Lessing, who remarked that people "commonly experience things they are afraid to admit to, being frightened of the label of 'insane' or 'sick'—there are no adequate categories for this kind of experience." They also discussed their mutual admiration of Colin Wilson, another mystically inclined British writer Joyce had met recently.

Unlike Drabble and Lessing, Colin Wilson was not well known in the United States, but Joyce had become "involved in a rapid-fire back-and-forth correspondence" with the young writer. He had sent Joyce several of his books, which she "admired immensely," and she had sent Wilson a copy of *Wonderland*. Both visionary and wildly productive, Wilson was a kind of soul mate, his prophetic stance speaking dramatically to Joyce's current preoccupation with transcendence: "Colin Wilson is a genius," Joyce told Gail Godwin, "and I didn't have the faintest idea. . . . Wilson is like someone writing from 2001, looking back at us now, summing a great deal up and indicating where we are going. Of course, I must admit I couldn't have understood him a year ago—I hadn't grown up out of my personal, private self—but more importantly I hadn't *known* that there are really higher levels of a quite sane self, reachable not through drugs or incantations but, evidently, just by completing one's personality." Joyce and Ray drove to Cornwall to visit Wilson, whom she found to be a "very nice energetic talkative soul (with 5,000 records in his house, and countless books)." She also found him to be quite sexist, however, directing most of his remarks to Ray and asserting "male chauvinist ideas about the inability of women to reason abstractly." Twenty years later, Wilson's attitude had changed very little. He remarked that he normally disdained women writers; they were "too concerned with themselves and their emotional problems." He insisted, however, that he had returned Joyce's admiration: "We immediately took to one another," he recalled. "I continue to think of her as one of the few really first-rate woman writers of the century." Despite her disappointment at Wilson's personal biases, Joyce continued to feel sympathetic toward him and admiring of his talent, and would later make energetic efforts to get his work published in the United States.

During this same excursion, Joyce and Ray spent a couple of days touring the rugged western countryside of England and visiting Stonehenge. They also called on another prominent British author, John Fowles, whose critically lauded, best-selling novel *The French Lieutenant's Woman* had appeared in 1969. Joyce and Fowles had an "excellent visit" in the novelist's eighteenth-century mansion in Lyme Regis, overlooking Lyme Bay and the Cobb, which featured so prominently in his novel.

Another brief trip Joyce and Ray took that spring, to visit Corpus Christi College at Oxford, also went well: she and Ray "loved everything there, including meals in a most dignified, aged dining hall, and walks along the streams and through the back-alleys of famous colleges. Perfection." Joyce's outgoing mood even extended to the part of her professional life that she liked least: giving interviews. She spoke with Frank Kermode in a broadcast for the BBC, and also gave a lengthy interview to Stanley Plumly for the literary magazine *The Ohio Review*. In sharp contrast to her previous exchanges with interviewers, Joyce spoke openly and excitedly to Plumly about her view of art and the function of the artist in society. Many of her comments reflected the extensive thinking and reading she had done since her visionary experience in December. The private self, she said, should not be "confused with the rather impersonal, inhuman flow of energy, which has nothing to do with an ego at all." She identified strongly, she added, with highly energetic and productive artists—Mozart, Picasso, Lawrence, and others—who attuned themselves to this inexhaustible field of spiritual vitality. (In her essay on Sylvia Plath, she argued that Plath had taken the opposite, tragic path of cutting herself off from any sense of a communal spirit, thus hurtling inevitably toward self-destruction.) Art, Joyce said, was "dream-like, springs from the dreaming mind . . . it's the effort of the Ego to communicate with a deeper self. Art is magnificent, divine, because it records the struggles of exceptional men to order their fantasies, their doubts, even their certainties, into an external structure that celebrates the life force itself, the energy of life."

Although Joyce felt that she had, in a very brief period of time, developed an optimistic new frame of mind, she continued to receive negative reaction in the literary press. *The Edge of Impossibility*, published in June 1972, received mostly respectful notices, but it was—like *Wonderland*—attacked in *The New York Times Book Review*. Wielding the hatchet this time was Roger Sale, who said the book was haphazardly put together, illustrating "a high intelligence at work carelessly." Joyce sent the *Review* a long letter of protest. She had written the essays slowly, she insisted, over a period of twelve years, and they had grown "out of a deep, meticulous concern with individual works of 'tragic literature.' " She went on to analyze Sale's review as exemplifying the "contemporary neurosis" that writers and critics must always be in competition, "a failure to see how we are all participating in a communal consciousness. There is a sense in which 'I' do not exist at all." Joyce said she looked forward to the day when literary people stopped "all this wasteful worrying over who owns what, who owns whom, who 'owns' a portion of art" and when "we will have again a truly communal art to which artists contribute anonymously." She asserted that "the cult of individual personality and 'ego' is no longer meaningful" and stated her firm position regarding critics who argued that she wrote too much and too quickly: "Since critics are constantly telling me to 'slow down,' I must say gently, very gently, that everything I have done so far is only preliminary to my most serious work."

Joyce's year away from Windsor, now almost over, had enabled her to communicate with her own "deeper self" and to heal her psychological wounds. Though she would miss London, she looked forward to communicating her ideas and her optimism to her students back home, to studying visionary literature and philosophy (especially the Eastern discipline of Zen), and to continuing her new surge of literary creativity. On August 2, she wrote excitedly to Kay Smith that "this year has been a transforming one. . . . I've been reading Whitehead, Teilhard, even Einstein (as best I can), even Eastern philosophy, mysticism, even cybernetics, plus dozens of novels and poets; I'm writing or planning half a dozen books at once—it's so much fun to be learning things." She incorporated her reading into her professional work as a reviewer, writing on such psychologists as R. D. Laing and Abraham Maslow, reviewing the work of her new British friends Margaret Drabble, Doris Lessing, and Iris Murdoch, and producing the *Saturday Review* essay "New Heaven and Earth," in which she attempted to summarize her changed philosophical position.

Interrupting this blaze of intellectual activity, Joyce and Ray regretfully left their beloved Belgravia penthouse on August 19, drove into the south of England, and set sail for America on August 25. They crossed on the S.S.

France, sharing meals with Robert Coover and his wife, who were also returning to the States after a lengthy European stay. Joyce spent most of her time
drafting several new short stories, writing in longhand since she had no access
to a typewriter. Docking in New York, she and Ray spent a few days in the
city, where Joyce gave an interview to *Library Journal* that again expressed her
new interest in mysticism. She remarked that she wrote fiction "for people
who are sensitive and somehow related to a web of consciousness that extends outward from them, to other people."

Joyce and Ray then began the drive home, stopping at Saratoga Springs
and briefly visiting the famed Yaddo writers' colony. When they returned to
Windsor, Joyce was immediately besieged by job offers from other universities, but wrote to Gail Godwin that she and Ray "probably will not move for a
while." She was eager to return to teaching, and she startled her department
head—who had arranged for Joyce to teach only a handful of honors and
graduate students that fall—by requesting one class of beginning freshmen.
"He seemed to pale," she told Gail, "as if believing me mad, so now I have
30 or so freshmen and was correcting freshmen themes yesterday and enjoying it."

Shortly after getting settled into the fall term, Joyce had to confront the
reviews of *Marriages and Infidelities*. Like *The Edge of Impossibility*, the short
stories received mostly positive reviews, but increasingly it was Joyce's productivity, rather than her work itself, that received the most attention. "Does
Joyce Carol Oates ever eat or sleep?" began one review. Others raised the
charge that Joyce was publishing her work indiscriminately: "One could wish
that Miss Oates had not chosen to publish some of the stories in this new
book," wrote the reviewer for *The Nation*, who found *Marriages and Infidelities* an unsettling mixture of brilliant stories and extremely weak ones. As if
echoing the line in Joyce's letter to John and Sue Ditsky about her own
"death trip" having run out, the reviewer for *Time* magazine called Joyce "the
busiest coroner of the American soul." Similarly, Michael Wood in *The New
York Times Book Review* found that Joyce was groping "for themes and forms
in far too much of this book. But even her groping is worth looking at, reveals
returning preoccupations that will surely blossom into better work." Yet some
reviewers found Joyce's fourth collection to be her best. Writing in *Saturday
Review*, William Abrahams (her future editor at Dutton and, in his role as
editor of *Prize Stories: The O. Henry Awards*, a champion of her short fiction
since the 1960s) proclaimed that even in the least of the stories "there is a
prodigality of talent that places her among the most remarkable writers of
her generation, and, at their best, they reach a level of achievement that sets
her impressively apart. *Marriages and Infidelities* . . . confirms what has already been evident for some years: In the landscape of the contemporary

American short story Miss Oates stands out as a master, occupying a preeminent category of her own."

Rejuvenated after her year abroad and less concerned than ever with her own "ego," Joyce was equally unfazed by flattering and belittling reviews. In her letters to Gail Godwin and Liz Graham that fall, Joyce reflected on her time in England and the renewed energy and optimism it had brought her. She had no intention of slipping again into the mire of unwanted social obligations that she had found so victimizing a year earlier. "We've simplified our lives immensely—no second car, very little social life indeed," she told Liz. "London spoiled us, showing how lovely life can be if it is truly, systematically simplified." To Gail, she admitted that "for so many years I endured a long maniacal struggle that I thought was myself vs. the world (minus, of course, people I liked or loved) but was really myself vs. myself, a kind of fragmented ego bouncing around the room and colliding with parts of itself." She now believed that her paranoia and stress had resulted in an unwise resistance to exterior conflicts and the demands of others; she thought back upon "so many perverse, childish incidents in my past—my emotional reactions against whole facets of life because of some trivial prejudice that, upon examination, hardly exists." Now she felt that "there isn't any struggle, essentially" and that "the only significant thing is how we enjoy the moment." Even negative experiences, she insisted, could be enjoyed within this liberated consciousness of the world not as inimical to the self but as an enveloping web of consciousness that includes all selves and all reality. She had been rereading such writers as Jung, Whitman, and Thoreau, seeming to understand their affirmative themes for the first time.

She had also begun an intensive study of Zen Buddhism, the focus of an extraordinary letter she wrote to Liz Graham on November 20, shortly after the two friends had visited. This unusual letter deserves extensive quotation. Carefully handwritten, many pages long, and focusing earnestly on a single topic, it is dramatically different from Joyce's usual chatty, typewritten letters. She wrote:

> Forgive me for being "personal"—since in a way I don't much believe in the personal or unique, knowing that everyone *is* fundamentally the same, and I suppose my concern is paradoxical—but I hadn't any opportunity on Wednesday to develop various strands of conversation that were begun. Zen Buddhism is a *part* of one type of Buddhism (Mahayanna)—there is an entirely other "way" (Therarada)—entirely different. [. . .] These are only *ways*. (The "Way of the Cross"—Christianity—is another way, alas, so diluted and popularized that it is almost meaningless to all but a few.) Psychoanalysis

should have developed into a strong, reliable, nonsensical way of liberation also, but seems to have failed or to be at an impasse. [. . .]

Zen Buddhism appeals to Western intellectuals because it is
so meta-intellectual. It is—like Hinduism and Buddhism—totally
compatible with the post-Einsteinian cosmos. [. . .] Unfortunately,
our culture hasn't much tradition for liberating the superior self—
instead of accepting the "Great Doubt" and plunging through despair into a higher consciousness, modern people try to stupefy their
minds with pills or alcohol. Or they go to be "psycho-analyzed" (i.e.,
adjusted to a trivial, shallow, and—frankly!—doomed civilization).
But there are innumerable ways to liberate oneself—not only the famous ways. [. . .] Gautama the Buddha taught just what Christ did
(earlier than Christ, of course—450 BC or so) and though Gautama's
teachings are, for me, quite believable and only common-sense, they
would probably disturb you. He denies the Ego, and the Ego (that
stronghold of neuroses!) is awfully stubborn in the West. Christ also
denies the Ego, but I suppose one could attach oneself to *Christ's*
ego, and thereby cross over. Christianity is certainly not *my* way, but
probably yours. If you feel uneasy in our society—well—wouldn't
Christ?— If you have inside you a potential saintliness, shouldn't
you be, at present, divided? Your obvious rejection of much of
your life is only normal. And wise. A materialist, capitalist, Ego-
infatuated society is totally at odds with any sensitive person, who
yearns to develop himself spiritually. This is an *instinct*—not a
chimera, a fad, or a whim.

[. . .] If you concentrate *entirely*—even for a half-second—that
is Zen. If you expand this to a full minute, in utter absorption,
that is Zen. If you expand such minutes to great blocks of time—
that is Zen. But if you sigh, sink back into cynicism, and are *quite*
bored—even then that is Zen, if you could experience yourself as
behavior, and not as an ego. Mystics East and West all agree that
men *are* already "saved" (i.e., enlightened—"Buddha" only means
'enlightened one'), are already divine, but fear acknowledging their
own potential for perfection. So, in a sense, even the divided self "is"
saved. But, within that self, in that enclosed ego, life does not appear to be holy. So I believe that—for me, at least—it is inside the
ego that we should help one another.

The "enlightenment" through which Joyce had saved herself from a potential breakdown dictated that she continue in her roles as a teacher and
writer, but with a new awareness of her relationship to other people and to
the cosmos. Returning from England, she knew there would be few problems
with others' demands: she had decided quite simply, she later said, never

again to do anything she did not want to do. "Did I tell you that I've eliminated nearly all social life?" she wrote to Gail. Though she and Ray still had a telephone, they'd announced to everyone that they hadn't reconnected their service, "and consequently no one calls. It's amazing, that Thoreau should be so totally right—simplifying one's life is wonderful." She added that she was sleeping well and had begun gaining weight.

Joyce's newfound serenity would not immediately be apparent in her fiction, since she still believed her artistic mission was to dramatize the painful conflicts of her era. "There's no need to write about happy people, happy problems; there's only the moral need to instruct readers," she said, "concerning the direction to take, in order to achieve happiness (or whatever: maybe they don't want happiness, only confusion)." In a brief essay published in *The American Scholar*, she noted that many American writers were dreamily lost in a self-obsessed view of art that was "passive and deathly"; only Norman Mailer and Saul Bellow, she said, had "struggled quite nobly to define a self in the center of chaos." She added that her year in England had allowed her "to think dispassionately about what is happening back home, about the kind of writing that is being turned out and applauded, and about my own career up to this point. I can see in amazement that I have only haphazardly and instinctively, never consciously, broken through that dreaminess myself, and that the whole range of my writing so far has dealt only with one phase of the personality and its possibilities."

Clearly, Joyce was eager to begin a new phase. In addition to her usual stories and reviews, she had begun a lengthy new novel. The characters in her fiction were no happier than before, but the person doing the writing was happy indeed. Ray, too, had never felt better. On November 23, Joyce noted to Gail that this was the twelfth anniversary of her and Ray's engagement: "good God!" she exclaimed, with the kind of incredulity she expressed often that fall at the dramatic transformations that had occurred in both their lives. "Who *were* those people?" During the next few years, Joyce's artistic challenge would be to articulate her mystical perceptions regarding personal identity and spirituality, and to integrate them into her larger view of American culture and its destiny. Whereas *Wonderland*, for all its narrative brilliance, had represented a kind of philosophical dead end, she now hoped to write more fiction that could, like *Do with Me What You Will*, suggest "the inevitable transformation of our culture."

10

The Visionary Gleam
1973–75

I have a glimmering of a reality that is continuous and far more substantial and autonomous and profound, than ordinary waking consciousness . . . but of course the writer must have faith in his own imagination, in order to write.
—letter to Bob Phillips,
June 1, 1974

> *the angels direct their fire*
>   *to pierce*
> *our eyelids*
> *and penetrate the old selfish*
>   *tightness*
> *of our single selves. . . .*
> —"Angel Fire" (1973)

The years after Joyce's return from London were a time of retrenchment and reflection. She firmly maintained her resolve, in both her social and her professional life, not to accede to the demands of other people merely for the sake of pleasing them. Declining social invitations except those from close friends, shunning publicity except for an occasional, carefully controlled interview, she focused her energies almost wholly on writing and teaching. In the argot of the time, she had become "centered," and she practiced meditation as a way of maintaining her new equilibrium. Another ritual she established at this time served a similar function: on New Year's Day, 1973, she began keeping a personal journal, a random but invariably thoughtful account of her psychological states, her dreams, her writing projects, her personal relationships. Eventually she hit upon a title for the journal, *The Invisible Woman*, since she cherished the simplified life and newfound sense of privacy she had found apart from her fame as "Joyce Carol Oates." In the coming years, she would type out several thousand pages of journal entries, often meditating on the disparity between her public persona and the private, "invisible" self she had found through her mystical experience, her numinous dreams, her meditation, and her writing.

One of the earliest entries in the journal, dated January 7, succinctly expresses Joyce's new conception of her own consciousness:

> Fascinating, the human mind; unfathomable. To think that we inhabit the greatest, most ingenious work in the universe . . . that is, the human brain . . . and we inhabit it gracelessly, casually, rarely aware of the phenomenon we've inherited. Like people living in a few squalid rooms, in a great mansion. We don't even know what might await us on the highest floor; we're stuck contemplating the patterns in the floorboards before us. Once in a while a truly alarming, profound dream/vision cracks through the barrier and we're forced to recognize the presence of a power greater than ourselves, contained somehow within our consciousness.

Meditating on her "dream/vision" in London, she asked herself, "Did I die, in a sense, back in December of 1971 . . . ? A peculiar experience which I'll never quite comprehend, though I've brooded over it constantly. I can say without exaggeration that a day doesn't pass without my contemplating of *it*." Joyce knew that her former self had departed forever, but "if I am dead from one point of view I'm still alive from another. It isn't 'my' life here, typing out these words; it's 'a' life, someone's life, someone both myself and not quite myself." As she had done with Liz Graham, she gradually began to share with others the turning point she had experienced and the new ideas it had inspired, but in her letters to such friends as Gail Godwin and Bob Phillips she confessed—as she did in her journal—that she might "try again and again to express this utterly simple experience (it lasted only about 10 minutes) in words, and I always fail."

Joyce's most congenial mode of expression had always been her fiction, and as she had done with the Fernandes stories, she allowed her visionary experiences to feed into her work: one night she dreamed of a weeping teenage girl, and over the next couple of days wrote "Honeybit," a story based on the dream. Finishing the story at four in the afternoon, she felt "besieged" as another "dream-image" intruded. Though exhausted from her work on "Honeybit," she immediately began the new story, "The Golden Madonna." In her journal, she described this creative intensity: "I was writing until 7:30 and it was time to start dinner and I was exhausted, completely exhausted, my vision blotched, my head aching. It would have been perfectly possible to put off 'The Golden Madonna' until tomorrow; it isn't *that* urgent. But once one is writing it's almost easier to continue than to stop." A note of self-chastisement would appear often in Joyce's journal over the years, since the obsessive intensity of her work habits at times seemed overwhelming. But like D. H. Lawrence and the other highly energetic, visionary writers with whom she identified, she gave her primary energies to art, consoling herself with the knowledge that other, negative aspects of her former life were now less of a risk to her psychological and physical health. Two years earlier she had been anorexic, weighing a skeletal 98 pounds. Now she weighed 108; though this was still a dangerously low weight for a woman of her height, she felt that she had "gained just enough: feel fine."

She had already begun work on a new novel that was partly inspired by her own recent transformation. As she had done with *Do with Me What You Will*, she conceived of the book, which she titled *How Lucien Florey Died, and Was Born*, as a complex "mandala," describing it as "a long complicated novel that takes place in California—a state that is a mixture of states of the soul, almost an entire nation in itself, a microcosm far more complex than people who read only the Hollywood or the atrocity stories. I believe that out of California, out of the West, some new model of the nation is about to flower." The two major characters, Jacob and Corinne, bore her own initials, representing a "synthesis of two poles of consciousness resulting in the (miraculous) birth." The initials "J. C." also suggested a religious dimension, of course, and the title character's name, "Lucien," evoked the novel's primary theme of enlightenment. Throughout 1973, Joyce worked steadily at the manuscript, producing over 1,000 pages in the first draft, then cutting the novel back to 616 pages in revision. But the book was never published, though a substantial excerpt, entitled "Corinne," appeared in *North American Review*. Years later, in 1989, Joyce destroyed the manuscript, finding the material "too raw, unassimilated," and not wanting to revisit "that period in my life when I'd needed to write that particular novel because of a particular conversion of the soul." She added that "I am another person now and I want the record of it, simply, gone."

Despite her recent "conversion" and the vastly altered quality of her interior life, Joyce's external routine had changed very little. Before beginning the spring 1973 term, Joyce and Ray had embarked on another of their lengthy car trips, driving first to the western coast of Florida, as they had done two years before, then touring the deep South. Returning home, they felt refreshed and ready to begin the spring term. "We enter a kind of vacuum, an aesthetic-spiritual retreat on our vacations," Joyce wrote to Gail Godwin, "and return to piles of mail and new scandals and gossip." Joyce had also returned to a new onslaught of public attention, since *Newsweek* had published a cover story on Joyce and her work in its December 11, 1972, issue. (Knowing the publicity meant a great deal to her publisher, Joyce had agreed reluctantly to cooperate, submitting to an interview and photographs; but she had first suggested to the *Newsweek* editors that Eudora Welty was more deserving of the attention.) The story was sympathetic and factually accurate, but there were always negative results from publicity. Joyce was flooded in the early months of 1973 with job offers, countless requests for public appearances, and a steady stream of fan mail—the kind of attention that would please many writers but that always made Joyce uneasy.

She pointedly averted even friendly inquiries about her increased level of success and visibility. When Bob Phillips asked about her job offers and congratulated her on her recent promotion to full professor at the University of Windsor, Joyce responded, "Do you know, these things mean almost literally nothing to me . . . ? So much so that I didn't even mention the promotion to Ray until a few days later." She also insisted that she had become indifferent to reviews of her work: "They are people's opinions; no more, no less." Similarly, when Joyce's former Syracuse professor Walter Sutton invited her to speak at the dedication ceremony for the university's new library and offered to send a car, she composed a message to be read at the ceremony by someone else, remarking to Sutton that "frankly, personally, I am somewhat at a loss as to why I am so important, why on earth anyone anywhere should desire to send a car for *me*."

As public estimation of "Joyce Carol Oates" grew, Joyce's sense of her personal significance continued to decline, as though her own identity were suffering the same extreme transmogrifications that, as a little girl, had frightened her in Lewis Carroll's Alice books. She noticed this phenomenon again in March: when the Detroit River flooded Joyce and Ray's neighborhood, propelling logs through their backyard, they considered evacuating the house but decided to stay; when the storm abated, Joyce felt a peculiar "indifference to the house and our possessions, except for things like my grandmother's ring and a few other pieces of her jewelry." As time passed, Joyce grew more confirmed in her belief that the individual ego—its achievements, its possessions, its "fame"—had relatively little importance. She told Gail Godwin that she had entered "that curious state the Zen Buddhists call *chin*"; having "come to the end of a certain kind of emotion, in this lifetime at least, I just don't feel a wide range of emotions any longer."

But with the publication that spring of Joyce's third volume of poems, *Angel Fire*, she found that she was still quite vulnerable, after all, to negative assessments of her work. Since her first volume of poetry, *Anonymous Sins*, appeared in 1969 (it was followed quickly by *Love and Its Derangements* in 1970), Joyce's poetry had been harshly reviewed. As a fiction writer, she had been publishing for more than a decade: behind her early novels lay a solid foundation of at least twenty "practice" novels and more than a hundred short stories. But as a poet, Joyce was a relative beginner, and in *Anonymous Sins* and *Love and Its Derangements* she was essentially publishing her apprentice work in the genre, a situation made possible by her fame as a novelist. Her early poetry depended far too heavily on abstraction and on flat, philosophical statement; it was awkward in its use of poetic form and image; and unlike her fiction, the poetry had not achieved a distinctive "voice," seeming instead an unassimilated miscellany of random thoughts and passionate but vaguely articulated emotions. As her friend Larry Goldstein, editor of *Michigan Quarterly Review*, later remarked, "Some of her early work would perhaps better have remained uncollected, for it gave her a bad reputation as a poet, so that readers have not looked into the much more skilled later work."

For *Angel Fire*, L.S.U. Press had printed a handsome dust jacket featuring a photograph of Joyce, but she had written to Charles East, her editor, that she wanted the cover changed; even the copies sent to reviewers should be replaced. "I am horrified at the prospect of *myself* on a serious book," she wrote, "not just the evident vanity and the misery of self-consciousness but a terrible realization that my image simply betrayed the poems inside the book. I *know* this—I feel it. That person on the dust jacket detracts from the poems, which are serious and meant to be somehow visionary, especially the last section—that is, impersonal." Joyce also directed Blanche Gregory to call East and plead with him to change the cover. East regretfully informed both Joyce and Blanche that it was too late to change the first edition; the cover would be changed, however, for later printings.

Angel Fire received some positive notices in *Library Journal* and *Choice*, but for the third time in two years (after *Wonderland* and *The Edge of Impossibility*) a new book of Joyce's was savaged in *The New York Times Book Review*. Even worse, the attack came from Helen Vendler, one of the country's most influential poetry critics. Noting that only a handful of novelists had succeeded as poets—Melville, Lawrence, Hardy, and Emily Brontë—Vendler insisted that Joyce's poems were overly abstract and, more damningly, "untruthful": "I often cannot bring myself to believe a word of the story a poem is telling me," she wrote. The poems also lacked art, suffering from "an ungainly structure, an incoherence of parts, and a lack of conclusiveness in the whole." Joyce, who had adopted the unfortunate habit of firing off letters to the editor in response to negative reviews, accused Vendler of "wasting [her] intelligence on destructive activities." In rebuttal, Vendler insisted that criticism was "a natural human activity" and that Joyce's poetry was "frigid and inanimate."

Only a year before, Joyce had met Helen Vendler in London, at a party given by John Gardner, and though the two women did not have much in common, Joyce had felt they'd gotten along fairly well. Vendler had been the source of one of Joyce's recent job offers, having arranged a visiting professorship at Boston University, where Vendler was then teaching. Joyce had declined, and now felt that Vendler's attack on *Angel Fire* was personally motivated. She confided in her journal that "I can't take her dislike for my writing very seriously." Still, the criticism had stung. Joyce's sensitivity came through clearly in an April 5 letter to Evelyn Shrifte, who had written to console Joyce about the review: "I wonder if you might . . . in the future . . . try not to make references to such things . . . ?" Joyce asked. She wanted "not to think or dwell upon negative things, especially when I'm working on something new or about to go teach a class." She added that "Helen Vendler and I know each other—she simply doesn't like me."

Another incident that spring revealed Joyce's sensitivity to incidents or people she considered destructive. She had accepted an invitation to visit a literary symposium at Ohio University, where the other guests included the critic Leslie Fiedler and the poet Robert Bly. During a panel discussion featuring all three writers, an audience member (ironically, a psychology professor, whom Joyce considered "near-deranged") began attacking the panel "in a tiresome, really mean way." The level of discourse among Joyce's fellow panel members quickly descended to the same level, much of the venom directed unexpectedly at her. Joyce recalled the moment when she'd had enough: "it crossed my mind that I would simply get up and leave—and I did; I walked off-stage a few minutes before the panel would have disbanded. So much for literary high-flying talk in Athens, Ohio." Recounting the incident to Gail Godwin, Joyce said this unpleasant incident caused her "the most emotion I've felt in over a year." During the panel discussion, she had felt "waves of hatred" coming toward her, and "if anyone had tried to stop me I believe I would have just broken into a run." One of the English department hosts, Stanley Plumly, followed Joyce outside and into the parking lot, trying to console her, but Joyce kept walking. In a letter to the poet Anne Sexton, Joyce confessed that she had left the symposium in tears, but the next day "it all seemed to me funny."

The incident suggests, however, that Joyce had been mistaken in her belief that she had "transcended" the sphere of her personal ego and its emotions. Her vulnerability to what she perceived at the symposium as "waves of hatred" recalls her childhood fear of the sexual predators and unfriendly teachers who had terrorized her. (Despite her fame, the Athens appearance was only the third time she had agreed to read her work in public. "I'm really new at this," she told a local journalist.) Joyce's style of responding to social and public situations had been conditioned by her early experiences with a world she perceived as hostile and potentially violent. In this case, however, her feelings of victimization were justified. According to a well-known poet who attended both the symposium and a local party the night before, "she was a victim of Robert Bly. He and Fiedler stood in the kitchen to plot how they would attack her, which they did on the stage of the auditorium the next day. And on the morning of the next day I watched Bly, in the living room of Stan

Plumly's house, excoriate her in savage terms for what seemed to be the offense of being popular and writing a lot. . . . I've seen writers treat each other badly but never so badly as she was treated—and she had every reason to walk off stage and leave town."

She and Ray left Athens with an enormous sense of relief, and when she got home she wrote a long, satirical story, "Rewards of Fame," loosely based on the incident. Joyce resolved to pick and choose her speaking engagements more carefully, and used such forums to discuss her new thinking about literature, psychology, and transcendence. In March, she gave a talk to the Michigan Association of Psychoanalysts called "The Visionary Experience in Literature." She found the psychoanalysts a "congenial, lively group" who responded positively to her ideas. Though most were Freudians, she noted that they sounded more like Jungians. "Of course I didn't say that I consider psychoanalysis doomed," Joyce observed wryly in her journal. "And Freud a tragically limited human being." Though invited as an authoritative speaker to such events, Joyce stressed to Kay Smith that she viewed herself primarily as a student and insisted that she was now learning more than ever. In addition to her teaching and her work on the *Lucien Florey* manuscript, she was taking a class in Buddhism and attending a lecture series in psychology.

As the hectic spring semester drew to a close, she and Ray were looking forward to another trip to the western United States, the setting of Joyce's novel-in-progress. They left Windsor in late June, and by July 6 Joyce was reporting to Kay that they were having "a glorious time," exploring California and discovering regions they hadn't visited during their previous trip. Joyce was particularly impressed by the Carmel Valley, the Lake Tahoe region, and the Sierra Nevadas. They also stopped for a few days near Stanford University, where both she and Ray enjoyed using the impressive library and taking long walks around the campus. Throughout the trip Joyce was avidly taking notes for *Lucian Florey*, hoping she could capture the mystique of the California landscape. "Unless you see the coast along Highway 1 and the Sierra Nevadas and Mt. Shasta up in the Cascades," she wrote to Gail Godwin, "you have no idea of California, and its strange appeal."

Impressed as Joyce was with the countryside, she was disappointed by her visits to the Esalen Institute's Zen Center and Tassajara. In her journal, she wrote mockingly of the "mystical" practices at these institutions: "Such foolish, exhibitionistic people at Esalen!—and the stilted formalities of the Zen Center, where earnest young people wore heavy black Japanese-style robes in 95° heat, in a stifling canyon." The residents' devotion to Zen discipline, she complained, had not freed them from "local, limiting rules of conduct. What is appropriate for a Zen monastery in Japan simply isn't appropriate in California in mid-summer." Joyce found it absurd that a Zen Center bulletin board announced a suspension of *zazen* sittings because of a holiday: "I had always believed that to the Zen student *zazen* was a joyful experience, not a task; evidently I was mistaken." Yet she was moved that at both Tassajara and Esalen the people were "grimly hoping to find something to believe . . . *something* meaningful." Despite these disappointments, Joyce herself found something meaningful in another social experience during this western trip. She participated in a weekend seminar given by the anthropologist and linguist Gregory Bateson, and she enjoyed the weekend thoroughly. Bateson was "obviously a genius," she remarked.

Leaving California, Joyce and Ray drove through the Canadian Rockies, visiting British Columbia's Glacier Park, then reluctantly began the long drive back to Windsor. This month-long, eight-thousand-mile excursion had been such a positive experience that she and Ray "felt rather homesick when we got *home*." Nonetheless Joyce had gotten exactly what she needed from the trip, and in the following weeks continued "working furiously" on *Lucien Florey*. She joked to her friends about the novel's extraordinary length: to Gail Godwin, she observed that she was on page 442 of the current draft, and was only one-third of her way through the story, and she told another friend, in mock-despair, that she really didn't "want to write the longest novel in English—help!" She found that *Lucien Florey* was the "most uncontrollable" of all the novels she had written: the second draft, less a revision than a full-scale rewriting, bore little resemblance to the first, but she found this complex story "the most exciting" of her career, "partly because it's about half-buried emotions I evidently have, but never exactly articulated or comprehended before."

Now that September was approaching, the usual seasonal distractions helped divert Joyce's attention from her ballooning manuscript. As usual, she looked forward to teaching her fall classes, even though her literary fame and her reputation as an excellent teacher meant that the size of both her literature and writing classes had grown unusually large. The 1973–74 academic year, she said, "should be a complex, rich, lengthy, and exhausting one." Since her novel *Lucien Florey* dealt in part with the teaching profession, Joyce had been reflecting more than usual on her academic career. She told Gail Godwin that "it's my secret belief that teaching is more addictive than anything so mild as drugs." The only blot on her optimism about the coming year was an attack of tachycardia she suffered in early September. Though the seizure was alarmingly protracted, lasting more than an hour and bringing hallucinations and thoughts of death, Joyce reflected in her journal that her recent attacks were "not as frightening" as those she had suffered in college. "I lie down and wait for them to pass. They are quite infrequent—once a year, perhaps—and no longer have the power to terrify."

In addition to her teaching, Joyce had carefully selected some speaking engagements for the fall. In November, she visited Washington, D.C., and sat on a panel discussing "bio-ethics (who has the right to sterilize and manipulate whom, etc.)." Other participants included the renowned psychiatrist Robert Coles, whom Joyce greatly admired, and the conservative economist Lester Thurow, whose opinions Joyce found alarming. She recalled that Thurow "screamed at our panel words to the effect that 'subsistence' people had no place in modern society," and she decided that he was "a fascist." (The discussion had been so upsetting that Joyce's insomnia returned for the next few weeks.) The conference had been organized by the Kennedy Foundation, and Joyce had been personally selected as a participant by Sargent and Eunice Shriver, who admired her novels. While in Washington, Joyce and Ray were taken on a VIP tour of the White House, an event she found unexpectedly tedious; halfway through the tour, Joyce and Ray slipped under a velvet rope and escaped. Alluding to the Watergate scandal, Joyce remarked to Gail Godwin that "Ray kept looking around for Nixon scurrying down the corridor in his bathrobe," but "we saw no signs of life." Yet the trip had been pleasant in many ways. Joyce was impressed by the capital's physical beauty; she and Ray enjoyed visiting the National Gallery and taking their customary long walks in Washington's surprisingly warm November weather. Returning to Windsor, Joyce was pleased that her only other commitment that year was to the MLA convention in late December, where she had agreed to participate in a panel discussion of androgyny. She had also agreed to attend an MLA panel on her own fiction.

Another concern that fall was the gauntlet of reviews for *Do with Me What You Will*, which was published in October. Though response was somewhat mixed, the positive reviews far outnumbered the negative. As usual, reviewers' opinions were notably contradictory. In *The Atlantic*, the book was damned as "ungainly—an outpouring without a shape," while Walter Clemons in *Newsweek* found it "the most carefully shaped of her novels." The reviewer for *Time* found the passive heroine, Elena, "one of the most boring women imaginable" and Joyce's treatment of the legal system unconvincing, resulting in "one of her weakest books to date," while Calvin Bedient in *The New York Times Book Review* considered Elena's story a "hypnotic dramatization" that was "striking in its relentless and subtle pursuit of psychological observation." In general, reviewers were troubled that Joyce had chosen such a quiet, enigmatic heroine for this massive novel, and they believed she allowed herself, in some scenes, a melodramatic treatment of love and infidelity.

Again Joyce tried to remain indifferent to critical opinion, writing in her journal that she felt "unmoved by excellent reviews: this isn't normal. I can see that this past year of meditation is having the result of diminishing my emotions generally. Whether it's good or bad or merely necessary I can't know." But she admitted to Bob Phillips that when Evelyn Shrifte telephoned about the front-page rave in the *The New York Times Book Review,* she felt "relief. I had been prepared to be philosophically resigned, as usual, but must say I would rather be girlishly happy." Despite her current absorption in *Lucien Florey,* Joyce did, after all, still have an enormous emotional investment in *Do with Me What You Will.* She recalled to Gail Godwin that "I loved writing it—I don't think I had ever loved writing a novel so much." She expressed gratitude when Gail insisted it was Joyce's best book: "I think so too," Joyce said, "and feel very attached, sentimental, even defensive of the characters." Long after completing the novel, Joyce continued to have dreams about Elena and Jack.

As the fall semester progressed, Joyce maintained her typically frenetic work schedule. In addition to teaching and finishing *How Lucien Florey Died, and Was Born,* she was preparing three other manuscripts for 1974 publication. (She had also hoped to bring out a group of three recent novellas in 1974, *Where the Continent Ends;* but like *Lucien Florey,* this book was displaced by other manuscripts and never appeared.) Her new collection of essays, *New Heaven, New Earth* and a volume of stories, *The Goddess and Other Women,* would both be published by Vanguard; and she had contracted with John Martin's California-based Black Sparrow Press for her collection of academic satires, *The Hungry Ghosts: Seven Allusive Comedies.* In her journal, Joyce noted that *New Heaven, New Earth* was her "least ambiguous book, very moral and very serious, absolutely 'my heart laid bare.'" Gathering essays on such disparate writers as D. H. Lawrence, Franz Kafka, Flannery O'Connor, Sylvia Plath, and Norman Mailer, she remarked in her preface that these visionary artists, "having experienced what seems to them as incontestably suprapersonal spirit that speaks through them, generally affirm all manifestations of this spirit and see the ordinary world's division of it into 'good' and 'evil,' 'objective' and 'subjective,' as fallacious." Such an affirmation clearly reflected Joyce's own current goals as a writer and suggested a highly personal, if idiosyncratic, thematic unity to *New Heaven, New Earth.*

Her short-story collection *The Goddess* was an even more personal book, since many of the stories were highly autobiographical (though braided with a considerable amount of fiction). She felt an "astonishment that *these words are going to be read by other people.* What upsets me because it is intimate, what pleases me because it is impersonal, art-work rather than journal, would appear to the reader unfamiliar with my life as more or less the same." Several of the twenty-five stories—"The Voyage to Rosewood," "The Dying Child," "Ruth"—made explicit use of her native countryside near Lockport, and some dealt with extremely personal themes: "Blindfold" centered on a young girl's sexual abuse, for instance, and "Concerning the Case of Bobby T." recalled Joyce's adolescent relationship with Roosevelt Chatham, her black junior high school friend.

Joyce's *Hungry Ghost* stories were in a deliberately lighter vein than either *New Heaven, New Earth* or *The Goddess*, but this book had a negative effect on her personal life, since she had assembled a collection that, one by one, dissected the foibles of her English department colleagues. In addition to the O. Henry Award–winning "Pilgrims' Progress," which included the unflattering caricature of Lois Smedick, and "Up from Slavery," which portrayed her only black colleague as a pompous womanizer, "The Birth of Tragedy" depicted a gay professor's sexual harassment of a terrified graduate teaching assistant, limning a real-life situation that had been a recent source of gossip in the Windsor English department. The collection also included another of Joyce's oddly prophetic tales, "Angst," which dealt with a woman novelist who attends a conference session devoted to her work. (After Joyce's own MLA session, she was amazed by how accurately she had dramatized her character's decidedly mixed emotions.) Although Joyce deflected attention from the objects of her satire through her use of literary allusion, her comical stance (she quoted Henry Fielding in her epigraph: "Surely a man may speak truth with a smiling countenance"), her tongue-in-cheek prefatory statement that "no resemblance to real persons is intended or should be inferred," and even by her choice of a relatively obscure publisher for the book, any publication by Joyce Carol Oates in 1974 automatically received wide press coverage. When it appeared, the book only intensified Joyce's controversial reputation among the Windsor faculty.

From Joyce's perspective, she had an altruistic motive in working with Black Sparrow, since she hoped to support small-press publishing; her own career had first thrived, after all, in the literary magazines. She had written to her agent, Blanche Gregory, that she wanted a less restrictive contract with Vanguard, so that she could submit work to small presses. She particularly admired John Martin and editors like him, whom she viewed as "working constantly, for love of what he does, for—I gather—not very much money." Martin, who had published in book form Joyce's long essay on D. H. Lawrence the previous year, recalled that he was making a particular effort at that time to publish unknown American poets, and that the expensive, autographed editions of Joyce's books he brought out did help to support his less commercial ventures. And he genuinely admired Joyce, considering her "the Dickens or Trollope, or even the D. H. Lawrence, of the latter half of the twentieth century." His only conflict with his most famous author came when he declined to publish her collected poems; Martin felt that his other poets would have resented him for publishing Joyce's poetry, which few readers considered equivalent in quality to her work in prose.

Joyce continued her involvement with smaller literary magazines as well. She agreed to write a regular column for the prestigious poetry journal *Ameri-*

can Poetry Review and used the column to publicize writers she admired, such as Colin Wilson and Philip Levine, and to get revenge on Roger Sale, the critic who had repeatedly attacked her work. Reviewing Sale's book *Modern Heroism*, Joyce wrote: "I read it to see if the high standards Sale uses to punish others are, in fact, observed by Sale himself in his own writing. They are not. *Modern Heroism* is an utterly commonplace achievement." She also used this forum to criticize the less savory features of the American literary establishment. One column recounted her unhappy experience at Ohio University, and another mocked the celebrity status given to certain writers, focusing on one particular "reward of fame" that had recently come her way. Describing a letter she had received from a university "special collections" curator who had gushingly proposed "a 'Joyce Carol Oates Collection' that would be a nucleus around which this university could build a great literary center," Joyce commented acidly: "How exciting!—to be a *nucleus*! Every infantile maniac's dream!"

Joyce had also ventured into other types of literary activity. She had conceived of a literary magazine, *Ontario Review*, which she and Ray would edit from their home as an additional way of supporting contemporary literature. This ambitious new project had also been the product of Joyce's visionary imagination: she told her colleague Gene McNamara that one day she was simply daydreaming, staring out the window, and the sight of a white bird soaring through the air seemed to her the ideal logo for a magazine. At that moment, she decided to undertake *Ontario Review*, sketching the bird logo herself. She wrote to Evelyn Shrifte that the magazine would appear twice yearly, "about 150 pages, of fiction, poetry, essays, and reviews, the emphasis to be upon American/Canadian work." Joyce saw the magazine as another way of paying back the small-press establishment that had helped launch her career; she and Ray took a special interest in finding and nurturing new, unpublished writers.

Apart from her prolific output in virtually every literary genre, her full-time teaching, and her efforts with the new magazine, Joyce was turning down few opportunities to communicate with other writers and scholars, especially in the wake of her broadened spirituality and its effect on her thinking and writing. After her appearance before the Michigan Association of Psychoanalysts, an analyst named Dale Boesky initiated a correspondence with Joyce about "the methodology of applied psychoanalysis and literature." In September and October of 1973, Joyce wrote long, extraordinary letters to Dr. Boesky outlining her views. Despite her frequently troubled characters, she said that she didn't believe in "neuroses" but rather saw them as "symptoms of restlessness, a normal and desirable straining against the too-close confines of a personality now outgrown, or a social 'role' too restrictive." In her fiction, however, she insisted that "nothing must be denied or softened or feared; all must be accepted. By a constant deflation of the Unconscious, with an awareness that the Unconscious is wilder, older, more dangerous, more idiosyncratic, more generous and more therapeutic than the ego, the ideal artist hopes to synthesize the ostensible contradictions of life and experience it as a seamless unity." Dr. Boesky found Joyce's letters so brilliant and stimulating that he published them in *The International Review of Psychoanalysis*, thus adding yet another, unexpected item to Joyce's long list of publications.

Though Joyce found her involvement in these various projects energizing rather than depleting, sometimes she felt no less astonished than her critics and readers at the amount of work she was producing. In a journal entry for December 18, she noted her and Ray's plans for *Ontario Review* (its first issue would appear in fall 1974) and took the opportunity to reflect on her work that had appeared in the past year—*Do with Me What You Will*, the small book on D. H. Lawrence, an off-Broadway play, and shorter work in more than a dozen magazines. "This is really too much," she told herself. "When did I write all these things . . . ?"

Joyce's happily productive year closed with a bizarre, upsetting incident in Chicago, at the 1973 MLA convention in late December. Though she enjoyed most of her activities, her panel on androgyny was unexpectedly attended by her estranged Detroit friend, Dan Brown. She recalled that Dan "looked pale, haggard, bitter. Murderous." At the end of her talk, Dan made his way through a group of people surrounding Joyce and thrust a small box into her hand, saying, "Here's a present for letting me *starve* in London!" Recoiling, Joyce let the box fall to the floor; she never retrieved it, and later was told it had contained a razor blade. (But according to Dan, the "present" was intended as a joke, not a threat of violence: the box contained a package of condoms.) Brown left immediately; when Joyce got back to her room, she phoned various hotels in the area, trying to locate him, but could not. The critic Leslie Fiedler was also attending the convention, and he told Joyce that Dan had recently initiated a slanderous letter-writing campaign against her and that he should be considered dangerous. Dan had also written to various other people, including several New York book and magazine editors, sometimes enclosing a story he had written called "Why I Killed Joyce Carol Oates: A Memoir." In this manuscript, later published as "Hatred" in a collection of Dan's stories, the narrator discusses his troubled relationship with a famous woman writer whom he finally murders by bashing in her head with a shovel. Dan also wrote angrily about Joyce to Blanche Gregory, who was no longer his agent, calling Joyce a "despicable bitch" and warning that she should stay away from him.

After hearing about the incident in Chicago, Blanche sent a worried letter to Ray Smith at his campus address, not wanting to alarm Joyce any more than necessary. She enclosed the letters she'd received from Dan, and expressed her concerns about Dan's state of mind. Blanche, Joyce, and Ray were relieved, at least, that Dan had returned to the Far East, teaching U.S. soldiers stationed in Thailand. Back in Windsor, Joyce tried to handle the situation by writing directly to Dan. She explained again why she hadn't been able to review Dan's novel, saying she was astonished that he still harbored such resentment. She also threatened legal action if Dan continued his letter-writing campaign and suggested he consult a lawyer. But this only fueled Dan's rage: addressing her as "Injured Innocence," he wrote a long letter attacking Joyce for refusing to help him and ascribing his inability to publish further novels to the same homophobic literary "mainstream" that had made Joyce wealthy and famous. "You threaten me now with a court suit," Dan fumed. "It isn't enough that you inflicted enormous pain on me, not once but several times. Is this just one more manifestation of your terrible temper, your temper tantrums?" He concluded by exclaiming, "Push this slander case, why don't you!"

In response, Joyce insisted that she had no prejudice against homosexuals and, if a court case was necessary, she would be happy to donate any amount she might receive to the gay liberation movement. In a second letter, she tried commiserating with his difficulties and simply wished him well, but this olive branch had no effect: Dan only accelerated his hostile activities, continuing his letter-writing campaign and occasionally remarking that Joyce's many letters to him represented "a literary gold mine" (according to Dan, his new agent had suggested this idea). By April, Joyce had had enough. She sent Dan a curt note, saying she would now have to take extreme measures. One of these measures had been to write a letter to *The New York Times Book Review*. Published on April 14, the letter did not identify Dan but noted that an individual writing from the Far East had begun attempting to sell her correspondence. She warned that "a legal action of some kind would be brought against any magazine that published this material." She then recounted, "as instruction to other writers," the general situation that had caused the feud with her former friend. "This man is, I believe, as much a victim of our culture's unfortunate emphasis upon fame, as he is of his own emotions. He might have chosen anyone to threaten: 'Joyce Carol Oates' was simply the only writer he knew well enough. The letters I wrote him represent only my futile attempt to reason with a most unreasonable individual."

Now that Joyce had cut off their correspondence, Dan tried a new ploy. On May 9, he sent a fake letter purporting to be from an official at the "Far East Division" of his university. Ostensibly written by one "Dr. Carl T. Arnow," the letter began: "Dear Ms. Oates, Unfortunately your letter of April 16th did not reach Dr. Daniel R. Brown of the University of Maryland. He committed suicide in Ubon, Thailand. Word has only just reached us here in our office."

According to the letter, Dan had died because of ill-treatment he suffered by Joyce and had left a suicide note that concluded, "Nobody can sue a dead man." Extremely upset, Joyce wrote "Arnow" a long letter, defending her actions and recounting Dan's emotional problems. Continuing the fiction, Dan sent another letter from "Arnow," defending his late friend Dan Brown and remarking that Dan's "effects" had been placed in his care. The letter concluded sarcastically: "Enclosed is a check for the balance left in Dr. Brown's savings and checking accounts: $12.69. I am sure that he would have wanted you to have it."

Joyce and Ray had quickly discerned that the letter about Dan's suicide was a hoax, and decided simply to ignore the situation. Dan and Joyce never corresponded again, though each later wrote "letters to the editor" when attacked by the other in print. In 1984, when Dan (who still used the pen name "Daniel Curzon") was interviewed by the gay magazine *The Advocate* and made some derogatory remarks about Joyce, she wrote promptly to the magazine's editors: "Curzon's strategy in regard to promoting himself is, simply, to cry 'homophobic' when people recoil from his inflated assessment of his own talent." In 1993, when Joyce was interviewed by *Playboy* and mentioned the feud with her former "acquaintance," Brown sent a long letter to the editor, narrating his own version of the feud and adding that the magazine could reprint the story originally titled "Why I Killed Joyce Carol Oates" at no charge. *Playboy* declined the offer.

Although Joyce would later dismiss her relationship with Brown and their conflicts as relatively insignificant in her life, both the loss of this once-close friendship and the ugly manner of its ending had clearly upset her deeply. Several of her short stories dramatized facets of the relationship: "The Betrayal," "Love. Friendship.," "Paradise: A Post-Love Story," and others. She also wrote several poems about the incident, such as "From the Dark Side of the Earth" (a reference to Dan's teaching assignment in Thailand), which attempts to see the situation from Dan's viewpoint. Joyce's next novel, *The Assassins*, would feature an obsessive homosexual character named Hugh Petrie, many of whose observations and emotional difficulties were based on Joyce's assessment of Dan's personality. As she told the *Washington Post*, "It was such an experience knowing there was somebody out there who would like me to die. It was very interesting. I really got a lot out of it, several stories, a novel." (For his part, Dan also pursued literary versions of this personal debacle—several short stories and a significant portion of his memoir were devoted to Joyce—and, like Joyce, simply moved on with his life, eventually relocating to San Francisco and achieving a significant reputation as a gay fiction writer and playwright.) While writing *The Assassins* in November 1974, Joyce chalked up the disastrous end of her relations with Dan to "my own bad judgment in terms of friendship." She later felt that Dan's personal difficulties had simply caused him to blow the entire relationship out of proportion: "I think of us still as friends, essentially," she wrote. "This 'misunderstanding' should [have been] over in a few days."

Balancing such negative incidents in Joyce's life was the new excitement she felt about her teaching. Her recent absorption in visionary literature had inspired a more innovative method in the classroom; she had begun stressing an interdisciplinary approach to literary study that incorporated readings in psychology, philosophy, and mystical writings, in addition to fiction and poetry. She had recently taught a course entitled Aspects of Consciousness, whose bibliography included dozens of titles, ranging from works by Whitman, William James, Carl Jung, and Teilhard de Chardin to contemporary books such as Abraham Maslow's *Toward a Psychology of Being* and Carlos Castaneda's *A Separate Reality*. She had also initiated a freshman course entitled Literature and Psychology, which filtered literary texts through the psychological theories of Jung and Maslow. (Joyce now considered Jung the greatest of all psychologists: "his wisdom stretches out to infinity," she wrote to her friend Gloria Whelan.) This became one of Joyce's most popular courses and dramatically increased her workload, the class size swelling to accommodate more than a hundred students.

But the public highlight of the year came not in Joyce's Windsor classrooms but at the Humanities Institute in Aspen, Colorado, where she was writer in residence for a week in July. Joyce's time there went "without a hitch," she wrote to Kay Smith. She met scholars from various fields, mainly government, history, and science, and found the Institute "a most interesting place altogether, as if Mann's magic mountain were given over to a think tank." Her time in Aspen went so well that she jokingly suggested this should be her last public appearance: "I'll quit while I'm ahead." But in October she accepted a two-day stint at Yale: signing the guest book at Calhoun College, she noticed that previous guests had included W. H. Auden, Northrop Frye, and Norman Mailer. Joyce wrote that she was "impressed (as one must be)," but she was not impressed by the place itself, where there was "incessant banging overhead, noise on the stairs and in the courtyard—endearingly drunken undergraduates—phonographs turned up high. . . . Is *this* the reward of a kind of fame? And how did Auden like staying here?" After one miserable, sleepless night, Joyce and Ray moved to the Sheraton-Hilton.

Despite Joyce's reputation as a reclusive, unapproachable writer, she had always believed that "we are on this earth to communicate with one another"; though she declined almost all interview requests geared solely toward publicity, she continued to participate actively in American literary culture through her campus readings and conference panels, her book reviewing, and her growing number of literary friendships. Apart from close friends such as Gail Godwin and Bob Phillips—she continued an avid, lively correspondence with both writers—she had expanded her acquaintance to include most of America's major literary figures of the 1960s and 1970s. (In Aspen, she'd been disappointed to miss meeting Saul Bellow by only a few days.) Joyce's tendency toward hero worship that she'd mentioned after meeting Doris Lessing in London was still apparent whenever she encountered older, revered writers such as I. B. Singer, Eudora Welty, and Lillian Hellman. (Before meeting Singer, she bought his latest book and, like the many other fans attending his reading, asked for his autograph.) But Joyce knew herself equal in reputation to her own generation of writers, and enjoyed meeting and exchanging ideas with fellow novelists such as John Gardner and Philip Roth.

Gardner, known for his prickly, combative personality and his outspoken criticism of many of his contemporaries, had admired Joyce's work since the early 1960s when, as an unknown writer and fiction editor of the literary magazine *MSS*, he had printed her early story "The Death of Mrs. Sheer" and had accepted her novella version of *The Sweet Enemy* (later he returned it, because of the magazine's financial problems). By 1974, Gardner was almost as famous as Joyce, having enjoyed both critical and financial success with his best-seller *The Sunlight Dialogues*. Though very different in temperament—Gardner was flamboyantly egocentric and a heavy drinker—the two writers enjoyed occasional visits and exchanges of letters. Both believed in the moral and social relevance of realistic fiction at a time when such metafictional writers as John Barth and Donald Barthelme (whose work Gardner despised) were having their vogue. During one lengthy, intense evening together, however, Gardner told Joyce that they were "antithetical." In her journal, Joyce reflected: "perhaps we are . . . he believes that art can be 'directed' far more than I allow; he believes one can more or less determine, program, what one will write." Gardner suggested that Joyce try writing a story "in which things go well, for a change," advice that made Joyce bristle: " 'I,' Joyce Smith, Joyce who is his friend, Joyce the conscious being, would gladly write such a novel for the edification of all; but, unfortunately, that self does not handle the writing, and will accept no assignments."

Another, more low-keyed writer whom Joyce admired was Philip Roth, with whom she shared a dislike of publicity and a monastic literary discipline. The two writers met in May, while Joyce was in New York for the NYU-Esalen conference. (Joyce had recently done an "interview-by-mail" with Roth, which she and Ray published in the inaugural issue of *Ontario Review*.) Joyce and Ray, she wrote to Bob Phillips, "had a very enjoyable lunch with Philip Roth, and afterward a walk in Central Park that lasted for hours; he's totally unpretentious, well-spoken, enormously well-read, and probably quite shy"—not the temperament she expected from the author of *Portnoy's Complaint* and *My Life as a Man*. Like Joyce, whose public shyness and fragile appearance seemed at odds with her ambitious, dynamic fiction, Roth seemed the antithesis of his sexually charged and flamboyant novels. Joyce also noted major differences between herself and Roth: unlike Joyce, who didn't own a television set and no longer read newspapers, Roth was an avid observer of the American political scene, especially in the wake of Watergate. Joyce told Roth that she and Ray learned all they needed about "the news" from "simply looking at headlines on the newsstands as we walked by. I must have sounded heretical to him." ("Must make an effort to know at least vaguely what is going on!" Joyce instructed herself, in her journal. "[President] Ford could have been assassinated a few days ago, for all we know.")

Not all of Joyce's encounters with her famous contemporaries had been pleasant, however. Some writers had been content to criticize her from afar: Susan Sontag called Joyce's relationship to her fictional characters "vampiristic," and, according to the *Newsweek* cover story, "one big female literary name" had sniffed that Joyce was "not our sort." That same year, Joyce and the prominent *New Yorker* writer Donald Barthelme had conducted, through the press, a kind of minor feud. Writing in *The New York Times Book Review*, Joyce had criticized a line from a Barthelme story—"Fragments are the only forms I trust"—taking it to represent Barthelme's fictional aesthetic. Joyce wrote: "This from a writer [. . .] whose works reflect the anxiety he himself must feel, in book after book, that his brain is all fragments." Interviewed by *Newsweek* a few months later, Barthelme returned the compliment, saying that reading Joyce's fiction was "like chopping wood" and that her work was only "at a slightly higher level" than Jacqueline Susann's. In a later interview, he said that his quotation about fragments had been "richly misunderstood . . . by my colleague J. C. Oates" and that the statement had represented a character's viewpoint, not his own. But by 1974, the feud had been tempered by humor. Barthelme concocted a facetious news story that might, he said, appear in *Women's Wear Daily* with the headlines "WRITER CONFESSES THAT HE NO LONGER TRUSTS FRAGMENTS . . . Trust 'Misplaced,' Author Declares . . . Discussed Decision with Daughter, Six . . . Will Seek 'Wholes' in Future, He Says." Barthelme's tongue-in-cheek article began: "Donald Barthelme, 41-year-old writer and well-known fragmatist, said today that he no longer trusted fragments. He added that although he had once been 'very fond' of fragments, he had found them to be 'finally untrustworthy.' "

Not to be outdone, Joyce composed her own mock news story, which she mailed to Barthelme as "partial restitution for having attacked him." Joyce's headlines read: "AUTHORESS SHIFTS LOYALTIES ... FORMERLY HOLISTIC & VIRTUOUS ... NOW ADMITS SECRET FRAGMENTARY ALLIANCE." Her story read: "Joyce Carol Oates, lady writer said to be 'prolific,' announced today that she may have acted 'in haste' in expressing delicately horrified distrust of 'fragments.' Some of her closest acquaintances are, she noted, 'fragments' in their own right." The story added that Oates was "known in the area for her reticence, and for hiding away in a house routinely disguised by huge banks of snow," but from her seclusion had issued a statement to the press: " 'Holistic' visions are simply too large to keep in a house this size,' Ms. Oates claimed." Barthelme also apologized. Referring to the "chopping wood" remark, he wrote to Joyce: "I said it, in a fit of grandiosity, and I guess I'm stuck with it. I'm sorry I said it, most uncolleguely of me. . . . I do find your work hard going, it's true, but give me this—I'm still reading. At the moment, *Do with Me What You Will*. When I am stoned to death for bigmouthedness, I will save two front-row seats for you and John Gardner." A few years later, Joyce finally met Barthelme in New York and the two became friendly correspondents.

Throughout 1974 and into the winter of 1975, Joyce's new manuscript *The Assassins* became the obsessive focus of her life; she worked exclusively on the novel until it was completed. Previously, she had often alternated a book chapter with a short story or a critical essay, but *The Assassins*, she noted, "will be the first novel I have written without any distractions in the form of columns, poems, short stories. The first full-length work I will have done that is a complete, constant meditation. It is safe to say that I am *never* apart from it." Beginning shortly after the assassination of a right-wing senator, Andrew Petrie, the narrative focused on three surviving relatives: his brother, Hugh; his widow, Yvonne; and his youngest brother, Stephen. When Joyce began the book in spring 1974, its working title had been *Death-Festival*; by August, she'd accumulated "a small mountain" of notes, totaling over 1,000 pages, and in November she completed the first section, a 220-page monologue by Hugh Petrie, a professional caricaturist who has bitterly resented his more attractive and famous brother and who has become obsessed—despite his homosexuality—with Yvonne Petrie. Though Hugh was based loosely on Dan Brown, Joyce gave Hugh some of her own traits as well. He suffers from tachycardia, is afraid to fly, and makes an aesthetic pronouncement that is taken verbatim from one of Joyce's prefaces: art "is not meant to be understood, but to be experienced." Yet the parallels with Brown are striking. When Hugh's work is rejected, he rails against the artistic establishment: "bastards uniting against me—persecuting me—trying to pressure me into conforming." Also like Dan, Hugh produces a document reporting his own suicide. In a New York novelty shop, he has a fake copy of the *New York Times* printed with a headline that declares: "Hugh Petrie, Prize-Winning Caricaturist, Dead By His Own Hand." The MLA incident is recast when Yvonne Petrie is presented an award given posthumously to her husband, and "a man ran up to the stage and threw something at her." At the end of Hugh's section, he attempts suicide in a Manhattan restaurant, firing a gun into his temple, but survives to endure the rest of his life as a helpless, blinded, totally paralyzed deaf-mute.

In parts two and three of the novel, Joyce switched to third person for the equally grim narratives focused on Yvonne and Stephen. Intellectual and reserved, Yvonne shares many traits with the outwardly composed but emotionally desperate women Joyce had created in her short-story volumes *Marriages and Infidelities* and *The Goddess and Other Women*. Finding herself in a kind of limbo after her dynamic husband's death, with little to do but sort out his papers and represent him at political conferences, Yvonne, like Hugh, is trapped inside her ego, and fantasizes her own brutal murder at the end of her section: two "assassins" wound her with gunshots, then hack her body to pieces with an axe. By now, it is clear that each of the surviving characters is his or her own "assassin," and the novel itself an extended meditation on the necessary death of an American view of selfhood and success focused upon the individual in isolated combat with other people and the world. This theme clearly grew out of the new philosophical outlook Joyce had developed after her mystical experience in London. In the novel's final, considerably shorter section Joyce introduced Yvonne's brother-in-law Stephen, a spiritually inclined young man who brings a religious, or visionary, dimension to the novel; yet he is a largely ineffectual character who drifts vaguely through life, uninvolved in the internecine squabbles of the wealthy Petrie clan but also unable to create a meaningful selfhood.

The story as a whole had been conceived, Joyce noted, out of Dan Brown's "threats against my life, or rather out of the emotions they engendered in me." The conference on "bio-ethics" she had attended in Washington had also helped inspire her political and moral themes; representing her late husband, Yvonne Petrie attends such a conference and finds it an upsetting experience. Describing *The Assassins* as a "difficult, teasing novel," Joyce found it her most draining writing experience since *Wonderland*. But unlike that novel, which she wrote at an intense, sometimes galloping pace, *The Assassins* was composed with a new, almost plodding deliberateness. In her journal, Joyce observed that her method of producing a long manuscript had changed dramatically in the years since her return from London and her burgeoning interest in Zen and in visionary literature. In her twenties and early thirties, she had disliked revision, since her original creative impulse had been spent and her imagination was already engaged with the next book. But now, she observed, "writing a novel is a *process*. It is an experience that evolves. The novel *is* its own experience and its subject is always the evolving of consciousness . . . that of the reader, the author, the characters." She was now writing, she claimed, from "a vantage point of total transcendence, liberation from blindness, freedom from snarls, restraints, ignorance, *sin*, whatever it might be called (mortality?) and begins at that point, with everything accomplished." Joyce now viewed her fiction not as linear, plot-driven narrative but as a "timeless or ahistorical vision." She found herself constantly rereading her work-in-progress, rewriting as she went along, becoming almost more involved in ceaseless revision than in moving the book forward.

Joyce's new emphasis on revision would only increase in the later 1970s and 1980s. By then, the method inaugurated with *The Assassins* of taking voluminous notes before starting to write, drawing elaborate maps of settings and family trees that traced back her characters' lineage for hundreds of years, and revising constantly once she did begin writing, would become a confirmed habit. The notion of creating a novel grounded in a specific chronology but that also achieved a lyrical, fluid meditation on large swaths of American history would come to fruition in experimental works such as *Childwold* (1976) and especially *Bellefleur* (1980). Heralding a new direction for her writing, *The Assassins* was in many ways Joyce's most ambitious novel to date: its layering of symbolism and literary allusion, its combination of psychological realism and dark, absurdist humor, and its larger vision of three isolated selves, each hopelessly embalmed in a monstrous subjectivity and together representing the random chaos and violence of an American society composed of people like them, constituted an intellectually formidable achievement.

Yet the "timeless" vision of *The Assassins* precluded its achieving some of the important qualities—dramatic tension and dynamic momentum, especially—that had distinguished *them, Wonderland,* and *Do with Me What You Will*. A more serious problem lay in Joyce's choice of protagonists, for unlike Jules and Maureen Wendall, Jesse Harte, or Elena Howe and Jack Morrissey, none of the three principal characters in *The Assassins* engages the sympathy or interest of the reader. For all its dazzling complexity this highly calculated novel lies inert on the page, a slow-moving morass of death-haunted perceptions and details that seldom achieves the hypnotic power of Joyce's other mature novels. Hugh's protracted monologue (which had been even longer in early drafts) is particularly frustrating, since for most readers the suicide attempt by this hate-filled, deranged man cannot come soon enough. ("Why do you talk so much?" one of Hugh's cousins asks him.) Though Joyce had "felt some anxiety" after finishing Hugh's section, she concluded that "he must be allowed his fate—his necessary destiny—the fulfillment of the pattern." By indulging her characters, however, Joyce lost even her most sympathetic readers. In the context of literary history, *The Assassins* is analogous to Melville's *Pierre* or Faulkner's *A Fable*, a far-reaching work by a major writer that nonetheless goes hopelessly awry.

As Joyce worked on the novel, three of her other books appeared, and their reception did not augur well for *The Assassins*. Just as the groundswell of critical praise early in her career had culminated in a National Book Award for *them*, a critical backlash was now in full swing. All three of Joyce's 1974 titles—*The Hungry Ghosts*, *The Goddess*, and *New Heaven, New Earth: The Visionary Experience in Literature*—received mixed responses. While some critics enjoyed the humor in Joyce's academic satires, others found them trivial and mean-spirited. The most wounding review, in *The New York Times Book Review*, bore the headline "Joyce Carol Oates is frankly murderous." Josephine Hendin called the satires "small situations of malice that so level every impulse toward escape, nobility, generosity or life that they exemplify the faults they claim to expose. What they invariably expose is Joyce Carol Oates's raw spleen."

Joyce's other, more ambitious volume of stories published that year, *The Goddess and Other Women*, was seen by many as less accomplished than her previous collections. This new book, John Alfred Avant complained, represented "Oates at her worst." He argued that she was repeating herself: the fictional situations were stale, the prose itself "dead on the page." Even Joyce's old friend Bob Phillips, writing in *Commonweal*, found the collection "unrelieved by humor or optimism," though he finally viewed *The Goddess* as "a thought-provoking document on love, hate, and pain in women's lives" and "art of a high order." The Canadian writer Marian Engel similarly praised the volume for its insight into women's "dark hearts." Although Joyce's critical essays typically received less widespread attention than her fiction, several critics did review *New Heaven, New Earth*, which was also viewed as an intriguing but often bewildering book. Some found the essays more interesting for their insight into Joyce's own evolving fictional practice than for their views on Lawrence, Kafka, Plath, and the essays' other ostensible subjects.

Although Joyce had now trained herself to pay as little attention as possible to reviews, her relationship to her critics would remain tense and unresolved; she adopted a policy of deliberately not seeking out reviews, yet her journal consistently recorded anxiety about the publication of each new book and the attendant onslaught of praise or blame. Dickens had called literary journalists "the lice of literature" and John Updike considered book critics "pigs at a pastry cart," but Joyce's journal entries on the subject were typically thoughtful rather than dismissive or cavalier: "How is a writer to contemplate his critics?" she asked herself. "To ignore them, to take them very seriously, to pick and choose among them? It would be a pity to banish all criticism simply because some of it, or most, is worthless; there are very intelligent, sensitive people writing criticism today. But just as I don't read student evaluations of my classes at the university . . . I think it's a good general principle not to read most of the criticism and reviews written about me. If Evelyn is especially delighted with a review, or if I open the *Times* and come upon a review, naturally I'll read it; but it's prudent not to seek out such things." To Bob Phillips, she admitted that "no notice at all is, in my opinion, better than the kind of contemptuous and even angry dismissals I often receive."

Joyce finished *The Assassins* in February 1975. After the spring term ended in late April, she and Ray took a two-week trip with stops in Washington, D.C., New York City, and several smaller New York towns: Brockport, where she visited her friends Bill and Han Heyen; Katonah, where Bob and Judy Phillips were now living; and finally Millersport, where she visited her parents.

Joyce made the most of her two days in Manhattan. She went to lunch with Lillian Hellman, whom she found "a gracious, frank, amusing, brilliant woman." The two had exchanged several letters before getting together: ironically, each was shy of approaching the other, though Hellman had repeatedly invited Joyce to come visit her either in New York or at her summer home on Martha's Vineyard. It was Hellman who finally initiated their luncheon meeting. Joyce also had a visit with Philip Roth and, at a party given by Joyce's friends Dan and Gloria Stern, she met Cynthia Ozick, whom she described as "gentle, sweet, lovely." Ozick had been an admirer of Joyce's fiction since her first book: "I reached up and removed it from the shelf of New Books at the New Rochelle Public Library," Ozick recalled, "studied a few paragraphs, and thought: ah. Ah. There is something here. . . . I felt she would be heard from." Ozick remembered that during the Sterns' party they discussed Joyce's interest in mysticism: "I found myself marveling, amazed: since in life (if not in fiction) I am myself an inflexible rationalist." A few days later, visiting the Phillipses in Katonah, Joyce also met the Texas writer William Goyen, whose fiction she greatly admired.

In Washington, Joyce had been invited to read her poetry at the Library of Congress, where she was given a gracious introduction by Stanley Kunitz, then serving as the library's poetry consultant, and was "treated like a queen." But she was handled less royally by Sally Quinn, to whom Joyce gave an interview for a story published two days later in the *Washington Post*. Quinn's article began ominously—"There is something about Joyce Carol Oates that annoys people"—and trotted out the shopworn image of Joyce as a timid nonentity. Quinn offered a detailed, rather catty critique of Joyce's hair, makeup, and "not particularly fashionable" dress, but of the reading itself acknowledged only that it was "a brilliant study in simplicity and perception." To Quinn, Joyce's lack of ego represented a "puzzle." Once again, Joyce patiently explained her indifference to publicity and to popular culture generally. Observing that she and Ray never watched television, she added: "When we got here at the motel we turned it on and it was as though we were a couple of aborigines. I said, 'Oh, look honey, this is what we're missing.' And then we saw all the deodorant ads." Joyce claimed that she no longer had any interest in winning awards for her work, remarking that the kind of egotism requiring fame and prizes was "just a phase of people's lives." Describing her own temperament, she told Quinn, "I don't think I get depressed or feel emotions like other people do. I think I have worked my way through all that."

Quinn's article annoyed Joyce. The continual frustration she felt at the distortion of her work and her personality in the press encouraged ongoing meditations on her own identity and only intensified her longing for a state of "invisibility." Now that *The Assassins* was completed and mailed off, she undertook a new literary experiment that reflected this longing: she began a series of short stories under a pseudonym, mailing them out herself to literary magazines around the country. Joyce didn't adopt the pseudonym— "Rae-Jolene Smith," a blending of her and Ray's names—to publish a different kind of fiction, her motive in the 1980s for choosing the name "Rosamond Smith" for a series of suspense novels. Rather she simply enjoyed the anonymity, as well as the sense of mischief and deception, involved in this effort, especially after her protracted, sometimes agonizing work on *The Assassins*.

To her delight, the stories were accepted by prestigious magazines such as *North American Review* and *Yale Review*. The latter magazine accepted a "Rae-Jolene" manuscript within days of buying an Oates story submitted by Blanche: "Had I known she had sent them a story," she wrote, "I wouldn't have sent them the other . . . ! A coincidence; how interesting it would be if both appeared in the same issue." (They did not.) Eventually Joyce produced enough stories under her pseudonym to consider collecting them—a contents page for this projected volume is in the Oates Archive at Syracuse University—but she finally abandoned this idea along with the pseudonym itself. Almost none of Joyce's friends discovered her game, even though John Ditsky, who knew Joyce's style intimately, published a poem in the same issue of *North American Review* that contained Rae-Jolene Smith's "The Disappearance." To Joyce's knowledge, only her friend Ruth Reed had recognized the imposture: "One Saturday morning, I was reading casually in the *Yale Review*," Ruth recalled, "and I read a short story by someone called Rae-Jolene Smith, and I finished the story, picked up the phone, called Joyce and said, 'Do you know anyone named Rae-Jolene Smith?' And she started to laugh—

she was absolutely delighted to have been found out at being under a pseud-onym. She was pleased that someone could recognize her work that way, I think, but she also liked the game of it."

Since returning from her trip to New York and Washington, Joyce had been pondering another serious and ambitious longer work. Apart from visiting with her parents, she had returned home to Millersport to immerse herself in the rural world of her childhood. She had begun having "stray unformed excit-ing thoughts about another novel" in March, only weeks after sending *The As-sassins* to Blanche. She knew only that the story would focus on a family living in the area she called Eden County and that the narrative would be diffracted through several of the major characters' viewpoints. Her working title was *Bro-ken Reflections*, and she spent the next few months simply taking notes for the novel, which she saw primarily in lyric rather than dramatic terms: "A prose-poem it seems," she wrote in late July, "but perhaps I can disguise it as a novel." Again Joyce concocted an elaborate family tree, since the story traced several generations of a farm family, the Bartletts, focusing on the teenage Laney; her older brother, Vale; her mother, Arlene; and her grandfather, Joseph. The fifth viewpoint character was Fitz John Kasch, the descendant of a powerful local family; a middle-aged intellectual, Kasch returns to the town of Childwold and becomes obsessed with the fourteen-year-old Laney.

Additional inspiration for the novel had come during another long trip Joyce and Ray took that summer: on the road for three weeks, they visited Toronto, Montreal, and Quebec City; Bar Harbor, Maine; Boston; and Lake Placid. It was during this trip that Joyce saw the name "Childwold" while driving along a mountain road, and this "richly suggestive" word "stung, stayed, grew, demanded room in my consciousness," partly because the novel re-created the "child's world" Joyce had known in Millersport. By August, Joyce began to feel overwhelmed by the stack of notes she had accumulated, recalling that this same process had preceded her composition of *The Assas-sins*. But once she began writing, in the middle of the month, the prose came swiftly. The first draft took six weeks, and by late September the manuscript, originally intended to be about 180 pages long, had reached over 300 pages. On October 15, she recorded in her journal that the novel was complete. Al-though she had done extensive cutting and rewriting, the final draft was 321 pages. Joyce had also produced an illustration—a sketch of a yew branch—for Vanguard to use on the dust jacket.

During these same weeks, Joyce had read galleys for *The Assassins*, which she and Evelyn had decided should displace Joyce's earlier long manuscript, *How Lucien Florey Died, and Was Born*. Joyce hoped fervently that her new novel would be well received, and for the first time suggested that Evelyn seek prepublication blurbs from other writers. "*The Assassins* is probably the most interesting book of mine I will be publishing for a while," she wrote, "so it wouldn't hurt to try promoting it in this manner." She was annoyed that the Vanguard copyeditors had made countless suggestions for revision, many of which she rejected: "One can query nearly every line of any manuscript," she told Evelyn, "but it's disheartening for the author to deal with it, since it assumes the author's general incompetence." Joyce had worked harder on this manuscript than on any she had written; despite its experimental nature and its eccentricities of style, she wanted the novel published as it was.

Joyce's withdrawal from press coverage of her work was now such that she hadn't even seen the notices of two relatively minor collections of her stories that had appeared during the summer. She and Ray didn't read the *New York Times*, so she was "astonished" to learn that a review by Elizabeth Pochoda of *The Poisoned Kiss* and *The Seduction and Other Stories* had appeared in the *Times Book Review*. "Vanguard usually informs—or warns—me of such things," Joyce noted. *The Poisoned Kiss* was a gathering of Joyce's "Fernandes" stories, her earlier foray into a pseudonymous identity, and *The Seduction*, published by Black Sparrow Press, brought together a group of recent stories that hadn't been appropriate for her last Vanguard collection, *The Goddess*. Joyce had risked incurring critical wrath by the near-simultaneous publication of two collections, and Pochoda did dismiss *The Poisoned Kiss*, suggesting that Joyce's mediumlike transcriptions of the Fernandes tales represented "automatic writing." But Pochoda praised the more familiarly Oatesian stories in *The Seduction* for "honoring the complexities of the real world." Though the collection was uneven, the weaker inclusions detracting from excellent stories such as "6:27 P.M." and "Passions and Meditations," it contained "some of [Oates's] best revelations of complexity in lives ordinarily thought to be without depth or value."

But *The Assassins*, the book Joyce considered her "best novel," received negative and even jeering reviews when it appeared in the fall. In *Newsweek*, Peter S. Prescott claimed that Joyce had written "a very bad, nearly incoherent novel," and *Time* called it her "roughest, most repetitive read." J. D. O'Hara, writing in *The New York Times Book Review*, complained that Joyce's characters lacked intelligible motivation: "these suspicious, isolated, hysterical victims merely flounder as their sickness bids." Even reviewers inclined to be sympathetic to Joyce's aims found it difficult to praise the novel. The feminist critic Suzanne Juhasz found the book undermined by repetition: "The novel is vivid but too long; insightful but lacking an underlying intellectual clarity." Like Juhasz, Patricia S. Coyne considered *The Assassins* well written—"Stylistically, she is irreproachable"—but felt that it constituted "a failure of vision." Coyne insisted, however, that critical hostility to Joyce's productivity was partly responsible for the book's negative reception. Had it taken years to write, she suggested, "it would have been greeted with boundless critical enthusiasm." But the literary establishment, for the time being, had had enough books by Joyce Carol Oates. "Her name," Coyne wrote, "once mentioned with reverence among the literati, is now increasingly spoken in jest."

As if the harsh reviews of *The Assassins* hadn't been difficult enough to bear, Joyce learned soon after the novel was published that the writer and film director Elia Kazan was threatening a lawsuit against her and Vanguard, alleging that since Kazan had published a best-selling novel entitled *The Assassins* in 1972, Joyce and her publisher were infringing on Kazan's property rights. (The lawsuit was never filed, since titles cannot be copyrighted under U.S. law.) At the same time, Joyce's longtime British publisher, Gollancz, abruptly dropped her; Joyce was particularly dismayed in that she and Livia Gollancz, head of the firm, had become friendly during Joyce's year in London. But Livia Gollancz, Joyce remarked in her journal, had disliked *The Assassins* so intensely that she could not bring herself to publish it.

Joyce remained stoically philosophical about the decline in her reputation. "Since I am a woman," she wrote, "and quite realistic, I must accept the fact that in choosing to write about subjects generally claimed by men I will be violently resented by many people—men and women both—and that I will never enjoy the kind of quiet, near-universal acclaim Eudora Welty has earned. It must be nice to have that sort of reputation. [. . .] However, Eudora Welty is Eudora Welty and I can only be myself; I have no choice but to continue with what I am doing." She had given up, she added, on the "public aspect of 'Joyce Carol Oates,' " feeling more strongly than ever the attractions of "invisibility." Like William Faulkner, who had remarked after *Sartoris* was rejected by his publisher that now he could write solely to please himself, Joyce reminded herself that her primary focus was her writing, not what others thought about it. With a poignant air of finality, she added that "I seem to be more concerned with my actual work than I am with my public reputation . . . which I believe to be more or less finished by now."

11

Invisible Woman
1976–77

*I suppose I am detached from my finite, personalized
self; I identify with another, deeper region of being. . . .*
—*Journal*, January 4, 1977

Apart from her writing, Joyce had other personal satisfactions that helped
sustain her through difficult periods in her life. Her teaching, her several
valued friendships, and her long and stable marriage to Raymond Smith had
served for years as important compensating factors during times of stress and
discouragement. She had remarked to friends and interviewers that without
her writing, and the release it provided for her powerful and intense imagination, she would probably "go crazy." But while writing especially ambitious
and problematic novels such as *Wonderland, The Assassins*, and the new
manuscript she began in 1976, *Son of the Morning*, her normally therapeutic
creativity could itself become a destructive force, causing anxiety, insomnia,
and weight loss. Although Joyce had always enjoyed teaching, during these
trying periods her work with students and her friendly relations with colleagues were an especially welcome respite from the long hours spent alone
at her desk, working or simply brooding. Such external concerns, she said,
helped to keep her from "spinning completely off into the dark, into the abstract universe."

After the harsh critical reception given to *The Assassins*, which represented the nadir of her public reputation, Joyce cherished more than ever her
status as an "invisible woman," avoiding publicity and frequent attempts to
coax her into the limelight. (She routinely declined honorary degrees, for instance, even when offered by her fondly remembered alma mater; by using

her name in their brochures and continually pressuring her to attend campus functions, even Syracuse University officials, she felt, had begun trying to exploit her.) Yet the sociable and gregarious side of Joyce's personality found a congenial outlet in her teaching; still known as "Mrs. Smith" on the Windsor campus, she seldom referred to her writing career during her classes. Although now a tenured full professor, Joyce still taught three courses per semester: a writing workshop, a small graduate seminar in the Modern period, and her large undergraduate Psychology and Literature class, which had grown so popular by the spring 1976 term that over 115 students had registered. Despite her hectic schedule, Joyce got to know her students well, especially her teaching assistants and others enrolled in the graduate program. "There is a closeness between students and faculty at Windsor that is very rewarding," she remarked. Sometimes it could also be trying. Although Joyce occasionally had brilliant students, many were beset with drug problems and emotional difficulties—as were certain of her colleagues, also. There was an aura of hothouse melodrama about university life that belied the stereotype of the ivory tower, a fact that particularly disturbed Joyce, who had always sought a kind of safe haven in academic life. She had discovered that teaching was "by no means a quiet, insular, retiring profession."

Yet she enjoyed the challenge of helping to shape young writers in her workshops and considered it a privilege to read the great modern authors— James Joyce, D. H. Lawrence, and W. B. Yeats were among her favorites— with a small group of graduate students. "Anyone who teaches knows that you don't *really* experience a text until you've taught it, in loving detail, with an intelligent and responsive class," she observed during the fall 1976 term. "At the present time I am going through Joyce's work with nine graduate students and each seminar meeting is very rewarding (and draining), and I can't think, frankly, of anything else I would rather do." She prided herself on attending responsibly to her teaching duties and on not having missed a single class in her nine years at Windsor. During the spring term, she'd suffered two bouts with the flu, but despite her "fever & misery" she'd met all her classes. On September 16, she noted in her journal that she had been teaching for fourteen years altogether, and that nothing else was "more effortless, more enjoyable. An odd sparkling unpredictable synthesis of the intellectual appetite & the social. One is buoyed along by the students' presences . . . by their response to the literature & to the questions I ask or the problems I pose."

Joyce had always viewed teaching as a spontaneous, exciting, quicksilver exchange between herself and her students. "She was a very popular teacher," Gene McNamara remembered. "People came here from far away, just to study with her." Sometimes her students' admiration reached the point of idolatry: after Gene and several other teachers had lunched in the Dominion House, a popular faculty hangout, one of Joyce's female students asked the waitress for Joyce's empty Coke can as a keepsake. Her students often gave her gifts: a piece of jewelry, a bouquet of red roses. One day Joyce came to her office and found a "Love Poem to Joyce Carol Oates" taped to her door.

Years later, Joyce's former graduate students remembered her as an exciting, inspiring, and sometimes demanding professor. During her first class meeting with Joyce, Marinelle Ringer was mesmerized "by those eyes, the steady tone of her voice. This mysterious creature—far from frail—threatened everyone in the room, or, rather, *challenged*. I had never encountered an imagination half so gripping." Joyce's teaching assistant during the 1976–77 year, Max Alberts, similarly remembered her as "an electrifying teacher: her lectures are fluid and dynamic and she is as funny as a stand-up comic." Another student, Rebecca Bragg, had come to Windsor solely to study with Joyce, even though she'd heard that her favorite writer was "reclusive." But if Joyce Carol Oates was reclusive, Mrs. Smith was not: "She was always available to her students," Bragg remembered. "She always came across as calm, relaxed and unhurried." Joyce stayed fully engaged in the seminar meetings, her teaching distinguished by "flashes of dry wit." This seemed all the more remarkable, Bragg observed, in that the strain of Joyce's intensive work habits was apparent: "she frequently showed the physical signs of not having had much, if any, sleep the night before. Her skin would be chalky and her eyes a little bloodshot, with dark circles underneath."

Another of Joyce's students from the mid-1970s, Sally Rosenbluth, recalled that Joyce's classes "were always quite formal. It seems to me that no relaxed, easy intimacy or camaraderie ever developed among the students," largely because the students "ranged so widely in our abilities." Joyce's classroom persona, according to Rosenbluth, was "reserved and rather dry," but "never condescending." Joyce treated the students as equals, yet maintained "a distinct distance" from them. Rosenbluth was particularly impressed by Joyce's lack of emotion: "She was like a tall, slender, singularly elegant bird picking her way carefully through the swamp, and when she spoke or made comments in class, she would gaze at us all the while from behind the huge lenses of her glasses; her expression was not so much guarded as solemn, and owlish. She never smiled—at least, I can't remember her smiling." But even though Joyce was "reserved, yes, and hard to know," she was also "kind, and generous with her time and energy." Rosenbluth was one of the few creative writing students whose work Joyce considered publishable. She put her student in touch with Blanche Gregory, and Blanche placed Rosenbluth's novel—which had been her thesis project under Joyce—with a major New York publisher, Atheneum.

Ringer, Bragg, and other former students noted that not all the young people in Joyce's classes inspired her sympathy and helpfulness. Her seminar on
D. H. Lawrence and James Joyce, for instance, had contained "a plodder,"
Bragg remembered, the type of student "Joyce couldn't abide. . . . One day,
this young woman had the temerity to disagree with an interpretation Joyce
had put forward on *Women in Love.*" The student had her facts wrong, however, and Joyce "was clearly irritated, and proceeded to reduce the poor plodder to a small puddle of woe. Joyce could be as unkind to people she didn't
like as she was kind to those she did. She danced intellectual circles around
this student, tripping her up again and again." Marinelle Ringer was present
on the same occasion: "I saw [Joyce] *deliberately* belittle a young woman
(who'd been in a car crash that had left one side of her face immobile, her expression permanently 'mediocre') to the point of tears: the girl dropped the
class." Ringer felt lucky that she was one of Joyce's favored students: "I could
do no wrong," she remembered. "That, essentially, was the kind of teacher
Joyce was. She chose her students. Once selected, there was never any question about the grade: you were an A." Ringer came away from Windsor with
"considerable respect for Joyce Carol Oates, but little affection."

Another of Joyce's graduate students, Dan Zins, had taken several of her
courses, beginning during the 1973–74 academic year, and had later served as
her teaching assistant. "Oates was a magnificent teacher, clearly the best one
I have ever had," Zins wrote, remembering her as both self-deprecating and
"viciously funny" when deflating certain "sacred cows" in American culture.
He considered Joyce's politics "left/liberal, but she was anything but doctrinaire in discussing literary and political topics. . . . She could be every bit as
critical of misguided or dogmatic leftists and radicals as she was of those who
blindly or selfishly supported the status quo." According to Zins, Joyce encouraged students to see their educational experience as an opportunity for
personal growth. "I'm here to liberate you," she once told the class, though
she emphasized that each student had to "find an individual path." Incorporating religion, mysticism, psychology, philosophy, history, and politics into
her discussions, Joyce adopted an interdisciplinary approach to learning that
stressed an imaginative, individual engagement with literature on the part of
each student. She de-emphasized the process of grading, and said that she'd
once given an exam in which the students made up their own questions.
Clearly, Joyce's attitude toward grading had grown more liberal since the Phil
London debacle several years earlier. "Real life is an open book exam," she remarked. When the students wrote tests, she would be looking for their intuitive insights into literature; by contrast, term papers were a way to attempt a
more thoughtful, ordered analysis. Yet she advised them not to strive for perfection, which could be "deathly," but to respond as spontaneously as possi-

ble to literary works. "I'm more interested in getting my class to think in new ways than in memorizing things," she told them. "Go where your passions lead you—trust your intuitions!"

As a whole, Joyce's former students offer a seemingly contradictory portrait: Joyce was reserved, yet energetic; she was funny in the classroom, yet "unsmiling." Any university professor who has read through the student evaluations of a particular class can testify that students often have wildly varying impressions of a teacher, largely because of the way they have perceived their personal relationship with him or her. In Joyce's case, especially bright students or those she liked personally clearly got the lion's share of her attention. As for her wit, she admitted that her humor was of the deadpan variety, understated and very dry. Some students "got" this quality of her temperament, while others did not.

Joyce now taught purely for enjoyment. She and Ray had saved more than half a million dollars from Joyce's royalties and movie options, and Joyce no longer even knew the exact amount of her university salary. But even though she loved teaching, there were frustrations at the University of Windsor that now prompted her to consider more seriously the offers from other institutions she was constantly receiving. Her undergraduate Psychology and Literature course, for instance, with its more than 115 students, had been assigned to an "ugly windowless fluorescent-glaring auditorium" with exposed pipes and poor acoustics, a setting that was "an affront to the eye and the spirit." Teaching this "oversized doomed class," Joyce had to speak at the top of her voice and sometimes felt "as if I were teaching a night course in an extension school." She pressed on, hoping "to wrest some enjoyment from it," but observed that "this is minimal living, minimal teaching." Even her graduate seminars were not always satisfying, since several students, she reported angrily in a letter submitted to the university administration, "came regularly in various states of 'alteration of consciousness'—alcohol, Librium, and Valium being the principal crutches, though an eerie combination of alcohol and amphetamines accounted for the vivacity of the seminar's most outspoken member." She wondered how such people "came to be allowed into a graduate program at all." One graduate student reminded her of "a brain-damaged sheep."

Joyce was also troubled by the petty, backbiting politics among poets and professors at Windsor; because Canadian writers received so little attention, she noted, their tendency to become spiteful or envious of one another was even greater than among literary people in the United States. "The Canadian literary 'scene' (to use a foolish term)," she observed, "is so in-grown, so claustrophobic. One thinks of a few scrawny chickens pecking in the dirt and fighting one another because there isn't quite enough feed to go around."

There was no literary community in Canada to which Joyce cared to belong. Although Windsor had provided a comfortable detachment from the chaotic atmosphere of larger American cities, she had always felt somewhat anomalous as a "landed immigrant" in Canada: "I seem rootless, homeless, without specific identity," she complained. Yet for all her reservations about Windsor, Joyce found it difficult to contemplate abandoning her settled, productive life. Early in 1977 she wrote in her journal, "We should leave Windsor but I don't suppose we will: our friends here, who mean so much to us (for *how* could we possibly make new friends and even if we did, they wouldn't be *these people*), the relative quiet that allows me to write without many distractions, the house and the river and the city itself are all too appealing."

In contrast to the draining social life that caused her near-breakdown and prompted her escape to London in 1971, she had now established a network of relationships that helped to counter the arduous isolation of her writing life. Mainly through lively, intense luncheon meetings, Joyce had kept up her friendships with Kay Smith, Marj Levin, Patty Burnett, Gloria Whelan, and Ruth Rattner, though she saw these women less often than when she'd lived in Detroit. "From what I could see of Joyce's life," Ruth Rattner said, "95 percent of her time was taken up with study and writing. I think maybe our lunches were a way of staying in touch with reality." In Windsor, Joyce socialized with her colleagues Gene McNamara, John Ditsky, and Alistair MacLeod, but these men—all writers themselves—respected Joyce's need for privacy and time to work. As she'd grown more established and comfortable in Windsor, however, Joyce had become more involved in the English department's social life. Joyce often joined Ray and her male colleagues in the pub-like atmosphere of the Dominion House, where they gathered after their classes. In October 1976 she noted that for the past couple of years she had entered a new, "extroverted" phase, and marveled at the "amount of time I spend with others, talking, chattering, gossiping, frankly & shamelessly wasting time." Most of the English faculty enjoyed drinking, and Joyce was usually the only teetotaler in the group, a situation that pleased her. "Though I don't drink myself I seem to like it that others do, in my company," she wrote. "I notice how much warmer and friendlier and wittier they are, how much laughter there is, how very *human* the experience becomes. I seem to take on some of the milder characteristics of intoxication myself simply by being in their presence." As they had done in Detroit, Joyce and Ray also entertained occasionally. In early November they invited thirty of their Detroit and Windsor friends for a party that lasted until 2 A.M. But even such a major effort did not interfere with Joyce's writing: after the party, she and Ray stayed up until five o'clock, cleaning the house; but Joyce rose at eight and had her usual full, productive day, "no exhaustion or weariness."

Nor was Joyce closed to the idea of new friendships: that same year John Ditsky introduced her to Betsey Hansell, a painter and *Detroit Free Press* writer. Like Patty Burnett, Betsey asked to paint Joyce's portrait, and from that point forward the two women saw each other frequently. Unlike Joyce's affluent, socially connected women friends in the Detroit suburbs, Betsey was brash and outspoken—qualities Joyce liked. Betsey recalled that John Ditsky had warned her to "be very careful" with Joyce, who had certain "rules" about conversation with friends; she was especially sensitive about her work and her literary career, which she didn't like to discuss. "If you broke one of Joyce's rules," John Ditsky told Betsey, "she wouldn't talk to you anymore." As a result, Betsey felt intimidated at first: "I was really given these 'rules' of how to talk with her," and she'd thought to herself, "What kind of a person is this who needs all these rules?" But when she actually met Joyce, she felt greatly relieved: "she really is very easy to be with. I loved painting her picture; she'd sit there very peacefully and she'd talk to me about the book [*Son of the Morning*] that she was writing." Betsey did become aware of an essential reserve in Joyce, however, a sense of barriers that could not be crossed. She never felt comfortable bringing up to Joyce the types of intimate issues—emotions, relationships, sex, and other topics—that she discussed freely and avidly with her other women friends.

Instead Betsey and Joyce usually talked about art and ideas. Betsey was sometimes amused by Joyce's absorption in her fiction. One day, Betsey received an unexpected call from Joyce, who asked if she could come visit Betsey's studio and have a cup of tea. This struck Betsey as odd, since Joyce was not usually one for spontaneous visits, preferring instead to arrange get-togethers far in advance, often by letter. Betsey's warehouse studio was located in one of Detroit's dangerous inner-city neighborhoods, but nonetheless Joyce gamely climbed the outdoor steps to the studio. Once inside, Joyce inspected the studio intensively, studying Betsey's worktables and the layout of the room. Then Joyce said, "Well, I don't think I have time for any tea, thank you," and abruptly departed. It was clear to Betsey that Joyce had simply wanted to see the studio for something she was writing. "I had to laugh," Betsey said, "because it was such a transparent excuse—you know, coming over for a cup of tea, and not even staying for it." In a letter to Ruth Rattner, Joyce later acknowledged that she had "borrowed Betsey Hansell's utterly squalid studio down near the John Lodge Expressway" for a scene in her novel *Cybele*.

Despite Joyce's preoccupation with her fiction, many of her friends singled out one quality they considered her most admirable: her generosity. Whenever possible, she helped her writer and artist friends with their careers (although she would withdraw her support quickly, as she had done with Dan

Brown, if she felt someone was trying to exploit her). Betsey Hansell recalled that Joyce was "so wonderfuly helpful in any way she could be," inviting Betsey to illustrate one of her books and reproducing her paintings in *Ontario Review*. "I feel so strongly about her generosity," Betsey said, "and her lack of thinking that she's a big shot—she's got humility." Ruth Reed agreed that Joyce "was always generous to other people," and didn't "tolerate fools, or people who are not as generous in her profession as she herself is." Joyce would often write unsolicited letters of support for her graduate students when they applied for jobs, and she put her writer friends in touch with potential agents and editors. Joyce felt a continuing sense of gratitude, at times mingled with disbelief, at the success she had enjoyed, and she felt the impulse to help lesser-known but deserving writers to get their share of recognition.

During social occasions, the quality of Joyce's her friends most enjoyed was her sparkling, often mischievous wit. Abandoning the shy persona she presented to reporters and to people she didn't know well, Joyce could be funny, animated, and even dominant in conversation with close friends. Gloria Whelan remembered Joyce's dinner parties: "Their house was right on the Detroit River so that as you sat at dinner the great freighters, lit up like birthday cakes, floated silently by so close you felt you could touch them. . . . But the real pleasure in those evenings was the conversation, which went on and on until late in the evening." When Joyce disagreed with an opinion expressed by a guest, Whelan recalled, Joyce's typical response was "a humorous riposte." John Reed noted that "Once we got to know her, we saw how playful she was, and it was a lot of fun to join in." Lois Smedick agreed: "She has an impish wit, one could say sometimes a wicked wit, and when Joyce is 'on,' there is nobody funnier." Joyce was a particularly good mimic, and did hilarious impersonations of her Windsor colleagues and of famous writers she had met.

Like her writerly curiosity about her friends' lives, Joyce's witty, performance-oriented brand of humor helped maintain a distance between her social persona and the private, "invisible" woman who did the writing. Joyce had always made a determined effort to keep her personal relationships and her writing career in two separate realms. Like Patty Burnett, Betsey Hansell noticed that Joyce would often shift conversation away from herself, focusing on the other person and preferring to ask questions rather than answer them. Though she dedicated books to her friends and sometimes presented them with gift copies, she seldom referred to her work-in-progress or discussed her writing in any detail. Similarly, she and Ray had agreed early in their marriage that Ray would not even read her work. Except for *Wonderland* and a handful of shorter pieces, he had indeed read very little. From someone as close to her as

Ray, Joyce feared that even a "raised eyebrow" suggesting criticism or disapproval would be upsetting. Close friends such as Kay Smith eagerly read each new book of Joyce's, but Kay, with her sunny disposition and warm affection for Joyce, offered only praise and encouragement.

With her colleagues at Windsor, however, the exigencies of art and friendship continued to represent a conflict. Though the controversy that had arisen over Joyce's 1974 collection of academic satires, *The Hungry Ghosts*, had died down, Joyce still insisted that she had the right to incorporate her experiences with other people into her fiction. One story Joyce wrote in 1976, "Gay," was set—like most of the *Hungry Ghosts* satires—at "Hilberry University," a thinly disguised portrayal of the University of Windsor. (In "Gay," one of the characters calls the university a "hotbed of mediocrity.") On January 1, 1976, Joyce had recorded in her journal an upsetting incident at a New Year's Eve party: Charles Murrah, one of her colleagues, had been drinking and made a scene, abusing his hosts and other guests. Joyce wrote "Gay" shortly afterward, focusing on both Murrah's drinking and his homosexuality. She showed the story in manuscript to several of her colleagues. Gene McNamara told Joyce that "Gay" was simply too close to the facts and would hurt Murrah; Joyce made some minor changes, but the story still contained details such as Murrah's real middle name and the location of his apartment. "We had an argument about it," McNamara remembered, "the only argument we've ever had. Her position was that she had the freedom, the artistic freedom to do it." In her journal, Joyce recalled the quarrel: "[Gene] doesn't think I have the right to assemble bits and pieces of people, for use in fiction. . . . The problem is that I sometimes write from my own experience, and my own experience necessarily involves people I know . . . otherwise, what on earth *would* I experience?" Joyce acknowledged that "Gay" was "a superficial story, hardly more than an anecdote, but a moral parable nonetheless." She never included it in any of her collections but, ironically, it was reprinted the following year in *Best American Short Stories*.

Joyce's colleague Colin Atkinson had also been upset by the story, especially since it appeared in a widely read magazine. He remembered that Joyce stopped by his office and said, with a mischievous expression, "Colin, I've been a naughty girl—I sold the story about Charles to *Playboy*." Atkinson felt that Joyce's use of Murrah's problems was cruel: "No one has a right to do that to other people. If you've got power, the obligation is on you. She did a job on Charles, and she did it deliberately." He had also been upset by Joyce's satiric portrait of their black colleague, Ed Watson, in "Up from Slavery." After "Gay," Atkinson decided he would never read any of Joyce's fiction again. For his part, Murrah considered taking legal action. None of his family members had known about his homosexuality, although Murrah confessed that he sent the story to one of his sisters himself and that otherwise she probably would never have seen the magazine. Other colleagues acknowledged that Murrah did enjoy his brief notoriety: "He sent copies all over the place," Atkinson recalled.

Charles Murrah, at least, had never been a friend of Joyce and Ray's, but Joyce's colleagues were shocked when Joyce used sensitive material from her close friend Gene McNamara's life the following year. In the early 1970s, McNamara had conducted an extramarital affair with a woman named Pat Lowther, whom he'd met after giving a poetry reading in Vancouver. Both Pat and her husband, Raymond Lowther, were poets with minor reputations in Canada. In October 1975, Pat Lowther was brutally murdered, beaten to death with a hammer, and her husband was charged with the crime and ultimately convicted. McNamara's former involvement with Lowther became public when he testified at Raymond Lowther's trial and acknowledged the affair. Because the story was reported in the *Windsor Star*, McNamara, a married man with five children, became a focus of local gossip during the trial. The facts of the Lowther case, which included such elements as jealousy, psychological derangement, violence, and "literary" characters, seemed ready-made as a Joyce Carol Oates story, and Joyce in fact found the material irresistible. After writing "Harriet Stillman: A Romance," which appeared in the Canadian magazine *Saturday Night*, Joyce noted in her journal: "The McNamara-Lowther situation as the core, the characters completely changed, the discovery of the body omitted from the story, other 'facts' altered. 'Gene' is not in the story at all."

But Joyce's colleagues felt that she had again unnecessarily appropriated a friend's unhappiness for her own uses. "She did a real job on [Gene]," Colin Atkinson remembered, "for no reason at all. They were good friends. He was going through hell . . . there was no need to do that." By the time the story appeared, in November 1978, Joyce and Ray had already left Windsor, but Gene McNamara took a kind of literary revenge by writing a satirical story about Joyce. McNamara's story, "The Art of the Novel," published in *Chicago* magazine, described a famous woman writer named Hazel Pyncheon as the scourge of her friends at "Tecumseh College": "Her colleagues discovered themselves in her fiction distorted into disorderly drunks, fools full of greed and lust, people small of spirit. In her stunted vision, her colleagues and students were grotesques and she had no sympathy for them. And so they were exhibited in the freak show she called her fiction." McNamara's protagonist attacked Pyncheon's prose style as "turgid, given to clots of undigested exposition and rhetorical questions. She was a devotee of the dot-dot-dot school . . . and the exclamation mark! Yet her work had been translated into 14 languages." He also mocked her productivity, describing her as an "inexhaustible word machine" who occasionally looked up from the typewriter "to observe the trees outside her window, trees destined to be cut for pulp." Elsewhere in the story, alluding to Hawthorne and his obsession with the Salem witch trials, he likened "Hazel Pyncheon" to "a Salem judge in the 17th century. All around her she saw concupiscence, her students and colleagues consorting with dark forces, breaking faith with her covenant, and she hardened her heart against these evil fallen creatures and condemned them to a perpetual hell of confinement in her fiction."

Although Joyce's other close Windsor friend, John Ditsky, never saw himself pilloried in Joyce's work, he also disapproved of her method and sympathized with his angry colleagues: "it would have been so easy to disguise the people that she was parodying," he complained, "but she didn't do it." When Joyce told him that her forthcoming novel, *Childwold*, was dedicated to him, Ditsky remembered that "I had about six nervous months after she told me this." He was greatly relieved when the novel appeared: "I didn't find a trace of myself there."

Joyce had written "Harriet Stillman: A Romance" in New York City while teaching a six-week summer course in creative writing at New York University. Staying in a pleasant apartment on Washington Square owned by the university, Joyce used the time to explore the city but also, having just turned thirty-nine, to contemplate her life, her marriage, and her career. She and Ray had continued to think about leaving Windsor, and two offers that had recently arrived were particularly tempting: Jim Tuttleton, the chairman of the N.Y.U. English department, had invited Joyce to teach the summer course, an undergraduate fiction-writing workshop, in the hope of convincing her to stay permanently as a member of the English faculty; and she had also been invited to visit Princeton University as writer in residence for the academic year 1978–79. Tuttleton remembered that he'd been trying to get approval for a graduate creative writing program at N.Y.U., and hoped that if Joyce could be persuaded to join the faculty that she might direct the new program; there would also be a position for Ray as a professor of eighteenth-century English literature. Joyce and Ray both mentioned to Tuttleton that they would like to leave Windsor. "I thought it would be a double coup," Tuttleton said, "if I could appoint both Joyce and Ray."

Joyce had hinted to John Ditsky that it was "going to be hard to return to Windsor," commenting that even with "lootings, fires, etc., NYC is NYC, unmatchable." But whenever she visited the city, she became aware that it simply held too many distractions and that its frenetic atmosphere would not be good for her writing. As always, stability and quiet were essential components of her Flaubertian wish to "live like a bourgeois." As she reflected on her life

that summer, she was aware that the most important stabilizing factor remained her long and placid marriage to Ray. On July 22, she wrote in her
journal that "my marriage has made my life stable. Ray is a center; perhaps
the center without which. . . . But it's useless to speculate." She described
her husband as "kindly, loving, sweet, at times critically intelligent, sensitive,
funny, unambitious . . . Ray is an extraordinary person whose depths are not
immediately obvious." The idea of living without him would be "like the end
of the universe, the obliteration of time. Unthinkable. If I survived his loss it
wouldn't be Joyce who survived but another lesser, broken person." Several
years earlier, Joyce had implicitly compared her relationship to Ray with the
marriage of Virginia and Leonard Woolf. After reading Quentin Bell's biography of Virginia, she had exclaimed, "How fortunate for Virginia that she had
Leonard—! Without him, who knows?"

Although Joyce's writing, her teaching, and her friendships all had their
difficult times, the harmonious relationship between Joyce and Ray had
stayed remarkably close and unchallenged; they had spent only two or three
nights apart since their marriage in 1961. They had always shared a deep love
of literature, but since Joyce focused on fiction and Ray on criticism, there
was little of the rivalry or resentment that sometimes plagued literary
couples. Like Joyce, Ray struck people as modest and self-effacing; he preferred a quiet daily routine focused on work and on domestic pursuits such as
gardening. Even the temperamental differences between Joyce and Ray were
complementary rather than conflicting: while Joyce was intense, strong-
willed, wildly productive, and prone to philosophical brooding, Ray had a
calm and flexible nature, and was a slow, methodical worker who had spent
many years on his slender critical study of Charles Churchill. In her journal,
Joyce had recorded a conversation with Ray that revealed their contrasting
dispositions: "I asked him if he thought very often of death—of life-and-
death—philosophical matters—the odd fact of human personality and
consciousness—these teasing things I am haunted by constantly, every hour
of my life. His reply was simple: 'No.' "

The only major change in their marriage had been, for Joyce, a positive
one. As a younger woman, she had sometimes felt emotionally dependent on
Ray to an almost perilous degree. During the 1960s, she had told Dan Brown,
she had considered her life wholly determined by her marriage, even though
that wasn't a fashionable viewpoint during the advent of the women's rights
movement. Being in love was a dangerous state, she added, because it was always possible that something could always go wrong. More recently, especially in the wake of her absorption in meditation and Eastern philosophy,
Joyce had enjoyed a firmer sense of selfhood and independence, even as she
continued to feel close to her husband and secure within their marriage. She

had particularly enjoyed their recent work on *Ontario Review* because they now had a project in common to which they were both devoted. At the same time, she continued to keep her writing life separate from her marriage, to the advantage of both. "Marriage necessitates a fantastic concentration of feeling upon a single individual," she observed. Extramarital relationships would be impossible for her, she said, since she could not contemplate "a fierce, erotic, wholly serious love that avoids marriage. . . . I rather doubt that I could bear such an experience for I need the stability of marriage, if I hope to explore my writing, if I hope to live happily." Conversely, she felt that literary achievement by itself, without her marriage, would have little value: "what would it profit me, really, to be a fairly successful writer and to write books that deeply absorb me, if I hadn't my life with Ray . . . if we hadn't our private, secluded, utterly secret life together."

Joyce had often noted the difficulty of evoking successfully, in fiction, the phenomenon of marriage: good fiction required conflict, so her stories, as in the collection *Marriages and Infidelities* and the novel *Do with Me What You Will*, tended to focus on adultery and betrayal as the necessary pathway to personal liberation. Her story "The Dead," portraying the drug-saturated, promiscuous writer Ilena Williams, had projected an alter ego, "a way I might have gone" without a stable life and marriage. But even the suicidal Ilena, with her series of failed relationships, acknowledged that "marriage was the deepest, most mysterious, most profound exploration open to man: she had always believed that, and she believed it now. . . . This plunging into another's soul, this pressure of bodies together, so brutally intimate, was the closest one could come to a sacred adventure."

Joyce's friends greatly admired the settled, congenial marriage Joyce and Ray had developed over the years. "At the time I knew them," Gloria Whelan recalled, "they cared a great deal for one another and their relationship was mutually protective and supportive." Marj Levin saw the marriage as "perfect for Joyce," and she viewed Ray as "an attractive protector" who served as a buffer between Joyce and the outside world. Ray, for instance, handled money matters, household repairs, and similar pragmatic details, freeing Joyce to pursue her literary work. Lois Smedick felt that "Ray, in certain areas, had confidence where Joyce didn't." Joyce lacked a certain "ground of assurance," Smedick said. "Unlike some people, who have family or social background to draw on, she was kind of lost, making it totally on her talent." Joyce particularly disliked confrontation. Smedick remembered that Joyce and Ray had an unexpected problem one day with a Customs agent while crossing the border from Michigan into Canada, and whereas Joyce became upset, Ray handled the problem deftly. Moreover, unlike some husbands of famous wives, Ray always seemed relaxed and sure of himself rather than threatened by the attention Joyce received. "He handled the whole situation remarkably well," Evelyn Shrifte recalled. "Somebody else might have been viewed as 'Mr. Oates,' but Ray always held his own ground."

In her journal, Joyce described the sense of equilibrium she had achieved both within herself and in her marriage to Ray. Despite the vicissitudes of her reputation and the unpleasant aspects of literary fame, she felt secure in her personal life:

> At the age of 39 I have come through, more or less. Even if my marriage were to collapse I wouldn't be lonely; I would not feel rejected or isolated or abnormal in any way, living alone. Marriage is only valuable in terms of Ray. Marriage in the abstract—to anyone else—would not appeal to me. Aloneness (which is not loneliness) rather appeals to me.

Since she had her writing career and "a reasonable amount of money for security," Joyce felt that she could do quite well on her own. With her working-class background, Joyce knew that an important component of her own freedom, as of any woman's or man's, was economic. She disagreed with feminists who felt that men were "the enemy," believing that "if all women exploited by men had their own sources of income they would at once, by magic, no longer be exploited by men (except emotionally—and one does conspire masochistically in that sort of exploitation): they would be free. Their identities would be their own." Yet Joyce's awareness of her own freedom came primarily through meditation and reflection upon her own personality, which she believed had remained essentially the same since childhood and had not really been affected by her marriage. Her periods of aloneness allowed her this recognition. "After 15 years of marriage & more or less continuous companionship," she wrote, "the experience of being alone is a very enlightening one. The *aloneness* awakens in me memories of similar times, similar emotions, many years ago. A very strong continuity of personality, then: I recognize myself as a girl seamlessly existing within my present self. . . . It's nonsense, as I have always believed, to imagine that one's personality changes very much over the course of years." As Joyce approached middle age, she observed that her economic freedom and her stable marriage had helped to nourish her sense of identity. They had also aided her in seeking the particular form of "invisibility" she craved—namely, "the protection of the unknowable, sacred, private self."

By the mid-1970s Joyce had reason to think of "protection," since she had a bewildered awareness of the envious hostility inspired by her literary fame and her prodigious output. Although Dan Brown's veiled threats against her were no longer an issue, there were troubling incidents closer to home that gave her concerns about her personal safety. On January 6, 1977, a middle-aged man from Detroit showed up in the Windsor English department and demanded of the secretary, "Where the hell is Joyce Carol Oates?" The next day, he came uninvited to Joyce's large Psychology and Literature class, insisting on talking with her and behaving strangely. He spoke, Joyce remembered, in "a sniggering mock-intimate voice." When Joyce explained that only registered students could attend her classes, the man responded, "You're very anti-man, aren't you," and left abruptly. Joyce was upset, since the man "gave off the unmistakable whiff of madness." Two days later, when Joyce arrived on campus for her next meeting with the class, she learned that her male teaching assistant had received a threatening call during the night from the same man. Referring to Joyce as a "skinny bitch," the man had shouted: "I'll kill her, I'll kill her, I'll kill her! I'll kill her and you'll help me— she hates us, she hates all of us [men]." It was decided that Joyce should not teach the class that day, and a short while later the Windsor police were summoned. For two hours, Joyce was closeted in her department chairman's office, answering questions. Joyce tried to see this as an "interesting experience," but she quickly became bored because "the detectives take down questions in longhand and are very, very slow and legalistic. Geoff Hayman, Special Investigation Division, is the man I'm supposed to call if the would-be murderer appears. I will crawl bleeding and gasping for breath to the nearest pay phone and dial Detective Hayman, ext. 20." A few days later, Joyce confessed in her journal that her attitude toward a possible attack was ambivalent, since she felt so relentlessly beleaguered by her own celebrity: "Detaching myself from the situation I can only conclude that one part of my mind desired a sudden, irrevocable *end* to the avalanche of work and responsibility and 'fame' (however minimal and however ironic—since it brings about such crude threats) . . . an infantile wish to bring things to a premature end."

Only two months later, Joyce had a similar experience: a would-be writer who had published a book with a vanity press phoned her, asking for advice, then wrote her a letter. Because she responded pleasantly both times, the man came to Windsor and requested a personal meeting, which Joyce declined. The man, who had been "smiling, very courteous," became suddenly angry and stalked away. He complained to the department chairman and to the dean, evidently wanting Joyce fired because she would not speak with him. Joyce was left to contemplate "one more crank in the area, seething with hatred for me. It was amazing how his smile vanished and a look of murderous rage appeared. Is my life to dwindle into a bad television melodrama . . . ?"

She was often the victim of crank phone calls, letters, and other forms of un-explained hostility from perfect strangers. This phenomenon would recur—in various and sometimes alarming forms—for many years to come. Her only way to combat the envious dislike of others was by keeping a sense of humor about her controversial reputation. When a literary acquaintance told her, in early 1976, that she was "the 'most hated' of contemporary writers," Joyce was incredulous. "I really lead a quiet and almost secluded life," she observed. "The resentment others feel toward me is an exaggeration, surely; if they could see me sinking beneath innumerable student papers perhaps they would take pity on me."

Despite such unpleasant distractions, Joyce kept her mind concentrated on her work. Within weeks after the hostile critical reaction to *The Assassins*, Joyce was already contemplating another large, ambitious novel. "As my nov-els grow in complexity they please me more and please the 'literary world' hardly at all—a sad situation, but not a paralyzing one," she told an inter-viewer that year. She was continuing with her informal examination of the major American professions: she'd already written about the world of medi-cine (*Wonderland*), the legal system (*Do with Me What You Will*), and poli-tics (*The Assassins*); her recent, unpublished manuscript, *How Lucien Florey Died, and Was Born*, had dealt in part with teaching (one of the major char-acters was a high school teacher) and she had also planned a novel centering on the business world. But now, fascinated by the phenomenon of funda-mentalist Christianity, which was enjoying a new visibility and popularity in the 1970s, Joyce wanted to focus on religious experience in America. She had already chosen her title: *Son of the Morning*, taken from a biblical passage about the fall of Lucifer.

Like *The Assassins*, this new project required months of reading, research, thinking, and note taking. While engaged in laying the imaginative founda-tion for *Son of the Morning* Joyce simultaneously wrote a shorter, less ambi-tious novel, an academic satire she called *Soliloquies* (the manuscript would not be published until 1979, under the title *Unholy Loves*). Finishing the first draft of *Soliloquies* on March 20, 1976, she described the novel in her journal as "so sane, so conservative in narrative technique and characterization, my most 'humane' novel but not my most dramatic. *Son of the Morning* will be more challenging." An accessible, briskly written example of psychological re-alism, *Soliloquies* explored a fictional English department at Woodslee Uni-versity, which is thrown into an uproar during the year-long visit of an elderly, world-famous British poet, Albert St. Dennis (based loosely on Stephen Spender). Following her usual practice, Joyce drew an elaborate map, which located the university and the homes of the various faculty members. The narrative focused on the tempestuous love affair between novelist Brigit

Stott and musician Alexis Kessler; as she had done in some of her academic
stories, Joyce used faculty parties for many of the scenes, set pieces that wittily explored the byzantine and frequently vicious complexities of academic
politics and the inevitable conflicts between personal need and professional
ambition. Throughout the novel, Joyce's prose maintained an arch, ironic
tone as she scrutinized the lives of her highly educated but emotionally troubled characters. The composition of *Soliloquies* proceeded smoothly: in the
interstices of long, ambitious novels, Joyce enjoyed writing in a deliberately
minor key, producing relatively unambitious books that served, in a sense, as
a warm-up for the more demanding work to come. Unlike *The Assassins*, she
found *Soliloquies* "enjoyable to write"; the first draft was produced in a matter of weeks, though she later put the manuscript through a typically elaborate revision.

Having finished *Soliloquies*, she still did not feel ready to begin the more
ambitious novel: "Am trying to think out a voice, a way of seeing, for *Son of the
Morning*," she wrote in her journal. "If I do the novel in third-person it will be
one sort of novel; if I do it in first it will be entirely different. I am reluctant to
choose a voice because that voice, once chosen, will exclude all the others."
Joyce had already done a vast amount of reading on all aspects of supernatural
experience, everything from classics such as St. Augustine's *Confessions* to recent books on the paranormal and studies of religious cults. She immersed
herself in the Bible, reading it daily for several months in the attempt to intuit
the worldview of her God-haunted protagonist, Nathan Vickery. "I wanted to
put myself in the place of a fundamentalist Protestant who could go to the
Bible every day for guidance and would not have any critical or historical pre-
conceptions," she said. She pondered her own childhood experience of attending Methodist services with a friend in Pendleton, New York, where she
had been so impressed by the emotional rapture she had witnessed. She'd also
had a recent opportunity to reflect on her own family's former Catholicism.
Joyce was furious that a group of Catholic cardinals had proclaimed that abor-
tion was unacceptable under any circumstances, "even to save the life of the
mother—since it was possible, they said, that the fetus could be male." Joyce
continued: "The Catholic Church. Its beauty. And then the Cardinals with
their ruling, their brutal diminishment of woman. The stupidity of these
'great' religions. Apart from forcibly organizing chaos, they are cruel in sense-
less, inhuman ways."

As *Son of the Morning* took shape in her mind, Joyce worked at other
projects. Her reading on the occult inspired her to write a long story called
"Night-Side," which dealt with the world of mediums and other "supernatural" phenomena in nineteenth-century Boston. This would become the

title story of her next collection, which explored philosophical and psychological themes related to various forms of religious seeking. She had also written a "decidedly minor" story which, as she wrote to Gail Godwin, "got out of hand" and became a 104-page novella entitled *All the Good People I've Left Behind*. She funneled her leftover writing energy into her journal: her entries for the first years of the journal, 1973 and 1974, had been fairly brief and sporadic, but in 1976 alone the entries totaled 165 typed, single-spaced pages.

When the spring 1976 term ended, Joyce put aside her writing briefly for another of her typically frenetic visits to New York, where she gave a reading at the YW-YMHA, spent time with Blanche Gregory and Evelyn Shrifte, visited bookstores and art galleries, saw Vanessa Redgrave in Ibsen's *The Lady from the Sea*, and met with a number of literary acquaintances: George Plimpton, Wilfrid Sheed, Donald Barthelme. Joyce now got along well with Barthelme, whom she found "high-spirited, sharp, intelligent, perhaps a little domineering—though in a charming way. Enjoys drinking. (Thank God Ray was along; I would have disappointed him.)" Like her friend John Gardner, Barthelme had a somewhat contentious personality. When Joyce mentioned that she'd seen his recent collection *City Life* on a best-seller's list, Barthelme "flared up, denied it, bet me $100 (wisely I declined the bet), called his editor Roger Straus at once & made me talk to the man, in order to be told that Barthelme had never had a best-seller, no, not once."

Joyce had another, even more enjoyable encounter during this trip: at long last, after several years of avid correspondence, she finally met her friend Gail Godwin in person. After visiting with Godwin, whom she found "even more charming and interesting than I had imagined," she was forced to reflect on the "riches the human world offers—the 'bright peopled world' beyond Windsor." In her journal and letters, the note of dissatisfaction with the relatively barren cultural life in Windsor appeared with increasing frequency.

After returning home, Joyce spent the summer writing short stories and poetry, reviewing books for various publications, and brooding incessantly on *Son of the Morning*. Since she wasn't actually composing a novel, an unusual circumstance for her, the short fiction manuscripts became especially numerous. On July 3, she apologized to Blanche for the number of stories she was sending, promising that a summer vacation she and Ray were planning would ease her agent's work load: "I'm sorry to be sending so much material your way—we're leaving tomorrow for a 2 or 3-week trip, so I won't be able to do much writing for a while." Joyce and Ray then embarked on a long, leisurely drive that encompassed Toronto, upstate New York, and New England. After visiting Fred and Carolina in Millersport, Joyce expressed relief that her father was enjoying his retirement after forty years of work in a fluorescent-lit factory. He and Carolina took leisurely rides in the country, did a great deal of reading and listening to music, and socialized with friends. Now that Joyce's autistic sister, Lynn, had been institutionalized, Carolina's life had also become less stressful. "No one deserves happiness more than my parents, who have worked so very hard most of their lives," Joyce noted. "Thank God they're really enjoying themselves now. All has turned out so well."

Another high point of the trip was Joyce's visit with John Updike and his wife, Martha, in Georgetown, Massachusetts. Over the years, Joyce had occasionally written to Updike and sent him gift copies of her books. Despite her reservations about some of his lesser work, he had remained the contemporary American writer she most admired: Updike's rural upbringing, his devotion to the art of fiction, his wide reading, and his amazing productivity resembled her own, even though the two writers' work could hardly have been more different in style and subject matter. Joyce and Ray took the Updikes to lunch and "spent a wonderful two hours or so talking of innumerable things." She found Updike "gentle, sly, clever, witty, charming, immensely attractive; and Martha seems to be his equal in every way." She also noted that Updike was "self-deprecating in a playful, understated way, the result perhaps of his early fame. Success has not spoiled him but, I suspect, made him nicer."

Updike had liked Joyce equally well, and a friendship gradually developed that would inspire several further visits and dozens of long, lively letters. Updike remarked that Joyce's "personal demeanor is refreshingly matter-of-fact and sensible, as Middle-American girls are. She also has that drollery and irony with which A-students ingratiate themselves and hide their intense ambitions." Like Joyce, he noted similarities in their backgrounds: "I myself am from a second-rank city like Lockport," Updike said, "and warmly respond to her images of high school, of mercantile striving, of thwarted aspiration." As a writer, he admired "her wonderfully productive, creative, experimental, fearless approach to the art of fiction. She gives life and drama to just those overlookable corners of American middle-class experience that attract me." He also thought highly of her literary criticism and appreciated her frequently kind remarks about his own writing.

Joyce had already published an appreciative essay on Updike's fiction in an academic journal and Updike would later write a glowing (and influential) review of her 1987 novel, You Must Remember This, in The New Yorker; but neither writer, in their private conversations and letters, showed much interest in sharing criticism or advice about the other's work. As time passed, they preferred trading literary gossip to talking shop. Updike recalled that he "once offered a few helpful (I thought) animadversions about a short story of hers and she dismissed them in a fraction of a sentence in her reply." Nor had Updike sought out Joyce's occasional criticism of his work, though she had quoted a passage in Updike's volume of essays and reviews, Picked-Up Pieces, that she considered sexist, and had told an interviewer that she had disliked his novel *Rabbit Redux*. But Updike observed that "a few demurs wouldn't trouble me," coming from Joyce; in any case, he added, "writers aren't terribly interested in rehashing done works."

After returning from her vacation, Joyce felt she was nearly ready to begin her major new project: in August, she began planning the structure of *Son of the Morning*. She had continued reading the Bible intensively, and felt "rather discouraged by the fundamental silliness of the Christ story: Christ's intolerance (threatening people with hell who merely don't listen to his disciples), his predilection for flattery (it's because Peter says 'Thou art the Christ, the Son of the living God' that Peter is given the keys to the kingdom of heaven), his ruthless sense of his own righteousness ('He that is not with me is against me'), . . . [and] his general obnoxious zeal, intemperance." Joyce felt she had discovered the source of the self-righteousness and cruelty that she believed underlay contemporary Christian fundamentalism: Christ "really wishes his 'enemies' (those who don't care to follow him) in hell, where they would suffer terribly; he lusted after complete dominion of men's minds." She speculated that Jesus Christ had "suffered what Jung might call an 'invasion' from the Unconscious: from that archetype that involves a sense of one's limitless capacity for being *right*, for telling others what to do, for saving the world."

Yet Joyce was not interested in satirizing the deeply held religious convictions of her protagonist. Though not sharing his worldview, she felt an "absolute kinship" with Nathan Vickery, whose obsessive spiritual quest formed an analogue to Joyce's ceaselessly energetic literary pursuits. As in *Childwold*, Joyce returned to Eden County for the early chapters of *Son of the Morning*, but within this densely textured naturalistic backdrop the child Nathan is a dramatic anomaly. Possessing the implacable serenity of the Christ child— throughout the book, Nathan's life and personality parallel Christ's in many ways—he greatly disturbs his own grandfather, Dr. Thaddeus Vickery, a pragmatist and agnostic whose absorption in medicine, in the reality of bodies and diseases, is dramatically opposed to his grandson's aloof, enigmatic spirituality. A sympathetic, powerfully drawn character, Thaddeus expresses Joyce's own mature, humanistic values of reason, skepticism, hard work, personal affection. Like Joyce, he reads the Bible in the effort to understand his grandson, and his reaction is a virtual paraphrase of Joyce's private journal: "[Thaddeus] could not believe what he was reading. . . . The Gospel according to St. Matthew presented a self-righteous, intolerant, wildly egotistical and even megalomaniacal personality—Jesus of Nazareth who confuses and bribes common people with miracles, who brags that He has not come to bring peace on earth but a sword, who threatens His enemies (those who merely choose not to believe in *Him* as the Son of God) with hellfire.... Why had Thaddeus believed that Jesus was fundamentally a loving person? It was not so; not so. 'The man was psychopathic,' Thaddeus whispered."

But Joyce grants Nathan Vickery his own undeniable power and charisma, engaging the reader's sympathy as Nathan struggles with the forces attempting to "possess" him—the world of eternity, of his visionary apprehensions; and the world of time-bound nature, of simple brute matter, which continually pulls him back, humbling and finally destroying his spirit. Joyce began the first section of the novel, "The Incarnation," with scenes embodying her characteristic vision of rapacious nature: for instance, Nathan is conceived through the brutal rape of his mother. The second section, "The Witness," charts Nathan's rise from a strange child haunted by visions into a sexually tormented young man, and finally into an enigmatic, powerful, and uncompromising religious leader. Forming his own church called the "Seekers of Christ," which Nathan's luminous spirituality and powerful oratory help build into a powerful, wealthy organization, Nathan indulges in a melodramatic self-punishment (for the sins of pride and lust) before his huge congregation and television audience, cutting out his own left eye in obedience to the biblical injunction, "If thine eye offend thee, pluck it out." Ironically, this incident only heightens Nathan's fame; a rapturous white-robed preacher, he begins touring the United States and preaching to crowds exceeding a hundred thousand people.

In "Last Things," the third and final section, Nathan's conflict with one of his own most fervent disciples, Japheth Sproul—whom Nathan casts out of the church when he suspects that Sproul harbors a homosexual attraction to him—leads to another climactic, violent scene. Maddened by his ejection from the Seekers for Christ, Sproul returns as a Judaslike figure and attempts to bludgeon Nathan to death with a crowbar. (The scene is clearly a deliberate echo of Dan Brown's conclusion to his story about Joyce, in which his protagonist beats a famous woman writer to death with a shovel.) Though Nathan survives, he now confronts the last in a series of visions he has endured throughout his life. But the vision, which Nathan interprets as a face-to-face confrontation with God, is not sacred but horrific; it is a glimpse of that unholy axis of reality that underlies all of Joyce's work, a voraciously hungry and indifferent natural universe that, as she phrased it in her later essay "Against Nature," is merely waiting "to swallow us up, books and all." Nathan sees God as "[a] great hole. A great mouth." Speechless with horror, he stares into the abyss: "He saw that the hole before him *was* a mouth, and that the writhing dancing molecules of flesh were being sucked into it, and ground to nothing, and at the same time retained their illusory being."

Nathan Vickery's ministry and his spiritual life end with this hellish vision, leaving him only with the knowledge that "his terror had just begun."

Joyce's long meditation on the novel had led her toward an innovative structure. Rather than making the agonizing choice between first- and third-person narration, she combined the two: the third-person narrative is framed by brief, interpolated monologues by Nathan himself, all addressed to an inscrutable God and suggesting that the novel is Nathan's own attempt to make sense of his experience. An aging, broken man, Nathan lives in exile, like Richard Everett typing out *Expensive People* alone in a rented room. While narrating his story, Nathan suffers a minimal, despairing existence, moving from one dilapidated rooming house to another, trapped in "a vast Sahara of time," an existential solitude and awareness that "my life is a horror." Yet, as Joyce told an interviewer after *Son of the Morning* appeared, "the whole novel is a prayer." She added that the book "begins with wide ambitions and ends very, very humbly" and that it is "painfully autobiographical in part." Not only is Nathan Vickery's rural background a mythologized transcription of Joyce's childhood environment in upstate New York; his philosophical disillusionment and his fall into language, into narrative, also parallel Joyce's own. As Joyce had written several years earlier, "The world has no meaning; I am sadly resigned to this fact. But the world has meanings, many individual and alarming and graspable meanings, and the adventure of human beings consists in seeking out these meanings." For Nathan, as for other of Joyce's obsessive seekers, language could articulate a personal if not a universal, objective truth. Nathan Vickery had continued to pray, therefore, just as Joyce Carol Oates continued to write.

Joyce began composing *Son of the Morning* in September—she wrote the first page on the first day of classes for the fall of 1976 term—and she worked at the manuscript with her usual doggedness. Once Joyce became involved in a project, virtually nothing could weaken the gravitational pull to her desk that she felt each morning. In early October, she underwent oral surgery for a deeply compacted wisdom tooth, and for several days suffered headaches, a swollen jaw, and constant bleeding. But although she felt "wretched physically ... weak, trembling, sickish, rather depressed," she forced herself to continue with the novel, typing with one hand and holding an ice pack to her jaw with the other. Her illness brought the recognition that she often took "so much for granted my own energy, which allows me to start work early in the morning and continue all day long and well into the night, sometimes until 11:30." Now her writing effort felt "like walking into a strong wind, stubborn & determined." She longed to sleep for a few hours, but "my Puritan sense of morality forbids such luxury." By October 20, she had finished the novel's first section.

Partly because she had allowed Nathan's story such a long gestation, she composed the remainder of the book even more swiftly. On December 12, she completed a first draft of over four hundred pages. Yet Joyce's interior sense of time continued to differ sharply from that of critics who accused her of "churning out" her fiction. Though the lengthy first draft had been completed in three months, in the midst of a full-time semester of teaching, she had complained on November 25 that she was proceeding "sluggishly" with the novel. Part of Joyce's chronic impatience with her progress related to her relentlessly fecund imagination: even as she was deeply absorbed in writing Nathan's story, the idea for her next novel, *Jigsaw*, had come to her. She looked forward to this new project, which she described as "a more human, more immediate & warm sort of novel" that would deal with a bachelor artist and his circle of friends in New York City. This less ambitious work would be a relief, she noted, after finishing Nathan Vickery's "odd, eerie, lengthy, rather mad story."

Although Joyce's intense creative life sometimes had the effect of blocking out the more external concerns of her career—she shared, to some degree, John Updike's lack of interest in "done works"—she was pleased that Blanche had sold her recent novella, *All the Good People I've Left Behind*, to *Redbook* for $8,000. There was also surprisingly good news about the recently published novel *Childwold* and the story collection *Crossing the Border*: Fawcett had paid $175,000 to reprint the two books in paperback. Joyce had considered *Childwold*, with its lyric rather than plot-driven structure, to be a particularly noncommercial work, and she'd originally suggested that *Crossing the Border* wouldn't interest Americans and should be published only in Canada.

The fairly strong sales of these books helped to compensate for their mixed reviews. Fortunately, both had fared well in *The New York Times Book Review*, Josephine Hendin saying of *Childwold* that "Joyce Carol Oates has written her best novel in years," and Anne Tyler giving a judicious, thoughtful notice to *Crossing the Border*. *Childwold* was also well reviewed in *The New Republic*, but *Newsweek* panned the book, insisting that it lacked clarity and suffered from a "rambling" structure. The review sounded a now-familiar note in Oates criticism, suggesting that the potential of *Childwold* had remained unrealized "because Oates these days is too busy turning out 'new novels.'" An equally damning review appeared in *The New Yorker*, a magazine that had virtually ignored Joyce's career in the past and that remained the only major, "slick" publication to consistently reject her short stories. The magazine's review of *Childwold*, by Susan Lardner, called it "an inconclusive mixture of sentimentality and disgust" that was weakened by "high-strung poetic prose."

In her journal, Joyce dismissed virtually all the reviews, remarking that Lardner's piece in *The New Yorker* resembled "a kind of 9th grade book report, expressing bewilderment." Even Josephine Hendin's glowing review, which Joyce considered "generous but not very perceptive," brought little satisfaction. She had begun to find the process of being reviewed "wearisome . . . I wish there were someone whose opinion I could honor." She found it ironic that *Crossing the Border* had fared better than *Childwold* with reviewers, since she considered the collection well written but "lightweight": "How strange, how perplexing, that a book I don't think very much of should be praised." The stories in *Crossing the Border*, several of them focused on a young American couple living in Canada, had been planned and written quickly, and like most writers Joyce valued most the ambitious, difficult works into which she poured, as she frequently put it, her "life's blood." In early 1977, she summarized her dissatisfaction with critical response to her writing:

> The banality of most of the criticism that has attached itself to my work. Hastily-written, incoherent, uncomprehending. What value? Very little. It isn't infrequent that reviewers get the plot wrong. Am I naive to have expected more consideration, am I naive to be disappointed . . . ? Even 'positive' criticism so often seems uninformed, ignorant. What to do? Keep on writing, I suppose; try to write better than in the past; remain stoic. At the very least it can be said that I've made a great deal of money—enough to be financially independent for life—if that's any consolation.

Joyce had taken another vacation to New York during the last week of 1976, a reward for having completed both the fall semester of teaching and *Son of the Morning*. This trip involved "a delirium of activity": as usual, she and Ray saw several plays and foreign films; they visited with Gail Godwin, Bob Phillips, and other friends. Joyce also attended to career matters, doing a signing at the MLA convention and attending a session on her work, where she listened patiently to critical analyses of her fiction that "didn't interest me very much." But she was pleased, at least, that "the majority of the people there seemed to *like* my writing." On such occasions, when Joyce emerged from her relative isolation in Windsor, she often experienced a jarring awareness of her own renown. It amazed her to see "all these people gathered together in an overheated room in the Americana Hotel because of *me*. Because of my writing."

After returning home, she continued taking notes for *Jigsaw*, a novel for which she had again planned an innovative structure. Her story of Claude

Frey and his relationship to a variety of sophisticated New Yorkers—including Max and Rhoda Brainard, whose four-year-old daughter, Lou-Lou, Claude adores—was based in part on Joyce's fascination with Lewis Carroll. Claude Frey enjoys inventing private games for Lou-Lou, in addition to the "adult" games he designs and sells to the world at large. This manuscript, never published and now stored in the Syracuse archive, showed Joyce at her sprightly and imaginative best: by dividing the narrative into numerous brief vignettes, resembling puzzle parts, she conveyed the excitement of New York life and the complex, "puzzling" jumble of relationships surrounding her likable hero. Moving among several narrative situations, employing both first- and third-person viewpoints, balancing plot-oriented and image-oriented chapters, and adroitly weaving the central motif of puzzle solving throughout the manuscript, she sustained an energetic and unpredictable narrative that constitutes a lively example of postmodernist gamesmanship.

During March and April, *Jigsaw* absorbed her completely; she found herself "absolutely enchanted with the development of the characters' relationships. . . . One piece of the puzzle of *Jigsaw* at once summons forth another, and still another." On March 22, she recorded a typical day in her journal: she would begin work early in the morning, stopping for "breakfast," her first meal of the day, around 3:00 P.M. While working on this novel, Joyce described her writing as "a drug, sweet and irresistible and exhausting." Just as she had composed *Son of the Morning* during the fall semester, *Jigsaw* was completed by the end of the spring term, on April 23. (Joyce's writing habits had changed very little since her college days when, as her creative writing professor Donald Dike had recalled, she'd turned in a novel each semester.) Joyce decided that she couldn't possibly submit *Jigsaw* to Blanche at this early date: "She would wonder at my 'industry.' " She longed to explain "that a writer lives and breathes his or her fictions," and asked: "Why are people so reluctant to understand that time is a different experience for all of us?" Ultimately *Jigsaw* was purchased by Vanguard, but it suffered the same fate as the *Lucien Florey* novel, bumped from the publisher's schedule in favor of other manuscripts.

In what had become a typical pattern for Joyce, ideas for further novels developed in her imagination even as she completed *Jigsaw*. Like the germ of her earlier novel *Wonderland*, one of these sprang directly from newspaper stories. (Joyce had resumed her old habit of eagerly scanning the newspaper each day.) In the spring of 1977, a string of brutal child murders in the Detroit suburbs had dominated headlines and inspired the most extensive manhunt in Michigan history. On March 27, Joyce had lunched with her women friends in Birmingham and they had discussed the fifth, most recent killing (of a ten-year-old boy, abducted from a parking lot). In her journal, Joyce wrote, "One is appalled by the crimes, mystified by the murderer's *driven-ness* . . . one murder followed by another by another by another and still an-other. . . . Yet the man can't be insane, in any obvious way. . . . When he's caught I suppose he will turn out to be one of those 'normal' 'ordinary' 'nice' 'polite' young men who routinely reveal themselves as desperate." The killer was never found, but Joyce continued to brood on the case, and would soon begin work on a novel she called *The Evening and the Morning*; the com-pleted 340-page manuscript would later be retitled *Graywolf: Life and Times*, since "Graywolf" was the name she had given the murderer. Like her novella *The Triumph of the Spider Monkey*, loosely based on Charles Manson, and her 1995 short novel *Zombie*, suggested by the case of Jeffrey Dahmer, the *Gray-wolf* project revealed Joyce's ongoing fascination with the criminal mind.

An even more ambitious idea for a novel occurred to her a few days later. In a journal entry for April 5, she first mentioned *Bellefleur*, the novel that would become her most ambitious work to date and that would absorb much of her imaginative energy for the next two years. "Licking about the edge of my vi-sion like gay golden crazy flames are the people of my next novel," she wrote. "Giants, seen from a child's point of view. . . . It should be a voluptuous, sprawling, 'undisciplined' expression of how the world, especially adults, ap-pears to a child's eye. It should be immensely enjoyable to write . . . !" She had already begun taking notes for the byzantine plot, though she discovered soon enough that *Bellefleur*, while often mesmerizing, would also be her most challenging novel, and not always "enjoyable."

During the remainder of the spring and summer, Joyce took notes for both *Graywolf: Life and Times* and *Bellefleur*, unable to hit upon a structure or narrative voice for either novel. As usual, she worked at short stories and reviews while waiting for a longer project to jell. The previous fall, she had accepted an invitation by Roger Rosenblatt, literary editor at *The New Re-public*, to begin reviewing regularly for the magazine, and she continued responding to the "bright peopled world" beyond Windsor. In April, an invi-tation she'd received from Princeton University merited only three brief sen-tences in her journal, but it would ultimately change the direction of her life: "Possibility of my going to Princeton for 1978–79. Awfully far in the future. It would be ideal, though: a lovely town, stimulating people, proximity to New York." While teaching at N.Y.U., she and Ray had driven down to Princeton, and she had reported to John Ditsky that it was "surely one of the paradisial places of the earth." Within the next few weeks, she decided to accept Princeton's offer of a one-year appointment as writer in residence; the Uni-versity of Windsor had agreed to grant a sabbatical for both Joyce and Ray, at full salary, enabling Joyce to test life outside of Windsor without losing the security of her permanent position.

In early May, she visited Baltimore for a reading at Johns Hopkins University. Her host for the visit was John Barth, whom she considered "a kindly, funny, erudite man, slim, attractive, conservatively well-dressed, far more hospitable than I had imagined." Joyce and Ray enjoyed Baltimore, a city they explored with their usual thoroughness. One day they lunched at the home of novelist Anne Tyler, whose Iranian husband, Tighe Modarressi, cooked "a delicious Persian shishkebab." Joyce had recently initiated a correspondence with Tyler, writing to thank her for the positive review of *Crossing the Border*. Tyler's observations had been "all the more meaningful," she wrote, "because they come from a practicing writer of considerable talent, whose writing I've admired for a long time." For her part, Tyler returned Joyce's admiration, both professionally and personally. "I remember being a little apprehensive about their first visit," Tyler said, "simply because I so respect Joyce's work (I do think that in the next century, people are going to wonder why we were not generally more aware of what a remarkable writer we had in our midst), but she was so unassuming and entertaining that both my husband and I felt we had known her for years." Like Joyce's other friends, Tyler noted how well Joyce and Ray's marriage seemed to work: "there was something appealingly delicate and fragile about [Joyce] that was nicely balanced by Ray's sturdiness, and we liked him fully as much as we did her."

During this trip Joyce and Ray also visited Washington: they attended a brunch at Roger Rosenblatt's home in Georgetown, visited the National Gallery, and took long walks around Capitol Hill. But even during this busy one-week vacation, Joyce's imagination stayed active. Although she was already pondering two ambitious novels, she had begun thinking about a possible novella, set in Maine, about a nineteen-year-old boy who falls in love with his beautiful cousin, a girl of fourteen. She thought excitedly about the "gradual infatuation; the sparring of adolescence; Duncan's tumultuous thoughts; his passion; Antoinette's provocative behavior, and then her fear, and anger; his rape of her; her hysteria; his wishing to silence her. . . ." She hoped to make of this tragic story "something quick and clean and spare and yet gripping, moving, terrible": the novella that eventually resulted, *A Sentimental Education*, would form the title piece of her next book of stories, published in 1980. She had already sent to Blanche a collection of recent stories entitled *Sunday Blues*, but with *Night-Side* scheduled for fall 1977 and *Son of the Morning* for 1978, *Sunday Blues* disappeared into what Joyce ruefully called her "logjam" of manuscripts and was never published.

Joyce's ongoing productivity disguised the fact that 1977 had been a restless, often unhappy year. In February, before starting *Jigsaw*, she'd complained to Gail Godwin that Windsor was "grayly the same" and that she was suffering "winter doldrums." Later that week, she wrote to Bob Phillips that she hadn't "felt very encouraged in recent weeks, for a variety of reasons which I won't go into." Joyce did not feel comfortable burdening even her longtime friends with her personal problems; instead she poured her frustration into her journal, which was "like an old friend—someone who will listen and not judge, someone who is always *there*."

Although she enjoyed her teaching at N.Y.U. during the summer, she confronted a bewildering impasse in her writing life. She spent the six weeks working at short stories—including one called "Washington Square," inspired by her New York apartment overlooking the square and by her recent reading of Henry James's novella of the same title—but none of the stories from this period are among her best, and though she published them in literary quarterlies she never collected them. The high-profile magazines like *The Atlantic* and *Esquire* that had once published her stories frequently now sent rejection letters instead. "I have been somewhat discouraged with the lack of acceptance of short stories of mine recently," she wrote to Blanche, "and wonder if I should simply stop writing them. . . . I have the feeling that many editors are simply 'off' my work right now and it wouldn't really matter what I wrote."

Throughout the summer and fall, her journal reflected her constant brooding on *Bellefleur*, but she could not find her way into the "oversized deranged novel," as she called it, that would represent such a dramatic departure from her usual mode of psychological realism. Though there had always been a symbolic and allegorical dimension to Joyce's work, her best-known novels, such as *them*, had been so firmly grounded in naturalistic detail and historical chronology that frequently she had been placed in the naturalistic tradition of Theodore Dreiser (a writer she had not yet read, and whom she found disappointing when she finally did read him). But *Bellefleur*, she recognized, would represent a bold leap into the kind of magical realism Gabriel Garcia Marquez had employed in *One Hundred Years of Solitude*. She felt equally frustrated when she meditated on *Graywolf: Life and Times*. She knew that the novel would focus on the love relationship of Johanna Benedict and James Fairfield, and that the presence of the murderer, Graywolf, would haunt both characters and cast a shadow over their romance, but even after taking more than a hundred pages of notes, she had no idea of how to begin. "I will never, never be able to translate into fictional terms, into *Graywolf* and *Bellefleur*, all that I feel," she complained on August 28. "All that I *know*. It simply eludes me, it's too intangible, too painfully subtle to be expressed in dramatic terms." She knew that Johanna Benedict would be a somewhat autobiographical character, a woman who was both intelligent and unhappy: on September 3, she wondered if Johanna were simply "depressed?—like me?" On another day she allowed herself a rare cri de coeur: "What am I doing with my life these days? My life? It seems to be melting away."

A few weeks earlier, she had noted that even when "events of good fortune" came her way, the good news she once would have celebrated now seemed routine. An unexpected royalty check for $85,000 had arrived in the mail, and she'd forgotten to tell Ray until the following morning; when she read a positive review of her work—*Night-Side*, for instance, received several excellent notices—she no longer felt elated but would "skim through it as though it were a review of anyone's book, of any book at all, not my own, not related to me." She remembered how excited she had been over the acceptance of her first book, and the first time one of her novels had been optioned for the movies. Now such things had become "almost ordinary events" and did nothing to alleviate the frustration over her current writing projects. Joyce often recorded her dreams in her journal, and one in particular suggested the irony of her present unhappiness:

> I am weeping with agonizing gratitude because someone (a woman, possibly a doctor) has given me some cards; birthday or Christmas cards; I am very lonely, and deeply moved by the fact that someone should think of me. A piteous dream, really: here I am with my 3/4 million dollars, my enviable marriage, house, position in life, career, friends, etc., weeping helplessly and shamelessly because some stranger has given me a few cards.

Although the beginning of school was often a time of renewed optimism for Joyce, the bustling start of the fall 1977 term did little to lift her melancholy spirits. She recognized that her impasse with her writing had coincided with the growing staleness of her personal life in Windsor. "One of my misfortunes is the fact that, increasingly, I have no one to talk to," she noted on September 16. Ten days later, she continued this theme. Feeling adrift in "one of those chartless formless moods in which everything is either too important, or not important enough," she longed to discuss her loss of direction, and the philosophical issues they raised, with someone: "My personal predicament is that there's no one—no one at all—whom I respect intellectually and spiritually and emotionally, and with whom I might discuss these things. . . . If I had the naivete to imagine that someone, not necessarily a psychoanalyst or a religious person, but someone, anyone, 'knew' more about these matters than I did I would feel such relief. But. Well. Alas, it's lonely here."

Later in the month, she finally felt able to begin writing *Graywolf: Life and Times*, and she worked at the manuscript throughout the fall, completing a first draft in December. But the novel never pleased her, even after elaborate revisions. She had found it difficult to modulate the symbolic, death-haunted aspect of the novel represented by the at-large murderer, Graywolf, and the more concrete, realistic story of Johanna, Fairfield, and their friends. (Her on-going indecision about two possible titles for the manuscript—she had taken the more myth-oriented title *The Evening and the Morning* from the book of Genesis—reflected her difficulty in bringing the material into focus.) As she later recognized, the unpublished novels of this period were produced partly because she wasn't yet ready to begin *Bellefleur*, and *Graywolf* in particular shows both her yearning to produce a symbolic work and her reluctance to abandon the durable realism she had practiced for so long. She was clearly in the throes of a major transition, a period of growth, but the process was bewildering and painful; she felt helpless as the confidence and sense of direction she had enjoyed earlier in the decade seemed to abandon her, negatively affecting both her personal and her professional life.

For the past five years, since her visionary experience in London, Joyce had felt that she'd transcended the kind of emotional strife and desperation so often suffered by her fictional characters. But while her meditation, and her absorption in mysticism and Jungian psychology, had enriched her interior life, they had also isolated her from the kinds of emotional connections that could support her in times of crisis. Even her relations with longtime friends like Kay Smith and her Windsor colleagues were "social" rather than intimate. Close relationships had often resulted in her feeling used and exploited, and for this reason she had lately felt more attracted to friendships with equally famous peers like John Updike. "I feel so good about knowing someone like Updike, *whom I cannot possibly help* because he is far beyond requiring any help, by anyone, toward any end. So his liking for me is totally disinterested." Yet such friendships, ironically, were conducted almost entirely by letter, and were not close in any deep, emotional sense. By the end of 1977, she'd begun to recognize that her generalized emotional detachment of the past five years, her introversion and invisibility, had led not to liberation but to painful isolation. She had reached a turning point that, within a few months, would prompt her adventurous plunge into a new creative and personal life. She wrote:

> I *want* to be open to wounding, to shock and despair: otherwise I won't be living. I *want* to be susceptible to hurt. Some years ago . . . 1972 or thereabouts . . . I had achieved an uncanny, chilling, and certainly premature "detachment" which seemed to me marvelous at the time; but it wasn't marvelous. It wasn't marvelous at all.

12

"Moving to Princeton, Moving to *Bellefleur*" 1978–80

Normality is my lot: I may be a maniac disguised as a bourgeois woman, but it is a quite thorough and convincing disguise.

—*Journal*, February 28, 1980

During the spring and summer of 1978, Joyce and Ray Smith looked forward to their planned one-year stay in Princeton. These months represented a major transition in Joyce's life: she was undertaking her first long-distance move since 1962, she was consciously preparing herself to write an entirely new kind of fiction, and in June she marked her fortieth birthday. Yet her letters and journal entries of this period reflect an easing of the melancholy that had plagued her the previous year. She maintained her usual teaching and social activity, but for the most part she had withdrawn contentedly into a private world of artistic pursuits and quiet reflection. She described this haven in the personal journal she now kept faithfully, writing long entries several times each week. More than ever, she felt the "impulse to retreat, to go into hiding," and she noted her identification with Emily Dickinson, with whom she shared the urge "to live sequestered and protected." Joyce observed that "I am exactly the same: for with me the art comes first, must come first, and everything else is grouped around it, subordinated to it." She reported feeling "a thrill of panic at the prospect of what might await . . . in utter isolation. I have all I can do to contend with the images that rush forth, in the fullness and complexity of my ordinary days."

Although still unable to begin *Bellefleur*, she resolved not to hurry the process of daydreaming and note taking that always preceded work on a major novel. As usual, her fecund imagination had provided ideas for other, less ambitious projects that employed her writing time while she brooded over *Bellefleur*. She wrote several short stories (including "Queen of the Night," which would remain one of her personal favorites), and she worked slowly and meticulously on a brief, carefully constructed novel she called *Cybele* (alluding to the Asian goddess of fertility). She also pursued other interests, resuming piano lessons and playing the works of her favorite composer, Chopin, for hours each day. She collected rare first editions, including books by Henry James and T. S. Eliot; and, aided by her artist-friends Betsey Hansell and Ruth Rattner, she learned more about contemporary painting, frequently visiting museums and galleries, occasionally purchasing a work for her own collection. But literature came first, as always. Apart from her work on *Cybele* and her usual reading and reviewing, she began an intensive study of contemporary Russian literature, in preparation for a Soviet-American Writers' Conference held at New York University in April 1978. She had agreed to serve as a judge for the National Book Awards and to edit the 1979 volume of *Best American Short Stories*. Despite her love of privacy, she also made several public appearances during these months (at Northwestern and the University of Michigan, as well as N.Y.U.), and gave interviews to *Publishers Weekly*, *U.S. News and World Report*, and even *People* magazine. She also overcame her disinclination to appear on television: she was featured on half-hour shows hosted by the Milwaukee Public Library and, later in the year, by Dick Cavett in New York.

The famous writer who consented to these public appearances, however, was "Joyce Carol Oates," a person still quite distinct in Joyce's mind from the private, invisible writer who conducted, again like Emily Dickinson, a richly rewarding interior life at home. Joyce's only apprehension about the move to Princeton, in fact, was feeling "doomed to perform in the role of 'Joyce Carol Oates,'" whereas in Windsor she had felt comfortably anonymous as "Joyce Smith." Two years earlier, she had chafed at the occasional "restriction to a few cubic feet of consciousness: Joyce Carol Oates," feeling herself "fated to spend hours as a kind of secretary to that person, answering her mail, turning down requests politely. . . . As Oates' public fortunes rise, mine must necessarily fall; as hers level off or decline, I gain." The media phenomenon of "Oates"—the timorous, enigmatic writer with a little-girl voice and enormous eyes "burning in a dove's face," as one feature writer had gushed—had increasingly little connection with the passionate, curious, vitally engaged artist Joyce knew herself to be. Yet she had resigned herself to this dichotomy and, to a degree, had even come to appreciate it. If her public mask seemed, at times, an unrecognizable caricature, it also provided a shield behind which she could live her own life quite peacefully. In this way, as she phrased it in her journal, "My life protects my soul."

The degree to which Joyce lived for art is nowhere more apparent than in the journal entries written during her last months in Windsor. Although she listed her personal values as "Love. Friendship. Art. Work.," a long entry of June 1 again stressed that art was paramount. "If life is random and accidental and refuses to 'arrange' itself aesthetically," she asked herself, "what relationship has art to it at all?" She provided a definitive answer:

> I think of art as a form of communication, the very highest form of communication. One soul speaking to another (as in Chopin's music). For personal reasons I write because writing is hard work, and challenging, and I love hard work and challenge and all that. . . . But, still. What *is* the relationship? The artist imposes his vision upon his material, and he necessarily distorts it because he cannot include everything; he must exclude. Rigorously. All this is a means, perhaps, to liberate his deepest self . . . which is a voice, a style, a rhythm. The "plot" of the novel or story is a structure upon which the writer's voice hangs, or by which it is given its freedom. Consequently it is a pragmatic thing, a device. But much more: it is emblematic, since it is never realistic. One's instinct is to experience the highest art in a religious sense, and this instinct though dimly understood is a wise one.

As for indulging in "theory" about literature, she added, "We will let the pedants do that for us."

Joyce's absorption in music that spring arose from a similar desire to nourish her "soul"—a word she now used often, in the wake of her extensive reading and thinking about spiritual matters. While playing the piano, she observed, "everything is idyllic: *that other dimension* is entered." At times, she could even have fantasies of giving up writing altogether in favor of playing piano, even though she had little musical talent: "I work at the piano," she wrote to Gail Godwin, "far longer than I work at my desk now. I wish I had the interest in prose fiction that I have in music." Chopin had become a kind of soul mate because his art, like Dickinson's, combined intense spirituality with equally intense discipline. "I want to hear only Chopin," Joyce wrote. "I am so deeply touched by the music I've been struggling with [. . .] and by Chopin's genius. . . . That he was as frail as I, and even weighed a bit less, makes the mystery all the more profound." Several months later, she added that if she could meet any great artist out of the past, it would be Chopin—not to speak with him personally ("I'm not equal to it") but "simply to listen. To be a witness." The bodiless nature of music, like the indefinable "voice" of great poetry or prose, particularly answered to Joyce's spiritual longings.

Joyce's puritanical focus on work was still conjoined, in fact, with a simultaneous longing to nourish her spirit and to "mortify" her flesh, especially through fasting. The previous year, assigned to review a collection of writings by the French mystic Simone Weil, Joyce had conducted in her journal a lengthy, complex argument with Weil's ideas and her way of life. Weil, who had literally starved herself to death in the effort to lead a purely spiritual existence, struck Joyce as hopelessly deluded, a self-appointed martyr, but the intensity of Joyce's engagement with Weil's writing suggests that she felt a discomforting identification as well. (This same discomfort crept into Joyce's frequent but curiously begrudging discussions of Flannery O'Connor, another woman artist with intense spiritual ambitions and a monastic way of life.) Several years later, after learning that her friend Susan Sontag admired Weil, Joyce would write in her journal: "I must reread Simone Weil to discover why I seem to dislike her so much. Or to disapprove of her."

Joyce had remarked that she resented the basic physical needs of her body: she considered sleep a waste of time and continued to speak about food with an anorexic's revulsion. (Chopin's tubercular thinness, his having weighed even less than she, surely intensified her attraction to him.) One journal entry that spring confessed that it was 6:00 P.M. and she'd consumed only an apple and some tea, but "to force myself to eat more would not only be unpleasant but a waste of time." She resented "the time I waste eating. When I could be playing piano. Or writing. Or reading." When she neglected to eat, she would feel "flashes of light-headedness" that suggested "a pure tuning out, a disappearance of self. . . . As if I could suddenly slip away, vanish; and not even pain or fear would remain." A month later, she again ate only an apple one day, and "even that apple a nuisance to eat when I hadn't any appetite." Although she faithfully made dinner for herself and Ray each evening, she speculated that if she lived alone she would never sit down to a meal but would eat as minimally as possible, while reading or working.

Aside from the usual stock taking most people undertake when they reach forty, Joyce's reflectiveness at this time also provided her with greater clarity about the necessary balance between her private and public identity. Unlike Emily Dickinson at the same age, Joyce was a world-famous writer who enjoyed socializing with her literary peers and who had gradually increased her participation in the everyday workings of literary culture. Whereas she had once avoided serving on prize juries, she now became avidly involved in her work with the National Book Awards (in the Contemporary Thought category). Contrary to her image as shy and withdrawn, she sometimes took a strong, even angry stand against inequities she perceived in the New York–based literary power structure. She resigned her National Book Critics Circle membership, for instance, when the organization sent a list of potential nominees it called a "voter's guide"; noting the abundance of New York writers on the list, and the disproportionate number of titles from publishers such as Knopf, Joyce considered the "guide" a blatant attempt to manipulate the vote. With her friends, she was similarly outspoken about writers she thought overrated, such as William Gass (whose prose she called "frankly gaseous"), and she considered Gordon Lish, risibly proclaimed "Captain Fiction" in the New York press, untalented as either an editor or a writer. Not surprisingly, when Joyce learned early in 1978 that she had been elected to the American Academy of Arts and Letters, her pleasure in receiving this recognition was mixed with skepticism about the number of academy members affiliated with *The New Yorker*, some of whom she considered lightweight talents. The academy, in fact, resembled in some ways her despised sorority at Syracuse, manifesting the same pretentiousness, cronyism, and inflated self-regard. Although Joyce attended a few academy functions soon after her election, she seldom attended meetings and gradually withdrew from participation in membership activities.

Joyce's move to Princeton and her appearances at international conferences did reflect, however, her increasing desire to involve herself in literary culture at the highest levels. She now recognized acutely, and sometimes painfully, the "provincial" nature of the University of Windsor: in March, when a prominent media critic from N.Y.U. came to lecture, she winced when one of her colleagues gave a "vapid and brainless" introduction that referred to New York City as "home of the hot dog and the Bronx cheer." ("Oh God," Joyce noted in her journal. "What embarrassment.") By contrast, she greatly enjoyed the Soviet-American Writers' Conference at the end of April, which was attended by her new friend John Updike and other writers such as William Styron, Elizabeth Hardwick, and Edward Albee. She felt heartened that "the Soviet delegates are genuinely interested in talking about literature—they want to know about the contemporary American novel in particular, are touchingly curious, even eager to learn." (There were also lighter moments, as when Updike presented her with a page of cartoon drawings and doodlings he had produced during one of the less edifying Soviet speeches, inscribing it, "For Joyce, in memory of yukking it up with the Bolshis, Love, John.") In all, the event had been inspiring: when she returned home, she began working on a story called "Détente," the first of several based on her exhilarating but baffling exchanges with the Russian writers and critics. "At heart it's an old, elemental paradox," she wrote in her journal, "How can people whom you like, for whom you feel actual affection [. . .] not be people of whom you approve. . . . How can you *like* someone who is, or might easily be, repressive, cruel, even murderous."

Joyce's anticipation of her year in Princeton, which would afford her similar opportunities to meet with intellectuals and artists from many fields, coincided with her decision that she should change publishers. For years she had felt a strong loyalty to Vanguard and especially to Evelyn Shrifte; her publisher had taken a chance on Joyce as an unknown writer, and had brought out several of her books before turning a profit. She also liked Evelyn Shrifte personally, even if she sometimes doubted her perceptiveness as an editor. In 1972, Joyce had angrily defended Vanguard when the journalist Richard Kostelanetz, in an essay published in the PEN newsletter, suggested that Joyce's publisher was a moribund company run by "older women." But by the late 1970s Joyce had begun to feel taken for granted: Vanguard no longer did an effective job of promoting her books, to the extent she sometimes joked that a new novel of hers had been published "secretly." Recent developments had intensified Joyce's frustration. She had been approached by the University of Texas and other institutions about creating an archive for her papers, but for more than a year Vanguard refused to return the manuscripts it had published.

Even more upsetting was a new, five-book contract Vanguard had recently offered that stipulated the same, relatively small advance as her previous contract. "I would be embarrassed to tell anyone of the terms which I accept, especially for so many books," Joyce complained to Blanche, explaining why she had not signed the contract. Joyce knew that her books were not "commercial," but neither did she intend to give her work away; she considered the new contract "appalling." Yet Evelyn refused to offer more money. The final breach came when Evelyn abruptly rejected Joyce's most recent novel, *The Evening and the Morning*, claiming it was "too experimental." "It was quite a blunt rejection," Joyce told Gail Godwin, "without suggestions for revision or anything, and I lost confidence utterly in Vanguard, or in their confidence in me." Evelyn apparently felt that she could afford to be selective: with the upcoming *Son of the Morning* and three other novels (*How Lucien Florey Died, and Was Born, Jigsaw,* and *Unholy Loves*) waiting in line for publication, not to mention two collections of stories and one of essays, there was hardly a shortage of Oates manuscripts.

Joyce now authorized Blanche to approach other publishers. "I feel that while I am fond of Vanguard people, especially Evelyn, there is a highly unprofessional quality to Vanguard that is most taxing," she wrote. Soon Blanche heard from Henry Robbins at E. P. Dutton, who offered $215,000 for the unpublished novels, more than doubling Vanguard's offer. Alarmed, Evelyn quickly became more generous, suggesting a payment of $350,000, even though Vanguard would have to borrow money to make such a large advance. A bidding war between Dutton and Vanguard resulted in Joyce signing with Dutton, though Vanguard had finally offered the higher price. Joyce felt guilty about leaving her longtime publisher—"I know I've hurt Evelyn badly"—but she knew the time had come. Apart from the improved contract, Joyce was delighted with Henry Robbins, whom Joan Didion had called "the best editor in America." Certainly one of the most respected editors in New York, Robbins had worked with an impressive roster of authors that included Didion, John Irving, Wilfrid Sheed, and Walker Percy. Robbins told Joyce that he now wanted to immerse himself in her unpublished work; he soon responded enthusiastically to *The Evening and the Morning* and asked to discuss revisions with his new author. As she got to know Robbins, Joyce found him "one of the sweetest, most sensitive, intelligent, and civilized of editors anywhere."

Years later, Evelyn Shrifte recalled that she was indeed "heartbroken" at the loss of Joyce's work, and suggested that Joyce's agent had been responsible for the misunderstanding: "Blanche never said anything about wanting more money," she insisted. It seems likely that Blanche, like Evelyn, had simply become accustomed to business as usual, especially since Joyce seldom showed much interest in financial matters. In fact, Joyce had recently begun thinking about changing agents as well. Blanche was now in her late seventies and seemed out of touch with current publishing trends. Some of Joyce's writer friends, and even Ray, believed she should find a new agent. Joyce knew they were right, reflecting that "indifference to money and simple inertia have kept me in place." Joyce did interview a well-regarded, much younger agent, but finally decided that she could not make the change. "I can't leave Blanche: I simply can't hurt her feelings," she wrote. She was grateful that apart from the book manuscripts, Blanche and her associate Gert Bregman had patiently handled hundreds of Joyce's short stories over the years, even though the majority of these were placed with low-paying or even nonpaying literary magazines. "Such consideration doesn't go unnoticed," Joyce had told Blanche.

Whenever Joyce considered undertaking a major alteration in her life—changing jobs, publishers, or agents—she tended to feel doubtful and apprehensive rather than viewing the change as an exciting opportunity. As always, she craved the stability that her writing life required and preferred to err on the side of excessive caution, tolerating imperfect but familiar situations, rather than risk a plunge into the unknown. So it was all the more remarkable that by moving to Princeton and leaving Vanguard she undertook two major changes simultaneously. As she noted in her journal, 1978 was a "watershed" year.

In the midst of these changes, however, other factors had brought Joyce "a sense of tranquility, rest, balance." These included such career milestones as her election to the American Academy and, more important to her, the July publication of *Son of the Morning*, her most ambitious book in years. Although she felt "dread" at the idea of a best-seller, since she "couldn't tolerate the unwanted attention & curiosity," she had a particular hope that this novel, into which she had poured so much emotion and effort, would be read widely and sympathetically by serious readers, and it was for this reason that she consented to an unusual number of interviews that summer to promote the book. It would have been embarrassing, she said, to arrive in Princeton if *Son of the Morning* had received the kind of jeering, hostile reception that had greeted *The Assassins* three years earlier.

But Joyce's fears were soon allayed: *Son of the Morning* was widely and enthusiastically praised as one of Joyce's finest books and a thoughtful, at times searing portrayal of religious experience in America. "With its unrelenting dark prose and tragic aura, this is Oates at the passionate and compassionate peak of her powers," read one typical review. In the *Washington Post Book World*, Joyce's friend and longtime admirer Anne Tyler wrote that *Son of the Morning* was "rich and dark and convoluted . . . the writing is so powerful that I felt literally pulled along by it." Equally heartening was Victoria Glendinning's unqualified praise in *The New York Times Book Review*. Glendinning wrote that *Son of the Morning* was "a hugely ambitious novel" that "explores the phenomena of 'revelation' and mystical experience with an extraordinary imaginative thrust." Glendinning also addressed the "backlash" against Oates's work in recent years, the widespread insistence that Oates wrote too much and too carelessly. "Can so regular a flow of novels, stories, poetry and criticism all be in the first class?" Glendinning asked. "Of course they can. Costiveness is not necessarily a literary virtue." To Joyce's delight, the *New York Times* had published the review twice, once in August, in the daily *Times*, and again in November, in the *Book Review*. Clearly, the backlash was over.

In late August, Joyce focused on the details of her move to Princeton; she would be so busy that she "made a vow not to write fiction—for several weeks," even though she continued to meditate obsessively on her next major novel, *Bellefleur*. (Ten days after making this vow, however, she had embarked on a full-scale revision of *Unholy Loves*, readying it for publication in 1979.) Since Joyce and Ray still planned on returning to Windsor the following year, they had leased their beloved home on Riverside Drive and had made a quick trip to Princeton in May to look for a rental. They'd been helped in this endeavor by a new friend, Richard Trenner, who had heard that Joyce Carol Oates was coming to teach and had written to offer his assistance. Then a graduate student at Rutgers, Trenner had attended Princeton as an undergraduate and knew the area well. Though he'd never met Joyce, he had long admired her fiction and had written her several fan letters over the years. When Joyce and Ray arrived for house hunting, she found Trenner "a sort of Jamesian young man; sensitive, intelligent, 'literary,' wonderfully generous." She was pleased to have found this "very helpful young friend," since the Creative Writing Program had not offered Joyce any assistance in making the transition.

Trenner put Joyce and Ray in touch with a real estate agent, but since the few rentals available were not suitable, they impulsively decided to buy a house. The agent showed them five properties, one of which immediately struck a chord: "As soon as we saw the house [. . .] we wanted it," Joyce wrote. Located in an affluent, densely wooded area where white-tailed deer frequently trotted through the backyards, the secluded house reminded them of their Windsor home. "A beautiful house, difficult to describe," Joyce noted at the time. "Glass walls, modular ceiling, an atrium-courtyard, a flagstone terrace, brook and pond, innumerable trees . . . an elegant atmosphere altogether. Good setting for art." Later Joyce observed that even though she was normally a deliberate, cautious person, she had made two of the most important decision of her life with intuitive quickness: becoming engaged to Ray after knowing him for only three weeks, buying the Princeton house in a matter of hours.

The move itself went less smoothly: the previous owners had left the house filthy, and it took several days of backbreaking work to make it livable. Joyce and Ray made endless shopping trips, buying everything from a Baldwin piano to small items of furniture, hanging plants, and "all sorts of unnecessary items." Joyce tried to keep writing, but she and Ray felt "exhausted, defeated," and "all because of trivia . . . an avalanche of trivia." Virtually everything went wrong: their furniture was two weeks late in arriving, and when a box of mail was finally forwarded, they learned that the Princeton post office had mistakenly sent it back to Windsor. The move was so traumatic that Joyce wrote decisively in her journal on September 6, "I don't *want* to move again. I *want* to stay here permanently."

After settling into their new home, Joyce and Ray began exploring their surroundings, taking long walks around the campus and bicycling through the lush countryside in their neighborhood. Joyce's apprehension that she would now be known as "Oates" had been well-founded, as people came up to her on the street, or in the grocery store, and shyly asked, "Are you Joyce Carol Oates?" In this way, Joyce met two of her colleagues that year, fiction writer Reginald Gibbons and poet Charles Wright. With few exceptions, Joyce liked all her new colleagues: Edmund Keeley, called "Mike," the novelist and translator who directed the Creative Writing Program; the distinguished poet Stanley Kunitz; and fiction writer Stephen Koch. Joyce told Bob Phillips that the program, "being so small, is very communal. It promises to be an exceptionally fine, and demanding, year."

Joyce's first semester was more demanding than she had hoped: she was given three fiction-writing workshops of ten students each, plus several tutorials. There were also numerous social events, readings, and lectures that kept her constantly busy. "How *intense* life at Princeton is!" she exclaimed. Her circle of acquaintance quickly expanded beyond the writing program: at a party in late September, she met the poet Daniel Halpern, who had frequently published Joyce's work in the literary magazine he edited, *Antaeus*. Halpern, a gregarious man with a wide range of interests, would become one of Joyce's closest Princeton friends. He taught at Columbia, and during their first meeting Joyce was amused when Halpern "implored me to come to Columbia next semester to teach a graduate seminar in fiction—is this how faculty are recruited?—at parties?" (Joyce declined the offer.) She also met the distinguished classicist Robert Fagles and the Nietzsche scholar Walter Kaufmann, whose work Joyce had known since her Nietzsche-besotted undergraduate days at Syracuse. Despite her hectic schedule, she began auditing a course Kaufmann was teaching called the Philosophy of Religion, and enjoyed sitting in the back and playing the role of a student. Kaufmann liked Joyce immensely, and soon the two were having frequent lunches together. Joyce had always felt a strong attraction to older men of high literary or scholarly achievement, viewing them as intellectual father figures; she had felt an immediate rapport with both Fagles and Kunitz as well. Donald Dike had served this function during her undergraduate years, and her new editor, Henry Robbins, would soon play a similar role. Joyce viewed her friendship with Kaufmann in Jungian terms, believing herself a kind of "anima" figure in the older man's eyes. Gratified that Kaufmann sought her company so often, she wrote: "Anima is an image-bearer. Not necessarily a distorted image. . . . But we feel ourselves invisible (I certainly do) & require others to reflect us, mirroring the intangible."

Joyce soon found her three courses almost unmanageable in the hectic swirl of the university's social and intellectual life, and especially now that she was about to begin *Bellefleur*, a novel she expected to run more than eight hundred pages. She noted with some dismay that she had taken a substantial pay cut from what she'd made at Windsor but was worked much harder at Princeton. When Mike Keeley approached her about staying for a second year, she agreed, but with the stipulation that her course load be reduced substantially. Yet in other respects Princeton had met and exceeded all her hopes for "a more stimulating community" than she'd known in Windsor. Her journal entries that fall were peppered with almost childlike exclamations of delight: "What a crammed, accelerated life!" "O Rare Princeton. Was there ever a paradise equal to it?" Writing to her friends back in Detroit, she was similarly ebullient: "Princeton is superb," she told Kay Smith, "a continual delight." To Liz Graham she wrote, "This is such an incontestably *lovely* part of the country. . . . The University is as marvelous as legend would have it."

Clearly, Joyce had found her element. Like her marriage to Ray, her accep-

tance of the Princeton appointment and her impulsive purchase of a new
home had been among the wisest decisions of her life.

With the start of the fall 1978 term, Joyce and Ray settled into a comfortable, if sometimes hectically busy, routine of teaching, writing, and enjoying
their new surroundings. Ray had accepted an offer from N.Y.U. to teach
eighteenth-century English literature, so he commuted by train to the city
once a week and spent the rest of his time editing *Ontario Review*. As she had
done with *The Assassins*, Joyce devoted virtually all her writing time to *Bellefleur*, seldom distracting herself with reviews, short fiction, or other projects.
After such a long period of gestation, Joyce was elated that she'd actually begun writing the novel. She found her absorption in this enormous Gothic
tale an ideal counterbalance to the intense social and intellectual life of
Princeton.

The composition of *Bellefleur*, carefully chronicled in her journal, illustrated clearly her ability to concentrate on a single, obsessive task while simultaneously conducting a busy, multifaceted life outside her writing. Despite
the onerous load of coursework, the flood of student fiction, and almost daily
social engagements, she completed the 820-page first draft in less than six
months. As usual, her sense of time accelerated sharply once she began the
novel. In this case, her unusually intense perception of time related to the
story itself, since its central figure, the child Germaine, grows only to the age
of four, even as she witnesses many tumultuous decades of her family's history. (Joyce took her epigraph from Heraclitus: "Time is a child playing a
game of draughts; the kingship is in the hands of a child.") Although Joyce's
progress, by any objective standard, was amazingly swift, for the writer herself
time seemed to be running out. Only a few days after beginning this immense
novel she wrote in her journal, apparently with a straight face, "I am accursed
with a superficial, lazy temperament, which no one will quite believe, and
don't know whether to be angry or amused at myself. I *must* get to this novel,
I have only one day of the weekend remaining!" Two weeks later, she felt that
the novel was going "slowly, amazingly slowly, as if I were crawling along on
my hands and knees." Divided into five parts, the story was further divided
into dozens of brief, carefully crafted chapters, each taking up a different
strand in the complex Bellefleur tapestry of multigenerational family conflict,
romantic passion, and Gothic fate; Joyce tried to complete one of the chapters each day. By late October, she was frequently experiencing exhaustion
but, even more often, exhilaration: "Writing for hours yesterday, lovely unin-
terrupted intense exhausting marvelous fruitful hours, hours, hours. And today I feel free, and very cheerful. Except, a sobering thought: I am already at
page 100 and my heroine hasn't gotten herself born."

By the end of the fall term, Joyce had written more than 300 pages; there had been days of complete frustration ("it felt, yesterday, as if I were crawling on the floor, pushing a bean with my nose") alternating with days of wholly pleasurable absorption ("nothing is more richly, lavishly, lushly rewarding"). Even more than in the past, writing had become her anchor; by contrast, her busy teaching and social life receded in importance. Her colleagues recalled that Joyce seemed a bit awkward and self-conscious during her first year at Princeton, and she admitted that she felt pressured by the constant, frenetic socializing and intimidated at the prospect of "entertaining" in the elaborate, sophisticated way that seemed the norm there. But it was also the case that she was so preoccupied with *Bellefleur* that the demands of social life seemed relatively trivial and uninteresting. (Noting that she lacked "the skill as a hostess and cook" necessary to requite her many dinner invitations, she added, "Nor do I want that particular sort of skill. Life is too short to waste it on such things!") Once again the longing for "invisibility" appeared in her letters and journal. "Why, I wonder, don't we all sink into our obsessions, and disappear from view?" she remarked on December 12. "As my 'renown' grows," she had observed a few weeks earlier, "my 'invisibility' deepens."

Occasionally Joyce did allow herself a brief distraction from her obsessive work on *Bellefleur*. In early November, Joyce and Ray saw two tiny kittens abandoned on the side of the road and decided to bring them home: these additions to the family, Muffin and Tristram, brought the number of household cats to four (in addition to their adult cats Miranda and Misty, Joyce and Ray also owned a parakeet, Ariel). Amused at her own impulsiveness, Joyce asked herself: "How do people become eccentric? Quite by accident!— we never intended to have *four* cats." Joyce's fondness for cats had only increased with time, especially now that her new novel featured a supernaturally beautiful cat named Mahalaleel, who scaled the walls of Bellefleur castle in the opening chapter. (Joyce would later use the incident of finding the kittens in a short story, "The Seasons," collected in *Raven's Wing*.) She also took time out in late November to write a story inspired by the publication of Flannery O'Connor's letters, *The Habit of Being*, which she was reading for review. As she planned the long, "Southern Gothic" narrative she called "The Bingo Master," Joyce described her ambition "to write the one story [O'Connor] could never have written."

Although Joyce allowed herself a brief trip to New York during the Christmas break, she spent most of the vacation working on *Bellefleur*. During the winter, her obsession with the novel only deepened. After many years of writing psychological realism, she felt a euphoric sense of liberation from the traditional constraints of narrative chronology and mimetic characterization. Enthralled by the fantastic, "magical" elements of the story, she called *Belle-*

fleur "my waking dream" and gloried in its "exuberant shameless playfulness."
In a telling metaphor, she called the novel "[a] vampirous creation. Feeding
it, daily, I am necessarily feeding myself—or am I?" (Even as she nourished
herself with work, she noted that she wasn't yet entirely free of the psychological urge toward anorexia, "a tiny nugget or kernel, still with me, no longer
dominating my thoughts but still available.") She veered between seeing the
novel as an intensely personal document dealing with her own ravening
imagination (she remarked to Dick Cavett that *Bellefleur* was an autobiographical novel written "in code"), and as a sprawling examination of American history and culture (she told *The New York Times Book Review* that her
new novel was "a critique of 'the American dream,' or a parody thereof"). Of
course, it was both. Inspired by the haunting image of a walled garden, Joyce
had originally seen the novel as a metaphor for the "unfathomable mysteries"
of human imagination, but had also intercalated numerous historical events
such as the war of 1812 and the building of the Erie Barge Canal. The Belle-
fleurs became the archetypal American family, with the patriarch Gideon and
matriarch Leah ultimately viewed as mythical, Adam-and-Eve figures in
Joyce's autonomous fictive world. Pondering the huge narrative structure she
was amassing, she asked herself: "What *is* this bizarre novel about? Only the
imagination? Childhood? Magic? Terror? [. . .] It's history . . . the beginning
of the world as transcribed long after the end of the world."

As she neared completion of the manuscript, she received further ac-
knowledgment of her international stature as a literary figure, learning that
she had been nominated for the Nobel Prize in Literature. At the age of forty,
she was exceptionally young to be considered for the prize, which typically rewards writers near the end of their careers, but a flurry of Nobel-related publicity would become an almost annual October ritual for Joyce. Each year, in
the days before the prize announcement, journalists would telephone the
Princeton English department with rumors that Joyce was a likely winner. As
head of the writing program, Mike Keeley remembered a request from one of
the major television networks to set up a "media room" and prepare for an
onslaught of reporters. On one occasion, Joyce received a phone call from a
reporter at four in the morning, informing her that the news had just come
"on the wire": she had won the Nobel. Asked for a comment, Joyce prudently
declined, deciding to await official word and then learning, later in the day,
that she had not won. Although Joyce could not avoid feeling hopeful each
time she was nominated—she knew that her parents, especially, would be
thrilled if she won—the annual publicity was also distracting. She did not
write for prizes or money, she often remarked; if artistic activity were not its
own reward, then it wouldn't be worth the effort and dedication involved.
Shortly after completing *Bellefleur*, she noted that her writing brought "a

sense of extraordinary self-worth," since it was "only by way of *this* self, and with a great deal of labor, that the art-work can take its place in the world."

Whenever Joyce finished a novel, she felt an immediate sense of exclusion, a "homesickness" for the exciting process of composition. The letdown was especially acute after *Bellefleur*. To offset depression, she turned immediately to another task: writing the introduction to the *Best American Short Stories* volume. In addition to her work with the National Book Awards, she had spent much of her reading time during the past few months poring over the hundred stories selected by the series editor, Shannon Ravenel. Joyce also began an immediate revision of *Bellefleur*, which she wanted to deliver to Blanche during a planned trip to New York in mid-April. At the same time, she was putting the finishing touches on *Graywolf: Life and Times* (she had again discarded her alternate title, *The Evening and the Morning*). The two manuscripts were so bulky that she joked about renting a U-Haul trailer to get them to New York.

During May and June, Joyce's new editor went through the manuscripts carefully; Robbins was especially taken with *Bellefleur*, and suggested a spring 1980 publication. Although Joyce was doubtful about publishing the book only a few months after *Unholy Loves*—the last of her works to be published by Vanguard—she trusted her editor's judgment, and quickly set to work on the revisions he suggested. He'd come out to Princeton for lunch one day in late June to discuss the book, telling Joyce that it could be made even stronger if it were shortened somewhat through a tightening of the prose and elimination of a few chapters he considered unnecessarily digressive. Joyce appreciated the suggestions; each time they met, she felt an enhanced respect and admiration for her new editor. "How much I like Henry!" she exclaimed in her journal. "Sensitive, widely-read, soft-spoken, sweet, intelligent, ah what an ideal editor . . . what an ideal *person*."

Joyce delivered the revised version of *Bellefleur* to Robbins on July 18, but her pleasure in this new editor-author relationship was tragically short-lived: less than two weeks later, Robbins suffered a fatal heart attack one morning on his way to work. (Though only fifty-one, Robbins had a history of heart problems.) Joyce was grief-stricken. She had looked forward to a long and rewarding relationship with Robbins not only as an editor but as a friend. "I wanted him so badly as a friend," she wrote, "someone I would perhaps not see often, but would think about often, and constantly, in connection with my writing." Her sense of euphoria at having brought *Bellefleur* into its final, polished form now seemed ludicrous as she pondered the "pointlessness of it, our activities: writing, the 'literary' life: Henry so suddenly wiped out, erased." She consoled herself by making an elaborate record of each meeting and conversation she'd had with Robbins, as a personal memorial to their brief but promising relationship. As a gesture of respect and affection, she also dedicated *Bellefleur* to the "memory of Henry Robbins (1927–79)."

One key to Joyce's intense productivity had always been her ability to continue writing even in times of exhaustion, illness, or depression; in her *Paris Review* interview, she had remarked that she sometimes forced herself to begin writing even when "nothing seems worth enduring for another five minutes," since art was a transcendent activity and the act of writing itself raised her spirits. By the time of Robbins's death, Joyce had already enjoyed a spectacularly productive year: not only had she produced the second half of *Bellefleur* and carefully revised the entire novel, and done revisions for *Graywolf: Life and Times*, and completed her National Book Award judging and her editorial work for *Best American Short Stories*, not to mention the occasional essay-review for *The New Republic*; she had also decided to transform her novella *The Triumph of the Spider Monkey* into a full-length play and had begun work on yet another novel.

The new book, *Marya: A Life*, began with a short story she had written some years before called "November Morning." In the original version, the story had centered on a young boy, but she now saw the possibilities for a longer, more autobiographical narrative and her character became a girl, Marya Knauer. In early May, Joyce began a series of short stories that would form an episodic novel relating key incidents in Marya's life. Joyce combined major swaths of her own experience—her upstate New York background, her sorority life at Syracuse, her passionate devotion to writing—with elements of her mother's life. (Like Carolina, Marya is "given away" by her real mother and raised by an aunt.) But, as she pointed out in a preface to the novel, the superficial resemblances between Joyce and Marya were less important than their common personal quest: "What is most autobiographical about the novel is its inner kernel of emotion—Marya's half-conscious and often despairing quest for her own elusive self."

On May 10, Joyce had announced in her journal her intention to "create, in Marya, an alternative self; an alternative life. A personality that is, and isn't, my own." Once the project was under way, Joyce produced one Marya story after another, completing a first version of the novel by mid-July. Joyce's description of her own creative intensity mirrored similar passages about Marya that were included in the novel. On July 14, she wrote in her journal: "The headachey delirium of one day (yesterday, for instance, when I wrote hour upon hour upon hour, all day long, until 10 PM), the detachment of the next (today, for instance, when I revised and coolly rearranged what I'd done in yesterday's debauch).... Quite clearly I require the poor struggling creature who writes until her head swims and her eyesight blotches and she can barely remember who she is ... though I much prefer the activity of today . . . sorting things out, retyping pages, Xing out passages, in general having a thoroughly enjoyable time with Marya and her fate."

In the months after Henry Robbins's death, Joyce worked at new projects: during the remainder of the summer, she produced a miscellany of new short stories ("West," "Ballerina," "Minor Characters"), though none were among her best and she never collected them. Instead, she longed to become involved in another long, complex novel. By late August, she was contemplating the Washington-set political novel she would call *Angel of Light*. As she had done with *Bellefleur*, she wanted to allow the necessary time for the story to develop fully in her mind, "taking notes without any sense of pressure" and "trying to envision the central scenes from the points of view of each character involved." As the weeks passed, however, she became uncomfortably aware that she was blocked: the narrative voice and structure of *Angel of Light* remained out of focus. She continued working as usual on the occasional short story, poem, or review, and periodically she would do further revisions to the completed manuscripts of *Bellefleur* and *Jigsaw*; but the nagging concern over her next long novel would shadow her creative life for the rest of the year.

In Princeton, there was always an abundance of stimulating social life to counter Joyce's hours of solitary brooding. As she began her second academic year, her circle of acquaintance continued to expand. Among her colleagues in the writing program, she became particularly close to the novelist and critic Stephen Koch, a witty New Yorker with whom Joyce developed the kind of close, playful, "brother-sister" relationship she had conducted with her friend John Ditsky in Windsor. Koch also served as the model for Constantine Reinhart, the central character in a series of short stories Joyce wrote that fall. As in the Marya stories, she envisioned those focused on Constantine as a loosely structured novel; but even though most of the stories were placed in magazines—one of the best, "The Sunken Woman," appeared in *Playboy*—the novel was never published. Like *Marya: A Life*, the Constantine stories mined Joyce's fascination with identity, especially the phenomenon of the doppelgänger that for Joyce had such personal relevance in her acutely felt split between her private, invisible self and the public Joyce Carol Oates. (She would explore this theme even more elaborately, in the late 1980s and 1990s, in her pseudonymous "Rosamond Smith" novels, which deal with literal twins and other symbolic manifestations of the divided self.) In the case of Constantine, the crux of his dual nature was his bisexuality; Joyce saw him "fluctuating between the two 'halves' of his personality." But Joyce also worked autobiographical material into his character, since Constantine is a celebrated critic frequently asked to give lectures and "perform" in public, creating a mask that is markedly different from the wounded, rather private man who remains hidden even from his lovers and friends. Like the Marya stories, those dealing with Constantine came swiftly, and she completed the cycle before the end of the fall semester. They were written, she noted, in an "easy, conversational, discursive style," and unlike the major novel still troubling her imagination, they caused her little tension or anxiety. Like *Unholy Loves*, the Constantine narrative was a relatively minor enterprise that employed her writing energies while she remained blocked in her progress toward a longer work.

It seems likely that during Joyce's first years in Princeton, as she adjusted to her exciting but often distracting new environment, she gravitated naturally toward episodic, loosely structured works: *Bellefleur, Marya: A Life*, and the Constantine narrative reflect, in this sense, the frenetic pace of her new life, which contrasted so dramatically with the quiet insularity she had known in Windsor. By the fall 1979 term, it was not uncommon for Joyce and Ray to have eight or ten social engagements in a single week. There were stimulating visits with Eudora Welty, John Updike, and the composer Ned Rorem; there were new friendships with writers teaching temporarily in the Princeton writing program, such as poet Maxine Kumin and novelist Richard Ford. (But Joyce's enthusiasm for her brilliant new friends was not always reciprocated: Ned Rorem, in a diary entry for December 1, 1979, noted crisply: "Joyce Carol Oates last night, and husband Raymond Smith.... They are Midwestern, not glib and New Yorkish, a touch bland, hard to talk to insofar as they are anxious not to offend." Joyce had once expressed private gratitude that she'd never been mentioned in Rorem's ongoing, published diaries, but her luck had run out.) Joyce and Ray had also become friendly with another couple, the poet Michael Goldman and his wife, the writer and film director Eleanor Bergstein, both of whom Joyce liked immensely. And in October, at a dinner given by Richard Trenner, Joyce had met the feminist scholar Elaine Showalter, then chairperson of the English department of Douglass College at Rutgers. Elaine, an energetic, enormously well-read woman who had long admired Joyce's work, would later join the Princeton faculty and become one of Joyce's closest friends.

Joyce gradually adjusted to the frantic pace of Princeton life, though she found its social demands more burdensome than exhilarating during her early years there. At the same time, she knew that Princeton was a far more appropriate environment for her than any she had known in the past. Unlike the social treadmill in Detroit that she had fled to England to escape, Princeton offered a more intellectual and artistic group of people. Although she and Ray still had not severed their ties with Windsor—the University of Windsor had agreed to grant Joyce a sabbatical with full pay for the following year—they felt increasingly settled in Princeton. They undertook a major renovation to their home that fall, converting the garage into a large study and guest room.

One anchor that helped Joyce navigate her busy Princeton days was her teaching. Now that her course load was lighter, she looked forward to each workshop meeting and discovered talented students almost every semester. A November 1979 article in the *Princeton Alumni Weekly* provided a glimpse of Joyce's classroom personality: the visiting reporter described Joyce as "a tall, slender, graceful woman, uncomfortably aware that she is a presence." Joyce's method was to combine a consideration of major writers and their techniques (during a ninety-minute class, she incorporated Hemingway, Faulkner, Flannery O'Connor, Pinter, Ionesco, and Updike, all "apparently with total recall, mentioning specific passages or stories") with a careful, line-by-line critique of the students' own fiction. Joyce told the workshop members that she saw her role "neither as flattering and humoring people nor being so critical that you give up." Even at Princeton, she said, people were too often "humored"; instead she "wanted to inject a reality principle from time to time, so long as it's not depressing."

By the end of 1979, Joyce's own mood had become less buoyant. She felt an increasing sense of isolation in her new surroundings. Despite her new, much-valued friendships—with Walter Kaufmann, Stephen Koch, Elaine Showalter, and others—Joyce still felt the lack of a like-minded confidante with whom she could discuss intimately the literary, philosophical, and personal issues that troubled her, and about which she wrote so copiously in her journal. She had been searching for this ideal friend, she noted, for much of her adult life. Her loneliness was palpable in a moving journal entry of November 22: "I've never found this person. He or she, or they, would have to be writers too . . . or poets. . . . But it's clear that they don't exist. Joyce's 'community' is an empty category, a mere sentimental ghost."

One of her consolations was the renewed respect given to her work. Like *Son of the Morning,* her recently published novel *Unholy Loves* received wide and positive attention. Joyce found it somewhat ironic that her least ambitious novel should be so warmly received, but the notices were heartening nonetheless. The noted writer Alice Adams gave the novel a glowing review in the *Chicago Tribune,* and in *Newsweek,* Walter Clemons described it as "fecund with ideas and highly enjoyable," and distinguished by "rapt, inspired passages." In *The New York Times Book Review,* A. G. Mojtabai praised the "wealth of trenchant social and psychological observation" and the "ferocious social comedy." Mojtabai found the novel uneven, however, and resuscitated the old stereotype of Joyce Carol Oates as a woman writing "in a fever of possession." Joyce fired off an exasperated response, which appeared in the *Review* several weeks later: "Contrary to the outlandish speculation in A. G. Mojtabai's review of my novel 'Unholy Loves,' I hardly write 'in a fever of possession'. . . . I revise extensively. I am passionate about the craftsmanship of writing. I am perfectly conscious when I write, and at other selected times.

Will I never escape such literary-journalism drivel? Year after year, the same old cliches. . . ."

By now, Joyce had become expert at delivering counterpunches to her critics: rather than accept insults or inaccuracies in silence, she would respond sharply to negative press (especially to the *New York Times*, which was read avidly by her Princeton friends). Then, believing that to dwell on such matters would be counterproductive, she would simply put the experience behind her. A journal entry for the last day of 1979 succinctly expresses Joyce's temperamental inclination to *move forward* into the next project, the next experience, the next phase of being. "Sometimes it seems that my life, my pulse, simply beats too quickly," she wrote, "and with the most extraordinary childlike eagerness!—a burning eagerness—to know, to learn, to absorb, to *be*—to pass out of myself and into . . . into not people so much as experiences, states of mind, *their* transformations." Joyce's accelerated sense of time (imaged physically in her bouts of tachycardia, when her heart would race as quickly as 150 beats per minute), in combination with her intense curiosity and addiction to work, prevented her from either becoming discouraged by hostile reviews or resting on her laurels. (Part of her eagerness to finish each novel-in-progress, she confessed, was her sense of mortality, her fear that she might not live to complete it.) In many ways, the next year would typify the extraordinary range of her activities and interests, and would continue the sea change in her public reputation, culminating that summer with the publication of her most ambitious novel to date, *Bellefleur*.

In a surprising shift, Joyce turned to playwriting in the early months of 1980. Most of the plays were dramatic versions of recent short stories such as "The Widows," "Night-Side," "The Changeling," and "Presque Isle." Since her unhappy early experience with *The Sweet Enemy*, Joyce had written relatively few plays, and with one exception they had been harshly reviewed. In 1967 her second play had been produced by Frank Corsaro at the Actors Studio; entitled *Sunday Dinner*, it had been adapted from a novella of the same title published in *Triquarterly*. When it was panned by the New York critics, Joyce confessed to Liz Graham that the reviews "served to convince me, absolutely, that I'm not a playwright and had better stick with other forms of writing." Yet she had tried again in 1972 with *Ontological Proof of My Existence*, which had grown out of *Wonderland* and centered on Jesse's runaway daughter, Shelley, and her involvement with an egocentric drug dealer. For this effort Joyce did receive, at last, some encouragement: Jack Kroll of *Newsweek* had called the play "a firecracker of a closet drama . . . a direct eruption from her strange, disturbing, and powerful sensibility." Yet her next attempt, *Miracle Play*, staged the following year by the New Phoenix Repertory Company, was reviewed negatively in the *New York Times* and the *Village Voice*.

Her most recent play, *The Triumph of the Spider Monkey*, had been directed by Daniel Freudenberger at the Phoenix Theatre in 1979. Joyce had been apprehensive about transferring this bizarre psychological case study to the stage, but was elated that the lead actor, Philip Casnoff, had captured her "maniac" Bobbie Gotteson perfectly. Never before, she felt, had a stage version accomplished her dramatic intention so powerfully. In the early weeks of 1980, encouraged by the production of *Spider Monkey* and still unable to begin *Angel of Light*, Joyce had long, excited conversations about drama with her Princeton colleague Robert Fagles, whose translation of *The Oresteia* (which she greatly admired) would serve as an important source for *Angel of Light*, a novel dealing with political and familial vengeance. On January 29, she visited New York again, this time to attend rehearsals for a short play, "Daisy," based loosely on James Joyce's relationship with his schizophrenic daughter, Lucia. (The prose version of "Daisy," collected in *Night-Side*, was a personal favorite among her own stories.) On February 20, after dining with Susan Sontag and her son David Rieff, Joyce and Ray attended the premiere of "Daisy" at the Cubiculo Theatre. Again she admired the actors' performances and she considered the music exquisite. Yet "Daisy" also received devastating reviews. Although Joyce was disappointed, she showed her usual resilience: "My detachment or fatalism is such that I absorbed the disappointment fairly quickly," she wrote. "A reasonable person would give up writing plays, or at the very least slash his wrists; I simply keep going, perhaps out of momentum." She added that "fatalism translates into cheerfulness, and cheerfulness makes possible a sort of benign amnesia." More than a decade would pass, however, before Joyce would make serious efforts to revive her fitful career as a playwright.

Again putting her negative press behind her, Joyce turned back to her mountain of notes for *Angel of Light* in early March, but continued to experience an "anguish of frustration" at her inability to begin. She labored over the material for the rest of that month, forcing herself to write the first chapter even though she found the draft unsatisfactory. The opening pages were written "with so much idiotic labor," she noted grimly, "one would think they were committed in blood." But she persevered, intrigued by her own material. She had become increasingly fascinated by the complex phenomenon of Washington politicians and their incessant struggle for power. Her interest was only enhanced by her view of the power-seeking mentality as diametrically opposed to her own temperament: "For me the highest values are privacy, freedom, and anonymity," she said, "which would have to be surrendered if one took up 'power.'" Focusing on a pair of young teenagers who feel betrayed by the adult world after their idealistic father is murdered, Joyce planned to combine a complex family drama with an allegorical portrayal of intergenerational conflict in post-Watergate America.

As she had done in *Bellefleur*, Joyce devised a complex system of historical and literary analogues for her new novel: though set in Washington, D.C., in 1980, *Angel of Light* evoked the powerful story of John Brown and his abolitionist activities in the 1850s, which she saw as "very closely tied in, in many moral and political ways, with the 1960s." Part of her difficulty in constructing the novel was her desire to "artistically unite these two disparate but very similar decades in American history." (The novel's title came from Thoreau, who had called John Brown "an Angel of Light"; yet Joyce intended, as well, a reference to that other ill-fated "angel," the Lucifer of Christian mythology.) At the same time, she employed the Greek myth of the house of Atreus as an allegorical framework for the novel. Joyce noted that the Atreus myth related to a time when "it was felt that as the leaders, as the morality and private lives of the leaders went, so went the entire nation: that these are exemplary and representative people." In the era of Vietnam and Watergate, she saw the ancient myth as a way to explore America's national sense of betrayal by its political leaders.

As *Angel of Light* opens, the highly principled, loving, and seemingly incorruptible Maurice ("Maurie") Halleck is dead; his children, Kirsten and Owen—the modern-day Electra and Orestes—make a pact to avenge what they consider a murder plotted by their own mother, the glamorous Washington hostess Isabel de Benavente Halleck, and her lover, Nick Martens, a capable but opportunistic colleague of Maurie Halleck and his closest friend since their prep school days in the 1940s. If Kirsten and Owen's suspicions seem far-fetched at first, the novel's subsequent exploration of the tangled relationships among the principals—and especially its revelations of the moral character of both Isabel and Nick—suggests that their outrage and desire for revenge are justified and even, as Joyce would later argue, "a normal response." Yet the moral issues in an Oates novel are never clear-cut: both Kirsten and Owen are spoiled Washington "rich kids"; Kirsten has a history of emotional instability, while Owen, whose preppie exterior conveys both unwarranted self-regard and an underlying lack of substance, is weak-minded enough to be easily brainwashed by a terrorist organization later in the novel. The Halleck children possess the idealism and skepticism common to adolescence, but also the strident single-mindedness of their spiritual ancestor, John Brown; like him, they allow their sense of personal righteousness to justify acts of barbaric violence.

Structurally, *Angel of Light* is deliberately disjointed, each chapter carefully honed to present an image of the Halleck family's decline; Joyce gave titles to each of the nine sections and even to the brief chapters within each section, providing an image-centered focus for each narrative piece in this intricately designed psychological and political puzzle. As always, Joyce was ingenious at drawing specific experiences from her own life and weaving them into her fictional world. Her Princeton friends Ed Cone and George Pitcher recalled that Joyce attended the annual party they gave to observe their night-blooming cereus, a rare American cactus that blooms only once each year, late in the summer, and only at night. Section VII of *Angel of Light* is entitled "Night-Blooming Cereus," and when Cone and Pitcher read the chapter based on their party, they noted that Joyce had transcribed almost verbatim remarks people had made while the plant bloomed.

Having begun the novel at last, Joyce soon became "immersed" in its complex structure, despite the many distractions of Princeton's busy spring season. By the middle of April, she had written 138 pages, and recorded in her journal the fantasy of escaping all her obligations outside the novel: "quiet . . . peace . . . tranquility . . . anonymity . . . invisibility . . . *no dinner parties for a week! two weeks!* Could anything be more shameless, more gloriously and deliciously self-indulgent, than to fantasize *no dinner parties for two weeks!!!!*" And there was another, more substantial distraction looming on the horizon: on May 12, Joyce and Ray would leave for a six-week tour of Eastern Europe, under the auspices of the U.S. Information Agency. The itinerary included stops in Frankfurt, Warsaw, Budapest, Oslo, Stockholm, Helsinki, Brussels, Antwerp, and Berlin; she was scheduled to make sixteen public appearances during the trip. By May 11, the day before her departure, Joyce had completed 239 pages of *Angel of Light*, and she feared that the six-week interruption would break her momentum and prevent her from completing the novel.

Yet the European trip was productive in its own way. Her colleagues at various stops included Susan Sontag and the poet John Ashbery, and she met countless European writers, translators, and U.S. embassy officials. She wrote to Bob Phillips that the "innumerable luncheons, banquets, and receptions" constituted "almost too much ceremony," but that they'd "met *wonderful* people" throughout the trip. Fascinated by such sights as the Berlin Wall and the Warsaw ghetto, and by her manifold impressions of the extraordinary contrasts between Communist East Europe and the West, Joyce began avidly taking notes for a series of short stories that would form the core of her 1984 collection, *Last Days*. The novella "My Warszawa" (whose protagonist, Judith Horne, was a blend of Sontag and Joyce herself), the brief, parablelike "Our Wall," the highly experimental tale "Ich Bin Ein Berliner," and other stories in this group expressed Joyce's discomfiting fascination with Eastern Europe. Warsaw made a particular impression, since for the first time Joyce felt acutely her own part-Jewish heritage, her identity as the granddaughter of Blanche Morgenstern: "The 'Jewishness' of one's spirit in such parts of the world is a queer, queer thing," she noted. "Certainly I have *never* experienced it before."

After returning from Europe, Joyce found that her prediction had come true: she now felt detached from *Angel of Light*, and after completing the stories inspired by her trip she began thinking about another long Gothic novel in the manner of *Bellefleur*, this one to be focused on a family of five sisters growing up in nineteenth-century America. The novel that would become *A Bloodsmoor Romance* was another "dream narrative," and in fact began with an intense, complicated dream Joyce had about one of the sisters. A few weeks later, an eerie coincidence again brought the Bloodsmoor material to mind: she had imagined beginning the novel with one of the Zinn sisters' mysterious abduction in a helium balloon; to Joyce's astonishment, only a few hours after she'd jotted down this idea, a helium balloon did appear above the woods behind Ray and Joyce's house, "one of the helium-filled flame-empowered passenger balloons we first noticed two years ago when we came to Princeton, over Lake Carnegie." Yet she was hardly ready to begin this major new work: it had "no name" and "no focus" at present, representing only "a certain gravitational pull" in her imagination. Instead, she knew she should force herself to return to *Angel of Light*. "How sad, how abrupt," she noted, "to have left Maurie Halleck (in his early 20s) in the middle of a thought." Since Ray had begun teaching part-time at Rutgers University that summer, Joyce had undertaken "an experiment in solitude." When Ray was gone for the entire day, she would "start writing at 9 in the morning, and continue on through, more or less without interruption," until 11 P.M. She became so totally reimmersed in *Angel of Light* that "I am hardly aware of the passage of time, and never feel hungry, or even lonely."

Joyce's only major distraction from her novel-in-progress that summer was pleasant enough: the publication of *Bellefleur* on August 18 brought her considerable press attention, most of it heartening. Although her recent Vanguard novels had sold about 20,000 copies each in hardcover, Dutton launched its first Oates title with a printing of 35,000 copies and pledged $35,000 for advertising and promotion. Joyce had cooperated in the large-scale launch of *Bellefleur* by agreeing to cut her royalty rate so that the 558-page book could be priced as affordably as possible. According to John Macrae III, then publisher at Dutton, the house was "convinced Oates's book will appeal to a much wider audience in addition to her loyal fans." Macrae's projection was accurate. Despite the complexity and difficulty of *Bellefleur*, it became Joyce's first book to make the *New York Times* best-sellers list; it also appeared on other newspaper lists and reached the top-ten ranking for all the major bookstore chains. By September 1, the novel was already in its fifth printing, bringing the total to 75,000 copies; on the strength of such sales, Dutton was able to auction the paperback rights for $345,000. Although Joyce accurately predicted that the commercial success of *Bellefleur* would be a "one-in-a-decade" phenomenon, since "the books to follow are, to put it mildly, *not* commercial," she decided to "enjoy this while it lasts . . . why not?"

She also enjoyed many glowing reviews: both John Leonard in the daily *New York Times* and John Gardner in the Sunday *Book Review* praised the novel highly. The first paragraph of Gardner's front-page review, one of the most influential of Joyce's career, summarized many critics' view of the book: "*Bellefleur* is the most ambitious book to come so far from that alarming phenomenon Joyce Carol Oates. However one may carp, the novel is proof, if any seems needed, that she is one of the great writers of our time. *Bellefleur* is a symbolic summation of all this novelist has been doing for 20-some years, a magnificent piece of daring, a tour de force of imagination and intellect." Another reviewer remarked that the novel "delights with its opulence, its brilliant plotting, and its sheer strangeness"; in *Newsday*, Dan Cryer called the novel "a totally absorbing reading experience and a breathtaking tour de force." The only dissenters in major publications were Joyce's former champion Walter Clemons at *Newsweek* and the novelist Russell Banks, who wrote in the *Washington Post* that *Bellefleur* was "shockingly humorless" and poorly written, giving "the impression that what we are reading is an author's rough draft."

But the general response to *Bellefleur* remained overwhelmingly positive, and the novel ultimately sold more than one million copies in hardback and paperback. Appreciative of her new publisher's efforts, Joyce granted several interviews to help promote the book. The most influential and widely read was Lucinda Franks's sympathetic feature story in the *New York Times Magazine*. The two women sat on the flagstone terrace behind Joyce and Ray's house; Franks quickly recognized the backyard pond, the holly, the dragonflies, and Joyce's cat Misty from their transmogrified versions in *Bellefleur*. During the interview, Franks remembered, Joyce sat "tall and erect as a signal tower, fading in and out each time a blue jay or cat intercepts her attention. She looks somehow lost in time." Likewise, Joyce found Franks "wonderful to talk with." Joyce and Ray became friendly with Franks and her husband, New York attorney Robert Morgenthau.

As always, Joyce balanced her extreme absorption in work with a life that she had once called "a study in conventionality." If she were to lose her "ballast of presumed 'normality,' " she noted, she would have to "stop writing about the sorts of things I have been writing about for the past 20 years." She had always felt "defined and loved and cherished" by her family relationships: first by her parents and Grandmother Woodside, then by Ray. "I moved without any period of adjustment from being a 'daughter' and 'granddaughter' to being a 'beloved' and 'wife.' I might not have known who I was, but I knew what I was: the role was there, and is still here." Yet even within the cocoon of what she called her "disguise" as a bourgeois woman, her intense dedication to work often seemed shadowed by an alarming degree of self-abnegation; as in the past, this expressed itself in symptoms of anorexia. As she finished *Angel of Light*, remaining alone at home during those long days when Ray was away at Rutgers, she ate less and less. She told a friend that "I've come to the conclusion that food—eating—is totally a social phenomenon. . . . The very notion of 'appetite' is bound up with the social context of eating. Remove that context, and one simply isn't hungry."

Working intensely through the month of August, she completed *Angel of Light* on September 1, then immediately began extensive revisions; a few weeks later, she had begun the even longer and more ambitious *A Bloodsmoor Romance*. This obsessiveness exacted a physical toll: by mid-October, she noticed a "considerable weight loss; cessation of menstrual periods; hair coming out rather too freely." She was so exhausted that she felt an "absolute sickness, in the pit of the stomach," along with severe headaches. As she worked on the opening chapters of *A Bloodsmoor Romance*, her "head almost literally rang with the need to push on, to push on, to get everything in." She continued to have no appetite: "Eating is a problem when one would rather work; and then I eat so slowly, the process is tiresome. . . . If I'm with other people (as I almost always am) I would rather talk, or listen, and the food becomes a distraction. Absurd 'problem' as I know fully."

Yet she kept working, spurred by the "mesmerizing mad language of *A Bloodsmoor Romance*." By the end of 1980, she had completed more than five hundred pages of the novel. But these months were far from happy ones. The glorious Princeton autumn had been shadowed by her own fragile health and by the unexpected deaths of two friends. On September 4, her Princeton colleague Walter Kaufmann died suddenly of a cerebral aneurysm at the age of fifty-nine. Not only had Kaufmann, as an authority on Nietzsche, been one of the older, male intellectuals of the type Joyce typically admired; he had also seemed a mysteriously lonely figure who had engaged her sympathy. Arriving at the Kaufmann house to visit her friend's widow, she'd "felt suddenly that I couldn't continue; couldn't go through with the visit. To walk in that door and not be greeted by Walter's firm handshake, his kiss on my cheek, his ebullient manner. . . ." Her sense of loss was acute. "I admired him immensely," she wrote, "and always enjoyed his company."

Far more traumatic was the news Joyce received in October that her old friend Kay Smith was dying. Suffering from liver and kidney problems exacerbated by her continued use of alcohol, Kay had avoided seeking medical help for her illness, which suggested to her friends that her death was a form of suicide. By early October, her condition was untreatable, and she spent most of the month in the hospital, dying on October 30. Shocked by the news, Joyce remembered "Kay, like Walter Kaufmann, so vigorously alive; so imaginative; practical-minded too; gifted with a delightful sense of humor." When Liz Graham phoned to tell Joyce that Kay had lapsed into a coma, Joyce's reaction had been "absurd childish disbelief." In the last weeks of Kay's life, Liz reported, there had been only a "very thin veneer of the 'old' gay, spirited, energetic Kay, this fragile shell going through the motions."

The death of this vital, attractive woman, whom Joyce had loved deeply, would haunt her for years. She would later deal with Kay's death in fiction, most notably in portraying the alcoholic decline of Persia Courtney in *Because It Is Bitter, and Because It Is My Heart*, but initially Joyce had felt overcome by grief and an uncharacteristic sense of helplessness. "I've been so depressed by Kay's death," she wrote to Gloria Whelan, "that I feel inordinately cheerful—in an insouciant, pointless way." To Liz Graham, she remarked that "I am already caught up short to realize that she won't be sending a card, or any more of her newsy, cheery letters. Even if the letters were part of her continual persona, they *were* wonderful letters."

Joyce had been able to accept the sudden deaths of Henry Robbins and Walter Kaufmann as unavoidable, she told Gloria Whelan, but "Kay's death is hideous because it is so—peculiar. One feels anger along with grief. I know that Kay would have insisted that any one of us see a doctor if we were in her condition—she would have dragged us there in person." Joyce's journal entry of November 1 conveys her painful bewilderment: "I feel so angry about this. Numb, and angry. For God's sake why hadn't she seen a doctor, though everyone begged her! The waste, the loss. . . . I can't think, can't even type. Inchoate emotions. Numbed half-thoughts." Her friend's death painfully underscored a theme that had run consistently through Joyce's own fiction: the human personality is unfathomable, even "phantasmagoric," and true self-knowledge, much less knowledge of another person, is impossible. The familiar, ebullient Kay was herself revealed as having been, at her emotional core, an "invisible woman," unglimpsed even by her closest friends.

While Kay had escaped from her private anguish into alcohol and finally into death, Joyce turned to her work for solace. "Thank God for romance; for Bloodsmoor," she noted on November 28. Making steady progress on the new novel, she reflected on the degree to which her own writing represented "an idyll, a true 'romance' " to which she could always turn in times of pain and confusion. For Joyce, art was always the supreme consolation: "A vision on the page; the works' integrity; allowing me constantly to change form—and to slip free. My salvation."

13

The Gothic
Wonderland
1981–84

*Here, suddenly, is a mysterious door in a wall, and here
is the golden key that will unlock it, one has only to
summon forth one's courage and enter. Whatever
awaits will not only be strange and unexpected, it will,
in a way impossible to explain,* make sense; *and it will
be ours—as "reality" never is.*

—"Wonderlands" (1985)

Heartened by the commercial and critical success of *Bellefleur*, Joyce Carol
Oates devoted most of her writing time in the early 1980s to a series of
postmodernist Gothic novels that represented the most ambitious single
undertaking of her career. In *Bellefleur*, she had experimented with the long-
established novelistic conventions of the family saga, and soon she conceived
the idea of taking up other Victorian narrative modes—first the romance
novel in *A Bloodsmoor Romance*, followed by a Gothic horror novel (*The
Crosswicks Horror*), a detective story (*Mysteries of Winterthurn*), and a
"family memoir" (*My Heart Laid Bare*)—as a way of viewing key epochs in
American history and, at the same time, of playfully exploring the virtually
endless permutations of literary genre. In January 1985, having completed
this quintet of novels, Joyce summarized her motives and aspirations for the
series:

> Why "genre," one might ask? Does a serious writer dare concern
> herself with "genre"? Why, in imagining a quintet of novels to en-
> compass some eight decades of American history (beginning in the
> turbulent 1850s in *Bloodsmoor*, ending in 1932 with the election of
> FDR in "*My Heart Laid Bare*"), and to require some 2600 pages of
> prose—why choose such severe restraints, such deliberately confining

structures? But the formal discipline of "genre"—that it forces us inevitably to a radical re-visioning of the craft of fiction—was the reason I found the project so intriguing.

In her early forties, Joyce viewed this mammoth undertaking as a unique
chance to combine her still-youthful energy with her seasoned maturity as a
fiction writer: "The opportunity might not be granted me again, I thought,
to create a highly complex structure in which individual novels (themselves
complex in design, made up of 'books') functioned as chapters or units in an
immense design: America as viewed through the prismatic lens of its most
popular genres."

By February of 1981, she had finished the first draft of A *Bloodsmoor Romance*, which ran to almost nine hundred typewritten pages. This second
novel in the series, dominated by the rather prim, antiquated voice of its
nineteenth-century narrator, involved less structural complexity than the
maze of interlocking tales that had caused her such difficulty in *Bellefleur*,
yet she was well aware that *Bloodsmoor*, with its formidable length and eccentric style, was hardly a candidate to repeat the commercial success of the earlier novel: "It is surely the riskiest novel I've ever done," she observed. In
preparation, Joyce had read widely in nineteenth-century history (including
works on social customs, fashion, and the lives of women) and had immersed
herself in popular romances of the day by such writers as Susan Warner, Mrs.
Elizabeth Stuart Phelps, and Mrs. E.D.E.N. Southworth. It was "a sobering
and instructive experience," she later noted in an essay on Warner's *Diana*, to
read such works, with their Victorian sentimentality, Christian moralizing,
and emphasis on feminine duty and submissiveness. By choosing a pious,
garrulous spinster—a classic example of the unreliable narrator—to chronicle
the adventures of the five Zinn sisters, Joyce simultaneously exploited and
subverted the conventions of the romance genre, suggesting the degree to
which the fateful adventures of her five "little women" (Joyce wove countless
allusions to Alcott's famous novel through her own) served as emblems of female experience not only in the Victorian age but into the twentieth century
as well. (Not surprisingly, an excerpt from the novel appeared in *Ms.* magazine.) A feminist work, a playful experiment in literary genre, and a densely
textured evocation of nineteenth-century American culture, A *Bloodsmoor
Romance* is a demanding, often eccentric book that, as Joyce had perceived,
would appeal primarily to a small readership with academic interests in social
and literary history.

One feature of A *Bloodsmoor Romance* that Joyce had particularly enjoyed
was its relative lack of violence; the composition of her previous novel, *Angel
of Light*, had been shadowed by her dread of writing the brutal, climactic

scene in which Isabel Halleck is murdered by her own son. *Angel of Light*, Joyce wrote to Gail Godwin, had been "painful from the start, but became more painful still, as 'the' chapter approached (the murder of Isabel, with whom I so very clearly identified)"; as a result, she promised herself "I would write something with a happy ending next, if I survived." But Joyce felt caught in a double bind: she was criticized for the violence in her work, yet her lengthy nonviolent "romance" received a lukewarm response from critics and readers, and even from her own publishers. While *Angel of Light* had fetched $125,000 and *Bellefleur* $345,000 for paperback rights, *Bloodsmoor* brought only $50,000 after a disappointing performance in hardcover. The readership for Joyce's ongoing Gothic experiment would decline even more precipitously when *Mysteries of Winterthurn* appeared in 1984. In stark contrast to the success of *Bellefleur*, the inordinately complex *Winterthurn*, saddled with another eccentric, old-fashioned narrator, sold only a few thousand copies in hardcover, the same number as an average first novel.

Yet Joyce's shift away from the stark, sometimes violent contemporary realism of her earlier work and into the lush, romantic playfulness of Gothic conventions hardly signaled any relaxation into an easier, more "feminine" mode of writing. Partly due to the daunting ambition of her Gothic sagas, Joyce often suffered from stress and other health ailments as she worked on these books. Shortly after completing *Bloodsmoor*, she endured two agonizing tachycardiac seizures. During the first, in mid-April 1981, her palpitations and shortness of breath were so severe that Ray rushed her to the hospital emergency room; the symptoms subsided, but a second attack followed a few days later. Although she had become somewhat accustomed to these seizures, they represented an ongoing concern. Also contributing to Joyce's stress were the kinds of smaller but ongoing annoyances that had plagued her career for years. Just as she had resigned her membership in the National Book Critics Circle because she questioned the organization's ethics, she had recently told the editor of *The New Republic*, Martin Peretz, that she could no longer write reviews for him. After the magazine assigned Joyce a book by Maggie Scarf dealing with depression, and Joyce spent several days carefully reading the book and writing a negative review, Peretz informed her that he couldn't print the review because he and Scarf were old friends. Joyce was understandably angry, since she hadn't been informed that only a flattering review would be deemed acceptable. At about this same time, she'd begun feeling disheartened by the number of letters she had been receiving lately, after the success of *Bellefleur*, from some of her own "friends" who wrote only to ask for favors such as help in finding an agent or publisher, or the use of her influence as a book reviewer and member of the American Academy.

Nor had Joyce's move to bucolic Princeton affected her status as a favorite

target of the mentally deranged, who regularly sent crazed letters and, even
more disturbingly, sometimes showed up in person at her readings and lectures. Such people often bore striking similarities to the bizarre creatures she
invented for her Gothic novels, such as the impish dwarf in *Bellefleur* named
Nightshade. Writing to John Ditsky in March 1982, Joyce described some of
the strange letters she had received: "letter from a fan/would-be novelist who
describes himself as 4 feet tall with a bushy black beard and 'the noisiest
crutches in Manhattan' . . . a dwarf who has written a novel about a dwarf
he'd like me to read . . . he prefers 'hand delivery' since he doesn't trust the
mail. A gentleman, kindly or mad, who wants to make lunch with me a 'gift'
to his troubled wife. And so on." A month earlier, while giving a lecture on
the Princeton campus, Joyce had been interrupted by "a madwoman" who
approached the podium "whitefaced, visibly trembling, dressed in a long
black coat." The woman disrupted Joyce's lecture by shouting, "This has
gone on long enough! We came here to hear the poet, not you. To hear Professor Oates, not you." Joyce "tried to explain that I was 'Oates,' " but the
woman kept shouting angrily that Joyce was an impostor. Joyce's friend
Elaine Showalter, sitting in the audience, had noted apprehensively that the
woman kept one hand plunged deeply into her pocket, suggesting that she
might have a gun. In her journal, Joyce remarked that she felt "a secret sly
agreement with the madwoman's accusation: 'This has gone on long
enough. . . .' (Did I half-want her to pull out a gun and begin shooting? Was
I 'mildly disappointed' when she simply left . . . ?)" Joyce noted wryly that
she "could die as a 'sacrificial victim,' as a public event, even a public spectacle. . . . 'This solves the vexing problem of how to write my next novel,' I
might have said, sinking into lethal unconsciousness." Although she could
joke about these incidents, such "rewards of fame" were becoming increasingly nerve-racking. "I'm not particularly eager to give a talk or a reading soon
again," she confessed.

Joyce's dismay was only reinforced when such intense, puzzling hostility
issued from allegedly sane individuals. In an interview given by Truman
Capote at about this time, Capote expressed a vicious dislike of Joyce and
her work: "To me, she's the most loathsome creature in America," Capote
said. "She's a joke monster who ought to be beheaded in a public auditorium
or in Shea [stadium]." He recalled a letter Joyce had written him: "She's written me extreme fan letters. But that's the kind of a hoax she is. I bet there's
not a writer in America that's ever had their name in print that she hasn't
written a fan letter to." Joyce ascribed Capote's venomous remarks to his own
stalled career and his jealousy of younger, more productive writers who had
taken the spotlight from him. Capote's remarks were especially odd in that
many years earlier, after Joyce had sent him the admiring letter, Capote had

written a friendly response, suggesting that Joyce call him the next time she was in New York and offering to buy her dinner. Yet the two writers had never met.

As usual, neither her own occasional health problems nor the vicissitudes of her public reputation had even a slight impact on her fertile imagination, her writerly confidence, or her relentless productivity. In the spring of 1981, she had begun research for the third installment of her Gothic quintet, *The Crosswicks Horror*. While *A Bloodsmoor Romance* had dealt with the later decades of the nineteenth century, *Crosswicks* would focus on the early years of the twentieth, and would be set in Joyce's own environment. On May 1, she noted in her journal that she'd been "reading, with feverish interest, books about Princeton in the 1900's, the first decade." By the end of May, she had begun *Crosswicks*, after the usual weeks of note taking and uncertainty. She worked compulsively on the manuscript all summer, noting at one point that she "could write endlessly, scarcely rising to the surface to eat, or even breathe." The more deeply she proceeded into the story, the more clearly she recognized that its autobiographical core was her ongoing grief and bewilderment over Kay Smith's death the previous year: "Kay's death (the 'demon' gnawing away at her from the inside) is metamorphosed into very nearly the entire novel," she wrote. "The sense of Horror imminent, Horror absolutely mysterious, Horror that, for all our good intentions, *cannot be stopped*."

As if countering her sense of "the horror" with her own unstoppable energy, Joyce brought the eight-hundred-page manuscript to completion on September 29, having completed the first draft in four intense months. In November, she confessed that she had come close to "an awkward sort of collapse," and had begun suffering acutely from insomnia. As usual, Joyce's method of relaxation was simply to work in other genres, "writing trifling things" that included several short stories, essays, and book reviews—activity which, compared to the perilous intensity of writing novels, seemed relatively benign and superficial. But by the end of the year, she was already immersed in research for her fourth Gothic, *Mysteries of Winterthurn*. On December 10, she wittily summed up her addiction to the Gothic mode: "Once one has tasted blood, reform is virtually impossible."

Joyce's work on *The Crosswicks Horror* had represented a welcome escape from her public identity as "Oates." In June, she'd written that "I am infatuated with the *private life*, and with *anonymity*; perhaps even *invisibility*." The mischievous side of her character, which she had once called her "best-kept secret," had also been gratified in *Crosswicks*, since the novel offered a frequently satirical portrayal of the very institution and community that now sustained her. Even after several years' residence in Princeton, Joyce still felt like an outsider. In the early 1980s, as the usual parade of distinguished writers and intellectuals came to the campus as visiting lecturers—Shirley Hazzard and Francis Steegmuller, Harold Bloom, Carlos Fuentes, E. L. Doctorow, and many others—Joyce continued to feel that she hardly belonged in Princeton, despite her own literary fame. "Set beside these eloquent and unfailingly genial mandarins," she wrote, after the visit by Hazzard and Steegmuller, she felt "both sly and crude, like a proletarian spy, a Bolshevik, in the stronghold of the bourgeoisie."

On other occasions, Joyce suffered a disillusionment with the "elite" literary establishment to which she now belonged. In the spring of 1982, she attended a luncheon at the American Academy of Arts and Letters in New York, and had the misfortune to sit near the distinguished poet Howard Nemerov, who had been drinking heavily; without warning, he was overtaken by nausea and vomited into his plate. Joyce and the others at Nemerov's table tried to ignore his illness—a sharp-eyed waiter came over quickly and removed the plate—but Joyce was disturbed by the incident, which she recorded succinctly in her journal the following day: "Not the most felicitous image to retrieve from yesterday's sunny festivities, but there you are: a major American poet in the tradition of Frost, Stevens, Wordsworth, et. al. [sic], overtaken so suddenly by nausea that he couldn't leave his luncheon place . . . and vomited there, babyish, infantile, not overly apologetic though red-faced afterward."

If Joyce felt out of place among the sometimes elegant, sometimes ill-behaved literary elite, she continued to feel alienated from another group that should have embraced her. The feminist literary establishment, which had grown in power and prestige in recent years, had not always treated Joyce's work kindly. As a writer of extraordinary range and inventiveness, Joyce was sui generis, and though her recent novels had been more explicit than her earlier work in revealing a feminist sensibility, she felt put off by the unsettling exclusivity of the feminist perspective on literature. Even Joyce's close friend Elaine Showalter, the feminist scholar to whom Joyce had dedicated *Bloodsmoor*, had startled her by saying that she no longer read male authors; by contrast, Joyce's literary heroes had been mostly male, and she confessed to feeling "little kinship" with major women writers such as Flannery O'Connor, Virginia Woolf, Sylvia Plath, Charlotte Brontë, and Colette. (In 1984, Joyce would attend a lecture given by the feminist critic Nancy Miller, "Reading Women's Writing": Joyce observed that she wasn't sure why she'd attended the lecture, since "the subject really doesn't interest me.") "Most women writers have been narrow," she argued. "Some have been narrow and deep; but to be narrow and deep is still to be *narrow*." Joyce identified more strongly with the titanic ambitions of Balzac, Melville, or Faulkner.

Joyce had always felt sympathetic toward the women's movement, particularly its goal of economic equality, but at the same time she had resisted any suggestion that a woman artist should be engaged in writing feminist propaganda at the expense of her personal artistic vision. When a feminist journal, the *Women's Review of Books*, printed a dismissive review of her 1985 novel, *Solstice,* and called it a "Sadistic Lesbian novel," Joyce wrote the editors that she "did not in truth know such a genre existed." She concluded the letter by attacking the slanted, propagandistic responses of some feminists to literature by women: "If I want to write a novel about sadistic lesbians, however, I will. This is my prerogative as a writer. [. . .] And if the (woman) writer is forced to choose between being faithful to what might be called her personal artistic vision and feminist 'politics,' she will always choose the former."

Now vocal on this issue, Joyce had held this viewpoint privately throughout her career. Almost a decade earlier, after the publication of Philip Roth's *My Life as a Man,* Joyce had speculated in a letter to Roth on the criticism she might encounter if she wrote a book entitled *My Life as a Woman.* "Our current fashionable beliefs," she said, "seem to deny so much that is objectively obvious—not to mention sane—that for any woman to acknowledge or even hint at her 'womanness' in relationship to some Other gender, would invite all sorts of trouble." She added that it was "obvious in my personal life and to those who know me—that Man, men, love, maleness, whatever it must be called, mean so much to me as to be inextricable from my being itself." She also insisted that *Do with Me What You Will* had been a love story that "does honor men, but not any reviewers recognized this."

In Detroit and Windsor, Joyce had felt relatively isolated as a "woman writer." By contrast, her friendships in Princeton with Elaine Showalter, Sandra Gilbert, Alicia Ostriker, and other accomplished feminist authors had helped Joyce to view herself as part of a female literary community. Joyce felt that critical resistance to the violence in her realistic fiction and to the experimental nature of her Gothic series related, at least in part, to her gender. She had grown particularly weary of the complaints about her violent materials; early that spring, she composed a brief, angry essay for *The New York Times Book Review* entitled "Why is Your Writing So Violent?" This question, she insisted, was insulting, ignorant, and "always sexist." She noted that "serious writers, as distinct from entertainers or propagandists, take for their natural subjects the complexity of the world, its evils as well as its goods." She recalled the ironic fact that in Eastern Europe, the previous summer, she had been asked this question in such cities as Warsaw and Berlin, scenes of epochal twentieth-century violence and political turmoil. Any worthwhile writer, she argued, "bears witness" to the brutal realities of the age.

Her reputation had suffered, she believed, from the unexamined assumption that the province of women's writing was domestic and "subjective" experience (as typified by the novels of Jane Austen and Virginia Woolf);

after all, male writers such as Hemingway and Norman Mailer were not criticized for their frequently violent materials. (Ironically, Joyce's friend John Updike had sometimes been criticized for the *lack* of violence in his fiction, suggesting that the gender bias could cut in both directions.) The reception many critics gave to a writer's work clearly depended on the assumption—so deeply imbedded in the communal psyche that even the recent gains of the women's movement had done little to dislodge it—that men should write about the larger world of war, politics, and the intellect, while women properly concerned themselves with home, family, and personal emotions; moreover, only male writers (Flaubert, Henry James, James Joyce, and Faulkner were the great modern prototypes) experimented boldly with fictional technique, while women followed along at a quieter, more "conventional" pace. Not surprisingly, the few canonical exceptions to the rule—Emily Dickinson, Virginia Woolf—had often been discussed in the context of their alleged "madness." Joyce noted sardonically that some interviewers, rather than criticizing the violence in her work, would offer instead a backhanded compliment they perceived as "the highest accolade": "You write like a man." Or else she was presumed, like Dickinson or Woolf, to be mad. In June of 1982, she was interviewed by a newspaper book editor who remarked casually that everyone he knew "believed that Joyce Carol Oates was insane."

As early as 1969, Joyce had remarked on her own "laughably Balzacian ambition to get the whole world into a book," and her current series of postmodernist Gothic novels represented her most serious attempt to achieve that goal. Although, in early 1982, she was eager to begin *Mysteries of Winterthurn*, this novel required a lengthy gestation reminiscent of *Angel of Light* and *Bellefleur*. She had begun doing research the previous December, but six agonizing months of note taking and false starts passed before she began the novel in earnest. In late March, she described her frustration: "Groping, crawling on hands and knees, I don't really know where I'm going, haven't a voice yet, a styleless novel is an impossibility."

For Joyce, however, a creative block never led to inactivity; she simply turned to other projects. She employed the six months between finishing *The Crosswicks Horror* and beginning *Mysteries of Winterthurn* by writing a series of powerful short stories, some of which ranked among her best. Between November 1981 and March 1982 she wrote "Funland," "The Witness," and "Last Days," all of which would be collected in her 1984 volume *Last Days*; the title story was a powerful reworking of her experience with the troubled graduate student Richard Wishnetsky, about whom she had written almost two decades earlier in "In the Region of Ice." During those same months, she produced several strong, still-uncollected stories—"Hull and the Motions of Grace," "The Granite Springs Elegies," "The Victim," "Magic,"

"An Old-Fashioned Love Story," "Growing Seasons and Killing Frosts," and "The Bat," and two others that would appear in the 1986 collection *Raven's Wing*, "Harrow Street at Linden" and "Nairobi." The latter story, first published in *The Paris Review*, would be selected by John Updike for his edition of *Best American Short Stories*.

One of the ongoing paradoxes of Joyce's career was that despite pouring her "life's blood" into her long and ambitious novels, most critics and readers—including the majority of her Windsor and Princeton friends—considered her short stories to be her finest work, far superior to her longer fiction. Although her reputation as a novelist had remained controversial, few critics disputed her standing as one of the preeminent masters of shorter fiction. In the two annual prize anthologies, *Best American Short Stories* and *Prize Stories: The O. Henry Awards*, Joyce's work had appeared more frequently than that of any author in the history of either series. William Abrahams, then editor of the O. Henry Awards and a longtime admirer of Joyce's work, had created a special category, giving her a "Special Award for Continuing Achievement" as early as 1972 (he would grant her this recognition again in 1986). Joyce's career had gotten under way, after all, with her prize-winning story in *Mademoiselle*, and she had always written stories, Abrahams emphasized, "not as a diversion or spin-off from the writing of novels, but as a central concern in her work—a fortunate recognition that the shorter form is peculiarly suited to her." Exploiting her instinctive sense of form, the short story demanded the technical control and keen attention to language, rhythm, and image through which she marshaled her effects and intensified the emotional and intellectual power of her prose. The genre also provided the ideal vehicle for her experimental impulses. "Radical experimentation," she once remarked, "which might be ill-advised in the novel, is well suited for the short story. I like the freedom and promise of the form."

By the early 1980s, Joyce had published more than three hundred stories. They had long been featured in national magazines such as *The Atlantic*, *Esquire*, *Playboy*, and *Cosmopolitan*, and even more plentifully in America's most prestigious literary quarterlies, such as *The Southern Review*, *Paris Review*, *Prairie Schooner*, and *Yale Review*. Her agents, Blanche Gregory and Gert Bregman, were accustomed to Joyce's steady stream of short manuscripts; she continued to send apologies for "over burdening" the agency. Except for experimental work, which went directly to literary journals, most of Joyce's stories made the rounds of the high-paying New York magazines, where they often commanded larger than normal payments due to Joyce's established reputation.

Of all the major magazines, only *The New Yorker* consistently rejected her work (and would continue to do so until 1994, when the magazine printed

"Zombie"). Since many of these rejected stories later won major awards and were anthologized in textbooks as classics of the genre, Joyce and her agents came to feel that the magazine was somehow biased against her. (With only one exception, its reviews of her books had been snidely negative; Joyce took consolation from the fact that William Faulkner's novels had also been panned in the magazine.) At one point, Blanche and Gert even considered submitting Joyce's work to *The New Yorker* under a pseudonym. Getting an Oates story into the magazine became a crusade for Blanche, who told a reporter that "if I don't sell her to *The New Yorker*, I'm gonna eat my hat." But Joyce herself expressed an aloof indifference to the situation, noting that some *New Yorker* fiction was "a little breezy" and "the verbal equivalent of a yawn."

By now, *The New Yorker*'s disdain for Joyce's passionate stories had become a distinctly eccentric, minority opinion. In 1982, Joyce's stature as a preeminent writer of short fiction was again reaffirmed in John Gardner's edition of *Best American Short Stories*. Having surveyed the more than two thousand short stories published in 1981, Gardner announced that "the heavyweight is Joyce Carol Oates"; he chose her novella-length "Theft" (one of the Marya stories) as representative of her success in the genre, but acknowledged that in 1981 alone she had published several other stories that were equally "as powerful, original, and moving." Joyce's 1980 collection, A *Sentimental Education*, had received similarly enthusiastic praise from *Newsweek*, *The New York Times Book Review*, and other publications.

Ironically, despite her continued success in the short story genre, and the uncanny power of concentration that enabled her to write eight or ten superb stories within a few months, Joyce now felt less engaged by short fiction than in the 1960s and 1970s, a period when, as Abrahams had perceived, the genre had been "a central concern in her work." Even in 1977, in her *Paris Review* interview, she had noted that her interest in writing stories had declined: "I don't quite know why. All my energies seem to be drawn into longer works." By December of 1981, this feeling had only been confirmed: "My temperamental problem is," she wrote, "a surprising resistance to the form of the short story. It seems that I only want to write prose that finds itself in the service of a higher or larger or more generous meaning."

To Joyce, the short stories (like the occasional essays and reviews) increasingly became a way of "siphoning off" the energy left over from a long novel. During the months in early 1982 when she was unable to begin *Mysteries of Winterthurn*, she noted that "my writing is *not* going well," though she had recently completed close to a dozen masterful short stories. Clearly, the novel had become the form by which she judged her success as a writer. In an essay called "Notes on Failure," also written at this time and published in the summer 1982 issue of *Hudson Review* (it was collected the following year in *The Profane Art: Essays and Reviews*), Joyce remarked on the ironic disparity between the writer's view of his own achievements (the typical writer "inhabits failure," she argued, "but the terms of his failure are generally secret") and his public reputation:

> One must be stoic, one must develop a sense of humor. And, after all, there is the example of William Faulkner, who considered himself a failed poet; Henry James returning to prose fiction after the conspicuous failure of his play-writing career; Ring Lardner writing his impeccable American prose because he despaired of writing sentimental popular songs; Hans Christian Andersen perfecting his fairy tales since he was clearly a failure in other genres—poetry, play writing, life. One has only to glance at *Chamber Music* [a volume of poetry] to see why James Joyce specialized in prose.

In a later, uncollected essay, "The World's Worst Critics," Joyce admitted that "the writer's effort to detach himself from his work is quixotic. . . . We are all in the position of King Lear, who, holding absolute authority over his kingdom 'but slenderly knew himself.' "

The critical consensus that Joyce's short stories were her finest achievement had developed early and had grown more firmly entrenched as time passed; but by now she had also established herself as a highly respected literary critic. Her earlier volumes of criticism, *The Edge of Impossibility* (1972) and *New Heaven, New Earth* (1974), had been published at the height of her early fame, a time when reviewers had begun expressing angry bewilderment at the sheer quantity of books by Oates; her criticism had been discussed, even by friendly commentators, primarily as it reflected the concerns of her fiction. But Joyce's critical essays now appeared in such prestigious academic journals as *Critical Inquiry* and *Modern Fiction Studies*, and her carefully written reviews, published regularly throughout the preceding decade in *The New Republic* and *The New York Times Book Review*, had established her reputation as an uncommonly well read, thoughtful, and fair-minded reviewer. Her 1981 volume of essays, *Contraries*, published by Oxford University Press, showed her characteristically broad range of interests, including essays on Shakespeare, Dostoyevsky, Conrad, Lawrence, Joyce, and Wilde; *The Profane Art: Essays and Reviews*, appearing two years later, contained fully developed assessments of such diverse writers as Yeats, Faulkner, Emily Brontë, Lewis Carroll, and John Updike, in addition to a generous sampling of review-essays on Jung, Simone Weil, Flannery O'Connor, and many others.

The newer critical volumes, while hardly receiving the attention given to

Joyce's books of fiction, did attract the respectful notices appropriate to her stature as an established woman of letters. One typical review praised *Contraries* as "an original, deeply personal rereading" of classic works that contained "the insights of a committed writer." But more important than good reviews was the respect that Joyce's impeccable critical writing brought from her peers. After reading *The Profane Art*, her friend John Updike wrote that "all of the authors you treat, including me, benefit from an exceptionally equaniminous temperament and orderly mentality rather different, it sometimes seems, from that which produces your fiction." Updike remarked that William Maxwell, his editor at *The New Yorker* for many years, "used to speak of 'small-minded' and 'large-minded' people, feeling that most of the affairs of the world were run by the former. You, in these silver-bound pages of *The Profane Art*, are very comfortably one of the latter."

While Joyce naturally felt gratified by the respect accorded to her short stories and her criticism, the controversy surrounding her work as a novelist only intensified after the publication of *Angel of Light* in 1981 and *A Bloodsmoor Romance* in 1982. Like some of her earlier novels, both works attracted a puzzling mix of extravagant praise and vituperative dismissal. Updike, surveying his friend's critical reputation a few years later, would remark that Joyce had suffered, throughout her career, "some of the harshest scoldings ever administered to a major talent." *Angel of Light* was praised on the front page of *The New York Times Book Review* as "a strong and fascinating novel" that invested the Atreus myth with new energy and a sense of mystery, suggesting "that this prolific and various novelist is staking out new fictional ground." But other major publications, such as *Time* and *Newsday*, savaged the book. Even Walter Clemons, who had written the flattering cover story on Joyce for *Newsweek* and several positive reviews of her work, called *Angel of Light* "a serious, ambitious failure" that showed the author "trapped inside her own head, conscientiously writing away but unable to impose her imagination on us," resulting in "an unfulfilled work."

Critical response to *A Bloodsmoor Romance* was even more sharply divided. Many reviewers enjoyed Joyce's witty parody of the romance genre, and both Anatole Broyard in the daily *New York Times* and Diane Johnson in the Sunday *Book Review* admired *Bloodsmoor*'s energy and experimental spirit. Johnson labeled *Bloodsmoor* "an antiromance that provides the satisfactions of a romance," and marveled at its author's versatility: "Oates is able to assume any stylistic guise and to write about anything." But Joyce's detractors insisted that the novel was overlong and pretentious. An anonymous reviewer in *The New Yorker* mimicked Joyce's narrator, calling *Bloodsmoor* an "arbitrary amalgam which, at *six hundred and thirteen* pages, is—tho' not out of the ordinary for our prolific *Authoress*—grievously o'erlong." In *Newsweek*,

Peter S. Prescott praised the ingenious plot but complained that "the reader can't care for the characters" and that the first-person viewpoint was seriously flawed, since the elderly narrator was "somehow privy to the characters' most intimate thoughts." The reviewer for *Time* ascribed the "futility and tedium of Oates' novel" to the author's overzealous research and her "empurpled" prose.

A *Bloodsmoor Romance* also occasioned what Joyce termed a "hatchet job." Months before James Wolcott's article, "Stop Me Before I Write Again: Six Hundred More Pages by Joyce Carol Oates," appeared in *Harper's* magazine, she had noted in her journal: "Word is out that *Harper's* has commissioned a 'hatchet job' on me. Odd in that *Harper's* published a long poem of mine some months ago ... in fact, two poems, in different issues. Lois S[medick] says I should be 'flattered' by the attention; but I believe I would rather be spared, all things considered." The opening sentence of Wolcott's article set the tone: "Under the doorframe Joyce Carol Oates's A *Bloodsmoor Romance* insidiously creeps, oil-black and oozesome." Wolcott, though far from an elegant prose stylist himself, accused Joyce of sloppy writing ("a lot of flimsy, careless doodle") and a lack of artistic control (an "inability to turn off the babble"). Finally, Wolcott argued, she seemed "too self-mesmerized to tune out the racket in her head."

In her journal entries and letters to friends, Joyce admitted that such attacks stung her; but she remained philosophical about the ephemeral highs and lows of her reputation. Several years later, in a touching letter to Gail Godwin, Joyce would commiserate with Gail's own anxieties over reviews, reminding Gail of the number of times "Oates" had been attacked in the press. But she remarked that in Princeton, in fact, "everyone is under stress; and battered, even humiliated, in public from time to time. After all, if you are 'up' one year you'll probably be 'down' the next. I've had to accommodate myself to the wild fluctuations in JCO's fortunes over the years but it does help to think of 'JCO' and 'GG' as separate entities—or, rather, no entities at all, only names on dust jackets. What have they to do with you and me— blissfully domestic these winter days with our wonderful husbands and our almost-wonderful cats?"

Now in her fourth year at Princeton, Joyce was enjoying her life in the university community more than ever. Gradually she had effected a healthy balance between the quiet seclusion of her writing days, when she typically worked nonstop from early in the morning until midafternoon, and the gregariousness of her social evenings. Joyce and Ray had become close to several other couples in the area: Elaine and English Showalter, both of whom taught in the English department; Robert Fagles of the Comparative

Literature department and his wife, Lynne; Dan Halpern, poet and editor of Ecco Press, and his wife, Jeannie, an attorney and fiction writer; Alicia Ostriker, poet and Rutgers professor, and her husband, Jerry, a professor of astrophysics at Princeton; Mike Keeley, who continued to direct the Creative Writing Program, and his wife, Mary; Princeton professors Ed Cone (music) and George Pitcher (philosophy); and a Princeton couple Joyce and Ray had met in 1980, Henry and Leigh Bienen. At Princeton, Henry Bienen (now president of Northwestern University) had served as chairman of the Political Science department, director of the Center for International Studies, and dean of the Woodrow Wilson School, while Leigh commuted to her job in Trenton as an attorney with the Department of Public Advocacy for the state of New Jersey. Joyce had quickly become close to both the Bienens, calling them "endlessly provocative, charming" and "a couple (the only?) with whom we can talk frankly about things that matter to us, books, life, etc., virtually no time wasted in vague pleasantries or conventional exchanges." Lively, quick-witted, and highly accomplished, the Bienens personified the busy, extremely sociable Princeton world to which Joyce now belonged.

Like Joyce, Henry Bienen recalled that he and Leigh "became friendly very, very quickly" with Joyce and Ray. Contrary to Joyce's public image as reserved and preoccupied with work, he observed that "she networks a lot" and that Joyce and Ray socialized frequently at cocktail and dinner parties: "Joyce has a network of probably ten to twelve friends whom she sees like that," he said. Dan Halpern agreed that "she is very close to a small group. She depends on those people a lot for support. They are her social life—her life outside of writing." This group had become "so important to her because it's really her only contact with the world where she is comfortable." Joyce always made a special effort to maintain her friendships. Ed Cone, pointing out that Joyce and Ray "pick their social events carefully," added that "she values her friends a lot. When she hasn't seen us for several weeks, she lets us know." Robert Fagles commented on the "casual call that you receive—about your health, a (sweet) review of your work you may have missed, an anecdote you ought to hear—these calls speak volumes." He added that many people misperceived Joyce as "a chilly, distant customer, incapable of entertaining close friendships." He insisted that "she has a positive gift for friendship, and her friendships are as voluminous, committed and heartfelt as her writings."

Having learned from her unhappy experience, years earlier, with the uncongenial social milieu of the Detroit suburbs Birmingham and Bloomfield Hills, Joyce was now extremely guarded with people she didn't know well. She chose her friends with great care and had become skilled at declining invitations and other overtures of friendship from people she found unappealing. She did not "suffer fools or bores gladly," Elaine Showalter noted. Henry

Bienen made the same observation and added: "She will say, 'Such-and-such is a fool,' or 'What an ass.' " Several friends noted that Joyce disliked being the center of attention at larger functions: "She likes to be quietly on the fringes," Lucinda Franks said. Others remarked that Joyce would often introduce a controversial note into a group conversation, then personally withdraw and quietly enjoy the ensuing fireworks. Such scenes would often find their way into her fiction.

Among her close friends, however, Joyce was a lively, gregarious presence. Bienen remarked that "she's very witty. Joyce likes to laugh." Now that she had become accustomed to Princeton and made friends, her social personality had changed dramatically. Those who had known Joyce during her first couple of years, like Mike Keeley, remembered that she had seemed ill-at-ease at first and had been "slow to break the ice." Her Puritan streak had shown through more than once: when guests at a party, having had a few drinks, became loud and boisterous, or began telling "raunchy" stories, Joyce "would sometimes become visibly uncomfortable." (Gene McNamara recalled Joyce's frequently saying "Ray, honey, I think we should go now" during social occasions at Windsor whenever she became bored or uncomfortable.) At first, Keeley said, Joyce and Ray had seemed "fairly unsophisticated compared to Princeton people who gave great weight to the style of dinner parties, which at this time was not among Joyce's stronger talents or interests." Henry Bienen, like Maxine Kumin and other guests during Joyce's early years in Princeton, recalled that "Joyce would say, 'I don't want to spend a lot of money for food,' " refusing to hire caterers or to eat in expensive restaurants. But after a few years, Bienen said, Joyce and Ray "would think nothing of having twenty-five or thirty people for dinner, and having it catered." Keeley agreed that Joyce later became "socially much more comfortable" and frequently gave parties—to the extent that, as he and others observed, Joyce and Ray's home became a social and cultural center in Princeton. But Joyce felt most comfortable in situations and settings she could control. "In a group where she doesn't know people, she gets very stiff," Dan Halpern observed, and turns into "one very rigid human being." But "if she's comfortable she's warm, witty, and very funny."

Like Joyce and Ray's friends in Windsor, their Princeton circle observed that Joyce Oates and Ray Smith were a perfectly matched couple. Joyce clearly had the dominant personality and did more of the talking during social occasions. At the same time, Ray had become quite well liked. "I find Ray very smart and tremendously knowledgeable about fiction, and a very shrewd observer of the world around him," Henry Bienen said. Another close friend remarked that "Ray is as unusual, in his own way, as [Joyce] is. It must be a strange life for him. She's a star, and she remains a star even when there is a chance maybe for Ray to shine." Joyce was so accustomed to getting recognition that when Ray accomplished something—with the Ontario Review Press, for instance—Joyce found it difficult to give him credit. "She is such an achiever that she can't let anything go, like the kid in class who has to answer every question." One Princeton friend remembered that sometimes Ray, after staying quiet for a long while, "will start talking about something and Joyce will say, 'Can I *please* finish?' Whereas Ray had been pretty quiet until that moment." Joyce "doesn't like to be interrupted." Another friend recalled an occasion when Ray had quietly disagreed with Joyce over her version of an incident both Joyce and Ray had witnessed. Annoyed, Joyce drew back in her chair. "Are you contradicting me?" she asked, effectively concluding the discussion.

Yet Joyce's occasional displays of temper were the exception, not the rule. The longer she remained in Princeton, the more Joyce's friends recognized her value to the community both as a major writer and as a warm, unique personality. Even though Joyce was usually congenial, unassuming, and approachable, all her friends had developed a great admiration—at times verging on awe—of her extraordinary intellect. Jeannie Halpern remarked that Joyce could be "very girlish and playful," and yet she possessed "this incredible mind. She combines the two and the result is remarkable. She is very charming. She can charm you to death." Alicia Ostriker saw a similarly engaging, paradoxical quality in Joyce's personality: "Joyce's voice is soft, coy, girlishly breathless; her manners are gracious, polite, blandly social. She likes to express surprise and dismay at things that the novelist Joyce Carol Oates would hardly bat an eyelash at." Henry Bienen agreed: "I think Joyce is really an unconventional person who wears a very conventional exterior," he said. "But her mind is an unconventional mind." Elaine Showalter recalled that "in the midst of a quite ordinary conversation about news or television or the family," Joyce would insert a remark "whose philosophical penetration makes the rest of us feel like amoebas in the company of a more highly evolved life form. . . . She has the uncanny personal power of genius." Dan Halpern agreed that "she is really just a kind of odd genius. I mean, she is amazing in the way her mind works. . . . She is very unpredictable—talking to her, you don't know which direction she's going to go."

Virtually all Joyce's friends knew that her mental agility included a tendency to seize upon potential new material for her fiction. People in Joyce's circle understood that any Princeton scandal or intrigue would "eventually find its way into her writing," Mike Keeley said. "That's a 'given' with Joyce—that's part of the territory of knowing her." Joyce would sometimes press him to reveal personal matters even when he expressed hesitation: "she can be sort of insistent in that way." Ostriker remembered that after writing in a *Village Voice* article and in one of her poems about her experience of being raped, Joyce "asked me about it, and sure enough, transformed the story into one of her own ["The Knife"]. I wasn't a bit offended; the woman in the story was both like and unlike me, and Joyce's own take on terror and suspense was pure art."

Many of Joyce's friends observed that she loved to gossip. She "likes to whisper. She likes to gossip," Alicia Ostriker said, and Elaine Showalter noted Joyce's love of "gossipy lunches and long phone conversations with a wide circle of women friends." According to Lucinda Franks, Joyce had raised gossip to the level of an art form: "She is a wonderful gossip . . . I mean really juicy stuff, high-quality gossip." Dan Halpern observed that "she has a way of taking in information" and "she uses it in her books, sometimes more directly than you might want." Henry Bienen added, "Joyce likes to sop up lots of information. She's like a big sponge. Sometimes you have to be careful what you say around her."

Joyce's intensity of engagement with her friends' experiences reflected the inexhaustible energy she lavished on all aspects of her life. Although her writing and her socializing sometimes tended to push her teaching into the background, Joyce had to spend less time on her teaching than she had in Windsor, since she now taught only creative writing workshops rather than seminars that required extensive reading and research. Joyce had nevertheless developed a reputation as a strong and demanding professor. Her colleague Emory Elliott remembered that she once assigned a very low grade to a senior thesis being directed by another professor, who became "quite angry," Elliott recalled. As the director of undergraduate studies in English, Elliott "had to negotiate a settlement, and I wrote Joyce a long letter explaining our usual grading was less demanding than hers; she was very understanding about it." Joyce was pleased that the creative writing workshops were graded on a pass-fail basis. "She said that creative work either succeeds or fails, so that there is no such thing as a B− novel or poem."

One of Joyce's close friends, George Pitcher, had firsthand knowledge of her classroom persona. Having retired from his position in the philosophy department, Pitcher enrolled in four of Joyce's undergraduate fiction-writing workshops in the early 1980s. He remembered that when a student would read a story, "Joyce went around the room and everybody gave their comments. Then Joyce gave her comments at the end." She treated the students as if they, too, were professional writers: "there was no condescending." He recalled that Joyce's criticism could be blunt—"this iron fist under the glove was very much there"—but that her remarks were always on target. "She was receptive to a lot of different styles," Pitcher added, "and could also be very intimidating. But she called it the way she saw it. If she thought something was good, she said so, and she said why. If something was bad, she said so."

Another student from the early 1980s was Pinckney Benedict, an aspiring young writer from West Virginia whose strong talent Joyce perceived at once. Joyce and Ray would later publish Benedict's first, widely acclaimed volume of short stories, *Town Smokes*, with Ontario Review Press, thus launching a promising career. Benedict first signed up for Joyce's workshop in the spring of 1983 and quickly thrived under her tutelage; like Pitcher, he took a total of four workshops from Joyce. His only disappointment was that the class met so seldom—only one ninety-minute session per week. He remembered that at the beginning of each semester she would hand out a list of "ground rules" for the class. One of the rules was to leave your ego at the door; the purpose of the workshop was to focus on the writing, not on the author. In the workshop, the goal was "to make the work into the best work it could be." Benedict felt that the most important lesson he learned from Joyce was to develop "a sort of dispassion in the editing phase." Revision had to be "cold and surgical," since the process was not "to salve your ego" but simply "to make a stronger story." He added that "she's a phenomenal editor, and she's very clear about what she is looking for and what her criteria are. She sits down in front of the class and runs through a story—sometimes on a very minute level—and explains what's good and what is not good. It's a little hard to take sometimes, because she can be extremely honest."

Some students in Joyce's classes, Benedict recalled, would become quite resentful of Joyce's high standards. One of her rules was that a student could not respond defensively while his or her story was being critiqued. One student protested: "I think it would be useful if we were allowed to respond to criticism," he told Joyce. They debated the issue briefly, and Joyce finally relented; the student began nervously defending his manuscript after each critical remark. But Joyce used the little controversy to make her point. Each time the student rebutted a suggestion for revision, Joyce would say sarcastically to the other student: "Well, I guess your criticism is worthless." The defensive student became increasingly uncomfortable and embarrassed. "It was an unnerving incident, but it really put an end to that whole debate," Benedict said.

Even though Benedict was a favored student, he too could be the object of a withering remark from Joyce. "One time," he remembered, "I had a story that I had written, which she had critiqued and hadn't particularly liked, and I rewrote it and turned it in a second time. We were all sitting around before class one day, and she was talking to somebody and she turned to me and said, 'Pinckney, do you know the expression "money down a rathole" '? I said I did, and she said, 'Good,' and turned away and left me to think about that.

I didn't ever pick that story up again." But if Joyce could be brutally honest, she was also sympathetic and encouraging; her "firm-but-gentle approach" was exactly what Benedict needed at that early stage in his development as a writer.

To Joyce, teaching remained an almost purely pleasurable part of her life, quite different from the anxiety-provoking process of writing fiction. She particularly valued the social aspect of teaching and the sense of community it provided; these were especially valuable to a writer, who struggled in solitude with creative work. "My students at Princeton are very lively, inventive, and imaginative," she said. "Teaching is the antithesis of writing, which is very solitary, a very slow process . . . the teaching is rather quicksilver, and alive, and social, with this admixture of different natures brought to bear around a seminar table, and you don't know what's going to happen from minute to minute."

The only negative aspect of her teaching life at Princeton was the insecurity of her position on the faculty. Although her initial one-year "visiting" appointment had been extended to a five-year contract, by 1982 the contract had almost expired. In March of that year, she wrote in her journal: "I should like a permanent position; a full-time position; a real department. Here, we are made to feel, or allowed to feel, peripheral." Mike Keeley acknowledged that the English department maintained a "snobbish" attitude toward the creative writing faculty and, in general, declined to grant them tenure. Joyce was still ineligible for tenure because her position was considered "part-time." She was given a second five-year contract, but she began seriously to consider the offers of tenured positions she frequently received from other universities. As much as she loved Princeton, her conservative nature and an awareness of her own stature as a writer contributed to her longing for the security and prestige of a permanent appointment. At times, she wrote, she and Ray wondered if she might "quit teaching on a formal basis, and journey out to give readings and lectures a few times a semester"; yet she felt " 'most myself' (whatever that phantasm is)" within the context of academic life. Only when Joyce appeared on the verge of accepting another offer would the Princeton University administration finally confront the issue of granting tenure to Joyce.

Some of her friends considered the treatment she received unconscionable. Alicia Ostriker remarked: "The fact that Princeton University for many years kept Joyce in an untenured status was outrageous. . . . She was more qualified to teach literature than 99% of the English professors in this country." In the spring of 1984, Joyce was again feeling restless, and wondered if she should have accepted an appointment Stanford University had offered the previous year. "Who knows!" she exclaimed. "I love Princeton, and yet. . . ." She had "a sense (erroneous, no doubt) that I 'know' Princeton and might now move on. But I couldn't bear another move. (Though Ray says *he* could.)" Finally she ascribed her restlessness to "spring fever." But her status on the Princeton faculty would remain an unresolved issue—and to Joyce, an unnerving one—for several more years.

Although Joyce felt uncertain about the future direction of her academic career, she had kept working on her series of Gothic novels with her usual energy and confidence. The mixed reviews and disappointing sales of A *Bloodsmoor Romance* had little effect on her progress: she had almost completed the fourth volume in the quintet, *Mysteries of Winterthurn,* by the time the second appeared. She had finally begun *Winterthurn,* after its long, agonizing gestation, in May of 1982, noting that "I *seem* to have the voice I want." While groping toward this voice, she'd also had difficulty in devising an appropriate structure. Originally she had hoped to include five different mysteries to be solved by her detective-hero Xavier Kilgarvan, but now recognized that three was "a more practical number." The newly conceived structure had the comforting advantage of familiarity, since several of her early novels also had been divided into three parts.

Just as she had done with *Crosswicks* the previous year, she worked hard at *Winterthurn* throughout the summer, making regular notes of her progress: by early June, she had written 133 pages; by early August, 345 pages; a month later, 500 pages. By November, she was working on revisions, and at the end of that month she took an unusual step: she asked Ray to read the 716-page novel in manuscript. For years Joyce had discouraged Ray from reading her work, but the intricate plot of *Winterthurn,* and the particular demands of the detective-mystery genre with its many clues, red herrings, and other devices, caused her some concern. "What particularly grates," she had complained, "is the relentless 'forward movement' of the plot . . . all plots are relatively arbitrary, even silly, but mystery plots are especially so, like creaking roller coasters that take off every five minutes." Happily, Ray's response was encouraging: "his intelligent comments and (evidently unfeigned) enthusiasm have been wonderfully gratifying," she noted. "To sit at dinner, at lunch, with so attentive a reader! . . . it's remarkable, really; and extremely helpful."

Joyce's new Dutton editor, Karen Braziller (who had been assigned to Joyce after Henry Robbins's death), also responded positively to *Mysteries of Winterthurn,* and ultimately she and Joyce would decide that it should displace *The Crosswicks Horror* as Joyce's next published novel. Karen had felt that the 930-page *Crosswicks* manuscript was far too long and needed major revisions. The pace was "too leisurely," she told Joyce, and the story "much too digressive"; she doubted that many readers would stay interested in a novel that included lengthy footnotes, detailed passages of exposition and description, and a long-winded historian-narrator whose sentences often wound along for more than half a page. Although Joyce undertook an extensive revision of *Crosswicks* and made significant cuts, the commercial failure of *Mysteries of Winterthurn* in 1984 would relegate its predecessor to the already sizable pile of Joyce's unpublished novels.

As usual, Joyce "relaxed" after work on a long novel by producing a new group of short stories. By January, she was working on "a 'novella-for-the-drawer' " called *Love and Friendship*. Published in 1985 under the title *Solstice*, this short novel dramatized an intense, symbiotic friendship between two women: a young teacher, Monica, who has moved to rural Pennsylvania after a painful love affair, and a temperamental painter, Sheila Trask. The introverted Monica and the brash Sheila represented Joyce's ongoing fascination with the doppelgänger, and she recognized at once that the two characters expressed important features of her own personality.

This intimate, highly charged subject matter had made the novella a "disturbing piece of fiction" to write; even for Joyce, the process of composition was extraordinarily intense. In Sheila, Joyce had created her most intimate and elaborate portrayal of her own creative life. The book was "starkly 'confessional,' " she wrote to Gail Godwin, "and makes explicit my intermittent (not constant) worry that the writing side of me is slowly destroying the other side of me, that they are locked in a struggle neither can control." A few weeks later, Joyce noted in her journal that there were "three 'JCO's'—at least": the "one who submerges herself to the point of exhaustion in certain fictional adventures, the one who ventures forth into society and gives parties, the one who is married to Raymond and lives a near-blissful life. Easing from one frame to the other to the other isn't difficult but altogether necessary, like breathing out and breathing in."

Another, less rewarding part of her life, perhaps representing a "fourth JCO," was the public persona that occasionally emerged from the comfortable cocoon of Princeton to give readings and lectures around the country. Before such an event, Joyce would joke to friends that she was leaving town for a day or two in order to "impersonate JCO." Often she enjoyed her visits to other campuses, but there were also times when the public aspect of her career seemed discouraging, even meaningless. In the spring of 1983, for instance, she visited Stockton College in nearby Pomona, New Jersey, and the experience was less than edifying. In her journal, she recorded the event with her usual economy and humor:

> A silly excursion the other day: to Pomona, NJ, one of the forget-
> table places of the world, Stockton College, built it seems in a kind

of marsh. Though I'd been drawn into accepting a reading engagement because early letters had been so friendly (do I mean flattering?—fawning?) it turned out, evidently, that no one in the college was very interested in my appearance . . . at least no one appeared. The audience was perhaps 80 people? 100?—and very nice, appreciative, they clapped a good deal, they were friendly, but the sense of utter futility struck me before, during, after the reading: what am I doing here? No classes to visit; no dinner; no reception after the reading; no one who knew me—I mean professionally; a woman who stumbled through an introduction—clearly unfamiliar with my work, from the French Dept., "they wanted a woman to introduce you," she said, half-embarrassed. "I was notified only three days ago. . . ." Long, long, rather dangerous drive in the dark, pelting rain; we left at 3 PM, arrived there around 6, located a fairly bad restaurant in the rain, got to the college at 8, I read at 8:15, it was all over by 9:20, we drove out at 9:25, $2000 check in my handbag, but I surely hadn't gone there for the money. . . . A comic experience; or was it depressing; or simply forgettable.

The experience was perhaps emblematic, for although 1983 was a typically productive year for Joyce, it was unusually fragmented. Unlike the preceding years, she worked on countless brief projects and never became immersed in a long novel: she would not begin the fifth installment of her Gothic quintet, *My Heart Laid Bare*, until December. Much of her work that year involved revision. In March, she revised *Mysteries of Winterthurn*, noting that she felt "homesick" for the novel: "Dear God, how I need another great long debilitating outlandish project . . . ! I love to be fatigued, malnourished, distracted, anxious & antic & high-strung, my mind racing feverishly." She added that she even missed the insomnia that inevitably came with a long, obsessive project. In May, she took up the short stories she had written about Marya Knauer and began transposing them into a novel. But later that month, she turned back to the *Crosswicks* manuscript for further revisions before returning to the Marya stories during the summer. While revising them, she recognized that Marya's story, like *Love and Friendship*, was highly autobiographical, a way of "inventing & re-inventing a form of myself. Certain losses, on-going puzzles, powerful heartrending images. . . . It's the pastness of the past I am enamoured of." She added that "Marya both is and patently is not 'Joyce.'"

In August, Joyce turned to yet another revision project. She began rewriting the stories based on her 1980 trip to Eastern Europe; they would be published the following year in her collection *Last Days*. She had maintained her interest in the concept of linked short stories that had governed her earlier collections *Crossing the Border* and *All the Good People I've Left Behind*. During the fall Joyce worked on another such collection, focused on the experiences of a character named Cecilia Heath; this group included a novella, written in October and never published, called *Gentle Passions*, as well as several shorter stories such as "The Orphan" and "Master Race" (the latter would be included in *Prize Stories 1987: The O. Henry Awards*). While working on these shorter projects, she had gradually amassed her usual pile of notes for the next long novel, *My Heart Laid Bare*, which would be focused on a family of confidence men named Licht. "My heart yearns to write the Licht novel," she noted in mid-October, as she worked on the Cecilia Heath stories, "but, it seems, I am not ready to begin. Many pages of notes assembled; a time-scheme; an outline of the novel; scribbled scenes, etc.—but I can't begin."

Joyce had also been frustrated that year by health problems: she suffered major attacks of tachycardia in early May and again in August. On both occasions, Ray rushed her to the hospital emergency room. During the first, "extremely violent" attack, which lasted about an hour, her "body was so wracked with an energy gone berserk, my breath so short, I myself couldn't feel much dread or simple nervousness." Her heart had been beating at the extraordinary rate of 150 beats per minute, "which must be a record for me." These attacks meant that she lived in "a sort of ubiquitous cloud of mortality" that gave an added urgency to all aspects of her life.

During the fall, there were further attacks of tachycardia, prompting visits to a cardiologist. Joyce remarked that the medication he prescribed was almost as bad as the illness, causing "side effects that last for about 24 hours: exhaustion, headache, depression, etc." One day, she reported that she'd taught a workshop on one of her bad days and "never thought I'd get through it—such a sense of unreality, pointlessness, real despair." But Joyce kept going, just as she'd done in Windsor during a bad case of the flu: she had taught the workshop "just to see if I could do it—and evidently no one noticed. Teaching is a healthsome profession." During these same months, Joyce sought medical advice for the extreme stress her workload and ill health were causing.

Near the end of the year, and seemingly motivated by thoughts of her own mortality, Joyce made a long entry in her journal that summed up her view of her personality, which often seemed dominated by the nagging riddle of her own "invisibility":

> Essentially I feel myself still in the making—an unformed "personality"—with a center but with no circumference. I haven't the tough elastic ego that allows me to delude myself into thinking that

my problems are significant or even exclusively mine; yet I can't rid
myself of the problems . . . however difficult they are to define.
(Sometimes I feel non-existent; vaguely apologetic; abashed; bewildered and embarrassed that anyone should be nice to me, kindly . . .
At other times I seem to think, For better or worse I *am* the person
I am, and with whom would I change places?) . . . I feel lonely; but
we see people often; have even been reluctantly turning down
invitations. . . .

Joyce often fell into this unmoored, vaguely bewildered state of mind
when she lacked the anchor of a long novel; she had just endured a particularly frenetic, distracted year. But by mid-December, a new energy and sense
of excitement arrived as she approached her next project. "How the rest of
my life is dwarfed set beside the novel," she wrote. "Planning & writing the
Prologue of *"My Heart Laid Bare"* at last. My novel of confidence, impostors,
tricksters." Joyce read classics of the "trickster" genre such as Melville's *The
Confidence Man* and Mann's *The Confessions of Felix Krull*, and her mood
soared as she began her own novel: "Such excitement, the last several days,
hour upon hour, [. . .] my fingers actually going cold & numb w/the exhilara-
tion/dread of—getting things right. The hope of *getting things right*." Her
changed mood prompted her agreement with Emerson that "a person is what
he dreams all day long. In which case the novelist *is* his/her novel." The last
words of her journal for 1983 succinctly state the case: "My heart laid bare.
Oh yes."

Since beginning her Gothic project, Joyce had begun to worry that her literary reputation was declining. Her early books had been nominated almost
every year for the National Book Award and other prizes, but she had recently
observed to Bob Phillips that none of her novels had been up for a major
award since 1971. "And when I think of the books I've published, which seem
to me, to me at least, better than my earlier books—well, it *is* discouraging,
I must admit . . . *do* you think I am unreasonable to feel, well, something of
a failure, or a failure-in-process?" With each new novel, she ran the risk of a
possible critical assault, like the sarcastic "review" of A *Bloodsmoor Romance*
that had appeared in *Harper's*. Yet she had advised Gail Godwin to ignore the
critics, and in her journal she offered similar advice to herself: "I have been
discouraged off and on over the years, I should remember. Going back, very
likely, to the beginning . . . to *before* the beginning! . . . so this present state
isn't all that new."

Early in 1984, she had reason to feel discouraged: Harvey Shapiro, editor
of *The New York Times Book Review*, had telephoned to warn her that the

magazine's review of *Mysteries of Winterthurn* would be negative. Other major reviews of *Mysteries of Winterthurn* were also disappointing. *Newsweek* called the novel "an ornate period piece replete with dungeon, swooning virgins, smelling salts and—most annoying—an overabundance of arch, archaic prose." *The New Yorker* was typically dismissive: "Miss Oates' plots are an odd admixture," the anonymous reviewer sniffed. "If she has a serious purpose— one beyond mimicry—it is sunk in the quicksand of her prose." In the daily *New York Times*, Michiko Kakutani complained of "heavy, archaic prose" in which the "element of suspense is missing." Yet some reviewers praised the novel, insisting that the detective-mystery genre had inspired a more disciplined approach than had been evident in *Bellefleur* and *A Bloodsmoor Romance*. Alan Ryan in the *Washington Post Book World* argued that *Winterthurn* was the best of the three Gothic novels, "allowing full play to the author's style and storytelling skill."

As usual, Joyce tried to focus on the positive notices and, most important, on her progress with the final novel in her quintet. Like the previous four, *"My Heart Laid Bare"* was completed in about six months: she had begun in December 1983 and announced her completion of the manuscript in a journal entry for June 30, 1984. Having now concluded her massive project, she reflected upon the time she had spent and the larger design of the quintet:

> The years, the years. I feel that I've been drained into them. Beginning w/ *Bellefleur*, a jumble of notes, a sensation, a 'walled garden.' And *"My Heart Laid Bare"* the return of the hero to the marsh; to his origins. I can see now that it is a birth and a death; the "birth" of Germaine (& the walled garden, the dreamy image) and the "death" of Abraham Licht. So I suppose it constitutes a dream-unity, apart from the various conscious & highly schematized thematic designs. . . .
>
> I loved writing the novels, it's true. Especially the re-writing. Best of all I love *Winterthurn*; it remains my favorite.

Looking back, she felt amazement at the ambition of her enterprise: "I surprised myself these past few years w/my stubbornness. And with sheer stamina. (Which my mirror-self belies. My photographed self. Oh why do I look so frail and tremulous when I feel so strong????)"

Joyce retained some hope that *The Crosswicks Horror* and *"My Heart Laid Bare"* might be published and received with sympathy, but since *Mysteries of Winterthurn* had succeeded with neither the critics nor the public, her editor at Dutton suggested that Joyce's brief novel *Love and Friendship* should be published next. Joyce preferred the idea of publishing the novel she had created from the Marya Knauer stories, a book she now called *Marya: A Life*, but Karen Braziller felt that the briefer *Love and Friendship* made "a more dramatic contrast" with the long novels. Finally Joyce agreed, returning to the manuscript and doing a final set of revisions. She also settled upon a new title, *Solstice*. As usual, she had found the revision process an intense one, and observed the degree to which her writing habits had changed over the years: "I wish I could retrieve my earlier younger self. I seem then to have found 'first drafts' less of a strain; it was revising that drained me, and counted as work. Now it's the absolute reverse. Doing revisions & rewriting is so intensely absorbing, so heady a pleasure there is almost a point at which one *has* to stop, for fear of simply turning the manuscript over and beginning again, to keep the process a process and postpone the day . . . when something new & difficult must be begun."

In February, Joyce had received the news that Karen Braziller would be leaving Dutton for a position with Persea Books. Joyce had been fond of Karen, but she was happy to learn that her new editor would be William Abrahams. As editor of *Prize Stories: The O. Henry Awards*, Abrahams had championed her work for many years, and coincidentally Joyce had recently decided to dedicate her 1984 collection of stories *Last Days* to him. He had been "so central, so crucial, in my career as a short story writer, I feel deeply grateful to him." A prominent Dutton editor with his own imprint, Abrahams (known to most people as "Billy") was an ideal editor for Joyce: seriously interested in literature and greatly enthusiastic about each new manuscript Joyce produced, he would become her loyal advocate and friend. Like so many of Joyce's readers, he particularly valued her short fiction, and ended one letter by remarking that "I can't imagine another author of stories so wide-ranging, of such intensity . . . well, I've been saying this for years and am more persuaded of it than ever!"

Though she and Billy Abrahams seldom met, since he worked from his home in California rather than in New York, the two spoke frequently on the telephone, and Joyce came to value and respect his advice. Almost two decades older than Joyce, he represented another in the series of experienced literary men she tended to admire. Having come to Dutton from Holt, Rinehart & Winston in 1984, Abrahams was known for his select group of authors; during his long career he had published Shirley Hazzard, John Knowles, Brian Moore, and other literary luminaries. According to Joyce, Abrahams was the sort of editor "every writer hopes for. He is bursting with enthusiasms and ideas. And he is a very careful, astute, and sympathetic reader. Billy combines the old-fashioned line editor's eye, looking at each sentence, with a larger view of literature, one might say a philosophical view." Billy Abrahams felt equally enthusiastic about Joyce; in fact, part of his moti-

vation for coming to Dutton was the chance to work with her. "The induce-
ment was irresistible," he said. "And as it's turned out, it is very challenging,
because Joyce writes so many books, *somebody* has to think about her very
carefully. Joyce herself is amazingly unconcerned with that sort of question.
It has apparently not crossed her mind that it might be a mistake to publish
three books in a three-month period. Her output is staggering. My main
problem is simply keeping up with her manuscripts as they appear."

But Abrahams doesn't hesitate to edit Joyce when he feels that changes
are needed. He has been especially influential in changing the titles of Joyce's
books when he felt her titles were inadequate. According to Joyce, Billy will
say: "Too modest, Joyce! This novel has more depth and scope and is more
important than that title." He inspired Joyce to find new titles for *The Green
Island* (which became *You Must Remember This*), *Song of Innocence* (*Because
It Is Bitter, and Because It Is My Heart*), and *Corky's Price* (*What I Lived
For*). He was also responsible for a major structural change to Joyce's 1996
novel, *We Were the Mulvaneys*. "His suggestions have been extremely valuable," Joyce remarked.

After completing *My Heart Laid Bare*, Joyce had little inclination to
consider another long project: instead she went in the opposite direction,
producing a series of very brief stories that she would come to call "miniature
narratives." They were "the size of a penny, a dime. Image-triggered narratives." Like the images that had resulted in *Bellefleur* and the other Gothic
novels, the visions that produced these short narratives seemed to spring directly from the unconscious. As she worked on the stories, she became aware
that her long immersion in the Gothic "wonderland" of her imagination had
intensified her sense of alienation from the tawdry reality of American life in
the 1980s.

In March of 1984 she confronted one of the darkest aspects of that reality
when she took a guided tour through a New Jersey prison facility. Although
the experience she had there was one of the most "humiliating" of her life
and she later admitted that a deliberate, long-term "amnesia" had blocked
out many of the details, she believed a professional acquaintance had invited
her to take the tour: "I've said yes to most invitations of a seemingly 'broad-
ening' and 'enriching' nature out of a dread of saying no to the crucial invitation that might make a difference in my life," Joyce wrote. Near the end of
the tour, which had been quite thorough, Joyce had felt that her impressions
of prison life were "disturbing, even depressing, but not annihilating, in no
way personal." That changed dramatically as she stood, along with several
other visitors (all male), observing a cell block in which about thirty male inmates were housed, free to walk about in a central "common room." Standing about ten feet above the common room, Joyce froze when she noticed

that two of the prisoners were watching her: "They were frowning at me, staring at me, as if they'd never seen anything quite like me before." Joyce made a tactical mistake—she smiled at them—and then a "ripple of excited interest passed among the inmates." Word quickly spread that a woman was present, and "like a match held to flammable material excited calls and cries spread through the cell block." Joyce, who had arrived as "a professional woman," now felt herself reduced to her "mere sexual identity": "A *woman: cunt*. What these eager men would do to me, if they could get hold of me: that was the promise of their eyes, their mouths." Joyce noted that "the episode could not have lasted more than a few minutes, and yet those few minutes were excruciating." Traumatized, Joyce quickly left the building, mentally blocking out the incident. She wrote a brief story, "Maximum Security" (collected in *The Assignation*), based on the prison visit, but she omitted her experience of sexual threat and humiliation from the story. Only in 1995, eleven years later, would she feel detached enough from the episode to write an essay, "After Amnesia," that described the terror she had felt during the prison visit. Clearly, the incident tapped into the reservoir of fear and anxiety remaining from her childhood sexual abuse, a trauma that inspired her career-long obsession with rape, molestation, incest, and other crimes of violence against girls and women.

A few months after this incident, on August 10, Joyce admitted that she'd been existing in "a time-machine, time-warp." Both her residence in affluent Princeton and her long immersion in nineteenth-century Gothicism had helped isolate her from the quotidian and sometimes violent realities of contemporary America. In this respect, Princeton had not stimulated her literary imagination as Detroit had done in the 1960s. One day in 1984, visiting the grocery store and examining the magazine rack, she'd confronted "things entirely alien to me. Not even *Time* or *Newsweek*. Magazines about soap operas, 'daytime t.v.,' rock stars, movie stars, homemaking, guns, action comics. My sense of total disengagement; disinterest. Have I lived too long? I wondered." She understood that she'd become similarly alienated from contemporary politics: "The Republicans, Reagan, etc. My sense of utter estrangement, as if I were from another country. An anthropologist perhaps. The God-toting name-dropping bullies. The party of privilege & 'Morality'— yes they're simply bullies. The most fearful thing is that they seem to believe in themselves."

Two months later, in October of 1984, Joyce would feel the first stirrings of a desire to apply her "anthropologist's" perspective to another, similarly conservative era in American politics: the 1950s. She first mentioned her thoughts about the novel that would become *You Must Remember This* on October 3: "Stray dream-images: a bed in which I can't sleep; or a character, unknown to me yet, can't sleep. Vague glimmering notions of Felix-the-cat. One instinct draws me to realism; the other, to something very different. I don't have a voice. Not the vaguest idea of a voice." The image of "Felix-the-cat" would lead to the major male character of *You Must Remember This*, the former boxer Felix Stevick; it would also lead Joyce to intensive research into the sport of boxing, which she saw as emblematic of the American code of masculinity, and ultimately to her nonfiction book *On Boxing*.

The novel took shape slowly in her imagination throughout the fall. Its working title was *The Green Island*: she'd decided that it wouldn't be "a political novel, and I want to resist splicing in all sorts of silly Fifties material." Rather, the book would be "an elegy of sorts, for that period in history/my life. Nostalgia is sentimental but I don't have any sentimental feelings about this. I feel clinical, detached, a little impatient." She had begun thinking of the novel's female protagonist, the teenaged Enid Stevick, whose intensely erotic affair with her Uncle Felix would represent a flagrant violation of sexual taboo during a notably conservative historical period. Five days later, she began the novel, noting that "the logistics of *The Green Island* are laid out. The skeleton, the master plan."

Joyce's exhaustion after completing her Gothic quintet had vanished quickly enough: her new novel represented an excited return to the intense realism of the early novels—*A Garden of Earthly Delights*, *them*, and *Wonderland*—that had made her name. Joyce's creative excitement as she began this new phase of her writing life is patent in a journal notation for November 6, 1984. Starting work on Enid and Felix's story, she wrote, was "like dousing the surface of the desk w/kerosene & lighting a match: flaring & blazing up: sheer delight."

14

Woman of Letters
1985–90

They say of course that it is the body that betrays; the self, the soul, remains inviolate; thus you are twenty years old so abruptly, so rudely, in a fifty-year-old body. And your journey has only now begun.
—American Appetites (1989)

Joyce's excited return to the realistic mode represented a major artistic turning point, one that is reflected in most of her fiction of the late 1980s and beyond. But the transition encompassed more than a simple reversion to her favored mode of psychological realism. Her Detroit fiction of the late 1960s and 1970s had focused on the social ills of contemporary America in the city Joyce considered a microcosm of the nation as a whole, and her Gothic quintet of the early 1980s had experimented with the aesthetic modes and American myths of the nineteenth century. In sharp contrast to these phases of her career, her work now became more directly autobiographical, returning again and again to the upstate New York world of her childhood.

This impulse would persist into the late 1990s. With few exceptions, her subsequent novels would be set in mythologized versions of the countryside she had known as a child and of the cities—especially Lockport and Buffalo—that had dominated her adolescent experience. *Marya: A Life* (1986), *You Must Remember This* (1987), *Because It Is Bitter, and Because It Is My Heart* (1990), *Foxfire: Confessions of a Girl Gang* (1993), and *Man Crazy* (1997) all feature female protagonists whose temperaments and ways of responding to a bewildering, often hostile environment mirror Joyce's own. Marya Knauer, Enid Stevick, Iris Courtney, Maddy Wirtz, and Ingrid Boone are highly intelligent, articulate girls who survive and bear witness to painful and even brutal early experiences. Like Joyce, they often find salvation in literary or academic achievement, seeing language as the means of ordering and, to some extent, transcending the past. Marya becomes a scholar, Iris marries into an academic family, Maddy records the achievements of the Foxfire gang, and only after Ingrid attends college does she cope with her horrific victimization and achieve a significant distance, both chronological and intellectual, from her nightmarish early life.

Despite the feminist themes in such novels, Joyce characteristically has not confined herself to depictions of female experience, placing male protagonists at the center of two major novels of the 1990s. Recalling Jules in *them* (1969), Jesse in *Wonderland* (1971), and Jack in *Do with Me What You Will* (1973), their names begin with the letter *J*, signaling their status as soul mates in Joyce's imagination. Years earlier, in the wake of completing *Wonderland*, she had suggested she might never again attempt to absorb herself into the soul of a man and attempt to "co-exist with him." Yet in *What I Lived For*, Jerome "Corky" Corcoran represents a deliberate attempt to identify and "co-exist" with a man as unlike herself as she could imagine. (A similar, less ambitious effort would result in the sexually tormented Jared in Joyce's 1996 novella, *First Love*; Joyce playfully included yet another permutation of her own name in this novella by calling her female protagonist "Josie Carolyn.") Yet even in Corky's portrait Joyce encoded many autobiographical details and throughout the novel strove to memorialize her own historical time and setting in exhaustive detail, tracing Corky's experiences in an upstate New York city between the 1950s and the 1990s. In *We Were the Mulvaneys* (1996), Judd Mulvaney is a more recognizably autobiographical character, a family historian who recalls the experiences of an Eden County farm family over more than two decades. Like the five novels featuring female protagonists, *What I Lived For* and *We Were the Mulvaneys* embody the familiar alternation of Joyce's imagination between the rural and urban features of her childhood world, each of which summoned up different but equally powerful forms of nostalgia. Taken as a whole, these seven novels suggest Joyce's obsessive interest in taking the Jamesian "backward glance," not only out of an impulse to honor and preserve the past but also, on a more personal level, to continue the effort of psychological healing undertaken by her narrators. Near the conclusion of *Man Crazy*, Ingrid Boone expresses her wish to have "every drop of poison squeezed from my blood," a line that recalls almost verbatim Joyce's journal entry about her inimical childhood environment and her attempt, "over the years, to draw out the poison drop by drop."

By 1985, Joyce's return to the realistic mode of her earlier writing was already under way: *Solstice* appeared early in the year, *Marya: A Life* was being readied for 1986 publication, and she was progressing steadily with her work on *You Must Remember This*. All three novels had a strong autobiographical basis: like *Solstice*, which examined the symbiotic and potentially destructive relationship between Joyce Carol Oates the artist and "Joyce Smith" the conventional, bourgeois woman, *Marya* and *You Must Remember This* pursued her familiar theme of the divided self, even as they evoked in meticulous detail the terrain of upstate New York. As an adult, Marya Knauer attempts to reconcile her backwoods origins with her mature identity as a successful writer and member of the intellectual elite, while Enid Stevick is torn between her identity as a "nice Catholic girl" of the 1950s and a wild, rebellious persona she calls "Angel-face," who ultimately becomes involved in an incestuous affair.

Joyce's autobiographical characters in these novels share an intermittent self-loathing that prompts suicidal impulses. In each case, the fictional character reflects Joyce's own personal struggles. Marya expresses a hatred of her own body that recalls Joyce's bouts with anorexia, the darker aspect of her yearning for "invisibility," and *You Must Remember This* begins with Enid's suicide attempt. This pattern spans Joyce's entire career; her obsessive concern with female identity has changed remarkably little during three decades of writing. *With Shuddering Fall* (1964), her first published novel, had ended with the mental breakdown of Karen Herz, another young Catholic girl masochistically obsessed with a hot-tempered man. Thirty-three years later, in *Man Crazy*, Ingrid's experiences are similar, though more extreme: after becoming involved with a murderous cult leader reminiscent of Charles Manson and enduring extremes of physical and psychological torture, she begins the process of recovery by producing her ironically titled memoir and making plans to marry her therapist. Similarly, in the novella *First Love*, the tormented Jared shows his cousin Josie some pornographic magazines featuring "hideous photographs of bound, tortured, naked female children." Interviewed shortly after *First Love* was published, Joyce remarked: "I believe there's a strong element of masochism in most women. Josie is a young woman involved in, and fascinated by, her own degradation." As always, Joyce remained anything but a doctrinaire feminist, insisting that both men and women, impelled by natural and little-understood impulses, often participate in their own victimization.

In her journal, and in interviews and letters, Joyce has often remarked on the deeply personal nature of works that might seem, to a casual eye, remote from her own experience. Many of her works were autobiographical, she insisted, even bizarre confabulations like *Bellefleur*, but the personal material was transcribed through images, in a kind of "code." Yet Joyce's novels since 1985 show her incorporating personal material with a new and sometimes unsparing urgency. In the early novel *them*, the split self-portrait of Jules and Maureen (Jules as Joyce's aggressive, adventurous alter ego, Maureen as her portrait of female victimization and its consequences) had been far less obvious than in the analogous brother-sister figures of Judd and Marianne in *We Were the Mulvaneys*, who serve similar functions: Judd as the professional writer and Marianne as Joyce's emotional self-portrait. Jules and Maureen had seemed figures in a social history, primarily, while Judd and Marianne are clear self-representations in what Joyce called "My valentine to that part of the world."

In the 1980s and 1990s, Joyce's secure position as a "woman of letters" combined with the increased self-knowledge of middle age has enabled this more intensely confessional impulse in her work. Intellectual and emotional distance from her own early traumas have given her the freedom to dramatize them more openly in her fiction and even to discuss them in interviews (with a frankness that would have been unthinkable to Joyce in her twenties or thirties). It also seems likely that Joyce's increasingly fragmented life during the 1980s and 1990s—stemming from her heightened visibility as a public figure and so different from her years of relative isolation in Windsor—has intensified her focus upon the distant past as a kind of emotional anchor, the essential core of her personal identity. In *Wonderland*, the brief portrait of Joyce as a small child with her parents had been a mere cameo, a rare autobiographical indulgence; but *We Were the Mulvaneys* and other novels of the past decade are filled with countless and remarkably specific details from Joyce's personal experience. (The same is true of her most recent volumes of poetry, *The Time Traveler* [1989] and *Tenderness* [1996], volumes that, in sharp contrast to the early, more impersonal work, contain elaborately detailed autobiographical and "confessional" poems.) The very phrasing of her titles—"you must remember this," "what I lived for," "we *were* the Mulvaneys"—suggests this backward-looking focus, as does the narrative technique in *Foxfire* and *Man Crazy*, both of which are deliberately constructed as "confessions." Whereas *them* and other early novels were "Balzacian," as Joyce herself pointed out, in their ambition as social chronicles, her most recent work is more "Joycean"— as in James Joyce—in its relentless focus upon language as a means of revisiting and memorializing the past.

As Joyce worked intensely on *You Must Remember This* during the winter and spring of 1985, she again complained of exhaustion, remarking to John Updike that "writing it so drains me of energy I'm left exhausted and dazed by 7 PM wondering how I can begin again in the morning." By early June she had completed the first draft; she worked with equal intensity at revisions and mailed the manuscript to Blanche Gregory by the end of the month. Yet her excavation of the 1950s was not quite completed: in order to write the scenes dealing with Felix Stevick's boxing career, Joyce had done extensive research into the sport. When an editor for *The New York Times Magazine* phoned to ask Joyce for an essay, she told him that she had become deeply involved in a study of boxing and doubted that his readers would care for an article on that subject by a woman. To her surprise, he said he would welcome such an essay. Far more surprising was the reaction from her friends, her literary peers, and the general public after "On Boxing" appeared on June 16.

Although few of Joyce's women friends were interested in the sport, she soon discovered the degree to which male writers identified with prize-fighters. Among those expressing admiration for Joyce's essay were her friend Russell Banks, who had joined Princeton's creative writing program in 1982; Richard Ford, who had also taught in the program; and Norman Mailer, who had written frequently about boxing. Joyce confessed surprise that so many male boxing aficionados (including professional sportswriters) should praise her essay, even if the praise was sometimes tainted with macho condescension. In September, introducing Joyce at a New York event sponsored by the writers' organization PEN, Norman Mailer proclaimed that Joyce's essay was "one of the most creative acts of feminism I've ever encountered." Even more amazing to Mailer, "On Boxing" was so good that "I said to myself, 'My God, I could have written this piece.' " When Joyce took the stage, she re-marked dryly that "there's nothing like that supreme accolade—to be told that you write like a man. And not just any man, but Norman Mailer."

Yet Joyce and Mailer were mutual admirers; although she had sometimes criticized his work in print, she had always acknowledged his extraordinary am-bition and talent. Joyce's boxing essay had genuinely intrigued Mailer—in the past, he had been known to dismiss the work of "women writers"—and for the next several years Mailer and his wife, Norris, invited Joyce and Ray to the large and boisterous parties they gave in their New York brownstone. In a letter to Eudora Welty, who had given a reading at the PEN event, Joyce wrote, "I'm so glad to be a friendly acquaintance of Norman's at this phase of his variegated career, aren't you? Now, rather than condemn women writers without having read them, he seems actually to have read some, even with enjoyment. Who could have predicted it?" But Joyce's and Mailer's interest in boxing had cre-ated a genuine bond between them: shortly after the PEN event, she wrote to him, "To speak of boxing is, for me, at least right now, to speak of something as infinitely provocative and rich and ambiguous and hopeless as life itself."

Joyce's interest in boxing had sprung from a number of sources: the Golden Gloves fights she'd attended as a young girl, with her father; the cultural sig-nificance of the sport during the 1950s, as Joyce came of age; her identification with the tough, working-class origins of most boxers; her innate fascination with drama, violence, and the power of the human will; and perhaps most important, her vision of the boxer as one who—like the serious, committed writer—gives his life's blood in artful opposition to all attempts to defeat him. Many writers were fascinated with boxing, she speculated, because of the sport's masochistic element: "contrary to stereotyped notions, boxing is primarily about being, and not giving, hurt. . . . To move through pain to triumph—or the semblance of triumph—is the writer's, as it is the boxer's, hope."

The seeming incongruity of Joyce's interest in boxing intensified public curiosity about her. For the next several years, whenever she made public appearances or gave interviews to promote her books, conversation would often drift away from Joyce's fiction and onto boxing (particularly if the interviewer was male). Critics had often said that Joyce's "frail" appearance seemed at odds with her violent fiction, and her expert knowledge of such a sport seemed even more surprising now that Joyce was a middle-aged Princeton professor who identified herself as a feminist. A few months after her essay appeared, a Doubleday editor suggested that she expand the piece into a book, and by October she was working with John Ranard, whose stark photographs of boxers and boxing matches would illustrate Joyce's 116-page monograph, *On Boxing*, published in 1987.

Joyce quickly became an acknowledged and much sought-after expert on the sport. In November of 1986, *Life* magazine flew Joyce and Ray to Las Vegas so that Joyce could cover the eagerly anticipated heavyweight match between Trevor Berbick and a then-rising twenty-year-old fighter named Mike Tyson. Joyce spent seven hours interviewing Tyson for her article and confessed surprise at "his really quite astounding knowledge of boxing history." Two months later, she visited Tyson's training camp and his home in Catskill, New York. In addition to becoming acquainted with Tyson, Joyce had developed a warm friendship with Jim Jacobs (Tyson's manager) and his wife, Loraine. In February of 1987, Joyce again flew to Las Vegas, this time as Jim Jacobs's guest, for another Tyson match, and again Joyce reported on the event (for *The Village Voice*). She had also participated in recent boxing-related interviews for *Sports Illustrated*, National Public Radio, HBO, and ABC's *Good Morning, America*.

For the remainder of the 1980s, Joyce's unexpected new career as a boxing expert at times threatened to overshadow her fame as a novelist. One morning, shortly after her first essay on the sport appeared, she received a telephone call from Dustin Hoffman: they talked for an hour, mostly about boxing, and Hoffman invited her to New York for a screening of his new film, *Death of a Salesman*, and a celebratory party at Lincoln Center. At the party, Joyce and Hoffman again discussed boxing, and the actor asked if she could collaborate on a film he wanted to make about Angelo Dundee, Muhammad Ali's former manager. (Joyce declined the offer.) Later Joyce became acquainted with another powerful Hollywood figure, the acclaimed director Martin Scorsese, who hoped to direct the film version of *You Must Remember This*. He asked Joyce to write the screenplay (Sean Penn and Ray Liotta were among the actors mentioned who might be cast as Felix), and this time she accepted. (Like most Hollywood properties "in development," the script was never filmed.) In the meantime, Joyce and her poet friend Dan Halpern, another boxing fan, had edited a collection of essays on boxing called *Reading the Fights*, which appeared in 1988. Joyce also attended boxing-related events, such as the annual Boxing Association Banquet in 1988 (to which she was invited by the sports department of the *New York Times*). In June of that year, her expertise in boxing had been acknowledged in an unexpected, somewhat bizarre way: a representative from New York Governor Mario Cuomo's office wrote to ask if she would be interested in serving as chairman of the New York State Athletic Commission, a job formerly held by Jose Torres. "Mischievous friends urged me to say 'yes,'" Joyce wrote to Russell Banks, "but common sense prevailed. Apart from being wholly unqualified, I don't even live in New York State and residency is required."

Yet Joyce's interest in the sport and, more important, her identification with certain boxers, remained intense. Though she seldom watched television otherwise, she would often join friends for pay-per-view coverage of important fights. In April of 1987, she was devastated by the middleweight championship match between Marvin Hagler and Sugar Ray Leonard. Confident that Hagler would win, she predicted his victory in *Sports Illustrated*, and in a letter to Russell Banks expressed her surprise that "so many quite responsible and knowledgeable people do think Leonard will win." To Joyce, Hagler was a proletarian hero whom she greatly admired, whereas Leonard was "just too sunny for me; too much a golden boy." Joyce watched the televised fight with Jim Jacobs, Kevin Rooney, and other boxing friends, and was shocked at the decision in Leonard's favor: "Hagler, our great champion, suddenly past tense. . . . When the decision was announced I had to get out of the room, couldn't make myself see the interviews. I had identified so strongly with Hagler."

In January of 1988, Joyce and Ray traveled to Atlantic City, again as guests of Jim Jacobs, for the heavyweight title match between Mike Tyson and Larry Holmes. In a letter to the fiction writer Mary Morris, Joyce described the evening as "another of those indescribably bizarre and anthropologically rich events—millionaire celebrities (like Jack Nicholson, [. . .] and Don Johnson and Barbra Streisand holding hands) in ring-side seats watching the extraordinary Mike Tyson 'defend' his title against an aged (38) and rather frightened-looking Larry Holmes." Another celebrity among the sixteen thousand spectators had been Muhammad Ali, whom Joyce considered the greatest heavyweight fighter in history. As she and Ray sat eating breakfast the next morning in the Trump Plaza hotel, she was amazed to see Ali, with two other men, seated at an adjacent table. There was a steady stream of autograph-seekers approaching Ali, so the idea occurred to Joyce: "Do I dare get his autograph?" she asked Ray, who responded, "Of course." She later recalled the incident, which took an unexpectedly poignant turn:

> I had never done anything like this in my life . . . but since Ali loves being approached, and no white woman had yet, that morning, come to his table, I summoned my courage and went over, and he signed a sheet of paper ("To Joyce, from Muhammad Ali"—I had to tell him my name, of course, and supply the date). I had intended to tell him, should he not, by now, know it, "You are the greatest heavyweight fighter in history and the most courageous man" but I got only half the sentence out—unaccountably, helplessly, I started crying; it was a sudden and wholly unexpected thing—as if the tears sprang from my eyes of their own volition. Up close, Ali's skin looked warm, rich, mahogany-dark, and his eyes weren't lustreless, and I'd seen a tape of him boxing only a few nights before, so somehow the two times conflated, and I suppose I was crying for myself primarily . . . which is what most tears are. Thus, my encounter with the great Muhammad Ali.

For all the high-toned, intellectual ruminations on boxing Joyce had committed to print, nothing speaks more eloquently of her profound identification with boxing than this tearful, near-wordless meeting with Ali.

Joyce's international fame now brought her into contact with many of the world's most celebrated people. Occasionally a major public figure would request a meeting with Joyce, out of admiration for her work. Such was the case with Jacqueline Kennedy Onassis, who had wanted to meet Joyce for several years and had extended a standing luncheon invitation to Joyce and Ray in the fall of 1987. Joyce had put off the meeting for several months—a trip to New York usually meant the loss of a day's writing—but finally she accepted. On February 4, 1988, Joyce and Ray drove into the city through pelting rain. Mrs. Onassis took them to the exclusive Manhattan restaurant Raphael's, on West Fifty-fourth Street, for what Joyce described to John Updike as "a cheery (though a bit humbling) luncheon." Joyce found Mrs. Onassis "very charming and very nice and clearly cultured but not at all 'literary.' " Despite her work as a Doubleday editor, she avoided talking about books. "When I asked who her writers were, a question all editors adore, I'd thought, she smiled and looked a bit vague and said, 'Oh—it's hard to remember names . . . their names escape me,' and we switched to talking about the new production of *The Cherry Orchard*." Mrs. Onassis also talked at length about horses, an interest dating back to her childhood. Joyce marveled at the former first lady's ability to ignore the stir she inevitably created in public, "the numerous stares sliding in

her direction and the excitedly attentive service of the waiters." On the whole,
Mrs. Onassis seemed "warm, enthusiastic, very accessible," even if Joyce was
somewhat surprised that she never mentioned Joyce's writing. "Thus, it all
seemed humbling; yet quite enjoyable," Joyce said. "We are led to take ourselves so very seriously, it's refreshing to be reminded how unseriously others
take us, which is a good thing."

Another unexpected invitation had also arrived in the fall of 1987: late one
night, Joyce received a call from the Soviet Embassy inviting her to a reception in honor of the Gorbachevs. During their visit to the United States, Gorbachev and his wife had expressed a particular interest in meeting some
prominent American intellectuals and artists. Characteristically, Joyce declined the invitation, saying she was too busy ("the introvert's habitual response," she later called it). But Ray, "appalled, talked me out of it, so I called
back the next morning to accept." (In the days before the reception, Joyce
and Ray were aware that their telephone was wiretapped, presumably for security reasons.) When Joyce arrived at the Soviet Embassy in Washington,
she gravitated toward others from the invited "cultural group": William Styron, Norman Mailer, Paul Newman, Yoko Ono, John Denver, and Sydney Pol-
lack. During Gorbachev's speech, Joyce was surprised—and somewhat
alarmed—to find herself seated at a table next to Henry Kissinger. In *Angel of
Light* (1981), Kissinger had been portrayed quite negatively, "but surely, I
thought, he had not read those paragraphs? Surely he had never read a word
I'd written." When she and Kissinger were introduced, "Kissinger said, unsmiling, 'Of course I know who you are' "; but after this awkward introduction, he "became for the duration my buddy, and I got along with him quite
well." The most surprising moment came when Mrs. Gorbachev warmly
squeezed Joyce's hands, "telling me she admired my writing, actually naming
book titles, and getting them right."

Joyce had been impressed by Gorbachev: she came away from the reception, she said, "with the visceral certitude that this is a person of surpassing
integrity; a man of the utmost sincerity; somewhat larger than life, perhaps.
And so brimming with energy! And a sense of his own historic worth!" In the
"elegantly Old World" setting of the Soviet Embassy, Gorbachev spoke to the
elite group of American intellectuals "with disarming candor of domestic Soviet problems, economic and moral; of the political necessities that brought
glasnost into being; of his many-times-reiterated hope for world disarma-
ment and peace." Joyce noted admiringly that Gorbachev spoke for half an
hour without pause, seldom glancing at his notes: "he is so practiced and
charming a speaker that those of us who are usually stupefied by speeches remained attentive, even rapt, throughout."

During 1986 and 1987, Joyce had become friendly with a prominent political figure in her own country: New Jersey Senator Bill Bradley, often named as a potential candidate for the Democratic presidential nomination. In March of 1986, Joyce had been surprised to receive an invitation from Bradley and his wife, Ernestine, to a brunch at their home. "Precisely why we were invited I don't know," Joyce wrote, but she accepted the invitation and found Bradley enormously intelligent and likable. In fact, she wondered if he might be "too intelligent and thoughtful" to be a successful presidential candidate. "He has the tolerance, even appetite, for ambiguity usually associated with literary types," she added. Several months later, Joyce and Ray reciprocated the Bradleys' invitation by giving a large luncheon party in honor of the senator and his wife. In the meantime, Joyce had read and greatly admired *Life on the Run*, Bradley's memoir dealing with his career as a professional basketball player.

Just as Joyce's literary fame offered her the opportunity to meet and exchange ideas with public figures, her residence in Princeton continued to provide an exciting and challenging intellectual atmosphere. Yet by 1986, her ninth academic year of teaching at the university, the issue of her permanent status as a faculty member remained unresolved. She had grown increasingly impatient with the situation and began seriously to consider the offers from other universities that often came her way. In January, she received a particularly tempting offer of a "Distinguished Professorship" from Queens College in New York. The job "would pay considerably more than Princeton gives me for the same general duties," Joyce told Bob Phillips. "It would also involve tenure. Except for the long, long commute I'd be seriously tempted to consider it; I do feel the need for a change." By early March, she was writing in her journal that the Queens position seemed like "an excellent idea." Joyce had let Russell Banks and her other colleagues in the writing program know that she was on the verge of resigning, a prospect that finally impelled the administration to act in Joyce's favor. In late April, Princeton offered her "a 'continuing appointment'—not tenure, legally speaking, but evidently identical," Joyce told Mike Keeley. University officials would also launch an effort to establish an "endowed chair" for Joyce in the near future.

Relieved, Joyce accepted Princeton's offer, and by the spring of 1987 a donor for the endowed chair had been secured: Roger S. Berlind, a former investment banker, had recently enjoyed enormous success as a stage and film producer (he had coproduced the Broadway musical *Cats*). On April 11, Joyce announced proudly to Bob Phillips that "I am the first 'Roger S. Berlind Distinguished Lecturer at Princeton.'" In the fall of that year, she received further good news: the university raised her rank to that of full professor. "My duties remain the same," she told Phillips, "but my salary has taken an alarming leap upward—don't ask me why, because I don't know, but they've decided to pay me a full-time salary for my two-thirds teaching."

Despite the matter-of-fact tone of this letter, Joyce was deeply moved by Princeton's unanticipated gesture. When she received the news from an administrative official, she had just returned from one of her writing workshops. She recorded the scene in her journal: " 'Thank you,' I said, 'I'm very moved . . .' feeling tears spring into my eyes." She returned home "with this unlikely gift, which baffles me still, though I *am* pleased; and I *am* grateful." She paused simply to savor "for today, for now, this UNMATCHABLE moment." Although happy with her raise of $25,000, she added that "money does not make much difference, except as a gesture (as I suppose they mean it to be, in this instance) of recognition and generosity." Joyce's annual income from her writing, after all, far exceeded her university salary. What mattered to Joyce, former denizen of a one-room schoolhouse and scholarship girl from Syracuse University, was the recognition and prestige that her new status as an Ivy League "Distinguished Professor" represented.

Joyce's Princeton friends and colleagues noted the delight she took in becoming the holder of an endowed chair. Russell Banks suggested that "it's comforting and securing to Joyce, coming from the world she came from as a child, to be able to have a distinguished connection to a distinguished university." Perhaps uniquely among Joyce's Princeton friends, Banks could understand Joyce's gratitude for the university's somewhat delayed recognition: the two novelists had developed a "siblinglike" relationship, Banks said, partly because they shared a working-class background in the northeastern "rust belt." Both viewed themselves as outsiders within Princeton's long-established, genteel, affluent, and somewhat insular community, a perception that accounted for Joyce's extreme surprise at the high rank the university had now given her. "There are days," Banks said, "when [Joyce] wakes up just delighted by the idea that she's the Berlind Chair. She just takes pleasure in it."

For all the importance Joyce attached to her status and prestige at Princeton, she was amused by the solemn rituals of the academic world. Early in 1989, the university held a special ceremony for its new chairholders, an event Joyce described ironically in a letter to John Updike: "The other evening here in Princeton, there was an elaborate university ceremony—Toni Morrison and I were, almost literally, 'installed' in our specially endowed chairs. The University takes its ceremonies more seriously than I can bring myself to take JCO, thus I was not prepared for the speeches, preposterous praise, waves of seemingly genuine affection, and the like." Later that year, writing to Richard Ford, Joyce noted a further irony in her situation as a Princeton chairholder: "I've always thought that if Princeton people really read my books, especially the administrators, they would not want me here at all; since they've invited me to stay permanently, it's evidence that they have not read my books, or haven't read them very thoughtfully." Even now, taken into the very bosom of the academic establishment, Joyce knew that her conventional exterior continued to shield the boldly imaginative "invisible writer" from public view.

Joyce's academic prestige at Princeton, though personally gratifying, had little effect on the critical reception of her books; if anything, her cozy, "establishment" status helped fuel the occasionally vituperative attacks on her work. As John Updike shrewdly observed, "New York critics were in awe of anyone who could live near Detroit, but felt they owed nothing to a resident of bucolic New Jersey."

Yet Joyce's return to the realistic mode in her novels had prompted, in some quarters, a renewed appreciation of her ability to convey the seething social tensions and psychological pressures of American life. *Solstice, Marya: A Life,* and *You Must Remember This* all had their ardent and outspoken admirers. Robert Jones in *Commonweal* argued that "*Solstice* is her best novel, a macabre comedy about coming of age in a world where innocence exists as a failure of intelligence." In *The New York Times Book Review,* Rebecca Sinkler called *Solstice* "a disturbing and unsparing story of the friendship between two unforgettable women." The novelist Mary Gordon reviewed *Marya: A Life,* also in the *Times Book Review*: "I am glad to see Miss Oates back in . . . the territory of *them* and her powerful Detroit stories; I find *Marya* her strongest book in years." Another reviewer wrote that "unlike Oates's recent gothic and Victorian excesses, *Marya* is a fairly straightforward narrative. . . . Constructed on a more intimate scale than those books, it is a stark, well-drawn portrait of the title character."

Joyce's long, ambitious novel of the 1950s, *You Must Remember This,* drew even more gratifying praise. Walter Clemons in *Newsweek* called the novel "one of her most powerful" and James Atlas, writing in *Vanity Fair,* proclaimed it "an American masterpiece," adding that "Oates's sprawling novel is the definitive history of an era." But the most influential response was John Updike's lengthy review in *The New Yorker.* Updike wrote that Joyce's novel "rallies all her strengths and is exceedingly fine—a storm of experience whose reality we cannot doubt, a fusion of fact and feeling, vision and circumstance which holds together, and holds us to it, through our terror and dismay." He added that "if the phrase 'woman of letters' existed, she would be, foremost in this country, entitled to it." Updike's praise, appearing in a magazine that had dismissed most of her work through the years, was perhaps the most gratifying and moving recognition Joyce had received in her entire career. After her friend Eleanor Bergstein called—fittingly enough, on Christmas day—and read the review over the phone, Joyce recalled: "I listened in shocked disbelief, and actually began to cry. Not that I believe the truth of what was said but simply that it *was* said, by anyone at all, but how very generously and richly by Updike, whose work I have admired for (could it be possible) almost 30 years." In her journal, she called Updike's notice "the most moving of all possible reviews, since Updike is of all living writers the one I most admire."

Joyce's publisher had shared Updike's enthusiasm for *You Must Remember This* and believed it had greater commercial potential than any novel Joyce had written since *Bellefleur*. Instead of the usual plain bound galleys, Dutton produced a glossy "Advance Reader's Edition" featuring the striking cover art that would appear on the hardcover, and planned an optimistic first printing of fifty thousand copies, twice the number ordered for her two preceding novels. In her journal, Joyce had noted her publisher's efforts with some apprehension, remarking on the " 'in house' excitement of a kind that bemuses, excites, upsets: for, after all, I am not a bestselling author and surely was not meant to be? I hate so much disappointing other people; not living up to their (commercial) expectations." Although the novel did have larger sales than either *Solstice* or *Marya: A Life*, Joyce's prediction was generally correct: *You Must Remember This* did not become a best-seller.

Among reviewers, her reputation remained controversial: some influential critics had attacked her recent novels as decisively as others praised them. Jonathan Yardley of the *Washington Post* found *Solstice* a "hysterical little novel . . . that reveals itself, beneath all the noise it makes, to have nothing at all to say." Dorothy Allison, writing in *The Village Voice*, called *Marya: A Life* "a less than satisfying psychological portrait" that was "frustratingly obscure." In the *Time* review of *You Must Remember This*, R. Z. Sheppard claimed that in attempting to write "a big novel" the author "overdoes it, as if in the grip of a writing demon. Frequently the book seems compiled rather than composed, facts and fiction accreting into a formidable but unshapely mass." Perhaps the most disappointing notice of *You Must Remember This* was Sven Birkerts's in *The New York Times Book Review*. Like the author's previous work, Birkerts argued, the new novel conveyed a sense of "futility and incipient violence," so that "when we finally close the book, we feel as though we were stepping from a cramped, overheated apartment." He found the conclusion of the novel rushed and unconvincing, and claimed that its tragic vision lacked "the decisiveness that the highest art demands."

After years of receiving a bewildering array of conflicting responses, Joyce knew better than to pay much attention to her critics. Yet she remained particularly sensitive to reviews appearing in *The New York Times Book Review*. When a negative review appeared there, she seldom failed to fire off a letter to the editors, objecting to inaccuracies or misrepresentations. In past years, such letters had been published in response to reviews of *The Edge of Impossi-*

bility, Angel Fire, The Hungry Ghosts, Unholy Loves, and *A Sentimental Education.* By now, Joyce was a powerful figure in the American literary establishment and she sometimes sent a letter directly to the reviewer, hinting at possible retaliation. Stung by Birkerts's review, she wrote to him: "Why do some reviewers sometimes misrepresent books in order to 'make a point' about them, thematic or otherwise; what grants them a sort of indulgence to treat, or maltreat, strangers, in a way that, very likely, they would never dream of treating friends, colleagues, neighbors, family . . . ? Since we live in a very small literary world, and I am forever entrusted with prize-, grant-, and fellowship-awarding, and your name will surely come up before one or another committee on which I serve, I would like to be able to speak with confidence about your integrity. It would be a pity for us to misunderstand each other further."

Asked by an interviewer why she bothered to answer her critics, Joyce replied with a characteristic boxing metaphor: "I'm a counterpuncher," she said. It was important to respond to misrepresentations or unfair attacks, she believed, in order to set the record straight. Probably Joyce had not written directly to the *Book Review* in response to Birkerts because, only a few weeks before, she had published another angry letter responding to an article by Jay Parini. In an essay discussing "prolific writers," Parini claimed that Joyce had written books worthy of being "tossed away." Joyce responded sarcastically: "Is this true only of 'prolific' writers? And what are the titles of these worthless books? Mr. Parini's confidence in his own literary powers should have nudged him to be specific since we are all eagerly awaiting his advice."

Joyce had done a fair amount of counterpunching recently. She wrote an even angrier letter to a magazine editor who had sent her a negative review of *Marya: A Life.* "Surely it is an act of gratuitous malice," Joyce fumed, "to send an author a negative review of a book on the very eve of publication; but in this case the insult is the more compounded by the shoddiness of the review itself." After detailing the review's many misstatements of fact, she remarked that "I am hardly lacking in insult, and don't need to be forcibly reminded of it." In 1989, feeling that Michiko Kakutani and Bruce Bawer had misrepresented her novel *American Appetites* in the *New York Times* and *Washington Post,* respectively, Joyce again wrote to her critics directly. "It is profoundly discouraging when a reviewer of your obvious intelligence and taste will misread a novel," Joyce wrote to Kakutani, "and convey this misreading in a crucial final paragraph, to millions of readers." (In 1993, after Kakutani savaged Joyce's novel *Foxfire: Confessions of a Girl Gang,* Joyce's publisher stopped sending Kakutani review copies of her books.) Her letter to Bawer reserved its knockout punch for the final paragraph: "I had nominated your Vendler essay for a Pushcart Prize; then, rereading it, decided that, apart from its virtues, it *was* simply too slapdash in part."

Whereas Joyce had once shunned power, declining to serve on awards committees, she now took a far more active—and at times, even aggressive—role in American literary culture. In 1988 and 1989, she served on juries for the National Book Award in fiction and the Pulitzer Prize in nonfiction, respectively, and plunged with her usual energy into the reading of nominated books and corresponding with her fellow judges. Part of Joyce's new willingness to exercise the power appropriate to her literary stature related to her increased involvement with feminist themes in her fiction and her essays. She had expressed this feminist consciousness in several of the essays published in her 1988 collection, (Woman) Writer: Occasions and Opportunities, which included considerations of prominent nineteenth-century women writers such as Emily Dickinson, Charlotte Brontë, and Susan Warner. (Joyce's earlier volumes of criticism had focused almost exclusively on male authors.) But her feminism emerged in practice as well as in the political theory underlying her criticism. Just as she no longer hesitated to retaliate against unfair reviewers, she responded angrily whenever she believed a journalist—almost always male—had written about her in a sexist or condescending way.

The most egregious example was an article by Richard Stern published in the journal Critical Inquiry (another magazine read avidly by Joyce's colleagues) in the summer of 1988. Stern was reporting on the PEN "Congress" held earlier that year in New York, which Joyce and Ray had both attended. Having watched them as they stood in a hotel lobby, Stern wrote: "They talked to no one, no one talked to them. There was a vividness of abandonment about them." Many of his observations focused on Joyce's physical appearance: "Oates herself is not vivid. If anything, she's the reverse. There are odd extrusions from her hunched thinness, a large Adam's apple, thick lips—darkened with lipstick when she appeared on a panel, but usually as colorless as the rest of her—immense, hyperthyroid dark eyes, usually screened by glasses, and a cap of light brown curls." After mentioning that he'd never finished a novel of hers, Stern returned to his less than flattering physical description: "In the lobby, she seemed so set apart, a creature from another medium. She gasped helplessly, away from the typewriter."

Not surprisingly, Joyce was furious, as were many of her friends and colleagues. Joyce wrote to the editor on August 8, insisting that the article had done "irreparable damage to my professional reputation." She added that the editor had "overstepped the boundaries of 'free speech' and [had] published libel." She reminded him that another journal, The Partisan Review, had been sued successfully after it printed a review that maligned a writer's professional integrity. Several of Joyce's prominent academic friends—Elaine Showalter, Sandra Gilbert, Susan Gubar, and others—wrote their own letters of protest to Critical Inquiry. Joyce admitted to Elaine that she wasn't serious about the lawsuit, but hoped to pressure the journal into printing a retraction. This strategy succeeded: the journal's editor agreed to print her response to Stern in the next issue. The letter displayed Joyce's ferocious eloquence at its best:

> No more grotesquely homosocial piece of writing—one can hardly call such a hodgepodge of impressions an essay—has appeared in *Critical Inquiry* than Richard Stern's "Some Members of the Congress." Is the punning title intentional?
>
> Most of the piece exudes gushing over men [. . .] By contrast, women are briefly and scornfully noted, dismissed in a line or two. [. . .]
>
> Naturally, I am most offended by the vicious portrait of me as a neurasthenic female. Since he did not trouble to hear my remarks at the PEN Congress, but seems to have merely stared at me in the lobby of the St. Moritz for a few minutes, Stern's vision of me bears about as much relationship to reality as science fiction does to science, or to fiction. If I have a prominent Adam's apple, thick lips, and light brown hair, it is certainly news to me; and if I do—so what? [. . .] As a Princeton professor and lecturer who travels a good deal, I am no more helpless away from my typewriter than my male colleagues, as Stern well knows. Would he dare heap any such assortment of trashy cliches on any man? And, if not, why on any woman? There is an animus here that shades into psychopathology.

Joyce concluded by accusing Stern of "a pig-souled sexism."

Later she and Stern exchanged letters: she suggested they call a truce and Stern agreed, remarking that he could send copies of his books as a peace offering. (Joyce declined the gift.) Several years after this imbroglio, Stern insisted that he hadn't intended to hurt Joyce, but suggested that her letter to *Critical Inquiry* "was meant to hurt me." He also recalled being "amused by Ms. Oates's claim that she knew nothing of me or my work." He insisted that Joyce's angry letter had contained "numerous distortions of my piece."

Despite Joyce's eagerness to set the record straight whenever she felt that she or her work had been maligned, she did not enjoy feuding with other writers, and even hesitated to write a negative review if she disliked a book. She knew firsthand how painful this could be to the writer, and she often pointed out that few people in America needed to be urged *not* to read a book. On one occasion, Joyce's willingness to accept review assignments placed her in an awkward dilemma. She had long admired the work of Saul Bellow, and when Anatole Broyard of *The New York Times Book Review* requested early in 1989 that she review Bellow's short novel *A Theft*, she agreed. On January 21, she wrote to John Updike that Broyard had suggested

"I was getting a reputation for only reviewing books I liked; then he asked me, if I didn't like this book, what would I do . . . so I said unthinkingly, 'Oh, I'll write it anyway.' " To Joyce's dismay, she found Bellow's new book uncharacteristically weak, but thanks to Broyard's "cunning" remarks, she could not avoid writing the review. "Now I suppose I have committed professional suicide," she told Updike. In fact, the review was a model of tact: Joyce softened her negative assessment of A *Theft* with high praise for Bellow's previous books and for qualities in the new novel that she did admire. Yet she honestly reported that A *Theft* was "underimagined" and lacked the kind of distinctive narrative voice Bellow had achieved in his earlier work.

Although Joyce had celebrated her fiftieth birthday the previous June and was now one of the world's most famous living writers, this incident showed that she retained the temperament of the enthusiastic teenager who had indulged in hero worship of much older, intellectual males, viewing them as spiritual father figures. She often remarked that she did not feel, intellectually or spiritually, like a middle-aged academic but retained the youthful, energetic mentality she appreciated in her Princeton undergraduates (she identified more strongly with them, she had recently told an interviewer, than with her famous peers or even with herself). In Joyce's mind, Bellow had long occupied the same Olympian category as her Syracuse professors, or great novelists such as Thomas Mann and William Faulkner (whom she had idolized in the 1950s, when both were still alive), or renowned scholars like Walter Kaufmann, whose classes she had audited when she'd first arrived in Princeton. Although she had clearly been joking when expressing the hyperbolic notion that she might be "committing professional suicide" in daring to criticize Bellow, the comment suggested her longing to maintain the intellectual universe of her youth and to leave her heroes untarnished. Months after writing the review of A *Theft*, she still felt the sting of regret. "It was painful to write," she remarked, "since I certainly do admire him, immensely."

Joyce's current position as America's preeminent "woman of letters" only intensified her awareness of the double-edged rewards of fame, especially in a country that made a cult of celebrity. She had reached a point in her career that, for some writers, could prove fatally distracting: it is far easier, after all, to fly around the country accepting awards and honorary degrees, reading to admiring crowds, and giving interviews, than to maintain the disciplined isolation necessary to create new work. But Joyce had become skilled at balancing the demands of her writing life with the perquisites and opportunities that now came her way as a public figure. She was well aware, for instance, that some "honors" were designed to benefit the donor more than the recipient: invitations to accept honorary degrees, she knew, were often a means of coercing a famous writer into making a public appearance for free. There was now such demand for Joyce's readings on college campuses that she declined far more invitations than she accepted. She had signed up with a lecture agency, the Cosby Bureau in Washington, to help deal with the logistics of travel and to negotiate her fees. Joyce now commanded as much as $10,000, plus travel expenses and accommodations, for a single reading or lecture, though she often accepted less from institutions that could not afford such a fee, or when a nearby engagement did not interfere greatly with her work schedule. She had overcome her fear of airplanes, however, and now actually enjoyed long flights, during which she could work uninterrupted for several hours; she had also learned to accept limousine service when it was offered, since she could work or read while being driven to and from her public appearances.

Russell Banks marvelled at Joyce's ability to work without distraction during such trips, her "uncanny ability to compartmentalize her attention." He noted that Joyce "can get into a car and start editing a manuscript the minute after a conversation has ended. . . . She can concentrate with extraordinary power." Unlike most writers, he added, Joyce never allowed herself "the leisure to back off and take a vacation from work, or regenerate herself in a kind of casual way. She has a kind of drive and work ethic that don't permit those kinds of lacunae." (Other friends such as Ed Cone and George Pitcher recalled their unsuccessful attempts to persuade Joyce to accompany them on vacations. Asked by an interviewer whether she wouldn't enjoy a vacation at the beach, Joyce responded: "I would go crazy. I could sit on the beach for maybe three minutes.") Yet a letter to Banks in April 1987 suggested that Joyce derived at least brief periods of relaxation within the hectic routine of her public activities: "I actually look forward to the several—I've lost track, how many—limousine trips I've had or am scheduled to have shortly, taking me to far-flung local places like Adelphi University, Queens College, East Brunswick library, the International Center for Photography [. . .], during which quiet time I can read, or look out of the window, or close my eyes." She added that "Impersonating 'JCO' is actually a good deal of fun since it rarely lasts long, and is about one-hundredth as difficult as working on my novel."

Virtually all of Joyce's traveling related in some way to her work. In the summer of 1987, she and Ray spent two weeks in Europe, but the days were filled with public appearances for Joyce: a visit to the Swedish Book Fair, a reading in the Netherlands sponsored by the U.S. Information Agency, and visits to the German cities of Hamburg, Heidelberg, and Frankfurt. (One of the side effects of travel was its heightening of Joyce's chronic insomnia; in hotel rooms she would occasionally work all night rather than sleep, producing poems with such titles as "Sleepless in Heidelberg.") Joyce enjoyed the European trip thoroughly. John Updike, Iris Murdoch, and Margaret Drabble also attended the Swedish Book Fair: as Joyce noted in her journal, "I was one of the foreign 'stars'—my lecture well-attended; a press-conference jammed; many Swedish 'fans.' "

Despite the high fees Joyce could now command for her readings, her hosts were seldom disappointed: she put her usual energy and intensity into talking with faculty and students, reading her work to large audiences, and gamely attending panel discussions, receptions, and dinners. The novelist Madison Smartt Bell, who had been a Princeton senior when Joyce arrived on campus in 1978, now taught at Goucher College; he recalled Joyce's brief visit to Goucher in the spring of 1985 for a three-day "residency." According to Bell, "the college really tried to get value" for its $10,000. "I saw Joyce's schedule for the three days and it was absolutely murderous," with events and appearances "from dawn till dark." Yet Joyce "went through the whole thing like a trouper, never seemed dismayed or even much fatigued, and actually seemed to enjoy it." Just before leaving for Goucher, Joyce had written to Alicia Ostriker that the event "should be fun—though they have scheduled me for nearly every minute (even my 'rest' periods are designated on the print-out)."

Other travels Joyce undertook related to her work in a different way. In 1986, she had published a new collection of short stories, *Raven's Wing*: the title story dealt with a small-time crook who hangs out at racetracks and becomes enamored of a thoroughbred. Published in *Esquire*, the story had been reprinted in Gail Godwin's edition of *Best American Short Stories*. Shortly before her trip to Europe, Joyce had received a letter from a man who had admired the story greatly. Alan Levitt, the owner of a horse farm called Lana Lobell in Bedminster, New Jersey, invited Joyce and Ray to visit; they went on August 9, a day when 143 horses were scheduled for auction. When Ray asked Levitt how one went about buying a racehorse, Levitt offered to buy a horse in partnership with Joyce and Ray. As they became caught up in the excitement of the auction, Joyce's characteristic frugality vanished: they spent $16,000, their half of the purchase price for a beautiful bay filly named Impish Lobell. (At $32,000, however, Impish Lobell was modestly priced; one of the horses auctioned that day sold for $260,000.) Describing the event in a letter to Mike Keeley, Joyce wrote: "In such episodes of extraordinary bidding it is the bloodline that is being bought." Their yearling was not yet trained, but Joyce eagerly began issuing invitations to her friends to accompany her and Ray to the racetrack. The following summer, Joyce and Ray visited the Meadowlands track and, to their delight, Impish won her qualifying heat; the filly came in first, Joyce wrote to Elaine Showalter, "over 13 other eager high-headed young pacers." In July 1989, Impish won $62,000 in her first high-stakes race, at a track in Yonkers. Yet Joyce's rather uncharacteristic venture into the world of horseracing was short-lived: she and Ray sold their interest in Impish a year later, after veterinary and feed bills became excessive. But just as her visits to Las Vegas had resulted in fiction and poetry on the subject of gambling, she culled a story from her experience with horse racing as well: "The Track" appeared in GQ magazine and was included in her 1996 collection, *Will You Always Love Me?*

Although Joyce traveled frequently, her trips were brief and carefully chosen, and she often expressed a preference for staying in Princeton and adhering to her usual routine. She had come to view her beloved home as a kind of sanctuary where she could avoid the public demands upon "JCO" and devote herself wholly to writing. As many of her friends noted, the unusual design of Joyce and Ray's home reflected the personality of its famous occupant: the house featured an extraordinary amount of glass, permitting the outward-looking curiosity about the world essential to a novelist, but at the same time it had a private, secluded quality, the entry doors enclosed within a private courtyard and the house itself set far back from the road and nestled among abundant trees. In a 1989 essay, "At Home," Joyce wrote that the house was "turn[ed] inward, showing no facade or face at all," corresponding to her own favored self-image as an "invisible" writer. She added that "such a house, with its air of being hidden, even reclusive, has the appeal of a child's paradise regained." When a friend would exclaim, "Your house is just like *you*," Joyce said that "I take it as a compliment and don't try to decipher it in terms of secrecy, or exposure (all that glass! so many needless doors!); let alone deception (sometimes visitors wander about the outside of the house, unable even to find the way into the courtyard, and, finding the courtyard, they stand indecisively pondering which of the four doors is 'the' door)."

Having now occupied the house for more than a decade, Joyce and Ray had developed a congenial arrangement: Ray, an avid gardener, maintained the exterior of the house, the lawn, and the pond; while Joyce did the housework and the cooking. Having added a handsome, light-filled study (which served as a guest room for out-of-town visitors) and a plant-filled solarium off the living room, they had successfully adapted the unusual house to their personal needs. (Built in 1962 by the Princeton architect Philip Collins, the original structure consisted of eight modules, each measuring twelve by sixteen feet and featuring a cathedral ceiling.) In her book-lined office, located directly across the courtyard from the new study, her desk faced a window that afforded a panoramic view of the fish pond, the downward-sloping back lawn with its tall ferns and dazzling array of wildflowers, and the luxuriant woods through which white-tailed deer trotted peaceably. Unlike the deliberately spartan work space she'd preferred as a young writer, she now permitted herself not only a view of natural beauty but a study covered with reproduced artworks (by Edward Hopper, Ansel Adams, René Magritte) and, on her windowsill, "the usual modestly talismanic objects writers set out for sentimental/superstitious reasons: small gifts, medallions commemorating 'honors,' family snapshots."

Despite Joyce's financial success, she never felt the impulse to hire outside help with cleaning or maintaining the house. Blessed with a short-range photographic memory, she could "proofread in my head" while vacuuming or cleaning the kitchen after dinner. She also edited her work during her and Ray's afternoon jogs and bicycle rides through the lush countryside nearby. The Delaware Valley, she wrote, represented a nourishing retreat from the "counter-world" of her imagination, an extension of her home environment. She and Ray had explored the area thoroughly. "The Delaware Valley is hardly our own personal discovery," she wrote, "but it has for us that kind of resonance. Perhaps its small towns and hamlets remind us of the past we've lost irretrievably." By now, she and Ray had "settled into Princeton with more of a sense of permanence, and of purpose, than we had settled into any previous phase of our lives, and it is now unlikely that we will ever leave."

Although Joyce viewed her home as a peaceful retreat and an ideal environment for her work, it was also a setting she enjoyed sharing with friends and family members. She and Ray had continued their practice of giving several large parties and numerous smaller dinners each year. The bulletin board in their kitchen was typically crammed with snapshots taken at these functions: along with pictures of their Princeton friends, there were shots of famous visitors such as E. L. Doctorow and John Updike. Joyce was particularly notable, in Princeton's extremely busy and self-absorbed intellectual environment, for reaching out to visiting writers and faculty who lacked local connections.

During the 1986–87 academic year, one of these was Tama Janowitz, a New York writer who had won the Hodder Fellowship, a competitive award that brought an accomplished writer or artist to the Princeton campus each year. Joyce helped sponsor Janowitz, who had recently achieved considerable celebrity with her book *Slaves of New York*. A young woman known for her trendy, attention-getting hairstyle, makeup, and clothes—a personal appearance more common in the hip New York club scene than in the somewhat genteel, tradition-bound ethos of Princeton—Janowitz felt uncomfortably out of place at first. Although pleased to escape her New York celebrity and a constantly ringing telephone, she soon found that she "wasn't that happy, because Princeton is not a friendly sort of town." But Joyce, a writer she had long idolized, welcomed her into the community: "Joyce was so kind to me," Janowitz remembered. "She organized dinners quite regularly and invited me, and often took me out. That was so wonderful. She was more than generous." Janowitz had been concerned that her controversial image might affect her reception in an Ivy League setting. But "[Joyce] didn't seem to pay any attention to what had been said about me or what people were saying. She just accepted me." Janowitz remembered that they talked often about Joyce's cats and about other writers they knew in common.

The many visitors to Joyce's home observed the special pleasure she took in making her parents, Fred and Carolina, feel welcome whenever they visited Princeton. Having been forced to drop out of school during the Depression, Joyce's parents lacked the educational advantages and cultural sophistication of their daughter's university colleagues, but Joyce invited Fred and Carolina to Princeton regularly and introduced them to her friends. Joyce's colleague Ted Weiss observed that "when her parents visit, good, sympathetic people that they are, if not literary, Joyce holds large parties for all her friends. Not many academics or writers that I know make parties with their parents at the center of them." In fact, Fred and Carolina's abundant intelligence, curiosity, and good humor made them extremely popular in Joyce's circle. Both Fred and Carolina were avid readers and had artistic inclinations that for many years had been stifled by their arduous work lives. Retired after forty years of factory work at Harrison Radiator, Fred at age seventy had begun taking music and literature courses at SUNY-Buffalo, and Carolina not only read her daughter's steady stream of books but enjoyed the fiction and poetry of Joyce's colleagues as well.

In a 1989 essay about Fred, Joyce meditated on the crucial importance of both her parents in her life and marveled at the ease with which Fred and Carolina had become part of her Princeton world. "How did the malnourished circumstances of my parents' early lives allow them to grow, to blossom, into the exemplary people they have become?" she asked. "The quality of personality they embody, their unfailing magnanimity of spirit, is so oddly matched with their origins and with the harsh and unsentimental world out of which they emerged." Fred and Carolina were extremely proud of their daughter's literary accomplishments, but Joyce observed to an interviewer that "they are so enthusiastic about everything they do. I mean, their enthusiasm is not just for their daughter, but for virtually everything. I get happiness from them, really. They have a real wisdom." She concluded her essay on Fred by remarking that "if there is one general trait I seem to have inherited from both my parents it's their instinct for rejoicing in the life in which they have found themselves. They remain models for me, they go far beyond me, I can only hope to continue to learn from them. 'Happiness is a kind of genius,' Colette shrewdly observed, and in this genius my parents abound."

Even during her parents' visits to Princeton, Joyce's work schedule remained intact: Carolina Oates observed that Joyce would put in a full writing day in her study "as if we weren't even there." While Joyce worked, Fred and Carolina would read in the sunny guest room, or Fred would help Ray with his gardening while Carolina cooked in her daughter's spacious kitchen. Joyce's parents enjoyed the break from their usual routine in Millersport and Joyce herself took great pleasure in their visits. In June of 1987, she wrote in her journal that Fred and Carolina had just departed "after a marvelous visit; one of our very warmest, most wonderful visits. [. . .] The house will now seem empty, and relatively unused, too quiet; our mealtimes too abbreviated, miniaturized. How I love my parents; but, more importantly, how wonderful they are in themselves."

Occasionally Joyce invited her parents along on one of her trips: they had attended some of her readings and had accompanied Joyce and Ray to several premieres of her plays. But the most ambitious trip came in August of 1989, when Joyce took her parents along for a seventeen-day trip through England, Scotland, and Ireland. "Our English visit went very well," Joyce reported to Russell Banks and his wife, Chase Twichell, "especially considering the difficulty of four people traveling together." In London, they saw *M. Butterfly* and David Hare's *The Secret Rapture*, and visited countless museums and galleries. They also toured the English countryside, driving through the Lake District and stopping to explore ancient monuments and castles. In Scotland, they attended a luncheon at Hawthornden Castle, a fifteenth-century structure that had been converted into a writers' retreat. As usual, the trip involved a grueling round of promotional stops for Joyce—her novel *American Appetites* had just been issued by her British publisher, Macmillan—but along the way she had stimulating visits with a number of prominent English and Irish writers: Germaine Greer, Edna O'Brien, Stephen Spender, Piers Paul Read, and others. The career-related activities during the trip were "certainly in the background, as far as I was concerned," Joyce told Richard Ford. What she most enjoyed was the new experience of traveling with her parents; in all, the trip "worked out wonderfully since it was very nice to do things as a family." Her Macmillan publicist and editor, Nick McDowell, and her English agent, Murray Pollinger, helped to make Fred and Carolina's first trip abroad particularly memorable. "We had the best time," Carolina recalled. "They treated us just like royalty."

Now that she had settled comfortably into middle age, Joyce's personal happiness seemed to refute W. B. Yeats's famous maxim that a writer could perfect either "the work or the life," but never both. Having explored the world of her childhood in *Marya: A Life* and *You Must Remember This*, Joyce drew the materials for her next major novel from the privileged life she now enjoyed: in fact, she chose her own "glass house" as the setting for *American Appetites*, a novel dealing with a highly intelligent, successful couple, Ian and Glynnis McCullough. Like Joyce and Ray, Ian and Glynnis are well established in an intellectual community: "Hazelton-on-Hudson" is a fictional portrayal of Princeton, New Jersey; Ian is a senior fellow in the "Institute for Independent Research in the Social Sciences," based upon Princeton's Institute for Advanced Study (then headed by Joyce's friend Henry Bienen), and editor of a political journal; Glynnis is a gourmet cook and the author of several renowned cookbooks. Joyce drew several key scenes in the novel directly from her own experience. The elaborate dinner party celebrating Ian's fiftieth birthday evoked the ebullient tone of Joyce and Ray's own parties; a scene in which Ian and Glynnis are awakened in the middle of the night by police pounding on their door in search of a teenage vandal (the officers have inadvertently approached the wrong house) replicates in virtually all its details a frightening experience endured by Joyce and Ray. Yet the novel makes an Oatesian swerve into violence when Glynnis, during an argument with Ian over a suspected infidelity, suffers a fatal fall, crashing through one of the house's numerous glass walls. Ian is charged with her murder, and the remainder of the novel details his trial along with the psychological repercussions of this incident that destroys forever the fragile equilibrium of the McCulloughs' lives.

In a televised interview with Charlie Rose given shortly after she completed the novel, Joyce stressed her awareness that the peaceful stability of her Princeton life could, like the McCulloughs', be shattered at any moment. "We've been lucky so far," she said, with the caution born of her bleak childhood environment. The novel was also a meditation on aging, she said, since both Joyce and Ian McCullough (she identified more strongly with Ian than with the doomed Glynnis) were confronting their fiftieth birthdays. And as the title suggested, the novel expressed Joyce's ongoing concern with the issue of food: "My secret (perhaps not so terribly secret) equation for the novel is food (an excess of, a fanaticism for) = (my) writing." As always, Joyce saw her work, rather than food, as her primary source of nurture; and the dark side of this equation, which she had dramatized in *Solstice*, was the ever-present danger that her extreme absorption in writing might drain her physical vitality, destroying the "normal" self she had projected into the characterization of Monica Jensen.

Joyce had an additional important motive in writing *American Appetites*, since she wanted to bring her own present world to dramatic life. *American Appetites*, she wrote to Mike Keeley, "has a good deal of food, cookery, and Princeton-like social life in it." In her journal, she observed that "*American Appetites* could not have been written anywhere else but in Princeton, of course. Though fiction, it is also a story unique to this world; to the middle-aged (consequently 'in power') personalities of this world." Although she admitted that her friend Henry Bienen "irradiates through the text here and there," she insisted he was "not *in* it; not at all." In July of 1987, Joyce wrote a letter to Henry and Leigh Bienen suggesting that although they would find certain details in the novel "that will be familiar to you [. . .] you will also see,

I'm sure, how purely (ethereally!) fictitious it all is." (To Joyce's amusement, several of her male Princeton friends, Bienen included, believed themselves to be the model for Ian McCullough.) But not surprisingly, Ian's primary significance lay in his identity as yet another of Joyce's male soul mates: an academic with a marked tendency toward philosophical introspection, Ian copes with issues of aging and professional "success" in his Princeton-like world, and like Joyce he considers himself a young person trapped in a middle-aged body. "If anyone, Ian McC. is myself," Joyce said. "A masculine version."

She had worked on the novel with her usual intensity, beginning in March of 1987 and completing a first draft only three months later, on June 15. (The first bound copies of *You Must Remember This* arrived on the same day: Joyce had continued her typical pattern of completing a new novel just as the previous novel was being published.) In fact, she was now working longer hours than ever before: on May 26, she wrote to Mike Keeley that she and Ray had altered their work schedules, resuming work after dinner and often continuing until midnight. She could now work quietly at night, since she had introduced another major change to her work routine: Ray had recently bought an IBM word processor and Joyce had taken to the machine with her usual avidity. But instead of making her writing easier, she found that "the word processor is demonic in stimulating ceaseless revision/recasting—so that now I seem to spend more time writing a single work than I have ever done in the past."

John Updike had recommended the machine to Joyce, mischievously suggesting that she could "double her output," but she told Updike that "I seem in fact to write more slowly." Nonetheless, she found the machine "mesmerizing; it makes all things, however improbably, seem possible." She told Elaine Showalter that the computer's mysterious workings felt like an extension of her brain waves. Yet Joyce used the machine for only a couple of years before returning to the typewriter: the computer and printer were always breaking down, and the monitor blocked the spectacular view outside her study window. She had found that the machine had stimulated revision to an extent that went "far beyond the point of being helpful, and into some strange self-hypnotizing realm of sheer language; it's a wonder I ever got to the point of printing anything out."

Even without a computer, the process of revision had come to dominate her writing life. After finishing *American Appetites*, she vowed immediately to "rewrite it completely," an activity that would represent "bliss" compared to the arduous work of composing the first draft. As usual, the novel had not come easily, and after its completion she felt exultant that she had, once again, survived an ambitious first draft: "how happy, how ecstatic, how pleased, how grateful, how, simply, surprised I am . . . that *American Appetites* turned out as it did; after so much uphill straining, more than the usual (except for *You Must Remember This*) perplexity, anguish. . . . Yes I am *very* amazed by it; and have only to glance through my early notes, now so groping, wrongheaded, blind, pathetic . . . to see what a problem I'd had; and to see how far (no matter what others may think) I managed to come."

That telling parenthesis, "no matter what others may think," suggested Joyce's usual anxiety over the critical reception of her work, particularly the long novels into which she poured so much effort. She was pleased, at least, that her publisher shared her enthusiasm about the novel: Dutton planned a first printing of 35,000 copies. In December of 1988, shortly before publication, Joyce noted hopefully that "Early reports of AA have been good, very enthusiastic, but who can tell what fate lies in store. Though 'fate' is too heavy a term, after all I've been through this before, and will go through it again." She had worried, she wrote to one friend, that *American Appetites* would be considered "a dangerously cerebral, possibly overly 'refined' novel, yet I see reviews that call it a thriller."

As usual, the response to her new novel was mixed. Apart from the infuriating reviews by Michiko Kakutani in the *New York Times* and Bruce Bawer in the *Washington Post* that had prompted her to write the two critics personally, there were also glowing notices. In the *Times Literary Supplement*, Patricia Craig noted that "*American Appetites* is a work of considerable richness and urbanity." Paul Gray wrote in *Time* that "Oates is here working at the very top of her form," adding that readers "who want to know what makes her important—as opposed to merely famous—could find no better place to begin than right here." Joyce wrote to Gray to thank him for the review: "This is just to say how much I was moved, and encouraged, by your generous and wholly unexpected review," she wrote. Joyce was also pleased when producer Dick Berg commissioned her to write the screenplay for the novel. (Earlier in the summer, she had completed the *You Must Remember This* screenplay for Martin Scorsese in a feverish thirteen days.) And the novel had been far from a commercial failure: the first printing sold out quickly and the publisher had ordered a second. But after Dutton threw a large publication party for the novel in January of 1989, Joyce wrote to Bob Phillips (who had been among the guests, along with such literary friends of Joyce's as George Plimpton, Shirley Hazzard, and James Atlas) that she "could wish for Dutton's sake that the novel were doing better (they always, *always* have their fingers crossed for a bestseller, you'd think by now they might know better)."

Following her usual pattern, Joyce had completed another major novel well before the publication date for *American Appetites*. In August of 1988, shortly after completing the *You Must Remember This* screenplay, Joyce noted that she'd "been working in a sort of trance of fascination or oblivion on a new novel." She had again returned to the 1950s: the new manuscript, with its working title *Song of Innocence*, would encompass the years 1956—"taking up, historically, where *You Must Remember This* left off "—to 1964. Based in part on the memories of her teenage friendship with Roosevelt Chatham, the novel focused on the relationship between the white teenager Iris Courtney and her black friend Jinx Fairchild, a gifted basketball player. Its final title, *Because It Is Bitter, and Because It Is My Heart*, came from a Stephen Crane poem that had haunted Joyce since she'd first encountered it in a college anthology. Writing to the prominent African-American critic Henry Louis Gates, Jr., Joyce recalled Chatham as "a black boy of my distant past, whom I knew in that glancing yet somehow close-up/magnified/even intimate way we know classmates in seventh or eighth grade [. . .] across whatever familial and social abysses." Like Marya Knauer and Enid Stevick, Iris is a gifted, sensitive girl who shares many traits with the young Joyce Oates: Iris escapes an unstable childhood environment (Iris's father was a gambler; her mother, an alcoholic) and attends a college that Joyce patterned closely on her memories of Syracuse University. But the novel was far more than codified autobiography: encompassing issues of race, class, and American history, along with the characteristic Oatesian theme of personal identity, it equaled *You Must Remember This* in its thematic scope and artistic ambition.

Joyce worked hard at *Because It Is Bitter* throughout the fall of 1988. On November 5, she wrote to John Updike: "After months of pushing a recalcitrant novel-in-progress uphill it has got to that point on the hill when it's beginning to go down, and gaining momentum." She completed the first draft on December 9. As usual, she felt "enormous happiness; enormous relief; enormous FAITH THAT I CAN DO IT in the face of what had seemed, no what surely was, crippling/paralyzing/suffocating difficulties. Those evenings, working late, in the guest room . . . typing & retyping . . . and near-sleepless nights, and early mornings."

Months later, after reading the novel in bound galleys, Joyce suggested (with more optimism than sound judgment) that it was "probably my strongest novel . . . at least it feels so to me. I'm still a bit entranced by it, in that aftermath of half-groggy sensation we all feel when finishing a big exhausting effort." When the novel appeared, Joyce was gratified by the positive reviews. In *The New York Times Book Review*, Marilynne Robinson admired the "complexity in the detail of [Oates's] prose" and hailed the novel's "extraordinary imaginative power." Her friend Henry Louis Gates, Jr., wrote in *The Nation* that "Oates renders the lineaments of racial resentment with precision. . . . At times we feel she has put everything she knows into a single page, each a cunning medley of grit and wit." Yet sales of *Because It Is Bitter* were disappointing. The paperback rights were sold for a much smaller sum than *Ameri-*

can Appetites had fetched the previous year. Joyce reported to her friend Bill Heyen that the book had been "a commercial failure, more or less."

Joyce was again suffering from exhaustion: during the winter of 1989–90, while *Because It Is Bitter* was being readied for publication, she had completed yet another novel of the 1950s entitled *Foxfire: Confessions of a Girl Gang*. Joyce called *Foxfire*, which was shorter and less ambitious than either *You Must Remember This* or *Because It Is Bitter*, an "odd little quicksilver novel." Again Joyce portrayed a sensitive adolescent girl, Maddy Wirtz, coming of age in upstate New York, and again she brought enlightenment to her protagonist through the crucible of violence. Maddy, like Margaret "Legs" Sadovsky and her other friends in the gang they call Foxfire, has suffered victimization at the hands of men, and the narrative included trademark Oatesian incidents of extreme brutality (including a gang rape). Like her other recent protagonists, Maddy was clearly an autobiographical character: as the "nice girl" in the gang, its intellectual member and official historian, Maddy was also the story-teller who preserved the gang's adventures long after Foxfire had burned itself out. As usual, Joyce was quick to complete her manuscript but reluctant to re-linquish it. On January 18 she told John Updike that it was "finished and should be mailed out of the house, but I keep leafing through it looking eagerly for a page that should be retyped another time, some justification for staying with this now-familiar and now-under-control material a little longer."

Joyce had continued her habit of working at shorter projects—book reviews, stories and poems, even novellas and plays—as a way of recuperating from the novels she found so draining. The genre that she found most consoling was poetry. After completing a novel, she would leave the room where she did most of her work and sit contemplatively at the long white Parson's table in the light-filled new study she and Ray had added to the house. There she wrote poems in long hand for a period ranging from a few days to ten weeks. In April of 1988 she went through a "poetry phase" of this kind, during which she produced much of the work that would appear in *The Time Traveler*. Alluding to the famous line by Sylvia Plath, Joyce wrote in her journal: "At such times I think, the blood-jet *is* poetry; why labor at prose . . . ?" Yet she could not imagine "the poet's life; this intensity day after day, year after year . . . poetry to me is a flame; a fire; an inferno; then a fire again; then a flame; then—it's gone. Anywhere from six to ten weeks & the extraordinary interlude is over."

Although she still wrote relatively little poetry compared to her output in prose, she had grown more confident and accomplished in this most difficult of all literary genres. The scathing review by Helen Vendler of her 1973 volume *Angel Fire* had marked a nadir in her reputation as a poet; other volumes she'd published in the 1970s, *The Fabulous Beasts* (1975) and *Women Whose Lives Are Food, Men Whose Lives Are Money* (1978), had received little attention. In

a 1978 *Paris Review* interview, she speculated that she might never again publish a collection, remarking that few people were interested in reading a novelist's poetry, and she had told her Detroit friend Philip Levine, the highly
regarded, American Book Award-winning poet, that her best energies had gone
into her fiction and that she was not really a poet—that is, a full-time, serious
poet—in the way that Levine was. Her poet friends tended to agree. "The
prose overshadows the poetry," Dan Halpern said. "You don't think of her as a
poet, even though she writes it." Larry Goldstein remarked that although he
enjoyed much of her poetry, "I've not found anyone else who admires it so
much as I do." The Pulitzer Prize-winning poet Maxine Kumin argued that
"the poetry, frankly, does not measure up to the fiction. It's too elastic, not as
highly plotted or curved, seems to serve as a safety valve for the prose."

Yet Joyce had maintained an active interest in poetry, reading and reviewing it regularly, and discussing the genre avidly with poet friends such as
Levine, Halpern, and Alicia Ostriker. Her 1982 volume, *Invisible Woman: New
and Selected Poems*, had represented an attempt to gather her stronger earlier
work (she did not include any poems from her weak first volume, *Anonymous
Sins*) and to suggest a new direction for her poetry. Many of the new poems,
such as "Tachycardiac Seizure," "Autistic Child, No Longer Child," and
"First Death, 1950," were highly autobiographical, dealing with personal and
familial recollections; they also partook of the impulse toward a nostalgic realism that characterized Joyce's fiction of these years. "Leavetaking, at Dusk"
expressed her emotions upon permanently leaving her home in Windsor, and
"The Present Tense"—published in *The Atlantic* and one of her personal
favorites of all her poems—attempted to summarize the frenetic pace of her
creative life.

But more important than the subject matter was her newly developed
ability to craft poems that varied widely in form, tone, and verbal texture. Of
her 1970 volume, *Love and Its Derangements*, she had admitted that "each of
the poems is a blur to me," an unrealized formal experiment that "in my frustration I somehow declared permanent." By contrast, her poems collected in
The Time Traveler were memorable, finely executed stays against confusion;
the newer work looked unflinchingly at the darker manifestations of time and
nature, but achieved a unifying voice that expressed a transcendent pleasure
and compensation in the mere act of bearing witness. Many of the poems,
like her novels of the 1980s and 1990s, were explicitly feminist in their concerns, and others were imbued with her characteristically intense nostalgia
for her childhood environment. The volume was an ample miscellany that
embraced many of the details of her present life as well. One poem responded to her travels through Eastern Europe, while another described an
encounter with heavyweight boxing champion Mike Tyson; "Makeup Artist"

and "Photograph Session" suggested moments transcribed from the life of a celebrated writer. There were several elegies: one for Joyce's grandmother, others for novelists John Gardner and William Goyen. Still others, such as "Waiting on Elvis, 1956" and "Roller Rink, 1954," had the character of sociological still lifes, brief looks at American social history of the kind that often appeared in Joyce's novels and stories.

Like Larry Goldstein, other friends insisted that Joyce had made remarkable progress in developing a distinctive poetic voice. Philip Levine saw *The Time Traveler* as "a high water mark of her career as a poet." In contrast to the uneven earlier volumes, virtually every poem in the book, he insisted, was a significant achievement. Alicia Ostriker suggested that Joyce's poems were "as unique as her prose—sharp, witty, compressed, mastering the idiom and the material phenomena of our time yet also probing the psyche. She has this extraordinary capacity to say things that are harrowing, with a perfectly deadpan manner. You would never mistake her voice for anyone else's—and that, of course, is what we can say of any outstanding poet."

In the summer of 1989, in a similarly brief but intense interlude, Joyce had ventured into yet another genre. In June, she produced one of her finest novellas, *I Lock My Door Upon Myself*; set in the late nineteenth century and dealing, like *Because It Is Bitter*, with the relationship between a white woman and a black man, the novella (which Joyce called a "peculiar balladic tragedy") had been difficult to write. Many false starts were required before she found the "right tone," enabling her to hear the narrator's powerfully nostalgic and lyrical voice. (The novella's title, she noted, was "very autobiographical in the sense that the writer locks her door upon herself in the obsessive enterprise of writing.") A few weeks later, she was hard at work on another novella, *The Rise of Life on Earth*, which returned to the Detroit setting of her earlier fiction. The story of a troubled nurse's aide who administers fatal drug overdoses to several of her patients, this novella was "absolutely riveting" but also, from Joyce's viewpoint, slow to take shape: "I seem to be working with glacial slowness," she wrote in her journal, "as if hacking my way through a thicket or burrowing (even) with my head."

Joyce recognized that these novellas were "utterly uncommerical & unmarketable"; they were too long for magazine publication and her primary book publisher, Dutton, was already bringing out an average of two titles a year by its most productive author. (In addition to the five novels by Joyce that appeared between 1985 and 1990, Dutton had published her collection of stories, *Raven's Wing*, in 1986; her gathering of essays, *(Woman) Writer: Occasions and Opportunities*, in 1988; and her volume of poetry, *The Time Traveler*, in 1989. By 1990, Dutton was readying two new books—*Twelve Plays* and *Heat and Other Stories*—for 1991 publication.) Yet Joyce did find homes for both novellas: her friend Dan Halpern happily accepted *I Lock My Door Upon Myself* for the fall 1990 list at Ecco Press (the 1988 Ecco volume of her miniature narratives, *The Assignation*, had sold quite well); and New Directions, a publisher hospitable to experimental works, agreed to bring out *The Rise of Life on Earth* in 1991. Halpern had been delighted to publish *I Lock My Door*, noting that critical response to the novella was "exceptional." Critics could have overlooked such a book, he remarked, since a novella issued by a small press normally would not receive many reviews. Halpern also believed that the timing was favorable, since *You Must Remember This* had been "a breakthrough book" for Joyce, inspiring new respect and attention for her subsequent books. Critics again seemed to realize, he added, that she was "a really original American writer, unlike anybody else who is writing in this country. From that point on, they really did take her more seriously."

Although Joyce had the ample confidence—and, as always, the near-limitless energy—required to pursue a variegated career as a fiction writer, dramatist, poet, critic, and teacher, she had felt increasingly beleaguered by her own reputation: even friendly reviewers, she felt, viewed her recent books in the context of her past work, so that an individual novel could not be assessed on its own terms. For an experimental writer who took seriously the term "novel," and attempted something genuinely innovative with each new book, it was particularly frustrating to encounter the same set of pre-programmed responses to her fiction year after year. As early as 1971, she had written to Gail Godwin of her desire to "arrange a funeral for 'Joyce Carol Oates' " and shed the stereotypical image attached to her name.

Other prominent writers had felt a similar frustration, and Joyce had been fascinated by the pseudonymous publications of Doris Lessing, Romain Gary, and others. In an essay called "The Art of Being No One," she observed that "In an ideal world uncontaminated by ego and individual 'identity,' all works of art, if not entertainment, might well be attributed to 'Anonymous.' These works would then be judged solely on their intrinsic merit; the attachment of specific creators, whether for the enhancement of the works or their detriment, would be irrelevant." While writing *Solstice*, Joyce had suggested to Blanche Gregory that the novel be submitted under a pseudonym, but Blanche had refused. One reason Blanche offered was that Joyce's style would be instantly recognizable to her readers. Surely another consideration was financial: an unknown writer could hardly claim as large an advance as a book by "Oates."

But in the summer of 1986, Joyce saw her chance to pursue a pseudonymous adventure. After completing *You Must Remember This*, she had felt her usual sense of depletion after a long novel, and decided to try a much briefer and less ambitious work. Her ongoing fascination with the "phantasmagoria" of human identity had prompted an interest in the phenomenon of human twins: two of her friends, the poet Phil Levine and her fellow boxing enthusiast Ron Levao, had identical twins, and she had discussed the phenomenon with both men. In her own life, Joyce had long been haunted by the peculiar version of the doppelgänger she saw in her autistic sister, Lynn. Sharing the same birthday but born eighteen years apart, Joyce and Lynn were intellectual opposites but shared a striking physical resemblance much closer than that between most siblings. In June of 1986, Joyce wrote to Elaine Showalter that she'd been doing considerable reading and research into twins, finding it "ever more fascinating but ultimately—as always—with any kind of research, I mean—it becomes vertiginous, as if all lines of research lead in and downward to one mysterious thing not to be named."

Joyce's research was for a brief, plot-driven novel—a "concept novel," as she termed it—to be called *Lives of the Twins*. The two-hundred-page manuscript, completed by the end of August, had been written "primarily as a diversion" and "in a mode or genre quite foreign to me: 'romantic mystery' it might be called." She added that "The subject is one that greatly interests me—identical twins, problems of 'identity'—but the treatment is not as deep or profound or, I suppose, as exhaustive as I would ordinarily give it." The very nature of her manuscript—focused upon a dual, or split, identity, as embodied in the twin psychiatrists Jonathan and James McEwan (further additions to Joyce's gallery of autobiographical, male characters whose names begin with J)—suggested the appropriateness of using a pseudonym, as a kind of literary "double" of her own. (And there was a more practical consideration: Joyce's contracts with Dutton for books under her own name stretched into the 1990s.) Since Blanche had strongly opposed the idea and since Joyce wanted, in any case, to keep the new venture as secret as possible, she approached another agent, a woman who lived near Princeton and whom Joyce already knew socially, Rosalie Siegel. Joyce pleaded with Siegel to tell no one—not even Siegel's husband—about the project. Siegel agreed to represent the manuscript, which she submitted to Simon & Schuster as a debut effort by an unknown writer. To Joyce's delight, *Lives of the Twins* was promptly bought for $10,000, the typical advance for a first novel. "When it was accepted," she recalled, "I felt the same excitement as when my first book was published."

Among her own associates, Joyce at first told only Ray and her old friend Bob Phillips about the forthcoming novel; in January of 1987, she mentioned in a letter to another friend, the poet Jana Harris, that she had written, "in one 6-week burst of possibly misguided energy, a pseudonymous novel about identical [male] twins." In retrospect, Joyce would feel that telling anyone at all had been a mistake. Even if her secret had been kept, she had surely erred in her choice of a pseudonym: like the name under which she had published several short stories in the 1970s, "Rae-Jolene Smith," the new pseudonym, "Rosamond Smith," echoed the name of her husband, Raymond Smith. It seemed only a matter of time before the ruse was uncovered.

Unfortunately for Joyce, her authorship of the novel was made public even before the galleys went out for review. Her hope of obtaining a "fresh reading" from the critics had been dashed. The news of Joyce's pseudonym had been leaked to Liz Smith, who published the information in her column, and the story was quickly picked up by the *New York Times* and *Newsweek*. Reporters began calling, and a chastened Joyce told them that she had merely "wanted to escape from my own identity." Both Blanche Gregory and Joyce's Dutton editor, William Abrahams, were taken aback by the revelation: "I'm quite stunned at this piece of news," Abrahams told the *New York Times*. "I'm in an odd position since I'm her editor and I should know what she's doing."

Joyce found the episode, including the unwanted publicity, particularly disagreeable in that she suspected Bob Phillips as the source of the leak. The incident came close to ending their thirty-year friendship. On February 21, 1987, she wrote to Phillips in an accusatory tone, saying that "you were only one of four people who knew." She concluded by saying that she'd been "hurt; very upset" and was "not in the mood to write letters, or even, much, to receive them." For his part, Phillips insisted that he had not betrayed Joyce's confidence: "Under the circumstances, you can only trust me that I told no one about your secret." He pointed out that the press stories had included information he had not known—for example, the name of Joyce's new agent. "I realize your note says you're not much in the mood to receive letters—so forgive even this note," Phillips wrote. "I just wanted—had to—go on record saying I told absolutely *no one*. And I didn't." A short time later, Joyce suggested they put the issue behind them, and Phillips agreed. Joyce never found out who had revealed her pseudonym.

Once this disagreeable episode had ended, however, Joyce enjoyed using her pen name to pursue her fascination with the doppelgänger theme. In the summer of 1987 she produced another brief mystery, *You Can't Catch Me*, about a genteel Southern book collector who confronts his own dark side after he is repeatedly mistaken for a profligate womanizer. (Though the second Rosamond Smith novel in order of composition, *You Can't Catch Me* would not be published until 1995.) Only a few weeks later, in early October, she was plotting *Soul-Mate*, which she completed in February 1988. Published the following year, it dealt with a scrupulous, intelligent young woman who becomes romantically involved with a psychopathic killer.

Around the time she was writing *Soul-Mate*, Joyce conceived the idea for *Snake Eyes*, a fictional recasting of a highly publicized incident. In the late 1970s, Norman Mailer had become acquainted with a prisoner named Jack

Henry Abbott, a convicted killer who had corresponded with Mailer from his cell. Abbott's writing impressed Mailer to the extent that the novelist helped secure Abbott's release from prison; in 1981, Abbott published an auto-biographical book, *In the Belly of the Beast*, but shortly afterward committed another murder and was returned to prison. The combination of psychopa-thology and literary talent in the Mailer-Abbott situation was irresistible to Joyce. In June of 1988 she wrote to Mailer, asking for updated information about the case. "I can't think of the Abbott affair," she wrote, "as anything less than tragic, considering the man's brilliance, his astonishing sensitivity (and in what a context!), and your generosity in responding to it, only to have the mat-ter blow up in your face." She did not inform Mailer that she planned to base a novel on the situation, saying only that "I am so curious about the continuation of this story, which haunted me years ago and still does." A few months later, Joyce decided to put the Mailer-Abbott story aside, since the situation "seemed to me too complex & tragic to treat in any way glibly." But she took up the idea again in the fall of 1990, and by December reported that it was "absorbing nearly all of my waking hours." In *Snake Eyes*, published in 1992, Jack Henry Abbott became Lee Roy Sears, a murderer on death row who is ultimately paroled due to the efforts of the attorney Michael O'Meara, another of Joyce's idealistic intellectuals living in a Princeton-like community in New Jersey.

Another Rosamond Smith story based on an actual incident, and one that struck much closer to home, was *Nemesis*, the most gripping and fully realized of Joyce's pseudonymous novels. In the fall of 1988, the Princeton English de-partment had been stunned when a male graduate student accused Thomas McFarland, the department's world-renowned specialist in Romantic literature, of sexually assaulting him. Joyce's friend Elaine Showalter, then serving as di-rector of graduate studies, had given a beginning-of-term party for faculty and graduate students, and after the party McFarland had offered the graduate stu-dent a ride. They stopped for a nightcap at McFarland's secluded home, where the student later claimed that McFarland abused him physically and sexually throughout the night, then drove him home sometime after 6:00 A.M. (The tall, burly professor outweighed the student by approximately eighty pounds.) Later that day, the student informed Elaine Showalter and a Princeton dean, Aaron Lemonick, of what had happened, then wrote a detailed account of his ordeal; but he declined to press criminal charges. After the story circulated among members of the English department, a further controversy arose over McFarland's "punishment": a one-year suspension from the university. Mar-garet Doody, a specialist in eighteenth-century literature, led an English faculty protest against what she viewed as the university's lack of moral leadership: "some professors for a very long time," she told *New York* magazine, "have seen students as a box of chocolates for their delectation." When university officials announced that McFarland would be allowed to resume his teaching duties the following year, Doody and several other faculty members resigned—including Joyce's friend Emory Elliott, the department chairman.

Although Joyce did not speak to the press about the scandal, she privately expressed disgust over the incident. At first, Princeton officials and faculty alike had kept quiet, and Joyce reported to Bob Phillips that "a shocking cover-up" was in progress. When McFarland returned after his suspension, she said, "he'll be assigned freshman courses, since no graduate students will enroll in his seminars, so he'll have 18-year-olds under his tutelage. And this is the Ivy League." She told her friend John Reed that "the University is too worried about public opinion, a possible retaliatory lawsuit, and other legal problems to permanently discharge [McFarland]." Like her colleagues who were resigning, Joyce was disturbed by the larger moral issues involved: "Not that I am a prim, self-righteous sort of person really," she wrote in her journal, "but it seems to me so strange & so . . . sad . . . that the administration has put forth no moral leadership; absolutely none. Just silence." In July of 1989, after the scandal was reported in a long *New York* magazine piece, Joyce wrote to Elaine Showalter that "the case so shamefully reveals the predilection of institutions for protecting psychopaths—so long as the psychopaths are white male academics with tenure." She thought that the magazine article had actually been too kind to the university administration: "Not enough was made," she argued, "of the attempts of the university to cover up the scandal."

By the spring of 1989, Joyce had decided that Rosamond Smith, unlike the university administration, would not be silent. She worked at *Nemesis* with her usual doggedness, typing out more than 1,000 manuscript pages before reaching a satisfactory 300-page first draft. She had kept many of the details of the McFarland scandal intact and had cleverly worked in Margaret Doody's comment about students who are viewed as candy by rapacious professors: the fictional villain in *Nemesis* dies after he samples a box of poisoned chocolates sent to his office. (McFarland's fate was less dramatic: he simply took early retirement from the university.) When *Nemesis* appeared in the summer of 1990, the reaction from Princetonians was mixed. Logan Fox, proprietor of Princeton's Micawber Books, argued that "Joyce has used a very unfortunate incident to make a point, but as every novelist does, she uses her world." Even a university spokeswoman was "delighted by the play of intelligence on this issue. Someone put this unfortunate event to entertaining use." But, according to a Princeton reporter, the English department faculty "refused comment on the book," though acknowledging that "everyone was talking about it." One anonymous Princetonian was "irate that Joyce chose just to show one side of the incident."

Unlike Doody and the other professors who had resigned, Joyce had characteristically chosen to make her point through writing rather than direct action. Joyce herself had not considered resigning, but she noted that "If I didn't feel some affection and very real loyalty for a few individuals [. . .] I would surely stir up trouble here, not just apropos such cynical episodes as the McFarland case but others as well." She'd decided to "continue as I am, taking my teaching very seriously, and writing what I can; and enjoying some remarkable friendships."

Despite the minor stir caused by the publication of Nemesis, Joyce's pseudonym and the fact that the mystery genre made the novel appear, to some observers, merely "entertaining," helped keep any serious controversy from developing. "Having recently discovered the pleasure of using a pseud-onym," she wrote lightheartedly to John Ditsky, shortly after the novel ap-peared, "I almost wish I'd used one from the start." This remark reflected Joyce's ongoing ambivalence about the attention her novels received: while she enjoyed hearing from readers and getting recognition for her work, the ap-peal of invisibility remained strong. Her desire to deflect attention from her individual personality and onto her work had become increasingly frustrated as her fame grew. Although she had largely abandoned the intense mysticism of the early 1970s that had sought to transcend the historical self altogether, her "Rosamond Smith" experiment represented another of her periodic at-tempts to escape the delimiting, stereotypical views of her career that were re-peated so often in the press. Like her alter-ego Ian McCullough in American Appetites, Joyce knew that "we are all in disguise from one another and from ourselves, souls glimmering like phosphorescent fire, hidden in the opacity of flesh." Through her ongoing experimentation as an artist, Joyce continued to discover and reveal further dimensions of her selfhood even as she often sought, as a public figure, to create new and ever more skillful disguises.

The increasing complexity of Joyce's professional life—she now published regularly under two names and was writing numerous plays and screenplays in addition to her usual volumes of fiction, poetry, and criticism—prompted her to make a long-dreaded decision in 1989. She had been represented by Blanche Gregory's literary agency since the beginning of her career, but Blanche was now eighty-eight; she vacationed frequently in Maine and Florida, and seemed wholly out of touch with current publishing trends. Joyce's sense of loyalty was strong, but both her husband and her editor Billy Abrahams urged her to make a change. Gail Godwin had highly recom-mended John Hawkins, a prominent agent who had represented Gail for many years. "My main concern is with making longterm plans that would carry me well into the late 1990's," Joyce wrote to Blanche on October 26, 1989. In this detailed, thoughtful letter, Joyce informed Blanche that all contracts negotiated by her agency would remain in force, but that Hawkins would be representing her future books, beginning with *Heat and Other Stories*. "Please understand that I am very grateful for our long association," she wrote. "I hope that the transition will be smooth and without emotion on both sides though I realize it is difficult." Joyce later said that her decision had been reached after "a good deal of guilty pondering," and that it seemed "unbelievable that, after 25 years, I won't be working with her any longer." But, she reasoned, "probably I am making too much of a necessary decision."

Both Blanche and her associate Gert Bregman were devastated by the news. Gert described her reaction after Blanche showed her Joyce's letter: "Surprise is putting it mildly—shock would be more apt." Although Joyce had been disappointed with the book contracts Blanche had negotiated in recent years, she felt especially bad about ending her association with Gert. "I'm truly sorry to have left Blanche," Joyce wrote to Gert in December. "I think *you* did an excellent job over the years with my stories!" Between 1964 and 1989, Gert had sold 392 of Joyce's short stories—a Herculean task of mailing, record-keeping, and negotiating that Joyce had acknowledged gratefully. At the John Hawkins agency, Gert's job of handling the stories now fell to an energetic young agent named Sharon Friedman.

If Joyce's change to a new literary agency marked a significant transition in her professional life, another step she took that same year also represented a kind of milestone. For several years, various university libraries had approached Joyce about the possibility of establishing an archive to house her manuscripts and other papers. In June of 1989, a professional appraiser spent eight full days in Joyce and Ray's home, methodically going through the countless manuscripts, letters, and journal pages Joyce had retrieved from the mildew-prone crawl space under the house (where much of the material had been stored for years) and from various jam-packed closets. Although gathering all her papers together was an "exhausting task," she felt enormous relief after the material—thirty boxes of it—was finally carted away. Joyce had been astonished to contemplate the sheer labor that had gone into her many books: the appraiser informed her, for instance, that she had produced over three thousand manuscript pages before arriving at the 340-page final version of *American Appetites*. "This makes me think, 'Oh my God,' " she wrote, "but swallow hard and think, 'Well—it was worth it.' " The sale of Joyce's papers was handled by Andreas Brown of the Gotham Book Mart: although other universities made higher bids, Joyce ultimately decided that the archive should be placed with her alma mater, Syracuse University.

Changing literary agents and establishing her archive were decisions appropriate not only to her stature as a prominent woman of letters but also to a writer who had reached the age of fifty—a symbolic birthday she had negotiated much more successfully than Ian McCullough had done in *American Appetites*. Joyce's current literary standing had been amply acknowledged in the past few years by numerous awards: the $25,000 Rea Award for the Short Story; the McGovern Award (given by the Cosmos Club); the Bobst Award in Literature; and an award from the American Association of University Women. Some awards, like the prize she had won for "Tone Clusters," were for specific works: her collection of miniature narratives *The Assignation* had won the Alan Swallow award for fiction at the University of Denver. Although Joyce admitted that she had not previously heard of some of these awards before learning that she'd won them, she found the recognition gratifying nonetheless.

At times, the honors heaped upon her verged on the embarrassing: in May of 1987, she had been invited to Lockport, New York, to help celebrate "Flotilla Day," the ceremonial opening of a new lock of the Erie Barge Canal and the dedication of the Lockport Canal museum. May 9 was proclaimed "Joyce Carol Oates Day": Joyce and Ray, accompanied by Fred and Carolina, rode in the lead barge as the flotilla progressed through the canal. The event culminated with fireworks, a chicken barbecue, and the mayor's presenting Joyce with the key to the city. (Writing to Mike Keeley, Joyce said that she kept the key on her window sill. She asked, "What does one do with the key to the city of Lockport?") Other forms of recognition were more significant: Joyce was especially pleased when *Because It Is Bitter, And Because It Is My Heart* was nominated for the National Book Award in 1990—her first nomination for a major award in almost two decades. "Awards are so strange," she wrote in her journal on August 17, 1990. "Not receiving them, you feel neglected; receiving them, you feel embarrassed & a bit guilty."

Even as Joyce enjoyed the recognition her awards brought her, she was mentally preparing herself for the next major challenge of her career. Her recent one-act plays, screenplays, and other short projects had come in the wake of her exhausting effort on *Because It Is Bitter*, after which she did not feel ready to pursue another ambitious novel for an uncharacteristically long time. In the late summer of 1990, however, she began to experience "Fragmented, exhausting dreams. A story begins, but ends swiftly." It seemed that "In my sleep, I am trying to write something, and to write I have to 'envision' something, and the effort becomes snarled, frustrating." Her confused dreams resulted in the opening paragraph of the novel she called *Corky's Price*, focused on a middled-aged man named Jerome "Corky" Corcoran. "This 'Corky Corcoran,' " she wrote, "will be the hero (?) of my next (?) novel. If I can organize it, if I can find the voice, if I'm naive enough to begin." The title *Corky's Price* would be changed to *What I Lived For* by the time the novel appeared four years later. During those years, Joyce's most audacious and ambitious novel would dominate her creative life.

15

What She Lives For
1991–98

These "moments" we live for that, unknown to us, con-
stitute a life. "Quicksilver—then gone."
—*Journal*, October 31, 1993

How we return to what we haven't known we've lost.
—"Off-Season" (1996)

Offering a "final chapter" to the biography of any living writer, particularly one possessed of the unflagging energy and invention of Joyce Carol Oates, has the feel of an arbitrary, even presumptuous gesture. In fact, the preceding chapters, for all their length, required the biographer to adopt a highly selective, even summary approach to many of the major experiences, relationships, and achievements of this extraordinarily busy writer, and to leave out others altogether. Any conclusions to be drawn about an experimental artist, especially one whose next work is likely to resemble nothing she has written before, are necessarily tentative, and certainly temporary. Before taking a backward glance at six decades of her life, we should remember that after another ten years, after she has published another twenty books, a second such glance will almost certainly yield a new and startling perspective.

As Joyce enters her seventh decade, her phenomenal creative drive shows no signs of abating. Her increasingly various, protean activity inevitably hampers the biographer's duty to summarize a writer's achievement or to predict the ways in which her work will be valued by posterity. As Anne Tyler once remarked, "A hundred years from now, they'll laugh at us for taking [Joyce] for granted." The aspect of her work, still underacknowledged, that will perhaps come to define her achievement "a hundred years from now" is its relentless experimentation, its readiness to tailor fictional form and technique to the kaleidoscopically ever-shifting American reality. In her sixties and seventies, it seems likely that Joyce, confronted by the rapidly changing landscape of a new millennium, will employ her art in radical, surprising ways, much as her predecessor Henry James developed an experimental, proto-modern style as he, too, crossed the symbolic barrier into a new century.

James, in fact, again serves as the literary precursor whose career seems the most appropriate analogue to that of Joyce Carol Oates. Except for him, virtually all major American novelists who lived past the age of sixty failed to sustain the brilliance of their earlier careers. Twain, Wharton, Dreiser, Cather, Faulkner, Hemingway, Baldwin, Welty, and Bellow, to name only a few, published relatively weak books in their later years; even Melville's *Billy Budd*, a work produced when he was about seventy (and published posthumously), long after he had abandoned a literary career, seems only a coda to the spectacular achievements of his young manhood. But Joyce Carol Oates continues to live unhampered by the failing health, family distractions, and flagging inspiration that have bedeviled other great American writers. Biography is an historical, not a prophetic, art; but it seems safe to assume that Joyce Carol Oates's writing will adapt to America's changing social and psychological terrain, metamorphosing in bold, unpredictable ways. The longevity of her career and the sustained excellence of her writing, in fact, may come to be seen as the qualities that set her apart most dramatically from her peers in American fiction. Her most recent long novel, *We Were the Mulvaneys* (1996), is one of her major achievements, and it seems entirely possible that her finest novel remains yet to be written.

In retrospect, however, it is possible now to describe several distinct phases in her career and to suggest her significance within twentieth-century American literary culture. Her earliest work clearly arose from personal feelings of alienation: the novels and stories dealing with Eden County dramatized forcefully the rural world near Millersport, Lockport, and Buffalo, which Joyce escaped (physically, if not emotionally) through her academic and literary achievements. The next major phase, spanning the years 1968 to 1972, was shaped largely by her Detroit experience, which encouraged her development from a somewhat derivative, Faulkner-inspired mythmaker to a major social chronicler in the tradition of her early idols Balzac, Dostoevsky, Mann, and James. Many critics and anthologists still consider the major works of this period—the novels *them* (1969) and *Wonderland* (1971), the stories collected in *The Wheel of Love* (1970) and *Marriages and Infidelities* (1972)—to be the fiction by Joyce Carol Oates that is most likely to endure. Although she has not produced another novel with the hypnotic power of *them* or the sustained intensity of *Wonderland*, the remainder of the 1970s saw her expanding her Balzacian exploration of American culture into the arenas of the law, politics, religion, and academic life. Of these novels, *Do with Me What You Will* (1973) and *Son of the Morning* (1978) stand apart as major achievements, equally successful as social chronicles and as masterly innovations in the art of fiction.

The next major phase of Joyce's career can be considered only a partial success. Residing comfortably in Princeton since 1978, Joyce has lacked any significant conflict with her own environment, a situation that permitted the playful experimentation and, some might say, the self-indulgent excess of her postmodernist Gothic quintet of novels that began with *Bellefleur* (1980). Although *Bellefleur* remains her largest-selling novel to date—partly because it was the first book published, and expensively promoted, by a new publisher—her readership declined precipitously with the next two volumes of the quintet. Whereas *Bellefleur* represented a bold reinvention of literary Gothicism, the succeeding volumes with their unsympathetic, long-winded narrators tempted Joyce into writing books which, with their richness of allusion and artifice, were relished by academic specialists but not by the more general readership that for years had looked to Joyce for unflinching, fully engaged portrayals of the contemporary American reality. The remainder of the 1980s and the 1990s, therefore, have seen a return to realistic, multigenerational family sagas—*You Must Remember This* (1987) and *We Were the Mulvaneys* are clearly the finest of these—interspersed with more experimental, sui generis works such as *Black Water* (1992), *What I Lived For* (1994), and *Zombie* (1995).

Joyce's Princeton environment, as more than one of her friends has observed, has been valuable personally to Joyce but has not inspired her best fiction, which has always been generated by intense and usually violent conflict. The relatively weak *American Appetites* (1989), her only long Princeton-set novel, confirmed that Joyce's most powerful writing arises from scenes of social upheaval—the poverty and random violence of post-Depression upstate New York, the epochal unrest of Detroit in the 1960s—and not from a world of poetry readings and dinner parties. (Not surprisingly, her best Rosamond Smith novel, *Nemesis*, grew out of the atypical Princeton incident of a professor allegedly raping a student; with characteristic speed, Joyce had seized upon this violent event at once.) Almost inevitably, therefore, Joyce's recent books have taken their subject matter from her distant past; or have continued her playful engagement with literary tradition, as in the Gothic stories in *Haunted: Tales of the Grotesque*; or, following her long-established practice, have been drawn from the increasingly sensational headlines of our national newspapers, mythologizing such events as Chappaquiddick and the Jeffrey Dahmer case in allegorical renderings of our Bosch-like American garden of hellish delights.

Although fiction has remained the genre to which Joyce is most committed and in which she succeeds most consistently, the past decade has seen an expansion, rather than a contraction, of her literary activity. Most of her plays date from these years, and she remains actively engaged in the theater; despite her prediction in the 1970s that she would not produce further books of poetry, her recent volumes *The Time Traveler* (1989) and *Tenderness* (1996) represent a major developmental leap in her skill and confidence as a poet; her wide-ranging essays, many of them gathered in her 1988 collection, *(Woman) Writer: Occasions and Opportunities* and many more still uncollected, display her increased poise and authority as a critic, cultural observer, and memoirist; and she remains more willing than ever to venture into wholly new territory, as witnessed by her enthusiastic work with composer John Duffy on the opera libretto based on her short novel *Black Water* and by the several screenplays based on her novels (none of them yet produced) that she has written in recent years. She has also expanded her work as an editor, having recently contracted to edit a book of fairy tales, an anthology of stories based on mother-daughter relationships, and a textbook for creative writing students. Her recent activity has only confirmed John Updike's assessment, more than a decade ago, that "if the phrase 'woman of letters' existed, she would be, foremost in this country, entitled to it."

It should not be surprising that beginning in the late 1980s Joyce's journal and letters voiced with increasing frequency the complaint that her wide-ranging professional commitments and her ongoing work in numerous literary genres made for an uncomfortably hectic and "fragmented" life. The desired solution to the problem, characteristically, was not to take a rest but simply to focus her energy on a single, ambitious, obsessive project. More than ever before, the prospect of working intensively on a long, complex novel represented an emotional anchor, since the imaginative counterworld of a new book provided a long-term source of personal stability and artistic fulfillment. As Joyce aged, the invisible writer increasingly sustained the public figure to which the name "Joyce Carol Oates" was attached. But her early progress on the novel she would finally entitle *What I Lived For* recalled the frustrating, familiar pattern of composition that had marked her work on *Bellefleur* (1980), *Angel of Light* (1981), and *You Must Remember This*. These books had required months and sometimes years of tentative groping toward an appropriate "voice," and her new novel likewise had a vivid life in her imagination long before she discovered its unique structure, tone, and idiom. Several years later, after *What I Lived For* was published, she recalled having "passed many months in a state of anger with myself, for not being able to do what my vision instructed. I had a definite vision of the novel. I knew emotionally what it was, but I'd sit down to work and I just couldn't seem to get it."

So when she announced to John Updike, in the spring of 1991, that she'd been taking "a vacation from novel-writing," the emphasis was somewhat misleading. For Joyce, any sort of vacation was still an unhappy prospect, and she often felt anxious and out of sorts when lacking a focus for her extraordinary creative energy. For many years, she had used such interim periods to work in other, less complex genres, and now she turned again to short stories, reviews, and poems, easily "navigable" projects that could employ her time productively and pleasantly while she waited for Corky Corcoran's story to take shape.

Yet the literary activity that most captivated Joyce during this period was her new and unprecedented immersion in play writing. Given the savage reviews her earlier plays had received and her decision to abandon the genre, she had plunged into writing plays with surprising enthusiasm. In the summer of 1989, she had exclaimed: "Now drama fascinates me! The idea of 'drama.' The stage as a place of ceremonial exorcism; appearances & (magical) disappearances." She recognized that the plays for which she'd begun excitedly taking notes were unlikely to be "successful" in worldly terms: "Playwriting *is* the excursion into failure. Knowing this beforehand I feel oddly intrigued; exhilarated." She observed good-humoredly to Dan and Jeannie Halpern that "there is no more futile enterprise than writing a play (at least, a play with my name attached)." Her endeavor was particularly noncommercial in that Joyce preferred one-acts to full-length plays. Like short stories, one-acts "get immediately to the drama," she observed.

By the fall of 1989, Joyce had completed a "little triptych" of short plays she called In Darkest America. These one-acts featured her characteristic subject matter: "Tone Clusters" dealt with the parents of a young weight lifter accused of murdering a fourteen-year-old girl and focused especially on the American media's fascination with such crimes; "The Eclipse" explored the relationship between a feminist and her aging mother. After completing the plays, Joyce remembered a letter she'd received in 1988 from Michael Dixon, literary manager of the Actors Theatre in Louisville, Kentucky; he had offered to commission a play from Joyce, suggesting a payment of $25,000. Busy at the time with her fiction, Joyce had declined. But now she submitted her new one-act plays to Dixon and was delighted to learn that "Tone Clusters" had been chosen as a cowinner in a competition sponsored by the theatre called the National One-Act Play Contest. Both "Tone Clusters" and "The Eclipse" would be produced during the 14th Annual Humana Festival of New American Plays, to be held in Louisville in April of 1990. (Joyce had dropped a third one-act, "How Do You Like Your Meat?," from her original triptych because the manuscript had grown longer than she had anticipated.)

Joyce quickly became involved in the production: she attended actors' auditions in New York and traveled to Louisville for rehearsals. She enjoyed the "communal atmosphere" of the theater: "I soon became caught up in the enthusiasm," she remarked. The schedule was pleasantly hectic and kept her "(literally) running from my apartment building to the theater, early in the morning, late (11 o'clock) at night, a distance of about a half mile . . . somehow it reminded me of student days, years ago, when you're afoot, virtually always in a hurry." She returned to Louisville in March 1990 for previews, and again in April for the Festival itself. Ray, Fred, and Carolina came along for the event, accompanying Joyce to seven plays in a dizzying three-day visit. Joyce was delighted that her plays had sold out for the entire six-week run.

She later recalled her Louisville experience as a turning point: "I never had much experience being in the theatre and working at rehearsals. Louisville got me started at that." Her success there had inspired her to continue writing plays that winter and spring: "Have been writing plays, I should say miniature plays, for weeks," she noted in her journal. "My favorite form is a sort of collage: the organization being that of a book of short fictions or poetry." In the past, she'd had many "phases" during which she wrote numerous short stories, one after another, and now ideas for new plays came in a similar flood. "My head is filled with plays!" she wrote to one friend. Most of the work that appeared in her 1991 collection *Twelve Plays* was written during these months, and several of the plays were produced at small theatres around the country. "The Eclipse" was performed again in New York by the Ensemble Studio Theatre (although Joyce found this production disappointing) in May; "The Eclipse" and "How Do You Like Your Meat?," along with a newer play, "The Ballad of Love Canal," were produced, also in May, at the Long Wharf Theatre in New Haven, Connecticut; and a brief "collage-play" called "I Stand Before You Naked" was presented by the American Place Theatre in July. In June, Joyce's Hollywood agent received a call from Steven Spielberg's production company, offering to commission a new, original play. The payment of $25,000 was "a good deal better than nothing," Joyce wrote to Mike Keeley, "for which I'd assumed I'd been writing plays all summer." She sent Spielberg's representatives a dramatic version of her futuristic allegory "Family," a story in *Heat and Other Stories*.

Without quite having intended it, Joyce had embarked on an entirely new literary profession, one she would pursue energetically in the coming years. Though continuing to brood about and take notes for *What I Lived For*, she had found a happy diversion in this captivating new venture: "Instead of writing short stories and poems," she told Gene McNamara in February 1991,

"I seem to be writing short plays—most of them one-acts, and some as short as a single page." Within the next few years Joyce's new commitment to the theater, encouraged by the warm reception given to her work by producers and directors around the country, led her to attempt several full-length plays as well. She enjoyed the collaborative nature of playwriting; though she could not attend all the rehearsals and openings for the numerous productions of her plays during these years, she traveled to as many as her schedule allowed, finding the process of working with actors and directors a pleasant alternative to her solitary writing life at home.

Joyce and Ray flew to Los Angeles in January of 1991 for a production of "Tone Clusters" and another one-act, "The Key," which was based on a chapter of Joyce's 1979 novel *Cybele*. The Los Angeles Theatre Works "staged reading" featured well-known actors—Edward Asner, JoBeth Williams, and Joyce Van Patten—and both Joyce and Ray enjoyed the experience thoroughly. They stayed in a luxurious hotel on the Santa Monica beach; the weather was balmy, in stark contrast to the frigid weather they'd left in Princeton, and they rose early every morning and jogged for miles along the water. "We found it paradisical," she said. Later that month, they went to New York for an Actors Studio reading of Joyce's short play "Greensleeves," directed by Tom Palumbo, in preparation for the Studio's festival of one-acts. Joyce particularly enjoyed seeing Frank Corsaro, whom she found very little changed since their previous collaboration on her first play, *The Sweet Enemy*, almost thirty years earlier.

In early April, Joyce traveled again to New York for an Ensemble Studio Theatre production of her one-act "American Holiday," and the following week she visited the Long Wharf Theatre in New Haven for its production of four of her short plays, directed by Gordon Edelstein. She found the Long Wharf production stimulating: "I was quite dazzled by the experience," she wrote, "and must admit that I could scarcely sleep at all the following night. There is something about the theatre—at least, about opening nights—that makes even a person as usually unemotional as myself tense and apprehensive."

One aspect of playwriting Joyce found especially nerve-racking was the possibility of a humiliating public failure. In 1992, she allowed a new production of "The Key" and "Tone Clusters" (under the title *Two by Joyce Carol Oates*) to be presented at Princeton's McCarter Theatre, although she was acutely aware of the risks involved. Disappointing as a failure in Louisville or Los Angeles might have been, the idea of suffering a major embarrassment in Princeton caused her considerable anxiety. She worried that her decidedly noncommercial plays could not succeed in a large theatre like the McCarter, and she envisioned endless rows of empty seats on opening night. But to her surprise, the

1,100-seat theater was sold out weeks in advance, and the production—again starring Edward Asner and JoBeth Williams—was well received. Fred and Carolina journeyed from Millersport for opening night: "What pleasure, to have my parents present; and to know that they were having a great time," Joyce wrote in her journal. In addition, there had been "many friends and familiar faces; much excitement; and all went well."

Productions of her one-acts had quickly multiplied, and 1992 became a kind of annus mirabilis for her theatrical career. In March, Joyce and Ray again flew down to Louisville, which was including her recent play "Procedure" in a festival of one-acts: New York's Ensemble Studio Theatre produced her one-act "Gulf War" a few weeks later. Also produced that spring were "Tone Clusters," at Chicago's Baliwick Repertory Theatre and at New York's SoHo Repertory; "The Floating Birches," at Harvard's American Repertory Theatre; and her full-length play from the early 1970s, *Ontological Proof of My Existence*, at the "Best of the Bronx Festival" at Lehman Center. Joyce continued to attend as many productions as she could, finding them enjoyable, "convivial occasions." The highlight of the year came on September 21, when Joyce participated in a staged reading (again at the McCarter) of a new full-length play she had written, a comedy entitled *The Perfectionist*, directed by Loretta Greco. This reading was in preparation for the full production already scheduled for the fall of 1993, to be directed by Joyce's friend Emily Mann. Encouraged by all this activity, Joyce had continued throughout the year to work on new plays, an activity she called "the most quixotic of pasttimes!"

The "convivial" nature of theatre work was a major part of its attraction for Joyce. She developed warm friendships with many of the directors with whom she worked—especially Tom Palumbo, Gordon Edelstein, and Emily Mann—and found in playwriting a literary activity that could unite, at least briefly, the serious writer long accustomed to working in disciplined solitude and the gregarious Princetonian who enjoyed dinner parties and other social occasions. Even after she succeeded in beginning *What I Lived For* in mid-1992, she stayed actively involved in her theater productions and avidly took notes for new plays. One of her brief respites from work on the new novel was particularly enjoyable: in November she went to New York for a rehearsed reading of her full-length play *Black*, directed by Tom Palumbo in association with The Women's Project & Productions. The female lead in this play (which dealt with a romantic triangle composed of a white woman and two men, one white and one black) was Norris Church, the statuesque wife of Norman Mailer. Joyce considered all the actors "outstanding," and she was also favorably impressed by Palumbo's direction. As usual, Joyce stayed involved in the process of bringing her dramatic vision into focus: shortly after the reading of *Black*, she sent a detailed letter to Palumbo with script revisions and suggestions for small changes in the production.

Joyce attended another production of *Black* in June of 1993, when the play was included in the Contemporary American Play Festival in Shepherdstown, West Virginia; she also saw two performances of her short play "The Rehearsal" at the Ensemble Studio Theatre in New York. But the reception of her plays remained a major concern, especially that summer as Emily Mann was readying *The Perfectionist* for its full-scale production at the McCarter in October. Again Joyce worried that the play would not succeed: she felt "both excitement & apprehension for I must confess I don't want to be the agent for my own (public) embarrassment. Of 1100 seats, how many are going to be empty night after night . . . ?" Yet Joyce enjoyed working on the production, especially since a trusted friend was directing. "Emily Mann is an exciting and inspiring director," Joyce wrote. Throughout the production she relied on Mann's expertise and agreed to the director's suggested cuts and alterations, which included the elimination of an entire scene. ("I am the most agreeable of playwrights," Joyce declared. Whenever Mann made a suggestion, Joyce gave a standard reply: "Just do it.") Joyce was also impressed by the cast, which included David Selby in the title role, Betty Buckley, and a promising young actor named Josh Rubins. She felt immense relief when the play became "a 'fabulous' box office success, as they say." The show sold out entirely during several of its performances. A romantic comedy that satirized the upper-middle-class Princeton milieu, *The Perfectionist* pleased audiences in a way that "a 'serious' play of mine would not," Joyce observed. On the whole, she found the play "a truly extraordinary experience in my life: the two performances we attended with my parents [. . .], so many friends, colleagues, such a dazzling sequence of events—the play itself greeted w/much applause, and the actors, so fine, so spirited."

Although Joyce's plays received mixed reviews, the number of new productions increased rapidly during the early 1990s. By 1995, more than sixty separate productions of her work had been mounted in theatres throughout the United States, including the Guthrie in Minneapolis, the Los Angeles Theatre Works, and the Playwrights' Theater in East Hampton, New York. The plays also drew attention in Europe: "The Secret Mirror" was produced in Edinburgh, "The Eclipse" in Vienna and Stockholm; "I Stand Before You Naked" had successful runs in London and Paris. The French reviews were ecstatic, and predictably quirky: a critic for *L'Express* called Joyce "the Bette Davis of the American literary world."

To Joyce, the ever-expanding horizon of her theatrical writing partook of the same experimental impulse that underlay her fiction. Some of her plays were recognizably "Oatesian" in their themes of power and victimization and

in their willingness to treat controversial subject matter such as race relations, AIDS, and crimes of horrific violence. The very titles of some plays—
"Gulf War," "The Ballad of the Love Canal"—suggested that Joyce had
continued to fulfill her role as an American social chronicler. Although she
thought of herself as a novice playwright, her work already showed a marked
eagerness to explore a wide range of experimental techniques. "The more
one is around the theatre the more ideas one gets for the stage," she said; her
three decades of reading and teaching great dramatic works likewise fueled
her appreciation for the myriad forms of theatrical writing. Critics who expected Joyce Carol Oates only to write plays about the gravest of social and
psychological problems, however, were taken aback by her unexpected venture into romantic comedy. In a lengthy 1994 article in *American Theatre*
magazine, Laurence Shyer marveled that Joyce could produce a skillful example of this genre: "The whole enterprise was rather unlikely and discon-
certing . . . and no less surprising is how Oates mastered the rudiments of
Broadway light comedy without ever having seen one."

After her success with *The Perfectionist* at the McCarter, Joyce continued
writing new and amazingly disparate kinds of plays. By the end of 1993, her
satiric comedy *The Truth-Teller* had been presented at the Circle Rep in New
York, and she had become fascinated with a new manuscript based on
Thoreau. She called the play *The Passion of Henry David Thoreau* and hoped
to present "Thoreau as I truly imagine the man to have been, especially the
young headstrong impulsive man. To break through the cliche of the
recluse/crank/bachelor/'naturalist' to the man inside. Thoreau's passion was
to create his soul." She reread *Walden*, Thoreau's journals, and several biogra-
phies of the writer. After completing the manuscript in January 1994, she
called it "the most intimate & indeed passionate play I've done." She also
knew it was "arguably the least commercial play I've ever written. And, at 95
pages, it's too long." Only a few weeks later she completed another manuscript entitled *The Woman Who Laughed*. Immediately afterward, she observed in her journal, "my head is flooded with a half-dozen *almost coherently
formed* little plays." The ideas were "more copious & alarming than ever," she
added. "The very *form & idea* of the theater is almost overwhelming!"

That same month, Joyce's play *Bad Girls* (based, like many of her plays, on
a short story of the same title) was given a staged reading at the McCarter,
with Emily Mann again directing. "Was there ever so *gifted & sympathetic* a
director?" Joyce exclaimed. "How strange, to see one's imagined 'bad girls'
there on the stage!" The play had been given "life—mercurial & unpredictable." A few days later, Joyce wrote to a friend that she'd been "writing
plays, and thinking/dreaming of plays, continuously for some time. I've
stopped 'thinking' in prose—or whatever it is, writers do. Now it's visual

scenes, oral exchanges." In the *American Theatre* interview, Joyce remarked that writing plays and writing novels were entirely separate disciplines: "It's the difference between swimming and jogging. Both are exercises and can be very rewarding, but they use completely different muscles. The challenge of the theatre is to make the characters vivid enough to be alive on stage and carry the weight of the action. The prose narrative voice doesn't require this; you're telling a story."

Despite the encouragement Joyce had received from directors and producers, the major reviewers remained unsympathetic to Joyce's plays. In *New York* magazine, John Simon attacked *The Truth-Teller* with his trademark nastiness, claiming "this elephantine farce could have sunk the *Titanic* faster than any iceberg." Jeremy Gerard panned the play in *Variety*, insisting that "Oates doesn't have a clue about how to breathe life into any of these characters," and Vincent Canby in the *New York Times* issued the familiar complaint about Joyce's "prodigious output," suggesting that she "hasn't the time to realize that her view of America isn't unique, or that many of her one-liners are worn sitcom thin." Outside the cliquish New York theatre world, however, Joyce often enjoyed positive notices. Douglas J. Keating in *The Philadelphia Inquirer* found much to admire, for instance, in Joyce's one-acts collected under the title *Here She Is!*: several of them were written "perceptively and vividly, and those qualities are reflected in the performances by a fine cast." After a major production of *The Woman Who Laughed*, starring Lucie Arnaz, at the 380-seat Sharon Stage in Sharon, Connecticut, a local writer called the play (which dealt with an elementary schoolteacher accused of sexual abuse) "a modern tragicomedy" comparable to Arthur Miller's *The Crucible*.

Joyce had become accustomed to mixed reviews for her plays: "this is more or less expected, I guess, in the theater," she wrote, "where one is never reviewed by a fellow playwright or writer, as in the literary world." She continued to enjoy attending the productions and was pleased when *The Woman Who Laughed*, like *The Truth-Teller*, enjoyed several sell-out performances. Joyce had been skeptical about Arnaz's casting for the demanding lead, but found that the actress "was actually quite touching in the role and received enormous applause."

Joyce's playwriting remained a genre that she pursued not because her efforts brought the kind of critical attention and prizes given to her novels and stories, but simply for the satisfaction and pleasure of the work itself. Even though her plays seldom achieved the power or originality of her best fiction, they represented yet another example of her willingness to explore new and challenging artistic terrain. Like the critics, many of Joyce's literary friends considered her dramatic efforts a minor achievement in comparison to her fiction. As John L'Heureux put it, "she is a great short story writer and a great novelist. Her poetry is lesser work, as is her drama." Yet, as her close friend Dan Halpern observed, even Joyce's less successful work was necessary to her full self-expression as an artist, and she needed to maintain a high level of productivity in a variety of genres: "She's got to move along and get a lot accomplished and cover a lot of area," Halpern remarked. "I think partly her writing has improved because of the fact that she has written as much as she has." Clearly, Joyce is the kind of artist who must continually test her limits, and it seems likely that her fiction can only benefit from the discipline required by writing for the stage.

Despite Joyce's frenetic theatrical activity in the early 1990s, she had continued to meditate incessantly on her novel-in-embryo. Her middle-aged male protagonist, Corky Corcoran, fascinated her, though for the moment her energy, she observed in April 1991, "might be more sensibly diverted elsewhere, like plays/short stories. Poor Corky! I envision the man perpetually in motion, yet, oddly, frozen, awaiting life." She admitted to John Updike that for all her involvement in writing plays and movie scripts, she remained in thrall to the novel: "I must be like one of those people who are alcoholics forever, whether they drink again or not; I always feel like a novelist, though even the thought of writing one again, organizing all that data, fueling the engine, pushing a narrative forward as if constructing a ship in a glass bottle, leaves me feeling faint and anxious."

Since the novel remained stalled, Joyce took on some major editing assignments: she had agreed to serve as the guest editor for the annual Ticknor & Fields anthology *The Best American Essays*, and had begun reading for an even more ambitious project, *The Oxford Book of American Short Stories*. For the Oxford anthology, she hoped to include excellent but unfamiliar stories by major writers, rather than the standard pieces that had already been anthologized countless times: "I've discovered little-known, in fact unknown, stories by people like Stephen Crane, Mark Twain, Jack London, Edith Wharton," she told one friend. "The contemporary section will give me the most difficulty—there are simply too many good writers, all sorts of excellent 'emerging' minority writers, plus my old, good friends who can't *all* be included; but will not like being left out."

But such editing projects often became a source of disappointment and even, on a couple of occasions, of disillusionment with the ethics of the publishing world. She became furious that spring when the publisher of *Best American Essays*, the now-defunct Ticknor & Fields, began pressuring her to include the publisher's own authors in her anthology. "I'm feeling a bit doubtful about this project," she wrote to Robert Atwan, who was assisting her with the book. Balking at the " 'special pleading' on the behalf of Ticknor & Fields to push one of their writers at the expense of another writer," a notion that Joyce found "unethical," she added: "This development calls into question, in my mind at least, the integrity of previous volumes of *The Best American Essays*, which one would like to think were determined solely by the guest editors." An even more dismaying project came a few years later, when Norton asked Joyce to assist R. V. Cassill as coeditor for *The Norton Introduction to Short Fiction*. Joyce exchanged numerous letters with Cassill and with the Norton editor, Carol Hollar-Zwick, and she worked hard to select material according to deadlines set by Hollar-Zwick. But once Joyce's work was completed, Cassill abruptly decided that he wanted no coeditor, and Joyce was dismissed from the project. When Joyce's agent, John Hawkins, intervened, Hollar-Zwick advised him to consult a lawyer; but ultimately Norton offered Joyce an alternative project, an anthology to be called *Telling Stories: An Anthology for Writers*, which she would edit alone.

Even when her edited volumes did come to fruition, the response was seldom what she had anticipated: although her writer-friends whose work she had included in *The Oxford Book of American Short Stories* were sent gift copies, most of them failed to acknowledge Joyce's efforts or to thank her for including their work. The book "seems to have fallen into a chasm deep as the Grand Canyon!" she exclaimed. There were few reviews in the American press, though British reviews were more numerous, and generally positive. But the reviews of *The Best American Essays* were disappointing: "the publisher must be seriously contemplating asking me for my fee back," she wrote ruefully to John Updike.

By late spring, Joyce was noting that 1991 had become "a very busy and fragmented year." *What I Lived For* remained in the note-taking stage, but another, much briefer novel intruded upon her imagination almost without her intending it. In May she had worked at a short story based on the tragedy of Chappaquiddick; it had focused on the final desperate hours of Mary Jo Kopechne. On May 27, she recorded her "delirious immersion in a story called 'Black Water.' The minutes/moments before death by drowning. [. . .] And, writing it, living it, I felt, yes, this is it, I know this is it, how horrible. The violation of the young woman's faith, too—in this unnamed masculine presence, so 'charismatic.' "

Writing the short story had proved such a powerful emotional experience that an ample treatment seemed necessary. For the next six weeks Joyce remained "immersed" in work on a 105-page manuscript, a novella designed to be read in two hours: exactly the length of time her heroine, Kelly Kelleher, stays alive after an unnamed "Senator" drunkenly crashes their car through a guardrail and into a ravine. Joyce had been fascinated by Chappaquiddick and had wanted to write such a story for years. The recent trial and acquittal on rape charges of William Kennedy Smith, along with the resignation of the liberal Justice Thurgood Marshall from the Supreme Court—events that seemed to symbolize the end of an era—impelled her to tackle this painful and controversial material. "I feel as if I have just emerged from a sustained horror/trauma," she wrote on July 7, after "several weeks of writing a short novel suggested by—but, as it turns out, very different from—the Chappaquiddick incident." Like so much of Joyce's work, *Black Water* had its genesis in a sense of moral outrage: "It's infuriating," she wrote, "when Ted Kennedy repeatedly refers to the incident as a 'tragic accident'—it was an accident that, while drunk, he drove a car into the water, but it was no accident that he allowed his passenger to drown. Imagine—he didn't report the accident for nine hours. Yet he wasn't charged with anything except leaving the scene."

Joyce assumed initially that her use of the novella form would preclude any commercial possibilities for the manuscript; she intended to send *Black Water* to a small publisher, as she'd done with her other recent novellas *I Lock My Door Upon Myself* and *The Rise of Life on Earth*. She sent a copy to her Dutton editor, Billy Abrahams, primarily as "a courtesy," but Abrahams loved the novel: "It just tore me apart," he said. "To me it was an amazing work of art, a masterwork." He wanted to publish *Black Water* as Joyce's next Dutton novel. (Joyce had earlier decided that the long-delayed fourth installment of her Gothic quintet, *The Crosswicks Horror*, should be published next.) Contrary to Joyce's initial expectations, her new agent, John Hawkins, saw enormous commercial potential in *Black Water*, partly because of its controversial subject matter, and decided to show the manuscript to several other publishers. "I was in terror of having to switch to another house," Joyce recalled. "The prospect of leaving Billy Abrahams was not a very pleasant one." But Hawkins's maneuvers resulted in Joyce's receiving three times the advance Dutton had originally offered. By January 1992, anticipating publication in May, the publisher was planning Joyce's lengthy book-signing tour for the short novel, the most extensive promotional effort yet undertaken for one of her books. Dutton had decided on an ambitious first printing of fifty thousand copies.

After she completed the tour, Joyce's life again took on the "fragmented" quality she had noted earlier in the year. Some of her distractions were less than pleasant. In July, she had been angered by a letter published in the *New York Times* by Joseph Epstein, editor of *The American Scholar*. Epstein had protested the encroachment of "political correctness" after being criticized for comparing feminists, in an essay published in *The Hudson Review*, to "pit bulls" and to "a wildly garish lesbian motorcycle club" known as "Dykes on

Bikes." Joyce found Epstein's remarks sexist and homophobic, and responded in a letter to the *Times* published on August 13 under the heading " 'Can't Take a Joke?' the Bigot Asks." Joyce pointed out that "the objects of bigotry do not commonly laugh at jokes made to humiliate them," noting that "Epstein speaks to those who find the comparison of feminists and pit bulls amusing, and the mere allusion to Dykes on Bikes hilarious." She saw such "humor" as "aggression, hatred and the wish to do harm," and insisted that because *The American Scholar* was the official journal of Phi Beta Kappa, which honors academic merit, "it is an embarrassment that Joseph Epstein should have been its editor for so many years. His resignation is long overdue."

After Joyce's remarks appeared, she received numerous supportive letters applauding her stand against Epstein. About half of the letters were from gay men. Epstein was notorious, Joyce recalled, for having stated publicly "that he would rather his son be dead than a homosexual. (Which means what, exactly? That all homosexuals should commit suicide?) The inexplicable cruelty of some presumably 'intellectual' people of our time is amazing." Those writing supportive letters included the prominent literary critics Richard Poirier and Edward Said. "My letter to the Times was written so quickly, with such anger and disgust, I dreaded actually seeing it in print," Joyce remarked to Said. "I'm glad it struck a chord with you and Dick Poirier, among kindred others."

In August, there were further distractions: for the first time in her life, Joyce had been called for jury duty. A Trenton drug dealer had been accused of assault against a woman he believed had informed on him (he was convicted of simple assault). Ever since the days when, as a college student, Joyce had observed courtroom proceedings in Lockport, she had wanted to serve on a jury. She found the experience both fascinating and exasperating. In her essay about the trial, "I, the Juror," Joyce wrote that she had viewed jury duty "as a privilege, very likely an adventure." She was pleased, too, that "it was 'Joyce C. Smith' and not 'Joyce Carol Oates' who had been called. Rare for me now, thus the more precious, any public experience in which I can be invisible, as if bodiless: that fundamental necessity for the writer." Yet her patience was tested by the frequent periods of waiting that jury service entailed and by the general slowness of the proceedings. At one point, Joyce began pacing in the basement holding area, "tracing elongated figure eights in the corridors, with a hope of forestalling early glimmerings of panic." When called into the courtroom, she identified herself as "a housewife and teacher." She knew that Princeton professors and artists were routinely dismissed by prosecuting attorneys for their presumed liberal bias.

The trial itself was often numbingly repetitious. There were only five witnesses, but the proceedings dragged on for several days. Joyce greatly admired the knowledge and professionalism of the judge, Judith Yaskin, but she was less impressed by her fellow jurors, who were, she wrote tactfully, "not thoughtful people; they were not, in a way, serious people." While sequestered in the jury room, Joyce noted in dismay, "most of the jurors chatted and laughed as if there were nothing much of import going on." Joyce's jury service was especially difficult in that she was suffering from a painfully infected finger, which required two minor surgeries during the trial, along with a regimen of antibiotics and prescription painkillers. "There were moments during the defense attorney's repetitive closing remarks when I was in terror of nodding off," she confessed in a letter to Judge Yaskin, "but I never actually did, and feel, now, tremendous relief." In retrospect, Joyce decided she was "grateful for my experience as a juror in Trenton, New Jersey, though it is not one I am eager to repeat." She noted wryly that she and her fellow jurors were paid five dollars per day for their service—"which, considering the contribution we made, seems about right."

Back at home, Joyce resumed her usual writing schedule, though the still-inflamed finger badly hampered her typing. She continued to work at short projects: since early in the summer, before the brief interlude that produced *Black Water*, she had been writing a group of short stories in the Gothic mode. Some of these began appearing in anthologies devoted to horror fiction with titles like *Meta-Horror* and *Sisters in Crime*; one story—under her pseudonym "Rosamond Smith"—even appeared in the pulp magazine *Ellery Queen's Mystery Magazine*. (Joyce gamely agreed to pose for the issue's cover photograph, holding a mask to symbolize her dual identity as Oates/Smith.) Other Gothic fabulations appeared in literary journals, like her reworking of Henry James's *The Turn of the Screw* called "Accursed Inhabitants of the House of Bly," published in *The Antioch Review*. (This was Joyce's second postmodernist "take" on James's tale, after her own story entitled "The Turn of the Screw," which had been collected more than two decades earlier in *Marriages and Infidelities*.) Many of Joyce's new stories were in what she called the "surreal mode," which she found "imaginatively stimulating and haunting. There is a theory that dreams are really generated by images, and that the stories or narratives are invented to contain the images; in horror fiction, this dominance of the image seems incontestable, relating the genre most vividly to the mysterious process of dreams."

Like *Bellefleur* and her other Gothic novels, this group of short stories—which would be published in 1993 under the title *Haunted: Tales of the Grotesque*—represented Joyce's periodic yearning to slip free of the constraints of realism. In a letter to Stephen King, she explained the process: "What so powerfully attracts me to the mode I call surreal—'Gothic,' 'horror,' 'psychological suspense,' 'dark fantasy,' whatever its somehow not helpful names—is the bold transposing of the 'real' into metaphor; the metaphor made 'real.' " By the end of the year, she had again assumed her pseudony-mous identity for work on a sixth Rosamond Smith novel, which had its gene-sis in her experience as a juror in Trenton. "I'd been intrigued by the title *Double Delight* (which refers to perhaps the most exquisitely beautiful hybrid tea rose I've ever seen)," she noted on December 28. "Rosamond is obsessively writing that, at the moment." (The novel appeared in 1997.)

During the early months of 1992, Joyce had more time than usual for her writing, since the university had granted her a paid leave for the spring se-mester. But there were other obligations: the Cosby Bureau had scheduled her for five readings in various parts of the country, and her ambitious tour for *Black Water* would begin on April 28. Although Joyce was now a practiced lecturer and continued to enjoy her visits to college campuses, the vicissi-tudes of travel could be trying. One of her worst trips came on January 30, when she was scheduled to speak at Auburn University in Alabama. She was booked on two separate flights, both of which were late, as was the limousine driver scheduled to meet her in Atlanta. "You can't imagine the desperation one feels," Joyce wrote, "arriving already late for an engagement, with no limo pickup in sight." As a result, Joyce missed a three o'clock class she was scheduled to visit, and arrived at the auditorium for her four o'clock public appearance, breathless and distracted, just two minutes ahead of time. Al-though her fee for the Auburn visit was $9,300, she noted that "I don't need the money, and in terms of stress, no money is worth it." As if the travel prob-lems weren't difficult enough, the jinxed Auburn trip had a dismaying con-clusion that seemed, in retrospect, almost comical: Joyce had read from her poetry, which went well enough, and had then followed the usual routine of signing books and attending a reception and dinner in her honor. But at the end of the evening, the professor who had organized the event approached her and remarked on the poetry reading Joyce had given: "We were so de-lighted to have you here, Miss Oates, but you know—this is a lecture series. The subject is 'the cultural effect of World War II.' " The booking had been scheduled more than a year earlier, and Joyce had forgotten that a special topic was involved. She then had a "dim recollection," she confessed in a let-ter to John Updike, that her booking agent had informed her of the topic. Chagrined, she "returned home the next day, and probably should not go anywhere ever again," she added. "I suggested that Auburn University invite you down; you'd surely do a more creditable job."

The grueling eighteen-day publicity tour Joyce had undertaken for *Black Water* in April 1992 achieved its aim: the novel reached the *Publishers Weekly* best-seller list, in addition to other lists in cities she had visited. The book was "selling better than any novel of mine since *Bellefleur*," she observed, "and, unlike *Bellefleur*, it's a novel people might actually finish if they pick it up." The book was also a critical success. In the *Los Angeles Times*, Richard Eder wrote that Oates had written "the ballad of Chappaquiddick. She has done it with startling success, without a lapse." Richard Bausch, writing in *The New York Times Book Review*, proclaimed that the novel was "as audacious as anything I know in recent fiction. . . . Taut, powerfully imagined and beautifully written, *Black Water* ranks with the best of Joyce Carol Oates's already long list of distinguished achievements." Among the major reviews, only Michiko Kakutani's in the daily *New York Times* was wholly negative: "for all its literary pretensions," Kakutani wrote, "*Black Water* is simply the latest example of 'faction,' an unfortunate genre of writing that evades the responsibilities of both history and fiction." The near-unanimous acclaim for this short novel Joyce had "never thought anyone would even notice" culminated in a nomination for the Pulitzer Prize in fiction.

Heartened, Joyce now returned to the material she had accumulated for *What I Lived For*. While waiting for the novel to jell, she had completed her new Rosamond Smith novel, *Double Delight*, and had also written the screenplay for her earlier Smith novel *Snake Eyes*; she had been paid $135,000 for the latter project and was pleasantly amazed that the Hollywood producers had "thrown so much money at me." Such commercial success hardly compensated, however, for her frustrating lack of progress with Corky Corcoran's story. For more than two years, the materials had remained intransigent, and she had now accumulated more than a thousand pages of notes, outlines, and brief scenes. The process of feeling her way into the novel, she observed in her journal, was like "dowsing, isn't it, yet without a dowsing rod / just really groping / tuning / for to choose the first sentence is to choose Corky's inner voice, the voice of the novel that looms up, in my imagination, far too large I suppose, partly because I have been carrying it about for so long now, uncertain or timorous of beginning."

Only gradually, as the summer wore on, did Joyce begin to feel the familiar "obsessive undertow" pulling her into the imaginative world of the novel; soon she was feeling the need "to break from it periodically, and to turn my thoughts elsewhere." By September she had produced 270 pages of a first draft and at last felt confident that she had found the narrative voice she had been seeking. As had happened with many of her earlier projects, her progress accelerated rapidly as her confidence grew. For the next six months, despite numerous distractions, she concentrated intently on the manuscript. In January 1993, she reported to John Updike that she had written 600 pages. "My new novel grows," she told him, "if not blossoms, like an immense bog,

devouring everything in sight." On March 20, the manuscript was complete
at 820 pages. "It seems impossible: I've finished," she wrote in her journal.
She then recalled the process of writing the novel, one she had repeated
often but that had proved especially exhausting this time, since the book was
so ambitious:

> First, the immersion to the point of obsession; the excitement in
> the work & anxiety when away from it; the sense of an irresistible
> forward-motion that both mimics and *is* the motion of Time. Then,
> afterward, a sense of profound loss & melancholy that is the loss of a
> *voice*—in this case Corky's voice, which seems to me somehow real
> & valid & even permanent apart from my invention. And then, the
> fear that nothing will ever mean quite so much again.

She concluded with a vow she had made often after completing a long project, and had many times broken: "this should be my last long novel. The effort was really exhausting." In an interview, she stressed the difficulty of this
project, recalling that "the quality of my life at that time was actually affected. I would be very depressed and despondent for days. I just don't want
to live that way anymore."

Already Joyce was pondering the reception her unusual story might receive. Having explored in such detail the consciousness of a crude, sexist, alcoholic man, she knew that there were "any number of people who would
detest him." Yet the character of Corky Corcoran represented the culmina-
tion of a particular skill Joyce had always possessed: the ability to occupy
convincingly the mind of a character who seemed—on the surface, at least—
wholly unlike herself. This time she had found the process of intuitive identification both exhilarating and surprising: "Immersed in Corky as I am," she
had observed as she neared completion of the manuscript, "I'm yet continually surprised by him—the swing of his mind, the absurdity of his 'insights.'
He's a fictional character yet I have absolute confidence that, in numberless
men, he exists." Male readers of *What I Lived For* would testify to the fidelity
with which Joyce replicated the thought processes and emotions of a man
like Corky. Not the least admiring reader was her editor, Billy Abrahams, who
considered the novel one of Joyce's finest achievements. "It is astounding,"
he said. "I don't know how she *knows* the things she knows, how she *does*
this." Joyce later recorded in her journal that "Billy, and others at Dutton, say
that this is my 'best' novel."

Like much of Joyce's recent work, *What I Lived For* represented a formal
experiment. She had abandoned her typical method of spanning many years
of her characters' experiences, focusing this immense novel on a mere four

days: the long Memorial Day weekend of 1992. This strategy contributed to the difficulty of composition, since the book, she said, was like "a great jigsaw puzzle": "Everything is interlocked, so that almost every sentence, and certainly every paragraph, hooks into other points of the novel." But by compressing the action so severely, offering a minute-by-minute rendition of Corky's thoughts, feelings, and experiences, Joyce was able to employ the kind of intensive psychological realism that characterized much of her best work, thereby dramatically evoking the passion, the relentless conflict, and the sheer energy of Corky's mental and physical life. Although the novel detailed Corky's romantic adventures, it also explored his traumatic family history and delved into his complex business and political dealings. In its larger contours, his story represented a powerful indictment of American culture, especially in its superficial vulgarity, its confusion of love and money, and its preoccupations with sex, material possessions, and social status. Corky Corcoran, who confesses that he is "not a guy comfortable inside his own head," suggested in many ways a typical male participant in this culture, an American everyman.

Yet *What I Lived For*, like her more recognizably autobiographical works of this period, also partook of Joyce's interest in lovingly re-creating the world of her own early life, following the example of James Joyce's *Ulysses* (to which she alluded throughout the novel), which had been written partly to memorialize Dublin at a particular historical moment. (It is surely no accident that the novel revolves around "Memorial Day.") Corky's urban environment, which Joyce calls "Union City," depends heavily on Joyce's early memories of Buffalo and Lockport. Corky's Irish identity also suggests a kinship: like Frederic Oates's ancestors, Corky's family emigrated from Ireland in the 1880s, and in middle age he feels out of place, despite his own success, in the elite, wealthy circles in which he now moves, recalling Joyce's own lack of identification with her Princeton environment.

But the novel was autobiographical in a more personal way: the similarities of Corky's sensibility to that of his creator are at least as striking as the more obvious differences. Joyce admitted that she viewed Jerome Corcoran as a kind of "brother"; she not only gave him her own initials but also referred to him in her journals and letters with the same affection she had expressed toward earlier male soul mates such as Jules in *them* and Jesse in *Wonderland*. Corky Corcoran is exactly Joyce's height, five feet nine; like her, he suffers from insomnia; he has a short-term photographic memory and a fast metabolism, so that he "never gained weight"; and in his conflicts with others, he considers himself a "counterpuncher," a word Joyce often used to describe herself. Not surprisingly, Corky also loves to "tell tales," and despite viewing women as "used kleenex," he is a liberal Democrat who sides with Anita Hill over Justice Clarence Thomas. Apart from his active involvement in Union City politics and business, he also shares Joyce's yearning for invisibility, spending time in a private "shadow-office" that he rents secretly; not even his trusted secretary knows its location. Corky relishes the hours he spends in the shadow-office because "nobody knows where he is." Even his penchant for reading mirrors Joyce's own, especially his fascination with science and the origins of the universe: "I read literature on these subjects continuously," Joyce observed, "and a number of the tiles Corky mentions are in fact part of my library."

As in other major novels, Joyce also used minor characters to express facets of her own temperament and experience. Corky's stepdaughter, Thalia, is a strong-willed anorexic who—like Shelley in *Wonderland*, Marianne in *We Were the Mulvaneys*, and Ingrid in *Man Crazy*—becomes in her emaciated physical body a deliberate, stubborn emblem of the emotional malnourishment she endured as a young girl. Like the earlier characters, she has transformed herself into a childlike, near-genderless person, cutting off her hair so that people "had to look twice to see was she a young woman, or a precocious boy." While at college she suffers a breakdown and is hospitalized, leaving her parents "shocked to see what Thalia had become—flat and wasted and deathly-white as an Auschwitz victim, a girl of twenty whose normal weight was 115 pounds (and this too, the doctor told them, was low) now weighing, even with the fluids pumped into her, 89 pounds."

Joyce's highly sexed protagonist, Corky, copes throughout the novel with his uneasy sexual attraction to his stepdaughter, a situation recalling numerous other incestuous relationships (often combined with rape and other abuse) in Joyce's fiction: the cousins Duncan and Antonia in *A Sentimental Education* (1980), the niece Enid and uncle Felix in *You Must Remember This* (1987), the cousins Jared and Josie in *First Love* (1996). Thalia is especially notable among this group of characters for the degree to which she rebels against her female role, even taunting Corky by luring him to her apartment and then slipping away after Corky has become sexually excited. Thalia's mother, Charlotte, also experiences Thalia's contrary, seemingly "unnatural" rebellion: "I'm so *exhausted*," she tells Corky, "with being a mother to a girl who refuses to be a daughter!" Like Joyce and many of her other characters, Thalia once rejected a doll she received as a gift, pointedly spurning the idea of her own potential motherhood.

Not surprisingly, Joyce concluded *What I Lived For* with a typically dramatic climax: Thalia, having stolen a gun from Corky (thus appropriating his male potency and predisposition to violent action), shoots him several times during a confused moment when she is seeking vengeance for a friend who has been raped and murdered. The scene suggests the sexual dynamic informing so much of Joyce's work: female vengeance against sexually predatory males. Powerful male figures in her novels, from Shar in *With Shuddering Fall* to Felix in *You Must Remember This* to Corky, are ultimately defeated by their own violent impulses, while female characters are left traumatized by passion, retreating into various forms of therapy and recuperation. Whether they seek direct retaliation, like Thalia and the Foxfire girls, or simply attempt to "draw out the poison" through self-examination and narrative reenactment, the pattern is essentially the same. Although rightfully praised for its verisimilitude in treating characters and themes seemingly removed from the author's own experience, *What I Lived For* also formed part of Joyce's ongoing obsession with her own geographical background and with her most personal and agonizing themes.

The distractions that occasionally had interrupted Joyce's work on *What I Lived For* were primarily agreeable ones. In the fall of 1992, she worked intermittently on the libretto based on *Black Water*, for which the composer John Duffy—affiliated with the American Musical Theatre in Philadelphia—was writing operatic music that Joyce found "ravishing." In early October, she had suffered through the annual ritual of media inquiries about the Nobel Prize for literature: once again she was rumored to be "on the short list." Before the winner was announced—it was Derek Walcott—she slept through the night, which she considered "a sign that I knew I would not win." (In the eastern standard time zone, news of the prize typically came in the predawn hours.) As usual, she was relieved that the tension of waiting, exacerbated by the usual flurry of phone calls from newspaper and television reporters, had come to an end.

In late October, Joyce and Ray made a promotional trip to Europe for *Black Water*, spending a total of twelve days in London and Paris. Joyce had not looked forward to the trip, with *What I Lived For* "weighing like cement on my chest," but she was impressed by the quality of the journalists and critics who interviewed her. She appeared on the French literary interview program *Caractères* and afterward was frequently recognized on the street and in the hotel: "how true it is," she observed in her journal, "that Parisiens respect those whom they perceive to be 'intellectuals.'" She told John Updike that "in the interstices of being asked how I write so much, why it's so violent, and so forth, we saw plays and museums and walked in the rain." On the whole Joyce found the trip delightful, partly due to the hospitality of her publishers, Macmillan in England and Stock in France: "they treated Ray and me so elegantly," she reported to Bob Phillips, "and put us up at lovely hotels out of all proportion to my obvious commercial worth as a writer." Joyce and

Ray made a point of returning home on November 2, in time to vote in the presidential election: she and Ray were "ecstatic" over Clinton's victory.

After Joyce completed *What I Lived For*, she had more time for socializing and for enjoying Princeton's stimulating intellectual environment. One of the contemporary writers she most admired, Robert Stone, visited the university in April, and Joyce attended a dinner given by Dan and Jeannie Halpern for Stone and his wife, Janice. Joyce was intrigued by Stone, whom she found "one of the most wildly/surrealistically funny people I've met." She considered him "a true talent, remarkably gifted & serious. There's hardly a line of his that doesn't ring with power." Stone had long appreciated Joyce's generosity to other writers, recalling that she had written him a letter praising his first novel, *A Hall of Mirrors*, in 1967. "I was very grateful to her," Stone recalled. "She was well known at that time and I was completely unknown." Through the years Joyce had "often sent me a note when she has liked something I've written." Stone was equally admiring of Joyce's work, especially *Wonderland*: he found its opening chapters "extraordinary," able to withstand comparison with "the best books ever written." By the 1990s, Stone considered Joyce an underrated writer: "I think she is a wonderful American realist," he remarked, particularly in her use of "realism that deals with American urban conditions in a clear-eyed and unsentimental way. It seems to me that nobody does it better."

Joyce socialized with other celebrated writers that spring. She and Ray gave one of their ambitious dinner parties in late April, with a guest list that included Toni Morrison and Mario Vargas Llosa, along with her university friends Russell Banks, Mike Keeley, and Sally and Jerry Goodman. She also attended dinner parties given that month for visiting writers Margaret Atwood and Jane Smiley. In her work life, Joyce had resumed the various professional activities that usually followed intensive concentration on a novel. Shortly after Robert Stone's visit, she was readying the manuscript of *Haunted: Tales of the Grotesque* for publication and thinking ahead to new projects. Noting the sense of "extraordinary freedom" she felt after finishing the novel, she wrote on April 13 that "even my dreams seem affected. And the excitement of being open to new work, new ideas and voices . . . its remarkable. All the world seems open!" And two weeks later: "So many ideas for stories! plays! flooding my head, since I've completed [*What I Lived For*]. It's amazing. It's dismaying— I'll never live to execute one-tenth of these promising gems. One-tenth—more like one-one hundredth."

Joyce was already preparing for another overseas excursion: she had agreed once again to participate in a tour sponsored by the U.S. Information Agency, her first since the arduous six-week trip to Eastern Europe in 1980. Although her May 1993 tour was considerably shorter at eighteen days, it was similarly ambitious. The itinerary included Spain, Italy, and Portugal; Joyce gave a total of thirteen lectures and readings, and participated in countless interviews, receptions, and ceremonial luncheons and dinners. She had her usual difficulties with insomnia (she used the sleepless hours to reread Thomas Mann's *Buddenbrooks*) and complained of "so many people, in so brief a space of time! And everyone wincing, hearing my schedule—how can you see Lisbon in one day? Milan in one afternoon? Palermo/Sicily in one day? Rome in two? Madrid in one afternoon & evening?" There were other problems: "these countries are too attractive to tourists, & overwhelmed with motorcycle/auto pollution, industrial development. The time to have visited them was probably 30 years ago." She and Ray were especially dismayed by Naples, which she found "one of the least attractive, graffiti-defaced cities we've ever visited." In Milan, she experienced the usual sense of unreality that attached to her identity as "Joyce Carol Oates," enduring a "preposterous introduction" before one of her lectures: "I sat there, as I had in Rome, staring into space as superlatives washed about me. *These people think I'm an immensely famous & successful American writer*. It all seems remote, improbable; comic."

Yet the trip had its pleasant moments: in Barcelona, where she helped promote the newly published Spanish translation of *Black Water* (*Aqua Negra*), she and Ray stayed at the five-star Meridian Hotel and visited museums featuring exhibits of work by Picasso and Miró. She found the countryside near the city "visually ravishing." In Granada, she took in "extraordinary sights— the Arabic architecture, the Alhambra, a luncheon ('in my honor') in a cliffside restaurant overlooking some of the stately buildings & walls of the Alhambra." She found Madrid a "beautiful, cosmopolitan city; *very* busy"; she gave an informal lecture on multiculturalism in America at Complutense University, an enormous campus serving 135,000 students. She also enjoyed visiting Portugal for the first time, having used the country as a setting for her 1975 collection of stories, *The Poisoned Kiss*. But she and Ray found Lisbon "not at all what we'd expected. Old, uniformly gray weatherworn buildings; a lustreless, anonymous 'downtown'; much construction; an undistinguished harbor & waterfront; miles of dreary city. . . . What a surprise! My romantic Lisbon!"

Although Joyce returned home to Princeton with a sense of relief, she and Ray left again, on July 22, for a leisurely car trip that included visits to Detroit and Windsor, where she saw her former academic colleagues and took sentimental journeys through her old neighborhoods; and to Lockport and Millersport, where she visited with her parents and her brother. These visits only intensified Joyce's recent tendency to ruminate about the distant past and to

imagine ways of dramatizing her memories in fictional terms. She particularly enjoyed visiting with her brother, Fred Jr., during her stay in Millersport.
Although they had never enjoyed a close relationship, she now observed that
Fred was "really *very* nice, intelligent, inquisitive" and exclaimed: "How little
I know my 'young' brother—my 'kid' brother, 49 yrs. old! Amazing." She considered his work in computer programming and design "most advanced &
imaginative."

While in Lockport, she also recalled a family member to whom she had
been much closer: she visited her Grandmother Woodside's former home
near the corner of Grand Street and Transit Road, noting that despite some
renovation to the houses, the neighborhood remained largely unchanged.
She wrote: "what emotional impact! I shut my eyes, imagine entering, ascending the stairs—the living room, the kitchen . . . (Ascending into what,
precisely? Mystery? Revelation? An old, lost child-self?)" Describing to John
Updike the poignant Lockport visit, she observed that "all the great, grave,
unanswerable questions (why are we here, what does it all mean, where is the
edge of the universe) I'd tormented myself with as a young adolescent still
wait for me in this somewhat melancholy city." By contrast, "how relatively
unreal and insignificant Princeton (where everyone is from somewhere else)
seems!" Not surprisingly, her next two novels, *We Were the Mulvaneys* and
Man Crazy, would focus not on her present life (which she had dramatized in
American Appetites) but would continue her relentless exploration of her
childhood world.

Only a week after returning from upstate New York, Joyce and Ray embarked on the two-week tour for *Foxfire*, departing on August 3. Like the
Black Water tour the previous year, Joyce's itinerary was ambitious: she made
promotional appearances in New York, Washington, D.C., Minneapolis, Portland, San Francisco, Los Angeles, and Denver. Even under ordinary conditions, such a trip would be difficult, but the tour became almost unbearable
on August 9, when Joyce "became alarmingly ill" at the Newark airport. The
next day, she was admitted to the Acute Care Center in Minneapolis, suffering from a blinding headache, a fever of 102, and severe chills. She was diagnosed with a blood infection, possibly the onset of Lyme disease. (Joyce had
worried for years about contracting the Lyme infection, since the woods behind her house were infested with ticks; she estimated that she had been bit-
ten at least twenty times that summer alone.) She began a regimen of
antibiotics, but the next few days were harrowing: during her Minneapolis
appearances, she suffered "migraine headache which left me near-blind";
participating in a radio show, she again felt "near-blind with head & neck
pain. The sickest I've ever been in public." Yet she was determined to finish
the tour. When she arrived on the West Coast, the antibiotics seemed to be

working, though she felt "dazed & fatigued" after a book signing in Portland. By the time she reached Palo Alto, she was actually enjoying the tour, which ended on an upbeat note with a dinner in Hollywood at which Al Pacino was a guest: Joyce found Pacino "*very* nice, dynamic, warm & funny." She considered him "one of these 'serious,' even literary-minded actors," she wrote to Russell Banks, "the kind who slip off to do Shakespeare when they can, who really are bright, sensitive, self-aware and ironic."

During the last few days of the trip, as Joyce recovered from her illness, her imagination lurched into new territory: she began contemplating a new novel to be called *We Were the Mulvaneys*. Her idea, she noted, was to write "a family tragedy of 'goodness.'" She imagined a "family-structured novel: moving from one of seven characters to the next, as the current of a narrative, though perhaps a double or triple narrative flows through them." *We Were the Mulvaneys* would become another novel-length obsession during the next two years even though, as usual at this early, note-taking stage, she worked primarily on shorter projects. At the end of August, riding in a limousine on her way to a bookstore signing, she experienced another "flood" of creative ideas: "so many images, plots! bizarre alternatives & situations!" She felt "almost too excited by these ideas to execute them & there are so many, too many of them—a virtual flooding of my brain so I find it difficult to sit still."

Joyce's new surge of creativity helped to compensate for the mixed reviews for *Foxfire: Confessions of a Girl Gang*. She had observed to John Updike that "my new novel has been strangely attacked—and as excessively praised." She viewed the entire process, she said, "like an out-of-the-body experience, watching from above somebody kicking with hobnailed boots one's own body." After the brilliant success of *Because It Is Bitter* and *Black Water*, a negative experience was perhaps not surprising: *Foxfire* was one of Joyce's weaker novels, shrill and unconvincing in some of its passages. Unlike the powerful sequences in *them* dealing with Maureen Wendall's victimization, which developed organically from the social ethos of that novel, *Foxfire* deployed its feminist rhetoric—idealistic, noble young girls versus piggish, predatory males—in a self-conscious and labored manner. Some of the reviews were indeed savage. In the *New York Times*, Michiko Kakutani found the novel "so contrived and portentous that the reader neither buys her simplistic message nor cares about her fictional creations." Yet *Foxfire* had its admirers: Carolyn See in the *Washington Post* called it "a wonderful novel," and in the *Philadelphia Inquirer*, Sheila Paulos argued that "this extraordinarily well-crafted book stands out even against the rich body of Oates's work." To Joyce, her new book seemed, "as I'm interviewed about it & read reviews, a different novel from the one I'd set out to write. My '*Huck Finn*' I'd thought it playfully & now people tell me, assure me, it's filled with anger/rage."

As the fall 1993 term began, rumors of an imminent Nobel Prize again reached Princeton, but this year the focus was not on Joyce but on her colleague Toni Morrison. After news of Morrison's prize was announced, Joyce exclaimed, "So, after all, the news media *did* come to [Princeton]—! Toni is so richly deserving of this award, however. Not only a brilliant writer, magical, impassioned, but a woman with a mission; a vision; indefatigable energy & ambition. A model, for all her uniqueness." By contrast, Joyce felt relatively invisible in her white skin: "I am only a *writer*—I have no socio/historical definition; no 'constituency'; I represent no one & nothing—not even (I suppose) myself. My 'self.' The unjust advantages of a white skin . . . privilege . . . breathed in unknowing & uncontemplated as the very air."

With media attention focused on Toni Morrison, Joyce quietly enjoyed her usual autumn pursuits: especially jogging, which had become almost an addiction. She stressed "how crucial to my life, how almost urgent, it is for me to get outside every day." Joyce's friend Dan Halpern noted that she pursued this activity even when she taught at the university. One day, he encountered her on campus and "she had her running shoes on, but she was also wearing a dress. She ran up and we had a little conversation, and then she kept running." He added that it was "very odd to see Joyce running in a dress at Princeton University." Joyce later insisted she had worn a casual blouse and skirt rather than a dress, but the incident was wholly characteristic: Joyce had few pretensions and paid little heed to Princeton's genteel code of behavior. If her teaching schedule permitted a brief jog across the campus, she happily seized the opportunity.

Although Joyce often conducted her daily life with a certain lack of self-consciousness—almost as if she were, in fact, invisible—she continued to cope with her identity as a literary celebrity. That fall, she felt apprehensive about an interview she had given to *Playboy* magazine, scheduled for the November issue. The interview had lasted for many hours, and when it finally appeared, she was dismayed that material she considered relatively inconsequential—a discussion of her tachycardia, for instance—was featured prominently, while her full-time teaching career at Princeton was not even mentioned. On November 3, she wrote to John Updike that she felt "thoroughly disgraced" by the interview, though as usual she tried to maintain a humorous perspective: "The only advantage is," she added, "now my reputation, so-called, is thoroughly shot, it can't get worse." Yet Joyce wrote tactfully to the interviewer, Lawrence Grobel, that he had managed to create "an interesting text" from their many hours of conversation; in the past, she noted, she had felt that most of her interviews were unfocused and tedious.

Other rewards of fame were far more unpleasant. For years, Joyce had been the target of various crank letter-writers from all over the country, and at times her mail was alarming. In October of 1993, Joyce wrote to her friend Richard Howard about the "lengthy, raving letters I've received from a prisoner in a Midwestern maximum security prison." She added that she often received "letters from disturbed individuals (90% of them male, for some reason)." (She used the prisoner's letters as a source for her poem "Like Walking to the Drugstore, When I Get Out," published in The Paris Review in 1995.) After Black Water appeared, an Illinois man returned his copy of the book directly to Joyce, claiming she had based the novel on him and that the experience of reading it had made him ill. That same year, another man wrote Joyce to inform her that he was being attacked regularly by alien life-forms.

Letters from women were sometimes equally bizarre: for several years, a Princeton woman had waged a letter-writing campaign and ultimately filed a lawsuit against Joyce, claiming that Joyce had broken into the woman's house, stolen her manuscripts, and fraudulently published them under the name "Joyce Carol Oates." (The woman also cited Stephen King, Norman Mailer, and other famous writers in her action.) As the court date approached, Joyce became apprehensive that she would actually have to confront the woman in court to refute this insane charge; finally Joyce wrote a pleading letter to the judge in the case, who then threw the woman's complaint out of court. Sometime later, a California woman began sending floral arrangements and telegrams to Joyce—accompanied by the ominous message "Spirit Rape"—along with a series of deranged letters. "There is a demonic certitude in such people quite lacking in the rest of us," Joyce observed. But disturbing as such letters were, they fed directly into Joyce's ongoing fascination with psychological derangement.

By the end of 1993, Joyce was avoiding such distractions by submitting, as usual, to "the gravitational pull" toward her work. "The nature of the work changes continuously," she wrote on December 16, "but the fact of it, never." During the next few months, she corrected the galleys of What I Lived For and continued to ponder the new novel, We Were the Mulvaneys. She was trying to imagine the "arc of their tragic/redemptive story," but her protagonist was "not yet in focus." A few weeks later, she put the manuscript aside in favor of a shorter, less ambitious "free-form novel" she had entitled Man Crazy. This manuscript consisted of "Vignettes, floating scenes. No strict chronology. I hope to bring my female protagonist from 1972, when she is 5 years old, to the present, when she is 28." This project was a departure from her usual method of careful note taking: "What is so wonderful about Man

Crazy, at least right now, is the ease of the voice. And I have so few notes!—
virtually nothing. So I will need to invent as I go along." She enjoyed the
bracing, improvisational quality of the new project, though within a few
weeks the work proved just as challenging as other novels she had written. In
sharp contrast to *What I Lived For* and *We Were the Mulvaneys*, however,
Joyce was able to complete *Man Crazy* (a fairly short novel at 227 manuscript
pages) in a mere eight weeks. The "ease of the voice" Joyce had found for this
brief but intense novel allowed for an absorbing and largely pleasurable writing experience.

Like most of Joyce's recent fiction, *Man Crazy* revisited the Eden County
terrain that had become the obsessive focus of her imaginative energy. A
loosely constructed, episodic narrative, *Man Crazy* is structurally similar to
earlier novels such as *Cybele* (1979) and *Marya: A Life* (1986), and particularly resembles *Marya* in its depiction of an upstate New York girl who survives early trauma and, as a young adult, comes to terms with her experience
through a selective and therapeutic process of memory. Like Marya's, Ingrid
Boone's early life is marked by the lack of emotional nurture that scars so
many of Joyce's autobiographical heroines. Tormented by her father's abandonment of the family, Ingrid sustains an emotional wound that later
prompts her to become involved with Enoch Skaggs, a Manson-like psycho-
path who recalls earlier counterculture monsters in Joyce's fiction such as
Noel in *Wonderland* and Ruby Red in the horrific story "Testimony." At
Enoch's hands, Ingrid suffers extremes of psychological and physical degradation, ordeals that reenact the pain of her early trauma. Drugged, tattooed,
sexually debased, locked in a cellar for days at a time when she "misbehaves,"
and forced to watch as a man is hacked to death with a machete and members of Enoch's "family" drink the victim's blood, Ingrid is slowly transformed into another of the emaciated female wrecks that populate Joyce's
fiction throughout her career, from Karen Herz in her first novel, *With Shuddering Fall* (1964), to Marianne in *We Were the Mulvaneys*. By the end of her
ordeal, Ingrid is "starved to 86 pounds," notes that her hair is "falling out in
handfuls," and is "mistaken for a child." Even after Ingrid comes through this
experience and confronts, in her midtwenties, her necessary maturation, her
anorexic impulses remain strong. Sharing a meal with her mother in the
concluding pages of the novel, Ingrid remarks: "The food was delicious and I
was very hungry but ate slowly as I needed to eat, not talking much. Each
mouthful chewed and premeditated, swallowed with caution lest my stomach will reject it for once my stomach had been so shrunken I'd screamed in
the agony of eating." Although Ingrid's experiences are far more extreme
than anything Joyce endured as a child, the specific details and working-out

of her trauma suggest that the novel became for Joyce yet another autobiographical, and perhaps cathartic, allegory of her own emotional history.

That spring and summer, Joyce worked intermittently on *Man Crazy* in
addition to book reviews and short stories. During the winter she had observed that "I haven't written a short story for so long . . . it's like losing track
of an old, close friend"; she was now writing several of the thoughtful,
densely textured stories that would appear in her 1996 collection, *Will You
Always Love Me?* Joyce also undertook several ambitious reviewing assignments, including an essay-review for *The New York Review of Books* on ten recent books dealing with serial killers. The project was a timely one, for earlier
in the year Joyce had written one of her most riveting short stories, "Zombie," dealing with a character who, like Jeffrey Dahmer, is a sexual predator
and murderer of young men. Although Joyce's work had featured violent
criminals as major characters in the past—most notably the "maniac" Bobbie
Gotteson in *The Triumph of the Spider Monkey*—nothing she had written
previously could quite match the eerie precision with which "Zombie" explored the deranged fantasies of a psychotic killer.

When Sharon Friedman, the agent who handled Joyce's short fiction, read
the story, she recognized immediately that it was an extraordinary piece. Like
Joyce's former agents, Blanche Gregory and Gert Bregman, she had submitted her client's stories to *The New Yorker* but without success. Friedman knew
that if she sent "Zombie" to Alice Quinn in the fiction department it would
be rejected out of hand. Instead she decided on a different strategy: she submitted the story directly to the magazine's adventurous new editor, Tina
Brown, who agreed that the story was brilliant and promptly accepted it. After
more than thirty years of professional writing, Joyce Carol Oates would finally
have a short story in *The New Yorker*. Although the magazine's legal department held up publication for many months—there were concerns that the
details drawn from Dahmer's case could provoke a lawsuit—"Zombie" finally
appeared on October 24, 1994. (Quinn and the other fiction editors had requested so many changes that Joyce, annoyed, compared them to "a swarm of
carnivorous gnats.") The magazine had taken the unusual step of sending out
a publicity release in advance of publication. "Do you think the editors felt
they should explain the story . . . ?" she wrote to one friend. "Its appearance
in their pages?" Despite the claim in the press release that *The New Yorker*
had a "tradition of publishing groundbreaking new fiction," many readers, including Joyce herself, had long considered the magazine's fiction relatively
thin, tepid, and conventional. After "Zombie" appeared, John Updike sent a
postcard with the jocular remark that the magazine's former editor, William
Shawn, must be "twirling" in his grave.

Not long afterward, Joyce had further problems with *The New Yorker*. The magazine had asked Joyce's biographer to edit a selection of her journals for a special issue devoted to fiction writers. At the last minute, however, *New Yorker* editor Alice Quinn refused to credit the biographer, who had worked with the journals for years, for editing the selections, insisting that readers should be given the false impression that Joyce herself had edited them. But Joyce had declined even to reread the journal entries, much less edit them: "Not only don't I reread the journal, I draw back from even thinking about it," she wrote. To make matters worse, when the journal selections were finally published, they were accompanied by a grotesque caricature of Joyce that was the visual equivalent of Richard Stern's insulting prose description in *Critical Inquiry*. Understandably, Joyce complained that the caricature was "frankly sexist, insulting."

By the time "Zombie" appeared in *The New Yorker*, Joyce had spent much of the summer expanding the story into a short novel of 145 typewritten pages. Like the short story "Black Water" on which she based her novel of the same title, the horrific tale of her deranged protagonist "Q.P." demanded a longer treatment. Aside from work on this novel, the summer of 1994 had been packed with a typical array of other short projects and travel plans. In early June, she visited Los Angeles for the American Booksellers convention, where she spoke at an enormous breakfast event—there were more than two thousand people in the audience—along with novelist E. Annie Proulx and Archbishop Desmond Tutu. The combination of speakers was rather awkward, particularly since the archbishop was "all hammy smiles for the camera, and very commandeering." During a photography session, someone suggested that the three speakers should "talk to one another, please." Joyce recalled that Archbishop Tutu asked, "in the most condescending way possible, 'And what kind of books do you write?' to Ms. Proulx and me; he wasn't even listening when I replied ironically, 'Oh, just novels.' "

Other parts of the West Coast trip were more enjoyable. Joyce and Ray had dinner with Ryan O'Neal, Farrah Fawcett, Diane Keaton, JoBeth Williams, and Joyce's friend Susan Loewenberg of the Los Angeles Theatre Works. Leaving Los Angeles, they stopped briefly in Las Vegas, where Joyce received the 1994 Bram Stoker Lifetime Achievement Award in Horror Fiction. (Her collection *Haunted: Tales of the Grotesque* had appeared earlier in the year.) "I'm not sure I deserved this," Joyce wrote, "in the context of career 'horror' writers," but she was touched by the recognition, a prestigious honor in the competitive field of horror fiction.

In the meantime, Joyce's publisher had been preparing another ambitious publicity campaign to launch its major new Oates novel. *What I Lived For* had been featured prominently by Dutton at the American Booksellers convention, and Joyce's editor was particularly optimistic. "Billy's hopes for my 'career' are unflagging," Joyce wrote appreciatively. "Billy *always* imagines that my next novel will be the breakthrough." Joyce herself was more skeptical, since she had been disappointed so often by both critical and public response to her books. In fact, she was preparing herself "for quite a beating this time," fearing that she would be condemned for "encroaching into male territory."

But *What I Lived For* was a virtually undisputed critical success. All the major newspapers praised the book, agreeing with James Carroll, who wrote in *The New York Times Book Review* that Corky Corcoran's story was "an engrossing, moving study of desperate, lonely and lost souls, of America itself in the midst of its decline." Carroll eloquently summarized the novel's achievement: "Joyce Carol Oates has written a vivid and continuous nightmare: a savage dissection of our national myths of manhood and success, a bitter portrait of our futile effort to flee the weight of the past, a cold-eyed look at our loss of community and family, a shriek at the monsters men and women have become to each other and a revelation of our desolate inner lives. *What I Lived For* is an American *Inferno*." In the *Atlanta Journal-Constitution*, E. J. Graff praised the novel's "breathtaking scope and insight," its ability to "transform the thriller into literary art." Although some reviewers reacted negatively to Corky Corcoran as a character—one headline read "Utter Pig: Oates' *What I Lived For* comes alive because of one"—even they admitted that the novel was a major achievement.

What I Lived For was nominated for a PEN/Faulkner award and for the Pulitzer Prize in fiction. As usual, Joyce did her best to help with promoting the novel, agreeing to yet another publicity tour. But Joyce's stepped up traveling in recent years had become wearing; more and more often, she returned home to her writing and to her university classes with a sense of relief.

In recent years, teaching had continued to represent a haven for Joyce, a source of intellectual refreshment: "Many a Princeton professor," she observed, "speaks warmly of teaching as the quiet, sequestered oasis of a beleaguered existence"; she enjoyed the "respectful concentration on good literature/literary matters, no interruptions." The course evaluations by Joyce's students in the 1990s provide a remarkably uniform portrait of her teaching style. Like her Windsor graduate students of the 1970s, her Princeton undergraduates found Joyce's comments on student work and on literature in general extremely stimulating and helpful. While some of the young writers saw Joyce as intimidating and aloof, complaining that class time was insufficient and that she was inaccessible outside of class, others spoke of her willingness to provide detailed and specific feedback on their work. As she had done in Windsor, Joyce singled out students she considered talented and left others feeling neglected and resentful. One of Joyce's senior thesis students, Scott Stein, remarked that her classes were often "polarized" between appreciative and disgruntled groups of students. But Stein found working with Joyce a wholly positive experience and benefited greatly from Joyce's editing ability. Virtually all her students praised the quality of her critical insights.

If Joyce spent less time with her students than she had when teaching in Detroit and Windsor, part of the reason lay in the increasingly fragmented nature of Joyce's writing life in the early 1990s. Not surprisingly, her near-simultaneous work on long and short novels, on long and short plays, and on her usual essays, short stories, and reviews did not prevent her from venturing into yet another genre. She had long admired the paintings of George Bellows, especially his boxing paintings, and she agreed to write a monograph on Bellows's work for a series published by Ecco Press called "Writers on Artists"; the brief book appeared in November 1995. Characteristically, Joyce had also scheduled two other books for 1995 publication: the Rosamond Smith novel *You Can't Catch Me*, published in the spring; and *Zombie*, which appeared in September.

With its controversial and, to some readers, distasteful subject matter, *Zombie* drew a predictably mixed response. In the *San Francisco Chronicle*, Michael Upchurch called it a "grisly, virulent gem of a book," noting that "readers with a taste for subversive fiction will be impressed." But Steven Marcus, writing in *The New York Times Book Review*, saw the novel as a "continuation of Ms. Oates's longstanding interest in the extreme, the gruesome, the bizarre and violent in American life." He found the writing "fluid, fluent, inflated and, finally, neither convincing in itself nor successfully dramatized as fiction." Again Joyce had expected a mixed response: "I do feel that I came through with a surprising minimum of virulent attacks for *What I Lived For*," she wrote, "so I'm prepared for a less friendly press with this one."

Joyce was absorbed in her new novel, *We Were the Mulvaneys*, by the time the reviews of *Zombie* appeared. Her work was proceeding "slowly, yet richly; *too* richly," she had observed in March. "I'm already at p.112 and have only covered about ¹/₁₀ of the story." In late May, her progress on the novel intensified after she gave a reading at Cornell University in Ithaca, New York, where some of her fictional scenes were set. "*Mulvaneys* is moving along with a definite stimulus after our Ithaca visit. What a beautiful campus Cornell is! But more than that, an interesting, even haunting place—its terrain, its creeks and deep gorges and 'plantations.' " Ithaca, she added, was "exactly the place for one of my characters, a brooding young man with a predilection for biology/evolutionary theory." By August, she was nearing completion of the novel, which had turned out "much longer than I'd hoped" at over 550 pages. Revising the manuscript in September, she felt her usual melancholy at the prospect of giving up a long-term, obsessive project, "a real reluctance to detach myself from the novel. It's almost literally like leaving a family . . . leaving home." The novel, which contained "great slices of childhood scenes, and landscapes," had taken "a chunk of my heart." By the time Joyce completed *We Were the Mulvaneys*, her schedule of publications for 1996 was set, following her typical pattern of bringing out two books with Dutton in addition to other, less commercial books with smaller presses: her Dutton collection of stories *Will You Always Love Me?* would come out in February; the novella *First Love* (another revisiting, this time in a Gothic mode, of the landscape surrounding Tonawanda Creek) would appear shortly afterward from Ecco Press, followed by *Tenderness*, a collection of poems from her and Ray's Ontario Review Press; and *Mulvaneys* was scheduled by Dutton for fall publication.

Joyce's obsessive desire to mythologize the vanished world of her childhood, so marked in her fiction of the late 1980s and the 1990s, had found its fullest expression in *We Were The Mulvaneys*, one of her strongest novels to date. This story of an upstate New York farm family traces the Mulvaneys' slow but inexorable expulsion from the Edenic setting of High Point Farm, where Michael and Corinne Mulvaney live between 1955 and 1980, raising four children. Moving the narrative viewpoint among all six family members, the novel focuses especially on three of the children—Patrick, Marianne, and Judd—and their coming of age in the 1960s and 1970s.

More than any other Oates novel, *Mulvaneys* depends heavily on a sense of place: in depicting the Mulvaney farm, Joyce avoided the stark realism of her early Eden County stories, choosing instead to re-create her childhood environment in a happier mode, composing what she called "my valentine to that part of the world." The Mulvaney homestead, which she called "a farm of the kind we'd never had," is depicted as a place of teeming, benevolent life—children, animals, constant bustling activity—whose centerpiece is the enormous lavender farmhouse that seemed "to float in midair, buoyant and magical as a house in a child's storybook." Many of these elaborate descriptive passages recall the mythmaking impulse Joyce had employed in *Bellefleur*, but here the myth is created not by metafictional experimentation but through the prism of the characters' memories, which include painful as well as "magical" recollections. Of all Joyce's previous novels, the one echoed most noticeably in the opening sequences of *Mulvaneys* is *Son of the Morning* (1978). Both novels use a marauding pack of wild dogs as an emblem of rapacious nature, and in both, the dogs' appearance is followed by an instance of human rapacity: like Elsa, Nathan Vickery's mother, Marianne Mulvaney is sexually assaulted, an incident that marks not only her own future life but that also alters the destiny of her entire family, forming the "tragic/redemptive arc" Joyce had described in her early notes for the novel.

Joyce used numerous details from her personal history in portraying the Mulvaneys. The name of her own Irish great-great-grandmother was Mary Mullaney (in *What I Lived For*, Corky Corcoran also has Irish relatives named Mullaney), and the children of Michael and Corinne represent important facets of Joyce's temperament. Marianne, their only daughter, is Joyce's empathetic portrayal of her own youthful vulnerability: after completing the novel, she admitted that of all the major characters she "felt closest to Marianne." Not only does Marianne, like Joyce, suffer a sexual assault; she also recalls the numerous other female characters in Joyce's novels—especially Shelley in *Wonderland*, Thalia in *What I Lived For*, and Ingrid in *Man Crazy*—whose victimization includes bouts with anorexia, an illness the sufferer views as a triumph of will over physical life but that actually becomes a self-destructive drama in which the woman "acts out" her own feelings of deprivation and emotional hunger. After Marianne, like Shelley Vogel, leaves her family and joins a hippielike commune, her brother Patrick finds her in the same condition in which the horrified Jesse Vogel found his daughter. Patrick feels appalled by "how thin she was. Upper arms no larger than his wrists. Collarbone jutting and breasts tiny as a twelve-year-old's." Marianne, like her ancestors in Joyce's fictional world, essentially starves herself into an asexual state, denying the femininity that her experience of rape has rendered undesirable. Not surprisingly, Marianne's doctor prescribes pills "to *help restore appetite*" but she refuses to take the medication: "that was Marianne's secret, one of her secrets."

Aside from presenting in Marianne her lifelong anorexic impulses, Joyce layered happier details into the portrait as well: like Joyce, Marianne has a deep and abiding love for animals, especially cats. When Marianne's cat Muffin (named for one of Joyce's most beloved pets) suffers a life-threatening liver ailment, she takes extreme measures—just as Joyce had done with her own Muffin—to prolong the animal's life as long as possible. Joyce provides a touching resolution to Marianne's peripatetic early life by having her fall in love with the kindly veterinarian who helps alleviate her pet's suffering.

Marianne's brother Patrick, by contrast, portrays Joyce's intellectual nature: her emotional reserve, her questing spirit, and her penchant for philosophical brooding. Like the young Joyce, Patrick attends church unwillingly, reads voraciously, excels in his studies and dreads giving a valedictory speech. (An unexpected rainstorm during her commencement exercises at Syracuse had helped Joyce avoid giving such a speech, while Patrick avoids his speech by setting off a "stink bomb" during his high school graduation ceremony.) Patrick's experiences as an undergraduate, like Marya Knauer's in *Marya: A Life*, recall the heady sense of discovery and the passion for intellectual life that Joyce had experienced at Syracuse. And, like Corky Corcoran, his interest in science reflects Joyce's own avid scientific reading.

The youngest Mulvaney brother, Judd, is a newspaperman who, like Maddy in *Foxfire*, recalls Joyce's identity as a writer: dispassionate yet sympathetic, Judd possesses the verbal ability and emotional detachment necessary to tell the story of his family's triumphs and tragedies during a thirty-year period. Like Nathan Vickery in *Son of the Morning*, he describes his own life in first person but uses third person to enter imaginatively into the personal histories of his siblings and his parents. Not surprisingly, Michael Mulvaney Sr. and his wife, Corinne, suggest some traits of Joyce's own parents, Fred and Carolina: like Fred, Michael struggles to provide for his family and is known for his hot temper; like Carolina, Corinne is a generous, energetic maternal figure who is the source of both physical and emotional nurture to her family. Also like Fred and Carolina, the Mulvaney parents move into a smaller, more modern ranch house after losing their farm, and now have "a country highway out front, diesel trucks thundering by." (Joyce does not, however, allow Michael and Corinne the peaceful old age that her own parents have enjoyed: after Michael loses his business and home, he suffers bankruptcy, the loss of his marriage, and ultimately death from alcoholism; the resilient Corinne must then create an entirely new life for herself.)

The Mulvaney family members come to terms with the loss of their "storybook past" in different ways. Both Patrick and Marianne leave upstate New York, spending years wandering the country in search of an adult selfhood outside the "garden" of their paradisical early life; they also seek to cope with the tormenting losses their family has suffered. As Patrick understands, "You can't exercise memory until you've removed yourself from memory's source." The pun on "exorcize" is surely deliberate. In the novel's concluding pages, he likewise echoes the "poison" metaphor Joyce had used in her journal and in *Man Crazy* to describe her painful childhood experiences: "it all just drained out of me. Like poison draining out of my blood. Like I'd been sick, infected, and hadn't known it until the poison was gone." For her part, Marianne gives herself fully to each new job and relationship as she moves from place to place—just as Joyce plunges wholeheartedly into the world of each new novel—but then abruptly leaves, reenacting the pattern of her original "banishment" after her rape. But also like Joyce, Marianne occasionally journeys back to visit her family and the countryside surrounding High Point Farm.

The poignant emotions arising from this return to the past dominate the concluding chapters of *We Were the Mulvaneys*, which stress not the diminished present or tragic past but the theme of reconciliation, the family members' ability to survive and adapt to the dramatic changes in their lives. At a family reunion in 1993, held appropriately on July Fourth—an event that suggests the Mulvaneys' independence as individuals even as it stresses their indissoluble family ties—the five surviving Mulvaneys come together along with their new spouses and children. Judd recognizes that their common experience of loss can't be expressed verbally—"For what are the words," he asks, "with which to summarize a lifetime, so much crowded confused happiness terminated by such stark slow-motion pain?"—but the final scene suggests a hardwon triumph of endurance and mutual understanding. Even though, as Corinne had once put it, "You never outgrow the landscape of your childhood," We Were the Mulvaneys insists that you can survive it.

When the novel appeared in the fall of 1996, critics agreed that it was one of Joyce's finest books and that its concluding scene of redemption and conciliation represented a new chord in her work. In the Los Angeles Times Book Review, Beverly Lowry noted that Joyce had "performed many a surprising, quick-change imaginative shift," and that with Mulvaneys "she veers dramatically away from the voice, tone and subject matter of her recent urban horror stories"; another critic observed that the novel "leads the Mulvaneys, and the reader, through darkness and into a light, and is unapologetically cathartic." In a glowing review, Valerie Miner in The Nation remarked that "Oates's unblinking curiosity about human nature is one of the greatest artistic forces of our time"; her only cavil about Mulvaneys related, in fact, to the positive ending, which she considered sentimental: "Is this really Joyce Carol Oates, intrepid archeologist in the dark, sticky folds of the contemporary psyche? Witnessing redemption on the Independence Day baseball diamond?"

Although this most recent of Joyce's long novels brings her work "full circle," in a sense, back to the Eden County landscape of her earliest fiction, and is imbued with the mellowed nostalgia of a seasoned novelist, it represents only a symbolic closure. Joyce Carol Oates remains as energetically committed to her art as she'd been in high school, when she wrote "practice novels" one after the other. After finishing Man Crazy and We Were the Mulvaneys, she moved with her usual alacrity into other modes and genres: editing a volume of Emily Dickinson's poems; revising and preparing her play about Thoreau for a staged reading at the McCarter Theater; completing a new screenplay, in collaboration with actor-director Jeanne Moreau, based on her 1985 novel, Solstice; reviewing books for the New York Review of Books and Times Literary Supplement; writing a spate of new short fiction; completing yet another Rosamond Smith novel entitled Starr Bright Will Be with You Soon; and soon thereafter completing another major new novel, tentatively entitled Broke Heart Blues, based on her high school experiences in Williamsville, New York.

Innovative and various as these recent projects have been, one of Joyce's major artistic challenges in the twenty-first century will be to reinvent herself as a novelist. Just as the cycle of Detroit novels came to an end in the 1970s, her nostalgic re-creation of her childhood world seems, with *We Were the Mulvaneys*, to have found its ultimate expression. Her obsessive renderings of sensitive, abused young girls, from Karen, Maureen, and Shelley in the early novels to Marya, Enid, Iris, Maddy, Marianne, Josie, and Ingrid in the more recent ones, inevitably grow less powerful with each repetition, despite the writer's resourcefulness in creating a unique voice and structure for each new book. In the early 1970s, after completing *Wonderland*, Joyce made a conscious effort to move away from despairing, tragic dramatizations of a nightmarish reality into what she called "a more articulate moral position" that could suggest ways of transcendence. The redemptive conclusion of *Mulvaneys* suggests that she may once again have reached such a crossroads and may choose to resist her fascination with the horrific abberation (serial killers, blood-drinking cults) in favor of more mature, complex fiction that dramatizes the arduous pathways toward healing and redemption. Joyce once bristled at John Gardner's advice that she write a story in which "things work out well, for a change"; she insisted that "happy endings don't work in my writing." But *Mulvaneys* suggests a possible change of heart, a maturity of vision, a fruitful new direction. If Joyce's future work were to emphasize themes of survival, resilience, and ultimate triumph, after all, it would certainly be true to the pattern of her own biography.

To her credit, Joyce has not allowed her comfortable Princeton life to weaken her identification with the insulted and injured in contemporary America. Nor has she ceased to be the controversial literary figure who often finds herself, for all her much-valued invisibility, at odds with the norms and expectations of her culture. Just as some critics in the 1970s found her violent subject matter and ambitious productivity to be objectionable, her fiction continues to disturb the conventional expectations of many readers. In 1997, for instance, her novel *Foxfire* was "banned" from high school reading lists in Toronto and elsewhere—inspiring considerable, mostly unfriendly publicity that Joyce found troubling—because arch-conservative parents' groups considered its language and subject matter offensive. Joyce found herself in the unanticipated position of being vilified as a "pornographer." "The ugly publicity does seem comical from a distance," she remarked, "and yet, when you're the object of such attacks, you do wind up feeling rather sullied. For of course almost no one will read the novel, only the attacks and the media coverage." Like many innovative novelists who likewise have been seriously engaged in closely observing and describing the world around them—the charges of obscenity suffered by Kate Chopin, James Joyce, and D. H. Lawrence come to mind—Joyce undoubtedly will continue in her role as a cultural radical and outsider, however well disguised she remains in her traditional role as a distinguished Ivy League professor and acknowledged woman of letters.

Despite Joyce's privileged and somewhat insular daily routine, the intellectual stimulation of Princeton has helped to broaden her academic interests, in turn enriching her work. Her friendships with Elaine Showalter and other feminist writers, for instance, surely prompted Joyce toward a clearer articulation of her own feminism, in both essays and fiction, than she would have achieved in Detroit or Windsor. At the same time, her academic vantage point has encouraged certain limitations in her work from the beginning: she pays little attention to television or movies, for instance, even though these media have been dominant in the United States for decades, and her work—unlike that of such contemporaries as John Updike, Norman Mailer, and Don DeLillo—lacks a sufficient awareness of the impact of popular culture generally on American life. On rare occasions, Joyce attends an art house film; but in 1975, after all, she made the humorous admission that she and Ray felt like "a couple of aborigines" when they watched television for a few minutes in a hotel room, and with few exceptions—a brief enthusiasm for the series *Hill Street Blues*, for instance—her attitude has changed very little. (When Ed Asner was hired to star in one of her recent plays and her friends excitedly congratulated her, Joyce was bewildered; she had never heard of Asner.) As she has often remarked, she remains a "print-oriented" person and would simply rather read than do anything else.

Despite her teaching and occasional public appearances, Joyce remains in essence the "invisible writer" she has been from the beginning of her career. Almost wholly absorbed in literary pursuits, she maintains the obsessive focus on work that has made Joyce Carol Oates the most prolific serious writer of the twentieth century and one of the most consistently inventive. Rather than depleting her energy, aging has only heightened her awareness that her remaining time is limited; as always, work seems only to whet her appetite for more work. As she wrote to one friend in late 1995, in a wholly typical remark, "So much energy after *Mulvaneys* has been finished. I feel like lightning yearning to strike."

NOTES

References to JCO's unpublished journal (housed in the Joyce Carol Oates Archive at Syracuse University) are noted by the abbreviation J. Interviews with JCO are identified by the interviewer: e.g., "Clemons interview"; interviews conducted by the author for this book are identified by the person interviewed: e.g., "Int. Carolina Oates, 1992."

Introduction

PAGE XV   "If you met her": Clemons interview, 1972.

PAGE XVIII   "staggeringly indolent": J, February 13, 1982.

"the social self, the person people encounter": letter from JCO to Elaine Showalter, July 17, 1989.

PAGE XIX   "the finest American novelist": Robert H. Fossum, "Only Control: The Novels of Joyce Carol Oates," *Studies in the Novel*, 7, ii (Summer 1975): 285.

"will quite naturally project": JCO, letter published in *The New Republic*, March 3, 1979.

PAGE XXI   "life's commitment": O'Briant interview, 1986.

PAGE XXII   "She Certainly Tried": "Stories That Define Me: The Making of a Writer," *New York Times Book Review*, July 11, 1982: 15.

"We work in the dark": James, "The Middle Years," *Scribners Magazine*, May 1893.

Chapter 1 In the North Country

PAGE 1 "sound flamboyant and colorful . . . Most of what was Hungarian . . . I think I am at home": "Budapest Journal: May 1980," *(Woman) Writer: Occasions and Opportunities.*

PAGE 2 "we carry our young parents within us . . . How ironic, as a writer . . . pulled back into that world . . . budged any further": "A Letter to My Mother Carolina Oates on her 78th Birthday, November 8, 1995," *New York Times Magazine,* May 12, 1996: 48.

"a daily scramble for existence": Franks interview, 1980.

PAGE 3 Bush family history: Int. Carolina and Frederic Oates, 1992.

PAGE 4 "a peculiar sort of Old World obstinacy": "Budapest Journal: May 1980."

"I was close to them . . . had moved up . . . there wasn't any closeness": Int. Carolina Oates, 1993.

PAGE 5 "John went to work in a steel foundry": Int. JCO, 1994.

"Lena would sometimes pour out part of the bottle": Int. Frederic Oates, 1993.

"began his day, at his early breakfast": "Food Mysteries," *Antaeus,* Spring 1992: 36.

"this goddamn coffee is too hot": Int. Frederic Oates, 1993.

"He had all the vices": Int. JCO, 1993.

"got drunk and started his Model-T": letter to Robert Phillips, October 10, 1985. Quotations from Robert Phillips' letters to JCO are courtesy of Department of Special Collections, Syracuse University Library.

PAGE 6 "who would give the shirt off his back": Int. Carolina Oates, 1993.

"If a horse tried to get away": JCO, "A Letter to My Mother": 48.

"First Death, 1950": *Invisible Woman: New and Selected Poems.*

"a simple woman with a 'peasant' mentality": Int. JCO, 1993.

PAGE 7 "rich, heavy, sour cream-dolloped goulashes": "Food Mysteries": 35.

"Carolina attended Erie County District School No. 7": Int. Carolina Oates, 1992.

"a small diner and beer joint called Hass Cafe": Int. Carolina Oates, 1992.

PAGE 8 "she was so angry with me": Int. Frederic Oates, 1992.

PAGE 9 "Beginnings": *(Woman) Writer: Occasions and Opportunities.*

PAGE 10 "area farmers started bringing people up from the South": Int. Frederic Oates, 1993.

"a strong memory of those migrant workers": Int. JCO, 1993.

"imperishable sense of reality": Clemons interview, 1972.

PAGE 11 "I have a great admiration for those females": Kuehl interview, 1969.

PAGE 12 "traverse its streets . . . the power to rend one's heart": "Preface to *You Must Remember This,*" *(Woman) Writer: Occasions and Opportunities.*

PAGE 13 "I drove by myself around the city . . . the kitchen! my grandmother's bedroom & sewing room!": J, Sept. 1985.

"the very image": letter from JCO to John Updike, January 11, 1988.

Oates family history: Int. Carolina and Frederic Oates, 1993.

PAGE 13 "shadowy young woman . . . penchant for secrecy": J, June 25, 1982.
PAGE 14 "just one notch above the blacks": Int. Frederic Oates, 1993.
"The man was no good": "Facts, Visions, Mysteries: My Father, Frederic Oates." Carolyn Anthony, ed., *Family Portraits* (New York: Doubleday, 1990): 153.
Morgenstern family history: Int. Carolina and Frederic Oates, 1993.
PAGE 15 "that sort of male-Irish-immature": letter from JCO to Russell Banks, July 13, 1992.
"he was a gravedigger": "Facts, Visions, Mysteries": 158.
PAGE 16 "They kept piling the work up on me": Int. Frederic Oates, 1992.
PAGE 17 "We couldn't find anything else": Int. Frederic Oates, 1993.
"Daddy's signs were always discernible . . . a strike or a layoff ": Int. JCO, 1993.
"I know, however, that the situation wasn't funny": J, August 24, 1977.
"It was the most beautiful sight": Int. Frederic Oates, 1992.
PAGE 18 "He and his flying buddies also enjoyed flying low": "Facts, Visions, Mysteries": 160.
"Abandoned Airfield, 1977": *Women Whose Lives Are Food, Men Whose Lives Are Money.*
"a friend of mine used to be in the Golden Gloves": Int. Frederic Oates, 1993.
"He was hurt very badly . . . gave me the sense of boxing being about failure": Int. JCO, 1994.
PAGE 19 "I found out who he was": Int. Frederic Oates, 1993.
"he had been rehired at Harrison Radiator": Int. Frederic Oates, 1992.
PAGE 20 "farmed out downstairs": Int. JCO, 1993.
"One winter, when Joyce was three or four": Int. Carolina and Frederic Oates, 1992.
"It's pretty bad, as a matter of fact": Kuehl interview, 1969.
PAGE 21 "Our Dead": *Mademoiselle*, April 1971: 166.

Chapter 2   "The Girl Who Wrote on the Edges": 1938–50

PAGE 23 "Sometimes I have such vivid memories!": J, August 15, 1978.
"My mind fixes upon old memories": J, June 25, 1982.
"They stopped just in time to witness a man's body": J, August 15, 1978.
"Christmas 1944 is, for me": "The Greatest of Gifts," *Life*, December 1990: 155.
PAGE 24 "by way of the snapshot . . . the lowly 'snapshot' yields!": "Cherished Moments," *Life*, Fall 1988: 153.
"I begin to see as I grow older": J, February 20, 1975.
"into a sort of part-middle-class": J, August 1, 1980.
"Fred had managed to get transferred": "Facts, Visions, Mysteries": 157.

PAGE 24   "Fred had owned a secondhand, canary-yellow Studebaker President":
          Road & Track, August 1989.
          "he continued to enjoy airplanes": "Facts, Visions, Mysteries": 160.
PAGE 25   "a plateau of enthusiastic incompetence": letter from JCO to John Up-
          dike, March 6, 1989.
          "I recall myself as a girl": J, May 27, 1991.
          "Because, I assume, I grew up in the country": letter from JCO to Mari-
          ana Torgovnick, July 3, 1993.
          "I have never found the visual equivalent": "They All Just Went Away,"
          The New Yorker, October 16, 1995: 179.
          "mud-brown churning water": "Sunday Drive 1948," *Traditional Home*,
          March 1995: 38.
          "To walk along the canal's high banks": "American Gothic," *The New
          Yorker*, May 8, 1995: 35.
          "I remember very little of [Joyce]": letter from Fred Oates Jr. to Greg
          Johnson, May 10, 1994.
          "My own brother and I": letter from JCO to David Shapiro, December
          26, 1987.
PAGE 26   "I remember it as if it had happened yesterday": J, Christmas 1987.
          "Her first and closest childhood friend": Int. JCO, 1993.
          "usually had more things than I did . . . fishermen would get very upset
          with us": Int. Jean Windnagle Fritton, 1992.
          "it was starting to rain and thunder": Int. Carolina Oates, 1993.
PAGE 27   "Until the relatively mature age of 11": "Trespassing," *New York Times
          Magazine*, October 8, 1995: 83.
          "one of my 'crystallizations-around-a-theme' essays": J, August 2, 1989.
          "a kind of seat, or swing": J, May 9, 1982.
          "The Molesters": *Where Are You Going, Where Have You Been? Selected
          Early Stories*.
          "Joyce was really afraid of the doll": Int. Carolina Oates, 1993.
          "Why Don't You Come Live with Me It's Time": *Heat*.
          "has its exact parallel in things I'd done": J, August 2, 1989.
          "I remember crawling on hands and knees . . . a dazed, headachy elation
          . . . So, this is how it is!": "Trespassing," *New York Times Magazine*, Octo-
          ber 8, 1995: 83.
PAGE 28   "The other students, particularly the boys": Grobel interview, 1993.
          "everybody intermarried": Franks interview, 1980.
          "I could run very fast": Int. JCO, 1992.
          "So many brutal, meaningless acts . . . simply didn't *know*": J, August 9,
          1975.
PAGE 29   "wasn't too wonderful": "Joyce Carol Oates: American Appetites": televi-
          sion interview with Tom Vitale, 1989.
          "dreadful place": J, April 6, 1976.
          "She was always above average . . . a nice matronly lady, and pleasant":
          Int. Jean Windnagle Fritton, 1992.
          "My very first impressions of Joyce": Int. Nelia Pynn, 1995.

PAGE 29 "a rough-hewn, weatherworn, uninsulated": "The Writing Life: Tales Out of School," *Washington Post*, March 16, 1997: X01.

PAGE 30 "very husky, very big": Int. JCO, 1994.
"[to] be dragged": "The Writing Life: Tales Out of School": X01.
"mauled . . . psychic violence primarily": Int. JCO, 1992.
"so vivid in my memory": J, September 19, 1993.
"ordered not to tell": Grobel interview, 1993.
"Blindfold": *The Goddess and Other Women*.
"Hostage": *Heat*.
"It was extremely important for me": Grobel interview, 1993.
"My father more or less protected us": letter from JCO to Robert Phillips, September 23, 1989.
"Such systematic, tireless, sadistic persecution": quoted in Stephan Salisbury, "For librarians, a mixed bag of views from Oates, others," *Philadelphia Inquirer*, July 12, 1982: D–1.

PAGE 31 "Carolina remembered that one time a drunken man": Int. Carolina Oates, 1992.
"Back Country": *Invisible Woman: New and Selected Poems*.
"In that world": Int. JCO, 1994.
"When you were a little girl": letter to JCO from Blanche Woodside, March 6, 1970.
"Snapshot Album": *Tenderness*.

PAGE 32 "Among my early childhood memories": letter from JCO to Jean Curtis, March 6, 1993.
"the first great book of my life": "Stories That Define Me: The Making of a Writer": 15.
"Carolina remembered that Joyce memorized whole sections": Int. Carolina Oates, 1992.
"I might have wished . . . happy endings": "Stories that Define Me: The Making of a Writer": 15.

PAGE 33 "I loved my crayolas": Int. JCO, 1994.
"several thousands of pages": "Stories That Define Me: The Making of a Writer": 15.
"Joyce often read in the poetry anthologies": Int. Frederic Oates, 1992.
"The letter and poem": ms. owned by Carolina and Frederic Oates.

PAGE 34 "This song has been written by Joyce Oates": ms. owned by Carolina and Frederic Oates.
"On one occasion Joyce wrote a story": Mary Wozniak, *Niagara Gazette*, August 1, 1987.
Jean Windnagle's autograph book: ms. owned by Jean Windnagle Fritton.

PAGE 35 "always working, always busy": Int. Carolina Oates, 1992.
"most of my games with Robin": letter from JCO to Carol North, August 12, 1959.

PAGE 36 "our firstborn, you know": Int. Frederic Oates, 1992.
"I was always, and continue to be": Phillips interview, 1978.

PAGE 37 "Where Are You Going, Where Have You Been?," "How I Contemplated the World from the Detroit House of Correction and Began My Life Over Again," "Small Avalanches": *Where Are You Going, Where Have You Been? Selected Early Stories.*

PAGE 37 "Testimony": *Raven's Wing.*
"there was no consciousness then": Grobel interview, 1993.

PAGE 38 "this was the hope that Joyce cherished": television interview, *The Originals,* 1989.
"Joyce Smith, a professor of English": Bellamy interview, 1972.

Chapter 3 The Romance of Solitude: 1950–56

PAGE 39 "Our household was traumatized": Grobel interview, 1993.
"my brother and I . . . surpassingly dull": Int. JCO, 1992.

PAGE 40 "they did allow . . . big dollar signs in his eyes": Int. Frederic Oates, 1993.
"Joyce's parents were against the marriage": Int. Raymond Smith, 1994.
"the numberless, so fatiguing and unrewarding Catholic masses": letter to Robert Phillips, April 3, 1994.
"I think people have been brainwashed": Grobel interview, 1993.
"In a 1993 essay": "The One Unforgivable Sin." *New York Times Book Review,* July 25, 1993: 3.
"You're very nice to write so temperately": letter to Father Torrens, August 9, 1993.

PAGE 41 "At the Seminary," "In the Region of Ice": *Where Are You Going, Where Have You Been? Selected Early Stories;* "Shame," *The Wheel of Love.*
"an ancient, wheezing, foot-pedal instrument": "And God Saw That It Was Good," *Southwest Review,* Spring/Summer 1995: 318.
"the raw, unmediated emotion": Int. JCO, 1992.
"the essentially 'adolescent' quality of the American national character": "Author Joyce Carol Oates on 'Adolescent America,'" *U.S. News and World Report,* May 15, 1978: 60.
"shattering experience": Applebaum interview, 1978.
"I would look around in church": Grobel interview, 1993.

PAGE 42 "Riding buses has been so much a part of my life": Int. JCO, 1994.
"Concerning the Case of Bobby T.": *The Goddess and Other Women.*
"very charismatic, unpredictable": letter to Henry Louis Gates, Jr., June 30, 1990.
"splitting him in two": Int. JCO, 1994.
"And I don't want to know": letter to Henry Louis Gates, Jr., June 30, 1990.

PAGE 43 "It's solely Lockport, NY": letter to Robert Phillips, September 1, 1985.
"enormously excited at once, extremely nervous": letter to Judith Wynn, August 10, 1987.
"The family always had chickens . . . Freddie's Doughnuts": "Food Mysteries": 35, 30.

PAGE 44 "Boxers don't feel pain quite the way we do . . . What's the point!": *On Boxing.*
"I wore a helmet and goggles": "Facts, Visions, Mysteries": 159.
"Joyce had taken a comic book along": Int. Frederic Oates, 1993.
" 'Tales of the Crypt' . . . *Dracula*": letter from JCO for Year of the Reader—Literacy Campaign, 1991.
"his ethnic exoticism": "Dracula: The Vampire's Secret," in David Rosenberg, ed., *The Movie That Changed My Life* (New York: Penguin, 1991): 65.
"We read a lot of literature . . . I'll tell you that": Int. Sara Glover, 1993.

PAGE 45 "Mrs. Glover asked Joyce to read a story": letter from Gordy Stearns to Greg Johnson, May 1996.
JCO's school records from North Park Junior High are courtesy of Carolina and Frederic Oates.
"Did I really live through that?": J, October 24, 1984.

PAGE 46 "Poor silly helpless Joyce!": J, January 4, 1977.
"First Death": *Mademoiselle*, June 1978: 188–94.
"You seem so alone . . . a sort of nightmarish delirium for months": J, January 9, 1977.

PAGE 47 "I remember my sickened feeling of guilt": J, January 4, 1977.
"drifted into simply not caring": J, January 9, 1977.
"really vicious . . . a period of extremes": Interview in *The Sunday Oregonian*, August 22, 1993.

PAGE 48 "mystery house": J, June 30, 1985.
"Little Wife": *Raven's Wing.*
"Thinking of the walk to and from school": J, February 1, 1977.
"selfless love, uncomplaining": J, August 27, 1973.
"marvelous zany invention": "Stories That Define Me: The Making of a Writer": 15.
" 'redeemed' by coming to live in the country": Int. JCO, 1992.
Background information on Williamsville Central High School and the town of Williamsville: Int. Frank Coward, 1993, and letter from Bruce Burnham to Greg Johnson, September 12, 1996.
"no expense had been spared": Int. George Kunz, 1993.

PAGE 49 "our school was much smaller": Int. Molly Eimers Dee, 1993.
"Here comes another bus": Int. Ellen Shapley Comerford, 1993.
"It had to be difficult": Int. Frank Coward, 1993.
"As a young girl I attached a great deal of importance to clothes": J, February 17, 1977.
"were solidly middle/upper-middle class": letter from JCO to Greg Johnson, July 3, 1993.

PAGE 50 "rail-thin with a tendency": Int. Frank Coward, 1993.
"a little eccentric": Int. Lee Cooke-Rente, 1993.
"the vision that comes to me": Int. Molly Eimers Dee, 1993.
"shy, almost apologetic": Int. Gail Paxson Mates, 1993.
"He seemed to be able to draw out Joyce": Int. Richard Gregory, 1993.

PAGE 50   "Quiet down, boys and girls": Int. Linnea Ogren Donahower, 1993.
"The class read such books": Int. Richard Gregory, 1993.
"to create, maintain, and extend": *The Searchlight*, Williamsville High School yearbook, 1956.

PAGE 51   "She was always very accommodating": Int. Faith Ryan Whittlesey, 1993.
"pretty exclusive": Int. Ellen Shapley Comerford, 1993.
"were pretty and had all the boyfriends": Int. Faith Ryan Whittlesey, 1993.
"We were all very good friends": letter from JCO to Greg Johnson, July 3, 1993.
JCO's course records are from her Williamsville High School transcript.

PAGE 52   "the quality of her writing": Int. Frank Coward, 1993.
"Another English teacher, Harold Stein": Int. Molly Eimers Dee, 1993.
"But Stein shared Joyce's love of writing": Int. Richard Gregory, 1993.
"a disproportionate amount of time": Int. Faith Ryan Whittlesey, 1993.
"had spoken of her great talent": Int. George Kunz, 1993.
"consciously training myself ": Phillips interview, 1978.
"I seem to have written them as a pianist practices": Int. JCO, 1992.
"a bloated trifurcated novel": Phillips interview, 1978.
"was taken at the time with Hemingway's style": Int. Gail Paxson Mates, 1993.
"accidentally opened a copy": "Stories That Define Me: The Making of a Writer": 15.

PAGE 53   "she met with a roadblock": J, April 3, 1980.
"Looking for Thoreau": *(Woman) Writer: Occasions and Opportunities*.
"Thoreau is mysteriously intimate": J, June 21, 1985.
"suffused with the powerfully intense": "Looking for Thoreau."

PAGE 54   "Senior Alphabet": *The Billboard*, June 11, 1956.
"she never gave it back to me": Int. JCO, 1994.
"strangely impressed": Terry Gross, "Fresh Air" interview, 1993.

PAGE 55   "Joyce would sometimes come to her house": Int. Linnea Ogren Donahower, 1993.
"Gail was an intellectual": Int. Faith Ryan Whittlesey, 1993.
"very nice people": Int. Carolina Oates, 1992.
"Lightning Bolt": *Road & Track*, August 1989: 58.
"the idea of dating": Int. JCO, 1994.
"My inclination toward chastity": J, September 24, 1977.

PAGE 56   "built into the female": J, July 31, 1977.
"Country & Western music": J, June 5, 1976.
"simply to be alone": Bellamy interview, 1972.

Chapter 4   Syracuse: 1956–60

PAGE 57   "the question, considering her background": television interview, *The Originals*, 1989.

PAGE 57 "she was among the fortunate 11 percent": "Seniors Win Scholarships," *The Billboard*, Williamsville High School newspaper, June 11, 1956. "Joyce felt she would probably become a teacher": Int. JCO, 1994. "Directory of Graduates": *The Billboard*, Williamsville High School newspaper, June 11, 1956.

PAGE 58 "in those years girls *hoped* to become engaged": "An Unsolved Mystery," in Mickey Pearlman, ed., *Between Friends* (Boston: Houghton Mifflin, 1994): 125–26. "The reputation of Syracuse was 'on the rise' ": Int. Dick Allen, 1993. "roomed with Joyce during part of their sophomore year": Int. Lori Negridge Allen, 1993.

PAGE 59 "less expensive and offered a more homelike, protective environment": Int. Sandy Gillan Dwenger, 1993. "an event of such psychic upheaval": J, November 23, 1974. "Carol was an English major": Int. Carol North Dixon, 1993. "If you lived under her room": Int. Sandy Gillan Dwenger, 1993. "the strange, inexplicable romance": J, September 6, 1976. "infatuated, my mind swirling with people": J, September 3, 1976. "Waking so very early": J, August 30, 1976.

PAGE 60 "The gym teacher almost fainted": Int. JCO, 1994. "It's like a mimicry of death . . . why I'm concerned with wasting time": Grobel interview, 1993. "I remember the excitement of each day at Syracuse": J, September 6, 1976. "Sandy Gillan remembered": Int. Sandy Gillan Dwenger, 1993.

PAGE 61 "practically traverse in my imagination": letter from JCO to Robert Phillips, December 12, 1988. "dressed in a blue reefer coat": Int. Walter Sutton, 1992. "may have bored the hell out of some students": Int. Arthur Hoffman, 1992. "she later credited her professor": Int. JCO, 1992. "The Decline of the Enjambed Couplet": "The Transformation of Vincent Scoville," *Crossing the Border*.

PAGE 62 "I was in awe": Int. JCO, 1994. "stories published in *Syracuse Review*": copies of Joyce's undergraduate stories were provided by Prof. Arthur Hoffman and by the Joyce Carol Oates Archive. "lowly regarded": Int. Lori Negridge Allen, 1993. "would look at me askance": Int. Carol North Dixon, 1993. "her enormous big brown eyes": Int. Robert Phillips, 1993.

PAGE 63 "a hawk among the pigeons": Int. Mary Marshall, 1994. "despairing": Phillips interview, 1978. "a mistake from the start": Int. JCO, 1992.

PAGE 64 "a large room": Int. Lori Negridge Allen, 1993. "We didn't get along": Int. JCO, 1994.

PAGE 64   "The Phi Mu house itself": Int. Sandy Gillan Dwenger, 1993.
"Joyce was more adamant": Int. Sandy Gillan Dwenger, 1993.
"enormously disturbing": letter from JCO to Lars Ake Augustsson, November 22, 1993.
"a powdered and perfumed alum": Phillips interview, 1978.

PAGE 65   "stuffing toilet paper into chicken wire": Int. Lori Negridge Allen, 1993.
"Instead of working with Nietzsche or Kant": Int. JCO, 1994.
"The racial and religious bigotry": Phillips interview, 1978.

PAGE 66   "smoking, screaming with laughter": Int. JCO, 1994.
"now the friend was losing interest": Int. Lori Negridge Allen, 1993.
"rather spoiled": letter from JCO to Carol North, August 6, 1958.
"She was very strong-willed": Int. Carolina Oates, 1992.
"a limited interest in friendship": Int. Sandy Gillan Dwenger, 1993.
"the sound of a typewriter": letter to Greg Johnson from Fred Oates Jr., May 10, 1994.
"Most of the time she sits at her desk": letter from JCO (as "Bethlehem J. Hollis") to Carol North, August 1957.

PAGE 67   "the Plague of Millersport": letter from JCO (as "Robin J. Oates") to Carol North, July 1958.
"Joyce was never heavy . . . Unless she read a book five times": Int. Lori Negridge Allen, 1993.
"I, Joyce Oates, have been on a diet": letter from JCO to Carol North, August 6, 1958.
"Joyce complaining that she was unprepared": Int. Lori Negridge Allen, 1993.
"turn in thirty pages": O'Briant interview, 1986.
"I am now in the midst of being de-Spinozaed": letter from JCO to Carol North, June 3, 1957.

PAGE 68   "The rumor on campus": Int. Robert Phillips, 1993.
"she very deliberately would put something over the manuscript": Int. Sandy Gillan Dwenger, 1993.
"With Dottie": Int. Lori Negridge Allen, 1993.
"Dick felt that Joyce and Frank's relationship": Int. Dick Allen, 1993.
"Much to my embarrassment": Int. Lori Negridge Allen, 1993.

PAGE 69   "surprised the daylights out of all of us": Int. Sandy Gillan Dwenger, 1993.
"We were fairly 'serious' about each other": Int. JCO, 1992.
"I was so vexed": J, May 10, 1979.
"I might be going to convert to Judaism": letter from JCO to Carol North, June 5, 1960.
"another Katherine Anne Porter": Int. Walter Sutton, 1992.
"Dike was positive": Int. Robert Phillips, 1993.
"Donald felt a very deep respect": letter to Greg Johnson from Sally Daniels Dike, January 30, 1993.
"one of those very creative people": Int. Carol North Dixon, 1993.

PAGE 70   "without bound": Int. Arthur Hoffman, 1992.

PAGE 70   "an overwhelming personality": Int. Robert Phillips, 1993.

"I had the uneasy feeling": Int. JCO, 1992.

"hung her head": Int. Robert Phillips, 1993.

"could do no wrong": Int. Dick Allen, 1993.

"so upset she confronted him": Int. Lori Negridge Allen, 1993.

"not nice": Clemons interview, 1972.

"they were shocked by some of their daughter's stories": Int. Carolina and Frederic Oates, 1992.

"gifts of the mind and the imagination": letter to Frederic Oates from Donald Dike, June 28, 1959.

PAGE 71   "by a kindly professor who pointed out": letter from JCO to John Updike, March 27, 1989.

"I remember the shock": J, July 30, 1977.

"Rapport": *Syracuse 10*, October 1958; "A Confession," *Syracuse 10*, May 1960; "In the Old World," *Syracuse 10*, March 1959; "Sweet Love Remembered," published in both *Syracuse 10*, March 1960, and in *Epoch*, Spring 1960.

PAGE 72   "two young men had murdered a man": Int. JCO, 1994.

PAGE 74   "Joyce's identification with him was so strong": Int. Carol North Dixon, 1993.

"Late adolescence is the time for love": "Literature as Pleasure, Pleasure as Literature": *(Woman) Writer: Occasions and Opportunities*.

PAGE 75   "If I had known they had published James Farrell": Int. JCO, 1994.

"Enclosed are the stories": letter from JCO to James Henle, August 11, 1958.

"Do go over to Vanguard": letter from JCO to Robert Phillips, August 6, 1959.

"extremely intelligent and mature": letter from Walter Sutton to Harvard Summer School admissions office, May 1, 1959.

"the most difficult in the English department": letter from JCO to Robert Phillips, July 26, 1959.

PAGE 76   "blundered into the library": letter from JCO to Robert Phillips, August 22, 1959.

"really fine, and an inspiration": letter from JCO to Carol North, July 1, 1959.

"If I had had a 'JCO' with whom to talk": J, October 24, 1990.

"though there were few women professors": letter from JCO to Greg Johnson, April 27, 1996.

"I am beginning to wonder about the wisdom": letter from JCO to Robert Phillips, July 26, 1959.

PAGE 77   "I would have one of my characters write you": undated letter from JCO to Carol North, circa 1957.

"I have the idea he is not my kind": letter from JCO to Robert Phillips, August 22, 1959.

PAGE 78   "the most capable undergraduate student": letter from Walter Sutton to David Savan, October 17, 1959.

PAGE 78 "Joyce should try to be assertive": Int. Mary Marshall, 1994.
"The committee was very sympathetic": Int. Walter Sutton, 1992.
"a 75 percent disadvantage": Int. JCO, 1994.
"she suddenly changed": Int. Arthur Hoffman, 1992.
"and trying to look a little prettier": Int. Carol North Dixon, 1993.
"incredibly strong": Int. Sandy Gillan Dwenger, 1993.

PAGE 79 "as soon as you begin speaking": letter from JCO to John D'Arms, June 2, 1992.
"such a sophomoric thing to do": Int. Sandy Gillan Dwenger, 1993.
"I don't want to give a speech": Int. Lori Negridge Allen, 1993.

PAGE 80 "I had by that time compromised myself": letter from JCO to Carol North, June 5, 1960.
"Joyce was giggling all the way": Int. Sandy Gillan Dwenger, 1993.

Chapter 5   New Directions: 1960–62

PAGE 82 "she had heard that Wisconsin was an excellent place": Int. JCO, 1994.
"the faculty at Wisconsin had been very good": Int. Raymond Smith, 1994.
"I have a single room": letter from JCO to Carol North, August 31, 1960.
"the climate of respectability": letter from JCO to Walter Sutton, September 14, 1960.
"I *was* Franz Kafka for a while": quoted in Paul D. Zimmerman, "Hunger for Dreams," *Newsweek*, March 23, 1970: 109a.
"where 'primary' materials . . . 'scholarly' ": J, October 10, 1976.

PAGE 83 "after innocent first year graduate students": letter from JCO to Robert Phillips, November 4, 1960.
"had produced 322 pages of a novel": letter from JCO to Carol North, August 31, 1960.
"he was very warm": Int. JCO, 1994.
"was an emotional and romantic one": Int. Raymond Smith, 1992.
"but when you hit it off with someone": Int. Raymond Smith, 1994.
"happened rather quickly": J, November 24, 1979.
"Ray had wanted to write fiction": Int. Raymond Smith, 1994.

PAGE 84 "she announced that she was a writer": Int. Raymond Smith, 1992.
"I have become fairly well acquainted": letter from JCO to Robert Phillips, November 4, 1960.
"My meeting him": letter from JCO to Robert Phillips, November 24, 1960.

PAGE 85 "cold, brief, emotionless": J, May 10, 1979.
"Ray's sense of humor": J, August 2, 1978.
"they decided to marry during the break": J, November 24, 1979.
"absolutely shocked": Int. Carol North Dixon, 1993.
"Joyce is getting married": Int. Frederic Oates, 1992.

PAGE 85   "Since Ray would be in Philadelphia": Int. Raymond Smith, 1994.
PAGE 86   "I went about afterward": J, November 24, 1979.
          "at dawn, leaving my sleeping husband": "Coming Home," *USAir*, May
          1995: 108.
          "at least the comfortable solidarity": letter from JCO to Robert Phillips,
          January 31, 1961.
          "turning into those people": Int. JCO, 1994.
          "She was *human*": J, October 10, 1976.
PAGE 87   "dozens of ideas . . . There has never been anything so brutal": letter
          from JCO to Robert Phillips, May 18, 1961.
          "had a very narrow concept of literature": Int. JCO, 1994.
PAGE 88   "They had to winnow out some people": Int. JCO, 1994.
          "My husband and I will both get our degrees": letter from JCO to Robert
          Phillips, May 18, 1961.
          "everyone thought we would crash . . . too far to drive": J, January 20,
          1975.
PAGE 89   "they spent a great deal of time talking about Lynn": Int. Raymond
          Smith, 1994.
          "She confided to Bob Phillips": Int. Robert Phillips, 1993.
          "my little sister, whimsical as always": letter from JCO to Carol North,
          June 5, 1959.
          "Lynn was never animal-like": J, March 21, 1979.
          "wouldn't know me": Terry Gross, "Fresh Air" interview, 1993.
          "That Lynn was born on my birthday": letter from JCO to Greg John-
          son, April 27, 1996.
          "Mute Mad Child": *Southern Review*, Spring 1983: 357–58.
PAGE 90   "Autistic Child, No Longer Child": *Invisible Woman: New and Selected
          Poems*.
          "By the time Lynn was fifteen": Int. Carolina Oates, 1992.
          "just the realization": letter from JCO to Robert Phillips, February 22,
          1993.
PAGE 91   "Joyce expressed horror": letter from Henry B. Rule to Greg Johnson,
          July 2, 1993.
          "they did not mix much": letter from Charles W. Hagelman to Greg
          Johnson, July 6, 1993.
          "suspicious, clannish": letter from Robert J. Barnes to Greg Johnson,
          August 1, 1993.
          "Joyce and Ray must have been as poor . . . the low grades were not his
          fault": letter from Henry B. Rule to Greg Johnson, July 2, 1993.
PAGE 92   "He teaches very well": letter from JCO to Robert Phillips, August 3,
          1961.
          "persistent chemical smell to the air": Int. JCO, 1992.
          "very provincial": letter from JCO to Walter Sutton, November 13,
          1961.
          "I've changed my mind . . . mailing out some three or four": letter from
          JCO to Robert Phillips, August 14, 1961.

PAGE 93   "Joyce took the bus to the campus": Int. JCO, 1992.
           "She was offered both a teaching fellowship and a graduate scholarship":
           letter from JCO to Walter Sutton, November 13, 1961.
           "I hadn't known about it": Clemons interview, 1969.
           "I have written at least a thousand stories": letter from JCO to Robert
           Phillips, March 12, 1962.
           "so poorly written": letter from JCO to Dan Brown, November 27, 1969.
PAGE 94   "were written to demonstrate": JCO's application for a Guggenheim
           grant, October 10, 1966.
PAGE 95   "an ostensibly ordinary letter": J, July 30, 1977.
           "wrote such a lovely little letter": Int. JCO, 1994.
           "Perhaps [Dike] happened to tell you": letter from JCO to Robert
           Phillips, April 9, 1962.
           "hid under the charming name J C Oates": letter from JCO to Robert
           Phillips, October 25, 1960.
PAGE 96   "only two women": letter from JCO to Robert Phillips, March 12, 1962.
           "Clyde was singlehandedly responsible": letter from JCO to Sue Craine,
           1991.
PAGE 97   "We had an interesting though hectic trip": letter from JCO to Robert
           Phillips, June 9, 1962.
           "we are enormously pleased": letter from JCO to Walter Sutton, July 19,
           1962.
           "When you're young and naive": television interview with Emory Elliott,
           1988.

Chapter 6   "An Entirely New World": Detroit, 1962–64

PAGE 98   "large-scale additions": Frank B. Woodford and Arthur M. Woodford, *All
           Our Yesterdays, A Brief History of Detroit*: 360.
           "the old, the very young, the black": B. J. Widick, *Detroit: City of Race
           and Class Violence*: 140.
           "Murder City, U.S.A.": "Visions of Detroit," *(Woman) Writer: Occasions
           and Opportunities*.
PAGE 99   "more or less carved into an old slum": letter from JCO to Robert
           Phillips, June 9, 1962.
           "The University of Detroit has an idyllic-looking campus": letter from
           JCO to Walter Sutton, July 19, 1962.
           "Craine was a native Detroiter": Int. Tom Porter, 1993.
           "At the urging of its young new president": Herman J. Muller, S.J., *The
           University of Detroit, 1877–1977, A Centennial History*: 337–38.
           "academic excitement": letter from James Holleran to Greg Johnson,
           November 3, 1993.
PAGE 100   "very pleasing and rewarding . . . I've finished a novel": letter from JCO
           to Robert Phillips, August 8, 1962.
           "his personality at home . . . About half an hour after we went to bed . . .

an academic novel . . .": letter from JCO to Robert Phillips, September 23, 1962.

PAGE 101   "as a threat to her continuing employment": letter from Jim McDonald to Greg Johnson, September 7, 1993.

"unbearably bad": letter from JCO to Robert Phillips, February 4, 1963.

PAGE 102   "a four-bedroom, two-story colonial": "Visions of Detroit."

"decided to be brave": letter from JCO to Robert Phillips, May 14, 1963.

"a wonderful change . . . The racial problem is a large one . . . long, long tedious Jamesian novel": letter from JCO to Robert Phillips, July 1, 1963.

PAGE 103   "somehow ordered, civilized": letter from JCO to Robert Phillips, September 5, 1963.

"like a separate apartment . . . never say anything to anybody": Int. Evelyn Shrifte, 1993.

PAGE 104   "Oh, her eyes were as wide . . . thought she was a genius": Franks interview, 1980.

"Established in 1926": Guy Henle, "Vanguard Press: 62 Influential Years," *The Authors Guild Bulletin*, Summer 1989: 13–15.

PAGE 105   "quiet, reserved, polite, and charming": letter from James Holleran to Greg Johnson, November 3, 1993.

"Obviously, none of this was Joyce's cup of tea": letter from Jim McDonald to Greg Johnson, September 7, 1993.

"We talked easily": letter from Dan Brown to Greg Johnson, April 21, 1995.

"liked his company as an intimate": Daniel Curzon, "Hatred," in *The Revolt of the Perverts* (San Francisco: Leland Mellott Books, 1978): 47.

"Sometimes she made me stammer": Dan Brown, unpublished memoir, 1986.

"of the locker room variety": letter from Jim McDonald to Greg Johnson, September 7, 1993.

PAGE 106   "of an egalitarian, sibling sort of atmosphere": Int. JCO, 1994.

"unapproachable . . . a defensive shield": letter from Jim McDonald to Greg Johnson, September 7, 1993.

"had selected me as a presentable young man . . . taken away by the gods": Dan Brown, unpublished memoir, 1986.

PAGE 107   "In story after story": Haskel Frankel, "Universals," *Saturday Review*, October 26, 1963: 45.

"contains some of the best stories": Father William T. Cunningham, "UD Teacher Clicks with First Book," *Michigan Catholic*, January 23, 1964: 12.

"attack large-scale emotion": Stanley Kauffmann, "Violence Amid Gentility," *New York Times Book Review*, November 10, 1963: 4.

" 'obvious' debt": letter from JCO to Robert Phillips, November 14, 1963.

"though briefly": letter from JCO to Robert Phillips, August 24, 1964.

PAGE 108   "I don't know what there is exactly about her": letter from JCO to Robert Phillips, November 14, 1963.

PAGE 108   "Is it really true": letter from JCO to Robert Phillips, August 24, 1964.
"professionalism of Miss Oates's prose": Louise Duus, "The Population of Eden: J. C. Oates' 'By the North Gate,' " *Critique*, 7, ii (1964): 177.
"reticent . . . not her own favorite subject": Edwina Schaeffer, "Author Shuns Spoken Word," *Detroit News*, January 15, 1964: 1–E.

PAGE 109   "I don't think any more of [Kauffmann's] positive remarks": letter from JCO to Robert Phillips, November 14, 1963.
"Through a U.D. colleague Joyce met Marjorie Jackson Levin": Int. Marj Levin, 1993.
"the largest and oldest club": letter from Marilyn Lyman to Greg Johnson, October 4, 1993.

PAGE 110   "I couldn't believe it": Int. Marj Levin, 1993.
"Don't let her mild, ladylike manner": letter from JCO to Robert Phillips, June 4, 1965.
"rather classy": Int. JCO, 1994.
"since I do not consider most of my stories": letter from JCO to Blanche Gregory, November 16, 1963.
"was rejected by three editors": agency records, courtesy of Blanche Gregory, Inc.
"I was just amazed": Int. JCO, 1994.
"because it isn't actually a bad story": letter from JCO to Robert Phillips, January 22, 1964.

PAGE 111   "wonderful news": letter from JCO to Blanche Gregory, January 22, 1964.
"in their usual state of non-communication": letter from JCO to Robert Phillips, December 22, 1963.
"Jamesian horror": letter from JCO to Robert Phillips, January 22, 1964.
"in a series of yawns": letter from JCO to Robert Phillips, November 14, 1963.
"Joyce had submitted two previous novels": letter from JCO to Blanche Gregory, January 3, 1964.
"About this same time": letter from JCO to Blanche Gregory, January 22, 1964.

PAGE 112   "a comedy of the absurd": Int. Gertrude Bregman, 1992.
"so many novels of mine": letter from JCO to Robert Phillips, December 22, 1963.
"My theme is one I feel very strongly about": letter from JCO to Blanche Gregory, April 5, 1964.
"people I've admired passionately": letter from JCO to Robert Phillips, June 5, 1964.

PAGE 113   "The Thief": *North American Review*, September, 1966: 10–17.
"psychological shock": J, November 17, 1974.
"they purchased a handgun": letter from JCO to Greg Johnson, June 1, 1995.

PAGE 114   "they're publishing my horrendous novel": letter from JCO to Robert Phillips, June 5, 1964.

PAGE 115   "I was working myself ": Kuehl interview, 1969.
           "an old, old bridge": "Sunday Drive 1948," *Traditional Home*, March
           1995: 38.
PAGE 117   "lacks a moral purpose": "Against Nature": *(Woman) Writer: Occasions
           and Opportunities.*
           "a dramatization . . . enthusiasm for": from JCO's application for a
           Guggenheim grant, October 10, 1966.
PAGE 118   "wouldn't have worked": Int. Ray Smith, 1994.
           "admired for years and years": letter from JCO to Robert Phillips, Octo-
           ber 10, 1964.
           "pretended to be cosmopolitan": Dan Brown, unpublished memoir,
           1986.
PAGE 119   "ferociously shy": Int. Frank Corsaro, 1993.
           "forgotten that she'd made the father": Dan Brown, unpublished mem-
           oir, 1986.
           "how much she had enjoyed": Christmas card from JCO to Robert
           Phillips, 1964.
           "Joyce received the annual 'Author of the Year' award: "U-D Instructor
           Named Author of the Year," *Detroit News*, Decmeber 9, 1964: 8–C.
           "I don't have much faith": letter from JCO to Robert Phillips, October
           10, 1964: 5.
           "One of the excellent qualities": John Knowles, "A Racing Car Is the
           Symbol of Violence," *New York Times Book Review*, October 25, 1964: 5.
           "hysterically incoherent": K. G. Jackson, "Books in Brief," *Harper's*, No-
           vember 1964.
PAGE 120   "Really the novel was most carefully planned": letter from JCO to
           Robert Phillips, November 12, 1964.
           "bowled over by Faulkner . . . Proust": Clemons interview, 1969.
           "a certain blindness toward excess": Kuehl interview, 1969.
           "a laughably Balzacian ambition": Clemons interview, 1972.

Chapter 7   "Violence All Around Me": Detroit, 1965–67

PAGE 121   "Detroit by Daylight": *Prairie Schooner*, 42, ii (Summer 1968): 126.
           "I've been writing like a fiend . . . millions of words!": letter from JCO
           to Robert Phillips, January 21, 1965.
PAGE 122   "just what the play is about": Jack Gaver, " 'The Sweet Enemy' Has Sour
           Press," *Detroit News*, February 16, 1965. C–3.
           "meaningless . . . should not have been foisted": " 'The Sweet Enemy,' "
           The Greenwich Villager, February 16, 1965: 12.
           "neither a theatre-of-the-absurd": James Davis, " 'Sweet Enemy' Poor
           Theatre," *New York Daily News*, February 16, 1965: C–2.
           "Miss Oates can be really funny": Richard Watts, Jr., "The Danger in
           Halloween Guests," *New York Post*, February 16, 1965: B–14.

PAGE 123 "It is difficult to distinguish": Howard Taubman, " 'The Sweet Enemy' Opens," *New York Times*, February 16, 1965: 39.

"I was talked into writing . . . Williams remarked that": Louis Cook, "Joyce Carol Oates: Success and Failure in the Big-Time," *Detroit Free Press* magazine, March 14, 1965: 6.

"was almost worth the horrendous reviews": letter from JCO to Robert Phillips, February 24, 1965.

"Joyce's fictional version": "The Sweet Enemy," *Southern Review*, Summer 1967: 653–720.

"flashes of mad humor": Associated Press review, quoted in the Louis Cook article.

PAGE 124 "a good writing day": Int. Jim Holleran, 1993.

PAGE 125 "along with most modern writers": letter from JCO to Robert Phillips, April 27, 1965.

"incidental novel": letter from JCO to Robert Phillips, July 21, 1965.

"write itself": letter from JCO to Robert Phillips, September 21, 1965.

"an established member of the department": Int. Tom Porter, 1993.

PAGE 126 "She would spend her lunch hour": Int. John Ditsky, 1992.

"We'd be making jokes": Int. JCO, 1994.

PAGE 127 "simply wandered into her university office one day": JCO's detailed recollections of Wishnetsky are taken from int. with JCO, 1994, and from JCO's essay "Richard Wishnetsky: Joyce Oates Supplies a Missing View," *Detroit Free Press*, March 6, 1966: 1–2, 12–13.

"his manic gleeful laugh": J, January 26, 1977.

PAGE 128 "Richard had left the classroom": letter from JCO to Dan Brown, July 15, 1965.

"he left school and was admitted": many of the facts about Richard Wishnetsky's life and death are taken from more than a dozen newspaper accounts of the murder-suicide published in the *Detroit News* between February 12 and March 12, 1966.

PAGE 129 "[Joyce] would be talking to him": Int. John Ditsky, 1992.

PAGE 131 "An early version": agency records, courtesy of Blanche Gregory, Inc.

"Worried that her negative portrayal": letter from JCO to Robert Phillips, May 23, 1966.

"what might I have done?": J, January 26, 1977.

"The confrontation between this deeply troubled boy": letter from JCO to Robert Phillips, May 27, 1967.

"In Memory of an Ex-Friend, a Murderer": *Literary Review*, Spring 1968: 391–93.

"an uncanny identification": J, February 24, 1982.

PAGE 132 "the poor feeble ghost of Richard Wishnetsky": letter from JCO to Greg Johnson, November 8, 1993.

"it was a lot of fun": letter from JCO to Robert Phillips, July 29, 1965.

"would be fine as a play": letter from JCO to Dan Brown, August 3, 1965.

PAGE 132   "an overly complex game": letter from JCO to Dan Brown, August 28, 1965.
"doddering": letter from JCO to Robert Phillips, November 1, 1965.
"a little disappointed": letter from JCO to Evelyn Shrifte, October 21, 1965.

PAGE 133   "I would prefer that it not be published": letter from JCO to Evelyn Shrifte, April 20, 1965.
"I hope that isn't too corny": letter from JCO to Evelyn Shrifte, November 8, 1965.
"an extravaganza": letter from JCO to Robert Phillips, December 24, 1965.
"the best thing I've done": letter from JCO to Robert Phillips, December 13, 1965.
"the usual economy-built . . . brought down the house": undated letter from JCO to Robert Phillips, circa January 1966.

PAGE 134   "I am working stolidly": letter from JCO to Robert Phillips, February 23, 1966.
"It's mainly daydreaming": Clemons interview, 1969.
"I wrote a first draft straight out": J, January 12, 1975.
"How did Fielding and Richardson . . . clatters on": letter from JCO to Robert Phillips, April 22, 1966.

PAGE 135   "While painters worked on the house": letter from JCO to Evelyn Shrifte, July 29, 1966.
"Those parties usually ended": Int. Ray Smith, 1992.
"Joyce expressed horror and alarm": Int. Tom Porter, 1993.

PAGE 136   "enigmatic and aloof ": Int. Marilyn Lyman, 1993.
"very exquisite": Int. Marj Levin, 1993.
"Kay aspired to write fiction . . . like an older sister . . . There was a side of Kay": Int. JCO, 1994.
"domineering to Kay": Int. Marj Levin, 1993.
"gave her no room": Int. Patricia Burnett, 1993.
"Kay would drink several Manhattans": Int. Marj Levin, 1993.

PAGE 137   "Blue Skies": Miriam Dow and Jennifer Regan, eds., The Invisible Enemy (St. Paul: Graywolf Press, 1989): 78–94.
"Cheeverland": J, June 19, 1982.
"Ray and I have acquaintances": letter from JCO to Robert Phillips, April 22, 1966.
"a kind of comedy": letter from JCO to Robert Phillips, August 14, 1966.
"had a lot of contacts": Int. John Ditsky, 1992.
"felt very faintly the tinges": J, February 18, 1975.
"these people": letter from JCO to Robert Phillips, April 22, 1966.

PAGE 138   "You're proposing a total revolution": Int. Patricia Burnett, 1993.
"mixed with envy": Daniel Curzon, "Hatred."
"got all fired up": letter from JCO to Robert Phillips, August 25, 1967.

PAGE 139   "I had noticed her sitting on this couch": Int. David Madden, 1993.

PAGE 139   "One of the first in-depth critical essays": "The Violent World of Joyce Carol Oates," *Studies in Short Fiction*, 4, iv (Summer 1967): 369–73.
"excellent, lengthy talks": letter from JCO to Robert Phillips, October 26, 1966.

PAGE 140   "Very amusing, and accidentally so": "Dear Editor," *The New Leader*, June 20, 1966.
"Accomplished Desires": *The Wheel of Love.*
"greatest pleasure of civilization": Bellamy interview, 1972.
"reading constitutes the keenest": "Literature as Pleasure, Pleasure as Literature," *(Woman) Writer: Occasions and Opportunities.*

PAGE 141   "I'm sorry": letter from JCO to Blanche Gregory, July 13, 1966.
"brilliantly written": Rita Estok, *Library Journal*, April 1, 1966: 1926.
"bizarre or horrifying": J. Kitching, *Publishers Weekly*, February 18, 1966: 90.
"Miss Oates as a storyteller": Millicent Bell, "Her Own Rough Truth," *New York Times Book Review*, June 12, 1966: 4.
"Joyce's second collection sold even fewer copies": letter from JCO to Robert Phillips, February 22, 1968.
"I hope you enjoy it": letter from JCO to Evelyn Shrifte, May 28, 1966.
"Opening in the 1920s . . . which is violence": Greg Johnson, *Understanding Joyce Carol Oates* (Columbia: University of South Carolina Press, 1987): 28–46.

PAGE 143   "for fun, I guess . . . I don't know why I always elect": letters from JCO to Robert Phillips, May 23, 1966 and August 14, 1966.
"my external career as a writer": from JCO's application for a Guggenheim grant, October 10, 1966.

PAGE 144   "very, very slow and inconsiderate": letter from JCO to Robert Phillips, November 22, 1966.
"quite unhappy": letter from JCO to Robert Phillips, September 3, 1966.
"since I have difficulties in seeing": letter from JCO to Evelyn Shrifte, September 29, 1966.
"did a truly marvelous job": letter from JCO to Blanche Gregory, November 22, 1966.
"with its surrealistic intermingling": letter from JCO to Evelyn Shrifte, November 21, 1966.

PAGE 145   "relentless, cyclical pattern . . . very sentimental about leaving U.D.": letters from JCO to Elizabeth Graham, September 15 and December 12, 1966.
"I don't have associates who are particularly interesting": letter from JCO to Walter Sutton, September 13, 1966.
"the schedule grew tiresome": J, September 16, 1976.
"so transparent . . . powerful feelings all around me": Clemons interview, 1972.
"animal terror": J, November 9, 1982.

PAGE 146   "in a constant state of agitation . . . a rebellion of people": B. J. Widick, *Detroit: City of Race and Class Violence*: 161, 166–68.

PAGE 146   "a large building": letter from JCO to Robert Phillips, August 9, 1966.

PAGE 147   "I am at work on various stories": letter from JCO to Elizabeth Graham, February 13, 1967.

"No more Jewish stories": agency records, courtesy of Blanche Gregory, Inc.

"Higher-income people are more sophisticated": Charlotte Slater, "Author on the Rise," *Detroit News*, October 29, 1967: C–12.

"incredibly eerie": Int. Marj Levin, 1993.

PAGE 148   "I find poetry entirely different . . . quite swiftly and breathlessly . . . I've stopped writing poems": letters from JCO to Robert Phillips, March 21, May 5, and June 1, 1967.

"I'm really afraid that he is mad": letter from JCO to Robert Phillips, August 14, 1967.

"a love story, sort of ": letter from JCO to Robert Phillips, July 10, 1967.

PAGE 149   "the energy to type it onto good paper": letter from JCO to Elizabeth Graham, August 14, 1967.

"the rioting is all over . . . I am very disappointed in it": letters from JCO to Evelyn Shrifte, August 12 and May 16, 1967.

"Detroit is a mess": letter from JCO to Robert Phillips, August 25, 1967.

"I am very disappointed in it": letter from JCO to Evelyn Shrifte, May 16, 1967.

"She wrote to Blanche that perhaps the two novels": letter from JCO to Blanche Gregory, September 29, 1967.

"This isn't the best book": Elizabeth Janeway, "Clara the Climber," *New York Times Book Review*, September 10, 1967: 5.

PAGE 150   "a magical naturalistic quality": "Hardscrabble Heroine," *Time*, September 22, 1967: 106.

"the book tends to trail off ": Raymond A. Sokolov, "Tobacco Boulevard," *Newsweek*, October 2, 1967: 94.

"these people are real": Granville Hicks, "Fiction that Grows from the Ground," *Saturday Review*, August 5, 1967: 24.

"I am pleased": letter from JCO to Evelyn Shrifte, September 27, 1967.

"I hope the reviews will bring you": letter from Evelyn Shrifte to JCO, September 5, 1967.

"I like Evelyn very much . . . a conservative and reasonable course . . . I think that ultimately I will remain"; letters from JCO to Blanche Gregory, September 29, October 20, and October 27, 1967.

"a hardy commuting trip": "Visions of Detroit."

"uneagerly looking forward": letter from JCO to Elizabeth Graham, January 8, 1968.

"addicted . . . suddenly I am there again . . . for better or worse": "Visions of Detroit."

Chapter 8   A House in Windsor: 1968–70

PAGE 152   "beating them back": letter from JCO to Robert Phillips, August 25, 1967.
"The party was quite pleasant": letter from JCO to Elizabeth Graham, October 2, 1967.
"The whole racial situation": letter from JCO to Robert Phillips, January 22, 1968.

PAGE 153   "I felt rather homesick": letter from JCO to Robert Phillips, October 30, 1967.
"It will be a tremendous relief . . . Would you believe": letters from JCO to Elizabeth Graham, January 8, 1968 and February 26, 1968.

PAGE 154   "we got along well": Int. Raymond Smith, 1994.
"there are several other first-rate": letter from JCO to Robert Phillips, January 22, 1968.
"how difficult it would be for a person of Joyce's gifts": Int. Lois Smedick, 1993.
"but just when you think you've got close": quoted in Betty Lee, "Tracking the elusive author," *Toronto Globe and Mail*, March 14, 1970: B–8.
"We seem to have a surplus": letter from JCO to Robert Phillips, September 10, 1968.

PAGE 155   "the best novels": letter from JCO to Elizabeth Graham, January 8, 1968.
"a kind of model": letter from JCO to Robert Phillips, January 10, 1968.
"She was struck": letter from Dan Brown to Greg Johnson, April 21, 1995.
"the great drama of capitalist society": "The Charmer Who Lost His Way," JCO's review of *Go, Said the Bird*, by Geoffrey Cottrell, The *Detroit News*, January 15, 1967: D–6.

PAGE 156   "I'm really a romantic writer": Kuehl interview, 1969.
"slowly and languidly": letter from JCO to Elizabeth Graham, February 26, 1968.
"with the speed of a glacier . . . in the current novel . . . I was astonished": letter from JCO to Robert Phillips, July 3, 1968 and undated letter, circa March 1968.
"immensely egotistical": letter from JCO to Elizabeth Graham, February 26, 1968.
"Evelyn managed . . . Evelyn was quite unhappy": letters from JCO to Robert Phillips, March 18 and May 14, 1968.

PAGE 157   "most gracious . . . for many minutes": letter from JCO to Elizabeth Graham, June 17, 1968.

PAGE 158   "And Joyce's agents continued to sell": agency records, courtesy of Blanche Gregory, Inc.
"Quite often, according to Gert": Int. Gertrude Bregman, 1992.
"quite small, with only two bedrooms": letter from JCO to Elizabeth Graham, May 14, 1968.
"The river (and surrounding waterways)": Int. Raymond Smith, 1992.

PAGE 158   "We love the new home . . . so many things to do": letter from JCO to
           Elizabeth Graham, July 3, 1968.
           "pretty impressed": Int. Father Norman McKendrick, 1993.
PAGE 159   "I was puritanical then, stubborn": JCO, "A Corner to Write In," *Elle*
           Decor, October 1991: 132.
           "We never really thought about it much": Grobel interview, 1993.
           "Certainly my work would not have precluded children": Int. JCO, 1992.
           "emotional room": Int. Marj Levin, 1993.
           "Your baby sounds delightful": letter from JCO to Robert Phillips,
           March 21, 1967.
PAGE 160   "I feel odd, almost apologetic": J, June 10, 1982.
           "she felt perplexed by the idea": letter from JCO to Dan Brown, Decem-
           ber 21, 1969.
           "I would imagine that not even Nabokov": from a letter quoted in San-
           ford Pinsker, "Suburban Molesters: Joyce Carol Oates' *Expensive Peo-*
           ple," *Midwest Quarterly* 19 (Autumn 1977): 89.
PAGE 161   "thinly codified secret . . . long unbroken mildly fevered sessions": "Af-
           terword" to paperback edition of *Expensive People* (Princeton: Ontario
           Review Press, 1990).
PAGE 162   "forty to fifty pages each day": Bellamy interview, 1972.
           "a blaze of activity": letter from JCO to Elizabeth Graham, September
           16, 1968.
           "finally managed to buy a dress": letter from JCO to Evelyn Shrifte,
           September 30, 1968.
           "I'm just not interesting": letter from JCO to Robert Phillips, Septem-
           ber 10, 1968.
           "a slender, soft-voiced young woman": Warren Bower, "Bliss in the First
           Person," *Saturday Review*, October 26, 1968: 34.
           "Joyce Carol Oates is completely her own woman": *Publishers Weekly*,
           August 12, 1968: 47.
           "She has proved": Granville Hicks, "What is Reality?" *Saturday Review*,
           October 26, 1968: 33.
PAGE 163   "brilliant . . . artificial": Louis T. Grant, "A Child of Paradise," *The Na-*
           tion, November 4, 1968: 475.
           "forte of frail, large-eyed women novelists": J. E. Bailey, "The Doomed
           and the Damned," *Time*, November 1, 1968: 102.
           "even more foolish": letter from JCO to Evelyn Shrifte, November 4,
           1968.
           "did pretty well": Int. Evelyn Shrifte, 1993.
PAGE 164   "the New York literary life": letter from JCO to Elizabeth Graham,
           March 15, 1969.
           "vibrating field of other people's experiences": Clemons interview, 1972.
           "larger and more significant than the sum": "Visions of Detroit."
           "very deeply into, very obsessed": *Ohio Review* interview, 1973.
           "participants in a vast social drama": McLaughlin interview, 1985.
           "her initiation . . . just before the 1967 riots": Greg Johnson, *Under-*

standing Joyce Carol Oates (Columbia: University of South Carolina Press, 1987): 77–87.

PAGE 166 "responded in a very weak, rather victimized way": Kuehl interview, 1969.

PAGE 167 "I was living like that": Phillips interview, 1978.

"a handsome book salesman": Dan Brown, unpublished memoir, 1986.

"bizarre paranoia": *Ohio Review* interview, 1973.

PAGE 168 "impossible to publish": agency records, courtesy of Blanche Gregory, Inc.

"very, very curious": Int. Patricia Burnett, 1993.

"One of the reasons": Int. Ruth Reed, 1993.

PAGE 169 "We consider her": quoted in William Silverman, "She Lets Her Fingers Do the Talking," *Detroit News*, February 2, 1969: 8.

PAGE 170 "unrealistic goals—autonomy without experience": JCO, "On the Student Revolution," *Detroit News Magazine*, February 16, 1969: 12.

"poems are nearly all lyric expressions . . . during a period of intense concentration": *Ohio Review* interview, 1973.

PAGE 171 "Some time ago": letter from JCO to Robert Phillips, February 9, 1970.

"I remember her sitting in my studio": Int. Patricia Burnett, 1993.

"She and Ray had taken up jogging": letter from JCO to Dan Brown, July 11, 1969.

"Ray and I have a new image": letter from JCO to Evelyn Shrifte, June 9, 1969.

PAGE 172 "spectrally thin": Paul D. Zimmerman, "Hunger for Dreams," *Newsweek*, March 23, 1970: 109A.

"unable to gain any weight . . . displays of food . . . a pleasant hobby": letters from JCO to Dan Brown, September 24 and October 3, 1969.

PAGE 173 Material on anorexia nervosa was taken from the following: Richard A. Gordon, *Anorexia and Bulimia: Anatomy of a Social Epidemic* (Cambridge: Blackwell, 1990); Hilde Bruch, M.D., *The Golden Cage: The Enigma of Anorexia Nervosa* (New York: Vintage Books, 1979); Susie Orbach, *Hunger Strike: The Anorectic's Struggle as a Metaphor for Our Age* (New York: Norton, 1986); and Joan Jacobs Brumberg, *Fasting Girls: The Emergence of Anorexia Nervosa as a Modern Disease* (Cambridge: Harvard University Press, 1988).

PAGE 174 "a very sensitive area": this source prefers to remain anonymous.

"it was so funny": Int. Ruth Rattner, 1993.

"there would be maybe half a canned peach": Int. Betsey Hansell, 1995.

"cared very little for food": Int. Maxine Kumin, 1993.

PAGE 175 "I love to be fatigued, malnourished": J, March 14, 1983.

"I should be a rational, contained person": Bellamy interview, 1972.

"there's this kind of empty blur": *Brockport Writers Forum* television interview, 1980.

"I don't really identify with my physical self": Grobel interview, 1993.

"had no appetite": J, April 5, 1979.

"Without appetite, steadily losing weight": "Food Mysteries": 28.

PAGE 176 "almost every minute of my life": Grobel interview, 1993.

PAGE 176　"a group of students occupied the Religious Studies building": Int.
Gene McNamara, 1993.
"a small clique of students": letter from JCO to Dan Brown, December
12, 1969.

PAGE 177　"created a climate of horror": Int. Gene McNamara, 1993.
"I was young, foolish, and rash": Int. Lois Smedick, 1993.
"The real 'Saul Bird' of the story": letter from JCO to James Dubro, November 5, 1970.
"Each novel calls forth hundreds": letter to *Mediums*, 1982: 19.
"had put the London affair": letter from JCO to Dan Brown, December 12, 1969.

PAGE 178　"a vehement, voluminous, kaleidoscopic novel": Robert M. Adams,
"The Best Nightmares Are Retrospective," *New York Times Book Review*, September 28, 1969: 4.
"that rarity in American fiction": "Urban Gothic," *Time*, October 10,
1969: 108.
"when Miss Oates's potent, life-gripping imagination": Calvin Bedient,
"Vivid and Dazzling," *The Nation*, December 1, 1969: 611.
"a fitfully realized character": L. E. Sissman, "The Whole Truth," *The
New Yorker*, December 6, 1969: 241.
"inability to perceive or create meaning": Benjamin DeMott, "The Necessity in Art of a Reflective Intelligence," *Saturday Review*, November
22, 1969: 73.
"violence in the head": Elizabeth Dalton, "Joyce Carol Oates: Violence
in the Head," *Commentary*, June 1970: 75.
"her classes were going well . . . she taught naturally": letters from JCO
to Dan Brown, December 12, 1969 and January 17, 1970.

PAGE 179　"Unwritten, untouched": J, November 15, 1974.
"she was pleased by the response . . . Fawcett paid $62,000": letters from
JCO to Dan Brown, December 21, 1969 and January 17, 1970.
"Gothicism, whatever it is": "Writing as a Natural Reaction," *Time*, Oc-
tober 10, 1969: 8.
"Joyce was 'visiting writer' . . . Evelyn Shrifte called to say": letters from
JCO to Dan Brown, March 2, 1970 and April 14, 1970.

PAGE 180　"Things like that happen every day": Paul D. Zimmerman, "Hunger for
Dreams," *Newsweek*, March 23, 1970: 109A.
"Writing fiction today": NBA acceptance speech printed in Mary
Kathryn Grant, *The Tragic Vision of Joyce Carol Oates*: 163–4.

PAGE 181　"relieved that the media frenzy . . . annoyed by the flood": letters from
JCO to Dan Brown, March 31, 1970 and April 14, 1970.
"I've lost about 20 pounds": Dudar interview, 1970.
"such a strain on both Ray and me . . . the first one hundred pages": letters from JCO to Elizabeth Graham, June 2, 1970 and April 22, 1970.

PAGE 182　"came to congratulate him . . . a field day . . . I received the beautiful
grandmother card": letters to JCO from Blanche Woodside, November
7, 1969; March 6, 1970; May 11, 1970.

PAGE 183   "I practically have to be carried home": letter from JCO to Elizabeth Graham, June 2, 1970.
"It was just like a hallucination": Aronson interview, 1971.
"Much of this novel": letter from JCO to Robert Phillips, September 16, 1970.
"while writing *Wonderland* . . . most despairing, unanswerable questions . . . might be my last novel . . . confusing atmosphere about it": Bellamy interview, 1972.

PAGE 184   "consciously re-thinking each scene": letter from JCO to Robert Phillips, September 16, 1970.
"domestic and demonic love": letter from JCO to Evelyn Shrifte, September 4, 1970.
"probably an immoral novel": Bellamy interview, 1972.
"With *Wonderland* I came to the end of a phase": Clemons interview, 1972.
"told me excitedly": letter from JCO to Elizabeth Graham, February 8, 1971.

PAGE 185   "Spanning the years 1939 to 1971 . . . tyranny raised to a level of grotesque insanity": Greg Johnson, *Understanding Joyce Carol Oates* (Columbia: University of South Carolina Press, 1987): 119–20.

PAGE 186   "inwardly tightening circles": Gordon O. Taylor, "Joyce Carol Oates: Artist in Wonderland," *Southern Review*, Spring 1974: 491.
"a fairly hectic three-day schedule . . . It's a lot of fun to re-imagine": letter from JCO to Elizabeth Graham, October 5, 1970.

PAGE 187   "one must really call Joyce Carol Oates": John Alfred Avant, *Library Journal*, September 1, 1970: 2829.
"create a verbal excitement": Richard Gilman, "The Disasters of Love, Sexual and Otherwise," *New York Times Book Review*, October 25, 1970: 62.
"powerful proof of her stature": Daniel Stern, "The Many Voices of Human Loneliness," *Washington Post Book World*, October 25, 1970: 4.
"seemed in therapeutic need": Pearl K. Bell, "A Time for Silence," *New Leader*, Nov. 16, 1970: 14.
"How Ray and I managed to get . . . I have my typewriter": letter from JCO to Robert Phillips, December 18, 1970.
"quite an adventure for us": letter from JCO to Elizabeth Graham, February 8, 1971.

Chapter 9   Transformation of Being: Hollywood and London, 1971–72

PAGE 188   "besieged by responsibilities": letter from JCO to Robert Phillips, March 4, 1971.
"at a loss to understand . . . intrude upon my life": letter from JCO to Elizabeth Graham, March 4, 1971.

PAGE 189   "excessive concern": letter from JCO to Kay Smith, February 9, 1971.

PAGE 189   "is spiritually exhausting and depressing . . . a nervous breakdown": letters from JCO to Elizabeth Graham, February 8 and July 27, 1971.
"self-conscious and abrasive": letter from JCO to Robert Phillips, May 28, 1971.
"had taken to coming out to visit me . . . really happened": letters from JCO to Gail Godwin, October 26, 1971 and February 18, 1972.

PAGE 190   "the most miserable winter": letter from JCO to Robert Phillips, Feburary 1, 1971.
"*please* write sometime soon": letter from JCO to Elizabeth Graham, February 8, 1971.
"after Ray and her family": letter from JCO to Dan Brown, February 3, 1970.
"I tried to keep up . . . literary likes and dislikes": "The Joys of Friendship Among Today's New Women," *Today's Health*, September 1974: 64.

PAGE 191   "it does seem that we have much in common . . . When I get into New York . . . an attempt to record . . . Yes, indeed": letters from JCO to Gail Godwin, December 8, 1969; September, 1970; May 1, 1972.

PAGE 193   "a way I could have gone": Clemons interview, 1972.
"some authentic details": letter from JCO to Gail Godwin, July 23, 1971.
"Enormous dosage . . . something dangerous": J, December 2, 1974.
"The Fact Is: We Like to Be Drugged," *McCalls*, June 1970: 69.

PAGE 194   "I've been writing stories . . . one typewriter . . . a new medium . . . we generally can't think of much . . . Kazin is very gentlemanly": letters from JCO to Robert Phillips, March 4, April 6, and April 16, 1971.

PAGE 195   "I liked him immensely": letter from JCO to Gail Godwin, July 23, 1971.
"shy, doesn't drink or smoke": Alfred Kazin, "Oates," *Harper's*, August 1971: 78.
"What a creative transformation": letter from Alfred Kazin to Greg Johnson, June 2, 1992.

PAGE 196   "like a character in a youth movie": letter from JCO to Gail Godwin, July 11, 1971.
"my head is filled with contrasts": letter from JCO to Gloria Whelan, April 30, 1971.
"her vision was seared": letter from JCO to Dan Brown, May 2, 1971.
"very nice": letter from JCO to Kay Smith, May 16, 1971.
"a blustering, mercenary man": letter from JCO to Gloria Whelan, May 18, 1971.
"Mr. Swanson is the number one Hollywood agent . . . our good luck": letter from JCO to Kay Smith, May 16, 1971.

PAGE 197   "intensity and rather aggressive people": letter from JCO to Gloria Whelan, May 18, 1971.
"I drove 50 desperate miles": letter from JCO to Robert Phillips, May 28, 1971.
"Things seem to get more hectic . . . sounds like inflation": letter from JCO to Elizabeth Graham, July 27, 1971.

PAGE 198   "very generous": letter from JCO to Evelyn Shrifte, April 13, 1971.

"she considered the figure unreal": letter from JCO to Dan Brown, May 19, 1971.

"I don't make many revisions": undated letter from JCO to Gail Godwin, circa late 1971.

"in a kind of trance": Bellamy interview, 1972.

"persona . . . but why?": J, May 30, 1976.

"I am so spiritually exhausted": letter from JCO to Gail Godwin, October 26, 1971.

"gotten to know": letter from JCO to Kay Smith, October 1, 1971.

"an extraordinary hour": letter from JCO to Gloria Whelan, September 28, 1971.

"glorious moments": letter from JCO to Robert Phillips, September 30, 1971.

"We realized . . . now and then": letters from JCO to Kay Smith, October 1 and December 15, 1971.

"How great it is to be in London": letter from JCO to Robert Phillips, September 30, 1971.

"Thank God . . . for the anonymity": letter from JCO to Gail Godwin, October 26, 1971.

"edgy, as always": letter from JCO to John and Sue Ditsky, October 19, 1971.

"Joyce was beginning to repeat herself": Peter S. Prescott, "Everyday Monsters," *Newsweek*, October 11, 1971: 96.

"Miss Oates loves to splash blood on us": Geoffrey Wolff, *New York Times Book Review*, October 24, 1971: 5.

"As time goes on": letter from JCO to Robert Phillips, November 12, 1971.

"It is so angry a review": letter from Evelyn Shrifte to JCO, October 22, 1971.

"reserved for Olympians": letter from JCO to John and Sue Ditsky, October 29, 1971.

"horrible and compelling": letter from JCO to Gloria Whelan, November 12, 1971.

"it's about one of *the* California experiences": undated letter from JCO to John Ditsky, circa November 1971.

"Joyce had been following newspaper accounts": Avant interview, 1972.

"Ellen Friedman has astutely noted": Ellen Friedman, *Joyce Carol Oates*: 119.

"a love story . . . evolution of her consciousness": Int. with the Literary Guild, 1993.

"central 'invisible' core": letter from JCO to Evelyn Shrifte, May 2, 1973.

"a 'positive' novel": letter from JCO to Gail Godwin, February 8, 1972.

"to move toward a more articulate moral position": Clemons interview, 1972.

PAGE 204   "someone in my novel": letter from JCO to John and Sue Ditsky, December 12, 1971.
"hit a snag": J, December 1, 1974.
"no idea how to deal with": J, December 2, 1974.
"She'd written to congratulate him": letter from JCO to Dan Brown, October 1970.

PAGE 205   A. M. Rosenthal: Joseph C. Goulden, *Fit to Print: A. M. Rosenthal and His Times*: 400.
"single, and last, meeting": letter from JCO to John and Sue Ditsky, October 19, 1971.

PAGE 206   "constant rain . . . exciting at first . . . vagrants . . . the very nadir": J, December 1 and 2, 1974.
"then I gave in": J, July 26, 1978.
"the experience of feeling": J, August 11, 1977.
"wildly transcendent experience": J, January 29, 1977.
"Transformation. Conversion": J, September 8, 1977.

PAGE 208   "I saw that the Void is primary": J, July 26, 1978.

PAGE 209   "I have just not felt right about *Wonderland*": letter from JCO to Evelyn Shrifte, January 6, 1972.
"approach the end of one segment": "New Heaven and Earth," *Saturday Review*, November 4, 1972: 54.

PAGE 210   "numinous dreams": J, August 11, 1977.
"I've disciplined myself ": letter from JCO to Gail Godwin, February 18, 1972.
"I find that I'm rising earlier and earlier . . . immediately rushed": letters from JCO to Robert Phillips, June 9 and May 29, 1972.
"I feel a completely new, exhilarated certainty": letter from JCO to Evelyn Shrifte, May 8, 1972.

PAGE 211   "in some strange mystical way": letter from JCO to John and Sue Ditsky, May 2, 1972.
"schoolgirl French": letter from JCO to John and Sue Ditsky, January 1972.
"an extraordinarily beautiful city . . . I realized . . . their new neighborhood was much quieter": letters from JCO to Gloria Whelan, February 3 and March 20, 1972.
"lovely—the way Greenwich Village" letter from JCO to Robert Phillips, May 29, 1972.
"a quaint crooked Englishy building": letter from JCO to Gail Godwin, March 28, 1972.
"spires, domes, chimneys . . . without any transition": letter from JCO to John and Sue Ditsky, April 1, 1972.

PAGE 212   "get along awfully well . . . effortlessly, generously": letter from JCO to John Ditsky, January 3, 1972.
"What impressed me most": Int. John L'Heureux, 1992.
"awfully nice . . . I had looked forward to meeting him": letter from JCO to Robert Phillips, February 11, 1972.

PAGE 212   *the* most unpretentious person": letter from JCO to Kay Smith, June 22, 1972.

"my children called her 'the thin lady' ": letter from Margaret Drabble to Greg Johnson, August 10, 1994.

PAGE 213   "I am a shameless hero-worshipper": letter from JCO to Gail Godwin, June 12, 1972.

"She is very warm, gracious": letter from JCO to Robert Phillips, May 29, 1972.

"I felt almost faint": "A Visit with Doris Lessing," *Southern Review*, Autumn 1973: 874.

"involved in a rapid-fire . . . countless books . . . excellent visit . . . Perfection": letters from JCO to Robert Phillips, July 4 and August 5, 1972.

"Colin Wilson is a genius . . . male chauvinist ideas": letters from JCO to Gail Godwin, July 3 and July 30, 1972.

PAGE 214   "too concerned with themselves": letter from Colin Wilson to Greg Johnson, November 8, 1994.

"confused with the rather impersonal": *Ohio Review* interview, 1973.

PAGE 215   "a high intelligence at work carelessly": Roger Sale, "A High Intelligence at Work Carelessly," *New York Times Book Review*, July 9, 1972: 23.

"out of a deep, meticulous concern": letter from JCO to *The New York Times Book Review*, July 30, 1972.

"this year has been a transforming one": letter from JCO to Kay Smith, August 2, 1972.

PAGE 216   "for people who are sensitive": Avant interview, 1972.

"probably will not move for a while": letter from JCO to Gail Godwin, September 18, 1972.

"Does Joyce Carol Oates ever eat or sleep?": *Publishers Weekly*, August 7, 1972: 40.

"One could wish that Miss Oates": Charles Lam Markmann, " The Puzzle of People," *The Nation*, December 4, 1972: 568.

"the busiest coroner": *Time*, October 23, 1972: 109.

"for themes and forms": Michael Wood, "Diminished People," *The New York Times Book Review*, October 1, 1972: 6.

"there is a prodigality of talent": William Abrahams, "Stories of a Visionary," *Saturday Review*, September 23, 1972: 76.

PAGE 217   "We've simplified our lives": letter from JCO to Elizabeth Graham, October 20, 1972.

"for so many years I endured": letter from JCO to Gail Godwin, September 18, 1972.

"Forgive me for being 'personal' ": letter from JCO to Elizabeth Graham, November 16, 1972.

PAGE 219   "There's no need to write about happy people": *Ohio Review* interview, 1973.

"passive and deathly": "Women's Liberation: What Will We Lose?" *The American Scholar*, Winter 1972–73: 144.

"good God!": letter from JCO to Gail Godwin, November 23, 1972.

Chapter 10   The Visionary Gleam: 1973–75

PAGE 221   "Fascinating, the human mind . . . and I always fail": J, January 19, 1973.
"I was writing until 7:30": J, January 9, 1973.
PAGE 222   "gained just enough": J, February 23, 1973.
"a long complicated novel": Batterberry interview, 1973.
"synthesis of two poles of consciousness": J, October 27, 1973.
"Corinne": *North American Review*, Fall 1975: 30–42.
"too raw, unassimilated": J, July 24, 1989.
PAGE 223   "Do you know, these things mean": letter from JCO to Robert Phillips, April 12, 1973.
"frankly, personally": letter from JCO to Walter Sutton, February 7, 1973.
"indifference to the house": J, March 17, 1973.
"that curious state": letter from JCO to Gail Godwin, May 2, 1973.
PAGE 224   "Some of her early work": letter from Larry Goldstein to Greg Johnson, June 22, 1992.
"I am horrified at the prospect of myself ": undated letter from JCO to Charles East, circa January 1973.
"untruthful": Helen Vendler, " The Ideas and Words, but Not the Surfaces and Cadences": *New York Times Book Review*, April 1, 1973: 8.
Letters from Oates and Vendler: *New York Times Book Review*, April 29, 1973.
PAGE 225   "I can't take her dislike for my writing": J, March 27, 1973.
"I wonder if you might": letter from JCO to Evelyn Shrifte, April 5, 1973.
"in a tiresome, really mean way": J, April 16, 1973.
"the most emotion I've felt": letter from JCO to Gail Godwin, May 2, 1973.
"it all seemed to me funny": letter from JCO to Anne Sexton, May 24, 1973.
"I'm really new at this": Dave Skal, "Joyce Carol Oates: Crazy Scenes and Demon Lovers," *The Post*, April 20, 1973: 3.
"she was a victim of Robert Bly": this source prefers to remain anonymous.
PAGE 226   "congenial, lively group": J, March 3, 1973.
"a glorious time": letter from JCO to Kay Smith, July 6, 1973.
"stopped for a few days near Stanford": letter from JCO to Evelyn Shrifte, July 12, 1973.
"Unless you see the coast": letter from JCO to Gail Godwin, October 1, 1973.
"Such foolish, exhibitionistic people": J, August 27, 1973.
PAGE 227   "obviously a genius . . . felt rather homesick": letter from JCO to Robert Phillips, August 13, 1973.
"she was on page 442": letter from JCO to Gail Godwin, October 1, 1973.
"want to write the longest novel . . . most uncontrollable . . . should be a complex . . . screamed at our panel": letters from JCO to Robert Phillips, September 12, August 13, and November 19, 1973.

PAGE 227   "it's my secret belief . . . Ray kept looking around": letters from JCO to
            Gail Godwin, October 1 and November 19, 1973.
            "not as frightening": J, September 7, 1973.
PAGE 228   "ungainly—an outpouring without a shape": Benjamin DeMott, " 'Now'
            Rituals," *Atlantic*, December 1973: 127.
            "the most carefully shaped of her novels": Walter Clemons, "Sleeping
            Princess," *Newsweek*, October 15, 1973: 107.
            "one of the most boring women imaginable": Martha Duffy, "Power
            Vaccum," *Time*, October 15, 1973: E3.
            "hypnotic dramatization": Calvin Bedient, "The Story of Sleeping
            Beauty and a Love That Is Like Hatred," *New York Times Book Review*,
            October 14, 1973: 18.
            "unmoved by excellent reviews": J, October 27, 1973.
PAGE 229   "relief. I had been prepared": letters from JCO to Robert Phillips, Octo-
            ber 12, 1973.
            "I loved writing it . . . I think so": letters from JCO to Gail Godwin, Oc-
            tober 1 and November 19, 1973.
            "least ambiguous book . . . astonishment that *these words* . . . Working
            constantly": J, November 19, 1974.
PAGE 230   "submit work to small presses": letter from JCO to Blanche Gregory,
            April 12, 1973.
            "the Dickens or Trollope": Int. John Martin, 1993.
PAGE 231   "I read it to see if the high standards": JCO, "Recent Books: Keithley,
            Levine, Sale, and Roth," *American Poetry Review*, May-June 1974: 45.
            "a 'Joyce Carol Oates' collection": "Haphazard Thoughts: From the
            Ridiculous to the Sublime," *American Poetry Review*, September-
            October 1973: 47.
            "one day she was simply daydreaming": Int. Gene McNamara, 1993.
            "extraordinary letters to Dr. Boesky": Dale Boesky, "Correspondence
            with Miss Joyce Carol Oates," *International Review of Psychoanalysis* (2)
            1975: 481–86.
PAGE 232   "This is really too much": J, December 18, 1973.
            "looked pale, haggard, bitter . . . should be considered dangerous": J,
            December 29, 1973.
            "despicable bitch. She'd better stay out of my way": letter from Dan
            Brown to Blanche Gregory, September 27, 1972.
PAGE 233   "astonished": letter from JCO to Dan Brown, January 4, 1974.
            "Injured Innocence": letter from Dan Brown to JCO, January 17, 1974.
            "no prejudice against homosexuals": letter from JCO to Dan Brown,
            January 24, 1974.
            "simply wished him well": letter from JCO to Dan Brown, February 1,
            1974.
            "a legal action of some kind": letter from JCO to *New York Times Book
            Review*, April 14, 1974.
            "Dear Ms. Oates": letter from "Dr. Carl T. Arnow" to JCO, May 9, 1974.
PAGE 234   "defending her actions": letter from JCO to "Mr. Arnow": May 21, 1974.

PAGE 234   "Curzon's strategy": letter from JCO to *The Advocate*, April 20, 1984.
"From the Dark Side of the Earth": *Women Whose Lives Are Food, Men Whose Lives Are Money*.
"It was such an experience": Quinn interview, 1975.
"my own bad judgment . . . in a few days": J, November 8, 1974.

PAGE 235   "his wisdom stretches out to infinity": letter from JCO to Gloria Whelan, January 28, 1974.
"without a hitch": letter from JCO to Kay Smith, July 22, 1974.
"a most interesting place": letter from JCO to Robert Phillips, September 3, 1974.
"I'll quit while I'm ahead": J, July 7, 1974.
"impressed (as one must be)": J, October 15, 1974.
"we are on this earth to communicate": television interview with Dick Cavett, 1980.

PAGE 236   "antithetical . . . will accept no assignments": J, February 11, 1975.
"had a very enjoyable lunch with Philip Roth": letter from JCO to Robert Phillips, June 1, 1974.

PAGE 237   "Must make an effort": J, October 22, 1975.
"vampiristic": Bellamy interview, 1972.
"like chopping wood," "not our sort": quoted in Clemons interview, 1972.
"WRITER CONFESSES": Int. with Barthelme by Jerome Klinkowitz, in Joe David Bellamy, ed., *The New Fiction: Interviews with Innovative American Writers* (Urbana: University of Illinois Press, 1974).

PAGE 238   "AUTHORESS SHIFTS LOYALTIES": letter from JCO to Donald Barthelme, 1974.
"I said it": letter from Donald Barthelme to JCO, January 9, 1974.
"will be the first novel I have written": J, January 16, 1975.
"a small mountain": J, August 7, 1974.

PAGE 239   "threats against my life": J, January 16, 1975.
"difficult, teasing novel . . . felt some anxiety": J, November 23, 1974.

PAGE 240   "writing a novel is a *process*": J, January 12, 1975.

PAGE 241   "Joyce Carol Oates is frankly murderous": Josephine Hendin, *New York Times Book Review*, September 1, 1974: 5.
"Oates at her worst": John Alfred Avant, "New and Notable Fiction," *The New Republic*, March 29, 1975: 31.
"unrelieved by humor": Robert Phillips, *Commonweal*, April 11, 1975: 58.
"dark hearts": Marian Engel, "Women Also Have Dark Hearts," *New York Times Book Review*, November 24, 1974: 7.
"How is a writer to contemplate his critics?": J, March 5, 1973.

PAGE 242   "no notice at all": letter from JCO to Robert Phillips, September 25, 1974.
"a gracious, frank, amusing": J, April 28 to May 10, 1975.
"I reached up and removed it from the shelf": letter from Cynthia Ozick to Greg Johnson, September 28, 1993.
"treated like a queen": J, May 10, 1975.
"There is something about Joyce Carol Oates": Quinn interview, 1975.

PAGE 243   "One Saturday morning": Int. Ruth Reed, 1993.
PAGE 244   "stray unformed exciting thoughts": J, March 23, 1975.
           "A prose-poem": J, July 26, 1975.
           "*The Assassins* is probably the most interesting": letter from JCO to
           Evelyn Shrifte, June 24, 1975.
PAGE 245   "astonished": letter from JCO to Robert Phillips, September 12, 1975.
           "automatic writing": Elizabeth Pochoda, "Joyce Carol Oates honoring
           the complexities of the real world," *New York Times Book Review*, Au-
           gust 31, 1975: 6.
           "a very bad, nearly incoherent novel": Peter S. Prescott, "Varieties of
           Madness," *Newsweek*, October 27, 1975: 99B.
           "roughest, most repetitive read": *Time*, February 23, 1976: 65.
           "these suspicious, isolated, hysterical victims": J. D. O'Hara, *New York
           Times Book Review*, November 23, 1975: 18.
           "The novel is vivid": Suzanne Juhasz, *Library Journal*, November 15,
           1975: 2174.
           "Stylistically, she is irreproachable": Patricia S. Coyne, "Thinking Man's
           Breakfast," *National Review*, September 3, 1976: 965.
PAGE 246   "disliked *The Assassins* so intensely": J, September 28, 1976.
           "Since I am a woman . . . finished by now": J, March 7, 1976.

Chapter 11   Invisible Woman: 1976–77

PAGE 247   "go crazy": Int. Marj Levin, 1993.
PAGE 248   "by no means a quiet, insular": letter from JCO to Robert Phillips, De-
           cember 12, 1977.
           "Anyone who teaches knows": Phillips interview, 1978.
           "She was a very popular teacher": Int. Gene McNamara, 1993.
PAGE 249   "One day Joyce came to her office": J, January 4, 1977.
           "by those eyes": letter from Marinelle Ringer to Greg Johnson, July 12,
           1995.
           "an electrifying teacher": letter from Max Alberts to Greg Johnson, Au-
           gust 6, 1995.
           "reclusive . . . dark circles underneath": letter from Rebecca Bragg to
           Greg Johnson, July 3, 1995.
           "were always quite formal": Int. Sally Rosenbluth, 1993.
PAGE 250   "Oates was a magnificent teacher": letter from Dan Zins to Greg John-
           son, 1992.
PAGE 251   "ugly windowless fluorescent-glaring . . . to wrest some enjoyment from
           it": J, January 21, 1977.
           "oversized doomed class": J, January 14, 1977.
           "came regularly in various states . . . classes were in session": "Dossier—
           Joyce Carol Smith, 1975–76, 1976–77," University of Windsor.
           "The Canadian literary 'scene' ": J, May 20, 1976.
PAGE 252   "I seem rootless, homeless": J, December 12, 1974.

PAGE 252   "We should leave Windsor": J, February 22, 1977.
"From what I could see of Joyce's life": Int. Ruth Rattner, 1993.
"amount of time I spend with others": J, October 20, 1976.
"Though I don't drink myself": J, April 1, 1976.
"no exhaustion or weariness": J, November 7, 1976.

PAGE 253   "be very careful": Int. Betsey Hansell, 1995.
"borrowed Betsey Hansell's utterly squalid studio": letter from JCO to
Ruth Rattner, September 1, 1981.

PAGE 254   "so wonderfully helpful": Int. Betsey Hansell, 1995.
"was always generous to other people": Int. Ruth Reed, 1993.
"Their house was right on the Detroit River": Int. Gloria Whelan, 1993.
"Once we got to know her": Int. John Reed, 1993.
"She has an impish wit": Int. Lois Smedick, 1993.

PAGE 255   "We had an argument about it": Int. Gene McNamara, 1993.
"[Gene] doesn't think I have the right": J, November 30, 1976.
"Colin, I've been a naughty girl": Int. Colin Atkinson, 1993.
"None of his family members had known": Int. Charles Murrah, 1993.

PAGE 256   "The McNamara-Lowther situation": J, August 2, 1977.
"She did a real job": Int. Colin Atkinson, 1993.
"The Art of the Novel," by Gene McNamara: *Chicago*, November 1979:
70–78.

PAGE 257   "I thought it would be a double coup": Int. Jim Tuttleton, 1993.
"going to be hard to return": letter from JCO to John Ditsky, July 16, 1977.

PAGE 258   "my marriage has made my life stable": J, July 22, 1977.
"How fortunate for Virginia": J, May 28, 1974.
"a conversation with Ray": J, December 12, 1974.
"wholly determined": letter from JCO to Dan Brown, May 19, 1971.

PAGE 259   "Marriage necessitates a fantastic concentration": J, December 6, 1976.
"what would it profit me, really": J, February 20, 1977.
"At the time I knew them": Int. Gloria Whelan, 1993.
"perfect for Joyce": Int. Marj Levin, 1993.
"Ray, in certain areas, had confidence": Int. Lois Smedick, 1993.

PAGE 260   "He handled the whole situation": Int. Evelyn Shrifte, 1993.
"At the age of 39": J, September 8, 1977.
"After 15 years of marriage": J, June 6, 1976.

PAGE 261   "Where the hell is Joyce Carol Oates?": J, January 6, 1977.
"interesting experience": J, January 8, 1977.
"smiling, very courteous": J, March 15, 1977.

PAGE 262   "the 'most hated' of contemporary writers": J, April 1, 1976.
"As my novels grow in complexity": Phillips interview, 1978.
"so sane, so conservative . . . enjoyable to write": J, March 21, 1976.

PAGE 263   "Am trying to think out a voice": J, April 29, 1976.
"I wanted to put myself": Applebaum interview, 1978.
"even to save the life of the mother": J, July 24, 1976.

PAGE 264   "decidedly minor": J, May 20, 1976.
"got out of hand": letter from JCO to Gail Godwin, June 7, 1976.

PAGE 264   "high-spirited, sharp, intelligent . . . beyond Windsor": J, May 20, 1976.
            "I'm sorry to be sending so much material": letter from JCO to Blanche
            Gregory, July 3, 1976.
PAGE 265   "No one deserves happiness more than my parents": J, July 22, 1976.
            "spent a wonderful two hours": J, July 22, 1976.
            "personal demeanor is refreshingly matter-of-fact": letter from John Up-
            dike to Greg Johnson, August 28, 1993.
            "her wonderfully productive, creative, experimental, fearless approach":
            letter from John Updike to Greg Johnson, August 7, 1993.
PAGE 266   "rather discouraged by the fundamental silliness": J, August 17, 1976.
            "absolute kinship": Phillips interview, 1978.
PAGE 267   "waiting 'to swallow us up' ": "Against Nature."
PAGE 268   "the whole novel is a prayer . . . autobiographical in part": Phillips inter-
            view, 1978.
            " The world has no meaning": " The Nature of Short Fiction; or, the Na-
            ture of My Short Fiction," preface to *Handbook of Short Story Writing*
            (Cincinnati: Writer's Digest Books, 1970): xii.
            "wretched physically": J, October 10, 1976.
            "so much for granted": J, October 14, 1976.
            "my Puritan sense of morality": J, October 20, 1976.
PAGE 269   "a more human, more immediate & warm sort of novel": J, November 1,
            1976.
            "Joyce Carol Oates has written her best novel in years": Josephine
            Hendin, *New York Times Book Review*, November 28, 1976: 8.
            "it lacked clarity": Paul D. Zimmerman, "Blurred Vision," *Newsweek*,
            November 15, 1976: 115.
            "an inconclusive": Susan Lardner, "Oracular Oates," *The New Yorker*,
            January 3, 1977: 74.
PAGE 270   "a kind of 9th grade book report": J, January 23, 1977.
            "generous but not very perceptive": J, November 26, 1976.
            "lightweight": J, June 27, 1976.
            "How strange, how perplexing": J, July 22, 1976.
            " The banality of most of the criticism": J, February 12, 1977.
            "a delirium of activity . . . my writing": J, January 1, 1977.
PAGE 271   "absolutely enchanted": J, March 24, 1977.
            "One piece of the puzzle": J, March 27, 1977.
            "a drug, sweet and irresistible": J, March 29, 1977.
            "She would wonder at my 'industry' ": J, April 23, 1977.
PAGE 272   "One is appalled by the crimes": J, March 27, 1977.
            "Possibility of my going to Princeton": J, April 12, 1977.
            "surely one of the paradisial places": letter from JCO to John Ditsky,
            July 5, 1977.
PAGE 273   "a kindly, funny, erudite man . . . gradual infatuation": J, May 4, 1977.
            "all the more meaningful": letter from JCO to Anne Tyler, July 22, 1976.
            "I remember being a little apprehensive": letter from Anne Tyler to Greg
            Johnson, August 28, 1993.

PAGE 273   "gradual infatuation . . . moving, terrible": J, May 4, 1977.
            "grayly the same": letter from JCO to Gail Godwin, February 3, 1977.
PAGE 274   "felt very encouraged": letter from JCO to Robert Phillips, February 9,
            1977.
            "like an old friend": letter from JCO to Gail Godwin, October 28, 1977.
            "I have been somewhat discouraged": letter from JCO to Blanche
            Gregory, October 31, 1977.
            "oversized deranged novel": letter from JCO to John Ditsky, June 23, 1977.
            "I will never, never be able to translate": J, August 28, 1977.
            "depressed?—like me?": J, September 3, 1977.
PAGE 275   "What am I doing with my life": J, September 1, 1977.
            "skim through it": J, July 30, 1977.
            "I am weeping with agonizing gratitude": J, August 29, 1977.
PAGE 276   "I feel so good about knowing someone like Updike": J, October 12, 1977.
            "I *want* to be open": J, December 2, 1977.

Chapter 12   "Moving to Princeton, Moving to Bellefleur": 1978–80

PAGE 277   "impulse to retreat": J, April 19, 1978.
            "to live sequestered and protected": J, June 5, 1978.
            "a thrill of panic": J, May 12, 1978.
PAGE 278   "doomed to perform in the role of 'Joyce Carol Oates' ": J, February 20,
            1978.
            "restriction to a few cubic feet": J, July 26, 1975.
            "burning in a dove's face": Aronson interview, 1971.
PAGE 279   "If life is random and accidental": J, June 1, 1978.
            "everything is idyllic": J, March 28, 1978.
            "I work at the piano": letter from JCO to Gail Godwin, June 23, 1978.
            "I'm not equal to it": J, July 28, 1978.
PAGE 280   "I must reread Simone Weil": J, January 7, 1982.
            "to force myself to eat": J, March 9, 1978.
            "even that apple a nuisance to eat": J, April 6, 1978.
PAGE 281   "Oh God . . . What embarrassment": J, March 11, 1978.
            "At heart it's an old, elemental paradox": J, May 3, 1978.
PAGE 282   "I would be embarrassed to tell anyone": letter from JCO to Blanche
            Gregory, September 25, 1978.
            "It was quite a blunt rejection": letter from JCO to Gail Godwin, De-
            cember 13, 1978.
            "I feel that while I am fond of Vanguard": letter from JCO to Blanche
            Gregory, September 30, 1978.
            "I know I've hurt Evelyn badly": J, November 12, 1978.
PAGE 283   "one of the sweetest, most sensitive": letter from JCO to Gail Godwin,
            December 13, 1978.
            "heartbroken": Int. Evelyn Shrifte, 1993.
            "indifference to money": J, September 26, 1978.

PAGE 283 "I can't leave Blanche": J, September 30, 1978.
"Such consideration doesn't go unnoticed": letter from JCO to Blanche Gregory, August 3, 1978.
"watershed . . . tranquility, rest, balance": J, June 17, 1978.
"dread . . . couldn't tolerate": J, July 5, 1978.

PAGE 284 "With its unrelenting dark prose": Janet Wiehe, *Library Journal*, August 1978: 1532.
"rich and dark and convoluted": Anne Tyler, *Washington Post Book World*, December 3, 1978: 14.
"a hugely ambitious novel": Victoria Glendinning, "Hungry for God": *New York Times Book Review*, November 26, 1978: 11.
"made a vow not to write fiction": J, August 11, 1978.
"Trenner had attended Princeton": Int. Richard Trenner, 1992.

PAGE 285 "As soon as we saw the house": J, May 21, 1978.
"I don't *want* to move again": J, September 6, 1978.
"being so small, is very communal": letter from JCO to Robert Phillips, September 14, 1978.

PAGE 286 "How *intense* life at Princeton . . . implored me to come to Columbia": J, September 22, 1978.
"Anima is an image-bearer": J, October 17, 1978.
"What a crammed, accelerated life!": J, September 30, 1978.
"O Rare Princeton": J, October 12, 1978.
"Princeton is superb": letter from JCO to Kay Smith, October 13, 1978.
"This is such an incontestably *lovely* part of the country": letter from JCO to Elizabeth Graham, October 12, 1978.

PAGE 287 "I am accursed": J, September 30, 1978.
"slowly, amazingly slowly": J, October 12, 1978.
"Writing for hours yesterday": J, October 27, 1978.

PAGE 288 "it felt, yesterday": J, December 24, 1978.
"nothing is more richly . . . Why, I wonder": J, December 12, 1978.
"the skill as a hostess": J, January 1, 1979.
"as my 'renown' grows": J, November 7, 1978.
"How do people become eccentric?": J, Christmas 1978.
"to write the one story": J, November 26, 1978.

PAGE 289 "my waking dream": J, January 25, 1979.
"A vampirous creation": J, February 19, 1979.
"a tiny nugget or kernel": J, April 5, 1979.
"What *is* this bizarre novel about?" J, February 6, 1979.
"Mike Keeley remembered": Int. Edmund Keeley, 1993.
"a sense of extraordinary self-worth": J, April 9, 1979.

PAGE 290 "How much I like Henry!": J, February 25, 1979.
"I wanted him so badly as a friend": J, August 1, 1979.
"pointlessness of it": J, July 31, 1979.

PAGE 291 "nothing seems worth enduring": Phillips interview, 1978.
"What is most autobiographical": "Preface to *Marya: A Life*": (*Woman*) *Writer: Occasions and Opportunities*.

PAGE 291   "create, in Marya": J, May 10, 1979.
         "The headachey delirium of one day": J, July 14, 1979.
PAGE 292   "taking notes": J, August 29, 1979.
         "fluctuating between the two 'halves' ": J, November 13, 1979.
PAGE 293   "easy, conversational, discursive style": J, October 26, 1979.
         "Joyce Carol Oates last night": Ned Rorem, *The Nantucket Diary of Ned Rorem, 1973–85*: 267.
PAGE 294   "a tall, slender, graceful woman": Margaret M. Keenan, "A Writing Workshop with Joyce Carol Oates," *Princeton Alumni Weekly*, November 5, 1979: 20.
         "I've never found this person": J, November 22, 1979.
         "fecund with ideas": Walter Clemons, *Newsweek*, October 29, 1979: 99.
         "wealth of trenchant social and psychological observation": A. G. Mojtabai, *New York Times Book Review*, October 7, 1979: 30.
         "Contrary to the outlandish speculation": letter from JCO to *New York Times Book Review*: October 28, 1979.
PAGE 295   "Sometimes it seems that my life": J, December 31, 1979.
         "served to convince me": letter from JCO to Elizabeth Graham, November 9, 1970.
         "a firecracker of a closet drama": Jack Kroll, "Action at the 'Cube,' " *Newsweek*, February 21, 1972: 99.
PAGE 296   "My detachment or fatalism is such": J, February 22, 1980.
         "anguish of frustration": J, March 8, 1980.
         "with so much idiotic labor": J, March 21, 1980.
         "For me the highest values": J, March 28, 1980.
PAGE 297   "very closely tied in . . . representative people": audio interview on *Angel of Light* with Tom Vitale, 1982.
PAGE 298   "quiet . . . peace . . . tranquility": J, April 14, 1980.
         "innumerable luncheons": letter from JCO to Robert Phillips, June 9, 1980.
         "The 'Jewishness' of one's spirit": J, July 7, 1980.
PAGE 299   "one of the helium-filled flame-empowered passenger balloons": J, September 7, 1980.
         "How sad, how abrupt": J, July 14, 1980.
         "an experiment in solitude": letter from JCO to Robert Phillips, August 11, 1980.
         "Dutton launched its first Oates title": "Oates Lowers Royalty to Help New Novel," *Publishers Weekly*, April 18, 1980: 75.
PAGE 300   "enjoy this while it lasts": J, August 13, 1980.
         "*Bellefleur* is the most ambitious": John Gardner, "The Strange Real World," *New York Times Book Review*, July 20, 1980: 1.
         "a totally absorbing reading experience": Dan Cryer, "A Critic's Choice for the Best of Literary 1980," *Newsday*, January 4, 1981: 20.
         "shockingly humorless": Russell Banks, "Joyce Carol Oates: In a Gothic Manor," *Washington Post Book World*, August 17, 1980: 14.
         "wonderful to talk with": J, May 3, 1980.

PAGE 301 "I've come to the conclusion that food": letter from JCO to Robert Phillips, August 11, 1980.
"considerable weight loss": J, October 17, 1980.
"felt suddenly that I couldn't continue . . . always enjoyed his company": J, September 5, 1980.
"Kay, like Walter Kaufmann, so vigorously alive": J, November 1, 1980.

PAGE 302 "very thin veneer of the 'old' gay, spirited, energetic Kay": undated letter from Elizabeth Graham to JCO.
"I've been so depressed . . .": letter from JCO to Gloria Whelan, November 7, 1980.
"I feel so angry about this": J, November 1, 1980.
"Thank God for romance": J, November 28, 1980.
"A vision on the page": J, November 13, 1980.

Chapter 13   The Gothic Wonderland: 1981–84

PAGE 303 "Why 'genre,' one might ask?": Afterword to *Mysteries of Winterthurn* (Berkley paperback edition).

PAGE 304 "It is surely the riskiest novel": letter from JCO to Robert Phillips, April 1, 1982.
"a sobering and instructive experience": "Pleasure, Duty, Redemption Then and Now: Susan Warner's *Diana*": *(Woman) Writer: Occasions and Opportunities*.

PAGE 305 "painful from the start": letter from JCO to Gail Godwin, September 19, 1981.
"sold only a few thousand copies in hardcover": Int. Billy Abrahams, 1993.

PAGE 306 "letter from a fan/would-be novelist": letter from JCO to John Ditsky, March 19, 1982.
"a madwoman . . . I'm not particularly eager": J, February 24, 1982.
"To me, she's the most loathsome creature": Lawrence Grobel, *Conversations with Capote*: 140–41.

PAGE 307 "reading, with feverish interest": J, May 1, 1981.
"could write endlessly": J, June 8, 1981.
"Kay's death": J, August 10, 1981.
"Once one has tasted blood": J, December 10, 1981.
"I am infatuated": J, June 7, 1981.

PAGE 308 "Set beside these eloquent and unfailingly genial mandarins": J, May 7, 1982.
"Not the most felicitous image": J, May 20, 1982.
"little kinship": J, May 31, 1982.
"the subject really doesn't interest me": J, November 6, 1984.
"Most women writers have been narrow": J, May 31, 1982.

PAGE 309 "Our current fashionable beliefs": letter from JCO to Philip Roth, February 25, 1974.

PAGE 309 "Why Is Your Writing So Violent?": *New York Times Book Review*, March 29, 1981: 15, 35.

PAGE 310 "believed that Joyce Carol Oates was insane": J, June 10, 1982. "Groping, crawling": J, March 28, 1982.

PAGE 311 "not as a diversion or spin-off": Abrahams, "Stories of a Visionary," *Saturday Review*, September 1972: 76.
"Radical experimentation": Schumacher interview, 1986.
"Except for experimental work": Int. Gertrude Bregman, 1993.

PAGE 312 "if I don't sell her to *The New Yorker* . . . It's their magazine": McCombs interview, 1986.
"the heavyweight is Joyce Carol Oates": "Introduction" to *The Best American Short Stories 1982* (Houghton Mifflin, 1982): xiv.
"I don't quite know why": Phillips interview, 1978.
"My temperamental problem is": J, December 5, 1981.

PAGE 313 "One must be stoic": "Notes on Failure": *The Profane Art*.
"the writer's effort to detach himself": "The World's Worst Critics," *New York Times Book Review*, January 18, 1987: 1.

PAGE 314 "an original, deeply personal rereading": *Publishers Weekly*, June 19, 1981: 94.
"all of the authors you treat, including me": letter from John Updike to JCO, July 28, 1983.
"a strong and fascinating novel": Thomas R. Edwards, "The House of Atreus Now," *New York Times Book Review*, August 16, 1981: 18.
"a serious, ambitious failure": Walter Clemons, "Wild Oates," *Newsweek*, August 17, 1981: 74.
"an antiromance": Diane Johnson, "Balloons and Abductions," *New York Times Book Review*, September 5, 1982: 1.
"arbitrary amalgam": *The New Yorker*, September 27, 1982: 145.

PAGE 315 "the reader can't care": Peter S. Prescott, "Romantic Agony," *Newsweek*, September 20, 1982: 92.
"futility and tedium": Patricia Blake, "Antimacassar," *Time*, October 4, 1982: 81.
"hatchet job": James Wolcott, "Stop Me Before I Write Again: Six Hundred More Pages by Joyce Carol Oates," *Harper's*, September 1982: 67–69.
"Word is out": J, July 13, 1982.
"everyone is under stress": letter from JCO to Gail Godwin, January 5, 1985.

PAGE 316 "endlessly provocative, charming": J, June 21, 1984.
"became friendly very, very quickly": Int. Henry Bienen, 1993.
"She is very close to a small group": Int. Daniel Halpern, 1992.
"casual call that you receive": Int. Robert Fagles, 1992.

PAGE 317 "Ray is as unusual, in his own way, as she is": this source prefers to remain anonymous.

PAGE 318 "Are you contradicting me?": this source prefers to remain anonymous.
"very girlish and playful": Int. Jeannie Halpern, 1993.

PAGE 318   "in the midst of a quite ordinary conversation . . . gossipy lunches":
            Elaine Showalter, "My Friend, Joyce Carol Oates: An Intimate Portrait,"
            Ms., March 1986: 45.

PAGE 319   "asked me about it, and sure enough . . . likes to whisper": Int. Alicia
            Ostriker, 1993.
            "She is a wonderful gossip": Int. Lucinda Franks, 1992.
            "has a way of taking in information": Int. Daniel Halpern, 1992.
            "Joyce likes to sop up lots of information": Int. Henry Bienen, 1993.
            "quite angry": Int. Emory Elliott, 1992.

PAGE 320   "to make the work into the best work it could be": Int. Pinckney Bene-
            dict, 1992.
            "she's a phenomenal editor": "Pinckney Benedict," in Michael Schu-
            macher, ed., *Reasons to Believe: New Voices in American Fiction*: 56.

PAGE 321   "My students at Princeton": television interview, *The Originals*, 1989.
            "I should like a permanent position": J, March 24, 1982.
            " 'most myself' (whatever that phantasm is)": letter from JCO to Robert
            Phillips, September 11, 1982.
            "Who knows!": J, March 19, 1984.

PAGE 322   "I *seem* to have the voice I want": J, May 15, 1982.
            "What particularly grates": letter from JCO to Robert Phillips, April 20,
            1982.
            "his intelligent comments": J, November 29, 1982.
            "too leisurely": letter from Karen Braziller to JCO, May 16, 1983.

PAGE 323   "disturbing piece of fiction . . .": J, February 11, 1983.
            "starkly 'confessional' ": letter from JCO to Gail Godwin, January 5, 1985.
            "three 'JCO's' ": J, March 5, 1983.
            "A silly excursion the other day": J, April 10, 1983.

PAGE 324   "Dear God, how I need another great long debilitating": J, March 14, 1983.

PAGE 325   "extremely violent": J, May 2, 1983.
            "side effects that last for about 24 hours": letter from JCO to Robert
            Phillips, November 18, 1983.
            "Essentially I feel myself still in the making": J, October 30, 1983.

PAGE 326   "How the rest of my life is dwarfed . . . Oh yes": J, December 11, 1983.
            "And when I think of the books I've published": letter from JCO to
            Robert Phillips, February 19, 1983.
            "I have been discouraged off and on": J, February 15, 1984.

PAGE 327   "an ornate period piece": Eloise Salholz, "Gothic Horrors," *Newsweek*,
            February 6, 1984: 79A.
            "Miss Oates' plots are an odd admixture": *The New Yorker*, February 27,
            1984: 133.
            "allowing full play": Alan Ryan, "Murder, Mayhem and Melodrama,"
            Washington Post Book World, February 19, 1984: 8.
            "I surprised myself": J, June 30, 1984.

PAGE 328   "a more dramatic contrast": J, March 19, 1984.
            "I wish I could retrieve my earlier younger self . . . grateful to him": J,
            May 2, 1984.

PAGE 328   "I can't imagine another author of stories": letter from William Abrahams to JCO, January 19, 1986.
"every writer hopes for": Joan Smith, "Word Perfect," *San Francisco Focus*, March 1995: 38.

PAGE 329   "Too modest, Joyce!": letter from JCO to Greg Johnson, April 27, 1996.
"the size of a penny": J, July 25, 1984.
"I've said yes to most invitations": "After Amnesia," unpublished essay, 1995.

PAGE 330   "things entirely alien to me": J, August 10, 1984.
"The Republicans, Reagan, etc.": J, August 24, 1984.
"Stray dream-images": J, October 3, 1984.

PAGE 331   "a political novel": J, October 24, 1984.
"The logistics of *The Green Island*": J, October 29, 1984.
"like dousing the surface of the desk": J, November 6, 1984.

Chapter 14   Woman of Letters: 1985–90

PAGE 335   "writing it so drains me of energy": letter from JCO to John Updike, March 1, 1985.

PAGE 336   "I said to myself . . . but Norman Mailer": quoted in "Bellow and Welty Read to Audience at Opening of PEN Celebrations," *New York Times*, September 19, 1985: C–18.
"I'm so glad to be a friendly acquaintance": letter from JCO to Eudora Welty, October 10, 1985.
"To speak of boxing is, for me": letter from JCO to Norman Mailer, October 1, 1985.
"contrary to stereotyped notions": *On Boxing*.

PAGE 337   "his really quite astounding knowledge": letter from JCO to Ron Levao, October 1986.

PAGE 338   "Mischievous friends urged me to say 'yes' ": letter from JCO to Russell Banks, June 22, 1988.
"so many quite responsible and knowledgeable people": letter from JCO to Russell Banks, April 3, 1987.
"just too sunny for me . . . so strongly with Hagler": letter from JCO to Russell Banks, April 23, 1987.
"another of those indescribably bizarre . . . I had never done anything like this": letter from JCO to Mary Morris, January 25, 1988.

PAGE 339   "a cheery (though a bit humbling) luncheon . . . a good thing": letter from JCO to John Updike, February 5, 1988.

PAGE 340   "appalled, talked me out of it": letter from JCO to Robert Phillips, December 13, 1987.
"the introvert's habitual response . . . attentive, even rapt, throughout": "Meeting the Gorbachevs": *(Woman) Writer: Occasions and Opportunities*.

PAGE 341   "Precisely why we were invited": letter from JCO to Robert Phillips, March 30, 1986.

PAGE 341   "would pay considerably more": letter from JCO to Robert Phillips, January 24, 1986.
"an excellent idea": J, March 7, 1986.
"a 'continuing appointment' ": letter from JCO to Edmund Keeley, June 23, 1986.
"I am the first 'Roger S. Berlind Distinguished Lecturer' ": letter from JCO to Robert Phillips, April 11, 1987.
"My duties remain the same": letter from JCO to Robert Phillips, October 26, 1987.

PAGE 342   " 'Thank you,' I said": J, October 6, 1987.
"it's comforting and securing": Int. Russell Banks, 1993.
"The other evening here in Princeton": letter from JCO to John Updike, March 6, 1989.
"I've always thought that if Princeton people": letter from JCO to Richard Ford, September 14, 1989.

PAGE 343   "New York critics": John Updike, "What You Deserve Is What You Get," The New Yorker, December 28, 1987: 119.
"Solstice is her best novel": Robert Jones, "Still Lost in the Maze," Commonweal, March 8, 1985: 150.
"a disturbing and unsparing story": Rebecca Pepper Sinkler, "Time and Her Sisters," New York Times Book Review, January 20, 1985: 4.
"I am glad to see Miss Oates back": Mary Gordon, "The Life and Hard Times of Cinderella," New York Times Book Review, March 24, 1986: 7.
"unlike Oates's recent gothic and Victorian excesses": Ann H. Fisher, Library Journal, March 15, 1986: 78.
"one of her most powerful": Walter Clemons, "A Kiss Isn't Just a Kiss," Newsweek, August 17, 1987: 68.
"an American masterpiece": James Atlas, Vanity Fair, August 1987: 140.
"rallies all her strengths": John Updike, "What You Deserve Is What You Get," The New Yorker, December 28, 1987: 119.
"I listened in shocked disbelief ": letter from JCO to David Shapiro, December 26, 1987.

PAGE 344   "the most moving of all possible reviews": J, December 25, 1987.
" 'in house' excitement of a kind": J, December 16, 1986.
"hysterical little novel": Jonathan Yardley, "Joyce Carol Oates on Automatic Pilot," Washington Post Book World, January 6, 1985: 3.
"a less than satisfying psychological portrait": Dorothy Allison, "Tame Oates," Village Voice, May 20, 1986: 56.
"a big novel": R. Z. Sheppard, Time, August 31, 1987: 62.
"futility and incipient violence": Sven Birkerts, "A Passion for Uncle," New York Times Book Review, August 16, 1987: 3.

PAGE 345   "Why do some reviewers sometimes misrepresent books": letter from JCO to Sven Birkerts, August 18, 1987.
"I'm a counterpuncher": "Joyce Carol Oates: American Appetites": television interview with Tom Vitale, 1989.

PAGE 345 "Is this true only of 'prolific' writers?": letter from JCO to *New York Times Book Review*, August 20, 1989.

"Surely it is an act of gratuitous malice": letter from JCO to *Show* magazine, February 25, 1986.

"It is profoundly discouraging": undated letter from JCO to Michiko Kakutani, circa December 1988.

PAGE 346 "They talked to no one": Richard Stern, "Some Members of the Congress," *Critical Inquiry*, Summer 1988: 882.

PAGE 347 "No more grotesquely homosocial piece of writing": "Response to Richard Stern," *Critical Inquiry*, Autumn 1988: 193.

"was meant to hurt me": letter from Richard Stern to Greg Johnson, August 24, 1992.

PAGE 348 "I was getting a reputation for only reviewing books I liked": letter from JCO to John Updike, January 21, 1989.

"she identified more strongly with them": television interview with Tom Vitale, 1989.

"It was painful to write": letter from JCO to Robert Phillips, March 18, 1989.

PAGE 349 "uncanny ability": Int. Russell Banks, 1993.

"I would go crazy": Grobel interview, 1993.

"I actually look forward to the several": letter from JCO to Russell Banks, April 26, 1987.

PAGE 350 "I was one of the foreign 'stars' ": J, August 25, 1987.

"the college really tried to get value": Int. Madison Smartt Bell, 1992.

"should be fun": letter from JCO to Alicia Ostriker, March 12, 1985.

"In such episodes of extraordinary bidding": undated letter from JCO to Edmund Keeley, circa August 1987.

"over 13 other eager high-headed young pacers": letter from JCO to Elaine Showalter, July 20, 1988.

"Impish won $62,000": letter from JCO to Russell Banks and Chase Twichell, July 23, 1989.

PAGE 351 "turn[ed] inward": "At Home," typescript essay from the Joyce Carol Oates Archive, Syracuse University.

PAGE 352 "The Delaware Valley is hardly our own personal discovery": "THE DELAWARE VALLEY: The Enchantment of the Counter-World," typescript essay from the Joyce Carol Oates Archive, Syracuse University.

"wasn't that happy, because Princeton isn't a friendly sort of town": Int. Tama Janowitz, 1993.

PAGE 353 "When her parents visit". Int. Ted Weiss, 1992.

"How did the malnourished circumstances": "Facts, Visions, Mysteries": 152.

"they are so enthusiastic": Mary Wozniak, "The parents behind a literary genius," *Niagara Gazette*: March 9, 1988.

"as if we weren't even there": Int. Carolina Oates, 1993.

PAGE 354 "after a marvelous visit": J, June 1987.

PAGE 354   "Our English visit went very well": letter from JCO to Russell Banks and
            Chase Twichell, September 7, 1989.
            "certainly in the background": letter from JCO to Richard Ford, Sep-
            tember 14, 1989.
            "We had the best time": Int. Carolina Oates, 1992.
PAGE 355   "My secret (perhaps not so terribly secret)": letter from JCO to Betty
            Fussell, December 2, 1988.
            "has a good deal of food": letter from JCO to Edmund Keeley, June 16,
            1987.
            "irradiates through the text": J, July 2, 1987.
            "that will be familiar to you": letter from JCO to Leigh and Henry
            Bienen, July 1987.
PAGE 356   "she and Ray had altered their work schedules": letter from JCO to Ed-
            mund Keeley, May 26, 1987.
            "the word processor is demonic": J, February 10, 1986.
            "I seem in fact to write more slowly": letter from JCO to John Updike,
            February 8, 1986.
            "rewrite it completely": J, June 1987.
            "how happy, how ecstatic": J, July 2, 1987.
PAGE 357   "Early reports of AA have been good": J, December 16, 1988.
            "a dangerously cerebral, possibly overly 'refined' novel": letter from JCO
            to Greg Johnson, December 21, 1988.
            "American Appetites is a work of considerable richness": Patricia Craig,
            Times Literary Supplement, September 15, 1989: 997.
            "Oates is here working at the very top of her form": Paul Gray, "Nice
            People in Glass Houses," Time, January 9, 1989: 64.
            "This is just to say how much I was moved": letter from JCO to Paul
            Gray, January 9, 1989.
            "could wish for Dutton's sake": letter from JCO to Robert Phillips, Janu-
            ary 22, 1989.
            "been working in a sort of trance": letter from JCO to Robert Phillips,
            August 23, 1988.
PAGE 358   "a black boy of my distant past": letter from JCO to Henry Louis Gates,
            Jr., June 30, 1990.
            "After months of pushing a recalcitrant novel-in-progress": letter from
            JCO to John Updike, November 5, 1988.
            "enormous happiness; enormous relief": J, December 9, 1988.
            "probably my strongest novel": letter from JCO to Robert Phillips, No-
            vember 12, 1989.
            "complexity in the detail": Marilynne Robinson, "The Guilt She Left
            Behind," New York Times Book Review, April 22, 1990: 7.
            "Oates renders the lineaments of racial resentment": Henry Louis
            Gates, Jr., "Murder She Wrote," The Nation, July 2, 1990: 27.
PAGE 359   "odd little quicksilver novel": J, December 17, 1989.
            "a commercial failure": letter from JCO to William Heyen, June 2, 1990.

PAGE 359   "finished and should be mailed out of the house": letter from JCO to
John Updike, January 18, 1990.
"At such times I think, the blood-jet *is* poetry": J, April 24, 1988.
PAGE 360   "The prose overshadows the poetry": Int. Daniel Halpern, 1992.
"I've not found anyone else": Int. Larry Goldstein, 1992.
"the poetry, frankly": Int. Maxine Kumin, 1993.
"each of the poems": *Ohio Review* interview, 1973.
PAGE 361   "a high water mark": Int. Philip Levine, 1993.
"peculiar balladic tragedy": J, June 21, 1989.
"very autobiographical in the sense": letter from JCO to Robert Phillips,
August 11, 1989.
"I seem to be working with glacial slowness": J, July 11, 1989.
PAGE 362   "a breakthrough book": Int. Daniel Halpern, 1992.
"In an ideal world": "The Art of Being No One," *New York Times*, July
22, 1996: A–10.
PAGE 363   "ever more fascinating": letter from JCO to Elaine Showalter, June 30,
1986.
"primarily as a diversion": letter from JCO to Rosalie Siegel, August 31,
1986.
"When it was accepted": *Newsweek*, February 23, 1987.
"in one 6-week burst": letter from JCO to Jana Harris, January 4, 1987.
PAGE 364   "I'm quite stunned": quoted in Edwin McDowell, "A Sad Joyce Carol
Oates Forswears Pseudonyms," *New York Times*, February 2, 1987: C–18.
PAGE 365   "I can't think of the Abbott affair": letter from JCO to Norman Mailer
and Norris Church, June 18, 1988.
"absorbing nearly all of my waking hours": letter from JCO to Robert
Phillips, December 17, 1990.
"the Princeton English department had been stunned": details of the
case are taken from two published accounts: Dorothy Rabinowitz, "Arms
and the Man: A Sex Scandal Rocks Princeton," *New York*, July 17, 1989:
30–36; and Wendy Plump, "Oates entwines fact and fiction in book
mirroring PU scandal," *Princeton Packet*, August 28, 1990: 1A, 8A.
PAGE 366   "a shocking cover-up": letter from JCO to Robert Phillips, December
23, 1988.
"the University is too worried": letter from JCO to John Reed, January
20, 1989.
"Not that I am a prim, self-righteous sort of person": J, May 7, 1989.
"the case so shamefully reveals": letter from JCO to Elaine Showalter,
July 17, 1989.
"Joyce has used a very unfortunate incident": responses to the novel are
taken from the *Princeton Packet* story.
PAGE 367   "My main concern is with making longterm plans": letter from JCO to
Blanche Gregory, October 26, 1989.
PAGE 368   "a good deal of guilty pondering": letter from JCO to Robert Phillips,
November 4, 1989.
"Surprise is putting it mildly": Int. Gertrude Bregman, 1992.

PAGE 368   "exhausting task": letter from JCO to Elaine Showalter, June 22, 1989.
            "This makes me think": letter from JCO to William Heyen, June 12, 1989.
PAGE 369   "Awards are so strange . . . Fragmented, exhausting dreams": J, August
            17, 1990.

Chapter 15   What She Lives For: 1991–98

PAGE 373   "passed many months": quoted in Greg Johnson, "A Reader's Guide to
            the Recent Novels of Joyce Carol Oates": 12.
PAGE 374   "Now drama fascinates me! . . . the writing *is* the reward": J, August 6,
            1989.
            "There is no more futile enterprise": letter from JCO to Dan and Jean-
            nie Halpern, August 12, 1989.
PAGE 375   "I soon became caught up": letter from JCO to Robert Phillips, Febru-
            ary 5, 1990.
            "Have been writing plays": J, April 16, 1990.
            "My head is filled with plays": letter from JCO to Emory Elliott, April
            22, 1990.
            "a good deal better than nothing": letter from JCO to Edmund Keeley,
            June 27, 1990.
            "Instead of writing short stories and poems": letter from JCO to Eugene
            McNamara, February 4, 1991.
PAGE 376   "We found it paradisical": letter from JCO to Greg Johnson, January 25,
            1991.
            "I was quite dazzled": letter from JCO to Arvin Brown, April 21, 1991.
PAGE 378   "both excitement & apprehension": J, June 17, 1993.
            "a 'fabulous' box office success": J, October 19, 1993.
PAGE 379   "The whole enterprise": Laurence Shyer, "The Sunny Side of Joyce
            Carol Oates," *American Theatre*, February 1994: 23.
            "the most intimate & indeed passionate play": J, January 4, 1994.
            "Was there ever so *gifted*": J, January 17, 1994.
            "writing plays, and thinking/dreaming of plays": letter from JCO to Greg
            Johnson, January 20, 1994.
PAGE 380   "It's the difference between swimming and jogging": Laurence Shyer,
            "The Sunny Side of Joyce Carol Oates," *American Theatre*, February
            1994: 24.
            "this elephantine farce": John Simon, "With Blunt Tools," *New York*,
            February 27, 1995: 115.
            "Oates doesn't have a clue": Jeremy Gerard, "Legit Reviews," *Variety*,
            February 20, 1995: 84.
            "prodigious output": Vincent Canby, "Free Spirit and Friend Confront
            Family Values," *New York Times*, February 10, 1995: C–3.
            "perceptively and vividly": Douglas J. Keating, " 'Here She Is!' is 9 Oates
            plays about women," *Philadelphia Inquirer*, March 14, 1995: E–1.

PAGE 380   "this is more or less expected": letter from JCO to Greg Johnson, February 14, 1995.

"was actually quite touching in the role": letter from JCO to Greg Johnson, August 18, 1995.

PAGE 381   "she is a great short story writer": Int. John L'Heureux, 1992.

"She's got to move along": Int. Daniel Halpern, 1992.

"might be more sensibly diverted": J, April 5, 1991.

"I must be like one of those people": letter from JCO to John Updike, May 23, 1991.

"I've discovered little-known, in fact unknown, stories": letter from JCO to Greg Johnson, January 25, 1991.

"I'm feeling a bit doubtful": letter from JCO to Robert Atwan, March 25, 1991.

PAGE 382   "seems to have fallen into a chasm": letter from JCO to Robert Phillips, October 13, 1992.

"the publisher must be seriously contemplating": letter from JCO to John Updike, October 21, 1991.

"a very busy and fragmented year": letter from JCO to David Shapiro, May 27, 1991.

"delirious immersion in a story called 'Black Water' ": J, May 27, 1991.

PAGE 383   "I feel as if I have just emerged from a sustained horror/trauma . . . except leaving the scene of an accident": letter from JCO to Greg Johnson, July 7, 1991.

"I was in terror of having to switch": letter from JCO to Robert Phillips, August 16, 1991.

"pit bulls": letter from Joseph Epstein to the New York Times, July 30, 1991: A–18.

PAGE 384   " 'Can't Take a Joke?' the Bigot Asks": letter from JCO to the New York Times, August 13, 1991: A–16.

"that he would rather his son be dead": letter from JCO to Robert Phillips, August 16, 1991.

"My letter to the Times was written so quickly": letter from JCO to Edward Said, August 24, 1991.

"as a privilege, very likely an adventure . . . seems about right": JCO, "I, the Juror," Witness, Vol, 5, #2, 1991: 9–10.

PAGE 385   "There were moments during the defense attorney's repetitive closing remarks": letter from JCO to Judith Yaskin, August 29, 1991.

"What so powerfully attracts me to the mode I call surreal": letter from JCO to Stephen King, October 22, 1991.

PAGE 386   "I'd been intrigued by the title Double Delight": letter from JCO to Greg Johnson, December 28, 1991.

"You can't imagine the desperation one feels": letter from JCO to Janet Cosby, February 2, 1992.

"We were so delighted to have you here, Miss Oates": letter from JCO to John Updike, February 1992.

PAGE 387   "selling better than any novel of mine": J, June 14, 1992.

PAGE 387   "the ballad of Chappaquiddick": Richard Eder, quoted in David Streitfeld, "Ballad for the Senator's Victim," *Washington Post*, June 17, 1992: B–8.
"as audacious as anything I know": Richard Bausch, "Her Thoughts While Drowning," *New York Times Book Review*, May 10, 1992: 29.
"never thought anyone would even notice": David Streitfeld, "Ballad for the Senator's Victim," *Washington Post*, June 17, 1992: B–8.
"thrown so much money at me . . . obsessive undertow": J, September 16, 1992.
"dowsing, isn't it": J, June 14, 1992.
"My new novel grows": letter from JCO to John Updike, January 12, 1993.

PAGE 388   "It seems impossible: I've finished . . . quite so much again": J, March 20, 1993.
"Immersed in Corky as I am": J, January 11, 1993.
"It is astounding": Joan Smith, "Word Perfect," *San Francisco Focus*, March 1995: 42.
"Billy, and others at Dutton": J, October 1993.

PAGE 390   "I read literature on these subjects": quoted in Greg Johnson, "A Reader's Guide to the Recent Novels of Joyce Carol Oates": 12.

PAGE 391   "ravishing": J, September 16, 1992.
"how true it is": J, October 31, 1992.
"weighing like cement . . . walked in the rain": letter from JCO to John Updike, November 23, 1992.
"they treated Ray and me so elegantly": letter from JCO to Robert Phillips, November 10, 1991.

PAGE 392   "one of the most wildly/surrealistically funny people": J, April 4, 1993.
"I was very grateful": Int. Robert Stone, 1992.
"extraordinary freedom": J, April 13, 1993.
"So many ideas for stories!": J, April 26, 1993.

PAGE 393   "visually ravishing . . . My romantic Lisbon!": J, May 1–18, 1993.

PAGE 394   "really *very* nice": J, July 27, 1993.
"what emotional impact!": J, July 29, 1993.
"all the great, grave, unanswerable questions": letter from JCO to John Updike, August 7, 1993.
"migraine headache . . . warm & funny": J, August 3–17, 1993.

PAGE 395   "one of these 'serious,' even literary-minded actors": letter from JCO to Russell Banks, August 21, 1993.
"family-structured novel": J, August 22, 1993.
"so many images, plots!": J, August 29, 1993.
"my new novel has been strangely attacked": letter from JCO to John Updike, August 7, 1993.
"so contrived and portentous": Michiko Kakutani, "Girls Who Hate Men and Act Accordingly," *New York Times*, July 16, 1993: C–18.
"a wonderful novel": Carolyn See, "Gang Girls Feel Their Oates," *Washington Post*, July 30, 1993: G–2.
"this extraordinarily well-crafted book": Sheila Paulos, "Gang that takes abuse into its own hands," *Philadelphia Inquirer*, August 1, 1993: N–1.

PAGE 395   "as I'm interviewed about it & read reviews": J, August 22, 1993.

PAGE 396   "So, after all . . . uncontemplated as the very air": J, October 12, 1993.
"how crucial to my life": letter from JCO to Robert Phillips, October 20, 1993.
"she had her running shoes on": Int. Daniel Halpern, 1992.
"The only advantage is": letter from JCO to John Updike, November 3, 1993.
"an interesting text": letter from JCO to Lawrence Grobel, September 19, 1993.

PAGE 397   "lengthy, raving letters": letter from JCO to Richard Howard, October 23, 1993.
"There is a demonic certitude in such people": letter from JCO to Robert Phillips, September 17, 1993.
"the gravitational pull . . . to create his soul": J, December 16, 1993.
"arc of their tragic/redemptive story": J, February 20, 1994.
"free-form novel": J, March 12, 1994.

PAGE 399   "I haven't written a short story for so long": letter from JCO to Greg Johnson, January 20, 1994.
"a swarm of carnivorous gnats": letter from JCO to Greg Johnson, September 27, 1994.
"Do you think the editors felt they should explain": letter from JCO to Greg Johnson, October 24, 1994.

PAGE 400   "Not only don't I reread . . . frankly sexist, insulting": letters from JCO to Greg Johnson, May 20 and September 12, 1995.
"all hammy smiles . . . I'm not sure I deserved this": letter from JCO to Greg Johnson, June 7, 1994.

PAGE 401   "Billy's hopes for my 'career' ": letter from JCO to Greg Johnson, July 29, 1994.
"for quite a beating this time": letter from JCO to Greg Johnson, October 16, 1994.
"an engrossing, moving study": James Carroll, "He Could Not Tell a Lie," New York Times Book Review, October 2, 1994: 7.
"breathtaking scope and insight": E. J. Graff, "Oates' latest etching goes from thriller to art," Atlanta Journal-Constitution, October 2, 1994: N–12.
"Utter Pig": Alan Cheuse, The Missoulian (Montana), January 1, 1995 (reprinted from the Los Angeles Times).
"Many a Princeton professor": letter from JCO to Greg Johnson, November 19, 1994.

PAGE 402   "polarized": Int. Scott Stein, 1996.
"grisly, virulent gem of a book": Michael Upchurch, "Oates Takes a Walk on the Psychopathic Side," San Francisco Chronicle, September 24, 1995: 5.
"continuation of Ms. Oates's longstanding interest": Steven Marcus, "American Psycho," New York Times Book Review, October 8, 1995: 13.
"I do feel that I came through": letter from JCO to Greg Johnson, October 4, 1995.

PAGE 402   "slowly, yet richly": letter from JCO to Greg Johnson, March 25, 1995.
"*Mulvaneys* is moving along": letter from JCO to Greg Johnson, June 1, 1995.

PAGE 403   "a real reluctance to detach myself ": letter from JCO to Greg Johnson, September 12, 1995.
"great slices of childhood scenes": letter from JCO to Greg Johnson, October 4, 1995.

PAGE 406   "performed many a surprising, quick-changing imaginative shift": Beverly Lowry, "Home is Where the Heart Breaks," *Los Angeles Times Book Review*, September 15, 1996: 3.
"Oates's unblinking curiosity": Valerie Miner, "Independence Day," *The Nation*, October 28, 1996: 63.

PAGE 407   "The ugly publicity does seem comical": letter from JCO to Greg Johnson, February 22, 1997.

PAGE 408   "So much energy after *Mulvaneys*": letter from JCO to Greg Johnson, October 24, 1995.

BIBLIOGRAPHY

This bibliography is highly selective. The listings of Joyce Carol Oates's uncollected work and of secondary sources in periodicals are limited to those cited in the text. For additional bibliographical information on primary and secondary material published before 1986, the reader should consult Francine Lercangée, *Joyce Carol Oates: An Annotated Bibliography* (New York: Garland, 1986). A more recent bibliography is located on *Celestial Timepiece*, a web site maintained by Randy Souther; the site address is given at the end of this listing.

Books by Joyce Carol Oates, 1963–1998

Novels

American Appetites. New York: Dutton, 1989.
Angel of Light. New York: Dutton, 1981.
The Assassins. New York: Vanguard, 1975.
Because It Is Bitter, and Because It Is My Heart. New York: Dutton, 1990.
Bellefleur. New York: Dutton, 1980.
Black Water. New York: Dutton, 1992.
A Bloodsmoor Romance. New York: Dutton, 1982.
Childwold. New York: Vanguard, 1976.
Cybele. Santa Barbara: Black Sparrow Press, 1979.
Do with Me What You Will. New York: Vanguard, 1973.

Expensive People. New York: Vanguard, 1968.
Foxfire: Confessions of a Girl Gang. New York: Dutton, 1993.
A Garden of Earthly Delights. New York: Vanguard, 1967.
Man Crazy. New York: Dutton, 1997.
Marya: A Life. New York: Dutton, 1986.
My Heart Laid Bare. New York: Dutton, 1998.
Mysteries of Winterthurn. New York: Dutton, 1984.
Solstice. New York: Dutton, 1985.
Son of the Morning. New York: Vanguard, 1978.
them. New York: Vanguard, 1969.
Unholy Loves. New York: Dutton, 1979.
We Were the Mulvaneys. New York: Dutton, 1996.
What I Lived For. New York: Dutton, 1994.
With Shuddering Fall. New York: Vanguard, 1964.
Wonderland. New York: Vanguard, 1971.
You Must Remember This. New York: Dutton, 1987.
Zombie. New York: Dutton, 1995.

"Rosamond Smith" Novels

Double Delight. New York: Dutton, 1997.
Lives of the Twins. New York: Simon & Schuster, 1987.
Nemesis. New York: Dutton, 1990.
Snake Eyes. New York: Dutton, 1992.
Soul/Mate. New York: Dutton, 1989.
You Can't Catch Me. New York: Dutton, 1995.

Short Stories

All the Good People I've Left Behind. Santa Barbara: Black Sparrow Press, 1979.
The Assignation. New York: Ecco Press, 1988.
By the North Gate. New York: Vanguard, 1963.
Crossing the Border. New York: Vanguard, 1976.
The Goddess and Other Women. New York: Vanguard, 1974.
Haunted: Tales of the Grotesque. New York: Dutton, 1994.
Heat and Other Stories. New York: Dutton, 1991.
The Hungry Ghosts: Seven Allusive Comedies. Los Angeles: Black Sparrow, 1974.
Last Days. New York: Dutton, 1984.
Marriages and Infidelities. New York: Vanguard, 1972.
Night-Side: Eighteen Tales. New York: Vanguard, 1977.
Oates in Exile. Toronto: Exile Editions, 1990.
The Poisoned Kiss and Other Stories from the Portuguese. New York: Vanguard, 1975.
Raven's Wing. New York: Dutton, 1986.

The Seduction & Other Stories. Los Angeles: Black Sparrow Press, 1975.
A Sentimental Education. New York: Dutton, 1980.
Unspeakable. New York: Dutton, 1998.
Upon the Sweeping Flood. New York: Vanguard, 1966.
The Wheel of Love. New York: Vanguard, 1970.
Where Are You Going, Where Have You Been? Selected Early Stories. Princeton, NJ: Ontario Review Press, 1993.
Where Is Here? Hopewell, NJ: Ecco Press, 1992.
Will You Always Love Me? New York: Dutton, 1996.

Selected Limited Editions

The Blessing. Santa Barbara: Black Sparrow Press, 1976.
Blue-Bearded Lover. Concord, NH: William B. Ewert, 1987.
Celestial Timepiece. Dallas: Pressworks, 1980.
Cupid and Psyche. New York: Albondocani Press, 1970.
Daisy. Santa Barbara: Black Sparrow Press, 1977.
Demon and Other Tales. West Warwick, RI: Necronomicon Press, 1996.
Dreaming America and Other Poems. New York: Aloe Editions, 1973.
Funland. Concord, NH: William B. Ewert, 1983.
The Girl. Cambridge, MA: Pomegranate Press, 1974.
Heat. New York: Library Fellows of the Whitney Museum of Art, 1989.
"JCO" and I. Concord, NH: William B. Ewert, 1994.
The Lamb of Abyssalia. Cambridge, MA: Pomegranate Press, 1979.
The Life of the Writer, the Life of the Career. Bennington, VT: Bennington College, 1995.
Luxury of Sin. Northridge, CA: Lord John Press, 1984.
A Middle-Class Education. New York: Albondocani Press, 1980.
The Miraculous Birth. Concord, NH: William B. Ewert, 1986.
Nightless Nights. Concord, NH: William B. Ewert, 1981.
Plagiarized Material. Los Angeles: Black Sparrow Press, 1974.
A Posthumous Sketch. Los Angeles: Black Sparrow Press, 1973.
Queen of the Night. Northridge, CA: Lord John Press, 1979.
Season of Peril. Santa Barbara: Black Sparrow Press, 1977.
A Sentimental Education. Los Angeles: Sylvester & Orphanos, 1978.
Small Avalanches and Other Stories. Helsinki: Eurographica, 1989.
The Step-Father. Northridge, CA: Lord John Press, 1978.
Such Beauty. Concord, NH: William B. Ewert, 1989.
The Time Traveler. Northridge, CA: Lord John Press, 1987.
Upon the Sweeping Flood. Logan, IA: Perfection Form Co., 1979.
Where Are You Going, Where Have You Been? Logan, IA: Perfection Form Co., 1979.
Wild Nights. Athens, OH: Croissant, 1985.
Will You Always Love Me? Huntington Beach, CA: James Cahill, 1994.

Women in Love and Other Poems. New York: Albondocani Press, 1968.
Wooded Forms. New York: Albondocani Press, 1972.

Novellas

First Love: A Gothic Tale. Hopewell, NJ: Ecco Press, 1996.
I Lock My Door Upon Myself. New York: Ecco Press, 1990.
The Rise of Life on Earth. New York: New Directions, 1991.
The Triumph of the Spider Monkey. Santa Barbara: Black Sparrow Press, 1976.

Poetry

Angel Fire. Baton Rouge: Louisiana State University Press, 1973.
Anonymous Sins. Baton Rouge: Louisiana State University Press, 1969.
The Fabulous Beasts. Baton Rouge: Louisiana State University Press, 1975.
Invisible Woman: New and Selected Poems 1970–1982. Princeton, NJ: Ontario Review Press, 1982.
Love and Its Derangements. Baton Rouge: Louisiana State University Press, 1970.
Tenderness. Princeton, NJ: Ontario Review Press, 1996.
The Time Traveler. New York: Dutton, 1989.
Women Whose Lives Are Food, Men Whose Lives Are Money. Baton Rouge: Louisiana State University Press, 1978.

Plays

I Stand Before You Naked. New York: Samuel French, 1991.
In Darkest America (Tone Clusters and The Eclipse). New York: Samuel French, 1991.
Miracle Play. Los Angeles: Black Sparrow Press, 1974.
The Perfectionist and Other Plays. Hopewell, NJ: Ecco Press, 1995.
Three Plays. Princeton, NJ: Ontario Review Press, 1980.
Twelve Plays. New York: Dutton, 1991.

Essays

Contraries. New York: Oxford University Press, 1981.
George Bellows: American Artist. Hopewell, NJ: Ecco Press, 1995.
The Edge of Impossibility: Tragic Forms in Literature. New York: Vanguard, 1972.
"The Hostile Sun": The Poetry of D. H. Lawrence. Los Angeles: Black Sparrow Press, 1973.
New Heaven, New Earth: The Visionary Experience in Literature. New York: Vanguard, 1974.
On Boxing. Garden City, NY: Doubleday, 1987.

The Profane Art: Essays and Reviews. New York: Dutton, 1983.
(Woman) Writer: Occasions and Opportunities. New York: Dutton, 1988.

Books Edited by Joyce Carol Oates

American Gothic Tales. New York: Dutton/Plume, 1996.
The Best American Essays 1991. New York: Ticknor & Fields, 1991.
The Best American Short Stories 1979 (with Shannon Ravenel). Boston: Houghton Mifflin, 1979.
The Essential Dickinson. Hopewell, NJ: Ecco Press, 1996.
First Person Singular: Writers on Their Craft. Princeton, NJ: Ontario Review Press, 1983.
Night Walks: A Bedside Companion. Princeton, NJ: Ontario Review Press, 1982.
The Oxford Book of American Short Stories. New York: Oxford University Press, 1992.
Reading the Fights (with Dan Halpern). New York: Henry Holt, 1988.
Scenes from American Life: Contemporary Short Fiction. New York: Vanguard, 1973.
The Sophisticated Cat. New York: Dutton, 1992.
STORY: Fictions Past and Present (with Boyd Litzinger). Lexington, MA: Heath, 1987.
Tales of H.P. Lovecraft. Hopewell, NJ: Ecco Press, 1997.
Telling Stories: An Anthology for Writers. New York: Norton, 1998.

Selected Uncollected Short Stories and Poems by Joyce Carol Oates

"Blue Skies." Miriam Dow and Jennifer Regan, eds., *The Invisible Enemy.* St. Paul: Graywolf Press, 1989. 70–94.
"Corinne." *North American Review,* Fall 1975: 30–42.
"Detroit by Daylight": *Prairie Schooner,* Summer 1968: 126.
"First Death." *Mademoiselle,* June 1978: 188–94.
"In Memory of an Ex-Friend, a Murderer." *Literary Review,* Spring 1968: 391–93.
"Mute Mad Child." *Southern Review,* Spring 1983: 357–58.
"The Sweet Enemy." *Southern Review,* Summer 1967: 653–720.
"The Thief." *North American Review,* September 1966: 10–17.

Selected Uncollected Essays and Reviews by Joyce Carol Oates

"American Gothic." *The New Yorker,* May 8, 1995: 35–36.
"An Unsolved Mystery." Mickey Pearlman, ed., *Between Friends.* Boston: Houghton Mifflin, 1994. 125–28.

"And God Saw That It Was Good." *Southwest Review*, Spring/Summer 1995: 318–30.

"The Charmer Who Lost His Way." Review of *Go, Said the Bird*, by Geoffrey Cottrell, *Detroit News*, January 15, 1967: D–6.

"Cherished Moments." *Life*, Fall 1988: 153.

"Coming Home." *USAir*, May 1995: 108.

"A Corner to Write In." *Elle Decor*, October 1991: 132.

"Dracula: The Vampire's Secret." David Rosenberg, ed., *The Movie That Changed My Life*. New York: Penguin, 1991. 60–75.

"The Fact Is: We Like to Be Drugged." *McCalls*, June 1970: 69.

"Facts, Visions, Mysteries: My Father, Frederic Oates." Carolyn Anthony, ed., *Family Portraits* (New York: Doubleday, 1990). 151–63.

"Food Mysteries." *Antaeus*, Spring 1992: 25–37.

"The Greatest of Gifts." *Life*, December 1990: 155.

"Haphazard Thoughts: From the Ridiculous to the Sublime." *American Poetry Review*, September–October 1973: 47–48.

"I, the Juror." *Witness*, Volume V (2), 1991: 9–20.

"A Letter to My Mother Carolina Oates on her 78th Birthday, November 8, 1995." *New York Times Magazine*, May 12, 1996: 48–49.

"Lightning Bolt." *Road & Track*, August 1989: 58.

"The Nature of Short Fiction; or, the Nature of My Short Fiction." Preface to Frank A. Dickinson and Sandra Smythe, eds., *Handbook of Short Story Writing*. Cincinnati: Writer's Digest Books, 1970. xi–xviii.

"New Heaven and Earth." *Saturday Review*, November 4, 1972: 51–54.

"On the Student Revolution." *Detroit News Magazine*, February 16, 1969: 14.

"The One Unforgivable Sin." *New York Times Book Review*, July 25, 1993: 3.

"Recent Books: Keithley, Levine, Sale, and Roth." *American Poetry Review*, May–June 1974: 43–45.

"Response to Richard Stern." *Critical Inquiry*, Autumn 1988: 193–95.

"Richard Wishnetsky: Joyce Oates Supplies a Missing View." *Detroit Free Press*, March 6, 1966: 1–2, 12–13.

"A Riddle Wrapped in a Mystery inside an Enigma." *The New Yorker*, December 12, 1994: 45–46.

"Stories That Define Me: The Making of a Writer." *New York Times Book Review*, July 11, 1982: 1, 15–16.

"Sunday Drive 1948." *Traditional Home*, March 1995: 34, 36, 38.

"They All Just Went Away." *The New Yorker*, October 16, 1995: 178–87.

"Trespassing." *New York Times Magazine*, October 8, 1995: 83.

"A Visit with Doris Lessing." *Southern Review*, Autumn 1973: 873–82.

"Why Is Your Writing So Violent?" *New York Times Book Review*, March 29, 1981: 15, 35.

"The World's Worst Critics." *New York Times Book Review*, January 18, 1987: 1, 30.

"Writers Draw." *Mediums*, 1982: 18–19.

"The Writing Life: Tales Out of School." *Washington Post*, March 16, 1997: X01.

Books About Joyce Carol Oates

Bastian, Katherine. *Joyce Carol Oates's Short Stories: Between Tradition and Innovation*. Frankfurt: Bern, Lang, 1983.

Bender, Eileen Teper. *Joyce Carol Oates: Artist in Residence*. Bloomington: Indiana University Press, 1987.

Bloom, Harold, ed. *Modern Critical Views: Joyce Carol Oates*. New York: Chelsea House, 1987.

Creighton, Joanne V. *Joyce Carol Oates*. Boston: Twayne, 1979.

———. *Joyce Carol Oates: Novels of the Middle Years*. New York: Twayne, 1992.

Daly, Brenda. *Lavish Self-Divisions: The Novels of Joyce Carol Oates*. Jackson: University Press of Mississippi, 1996.

Friedman, Ellen. *Joyce Carol Oates*. New York: Ungar, 1980.

Grant, Mary Kathryn. *The Tragic Vision of Joyce Carol Oates*. Durham, NC: Duke University Press, 1987.

Johnson, Greg. *Joyce Carol Oates: A Study of the Short Fiction*. New York: Twayne, 1994.

———. *Understanding Joyce Carol Oates*. Columbia: University of South Carolina Press, 1987.

Lercangée, Francine. *Joyce Carol Oates: An Annotated Bibliography*. Preface and annotations by Bruce F. Michelson. New York: Garland, 1986.

Milazzo, Lee. *Conversations with Joyce Carol Oates*. Jackson: University Press of Mississippi, 1989.

Norman, K. and Torborg, M. *Isolation and Contact: A Study of Character Relationships in Joyce Carol Oates's Short Stories, 1963–1980*. Göteborg, Sweden: Acta Universitatis Gothoburgensis, 1984.

Severin, Hermann. *The Image of the Intellectual in the Short Stories of Joyce Carol Oates*. Frankfurt: Peter Lang, 1986.

Showalter, Elaine, ed. *"Where Are You Going, Where Have You Been?"* New Brunswick, NJ: Rutgers University Press, 1994.

Sreelakshmi, P. *Elective Affinities: A Study in the Sources and Intertexts of Joyce Carol Oates's Short Fiction*. Madras: T.R. Publications, 1996.

Wagner, Linda M., ed. *Critical Essays on Joyce Carol Oates*. Boston: G. K. Hall, 1979.

Waller, G. F. *Dreaming America: Obsession and Transcendence in the Fiction of Joyce Carol Oates*. Baton Rouge: Louisiana State University Press, 1979.

Wesley, Marilyn. *Refusal and Transgression in Joyce Carol Oates: Fiction*. Westport, CT: Greenwood Press, 1993.

Selected Essays and Reviews About Joyce Carol Oates

Abrahams, William. "Stories of a Visionary." *Saturday Review*, September 23, 1972: 76, 80.

Adams, Robert M. "The Best Nightmares Are Retrospective." *New York Times Book Review*, September 28, 1969: 4–5, 43.

Allison, Dorothy. "Tame Oates." *Village Voice*, May 20, 1986: 56–57.

Atlas, James. Untitled review of *You Must Remember This*. *Vanity Fair*, August 1987: 140.

Avant, John Alfred. Untitled review of *The Wheel of Love*. *Library Journal*, September 1, 1970: 2829.

———. "New and Notable Fiction." *The New Republic*, March 29, 1975: 30–31.

Bailey, J.E. "The Doomed and the Damned." *Time*, November 1, 1968: 102.

Banks, Russell. "Joyce Carol Oates: In a Gothic Manor." *Washington Post Book World*, August 17, 1980: 4, 8, 14.

Bausch, Richard. "Her Thoughts While Drowning." *New York Times Book Review*, May 10, 1992: 1, 29.

Bedient, Calvin. "The Story of Sleeping Beauty and a Love That Is Like Hatred." *New York Times Book Review*, October 14, 1973: 1, 18.

———. "Vivid and Dazzling." *The Nation*, December 1, 1969: 609–11.

Bell, Millicent. "Her Own Rough Truth." *New York Times Book Review*, June 12, 1966: 4–5.

Bell, Pearl K. "A Time for Silence." *New Leader*, November 16, 1970: 14–15.

Birkerts, Sven. "A Passion for Uncle." *New York Times Book Review*, August 16, 1987: 3.

Blake, Patricia. "Antimacassar." *Time*, October 4, 1982: 78–79, 81.

Boesky, Dale. "Correspondence with Miss Joyce Carol Oates." *International Review of Psychoanalysis* (2) 1975: 481–86.

Canby, Vincent. "Free Spirit and Friend Confront Family Values." *New York Times*, February 10, 1995: C3.

Carroll, James. "He Could Not Tell a Lie." *New York Times Book Review*, October 2, 1994: 7.

Clemons, Walter. "A Kiss Isn't Just a Kiss." *Newsweek*, August 17, 1987: 68.

———. "Sleeping Princess." *Newsweek*, October 15, 1973: 107.

———. "Wild Oates." *Newsweek*, August 17, 1981: 74.

———. "Wild Oates in Academe." *Newsweek*, October 29, 1979: 99.

Coyne, Patricia S. "Thinking Man's Breakfast." *National Review*, September 3, 1976: 965–66.

Craig, Patricia. Untitled review of *American Appetites*. *Times Literary Supplement*, September 15, 1989: 997.

Cryer, Dan. "A Critic's Choice for the Best of Literary 1981." *Newsday*, January 4, 1981: 20.

Cunningham, Father William T. "UD Teacher Clicks with First Book." *Michigan Catholic*, January 23, 1964: 12.

Dalton, Elizabeth. "Joyce Carol Oates: Violence in the Head." *Commentary*, June 1970: 75–77.

Davis, James. " 'Sweet Enemy' Poor Theatre." *New York Daily News*, February 16, 1965: D–8.

DeMott, Benjamin. "The Necessity in Art of a Reflective Intelligence." *Saturday Review*, November 22, 1969: 71–73, 89.

———. " 'Now' Rituals," *Atlantic*, December 1973: 127.

Duffy, Martha. "Power Vacuum." *Time*, October 15, 1973: E3–E4.

Duus, Louise. "The Population of Eden: J. C. Oates' 'By the North Gate.' " *Critique*, 7, ii (1964): 176–77.

Edwards, Thomas R. "The House of Atreus Now." *New York Times Book Review*, August 16, 1981: 1, 18.

Engel, Marian. "Women Also Have Dark Hearts." *New York Times Book Review*, November 24, 1974: 7, 10.

Estok, Rita. Untitled review of *Upon the Sweeping Flood. Library Journal*, April 1, 1966: 1926.

Fisher, Ann H. Untitled review of *Marya: A Life. Library Journal*, March 15, 1986: 78.

Fossum, Robert H. "Only Control: The Novels of Joyce Carol Oates." *Studies in the Novel*, 7, ii (Summer 1975): 285–97.

Frankel, Haskel. "Universals." *Saturday Review*, October 26, 1963: 45.

Gardner, John. "The Strange Real World." *New York Times Book Review*, July 20, 1980: 1, 21.

Gates, Henry Louis, Jr. "Murder She Wrote." *The Nation*, July 2, 1990: 27–29.

Gaver, Jack. " 'The Sweet Enemy' Has Sour Press." *Detroit News*, February 16, 1965: C–8.

Gerard, Jeremy "Legit Reviews." *Variety*, February 20, 1995: 84.

Gilman, Richard. "The Disasters of Love, Sexual and Otherwise." *New York Times Book Review*, October 25, 1970: 4, 62.

Glendinning, Victoria. "Hungry for God." *New York Times Book Review*, November 26, 1978: 11.

Gordon, Mary. "The Life and Hard Times of Cinderella." *New York Times Book Review*, March 2, 1986: 7.

Graff, E. J. "Oates' latest etching goes from thriller to art." *Atlanta Journal-Constitution*, October 2, 1994: N–12.

Grant, Louis T. "A Child of Paradise." *The Nation*, November 4, 1968: 475.

Gray, Paul. "Nice People in Glass Houses." *Time*, January 9, 1989: 64.

"Hardscrabble Heroine." *Time*, September 27, 1967: 106.

Hendin, Josephine. "Joyce Carol Oates is Frankly Murderous." *New York Times Book Review*, September 1, 1974: 5.

———. Untitled review of *Childwold. New York Times Book Review*, November 28, 1976: 8, 30.

Hicks, Granville. "Fiction That Grows from the Ground." *Saturday Review,* August 5, 1967: 23–24.

———. "What Is Reality?" *Saturday Review,* October 26, 1968: 33–34.

Jackson, K. G. "Books in Brief." *Harper's,* November 1964: 151.

Janeway, Elizabeth. "Clara the Climber." *New York Times Book Review,* September 10, 1967: 5, 63.

Johnson, Diane. "Balloons and Abductions." *New York Times Book Review,* September 5, 1982: 1, 15–16.

Johnson, Greg. "A Reader's Guide to the Recent Novels of Joyce Carol Oates." New York: Dutton, 1995.

Jones, Robert. "Still Lost in the Maze." *Commonweal,* March 8, 1985: 150–52.

"The Joys of Friendship Among Today's New Women." *Today's Health,* September 1974: 63–65.

Juhasz, Suzanne. Untitled review of *The Assassins. Library Journal,* November 15, 1975: 2174.

Kakutani, Michiko. "Girls Who Hate Men and Act Accordingly." *New York Times,* July 16, 1993: C–18.

Kauffmann, Stanley. "Violence Amid Gentility." *New York Times Book Review,* November 10, 1963: 4, 61.

Keating, Douglas J. " 'Here She Is!' is 9 Oates plays about women." *The Philadelphia Inquirer,* March 14, 1995: E–1.

Kitching, J. Untitled review of *Upon the Sweeping Flood. Publishers Weekly,* February 18, 1966: 90.

Knowles, John. "A Racing Car Is the Symbol of Violence." *New York Times Book Review,* October 25, 1964: 5.

Kroll, Jack. "Action at the 'Cube.' " *Newsweek,* February 21, 1972: 99.

Lowry, Beverly. "Home Is Where the Heart Breaks." *Los Angeles Times Book Review,* September 13, 1996: 3, 9.

Madden, David. "The Violent World of Joyce Carol Oates." *Studies in Short Fiction,* 4, iv (Summer 1967): 369–73.

Marcus, Steven. "American Psycho." *New York Times Book Review,* October 8, 1995: 13.

Markmann, Charles Lam. "The Puzzle of People." *The Nation,* December 4, 1972: 566, 568.

Miner, Valerie. "Independence Day." *The Nation,* October 28, 1996: 62–64.

Mojtabai, A. G. "Poet and Teachers." *New York Times Book Review,* October 7, 1979: 9, 30.

O'Hara, J. D. Untitled review of *The Assassins. New York Times Book Review,* November 23, 1975: 10, 14, 18.

"Oates Lowers Royalty to Help New Novel." *Publishers Weekly.* April 18, 1980: 75.

Paulos, Sheila. "Gang that takes abuse into its own hands." *Philadelphia Inquirer,* August 1, 1993: N–1, N–2.

Phillips, Robert. Untitled review of *The Goddess and Other Women*. *Commonweal*, April 11, 1975: 55, 57–58.

Pinsker, Sanford. "Suburban Molesters: Joyce Carol Oates' *Expensive People*." *Midwest Quarterly*, 19 (Autumn 1977): 89–103.

Pochoda, Elizabeth. "Joyce Carol Oates honoring the complexities of the real world." *New York Times Book Review*, August 31, 1975: 6.

Prescott, Peter S. "Everyday Monsters." *Newsweek*, October 11, 1971: 96, 100, 101A, 102.

———. "Romantic Agony." *Newsweek*, September 20, 1982: 91–92.

———. "Varieties of Madness." *Newsweek*, October 27, 1975: 99B, 100, 100D.

Robinson, Marilynne. "The Guilt She Left Behind." *New York Times Book Review*. April 22, 1990: 7, 9.

Ryan, Alan. "Murder, Mayhem and Melodrama." *Washington Post Book World*, February 19, 1984: 8.

Sale, Roger. "A High Intelligence at Work Carelessly." *New York Times Book Review*, July 9, 1972: 23–24.

Salholz, Elaine. "Gothic Horrors." *Newsweek*, February 6, 1984: 79A, 79C.

See, Carolyn. "Gang Girls Feel Their Oates." *Washington Post*, July 30, 1993: G–2.

Sheppard, R. Z. Untitled review of *You Must Remember This*. *Time*, August 31, 1987: 62.

Simon, John. "With Blunt Tools." *New York*, February 27, 1995: 115.

Sinkler, Rebecca Pepper. "Time and Her Sisters." *New York Times Book Review*, January 20, 1985: 4.

Sissman, L. E. "The Whole Truth." *The New Yorker*, December 6, 1969: 238, 241–42.

Sokolov, Raymond A. "Tobacco Boulevard." *Newsweek*, October 2, 1967; 93–94.

Stern, Daniel. "The Many Voices of Human Loneliness." *Washington Post Book World*, October 25, 1970: 4–5.

Streitfeld, David. "Ballad for the Senator's Victim." *Washington Post*, June 17, 1992: B–1, B–8.

Taubman, Howard. " 'The Sweet Enemy' Opens." *New York Times*, February 16, 1965: 39.

Taylor, Gordon O. "Joyce Carol Oates: Artist in Wonderland." *Southern Review*, Spring 1974: 490–503.

Tyler, Anne. Untitled review of *Son of the Morning*. *Washington Post Book World*, December 3, 1978: 14.

Untitled, anonymous review of *Angel of Light*. *Publishers Weekly*, June 19, 1981: 94.

Untitled, anonymous review of *The Assassins*. *Time*, February 23, 1976: 65.

Untitled, anonymous review of *A Bloodsmoor Romance*. *The New Yorker*, September 27, 1982: 145–46.

Untitled, anonymous review of *Expensive People*. *Publishers Weekly*, August 12, 1968: 47.

Untitled, anonymous review of *Marriages and Infidelities*. *Publishers Weekly*, August 7, 1972: 40.

Untitled, anonymous review of *Marriages and Infidelities*. *Time*, October 23, 1972: 109, 112.

Untitled, anonymous review of *Mysteries of Winterthurn*. *The New Yorker*. February 27, 1984: 133–34.

Upchurch, Michael. "Oates Takes a Walk on the Psychopathic Side." *San Francisco Chronicle*, September 24, 1995: 5.

Updike, John. "What You Deserve Is What You Get." *The New Yorker*, December 28, 1987: 119–23.

"Urban Gothic." *Time*, October 10, 1969: 106, 108.

Vendler, Helen. "The Ideas and Words, but Not the Surfaces and Cadences." *New York Times Book Review*, April 1, 1973: 7–8.

Wiehe, Janet. Untitled review of *Son of the Morning*. *Library Journal*, August 1978: 1532.

Wolcott, James. "Stop Me Before I Write Again." *Harper's*, September 1982: 67–69.

Wolff, Geoffrey. "Miss Oates Loves to Splash Blood on Us." *New York Times Book Review*, October 24, 1971: 5, 10.

Wood, Michael. "Diminished People." *New York Times Book Review*, October 1, 1972: 6, 43.

Yardley, Jonathan. "Joyce Carol Oates on Automatic Pilot." *Washington Post Book World*, January 6, 1985: 3.

Zimmerman, Paul D. "Blurred Vision." *Newsweek*, November 15, 1976: 115.

Other Books and Articles Consulted

Bellamy, Joe David, ed. *The New Fiction: Interviews with Innovative American Writers*. Urbana: University of Illinois Press, 1974.

"Bellow and Welty Read to Audience." *New York Times*, September 19, 1985: C–18.

Bruch, Hilde, M.D. *The Golden Cage: The Enigma of Anorexia Nervosa*. New York: Vintage Books, 1979.

Brumberg, Joan Jacobs. *Fasting Girls: The Emergence of Anorexia Nervosa as a Modern Disease*. Cambridge: Harvard University Press, 1988.

Curzon, Daniel. "Hatred." *The Revolt of the Perverts*. San Francisco: Leland Mellott Books, 1978. 45–69.

Gardner, John, ed. (with Shannon Ravenel). *The Best American Short Stories 1982*. New York: Houghton Mifflin, 1982.

Gordon, Richard A. *Anorexia and Bulimia: Anatomy of a Social Epidemic*. Cambridge: Blackwell, 1990.

Goulden, Joseph C. *Fit to Print: A. M. Rosenthal and His Times.* Secaucus, NJ: Lyle Stuart, 1988.

Grobel, Lawrence. *Conversations with Capote.* New York: New American Library, 1985.

Henle, Guy. "Vanguard Press: 62 Influential Years." *The Authors Guild Bulletin,* Summer 1989: 13–15.

McNamara, Gene. "The Art of the Novel." *Chicago,* November 1979: 70–78.

Muller, Herman J. *The University of Detroit, 1877–1977, A Centennial History.* Detroit: University of Detroit, 1976.

Orbach, Susie. *Hunger Strike: The Anorectic's Struggle as a Metaphor for Our Age.* New York: Norton, 1986.

Rabinowitz, Dorothy. "Arms and the Man: A Sex Scandal Rocks Princeton." *New York,* July 17, 1989: 30–36.

Rorem, Ned. *The Nantucket Diary of Ned Rorem, 1973–85.* San Francisco: North Point Press, 1987.

Schumacher, Michael, ed. *Reasons to Believe: New Voices in American Fiction.* New York: St. Martin's Press, 1988.

Smith, Joan. "Word Perfect." *San Francisco Focus,* March 1995: 38–42.

Stern, Richard. "Some Members of the Congress." *Critical Inquiry,* Summer 1988. 688–730.

Widick, B. J. *Detroit: City of Race and Class Violence.* Chicago: Quadrangle Books, 1972.

"Women's Liberation: What Will We Lose?" *The American Scholar,* Winter 1972–73: 144–45.

Woodford, Frank B. and Arthur M. Woodford. *All Our Yesterdays, A Brief History of Detroit.* Detroit: Wayne State University Press, 1969.

Selected Interviews with Joyce Carol Oates

Joyce Carol Oates has given more than a hundred print, radio, and television interviews in the past thirty years, most of which have provided significant information and insights for this biography. Only interviews quoted directly and referenced in the Notes are cited below. Twenty-five of Oates's interviews from 1969 to 1989 are collected in Lee Milazzo, ed., *Conversations with Joyce Carol Oates* (Jackson: University Press of Mississippi, 1989).

Print Interviews and Feature Stories

Applebaum, Judith. "Joyce Carol Oates." *Publishers Weekly,* June 26, 1978: 12–13.

Aronson, Harvey. "Joyce, Joan, and Lois: woman's need vs. writer's ego." *Cosmopolitan,* January 1971: 102–3, 115–17.

"Author Joyce Carol Oates on 'Adolescent America.' " *U.S. News and World Report,* May 15, 1978: 60.

Avant, John Alfred. "An Interview with Joyce Carol Oates." *Library Journal*, November 15, 1972: 3711–12.

Batterberry, Michael and Ariane. "Focus on Joyce Carol Oates." *Harper's Bazaar*, September 1973: 159, 174, 176.

Bellamy, Joe David. "The Dark Lady of American Letters." *The Atlantic Monthly*, February 1972: 63–67.

Bower, Warren. "Bliss in the First Person." *Saturday Review*, October 26, 1968: 34–35.

Clemons, Walter. "Joyce Carol Oates at Home." *New York Times Book Review*, September 28, 1969: 4–5, 48.

———. "Joyce Carol Oates: Love and Violence." *Newsweek*, December 11, 1972: 72–77.

Cook, Louis. "Joyce Carol Oates: Success and Failure in the Big-Time," *Detroit Free Press* magazine, March 14, 1966: 6–8.

Dudar, Helen. "She Wrote About 'Them'." *New York Post Weekend Magazine*, March 14, 1970: 19–20.

Fitzsimmons, Kate. "Wild Oates: An Interview with Joyce Carol Oates." *San Francisco Review of Books*, October/November 1994: 26–28.

Franks, Lucinda. "The Emergence of Joyce Carol Oates." *New York Times Magazine*, July 27, 1980: 22, 26, 30, 32, 43–44, 46.

Grobel, Lawrence. "Playboy Interview: Joyce Carol Oates." *Playboy*, November 1993: 63–76.

Kazin, Alfred. "Oates." *Harper's*, August 1971: 78–82.

Keenan, Margaret M. "A Writing Workshop with Joyce Carol Oates." *Princeton Alumni Weekly*, November 5, 1979: 20–21, 28–29.

Kuehl, Linda. "An Interview with Joyce Carol Oates." *Commonweal*, December 5, 1969: 307–10.

Lardner, Susan. "Oracular Oates." *The New Yorker*, January 3, 1977: 74, 76.

Lee, Betty. "Tracking the elusive author." *Toronto Globe and Mail*, March 14, 1970: B–8.

McCombs, Phil. "The Demonic Imagination of Joyce Carol Oates." *Washington Post*, August 18, 1986: C1, C11.

McDowell, Edwin. "A Sad Joyce Carol Oates Forswears Pseudonyms." *New York Times*, February 2, 1987: C–12.

McLaughlin, Frank. "A Conversation with Joyce Carol Oates." *Writing!*, September 1985: 21–23.

O'Briant, Don. "A Little Wilder Joyce Carol Oates." *Atlanta Journal-Constitution*, April 23, 1986: C–1, C–6.

Phillips, Robert. "Joyce Carol Oates: The Art of Fiction LXXII." *The Paris Review*, Fall 1978: 199–206.

Plump, Wendy. "Oates entwines fact and fiction in book mirroring PU scandal." *Princeton Packet*, August 28, 1990: 1a, 8a.

Quinn, Sally. "Joyce Carol Oates: A Life Within." *Washington Post*, April 30, 1975: B1, B11.

Salisbury, Stephan. "For librarians, a mixed bag of views from Oates, others." *Philadelphia Inquirer*, July 12, 1982: D–1, D–7.

Schaeffer, Edwina. "Author Shuns Spoken Word." *Detroit News*, January 15, 1964: 1–E, 2–E.

Schumacher, Michael. "Joyce Carol Oates and the Hardest Part of Writing." *Writer's Digest*, April 1986: 30–34.

Showalter, Elaine. "My Friend, Joyce Carol Oates: An Intimate Portrait." *Ms.*, March 1986: 44–50.

Shyer, Laurence. "The Sunny Side of Joyce Carol Oates." *American Theatre*, February 1994: 23–26.

Silverman, William. "She Lets Her Fingers Do the Talking." *Detroit News*, February 2, 1969: 6–10.

Skal, Dave. "Joyce Carol Oates: Crazy Scenes and Demon Lovers." Ohio University *Post*, April 20, 1973: 3–4.

Slater, Charlotte. "Author on the Rise." *Detroit News*, October 29, 1967: C–12.

"Transformation of Self: An Interview with Joyce Carol Oates." *The Ohio Review*, Autumn 1973: 50–61.

"U.D. Instructor Named Author of the Year." *Detroit News*, December 9, 1964: 8–C.

Wozniak, Mary. "The parents behind a literary genius." *Niagara Gazette*, March 9, 1988.

———. "Oates." *Niagara Gazette*, August 1, 1987.

"Writing as a Natural Reaction." *Time*, October 10, 1969: 8.

Zimmerman, Paul D. "Hunger for Dreams," *Newsweek*, March 23, 1970: 109A.

Audio and Television Interviews

Cavett, Dick. *The Dick Cavett Show*. New York, 1980.

Elliott, Emory. "Contemporary American Literature with Joyce Carol Oates." Television interview, 1988.

Filardo, Francis R. *Brockport Writers Forum*. Television interview, 1980.

Gross, Terry. "Fresh Air." National Public Radio: August 3, 1993.

The Originals. "Joyce Carol Oates." A Screentime-Norflicks-Jillian Production, 1989.

Vitale, Tom. "Joyce Carol Oates: American Appetites." Television interview, 1989.

———. "A Moveable Feast." Audio interview, 1982.

Web Site

Randy Souther's web site on Joyce Carol Oates, *Celestial Timepiece*, is extremely helpful to anyone attempting to keep abreast of Oates's ever-burgeoning publications and other facets of her career. The address: http://www.usfca.edu/fac-staff/southerr/jco.html.

INDEX